AN INTRODUCTION TO SEARCH ENGINES AND WEB NAVIGATION

AN INTRODUCTION TO SEARCH ENGINES AND WEB NAVIGATION

MARK LEVENE
Department of Computer Science and Information Systems
Birkbeck University of London, UK

A JOHN WILEY & SONS, INC., PUBLICATION

Published by John Wiley & Sons, Inc., Hoboken, New Jersey

Published simultaneously in Canada

For general information on our other products and services or for technical support, please contact our Customer Care Department within the United States at (800) 762-2974, outside the United States at (317) 572-3993 or fax (317) 572-4002.

Wiley also publishes its books in a variety of electronic formats. Some content that appears in print may not be available in electronic formats. For more information about Wiley products, visit our web site at www.wiley.com.

Library of Congress Cataloging-in-Publication Data:

Levene, M. (Mark), 1957-
An introduction to search engines and web navigation / Mark Levene.
p. cm.
ISBN 978-0-470-52684-2 (pbk.)
1. Internet searching. 2. Web search engines. I. Title.
ZA4230.L48 2010
025.0425–dc22

2010008435

Printed in Singapore

10 9 8 7 6 5 4 3 2 1

To my wife Sara and three children
Tamara, Joseph and Oren

CONTENTS

PREFACE

MOTIVATION

Searching and navigating the web have become part of our daily online lives. Web browsers and the standard navigation tools embedded in them provide a showcase of successful software technology with a global user-base, that has changed the way in which we search for and interact with information. Search engine technology has become ubiquitous, providing a standard interface to the endless amount of information that the web contains. Since the inception of the web, search engines have delivered a continuous stream of innovations, satisfying their users with increasingly accurate results through the implementation of advanced retrieval algorithms and scalable distributed architectures. Search and navigation technologies are central to the smooth operation of the web and it is hard to imagine finding information without them. Understanding the computational basis of these technologies and the models underlying them is of paramount importance both for IT students and practitioners.

There are several technical books on web search and navigation but the ones I have seen are either very academic in nature, that is, targeted at the postgraduate student or advanced researcher, and therefore have a limited audience, or they concentrate on the user interface and web site usability issues, ignoring the technicalities of what is happening behind the scenes. These books do not explain at an introductory level how the underlying computational tools work. This book answers the need for an introductory, yet technical, text on the topic.

My research into web search and navigation technologies started during the beginning of the 1990s just before the internet boom, when, together with my colleagues, we began looking at hypertext as a model for unstructured (or semistructured) data connected via a network of links, much in the same way web pages are connected. Of particular interest to us was the infamous "navigation problem" when we lose our way navigating (or what has become known as "surfing") through the myriad of information pages in the network. Tackling this problem has provided continued impetus for my research.

In a wider context, the activity of information seeking, that is, the process we go through when searching and locating information in order to augment our state of knowledge, has been of major concern to all involved in the development of technologies that facilitate web interaction.

I have been using browser navigation tools and search engines since their early days, and have been fascinated by the flow of new ideas and the improvements that each new tool has delivered. One of my aims in this text is to demystify the technology underlying the tools that we use in our day-to-day interaction with the web, and another is to inform readers about upcoming technologies, some of which are still in the research and development stage.

I hope that this book will instill in you some of my enthusiasm for the possibilities that these technologies have and are creating to extend our capabilities of finding and sharing information.

AUDIENCE AND PREREQUISITES

The book is intended as an undergraduate introductory text on search and navigation technologies, but could also be used to teach an option on the subject. It is also intended as a reference book for IT professionals wishing to know how these technologies work and to learn about the bigger picture in this area.

The course has no formal prerequisites, all that is required is for the learner to be a user of the web and to be curious to know how these technologies work. All the concepts that are introduced are explained in words, and simple examples from my own experience are given to illustrate various points. Occasionally, to add clarity to an important concept, a formula is given and explained. Each chapter starts with a list of learning objectives and ends with a brief bullet-pointed summary. There are several exercises at the end of each chapter. Some of these aim to get the student to explore further issues, possibly with a reference which can be followed up, some get the student to discuss an aspect of the technology, and others are mini-projects (which may involve programming) to add to the student's understanding through a hands-on approach. The book ends with a set of notes containing web addresses to items mentioned in the book, and an extensive bibliography of the articles and books cited in the book.

Readers should be encouraged to follow the links in the text and to discover new and related links that will help them understand how search and navigation tools work, and to widen their knowledge with related information.

TIMELINESS

I believe that due to the importance of the topic it is about time that such a book should appear. Search and navigation technologies are moving at a very fast pace due to the continued growth of the web and its user base, and improvements in computer networking and hardware. There is also strong competition between different service providers to lock-in users to their products. This is good news for web users, but as a result some of the numerics in the text may be out of date. I have qualified the statistics I have given with dates and links, which can be found in the notes, so the reader can follow these to get an up-to-date picture and follow the trends. I do not expect the core technologies I have covered to radically change in the near future and I would go so far as to claim that in essence they are fundamental to the web's working, but innovation and new ideas will continue to flourish and mold the web's landscape.

If you find any errors or omissions please let me know so that I can list them on the book's web site. I will also be grateful to receive any constructive comments and suggestions, which can be used to improve the text.

ACKNOWLEDGMENTS

First I would like to thank my wife and family who have been extremely supportive throughout this project, encouraging me to put in the extra hours needed to complete such a task. I would also like to thank my colleagues at the Department of Computer Science and Information Systems at Birkbeck, who have read and commented on parts of the book. Special thanks to my editors at Wiley, Lucy Hitz and George Telecki, who have patiently guided me through the publication process. Finally, I would like to thank the reviewers for their constructive comments.

The people who have built the innovative technologies that drive today's web are the real heroes of the revolution that the World Wide Web has brought upon us. Without them, this book could not have been written. Not only in terms of the content of the book, but also in terms of the tools I have been using daily to augment my knowledge on how search and navigation technologies work in practice.

Mark Levene
London, June 2010

LIST OF FIGURES

CHAPTER 1

INTRODUCTION

"People keep asking me what I think of it now it's done. Hence my protest: The Web is not done!"

— Tim Berners-Lee, Inventor of the World Wide Web

THE LAST two decades have seen dramatic revolutions in information technology; not only in computing power, such as processor speed, memory size, and innovative interfaces, but also in the everyday use of computers. In the late 1970s and during the 1980s, we had the revolution of the personal computer (PC), which brought the computer into the home, the classroom, and the office. The PC then evolved into the desktop, the laptop, and the netbook as we know them today.

The 1990s was the decade of the World Wide Web (the Web), built over the physical infrastructure of the Internet, radically changing the availability of information and making possible the rapid dissemination of digital information across the globe. While the Internet is a physical network, connecting millions of computers together globally, the Web is a virtual global network linking together a massive amount of information. Search engines now index many billions of web pages and that number is just a fraction of the totality of information we can access on the Web, much of it residing in searchable databases not directly accessible to search engines.

Now, in the twenty-first century we are in the midst of a third wave of novel technologies, that of mobile and wearable computing devices, where computing devices have already become small enough so that we can carry them around with us at all times, and they also have the ability to interact with other computing devices, some of which are embedded in the environment. While the Web is mainly an informational and transactional tool, mobile devices add the dimension of being a location-aware ubiquitous social communication tool.

Coping with, organizing, visualizing, and acting upon the massive amount of information with which we are confronted when connected to the Web are amongst the main problems of *web interaction* [421]. Searching and navigating (or surfing) the Web are the methods we employ to help us find information on the web, using search engines and navigation tools that are either built-in or plugged-in to the browser or are provided by web sites.

In this book, we explore search and navigation technologies to their full, present the State-of-the art tools, and explain how they work. We also look at ways of modeling different aspects of the Web that can help us understand how the Web is evolving and how it is being and can be used. The potential of many of the technologies we introduce has not yet been fully realized, and many new ideas to improve the ways in which we interact with the Web will inevitably appear in this dynamic and exciting space.

1.1 BRIEF SUMMARY OF CHAPTERS

This book is roughly divided into three parts. The first part (Chapters 1–3) introduces the problems of web interaction dealt with in the book, the second part (Chapters 4–6) deals with web search engines, and the third part (Chapters 7–9) looks at web navigation, the mobile web, and social network technologies in the context of search and navigation. Finally, in Chapter 10, we look ahead at the future prospects of search and navigation on the Web.

Chapters 1–3 introduce the reader to the problems of search and navigation and provide background material on the Web and its users. In particular, in the remaining part of Chapter 1, we give brief histories of hypertext and the Web, and of search engines. In Chapter 2, we look at some statistics regarding the Web, investigate its structure, and discuss the problems of information seeking and web search. In Chapter 3, we introduce the navigation problem, discuss the potential of machine learning to improve search and navigation tools, and propose Markov chains as a model for user navigation.

Chapters 4–6 cover the architectural and technical aspects of search engines. In particular, in Chapter 4, we discuss the search engine wars, look at some usage statistics of search engines, and introduce the architecture of a search engine, including the details of how the Web is crawled. In Chapter 5, we dissect a search engine's ranking algorithm, including content relevance, link- and popularity-based metrics, and different ways of evaluating search engines. In Chapter 6, we look at different types of search engines, namely, web directories, search engine advertising, metasearch engines, personalization of search, question answering engines, and image search and special purpose engines.

Chapters 7–9 concentrate on web navigation, and looks beyond at the mobile web and at how viewing the Web in social network terms is having a major impact on search and navigation technologies. In particular, in Chapter 7, we discuss a range of navigation tools and metrics, introduce web data mining and the Best Trail algorithm, discuss some visualization techniques to assist navigation, and look at the issues present in real-world navigation. In Chapter 8, we introduce the mobile web in the context of mobile computing, look at the delivery of mobile web services, discuss interfaces to mobile devices, and present the problems of search and navigation in a mobile context. In Chapter 9, we introduce social networks in the context of the Web, look at social network analysis, introduce peer-to-peer networks, look at the technology of collaborative filtering, introduce weblogs as a medium for personal journalism on the Web, look at the ubiquity of power-law distributions on the Web, present effective searching strategies in social networks, introduce opinion mining as a way of obtaining knowledge about users opinions and sentiments, and look at Web 2.0 and collective intelligence that have generated a lot of hype and inspired many start-ups in recent years.

1.2 BRIEF HISTORY OF HYPERTEXT AND THE WEB

The history of the Web dates back to 1945 when Vannevar Bush, then an advisor to President Truman, wrote his visionary article "As We May Think," and described his imaginary desktop machine called *memex*, which provides personal access to all the information we may need [119]. An artist's impression of memex is shown in Fig. 1.1.

The memex is a "sort of mechanized private file and library," which supports "associative indexing" and allows navigation whereby "any item may be caused at will to select immediately and automatically another." Bush emphasizes that "the process of tying two items together is an important thing." By repeating this process of creating links, we can form a *trail* which can be traversed by the user; in Bush's words, "when numerous items have been thus joined together to form a trail they can be reviewed in turn." The motivation for the memex's support of trails as first-class objects was that the human mind "operates by association" and "in accordance to some intricate web of trails carried out by the cells of the brain."

Figure 1.1 Bush's memex. (Source: Life Magazine 1945;9(11):123.)

Bush also envisaged the "new profession of trailblazers" who create trails for other memex users, thus enabling sharing and exchange of knowledge. The memex was designed as a personal desktop machine, where information is stored locally on the machine. Trigg [647] emphasizes that Bush views the activities of creating a new trail and following a trail as being connected. Trails can be authored by trailblazers based on their experience and can also be created by memex, which records all user navigation sessions. In his later writings on the memex, published in Ref. 509, Bush revisited and extended the memex concept. In particular, he envisaged that memex could "learn from its own experience" and "refine its trails." By this, Bush means that memex collects statistics on the trails that the user follows and "notices" the ones that are most frequently followed. Oren [516] calls this extended version *adaptive memex*, stressing that adaptation means that trails can be constructed dynamically and given semantic justification; for example, by giving these new trails meaningful names.

The term *hypertext* [503] was coined by Ted Nelson in 1965 [495], who considers "a literature" (such as the scientific literature) to be a *system of interconnected writings*. The process of referring to other connected writings, when reading an article or a document, is that of *following links*. Nelson's vision is that of creating a repository of all the documents that have ever been written thus achieving a universal hypertext. Nelson views his hypertext system, which he calls *Xanadu*, as a network of distributed documents that should be allowed to grow without any size limit, such that users, each corresponding to a node in the network, may link their documents to any other documents in the network. Xanadu can be viewed as a generalized memex system, which is both for private and public use. As with memex, Xanadu remained a vision that was not fully implemented; a mockup of Xanadu's linking mechanism is shown in Fig. 1.2. Nelson's pioneering work in hypertext is materialized to a large degree in the Web, since he also views his system as a means of publishing material by making it universally available to a wide network of interconnected users.

Douglas Engelbart's o*n*-*l*ine *s*ystem (NLS) [205] was the first working hypertext system, where documents could be linked to other documents and thus groups of people could work collaboratively. The video clips of Engelbart's historic demonstration of NLS from December 1968 are archived on the Web,[1] and a recollection of the demo can be found in Ref. 204; a picture of Engelbart during the demo is shown in Fig. 1.3.

About 30 years later in 1990, Tim Berners-Lee—then working for Cern, the world's largest particle physics laboratory—turned the vision of hypertext into reality by creating the World Wide Web as we know it today [77].[2]

The Web works using three conventions: (i) the URL (unified resource locator) to identify web pages, (ii) HTTP (hypertext transfer protocol) to exchange messages between a browser and web server, and (iii) HTML (hypertext markup language) [501] to display web pages. More recently, Tim Berners-Lee has been

[1]Video clips from Engelbart's demo can be found at http://sloan.stanford.edu/mousesite/1968Demo.html.

[2]A little history of the World Wide Web from 1945 to 1995. www.w3.org/History.html.

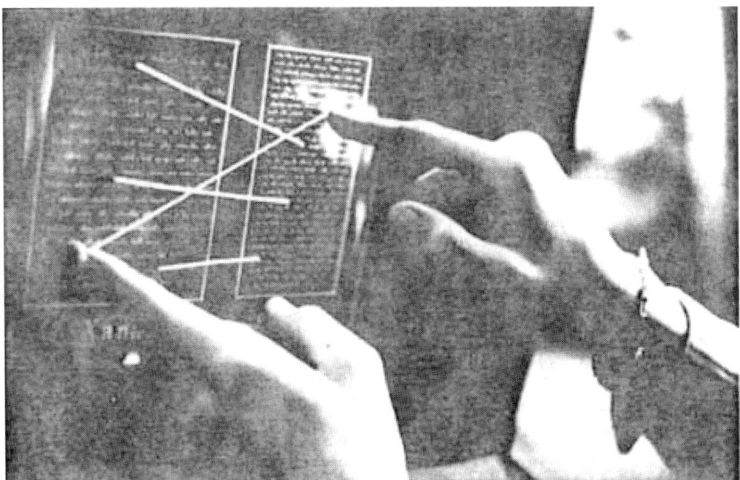

Figure 1.2 Nelson's Xanadu. (Source: Figure 1.3, Xanalogical structure, needed now more than ever: Parallel documents, deep links to content, deep versioning, and deep re-use, by Nelson TH. www.cs.brown.edu/memex/ACM_HypertextTestbed/papers/60.html.)

Figure 1.3 Engelbart's NLS. (Source: Home video of the birth of the hyperlink. www.ratchetup.com/eyes/2004/01/wired_recently_.html.)

promoting the semantic web [78] together with XML (extensible markup language) [259], and RDF (resource description framework) [544], as a means of creating machine understandable information that can better support end user web applications. Details on the first web browser implemented by Tim Berners-Lee in 1990 can be found at www.w3.org/People/Berners-Lee/WorldWideWeb.

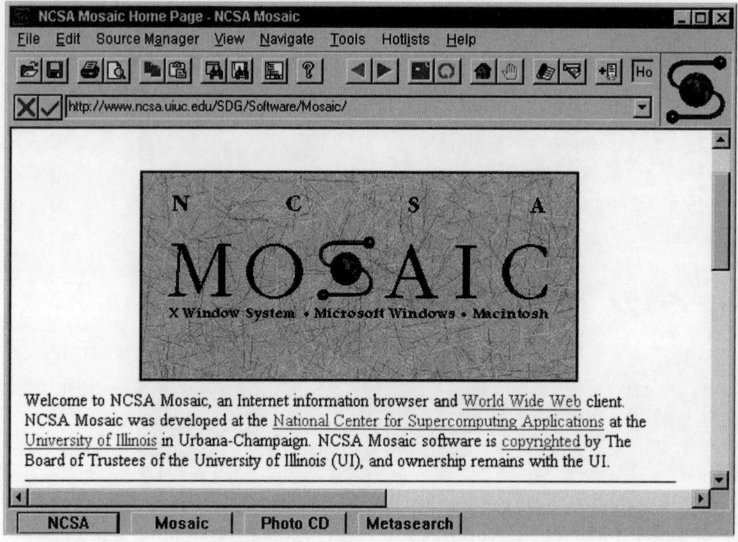

Figure 1.4 Mosaic browser initially released in 1993. (Source: http://gladiator.ncsa.illinois.edu/Images/press-images/mosaic.gif.)

The creation of the Mosaic browser by Marc Andreessen in 1993 followed by the creation of Netscape early in 1994 were the historic events that marked the beginning of the internet boom that lasted throughout the rest of the 1990s, and led to the mass uptake in web usage that continues to increase to this day. A screenshot of an early version of Mosaic is shown in Fig. 1.4.

1.3 BRIEF HISTORY OF SEARCH ENGINES

The roots of web search engine technology are in information retrieval (IR) systems, which can be traced back to the work of Luhn at IBM during the late 1950s [444]. IR has been an active field within information science since then, and has been given a big boost since the 1990s with the new requirements that the Web has brought.

Many of the methods used by current search engines can be traced back to the developments in IR during the 1970s and 1980s. Especially influential is the SMART (system for the mechanical analysis and retrieval of text) retrieval system, initially developed by Gerard Salton and his collaborators at Cornell University during the early 1970s [583]. An important treatment of the traditional approaches to IR was given by Keith van Rijsbergen [655], while more modern treatments with reference to the Web can be found in Refs 45, 68, 453, and 164. More recent developments, which concentrate on web technologies, are the probabilistic perspective on modeling the Web as in Ref. 46 and the data mining perspective on managing web information, which can be found in Refs 128 and 435.

Owing to the massive amount of information on the Web, right from the early days of the Web, search engines have become an indispensable tool for web users. A history of search engines detailing some of the early search services can be found in Ref. 659.[3]

Here, we will be very selective and mention only a few of the early and current search engines; see http://searchenginewatch.com/links and http://en.wikipedia.org/wiki/List_of_search_engines for up-to-date listings of the major search engines. More details on many of the current search engines are spread throughout the book.

- Yahoo (www.yahoo.com), which started up in February 1994, was one of the earliest search services.[4] Initially, Yahoo was only providing a browsable directory, organizing web pages into categories which were classified by human editors. Yahoo continues to maintain a strong brand and has evolved into a full-fledged search engine by acquiring existing search engine technology in mid-2003. (You can get some insight on the latest innovations in Yahoo's search engine from its weblog at www.ysearchblog.com.)
- InfoSeek, which started up in July 1994, was the first search engine that I was using on a regular basis, and as with many of the innovative web tools, users voted with their clicks and its reputation spread by word of mouth. In July 1998, Infoseek merged with Walt Disney's Buena Vista Internet Group to form Go.com, which was ultimately abandoned in January 2001.
- Inktomi, which started up in September 1995, provides search engine infrastructure rather than delivering the service from their web site. Until it was acquired by Yahoo in March 2003, it was providing search services to some of the major search engines.
- AltaVista (www.altavista.com), which started up in December 1995, was the second search engine that I was using on a regular basis. It was initially a research project in Digital Equipment Corporation, and was eventually acquired by Overture in April 2003.
- AlltheWeb (www.alltheweb.com) was launched in May 1999 by Fast Search & Transfer, and in a very short time was able to build a very large and fresh index with fast and accurate search results. It was also acquired by Overture in April 2003.
- Ask Jeeves (www.ask.com) started up in April 1996. It went public in July 1999, and is one of the survivors in the search engine game. Its strong brand and distinctive question answering facility have evolved into a general search service through its acquisition of Teoma in September 2001, which has enabled it to manage a proprietary search service and develop its own search technology. It was acquired by e-commerce conglomerate IAC (InterActiveCorp) in July 2005.

[3]See also, A history of search engines, by W. Sonnenreich. www.wiley.com/legacy/compbooks/sonnenreich/history.html.

[4]The history of Yahoo!—How it all started. http://docs.yahoo.com/info/misc/history.html.

- Overture (www.overture.com) started up as Goto.com in September 1997, and pioneered pay-per-click search engine advertising. It was renamed as Overture in September 2001 and was acquired by Yahoo in July 2003. In April 2005, Overture was rebranded as Yahoo Search Marketing (http://searchmarketing.yahoo.com).
- Bing (www.bing.com) is Microsoft's search engine that went online in June 2009. It replaced Live search, released in September 2006, which replaced MSN search, originally launched in August 1995, coinciding with the release of Windows 95. Initially, MSN search partnered with major search engines to provide the search facility for their site. Realizing the strategic importance of search to Microsoft's core business, Microsoft announced, in 2003, that it would develop its own proprietary search technology. The beta version of the search engine was released by MSN in November 2004, and in February 2005 MSN search was officially delivering search results from its internally developed engine. (You can get some insight on the latest innovations in Bing's search engine from its weblog at www.bing.com/community/blogs/search.)
- Google (www.google.com) was started up in September 1998, by Larry Page and Sergey Brin, then PhD students at Stanford University.[5] Google was the third search engine that I was using on a regular basis and am still using today, although I do consult other search services as well. It became a public company in August 2004, and, as of late 2004, has been the most popular search engine. You will find a wealth of information in this book on the innovative features that Google and other search engines provide. (You can get some insight on the latest innovations in Google's search engine from its weblog at http://googleblog.blogspot.com.)

[5]Google History. www.google.com/corporate/history.html.

CHAPTER 2

THE WEB AND THE PROBLEM OF SEARCH

"Basically, our goal is to organise the world's information and make it universally accessible and useful."

— Larry Page, cofounder of Google

TO UNDERSTAND the magnitude of the search problem we present some statistics regarding the size of the Web, its structure, and usage, and describe the important user activity of information seeking. We also discuss the specific challenges web search poses and compare local site search within an individual web site to global search over the entire web.

CHAPTER OBJECTIVES

- Give an indication of the size of the Web, and how it can be measured.
- Give an indication of the relative usage of search engines.
- Highlight the differences between structured data organized in tables, and traditional web data that does not have a fixed structure.
- Explain the bow-tie structure of the Web.
- Introduce the notion of a small-world network (or graph) in the context of the Web.
- Discuss different kinds of information-seeking strategies on the Web: direct navigation, navigating within a directory and using a search engine.
- Discuss the problems inherent in web information seeking.
- Introduce a taxonomy of web searches.
- Present the differences between web search and traditional information retrieval.

An Introduction to Search Engines and Web Navigation, by Mark Levene

- Introduce the notions of precision and recall used to evaluate the quality of an information retrieval system, and discuss these in the context of web search.
- Discuss the differences between search within a local web site and global web search.
- Highlight the fact that web search engines do not solve the site search problem.
- Make clear the difference between search and navigation.

2.1 SOME STATISTICS

The Web is undoubtedly the largest information repository known to man. It is also the most diverse in terms of the subject matter that it covers, the quality of information it encompasses, its dynamic nature in terms of its evolution, and the way in which the information is linked together in a spontaneous manner.

2.1.1 Web Size Statistics

As an indication of the massive volume of the Web, an estimate of its size, given by Murray of Cyveillance in July 2000 [487], was 2.1 billion pages. At that time the Web was growing at a rate of 7.3 million web pages a day, so according to this prediction there were already over 4 billion web pages by April 2001. Extrapolating forward using this growth rate, we can estimate that the Web would have over 28 billion web pages in 2010. As we will see, this estimate was very conservative as our size estimate for 2010 is about 600 billion, which implies a growth rate of 200 million web pages per day.

This estimate does not include *deep web* data contained in databases, which are not directly accessible to search engines [76]. As an example, patent databases such as those provided by the US patent and trademark office,[6] are only accessible through a tailored search interface. Thus, without direct access to such data, search engines cannot easily fully index this information.[7] It is estimated that the deep web (also known as the *hidden or invisible web*[8]) is approximately 550 times larger than the information that can be accessed directly through web pages. Other types of web data, which are ephemeral in nature such as train timetables (which may last months or years) and travel bargains (which normally last only weeks), or contain complex formats such as audio and video, are problematic for search engines and although not invisible, are difficult to deal with. Also, there are web pages which are literally not accessible, since they are not linked from other visible web pages, and thus are deemed to be part of the hidden web.

[6]United States Patent and Trademark Office home page. www.uspto.gov/patft/index.html.

[7]Google Patent Search. www.google.com/patents.

[8]The Deep Web Directory. www.completeplanet.com.

The deep web site is accessed through web query interfaces that access back-end web databases connected to a web server. Therefore, a deep web site may have several query interfaces connecting to one or more web databases. A study from 2004 estimated that there are approximately 0.30 million deep web sites, 0.45 million web databases, and 1.25 million query interfaces [290]. Through random sampling from these databases, they concluded that the three major search engines (Google, Yahoo, and Microsoft's Live rebranded as Bing) cover about one-third of the deep web. It also transpires that there is a significant overlap between the search engines in what is covered. So the deep web is not so invisible to search engines but what is hidden seems to be hidden from all of them.

For search engines, the issue of *coverage*, that is, the proportion of the accessible web they hold in their web page index, is crucial. However good the search engine tool may be, if its coverage is poor, it will miss relevant web pages in its results set.

In early 2004, Google reported that their index contained 4.28 billion web pages.[9] After an intensive crawling and re-indexing period during 2004, Google announced later in the year that it had nearly doubled its index to a reported size of over 8 billion web pages.[10] For comparison, toward the end of 2004 MSN Search (rebranded as Bing in mid-2009), which had then begun deploying its own search engine, reported an index size of over 5 billion web pages,[11] in April 2005, Yahoo search reported a similar index size of over 5 billion,[12] and Teoma, the search engine powering Ask Jeeves, reported an index in excess of 2 billion web pages.[13]

Older estimates of search engine sizes from the end of 2002, were as follows: Google had over 3 billion documents, AlltheWeb (now integrated with Yahoo Search) had 2 billion documents, AltaVista (also integrated into Yahoo Search) had over 1 billion documents, Teoma had over 1 billion documents, and MSN Search had access to over 1 billion documents.[14]

As we will see below, the Web has grown since 2004, and our current estimate of the accessible web as of 2010 stands at about 600 billion pages. This estimate may still be conservative, as each search engine covers only a certain fraction of the totality of accessible web pages [406], but it gives us a good idea of the scale of the enterprise. The exact number is evasive but our current estimate of 600 billion accessible web pages, approaching 1 trillion, is probably

[9]Google press release, Google achieves search milestone with immediate access to more than 6 billion items. February 2004. www.google.com/press/pressrel/6billion.html.

[10]Google's index nearly doubles, by Bill Coughran, November 2004. http://googleblog.blogspot.com/2004/11/googles-index-nearly-doubles.html.

[11]Microsoft unveils its new search engine—At last, by C. Sherman, November 2004. http://searchenginewatch.com/3434261.

[12]Internet search engines: Past and future, by J. Perdersen, Search Engine Meeting, Boston, 2005. www.infonortics.com/searchengines/sh05/slides/pedersen.pdf.

[13]Teoma Category Archive, Teoma 3.0, September 2004. www.searchengineshowdown.com/blog/z_old_engines/teoma.

[14]Search engine statistics: Database total size estimates, by G.R. Notess, Search Engine Showdown, December 2002. www.searchengineshowdown.com/statistics/sizeest.shtml.

not far from the truth; this not withstanding the issue of the quality of a web page and how often it is visited, if at all.

To measure the size of the Web, Lawrence and Giles [405] (see also Ref. [107]) had an ingenious idea based on a widely used statistical method to estimate the size of a population, which is called the *capture–recapture* method [680]. To illustrate the method, suppose you have a lake of fish and you want to estimate their number. Randomly select, say 100 fish, tag them, and return them to the lake. Then, select another random sample with replacement, say of 1000 fish, from the lake and observe how many tagged fish there are in this second sample. In this second sample, some of the fish may be selected more than once, noting that the chance of selecting a tagged fish will be the same for each fish in the second sample; that is, 100 divided by the total number of fish in the lake. Suppose that there were 10 tagged fish out of the 1000, that is, 1%. Then we can deduce that the 100 fish are in the same proportion relative to the whole population, that is they are 1% of the total population. So, our estimate of the number of fish in the lake in this case will be 10,000.

Using this method, Lawrence and Giles defined the following experiment with pairs of search engines to estimate the size of the Web. To start with, they tagged all the pages indexed by the first search engine as were the fish. They then chose several typical queries (575 to be precise) and counted the number of unique hits from the first search engine in the pair; that is, they counted the number of web pages returned from the first search engine. They then fired the same queries to the second search engine and measured the proportion of tagged pages from the results set; these pages are in the intersection of the results of the two search engines. As with the fish, assuming that the set of all tagged pages is in the same proportion relative to the set of all accessible web pages, as is the intersection relative to the results set of the second search engine, we can estimate the size of the accessible web. The resulting formulae is the number of pages indexed by the first search engine multiplied by the number of pages returned by the second search engine, divided by the number in the intersection.

Their estimate of the size of the Web from a study carried out in 1998 was 320 million pages, and around 800 million from a later study carried out in 1999. A further estimate from 2005 using a similar technique claims that the size of the indexable web has more than 11.5 billion pages [272].

A more recent estimate from the beginning of 2010, which is periodically updated on www.worldwidewebsize.com, put a lower bound on the number of indexable web pages at about 21 billion pages. The technique used by de Kunder to reach this estimate is based on the expected number of web pages containing a selected collection of words. Each day 50 word queries are sent to Google, Yahoo, Bing, and Ask and the number of web pages found for these words are recorded. The 50 words have been chosen so that they are evenly spread on a log–log plot of word frequencies constructed from a sample of more than 1 million web pages from the Open Directory (www.dmoz.org), which can be considered to be a representative sample of web pages. (The distribution of word frequencies obeys Zipf's law; see Section 5.1.3 and see Section 9.6.) Once the word frequencies are known, the size of each search engine index can be extrapolated.

The size of the overlap between the search engines is computed from the daily overlap of the top-10 results returned by the search engines from a sufficiently large number of random word queries drawn from the Open Directory sample. Finally, the overlap and index sizes are combined to reach an estimate of the Web's size.

This estimate is much lower than the 120 billion pages that the search engine Cuil (www.cuil.com) has reported to index in 2008.[15] Although Google has not been disclosing the size of its index, a post from its Web Search Infrastructure Team on the official Google blog from July 2008[16] reported that they process over 1 trillion unique URLs (10^{12}). This figure of 1 trillion contains duplicate web pages such as autogenerated copies, so on its own it does not tell us how many web pages there actually are. To get an estimate of the Web's size we can make use of the finding that about 30% of web pages are either duplicates or near-duplicates of other pages [218]. The resulting estimate of about 700 billion web pages is still a rough upper bound as some pages are created with the intent to deceive search engines to include them in their index and have little relevance to users, detracting from the user experience. The activity of creating such pages is known as *spamdexing*, and such pages when detected by a search engine, are considered as spam and therefore not indexed. Using a further estimate that about 14% of web pages are spam [508], we can conclude that the Web contains approximately 600 billion indexable web pages as of 2010.

Even more daunting is the thought of delivering a speedy search service that has to cope with over 500 million (half a billion) queries a day, which is about 6000 queries a second. The answer to the question, "How do they do it?" will be addressed in Chapter 4, when we dig deep inside search engine technology. Keeping up with the pace in this extremely dynamic environment is an uphill struggle. The Web is very fluid; it is constantly changing and growing. Many of its pages are dynamically generated such as news pages which are constantly updated and stock prices which are continuously monitored, and many pages are displayed differently to varying audiences; for example, depending on the browser used, or some contextual information such as the country of origin of the surfer (if this is evident from their domain name) or the time of day. These complexities often mean that the web pages are written in a scripting language rather than in HTML and thus are harder for search engines to interpret. On top of all this, there is a multitude of data formats to deal with,[17] which makes the search engine's task even more difficult.

In their 1999 study, Lawrence and Giles also reported that the degree of overlap between search engines is low, a result that has been confirmed time and time again since then [623]. This would imply that metasearch, where results from several search engines are aggregated, would significantly increase the coverage of a search service. Although, in principle this is true, the major search engines

[15]Cuil Launches Biggest Search Engine on the Web, July 2008. www.cuil.com/info/blog/2008/07/28/cuil-launches-biggest-search-engine-on-the-web.

[16]We knew the web was big. http://googleblog.blogspot.com/2008/07/we-knew-web-was-big.html.

[17]Wotsis's Format. www.wotsit.org.

are now blocking metasearch engines unless they pay for the service. Also, as the relative coverage of the major search engines increases, the benefits of metasearch are less clear. As gatekeepers of web information, the major search engines, predominantly Google, Yahoo, and Microsoft's Bing, are rapidly monopolizing the web search space and thus other issues, which may lead to regulation of search engines, are currently being raised and debated[18]; see Section 4.2.

A higher level measure of the size of the Web is the number of accessible web sites, rather than web pages. So, to estimate the number of web sites we need only identify the home page of each site as its representative. Researchers at the Online Computer Library Center (OCLC)[19] have conducted annual samples of the Web from 1997 to 2002 in order to analyze the trends in the size of the *public web*, which includes only sites that offer free and unrestricted access to a significant amount of their content.

Each web site can be identified by its IP (Internet Protocol) address. A random sample from the set of valid IP numbers is generated and each IP address is tested to check if it corresponds to an existing web site. The proportion of web sites within the sample is then used to extrapolate an estimate of the number of web sites from the total number of valid IP addresses. This extrapolation can be viewed as an application of the capture–recapture method.

In 1993 there were just 130 web sites[20] and the growth has been exponential until 2000, when there were about 2.9 million public web sites. In 2001 there were about 3.1 million web sites in the public web and in 2002 the number amazingly decreased to about 3 million [512]. This evidence suggests that the growth of the Web may periodically slow down in terms of number of web sites, which does not necessarily mean that the growth in terms of number of pages will follow a similar trend. One reason for the slowdown in 2002 is due to the fact that web technology had lost some of its novelty factor and we no longer witnessed the mad rush to buy domain names and gain web presence. On the one hand, organizations are spending more time in consolidating their web sites but on the other, due to the slowdown in the economy at that time, many web sites have literally disappeared.

Statistics regarding the number of registered commercial domains are also available, although many web sites own several domain names, implying that such statistics are an unreliable measure of the actual number of web sites. As of the beginning of 2010 there were about 113.90 million registered commercial domains compared to about 44.30 million in October 2004.[21] (Academic and government domains are excluded from this count.) It is interesting to note that although on the whole the number of registered domains is increasing, many domains are also deleted from the count (i.e., they are not re-registered when they expire).

[18]Google Watch. www.google-watch.org.

[19]Web Characterization OCLC Online Computer Library Center, Office of Research. www.oclc.org/research/activities/past/orprojects/wcp.

[20]Web growth summary. www.mit.edu/people/mkgray/net/web-growth-summary.html.

[21]Domain Tools, Domain Counts and Internet Statistics. www.domaintools.com/internet-statistics.

Netcraft (www.netcraft.com) performs a monthly survey of the number of web sites across all domains, reporting about 233.85 million sites as of December 2009 compared to about 66.80 million in June 2005.[22] Netcraft identifies the number of web sites by counting the web servers hosting a domain rather than by counting valid IP addresses.

An interesting point to make is that some of the web sites and web pages that have disappeared may be accessible through the Internet Archive,[23] which is a nonprofit company founded to build an "Internet Library" with the aim of offering permanent access to its digital collections. This is part of a broader agenda to archive web material, which is becoming a priority for the Web, since to a large degree the state of the Web at any given time represents a snapshot of our society and culture. Thus, there is value in preserving parts of the Web, so as to have access to its previous states. The issues relating to preservation and archiving of the Web are part of a larger concern regarding the lifespan of digital artifacts and the problem of having access to historical information.

So, how much information is out there? According to a study carried out in Berkeley in 2003,[24] if we include information in the deep web, the numbers add up to about 92,000TB (1 million million bytes) of information, which is 92PB (1000TB) of information. (The size of the surface web i.e., the World Wide Web, was estimated at about 170TB.) With the amount of information on the Web growing on a day-to-day basis it will not be long before we will be talking in terms of exabytes (1 million TB) of information. Of course, much of the content is irrelevant to us and of doubtful quality, but if it is out there and can be searched, someone may be interested in it. At the end of the day, search engines companies continually have to make a choice on which content they should index and make publicly available, and this will undoubtedly lead to some controversy.

2.1.2 Web Usage Statistics

The market share of the competing search engines is measured by companies that track the search and browsing behavior from a panel of several million users while they are surfing the Web.[25] We quote some statistics from late 2008

[22]Netcraft web server survey. http://news.netcraft.com.

[23]Internet Archive. www.archive.org.

[24]How much information? 2003, by P. Lyman and H.R. Varian. www.sims.berkeley.edu/research/projects/how-much-info-2003.

[25]There are several companies that collect information from a panel of several million users while they are searching and browsing the Web. To mention a few of the known ones: (i) Alex Internet (www.alexa.com) is a subsidiary of Amazon.com, (ii) Nielsen//NetRatings (www.nielsen-online.com) is a well-established information and media company, delivering, amongst other services, measurement and analysis of Internet users, (iii) comScore (www.comscore.com) is an internet information provider of online consumer behavior, (iv) Hitwise (www.hitwise.com) is an online measurement company monitoring internet traffic, and (v) Compete (www.compete.com) is a web analytics company that analyzes online user behavior.

and the beginning of 2009, noting that the percentages are only approximations obtained from sampling, and that the reported measurements are variable across the different information providers. The percentages given are indications of trends and thus, are subject to fluctuations.

The most visible trend is that Google's popularity in terms of audience reach has become increasingly dominant in the western world in the last few years, but its position is far from leading in the Far East. The rise of Google in the space of a few years from an experimental search engine developed by two research students in Stanford in 1998 is in itself an amazing story, which is told in depth elsewhere. It is hard to predict whether these trends will persist, and when making such predictions we should also take into account the fact that search engine loyalty is generally low.

In the United States, the popularity statistics show Google with 64%, Yahoo with 21%, Bing (Microsoft's search engine, rebranded as Bing from Live in mid-2009) with 8%, and Ask (also known as Ask Jeeves) with 4%. It is interesting to note that Google's market share is much larger in many of the European countries such as France (91%), Germany (93%), Italy (90%) and the United Kingdom (90%); similar figures are seen in South America. The global picture includes Baidu (www.baidu.com), the leading Chinese search engine which was launched in 1999, with 13% globally, but Google is still the global leader with 64%, followed by Yahoo with 15%, Bing with 4%, and Ask with 2%.

In the Far East, the story is somewhat different. In China the market share of Baidu is 57%, Google is 16%, and Yahoo is 5%. Major reasons for the big success of a local brand in China are the cultural and language differences. Baidu has a controversial policy (at least in the West), in that it provides searchers with links to music files that are available for download on the Web; there is an ongoing dispute between Google and Baidu on this issue. In Korea, a local web search engine called Naver (www.naver.com) which launched in 1999, is even more dominant with a market share of 75%. Surprisingly, in Korea the second most popular search engine, Daum (www.daum.net), which started in 1995 and was Korea's first web portal, is also local with a market share of 20%. In Korea Google's share is only 1.5%, coming behind Yahoo which has a share of 4%. Here also, major reasons for the success of the local brands are the cultural and language differences. In Japan, Yahoo with a market share of 51% is the leader, followed by Google with 38%. Yahoo had an early head start in Japan, incorporating there in 1996, less than a year after its parent company was formed; on the other hand, Google opened offices in Japan only in 2001. Yahoo Japan has a very localized strategy, with 40% of its shares being owned by the local telecommunications and media company Softbank. It has built a very local identity and is considered by many Japanese as a local brand. Russia is another country where Google is second with a market share of 21% behind the local web search engine, Yandex (www.yandex.com), with a share of 55%. Yandex was launched in 1997, and its success relative to Google, Yahoo, and Microsoft's Bing can be attributed to its handling of the Russian language.

How many people are surfing the Web? There were about 800 million internet users as of late 2004 and the number doubled to 1.6 billion in mid-2009 (which is approaching a quarter of the world's population).[26]

According to a report from late 2008,[27] there are about 400 million broadband subscribers, which covers about a quarter of the Internet users. The share of broadband subscription is highest in Western Europe (about 26%), North America (about 22.5%), and South and East Asia, which includes China and India (about 23%). Asia-Pacific has a much lower share (about 15.5%) and the rest of the world's share is even lower (about 13%). It is interesting to note that if we look at countries, then China has the largest number of broadband subscribers at about 81 million and has thus overtaken the United States, which at second place has about 79 million subscribers.

As the gap in pricing between broadband and narrowband continues to close, so will the trend of increased broadband connections continue to rise. In terms of trends as of 2010, mobile broadband is starting to take off in countries where the network infrastructure is available.

For October 2004, usage statistics indicate that users spent, on an average, 25 hours and 33 min surfing the net, viewing 1074 web pages, with an average of 35 min per session and viewing 35 web pages during the session. For comparison purposes, the statistics for February 2009 revealed that users spent, on an average, 34 hours and 17 min surfing the net, viewing 1549 web pages, with an average of 60 min per session and viewing 44 pages per session.[28]

This indicates that users are, on an average, spending more time surfing the Web and viewing more pages than before. It is worth noting that these statistics tend to fluctuate from month to month and that there are cognitive limits on what internet users may achieve within any surfing session.

In terms of search engine hits per day, Google has reported over 200 million during mid 2003.[29] The number of searches Google receives per day as of 2010 is elusive, but it is probably of the order of 3.5 billion per day which is over 40,000 queries per second [180]. If we are interested in the volume of queries for a particular phrase or keyword, we can obtain up-to-date figures by making use of the keyword tool provided by Google,[30] which is used by advertisers to find appropriate keywords to improve the performance of a campaign. For example, the tool shows that the average monthly volume in April 2009 for the query "computer science" was 673,000.

We mention the Pew Internet and American Life Project (www.pewinternet.org), which is a nonprofit "fact tank" that produces reports exploring the impact of the Internet on families, communities, work and home, daily life, education, health care, and civic and political life. Its reports are based on data collection

[26]Internet World Stats, Usage and Population Statistics. www.internetworldstats.com/stats.htm.

[27]F. Vanier, World Broadband Statistics: Q3 2008. http://point-topic.com/

[28]Neilsen//NetRating, Global Index Chart. www.nielsen-online.com/press_fd.jsp?section=pr_netv.

[29]Google Builds World's Largest Advertising and Search Monetization Program. www.google.com/press/pressrel/advertising.html.

[30]Google AdWords Keyword Tool. https://adwords.google.com/select/KeywordToolExternal.

from random phone surveys, online surveys, and qualitative research. This information is supplemented with research experts in the field of study. The project has produced reports on a variety of topical issues such as music downloading, online privacy, online banking, online dating, broadband users, Wikipedia users, mobile access to data and information, adults and social network web sites, cloud computing, and the future of the Internet.

We have all heard of road rage but now we have the phenomenon of web rage or search rage. A survey conducted by Roper Starch Worldwide in mid-2000[31] concluded that it takes on an average 12 min of web searching before the onset of search rage when users get extremely frustrated and lose their temper. A more recent survey commissioned in the United Kingdom by the Abbey National during the beginning of 2002[32] confirmed the previous survey showing a discernible gap between our expectations and the actual experience when surfing the Web. Apparently half of web surfers lose their temper once a week when surfing the Web, leading to extreme behavior such as the frustrated IT manager who smashed up an expensive laptop after a web page failed to recognize his personal details after six attempts. Some of the top irritations when surfing the Web are slow download times of web pages, irrelevant search results, web sites that have no search facility, unhelpful help buttons, poorly designed content, scrolling down a lot of information before getting the information needed, and ads. No doubt we have not heard the last of the web rage phenomenon.

Unfortunately as you are reading the book, some of these statistics will already be outdated but the World Wide Web is here to stay and the trends I have shown indicate that more people will be online with faster connections and more information to search. The URLs of the sites from which I have collected the statistics can be found in the footnotes. By following these links you may be able to get up-to-date statistics and verify the trends.

The trends are also indicating that e-commerce transactions, that is, the use of online services to conduct business, are on the rise.[33] Amongst the activities that many of us regularly carry out online are shopping, travel arrangements, banking, paying bills, and reading news.

2.2 TABULAR DATA VERSUS WEB DATA

Many of us have come across databases; for example, our local video store has a database of its customers, the library we go to has a database of its collection and the borrowing status of its items, and when we use a cashpoint (ATM) we connect to the bank's database, which stores all the information it needs to know about our financial situation. In all of these examples the information is stored in the database in a structured way; for example, the bank will store all your

[31]WebTop search rage study, by Danny Sullivan, February 5, 2001. http://searchenginewatch.com/sereport/article.php/2163451.

[32]Web rage hits the Internet, 20 February, 2002. http://news.bbc.co.uk/1/hi/sci/tech/1829944.stm.

[33]ClickZ Stats, Trends & Statistics: The Web's richest source. www.clickz.com/stats.

personal details and your credit information in a record format, not dissimilar to a spreadsheet. The Web can be loosely viewed as a database but it is a very different beast from the traditional (relational) database used by most medium to large corporations. (An authoritative book on relational database technology is Ref. [420].)

Let us highlight some of the differences. As can be seen on the left-hand side of Fig. 2.1, in a tabular or relational data representation, all the rows (or records) have the same predictable format. So, in this example each row representing a single employee contains three cells (or attribute values): the first has the employee's name, the second the employee's phone extension, and the third the employee's room number. Data in a web site, as shown on the right-hand side of Fig. 2.1 is arranged as a network of web pages each containing multimedia, such as text (natural language) and images (visual information), and hyperlinks which are embedded references linking web pages together. A company's employees may all have home pages within the web site but the internal structure of the individual home pages may vary from employee to employee.

A relational database is queried using SQL (Structured Query Language) while the web is queried using a search engine. When using SQL the target data required must be specified precisely in a logical manner, so we can ask the database queries such as "Who is the person in room 117?" or, "How many employees are there in the department?" All SQL queries have exact answers, so the person in 117 is Mark, and there are exactly four employees in this department. A query to a search engine is normally specified just as a bunch of keywords. It is free-text with little added syntax if any. Most web users can easily type in sensible queries to search engines but not many users can formulate correct SQL queries to a database without any training (although tools such as Microsoft Access make the formulation of such queries easier).

The resulting web pages returned by a search engine are given as a ranked list of the web pages it considers most "relevant" to the query. These returned

Name	Extn	Room
Mark	6711	117
George	6712	107
Alex	6705	122
Boris	6746	111

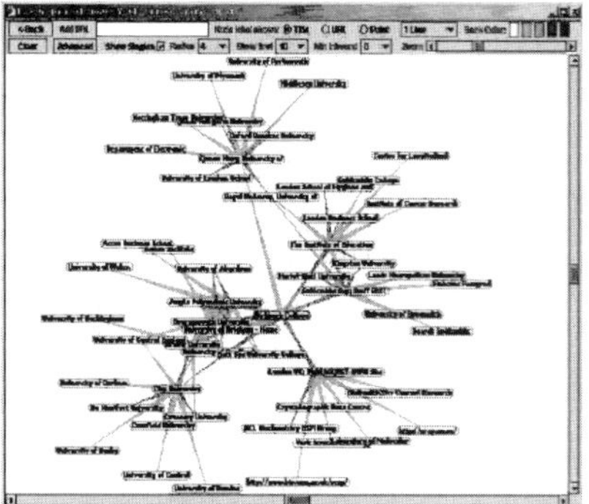

Figure 2.1 A database table versus an example web site. (Source: TouchGraph's GoogleBrowser (www.touchgraph.com/TGGoogleBrowser.html) display of web pages related to to the URL input to the tool, according to Google's `related` search operator.)

answers are not always precise, in the sense that the search engine is trying to find the "best" match for the query, and the person browsing the web pages returned must decide whether any specific page satisfies his or her query or not. Queries such as "How many employees work in the department?" are almost impossible to pose to a search engine but are standard queries to a relational database. First, the search engine may or may not have indexed all the employees home pages. Secondly, the search engine must recognize whether a given page is a home page or not and this in itself is a nontrivial matter. Thirdly, whatever the query may be, some of its results may not be home pages and some of the pages may be duplicated in the answer set, so it is almost impossible for the search engine to count the number we require.

The structure of a relational database does not change rapidly after the initial database design. So, for example, think of the massive database sitting in a bank storing all its customers' details, and all of the software that has been written for the applications that query the database. Each change in the structure of tables, say a change of an attribute, has major implications in terms of the maintenance of the software. On the other hand, search engines must adapt to many different data formats and be very flexible in order to accommodate for querying information that is changing all the time.

An error in a database is crucial. So, if a data value is corrupted, the database system cannot function and when you approach the cashpoint (ATM), you will get an error message. If some of the employee data is missing, we cannot estimate the answer to the query from the rest of the data. A search engine, on the other hand, does not depend on all the information being available. We have already seen that search engines cover only part of the Web, but we still get sensible results to many of our queries. Even if some of the search engine's servers are down for some reason, it can still function as we are not expecting precise answers. If we pose the same query to two search engines we will inevitably get different answers, and as search engine indexes are constantly changing, and they are continuously finding ways to improve their results, posing the same query to the same search engine will most likely give different results within relatively short time intervals [47].

2.3 STRUCTURE OF THE WEB

If we were to look at the Web from above as we view a metropolis when approaching it by air, we would see a complex network (or graph) of nodes and links that has the appearance of an emergent self-organizing structure. It might look something like Fig. 2.2 showing a partial map of the Internet (the physical network over which the Web is built);[34] the technique for generating such a map makes use of the traceroute tool, which traces the paths of packets through the Internet from a host to a given destination [100].

[34] See also Internet Mapping project. www.lumeta.com/internetmapping.

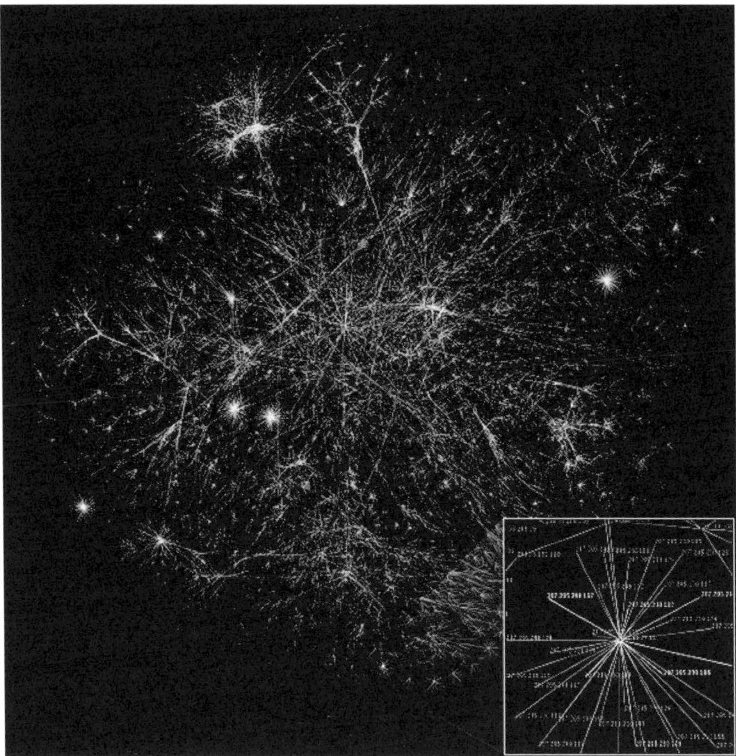

Figure 2.2 Partial map of the Internet (2005). (Source: Generated by the Opte project (www.opte.org/maps) in January 2005. http://commons.wikimedia.org/wiki/File:Internet_map_1024.jpg.)

If you further descend toward the Web, the picture will become clearer and you will be able to detect landmarks (which are the web pages) and roads (which are the links) connecting them together. A visualization of this descent, using Touchgraph's Google Browser (www.touchgraph.com/TGGoogleBrowser.html), is shown in Fig. 2.3, which depicts the web pages that are connected to the home page of the Department of Computer Science and Information Systems at Birkbeck (also known as SCSIS), via a similarity relationship computed by Google.

2.3.1 Bow-Tie Structure of the Web

To find out more about the structure of the Web, researchers from AltaVista, Compaq, and IBM performed a web crawl in May 1999 of over 200 million nodes and 1.5 billion links [108]. A web crawl is a task performed by special-purpose software that surfs the Web, starting from a multitude of web pages and then continuously following the hyperlinks it encountered until the end of the crawl. (We will discuss web crawling in Section 4.6.)

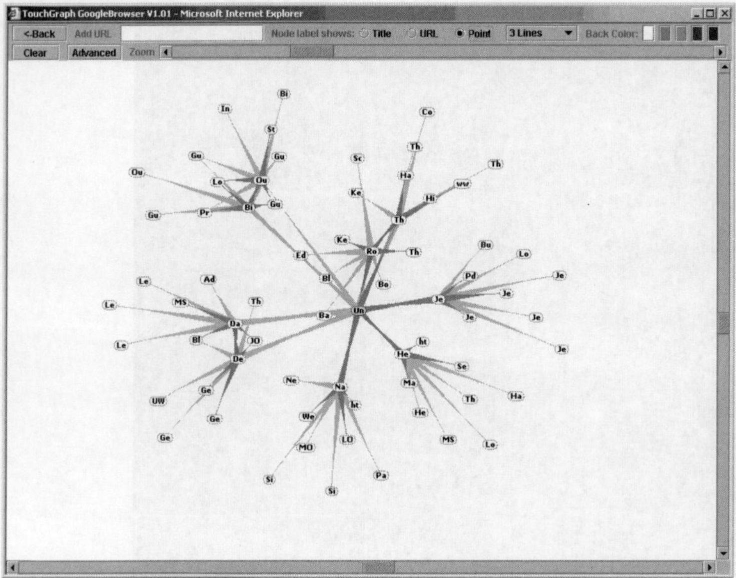

Figure 2.3 A view of web pages related to www.dcs.bbk.ac.uk.

One of the intriguing findings of this crawl was that the Web has a bow-tie structure as shown in Fig. 2.4. The central core of the Web (the knot of the bow-tie) is the strongly connected component (SCC), which means that for any two pages in the SCC, a user can navigate from one of them to the other and back by clicking on links embedded in the pages encountered. In other words, a user browsing a page in the SCC can always reach any other page in the SCC by traversing some path of links. The relative size of the SCC turned out to be 27.5% of the crawled portion of the Web. The left bow, called IN, contains pages that have a directed path of links leading to the SCC and its relative size was 21.5% of the crawled pages. Pages in the left bow might be either new pages that have not yet been linked to, or older web pages that have not become popular enough to become part of the SCC. The right bow, called OUT, contains pages that can be reached from the SCC by following a directed path of links and its relative size was also 21.5% of the crawled pages. Pages in the right bow might be pages in e-commerce sites that have a policy not to link to other sites. The other components are the "tendrils" and the "tubes" that together comprised 21.5% of the crawled portion of the Web, and further "disconnected" components whose total size was about 8% of the crawl. A web page in Tubes has a directed path from IN to OUT bypassing the SCC, and a page in Tendrils can either be reached from IN or leads into OUT. The pages in Disconnected are not even weakly connected to the SCC; that is, even if we ignored the fact that hyperlinks only allow forward navigation, allowing them to be traversed backwards as well as forwards, we still could *not* reach reach the SCC from them.

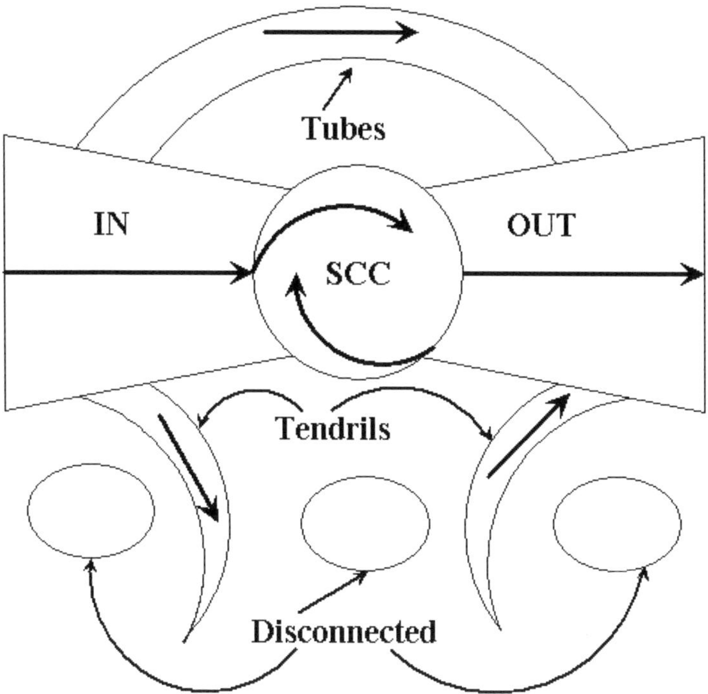

Figure 2.4 Bow-tie shape of the Web.

2.3.2 Small-World Structure of the Web

This study of the Web also revealed some other interesting properties regarding the structure and navigability of the Web. It turns out that over 75% of the time there is no directed path of links from one random web page to another. When such a path exists, its average distance is 16 clicks and when an undirected path exists (i.e., one allowing backward traversal of links) its average distance is only seven clicks.

Thus, the Web is a *small-world network* [674] popularly known through the notion of "six degrees of separation," where any two random people in the world can discover that there is only a short chain of at most six acquaintances between them. Well, not quite six degrees of separation for the Web, but on an average close enough if you consider undirected paths. Moreover, since in a small-world network the average distance between any two nodes is logarithmic in the number of pages in the network, a 10-fold increase in the size of the Web would only lead to the average distance increasing by a few clicks. (We will discuss small-world networks in more detail in Section 9.6.7.)

The *diameter* of a graph is the maximum shortest distance between any two nodes in the graph. It was found that the diameter of the SCC of the web graph is at least 28 but when considering the Web as a whole, the diameter is at least 500; this longest path is from the most distant node in IN to the most distant node in OUT.

Although the average distance between nodes in the Web is small, this does not imply that it is easy to find a path leading from any web page to another. In fact, Jon Kleinberg [376] investigated this problem in a setting where he assumed that the likelihood of adding a link from one page to another decreases with the distance, in the existing network, of the target page from the source page. He showed that in an idealized network structure, where the likelihood of adding a link between two pages is proportional to the inverse square of their distance, there is a simple algorithm that efficiently finds a short path to the destination page. The method follows the "greedy" heuristic, which implies that at each stage you should choose to follow the link to the page that brings you closest to the destination sought after. (We discuss Kleinberg's algorithm and its variants in more detail in Section 9.7.4.)

2.4 INFORMATION SEEKING ON THE WEB

What are the processes we might follow when trying to find information on the Web? The broad term we will use for this type of activity is *information seeking*. Depending on what information you need, the activity you intend to carry out, and your level of sophistication, there are several different strategies you may follow.

2.4.1 Direct Navigation

The simplest strategy is *direct navigation* when the web site address (or URL) is entered directly into the browser. This strategy is often successful for finding home pages of companies such as www.ibm.com, institutions such as www.mit.edu, e-commerce sites such as www.amazon.com, and services such as www.cnn.com. Direct navigation is less successful for finding products such as Apple's MacBook or HP's iPAQ, since these do not necessarily map directly to the required web addresses. The user can augment the direct navigation strategy with some surfing activity. So, to find information on the iPAQ, the user may first enter www.hp.com into his or her browser, follow the link to handheld devices, and then follow a further link to a relevant page.

In trying to pinpoint the information needed, the user will probably click on further links and make use of the back button to return to previously browsed pages. At all times when users are surfing they will pick up proximal cues such as snippets of text and images, which the web site designer put in place to help users orient themselves and find information. Sometimes to find a product, a fortuitous guess, in this case www.apple.com/macbook, will deliver the desired web page directly.

RealNames, now a defunct dot-com,[35] had the ingenious idea of mapping keywords to web addresses, so if HP purchased the keyword iPAQ, entering

[35]RealNames to close after losing Microsoft. http://searchenginewatch.com/sereport/article.php/2164841.

"ipaq" into the browser would direct the user straight to the relevant page in www.hp.com, or depending on the user's location to the relevant page within his or her local HP web site. This idea of navigation by keywords also has the advantage of allowing multilingual access, as the keywords could be entered in any language. However, there are also problems with this approach, some of which are common with domain names; for example, who should be allowed to own popular keywords such as "car" and "computer" and what about spelling mistakes and singular and plural forms. There may also be some confusion that could arise between domain names and keywords, since to be useful there would have to be some consistency between these two mechanisms of addressing web pages.

Another common direct navigation strategy is to make use of the bookmarks or history facilities, which are built into the browser. Both will be discussed in more detail in Section 7.2, when we introduce the different navigation tools that are available. In any case, the use of these tools may have to be augmented by surfing in order to locate the exact information we are seeking.

As URLs can be quite long, sometimes due to passing attributes in the URL within the query string, URL shortening can be quite useful. Two URL shortening services are: www.tinyurl.com and http://bit.ly. As an example, the tinyURL for www.dcs.bbk.ac.uk is: http://tinyurl.com/yldurb5 and the bit.ly URL is: http://bit.ly/v9dfJ. From a direct navigation point of view, although there is less to type in to the toolbar, the shortened URL will be hard to remember and obscures the target URL. (Also, if the service ceases to operate the shortened URLs will become stale.)

Browser features such as Firefox's *awesome bar* make it easier to directly navigate to web pages by allowing users to type into the browser a term in a URL, the title of a web page or a user-defined tag associated with the page, with the additional help of an auto-complete facility.

2.4.2 Navigation within a Directory

A *web portal* is a web site that provides a gateway, or an entry point, to other resources on the Web. Examples of portals are www.msn.com, www.aol.com, www.netscape.com, and www.yahoo.com. Web portals provide a broad range of features, services, and content. Of special interest to the information seeker are portals that are organized in the form of a subject directory such as Yahoo Directory (http://dir.yahoo.com) and the Open Directory (www.dmoz.org). Web directories consist of a topic categorization, including amongst other categories: Arts, Business, Computers and Internet, Entertainment, Government, News, and Science. So, to find information on search engines and directories from the Yahoo Directory, you will have to follow the topic hierarchy from the Computers and Internet category to the Internet, then to the World Wide Web, next to Searching the Web, and finally to Search Engines and Directories, which will give you several relevant sites and suggest several additional subcategories you can investigate to find what you need.

Directories organize the information in a natural manner, where the sites in the directory are compiled by human editors. *Navigating through a directory* as an information-seeking strategy is useful for a novice but may lead to frustration depending on how specific the information need is and how many different categories the user needs to navigate through. Also, there is the issue of coverage discussed earlier, as compared to the billions of web pages indexed by the main search engines, the Yahoo Directory lists only several million web pages.[36] To overcome the problem of coverage, directory services either partner with a web search engine such as Google to provide supplementary answers for their users' queries, or they power their own search using proprietary search engine technology.[37]

2.4.3 Navigation using a Search Engine

As web search engines' quality has been steadily increasing in the last few years, and with it the rise of Google as a leader in the field, more surfers are turning to search engines to provide them with an entry point web page to help them satisfy their information needs.

For the *search engine strategy*, a user seeking information on the Web will normally iterate through the following steps (Fig. 2.5):

1. *Query formulation*: the user submits a query to a search engine specifying his or her goal; normally a query consists of one or more input keywords.
2. *Selection*: the user selects one of the web pages from the ranked results list returned by the search engine, clicks on the link to that page, and browses the page once it is loaded into the browser.

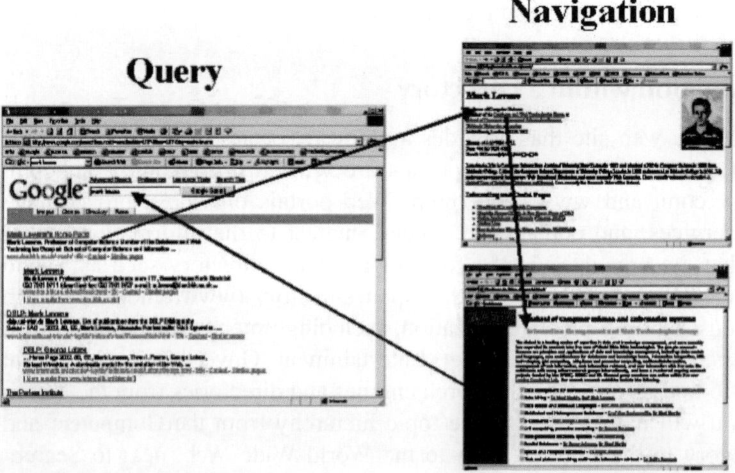

Figure 2.5 Information seeking.

[36]ODP and Yahoo size projection charts. www.geniac.net/odp.

[37]Who powers whom? Search providers chart, by D. Sullivan, July 2004. http://searchenginewatch.com/reports/article.php/2156401.

3. *Navigation (or surfing)*: the user initiates a navigation session, which is the process of clicking on links and browsing the pages displayed. The user surfing the Web by following links will use various cues and tools to augment his or her navigational activity.
4. *Query modification*: a navigation session may be interrupted for the purpose of query modification, when the user decides to reformulate the original query and resubmit it to the search engine. In this case, the user *returns* to step (1).

2.4.4 Problems with Web Information Seeking

There are several problems with information seeking on the Web. First, the Web is an open system which is in constant flux: new sites appear, old ones change or disappear, and in general the content is emergent rather than planned. This implies that results are not stable and that users may need to vary their strategy over time to satisfy similar needs.

Secondly, the quality of information on the Web is extremely variable and the user has to make a judgment. For example, if you submit the query "search engine tutorial" to any of the major search engines you will get many thousands of results. Even if you restrict yourselves to the top 10 ranked tutorials, the ranking provided by the search engine does not necessarily correlate with quality, since the presented tutorials may not have been peer reviewed by experts in a proper manner, if at all.

Thirdly, factual knowledge on the Web is not objective, so if you want to find out who is the president of the United States you may get several answers. In this case you may trust the White House web site to give you a correct answer but other sites may not be so trustworthy.

Finally, since the scope of the Web is not fixed, in many cases we do not know in advance if the information is out there. There is uncertainty hanging in the air that does not diminish after we do not find what we are looking for during the first search attempt. For example, if you are looking for a book which may be out of print, you can try several online second-hand book stores and possibly try and locate the publisher if their web site can be found. As another example, you may be looking for a research report and not know if it has been published on the Web. In this case, you may look up the author's home page, or the name of the report if it is known to you, or alternatively, you may try and find out if the institution at which the report was published maintains an online copy. In such cases, you will have to combine several strategies and several search sessions before you find what you are looking for, or simply give up.

The choice of appropriate strategy also depends on the user's expertise. Novice users often prefer to navigate from web portals which provide them with directory services. One reason for this is that their home page is by default set to that of their service provider, and being unaware of other search services they are content to use the portal put in front of them. Once a user learns to use search engines and becomes web savvy, he or she can mix the various strategies

I have described. As search engines make it easier to find web sites and pages with relevant information, more users are turning to web search engines as their primary information-seeking strategy. One interesting by-product of this shift to search engines is that users spend less time navigating within web sites and tend to jump from one site to another using the search results list as a guide from which to choose the next site to jump to.[38]

2.5 INFORMATIONAL, NAVIGATIONAL, AND TRANSACTIONAL QUERIES

A useful taxonomy of web searches was devised by Andrei Broder, the former vice president of research at AltaVista [106]. Broder argues that the "need behind the query" is often not informational, and divides queries into three categories:

1. *Informational*: when the user's intent is to acquire some information about a topic presumed to be present in one or more web pages.
2. *Navigational*: when the user's intent is to find a particular site from which to start surfing.
3. *Transactional*: when the user's intent is to perform some activity which is mediated by a web site, for example online shopping, or another web service such as news delivery, online library browsing, or some other specialist service.

Depending on the specification of the query and the quality of the search engine, the user issuing an informational or transactional query may satisfy his or her information need with minimal navigation and query modification. For example, if the user is interested in the details of a particular patent by a given author, he/she may find the information by first locating the site with the relevant patent database and then finding the patent through the tailored search interface.

Informational queries may be very wide such as "sports cars" or "London" or much more specific such as "e-type jaguar sports car" or "Tower of London".

As an example of a navigational query, suppose you intend to find out more about handheld devices and wish to compare the various models. This will definitely lead to a lengthy navigation session across several sites. Even if you can pinpoint a brand you are interested in, you may need to spend time surfing the manufacturer's and distributor's web sites, and possibly surf some independent consumer sites, to evaluate the different models that are available and their capabilities. From the search engine's point of view, the result of a typical navigational query will be the home page of the institution or organization most relevant to the query. So, the first result for the query "hp handheld" will typically be HP's home page for handheld devices, while the first result for the query "palm handheld" will be Palm's home page. When a navigational query is

[38]Information foraging: Why Google makes people leave your site faster, J. Nielsen, June, 2003. www.useit.com/alertbox/20030630.html.

accurately specified, a feature such as Google's "I'm Feeling Lucky" will bring you directly to the required home page.

As an example of a transactional query, the keywords "bargains online bookshop", would point the user toward online bookshops, where further interaction with the user will take place within the online bookshop rather than with the web search engine. In this case the user will probably interact with a search service local to the online bookshop, in order to pinpoint the bargain he or she is after and, in addition, may have to navigate within the bookshop's web site to find the information needed.

A generalization of transactional queries is the category of resource queries [576]. Such queries satisfy resource goals such as downloading a file, viewing some content such as a movie clip, interacting with a dynamic site such as a currency converter, or obtaining a map that can then be printed out.

2.6 COMPARING WEB SEARCH TO TRADITIONAL INFORMATION RETRIEVAL

Traditional IR systems normally index a closed collection of documents, which are mainly text-based and usually offer little linkage between documents. Traditional IR systems are often referred to as *full-text retrieval systems*. Libraries were among the first to adopt IR to index their catalogs and later, to search through information which was typically imprinted onto CD-ROMs. The main aim of traditional IR was to return relevant documents that satisfy the user's information need. Although the main goal of satisfying the user's need is still the central issue in web IR (or web search), there are some very specific challenges that web search poses that have required new and innovative solutions.

- The first important difference is the scale of web search, as we have seen that the current size of the web is approximately 600 billion pages. This is well beyond the size of traditional document collections.
- The Web is dynamic in a way that was unimaginable to traditional IR in terms of its rate of change and the different types of web pages ranging from static types (HTML, portable document format (PDF), DOC, Postscript, XLS) to a growing number dynamic pages written in scripting languages such a JSP, PHP or Flash. We also mention that a large number of images, videos, and a growing number of programs are delivered through the Web to our browsers.
- The Web also contains an enormous amount of duplication, estimated at about 30% [295]. Such redundancy is not present in traditional corpora and makes the search engine's task even more difficult.
- The quality of web pages vary dramatically; for example, some web sites create web pages with the sole intention of manipulating the search engine's ranking, documents may contain misleading information, the information on some pages is just out of date, and the overall quality of a web page

may be poor in terms of its use of language and the amount of useful information it contains. The issue of quality is of prime importance to web search engines as they would very quickly lose their audience if, in the top-ranked positions, they presented to users poor quality pages.

- The range of topics covered on the Web is completely open, as opposed to the closed collections indexed by traditional IR systems, where the topics such as in library catalogues, are much better defined and constrained.
- Another aspect of the Web is that it is globally distributed. This poses serious logistic problems to search engines in building their indexes, and moreover, in delivering a service that is being used from all over the globe. The sheer size of the problem is daunting, considering that users will not tolerate anything but an immediate response to their query. Users also vary in their level of expertise, interests, information-seeking tasks, the language(s) they understand, and in many other ways.
- Users also tend to submit short queries (between two to three keywords), avoid the use of anything but the basic search engine syntax, and when the results list is returned, most users do not look at more than the top 10 results, and are unlikely to modify their query. This is all contrary to typical usage of traditional IR.
- The hypertextual nature of the Web is also different from traditional document collections, in giving users the ability to surf by following links. On the positive side (for the Web), there are many roads (or paths of links) that "lead to Rome" and you need only find one of them, but often, as we will discuss later, users lose their way in the myriad of choices they have to make.

Another positive aspect of the Web is that it has provided and is providing impetus for the development of many new tools, whose aim is to improve the user's experience. This is one of the main topics I will address throughout. It is fair to say that the advances in the last 10 years in the area of web search are impressive.

2.6.1 Recall and Precision

Suppose we have a corpus of documents and we can mark the subset of those which are relevant to a given query. The retrieved set of documents by the search engine and its overlap with the relevant set is shown in Fig. 2.6. The *precision* is the amount of overlap divided by the number of documents retrieved and the *recall* is the amount of overlap divided by the number of relevant documents. Ideally, we would like the search engine's results to have both high precision, when it returns *only* relevant pages, and high recall, when it returns *all* the relevant results. In practice when we increase the recall, that is, we increase the number of web pages returned to the user, then the precision is decreased, since, overall, there will most likely be more irrelevant web pages returned.

For the Web, the measurement of recall is not very useful as such, especially as users will only scan few of the result pages. In a broad sense, recall on the

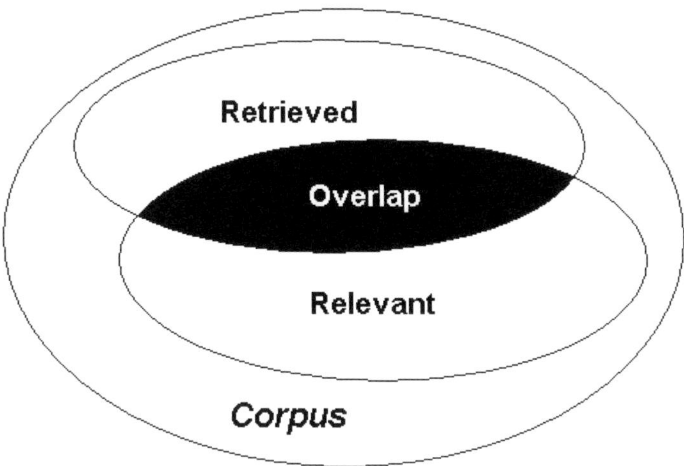

Figure 2.6 Recall versus precision.

Web is related to search engine coverage. If the coverage of the search engine is higher, that is, it indexes a larger proportion of the Web, and assuming that its search algorithms are of a satisfactory standard, it can achieve high precision. Moreover, a search engine with low coverage cannot expect to achieve high precision for a large variety of queries.

On the Web, precision is most important, and in particular, top-*n* precision, which is the number of relevant answers in the top-*n* ranked pages returned to the user. So, if users do not normally inspect more than 10 pages, measuring the top-10 precision makes sense. We will discuss these and other methods to evaluate search engines in Section 5.4.

To evaluate their search engines, the IR community has an annual competition organized by the National Institute of Standards and Technology (NIST). The Text REtrieval Conference (TREC),[39] as it is called, has been conducted since 1992 and the number of participating groups has grown over the years. For example, in 2003, 93 groups from 22 countries participated. For each TREC, data sets and queries are posted well before the conference, and the participants install the data sets on their computers and run the queries using their search engine. They then return the top-ranked retrieved results from their search engine to NIST, and NIST evaluates the results against predetermined relevance judgments. The TREC cycle ends with a workshop that is a forum for publishing the results of the competition. TREC is divided into several tracks, focusing on different types of retrieval tasks. The track that we are interested in is the web track, where the data set is a snapshot of web pages. One of the important tasks in the web track is home page–finding, since often, the best a search engine can

[39]Text REtrieval Conference (TREC) to encourage research in information retrieval from large text collections. http://trec.nist.gov.

do is bring the user to a relevant home page, which will be a starting point for a user navigation session.

The commercial web search engines have so far not participated in this competition. Admittedly, they have more to lose by not scoring well and there is the possibility of exposing some of the weaknesses in their system but there are probably other reasons. Running a commercial search engine is a serious business. Gone are the days when a leading web search engine can be managed by a few talented researchers in a well-funded lab. As we have seen, there are different kinds of information needs for different users and different queries. Although the corpus used for the Web TREC appears to have a structure similar to the Web as a whole [616], it is closed in nature and the relevance measurements do not necessarily reflect the variety of web users and tasks. These issues are being refined every year in TREC but it may be that the web search engines are just too busy to participate; still, their absence is noted.

2.7 LOCAL SITE SEARCH VERSUS GLOBAL WEB SEARCH

A Forrester report from June 2000 entitled "Must Search Stink?" [278] attracted attention to the fact that as individual web sites have grown in size, the quality of the site's search engine should be given higher priority. According to Nielsen "search is the user's lifeline for mastering complex web sites,"[40] and users often prefer using the search box prior to surfing within a site in order to save themselves time in locating the information they need, instead of following links from the home page.

To distinguish between local site search engines (often referred to as *enterprise search engines*) that operate on an individual web site and web search engines such as Google and Yahoo that provide global web search, we will refer to the former as *site search* and to the latter as *web search*.

It seems that poor quality site search is costing organizations millions of dollars per year and according to an IDC (international data corporation) bulletin from 2002 [213], every technical question that is answered automatically saves the company the $30 it would cost to pay a person to give the answer.

Studies of web sites are consistently telling us that well over 50% of queries within these sites are unsuccessful.[41] On the other hand, as web search is getting better,[42] user satisfaction when searching the Web as a whole is increasing well beyond the 50% mark. Admittedly, many web searches are "known item searches," which are informational and more specifically characterize the situation when we know exactly what we are searching for, and it is easy to verify

[40]Search: Visible and simple, J. Nielsen, Alertbox, May 2001. www.useit.com/alertbox/20010513.html.

[41]Why search engines fail, by C. Sherman, August 2002. http://searchenginewatch.com/searchday/article.php/2160661.

[42]NPD search and portal site study, by D. Sullivan, July 2002. www.searchenginewatch.com/sereport/article.php/2162791.

whether the answer satisfies the search criteria. Examples of known item searches are looking for a particular article by an author, looking for a particular type of car or looking for a piece of music by a known composer. But obviously, the site search problem is much easier than solving web search; for a starter, just consider the issue of scale faced by the web search engines. It may be the case that if one of the major search engines decided to spend more of their resources to tailor their search to individual web sites, then the situation would improve. There has been some effort in this direction, for example with the release of Google's search appliance,[43] but it remains to be seen if this tool on its own can turn tables on the bad reputation of site search. However, two advantages that Google's search appliance has over its competitors in this space are brand awareness and ease of use [519].

The rise and fall of site search engines is an ongoing saga and as new players join the market, older players either get swallowed up by the bigger players or disappear from the scene. More sophisticated enterprise search tools as delivered by Autonomy (www.autonomy.com), provide a more integrated solution with a company's content but are very expensive to deploy and the lock-in effect to the product is much greater than a simple search solution.[44]

So why has site search been neglected?

- It may be that our expectations from web search are lower than from site search. For example, if the web search engine directs us to the relevant home page within a relevant site, we may be satisfied with the search result and then blame the local site search engine for not directing us to the relevant page within the site.
  But regardless of the statistics that are hurled at us, there are other genuine reasons for the overall lack of good site search.[45]
- Many companies are not willing to invest in site search; maybe because they spend all of their web development budget on web site design and little cash is left in the kitty, or maybe they feel that since web search is free why should site search cost them anything. To some degree, good web site design, which includes useful navigation tools, can compensate for bad site search but for large web sites such as corporate, institutional, and government sites, this argument is very thin.
- There are other issues with site search that differentiate it from web search. Much of a web site's data may reside in searchable databases; that is, it may be part of the hidden web, and, moreover, it may not be straightforward to integrate this information into the site's search engine. This is part of the wider issue of content management and the integration of different types of content that are potentially searchable such as product data, company documents, and multimedia.

[43]Google search appliance. www.google.com/enterprise/search/gsa.html.

[44]Search on, by T. Kontzer, January 2003. www.informationweek.com/story/IWK20030117S0006.

[45]Why good sites lack search engines, by C. Sherman, August 2002. http://searchenginewatch.com/searchday/article.php/2160611.

- Another problem we have not mentioned is that of language. As the major web search engines are biased toward the English language, this is an undeniable opportunity for local language-specific search engines to flourish [49].
- There is also the problem of searching an *intranet*, which is an internal network that is used inside an organization and does not have a public face. Integrating all the intranet information including databases and e-mail, may demand more than a standard search engine and in addition, there are serious issues of security and authorization of information.

A paper presented at the World Wide Web Conference in 2003 studied the problem of intranet search at IBM [210]. One major difference between intranets and the Web as a whole, is that the structure and content of intranets is driven by the management of the company rather than by a democratic or chaotic process, and new content generally needs managerial approval. The aim of intranet documents is mainly for dissemination of information and internal procedures and therefore, a large number of queries may have a limited answer set. It was found that on the IBM site many of the queries used specific jargon, acronyms, and abbreviations, which need to be taken into account by the site's search engine. Another interesting complication that arose is that, in the situation where the intranet is geographically dispersed, as in the case with IBM, the answer to a query may be specific to a location.

- It has also been argued that site search should reflect the tasks that users wish to carry out on the site [291]. In particular, in many cases, to satisfy their information need, users will need to combine keyword search with surfing along links corresponding to the site's structure. So if the site is one containing cooking recipes, it may be organized into a directory structure much like Yahoo, according to some specific culinary categorization. Users can be provided with different interfaces to accommodate for different tasks within the site. There could be a basic keyword search interface for users to find a good starting point for navigation, an enhanced search following the directory structure of the site, and a browsing interface to allow users to navigate efficiently through and across categories. There is a good argument that search and navigation need to be combined, and we will delve deeper into this issue in Chapter 7, when we focus our attention on navigation.

In summary, there are various problems with site search that need to be addressed separately to web search as a whole, before users' satisfaction levels with the search box on web sites will reach acceptable levels. One conclusion is that a local site search engine should reach the parts of the site that the web search engines do not reach.

2.8 DIFFERENCE BETWEEN SEARCH AND NAVIGATION

Going back to the information-seeking strategy shown in Fig. 2.5 makes the difference clear. Suppose you are searching for information on Arthur Samuel's seminal work in machine learning. The overall information-seeking process is a search process, where complementary strategies can be deployed. In the context of the Web as a whole, the main search mechanisms are the use of search engines and surfing. So when we say "searching" the Web for information we mean employing a search engine to help us find the information we seek, and when we say "navigating" or "surfing" the Web, we mean employing a link-following strategy starting from a given web page, to satisfy our information need. The information-seeking strategy that is steadily becoming the most used and useful strategy on the Web is the search engine strategy, which combines search and navigation in a natural way.

To start your information-seeking session you may type the keywords "samuel machine learning" to a web search engine; this is search. The title of one of the web pages that appears in the top 10 hits returned is "Arthur Samuel", you click on the link (http://www-db.stanford.edu/pub/voy/museum/samuel.html) and get a web page about him and his pioneering work in machine learning. You learn that he developed a computer program to play checkers and that he wrote influential papers in the area, that are still worth studying. The process you have gone through to extract this information from the web page is called *browsing*. You add the keyword "checkers" to the search engine box and one of the top 10 hits on the results page leads you to a description of Samuel's artificial checkers player (www.cs.ualberta.ca/~sutton/book/11/node3.html). From that page, you can surf to a page about TD-Backgammon, which is a world-class backgammon program developed by Gerald Tesauro at IBM. If you haven't picked this one up already, Samuel was also working at IBM at the time he developed his checkers program. (Incidently, the chess computer Deep Blue that defeated world chess champion, Garry Kasparov, in May 1997 was also developed at IBM.) TD-Backgammon was heavily influenced by Samuel's machine learning research. In fact, if you dig a bit deeper, you will find that Samuel used a technique, later called *temporal difference learning*, that is an important form of reinforcement learning. You will have to do some more searching and navigating to find out that Samuel's seminal paper was called "Some studies in machine learning using the game of checkers," and that it was originally published in IBM's Journal of Research and Development in 1959. A little more effort and clicking will lead you to the web page within IBM's journals site, where you can download a PDF file containing the paper [584]. So by a judicious combination of search and navigation, together with browsing, you can learn many useful facts about Samuel's contribution to machine learning, one of them being the fact that Samuel's program was probably the first one that could improve itself without human intervention.

CHAPTER SUMMARY

- In 2004, the Web was estimated to have over 8 billion pages, based on the index size reported by one of the leading web search engines, Google. A more recent estimate from May 2005, that the size of the Web is more than 11.5 billion pages [272], uses the statistical capture–recapture method. As of 2010 our estimate of the size of the Web is approximately 600 billion web pages, much larger than what was thought a few years back, and it is still growing.

- As of 2009, about a quarter of the world's population is connected to the Internet. From a variety of statistics, we highlight that aggregated together, the most popular web search engines have to process billions of queries per day.
- As opposed to database tables, web data is organized as a network of web pages, with no fixed structure imposed on it. As opposed to a database query, which is a precise statement with a fixed answer, a search engine query is normally free-text, and the answers are returned in the form of a ranked list of pages the search engine considers to be the most relevant to the query.
- The Web has a bow-tie structure, its main components being (i) the SCC, where any two pages can reach each other by following links; (ii) the IN component, whose pages can lead to those in the SCC; and (iii) the OUT component, whose pages can be reached from those in the SCC. The Web is small-world network, in the sense that short paths exist between any two pages in the SCC, although these short paths may not be easy to find.
- There are several strategies for information seeking on the Web. In direct navigation, the site's address is entered directly into the browser. In navigating within a directory structure, such as Yahoo or the Open Directory, navigation is carried out within a topic hierarchy. In the search engine strategy, users take advantage of a search engine to help them find a web page that may satisfy their goals or provide a good starting point for navigation. Information seeking on the Web is problematic as the Web is continuously changing, the quality of information is is extremely variable and may be misleading, and there is often uncertainty on whether the information is even available on the Web.
- A useful taxonomy of web searches divides queries into three categories: informational, navigational, and transactional.
- Web search is different from traditional IR in several respects. The scale of web search is well beyond traditional IR, there is a large amount of duplication on the Web, which is not present in traditional corpora, the quality of web pages is very variable, and the range of topics it covers is completely open. Moreover, the Web is global, distributed, and hypertextual in nature, and the queries submitted to search engines are typically much shorter than those submitted to traditional IR systems, and devoid of advanced syntax.
- Recall and precision are the important metrics by which traditional IR systems have been evaluated. In the context of a search engine, recall is related to the coverage of the search engine and as users do not normally inspect more than a screen full of results, precision is normally measured only with respect to the top-n results, where n is between 10 and 20.

- Search within a local web site (site search) differs from searching within the global web (web search). While users are becoming more satisfied with web search, site search is lagging behind. Reasons for this are our expectation from web search may be lower than those from site search; many companies are unwilling to invest in site search; site search may involve searching through corporate databases and other data such as e-mail, which is in the domain of content management systems; there are also problems to do with language as most search engines are biased toward English; and finally, site search maybe more task oriented than web search and thus best be catered for by combining search and navigation.

EXERCISES

2.1. **(Discuss)**. One of the challenges in site search (also known as *enterprise search* (288, 485)) is to provide an integrated search facility over a diverse set of information sources including web data, internal databases, e-mail, and a multitude of documents in different formats.

Discuss the problems of such an integration, making specific reference to dealing with unstructured data versus structured data, and the different types of queries that users may pose to different types of information sources.

2.2. **(Miniproject)**. Choose a web site which has a site search facility. Select several queries and submit them to both, the site search engine and also to one of the major search engines using the "site:web-site-name" query syntax, so that the queries are searched within the web site you have chosen.

Compare the search results from the site search and web search with reference to the quality of the returned search results, the coverage of the index and freshness of the results, the user interface, and the user interaction.

2.3. **(Explore)**. The Internet Archive (www.archive.org) provides access to previous copies of web pages through the *Wayback machine*.

Find out more about this service and how it works. Then trace the history of a selected web page of your choice, and comment on how and why it has changed.

2.4. **(Explore)**. Investigate Touchgraph's Google Browser (www.touchgraph.com/TGGoogle Browser.html), which displays pages similar to the one whose URL is used as input into the tool.

Discuss the utility of such an interface in the context of information seeking on the Web, and suggest features you think would be useful to add to it.

2.5. **(Miniproject)**. Given a web graph (i.e., the set of URLs of pages and the links between them), how could you efficiently compute the average distance between pages in the graph? (Hint: use a breadth-first search strategy.)

Test out your procedure on a portion of the web graph of a web site of your choice.

2.6. **(Explore)**. Google's "browse by name" feature of its toolbar allows you to type a keyword or a phrase into the address bar of the browser, instead of a URL.

Find out about the behavior of this feature, and compare it to Google's "I'm Feeling Lucky" feature.

Discuss the merits and limitations of this feature as a form of direct navigation.

CHAPTER 3

THE PROBLEM OF WEB NAVIGATION

"We never, ever in the history of mankind have had access to so much information so quickly and so easily."

— Vint Cerf, Father of the Internet

WEB NAVIGATION, also known as *surfing*, involves browsing web pages and clicking on hyperlinks. Combined with the use of search engines this activity dominates information seeking. To support surfing, the navigation problem of "getting lost in hyperspace" must be dealt with. We argue that machine learning is a technology that can be used to improve user interaction, and that Markov chains are a natural model of web user navigation.

CHAPTER OBJECTIVES

- Explain how the navigation problem arises when we surf the web.
- Motivate the use of machine learning algorithms for developing technologies that can adapt to users' behavior and improve web interaction.
- Introduce the naive Bayes classifier and its application to automatic classification of web pages.
- Introduce the notion of trails on the web, and argue that trails should be first class objects that are supported by the tools we use to interact with the web.
- Introduce the notion of a Markov chain in the context of the web.
- Explain how Markov chain probabilities can be used to reason about surfers' navigation behavior.
- Explain how Markov chain probabilities can be used to measure the relevance of links to surfers.

An Introduction to Search Engines and Web Navigation, by Mark Levene

- Explain the potential conflict between the objectives of the web site owner and users visiting the site.
- Explain the potential conflict between the navigability of a web site and its business model.

3.1 GETTING LOST IN HYPERSPACE AND THE NAVIGATION PROBLEM

Let us go back to users' search engine strategy, which is central to our information seeking process. It combines search and navigation in an iterative loop where the user inputs a query, does some navigation, and repeats this process until the information is found or the user gives up.

Employing a search engine and surfing are two separate activities that dominate our information seeking quest. In a typical information seeking session, we jump to and from the search engine's results list, which makes the process more difficult. Also, when browsing a web page and in the midst of a navigation session, the search engine does not help us in choosing the best link to follow given the goal we wish to achieve. There is a strong argument here for providing a rich set of navigation tools that are aware of the user's goals; we will pursue the issue of navigation tools in Chapter 7. Unless the information need is very specific such as "find me a known document by a known author," the user will have to carry out some navigation. No matter how much search engines improve we cannot bypass the fundamental process of surfing, which is after all what makes the web unique. Even in cases where navigation is the dominant activity, search engines play a crucial role, since they are good at directing us to relevant home pages, which are usually relevant starting points for us to navigate from.

When surfing we pick up any cues available on the web page we are browsing, such as link text (also known as *anchor text*), in order to make an informed choice of which link to click on. So, if you are browsing the home page of HP (www.hp.com) and looking for information on the iPAQ computing device, you will probably first click on the link to "handheld devices" and then follow one of the links to "iPAQ Pocket PCs." It is easy to navigate when we know exactly what we want and the web site is helping us with relevant link text.

If we were surfing by randomly following links, then the probability of finding anything useful would be infinitesimal as the number of links on a web page is on an average between seven and eight [396]. So, a positive navigation experience depends on how focused our information need is, how we make best use of the tools available to us, and on the design quality of the web site we are surfing through.

If, for example, the search is quite broad, say finding out about "neural networks," we will quickly get frustrated unless we focus the search. This is especially true as we normally only scan through the first results page of a search engine, typically only navigate through a few web pages, usually between one and three, and do very little query modification if at all. Even if our query is focused, say we are looking for a multiauthor document, it may be hard to satisfy the query as that document could reside in several places, for example, on the home page of one of the authors or somewhere within the site of the institution one of them is working for, or on a publisher's web site.

All these factors mean that navigation is not always easy to carry out and often involves anxiety as a result of a feeling of disorientation. As another example, my wife and I were looking to buy a new mattress and got attracted to a recent innovation that uses a special type of foam instead of the traditional springs. We had some idea of the companies that were selling this mattress but wanted to find out more about the benefits, durability and price of the product. Our search ended up in very little new information; we did not glean from our local bricks and mortar store, as any useful facts that may have been out there were buried deep within web sites and not easily found by navigation. Our searches were either too specific or too general and surfing the, supposedly relevant, web sites did not yield many useful results.

This problem of users "getting lost in hyperspace" is one of the central unresolved problems of web interaction. It comes from a feeling of frustration of not finding the information we are looking for and from a feeling of disorientation within the web site we are surfing through.

Let us look at a simple concrete example to illustrate how the navigation problem may arise (Fig. 3.1). Suppose you are surfing the Department of Computer Science and Information Systems' web site looking for information on our research in the area of Web Technologies. You click on the following links starting from the Department's home page (SCSIS),

first Research *then* Activities *followed by* WebTech *and finally* My home page

There are many interesting links on my home page. You see a link to heuristic games and click on it. If you continue to be sidetracked and follow some of my game links you will very quickly feel the syndrome of being lost in hyperspace. You may find yourself reading an article on www.chessbase.com about a match between Kasparov and the chess program Fritz. But, this is way off what you set out to do, which was to find out about research in the area Web Technologies at Birkbeck. This is exactly the *navigation problem* we

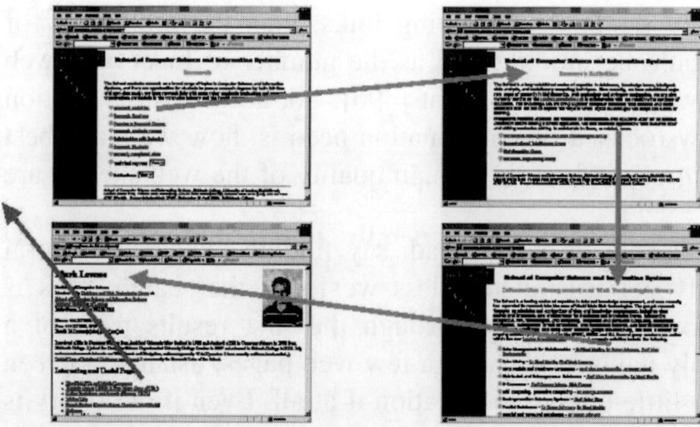

Figure 3.1 The navigation problem.

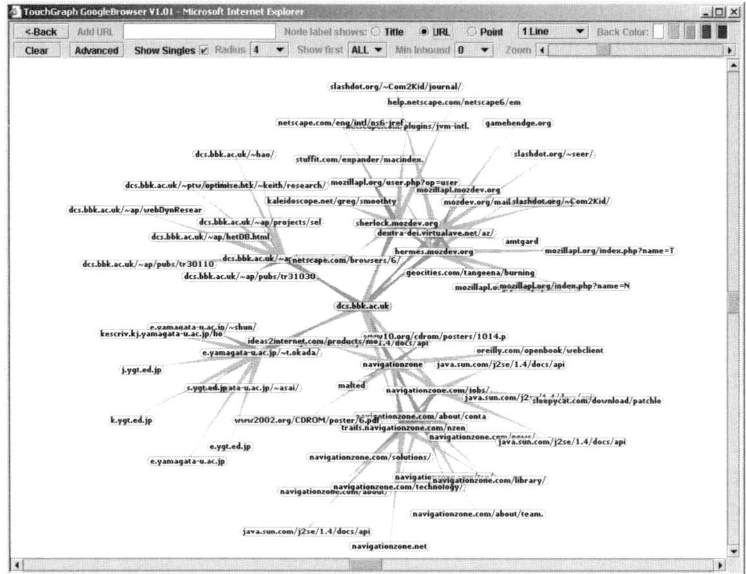

Figure 3.2 Being lost in hyperspace.

often face when we lose the context within which we are surfing, with respect to our original goal (Fig. 3.2, visualized using Touchgraph's Google Browser, www.touchgraph.com/TGGoogleBrowser.html).

When we are lost in hyperspace we are faced with the dilemma of what to do next. The first question we should ask ourselves is what was the original goal of our search session, and has this goal changed? Once we have established our goal, that is, our information need, we can ask ourselves three further critical questions [504]:

1. Where are we now relative to some landmark page such as the home page?
2. Where did we come from and can we return to a previously browsed page?
3. Where can we go to now from here and what should we do next to achieve our original goal?

A *landmark page* is a prominent page such as the home page or a resource list page that is central in terms of enabling the user to reach other relevant web pages.

- The first question is not always easy to answer unless there are some navigation tools to highlight the user's context within the current site that is being navigated through, and, more generally, within the context of the search session, which may span over several web sites.
- To answer the second question the history list and back button provided by the browser can come to our rescue. Again this is an issue of context, that is, knowing the past can help with the future. In our example, backtracking to the Web Technologies home page may be the most sensible option.

- Finally, to answer the third question the user first needs to establish what is the starting point for continuing his or her navigation. It may be that following a link on the currently browsed page is a good choice, or maybe first returning to a previous page, or even more drastically returning to the search engine's results page, if the navigation was initiated as a result of a query. Often, the best choice is simply to give up for now and have a break.

The navigation problem is becoming even more acute with the continuous growth of web sites in terms of their structure, which is becoming more complex, and their size in terms of the vast amount of information they intend to deliver. In contrast, users are not willing to invest time to learn this structure and expect transparent delivery of relevant content without delay. This problem needs to be tackled by orientation and navigation tools which improve user interaction, in analogy to the diverse set of tools ranging from road signs, the compass and map, to global positioning systems (GPS), all of which we use to orient ourselves in physical spaces.

3.2 HOW CAN THE MACHINE ASSIST IN USER SEARCH AND NAVIGATION

Our motto is that

> The machine should adapt to the user and not vice versa!!

Too many systems have been developed that demand us to plow through a myriad of help manuals to try and figure out what we can do and how to do it, and once we have figured this out the machine does not learn our preferences. I believe that the system should adapt to the user and not vice versa. Several machine learning techniques have matured in recent years and can provide a sound basis for improving the computer's understanding of the user who is using it and interacting with it. That is, the machine can learn from the user's interaction with it and adapt to their behavior and preferences.

3.2.1 The Potential Use of Machine Learning Algorithms

Arthur Samuel, mentioned in an earlier see section, was one of the pioneers of machine learning, who during the 1950s developed a checkers program that could improve its strength without human intervention by using reinforcement learning. Much like a human learning to play a game such as checkers or chess, Samuel's program could adapt its behavior so that the weights of positional features leading to the artificial player choosing good moves were increased relative to the weights of other features [306]. In the case of chess, features that are assessed may be material advantage, king safety, pawn structure, and so on. In the case of a personalization system using machine learning, the features are those contained in a user profile indicating the user's preferences. Some preferences may be demographic such as age, sex, occupation, and language of choice, and others may be related to the user's interests such as categories that provide a good match with his or her natural preferences and categories that can be gleaned from the user's surfing habits. Surfing habits can be measured, for example, from the average time spent browsing a page and the average number of keywords in queries the user entered into a search engine box. We defer a more detailed discussion of personalization to see Section 6.4, as one of the upcoming technologies that can improve many aspects of our interaction with the web.

We use the bookmarks tool to illustrate how adaptive technology can be useful. The bookmarks navigation tool is built into the browser to allow us to return to web pages that we have already visited and consider important enough to store as bookmarks. Most of us using the bookmarks tool keep on adding new URLs to the list at a much higher rate than we remove URLs from the list, implying that we find it difficult to manage our bookmarks. One problem that I have with my bookmarks is that, by default, the most recent one is added to the end of the list; that is, the bookmarks appear in reverse order of arrival. Using machine learning techniques the browser could readily learn which bookmarks are more popular and relevant to the user, and use this knowledge to filter these to the top of the list. (We discuss navigation tools in detail in see Section 7.2.)

As several machine learning techniques have matured in recent years, these can provide a sound basis for improving web interaction. With reference to personalization, the machine can build statistical models of the humans using it to improve its understanding of and reactions to the person it is interacting with.

We will not give details of the techniques available to web developers, but only list some of the key technologies: neural networks (NN), Bayesian networks, clustering, classification and decision trees (473, 455). Many of these techniques are already in use in web technologies under the broad banner of *web data mining* (128, 435), which is the topic of see Section 7.4.

3.2.2 The Naive Bayes Classifier for Categorizing Web Pages

The Yahoo directory, which contains several million web pages and over 150,000 categories, as of 1999 [399], is maintained by a team of human editors to ensure that new web pages match the criteria for inclusion and are slotted into the appropriate category.[46] Maintaining a human edited directory has several advantages, one of them being the human touch, which stands out positively in this age of the machine, and others to do with the overall quality of the directory. But the biggest problem of having human editors is to do with the scale of the operation. Although Yahoo does not disclose the exact number of editors it employs at any given time, it was commented in mid-2003 that on an average it uses "a building full

[46] A more recent estimate of the number of categories in Yahoo's directory has not been publicly available as of the beginning of 2010; see, Web Directory Sizes, by D. Sullivan, January 2003. http://searchenginewatch.com/reports/article.php/2156411.

of editors."[47] It is not known exactly how many full-time editors Yahoo employs, but the number is likely to be about 100 at any given time. In comparison to Yahoo, the Open Directory, which is a nonprofit project, contains, as reported on their home page at the beginning of 2010, over 4.5 million pages, over 590,000 categories and over 84,500 part-time editors all of whom are volunteers.[48]

This opens the door for machine text categorization techniques to be employed in order to widen the scope and size of web directories. A successful technique that has been widely deployed is the naive Bayes classifier, which despite making some simplifying statistical assumptions regarding the appearance of words in categories has proved to be as effective as more complex classification techniques.

The naive Bayes classifier is based on a statistical rule for computing probabilities developed by Reverend Thomas Bayes in the mid-eighteenth century in England. Consider the two categories "belief networks" (also known as *Bayesian networks*) and "neural networks", which are both subcategories of the "machine learning" category in the Open Directory. Suppose a new web page is submitted for inclusion in the machine learning category, then the editor must decide whether to classify it under belief networks (BN) or NN. If the document contains words such as "Bayesian" or "probability," it is more likely to be in the BN subcategory, whereas if it contains words such as "neural" or "perceptron" it is more likely to be in the NN subcategory.

Bayes rule allows us to assess the probability of a subcategory, say BN or NN, given the past evidence of previous documents that have already been classified under one of these subcategories, and tells us how to use this information to help classify new web pages such as the one that has just arrived. The previously classified documents in the category under scrutiny are called the *training set*. So, as an example, consider the probability that the new document (or web page) belongs to NN given the word "neural," and correspondingly the probability that it belongs to BN given this evidence.

First, we must consider the *prior* evidence, which is our belief that the document belongs to NN or BN before examining the detailed content of the training set. A simple estimation of our prior belief of the document being NN or BN could be the proportion of documents in the training set that are already classified as NN, or respectively as BN.

Second, we must compute the probability of the word, say "neural," appearing in a document belonging to a particular class. This probability is called the *likelihood* of the word given the class. In our case we can compute the likelihood of "neural" given NN, and correspondingly the likelihood of "neural" given BN, as follows. Count the number of times the word "neural" appears in the NN classified documents in the training set and divide by the total number of words appearing in the NN classified documents in the training set, including repetitions (so if a word appears 10 times in the document set it counts 10 toward

[47]The changing face of search engines, S. Olsen and J. Hu, March 2003, CNET News.com. http://news.com.com/2100-1032-993677.html.

[48]About the Open Directory project. www.dmoz.org/about.html.

the total number of words). That is, estimate the proportion of the word "neural" within the totality of words in NN documents from the training set, and similarly estimate the proportion of this word within the totality of words in BN documents.

Bayes rule now tells us that up to a normalization constant, the probability of a new document belonging to a given class, say NN, given that a word, say "neural," appears in this document is our prior belief of NN multiplied by the likelihood of "neural" given NN. Dividing the result by the normalization constant will ensure that the probability is between zero and one; the closer the result to one, the higher is its probability. Similarly, Bayes rule allows us to compute the probability of the new document belonging to BN given "neural."

Equation 3.1 describes Bayes rule more formally. C stands for the category, which in the above example is NN or BN, and f stands for a feature (or a set of features) such as the number of occurrences of a word in a document (or a set of such word occurrence counts) that are used to classify the document. $P(C)$ is the overall probability of the category C in the document space (the prior probability), $P(f)$ is the overall probability of the feature (the normalization constant), and $P(C, f)$ is the joint probability of C and f occurring; that is, of a document of category C having the feature f. $P(C \mid f)$ is the conditional probability of category C given the feature f occurring in a document and $P(f \mid C)$ is the probability of feature f given that the document's category is C (the likelihood).

Bayes Rule:

$$P(C \mid f) = \frac{P(C, f)}{P(f)} = \frac{P(f \mid C)P(C)}{P(f)} \tag{3.1}$$

The naive Bayes classifier makes the simplifying assumption that given a class, the words in a document are independent of each other. This assumption is not true in reality, since, for example, the term back propagation is a strong indication of belonging to NN; that is, the individual words "back" and "propagation" are not independent of each other. Nonetheless, assuming independence drastically reduces the complexity of computing the probabilities, and in practice naive Bayes has performed consistently well, often better than more sophisticated techniques [281].

Once we know the probability of a class given each word in the new web page being assessed for inclusion in the directory, the naive Bayes classifier can combine all the evidence by multiplying the probabilities together and choosing the class with a higher probability given the new web page. In our example, web pages containing words such as "neural," "back," "propagation," and "perceptron" will most likely lead to choosing NN as the appropriate subcategory, while words such as "Bayes," "probability," and "belief" will most likely lead us to choosing BN.

A formal statement of the simplifying assumption underlying naive Bayes classification is given in Equation 3.2; f_i, for $i = 1, 2, \ldots, n$, are the features such as the number of word occurrences in a document, and C is a class. The independence of the features given the class implies that the conditional probability can be evaluated as a product of the conditional probabilities of the individual features given the class.

Naive Bayes Assumption:

$$P(f_1, f_2, \ldots, f_n \mid C) = \prod_{i=1}^{n} P(f_i \mid C) \tag{3.2}$$

There is a subtlety that needs to take into account the situation of trying to classify a web page containing one or more words that appear in the training set of one of the categories but not in the other. The problem is that the probability of the word given the latter class may be zero, implying that combined probability for this class, computed using Equation 3.2, is also zero. A typical solution to this problem is to add *dummy* occurrences of such words to the training set so that these words have small, greater than zero, probability [473].

In summary, I believe that intelligent technology, based on machine learning, can deliver the next generation of search and navigation tools. (This is already happening to some degree as of 2010, but I hesitate at this moment in time to replace "next generation" with "current generation.") The idea is to shift to the machine more of the tasks that cannot be done manually due to their large scale, and to improve the interaction between human and the machine through personalization and collaboration technologies. The machine learning techniques must (i) *adapt* to changes in the environment, so if my interests change the machine should detect this; (ii) *learn* and improve its performance as more information becomes available from interaction; (iii) have *predictive* capabilities, so that it can anticipate what to do next; (iv) be *robust*, that is, continue to operate in the face of unexpected inputs; and (v) be *secure* and respect *privacy* [98].

3.3 TRAILS SHOULD BE FIRST CLASS OBJECTS

A *trail* is defined as a sequence of web pages through a web space. This definition of a trail is very general and effectively includes any sequence of web pages that a user has followed or can follow within a navigation session. A web space is normally a web site but in some cases may span over several sites, especially when the search engine's results list is guiding our choices or when we are using a resource list to find information.

Consider the simple web site shown in Fig. 3.3, which is a small subset of the Department's site. In Fig. 3.4, we highlight four trails starting from Mark's home page.

1. The first trail: *from* Mark *to* SCSIS.
2. The second trail: *from* Mark *to* SCSIS *then to* Staff *and finally back to* Mark.
3. The third trail: *from* Mark *to* SCSIS *then to* Research *then to* WebTech *and finally back to* Mark.

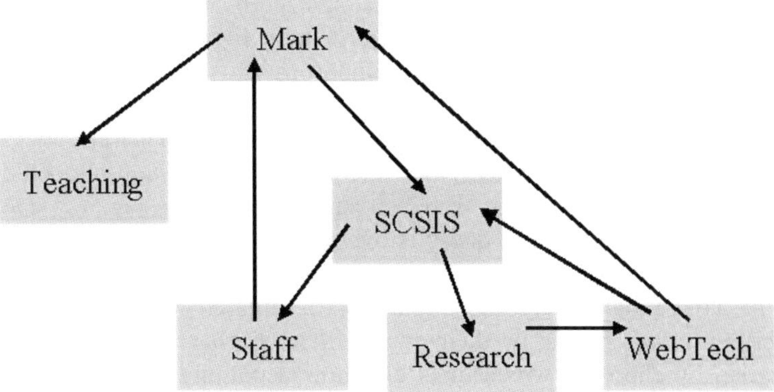

Figure 3.3 Example web site

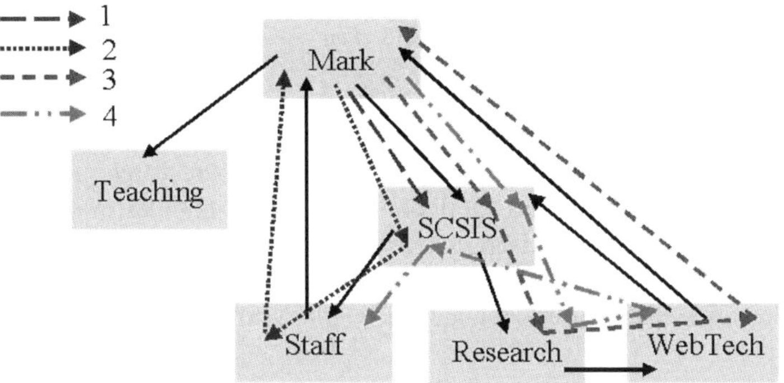

Figure 3.4 Four trails within the web site.

4. The fourth trail: *from* Mark *to* SCSIS *then to* Research *then to* WebTech *then back to* SCSIS *and finally to* Staff.

Trails can be created in several different ways. They can be *authored*, which means that they have been explicitly defined for a given purpose. Guided-tours are examples of authored trails, so the Department could author some trails which guide new students through key areas in its web site, and these can be enacted through some script followed by new students surfing the site. Trails can also be *derived* according to specific criteria, for example, as a result of a user query, or following the hierarchy of a web directory such as Yahoo. Finally, we have *emergent* trails that are created via repeated navigation through a web space. These may be *personal*, that is, trails that arise from an individual's activity, or *collaborative*, that is, trails that arise from a group activity through the space. So, for example, the trails in Fig. 3.4 could have emerged from navigation sessions of users who visited the web site and surfed it starting from Mark's home page.

In all cases *trails should be first class objects*, implying that the browser and the tools it supports should recognize trails. This is one of the central points that

I wish to make, and one that has already been recognized by Bush in 1945 and, over the years, by many researchers and practitioners in the hypertext community.

Search engines querying the web do *not* support trails as first class objects. So, for example, if you submit the query "mark research" to a search engine you will get a list of relevant web pages with little indication of what trails these pages may lead to. The highest ranked pages the search engine suggests could be Mark's home page followed by the WebTech page, as shown in Fig. 3.5, and some other web pages, assuming the query is over the entire Department's web site. This list, returned by the search engine, does *not* necessarily aid us in the intricate task of navigating through the Department's research web pages. It is left to the users to do the surfing on their own, without further assistance from the search engine, by choosing which links to follow according to the cues on the web pages being browsed.

In our example, a relevant trail for the query "mark research" may be the trail

> *starting from* Mark *then follow the link to* SCSIS *then the one to* Research *and finally the one to* WebTech

as shown in Fig. 3.6. This derived trail will guide the user from Mark's home page to the home page of the Database and Web Technologies research group.

To address the above mentioned shortcoming of search engines, a simple model of keyword search can be devised, where trails are first class objects. For a search engine, a web page that is returned should reasonably contain all the keywords that the user entered, and for a *trail engine* a trail that is returned

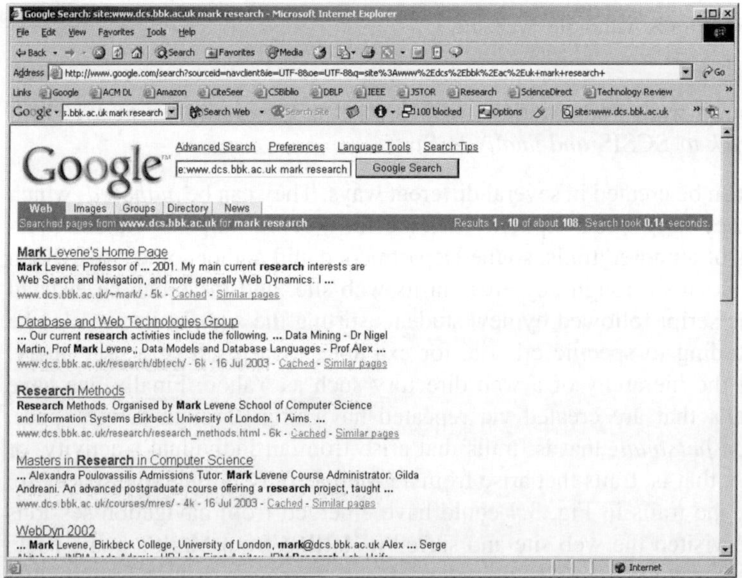

Figure 3.5 Search engine results for the query "mark research" submitted to Google.

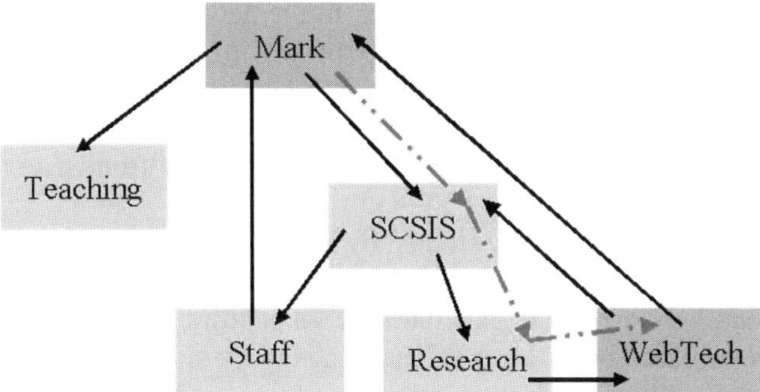

Figure 3.6 Relevant trail for the query "mark research."

could be such that each keyword appears in at least one of the pages in the trail. Note that a search engine query is a special case of trail engine query, where the returned trails are of length one. We consider the inner workings of a search engine and a trail engine in later chapters but for now let us consider how a trail engine can make sense of the tangled web of pages and links in order to form relevant trails for the user.

As we have mentioned earlier if we were to try and find trails by randomly surfing along links as we encounter them, then there would be no hope of finding anything useful. The trail engine needs to be a bit more intelligent and use some heuristics, or rules of thumb, which will allow it to search for relevant trails in a more guided manner. One important rule of thumb is to use "cues" present on the web pages and on the link text, which can help it "guess" what the next relevant link to click on maybe. The process of guessing can be viewed in terms of probabilities [279], where a guess is the result of tossing a biased dice with as many sides to it as there are links on the web page the surfer is browsing. The crucial issue here is how to bias the dice so that the guided search is more likely to visit relevant pages, or in other words what probabilities should be attached to the links so that relevant trails are more likely, and thus can be found effectively. We will address this issue in the next section.

3.4 ENTER MARKOV CHAINS AND TWO INTERPRETATIONS OF ITS PROBABILITIES

Markov chains are named after the Russian mathematician Andrei Andreyevich Markov who proposed them at the beginning of the twentieth century as a basic model of a stochastic process; that is, one involving chance.

3.4.1 Markov Chains and the Markov Property

A finite Markov chain may be described in brief terms as follows [365]. The Markov chain has a network structure much like that of a web site, where each node in the network is called a *state* and to each link in the network a *transition probability* is attached, which denotes the probability of moving from the source state of the link to its destination state. The process attached to a Markov chain moves through the states of the networks in *steps*, where if at any time the system is in state i, then with probability equal to the transition probability from state i to state j, it moves to state j.

Markov chains have been extensively studied by statisticians and have been applied in a wide variety of areas ranging from biology and economics to computing, linguistics, and sociology. Concrete examples are as follows: (i) branching processes, which are a special type of Markov chain, acting as models of population growth; (ii) random walks, which are also a special type of Markov chain, acting as models of stock market fluctuations; (iii) queueing theory, which builds on Markov chains; and (iv) simulation using Markov chain Monte Carlo methods.

In our case, we will model the transitions from one page to another in a web site as a Markov chain. The assumption we will make, called the *Markov property*, is that the probability of moving from a source page to a destination page does not depend on the route taken to reach the source. This assumption often holds in practice but can be relaxed when necessary.

Equation 3.3 formalizes the Markov property, where S_i, for $i = 1, 2, \ldots, t$, are states of the Markov chain. It says the probability of being in state S_t—given that at time 1 the Markov chain was in state S_1, at time 2 it was in state 2, and so on until time $t - 1$, when it was in state S_{t-1}—is independent of the *history* of the Markov chain prior to time $t - 1$. That is, the conditional probability of being in state S_t at time t is conditional only on the state S_{t-1} that the Markov chain was in at time $t - 1$.

Markov Property:

$$P(S_t \mid S_{t-1}, S_{t-2}, \ldots, S_2, S_1) = P(S_t \mid S_{t-1}) \tag{3.3}$$

3.4.2 Markov Chains and the Probabilities of Following Links

Let me explain how the process works in the context of surfing the web, and consider, in particular, the web site shown in Fig. 3.3. Mark, who is an experienced surfer, normally starts his navigation session from his home page, especially when he is surfing the Department's web site. Although Mark supposedly knows why he chose to follow a particular link, say leading to the Department's home page (SCSIS) rather than to the Teaching home page, all an observer of Mark's navigation sessions can say is that 70% of the time Mark clicked on the link leading to SCSIS from his home page, and 30% of the time he clicked the link leading to Teaching from his home page. If the statistics are stable, then given that Mark is browsing his home page, the machine can make a guess at which link Mark will follow by tossing a biased coin whose outcome will, on an average, be SCSIS 70 out 100 tosses and Teaching for the remaining 30 out of 100 tosses. Filling in the transition probabilities for each link in the web site that Mark has followed after observing his surfing behavior over a period time may lead to the Markov chain shown in Fig. 3.7.

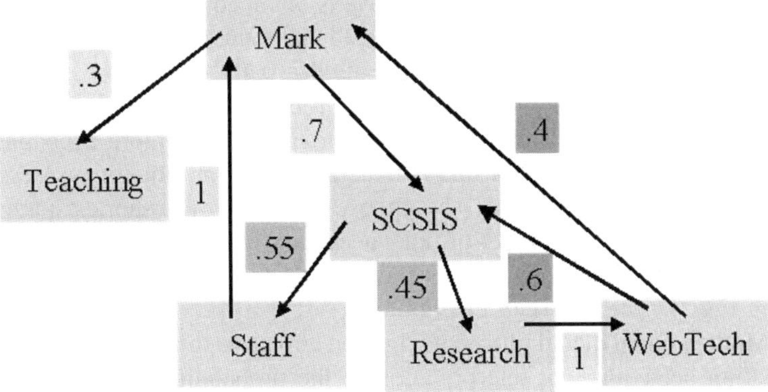

Figure 3.7 Markov chain for example web site.

Consider the two trails, the first one,

> *starting from* Mark *to* SCSIS *then to* Staff *and finally back to* Mark

and, the second one,

> *starting from* Mark *to* SCSIS *then to* Research *then to* WebTech *and finally back to* Mark

as shown in Fig. 3.8. In both trails, 70% of the time the surfer moves from Mark to SCSIS. Then, 55% of the time the surfer moves to Staff, which is on the first trail, and 45% the surfer moves to Research, which is on the second trail. Then, if on the first trail, the surfer, continuing his or her navigation session, will always move back to Mark's home page. On the other hand, if on the second trail, he or she will always continue to the WebTech page, and then 40% of the time return to Mark's home page before reaching the end of this trail.

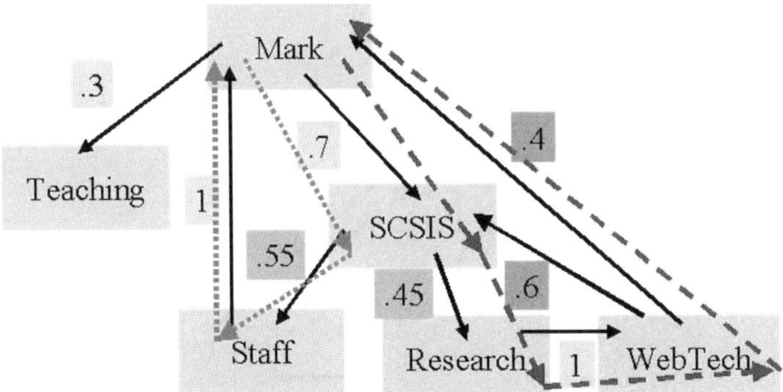

Figure 3.8 Two trails in the Markov chain.

The overall probability of the first trail above is obtained by multiplying the probabilities 0.7 and 0.55 to get 0.385 or 38.5%, and using this multiplication rule for Markov chains for the second trail—multiplying 0.7, 0.45, 1, and 0.4—we get 0.126 or 12.6%. We note that the first trail is more probable than the second trail, and, in general, due to the multiplication rule, shorter trails are more probable than longer ones. One explanation for this is that, generally, but not always, less effort is needed from the user if he or she chooses to follow the shortest path; that is, the one having the least number of links necessary to get from one page to another. The probabilities for the four trails shown in Fig. 3.4, given the Markov chain shown in Fig. 3.7, can be seen in Fig. 3.9.

So, our Markov chain model of web navigation allows us to reason about the surfer's navigation behavior. Our interpretation of the probabilities, as we have just outlined, is the proportion of times a user has followed a link. The usage information regarding link following statistics can be collected from web server logs and analyzed with *web usage mining* techniques, which we will discuss in see Section 7.4.

3.4.3 Markov Chains and the Relevance of Links

Another interpretation of probabilities attached to links is that they measure the strength of the relevance of following a link with respect to some specific surfer's goal. As mentioned earlier, a search engine query is one way users can specify their goal. For example, the two trails shown in Fig. 3.8 can also be related to a user's query such as "mark research" by scoring the web pages in the site using a search engine, and interpreting the score of the destination page that can be reached by clicking on a link, as the strength of association linking one web page to another.

Assume the sample web site that we have been examining and some particular unspecified query, not necessarily "mark research." The scores that the search engine attaches to the individual web pages could be as shown in Fig. 3.10

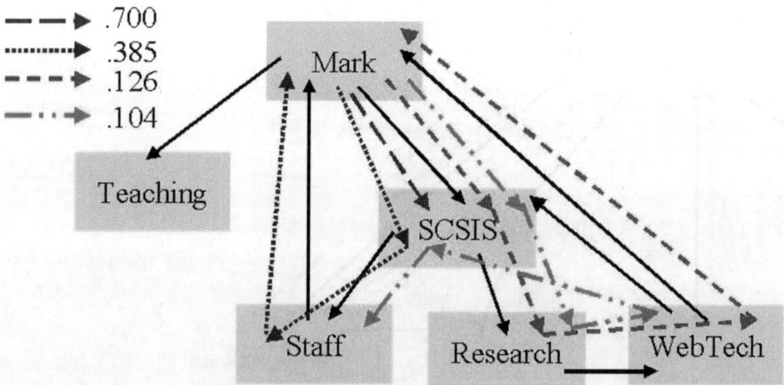

Figure 3.9 Probabilities of the four trails.

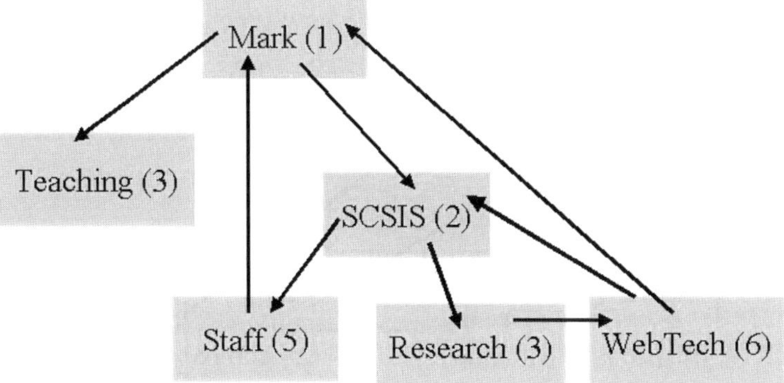

Figure 3.10 Scoring web pages.

in parentheses near the title of each page. Once we have chosen to start the navigation from Mark's home page where should we go to next?

In other words, what are the transition probabilities that can be deduced from the search engine's scores.

The search engine attached the score of 3 to Teaching and the score of 2 to SCSIS. So, according to our Markov chain interpretation 60% (or 3/5) of the time we should click on the link leading to the Teaching page and 40% (or 2/5) of the time we should click on the link leading to the Department's home page (SCSIS). Overall, we would say that with respect to the content of the web pages, the trail

from Mark *to* Teaching

scores higher than the trail

from Mark *to* SCSIS

Assuming the surfer has clicked on SCSIS, where will he or she go next. We note that if the surfer clicks on the link leading to the Research home page, there is only one link to be followed from there leading to the WebTech home page, so we lump the Research and WebTech pages together. We aggregate the scores of the pages in a lump by reducing the influence of pages which are further away. In this case, we have chosen the decay factor to be 3/4, so the aggregate score is $3 + (0.75 \times 6) = 7.5$. The justification for decaying the influence of pages is that the worth to the user of browsing a page diminishes with the distance of the page from the starting point. This assumption is consistent with the experiments carried out on web data sets [317]. So, according to our Markov chain interpretation, when we are browsing the Department's home page, 60% (or 7.5/12.5) of the time we should click on the link leading to the lumped pages, Research and WebTech, and 40% (or 5/12.5) of the time we should click on the link leading to Staff. Computing all the transition probabilities for each link in the web site, in this manner, results in the Markov chain shown in Fig. 3.11.

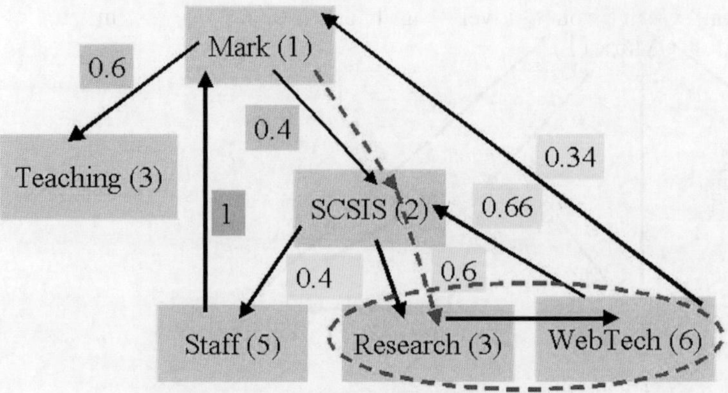

Figure 3.11 Constructing a Markov chain from scores.

To summarize, the Markov chain model we have presented aids our understanding of users surfing the web and supports two different interpretations of the transition probabilities attached to hyperlinks. In the first interpretation, a transition probability denotes the proportion of time the user followed the link, when faced with the choice of which link to follow from the link's source web page; that is, the probability is interpreted as the *popularity* of the link. We use the term *popularity* in its most generic sense, as the probabilities can be aggregated for a group of users rather than just for an individual, supporting not only personalization but also collaboration; collaborative aspects of surfing will be dealt with in Chapter 9. In the second interpretation using the scores attached to web pages, the transition probability denotes the worth or utility to the user of following the link and browsing the page reached; that is, the probability is interpreted as the *relevance* of a link to a user. These two interpretations are not mutually exclusive from the surfer's point of view as both popularity and relevance have an effect on the choices we make when navigating the web.

3.5 CONFLICT BETWEEN WEB SITE OWNER AND VISITOR

The owner of a web site has objectives, which are related to the business model of the site. If it is an e-commerce site such as www.amazon.com or www.expedia.com, its main aim is to sell you the products they offer. On the other hand, if it is an organization such as government (e.g., www.firstgov.gov) its aims are mainly informational, or if it is institutional such as a university (e.g., www.bbk.ac.uk) or a national museum (e.g., www.thebritishmuseum.ac.uk) it has informational objectives but also would like to attract potential students in the case of a university and visitors in the case of the museum. The owner of a web site may also be a service provider of some sort such as a portal (e.g., for media such as www.bbc.co.uk, or for general web access such as www.yahoo.com) or a search engine, whose main objective, if it is commercial, is to make profit, often through advertising, but it must also have a mission to provide a quality service to its community of users. One measure of success for a web site is the number of unique visitors to the site, which can be inferred for the clickstream data, but even more important is the conversion rate from visitors to customers, or in the case of advertising the correlation between the clickstream data and the revenue generated.

Visitors to a web site have different objectives related to their information needs, which we have discussed in detail earlier in the chapter. Often visitors to an e-commerce web site would like to gather some information, and their experience when surfing the site will probably have an effect on whether they will be converted to customers at some later date.

Often the objectives of the user and the owner are in conflict. The web site owner would like to know as much as possible about its users but users often prefer to remain anonymous for privacy reasons. To identify its users web sites may demand the user to register in return for providing them with some information, or they can store HTTP *cookies*[49] on the user's machine. A cookie is a piece of text that a web site can store on the user's machine when the user is browsing the site. This information can be retrieved later by the web site; for example, in order to identify a user returning to the site. Cookies raise important issues relating to web privacy, which are controversial when users are unaware that their movements are being tracked on an individual basis. In the interest of privacy, browsers allow users to view, enable, and disable HTTP cookies from selected or all web sites.

Another type of cookie, which is stored as by Adobe flash applications, is called a *flash cookie*.[50] Flash cookies are less known than HTTP cookies and are more resilient to deletion, as they are stored in a different location on the user's computer. Flash cookies have become a convenient way to track users when HTTP cookies have been removed. Often, a small 2kb invisible flash module is loaded into the web browser with a web page in order to record the visit with the aid of a flash cookie. Analysis of flash from 100 popular web sites revealed that more than half of the sites are using flash cookies [618]. On several sites, flash cookies are used as backup for HTTP cookies, which may be deleted. A tighter integration between browser tools and flash cookies would allow users to block such cookies in the interest of privacy. This statement also applies to other forms of user tracking, where for privacy reasons the user should be allowed to opt out by blocking the tracking mechanism.

A long-standing court case against the online ad provider Doubleclick (acquired by Google in 2008) for failing to disclose its use of cookies in targeted advertising to individual users eventually forced the company to adopt privacy related restrictions that include disclosing their activities to users.[51] With web usage mining techniques, discussed in see Section 7.4, we will see that by

[49]How internet cookies work, by M. Brain. www.howstuffworks.com/cookie.htm

[50]What are local shared objects? www.adobe.com/products/flashplayer/articles/lso.

[51]DoubleClick loses its cookies, Wired News, August 2003. www.wired.com/news/business/0,1367,54774,00.html.

using the server data logs that record the activities of visitors to a web site, the site's administrator can analyze how users are surfing through their site without identifying them individually.

Visitors using a search engine or directory service are interested in an efficient and accurate search service that will satisfy their information needs. They will be put off by a search engine home page that is cluttered with advertising, where the ads cannot be distinguished from genuine content, where pop-ups keep flying in their face, and where the search box is hardly visible. The clean, uncluttered search engine user interface pioneered by Google has gained it many followers, and has forced many of the other search engines to follow in suite. Finding the right balance between the users needs and the commercial needs of the service provider is an ongoing concern that may even lead the web site to change its business model.

Netscape's home page was one of the most visited during the heyday of the company, whose browser changed the face of the web during the mid-1990s. In 1996 Netscape's share of the browser market was about 73%, dropping to just over 30% in 1999, and to just under 4% in 2003. On the other hand, Microsoft's Internet Explorer's share of the market was about 20% in 1996, rising to just under 68% in 1999, and to nearly 96% in 2003.[52] In late 2009, Netscape's browser was already hardly visible.

Netscape was founded as a software firm with browser technology being at the center of its operations. Netscape's site was one of the web's hottest properties as visitors flocked to the site to download its browser. By mid-1997, it reported having over 100 million visitors per day, making Netscape one of the main gateways to the web at that time. As the browser war with Microsoft heated up and Netscape was losing the battle, the commercial potential of their home page as a gold mine for advertising was recognized. Turning their home page into the Netcenter portal resulted in revenues of over 100 million dollars from advertising and partnerships through their web site, as reported in 1997. Netscape had then become a media company in addition to being a software company. The fascinating story of the rise and fall of Netscape has been told elsewhere [169]. On the one hand, it illustrates the power of the service to attract users, and, on the other hand, the power of the users to effect the service itself.

As an epilogue to this story, the browser wars may be back, as late in 2004 Mozilla released its open source browser Firefox www.mozilla.org/products/firefox, which promised to fix some security flaws in Internet Explorer and provide some new features.[53] Firefox has gained much ground since its release, and as of late 2009 had a market share of about 32% compared to

[52]Browser wars: High price, huge rewards, by John Borland, CNET News.com, April 2003. http://zdnet.com.com/2100-1104-996866.html.

[53]The browser wars are back, according to Netscape's founder, by J. Hu, October 2004, CNET News.com. http://news.zdnet.co.uk/internet/0,39020369, 39169278,00.htm.

Microsoft's Internet Explorer's declining share of about 56%.[54] In the meanwhile Google have released late in 2008 an open source browser, called *Chrome*, which has already gained a market share of about 4% by late 2009.

3.6 CONFLICT BETWEEN SEMANTICS OF WEB SITE AND THE BUSINESS MODEL

The web sites of the e-commerce giant Amazon have consistently been amongst the most popular sites on the web. When you visit Amazon you may have an informational need, for example, to find out what Amazon has to say about this book; a transactional need, for example, to buy this book from Amazon; or a navigational need, for example, to explore the range of books available about search engines. A commercial site such as Amazon must convert visitors to customers to maintain its business, but on the other hand to keep both its customers and potential customers happy, it must also provide solutions to informational and navigational queries.

The book section of Amazon is divided into categories such as science, travel, sports, and computers and internet. Users may browse through these categories as they would browse through categories within the Yahoo Directory. With the aid of the site search engine provided by Amazon, users can pursue the search engine strategy we have explored earlier, when users alternate between querying the search engine and navigating by following links. Even when trying to satisfy an informational or navigational need, Amazon keeps its business model in mind by recommending books to you and providing links to the checkout to get you closer to the conversion from surfer to customer.

The conflict here is more of a balancing act between the business objectives, that is, to increase the conversion rate, and the web site navigability from the user's point of view. This tension between the natural semantics of the web site in terms of some hierarchical structure that eases users ability to navigate the site to satisfy their information needs, and the ability of the web site owner to design transparent trails through the site that make it easier for users to convert their need to a transactional one, is an ongoing issue for all web designers to consider seriously.

Another related issue is that of web search engines finding product pages within e-commerce sites, in situations when users start their information seeking from a web search engine. A study conducted by researchers at CSIRO (Australia's Commonwealth Scientific and Industrial Research Organisation), which concentrated on finding books through web search engines, showed that many of the product web pages were buried deep within the online hierarchy of the bookstores, making it difficult for web search engines to index these pages [651]. From the web site's point of view, the conclusion here is that it should take into account the fact that many of their customers will arrive at their web site from a web search engine, and therefore they should make the product information

[54]StatCounter, Global Stats. http://gs.statcounter.com.

more visible and easy to navigate to, which will result in increased traffic to their site.

CHAPTER SUMMARY

- The navigation problem of "getting lost in hyperspace" as a result being disoriented and frustrated when following links is one of the central unresolved problems of web interaction. When we are lost we should ask ourselves what our information seeking goal was, and whether it has changed? We should then try and answer three further questions before deciding what to do, they are where are we, where did we come from, and where are we going to?
- Machine learning has the potential to improve web interaction by building a statistical model of the user's preferences, which is adaptive in the sense that it changes in time as the user's behavior changes. The naive Bayes classifier is an example of a machine learning technique, which can be used to automate, or at least to semiautomate, the categorization of web pages, thus saving human effort, and coping with the problem of scale.
- A trail is a sequence of web pages through a web space, and can be viewed as the pages a surfer visits during a navigation session. Trail can be authored, derived, or emergent, the last type being either personal or collaborative. It is argued that the browser and its tools should support trails as first class objects.
- Markov chains were introduced as being able to model the probability of transition from one page to another within a web site, the probability having two different interpretations. It can denote the relative frequency that surfers followed the link from the source page to the destination, that is, the popularity of the link, or it can measure the utility to the user of following the link, that is, its relevance.
- The owner of a web site has objectives related to the business model of the site, while the visitors to the site have a different set of objectives related to their information need. Finding the balance between the users needs and the commercial needs of the service provider is an ongoing effort that effects the provider's business model.
- There is a potential conflict between the navigability of a web site and its business model. In an e-commerce site, a conflict may take place between users trying to satisfy informational or navigational needs and the intent of a web site to increase the conversion rate of its visitors.

EXERCISES

3.1. (Discuss). Discuss some of the reasons why information seeking cannot be satisfied solely by the use of search engines, that is why the process needs to be augmented with navigation, that is, link following.

Give examples from your own experience to illustrate your points. (See Ref. 110 for a personal account of reasons for being disgruntled with searching on the web using current search technology.)

3.2. **(Miniproject).** Choose two subcategories at the bottom level of the Open Directory (www.dmoz.org) hierarchy, that is, ones that do not have any further subcategories, and save the web pages in these subcategories on your computer.

Build a naive Bayes classifier to discriminate between your chosen subcategories using the saved web pages as the training set. (You may ignore the HTML tags, treating the pages as simple text files.)

Test your classifier on web pages you have retrieved using a search engine, with queries that characterize each of the categories you have chosen.

3.3. **(Discuss).** Why are Markov chains a useful model of users surfing the web?

How do you think a Markov chain model could be used to rank web pages by popularity?

Argue for and against the Markov property as an assumption regarding surfers' navigation behavior.

3.4. **(Miniproject).** Obtain the network structure (i.e., the set of URL of pages and the links between them) of a small web site or a portion of a larger site of your choice. You should identify the site's home page and add a link from each page back to the home page if not already present.

Treat the network as a Markov chain, assuming that the probabilities of links from any page are uniform; that is, if there are n links on a page, then each has a probability of $1/n$ of being chosen.

1. Compute through simulation the probability of passing through each page during a very long navigation session, starting from the home page.
2. Change the assumption of uniform link probabilities so that probability of a link reflects its popularity, and repeat the simulation to revise the probabilities of visiting a page during a very long navigation session.

   Comment on your findings.

3.5. **(Explore).** Although cookies can identify a user, they cannot on their own be used to identify any personal details about the user.

Explain this statement with reference to concerns that cookies violate a user's privacy.

Have a look at the privacy policy of two web search engines of your choice and summarize your findings explaining how these search engines make use of cookies.

CHAPTER 4

SEARCHING THE WEB

"The internet has been the most fundamental change during my lifetime and for hundreds of years."

— Rupert Murdoch, Media owner

WE INTRODUCE web search by presenting the major search engines that are battling for our clicks. We look at some statistics derived from search engine log files, giving us insight into how users employ search engines to answer their queries. We describe the components of a search engine and how search engines make use of special crawling software to collect data from web pages and maintain a fresh index that covers as much of the Web as they possibly can.

CHAPTER OBJECTIVES

- Detail the various aspects of a typical search session.
- Raise the political issues that arise from search engines being the primary information gatekeepers of the Web.
- Introduce the main competitors, Google, Yahoo, and Bing, involved in the ongoing search engine wars to dominate the web search space.
- Present some search engine statistics generated from studies of query logs.
- Explain the implications of using different query syntax, on search results.
- Present the most popular search keywords found from studies of query logs.
- Present a generic architecture for a search engine and discuss its various components.
- Explain how the search index organizes the text found in web pages into an inverted-file data structure.
- Explain how hyperlink information pertaining to URLs is stored in a link database.
- Explain the roles of the query engine and how it interfaces between the search index, the user, and the Web.

An Introduction to Search Engines and Web Navigation, by Mark Levene

- Explain the roles of the query interface.
- Explain the task of a web crawler.
- Explain how the basic algorithm of a crawler works.
- Discuss the problems involved in crawling and highlight different crawling strategies.
- Discuss the issue of how often a crawler should refresh a web page.
- Explain the use of the robots exclusion protocol.
- Explain the meaning of a spider trap in the context of web crawling.
- Detail the logistics of delivering a continuous, round-the-clock, global search service in terms of resource implications and software and hardware architectures.
- Explain the process of serving a Google query.
- Describe Google's distributed architecture based on the Google File System, the MapReduce algorithm, and the BigTable database system.

4.1 MECHANICS OF A TYPICAL SEARCH

Nowadays, it is practically impossible to find anything on the Web without employing a search engine to assist us. As I have discussed in the previous chapter, in order to satisfy our information-seeking objectives we, most often, need to combine search with navigation in a judicious manner. The search engine's role in this process is to narrow down the vicinity of web pages that could contain the information required and to provide alternative entry points for the user to initiate a navigation session from.

A search engine is like a radar homing onto web pages that help the user find relevant information. Once the search engine locks onto a relevant page, it presents a summary of that page to the user. The user may then choose to browse the page, and will decide whether to navigate from that page to other pages by following links, or to inspect the summaries of other pages the search engine presents for the query.

Let us look at the mechanics of user interaction with a search engine using Google, which is currently one of the dominant players in the search space, as our typical search engine. Archie Searcher is our archetypal user. He regularly starts searching from Google's home page at www.google.com. The large search box and the simple, uncluttered user interface are appealing to him. When typing in his query, Archie rarely uses any of the advanced features but when he does, he goes to the advanced search interface and occasionally consults the help feature. I encourage you to investigate these features in your own time, and possibly consult a recent book called Google Hacks, which is full of tips and tools for Googlers [154]. Apart from standard web search, search engines offer other search services such as image search, video search, news search, blog search, and product search. The current search engine wars will mean that there will be fierce competition between search engines to lure users to use their services, which is good news for the consumer of search, at least in the short term.

For the moment, let us concentrate on web page search. Archie is interested in Computer Chess so he initiates a query by typing the keywords "computer chess" into Google's search box as shown in Fig. 4.1. Google responds almost instantly, in about 0.20 secs according to its calculations, with a screen full of results, as shown in Fig. 4.2. Google also informs us that it has found 3.69 million results that are relevant to our query, as part of the number games that search engines play. The results are ranked from the most relevant hit at the top of the page to the least relevant hit at the bottom of the page.

Search engines often display sponsored links among their results, which are ads paid for by companies wishing to advertise their products. These are marked as sponsored by the search engine, to distinguish them from free results, also known as organic results. It is notable that for some search engines, such as

Figure 4.1 Query "computer chess" submitted to Google.

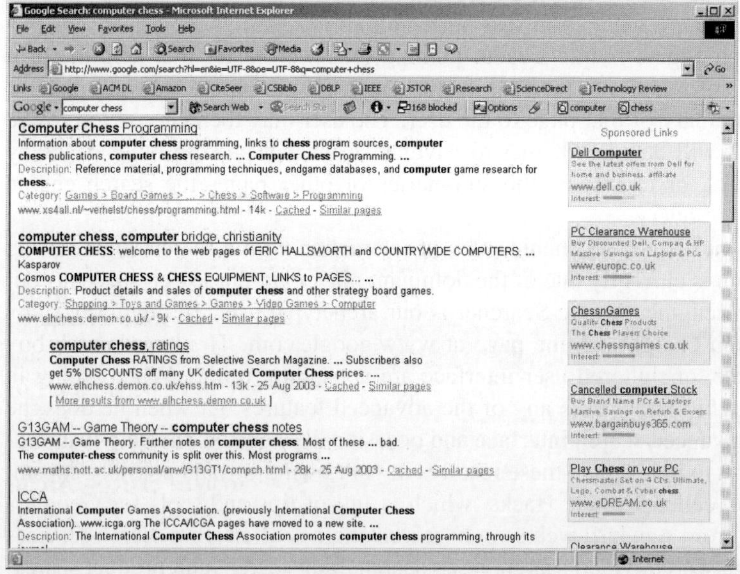

Figure 4.2 Results for "computer chess" from Google.

Overture which was subsequently acquired by Yahoo, the number of sponsored links dominate the results list. From the search engine business point of view, the importance of these ads cannot be underestimated since advertising is their major source of income. (The other main revenue stream for search engines is, of course, providing search services.) In a nutshell, a sponsored link is displayed on the results list when keywords chosen by the customer match one or more of the keywords in a user query. The customer is normally billed for the ad on a pay-per-click basis, meaning that each time a web searcher clicks on the ad the customer has to pay.[55] The way in which advertising is combined with search results is important to understand, since as it is big business, we will see much more of it as the search engine wars commence; we discuss search engine advertising in detail in Section 6.2.

Archie is now considering an organic result, that is, one that is *not* sponsored; in particular, he is concentrating on one of the highest ranking results. Its title is "Computer Chess Programming," and clicking on the title will cause the browser to load the web page for viewing. Below the title there is a summary and a description of the web page, containing several key sentences and phrases for the page pertaining to the query. The summary is dynamic; that is, it is specific to the query "computer chess." When this web page is in the results list for a different query, it will have a different summary. So, for the query "computer chess" we get the summary,

> Information about *computer chess* programming, links to *chess* program sources, *computer chess* publications, *computer chess* research. ... *Computer Chess* Programming. ...

for this high ranked result, and for the query "computer game research," we get the different summary

> ... *Computer Game Research*: *Computer Game Research* Groups and People. Other *computer* chess related links. *Computer* Chess Championships: ...

for the same web page, now ranked at a different position on the results list.

Other features that appear for web pages on the search engine's results list are its URL; that is, the web page address at the other end of the link, the size of the result page, its Open Directory category if this page exists in the directory listing as shown in Fig. 4.3 (this feature was disabled in 2004 when this screenshot was taken, and will be useful when resurrected), a cached version of the web page, and a "similar pages" feature which may have been based on an algorithm codeveloped by Monica Henzinger [182], who (as of 2010) is a research director at Google.

If, instead of entering the individual keywords "computer chess," Archie enters the phrase "computer chess", by combining the keywords using double

[55]Google Advertising. www.google.com/ads/index.html. Yahoo! Search Marketing. http://searchmarketing.yahoo.com.

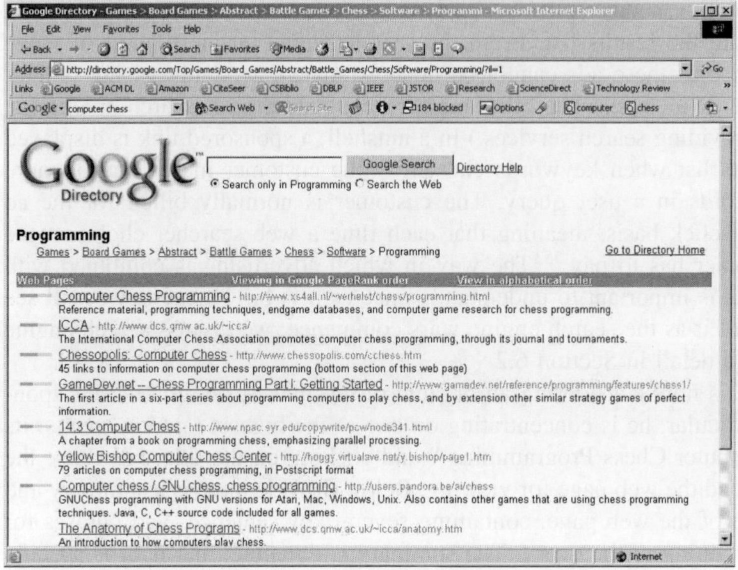

Figure 4.3 Relevant category from the directory for "computer chess" from Google.

quotes, Google will respond with the results as shown in Fig. 4.4. It is most interesting to note that the results list differs from the previous one. After you have read the next chapter, and you have a better understanding of the internal working of a search engine, you may wish to hypothesize about why there is such a difference. It suffices to say at this stage that phrase matching insists that the whole phrase, that is, "computer chess" be matched, rather than the individual keywords, computer and chess, so it is a more stringent requirement on the matching process.

4.2 SEARCH ENGINES AS INFORMATION GATEKEEPERS OF THE WEB

Search engines are currently the primary information gatekeepers of the Web, holding the precious key needed to unlock the Web both, for users who are seeking information and for authors of web pages wishing to make their voices heard. The search engine box from which we can launch a web query is present not only on the search engines' home pages but also on the pages of portals and web directories, which may offer alternative, specialized search services. The web search box is almost omnipresent, if we are to consider the search engine toolbar utility that plugs into the browser allowing us to access web search engines directly without going to the search engine's home page.[56] Looking back at

[56]Search toolbars & utilities, by Chris Sherman, May 2003. www.searchenginewatch.com/links/article.php/2156381.

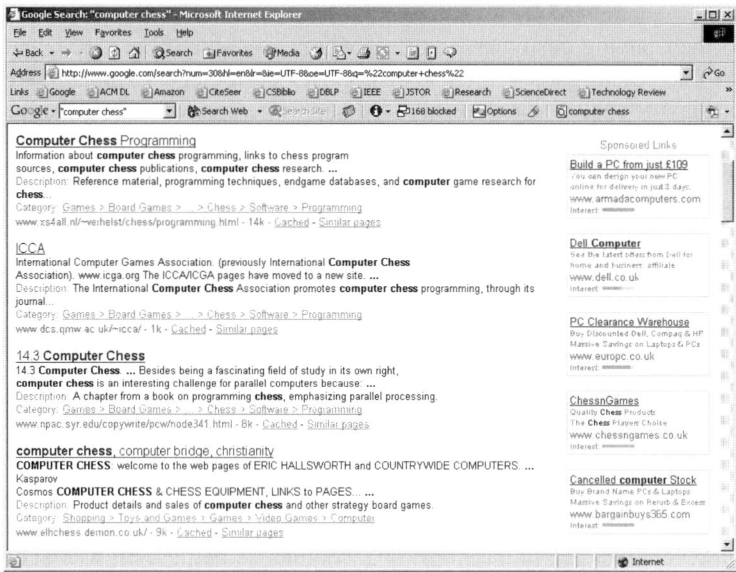

Figure 4.4 Results for phrase "computer chess" from Google

Fig. 4.2 you can spot that Google's toolbar has been installed on Archie's browser with the query "computer chess" already typed into the toolbar search box, noting that Archie can invoke a search from the toolbar while browsing any web page whatsoever. Millions of users have already downloaded the Google toolbar[57] and other search engine toolbars, allowing the search engine of their choice direct access to the information-seeking behavior of its users including Archie.

As information gatekeepers, web search engines have the power to include and exclude web sites and web pages from their indexes and to influence the ranking of web pages on query results lists. Web search engines thus have a large influence on what information users will associate with the Web.

Imagine the following futuristic scenario, when the search engine wars are over and a single search engine dominates the Web; let us call this search engine Dominant-SE. As the monopolizer of web information, Dominant-SE can determine how we view the Web, since without its lens we are almost blind when it comes to finding anything useful on the Web. Dominant-SE can make or break any business whose livelihood depends on web visibility, and feed us with any information it chooses as answers to our queries. Dominant-SE will most likely be able to track our individual queries and feed us with a personalized version of the Web, tailored to maximize its profit. These are indeed political issues with serious legal ramifications for a democratic society with a free economy.

Search engines are aggregators of information rather than media companies in the traditional sense. However, the main web search engines are for-profit corporations and as such, are similar to media companies in that advertising is

[57]Google gets souped up toolbar, June 2003. www.wired.com/news/business/0,1367,59418,00.html.

their core business model [654]. As commercial enterprises, search engines are responsible to their paying customers, most of whom are advertisers [305], and make editorial choices to satisfy their audience and customers. Examples are omitting to display offensive search results and suppressing politically sensitive results. There is also editorial control in the selection of ads; for example, choosing not to have "gun-" or "drug-"related advertising. The choices made by the main search engines vary, and it is still unclear what this bias means from the perspective of democratic discourse [184].

There is an increasing voice supporting regulation of search engines due to possible commercial bias, where the rich and powerful can use their influence and dollars to determine what a search engine can retrieve. Introna and Nissenbaum [323] argue that the Web is a public good and thus its resource should be distributed in accordance with public principles rather than market norms. They call not only for more argument and discussion on these issues but also for policy and action.

As a first step, they propose that search engines disclose their underlying algorithms in a full and truthful manner. This does not seem to be a practical demand as search engines are in the midst of a continuous battle with web sites that use their understanding of a search engine's ranking mechanism to try and artificially manipulate the ranking to their advantage. Moreover, advertising fraud is a serious problem for search engines [200], and sharing their methods would make it easier for fraudsters to defeat their system.

Search engine optimization and visibility is currently big business with many companies offering ways to improve your web site ranking and to counter unscrupulous methods, search engines are continuously upgrading their ranking algorithms, which are kept under lock and key, to protect themselves from offenders. (In Chapter 5, when I explain the ideas behind search engines' ranking methods I will return to the issue of search engine optimization.)

The whole issue of "fairness" with regards to appearance on a search engine's listing does not have an agreed upon legal interpretation, so search engines have a difficult dilemma to deal with when they wish to exclude a web site; for example, due to racism, pornography, copyright infringement or rogue search engine optimization.

The decision by Google to exclude some web sites from their index has been called the "Google death penalty" by Zittrain from the Berkman Center for Internet & Society at the Harvard Law School ([707], p. 218), since, due to the current dominance of Google, these sites are effectively cut off from their intended audience. Zittrain together with Edleman, also from the Harvard Law School, have been studying search result exclusions,[58] and the wider issues related to internet filtering, where organizations or countries seek to restrict access to certain web sites from within their premises and territories.[59]

[58]Localized Google search result exclusions Statement of issues and call for data, by J. Zittrain and B. Edelman, October 2002. http://cyber.law.harvard.edu/filtering/google.

[59]Documentation of Internet filtering worldwide, by J. Zittrain and B. Edelman, April 2003. http://cyber.law.harvard.edu/filtering.

In 2003, Google was nominated for the Big Brother award which is presented by the nonprofit organization Privacy International[60] to companies which have done the most during the past year to invade our privacy. Anyone can be nominated for this award and at the end of the day, Google was not one of the finalists, but the publicity this nomination has been given in the technology press has raised some important questions regarding search privacy. (Google was also nominated for the Big Brother award in 2007, as the most invasive company, but again failed to win the award.)

The 2003 nomination was made by Google-Watch (www.google-watch.org), who is claiming the Google's search mechanism is invading our privacy by retaining all our search information. When Archie first visited Google, a cookie (see Section 3.5) was sent from Google to Archie's computer, allowing Google to store Archie's preferences and to identify Archie each time he searches using Google. Although Archie can set his browser to refuse cookies, like most web surfers, he is aware that this may limit the functionality of the service, and he has not had the time nor the inclination to dig deeper into this issue, and weigh the pros and cons of cookies. Google[61] and other search services such as Yahoo[62] make their privacy policy clear to counter any allegation that they are using Big Brother tactics.

One point which is important to know is that the information present in cookies is not, generally, sufficient on its own to identify you personally. A cookie can be used to associate a web address with your searches, but any further information about you can only be obtained if the service provider gets you (i.e., the user) to register with them in return for some additional benefit, or if the service provider uses a data mining program to try and puzzle together the web address with a user. The normal use of cookies is anonymous, and on its own would not be sufficient evidence to tarnish the reputation of a search service. Danny Sullivan, the creator of Search Engine Watch and more recently Search Engine Land, has written at length about this issue[63] stating that there are privacy issues that we should be aware of regarding all search engines but in most cases users cannot be personally tracked, unless they are registered and signed in.

One issue which is of prime importance when we are using an online service, be it a search engine or an e-commerce portal, is that of trust. The challenge of any such service is to build a relationship of trust between the provider of the service and their users, and to combine it with an open and clear privacy policy.

As advertising is currently the bread and butter of search services, they wish to personalize ads to increase the click-throughs on which their revenue depends. This form of advertising where users are shown ads according to their personal preferences is known as *behavioral targeting*, discussed in Section 6.2.4;

[60]Privacy International. www.privacyinternational.org.

[61]Toolbar privacy policy. http://toolbar.google.com/privacy.html.

[62]Yahoo! Privacy Policy. http://privacy.yahoo.com. http://searchenginewatch.com/sereport/article.php/2189531.

[63]Search privacy at Google & other search engines, by D. Sullivan, April 2003.

Google prefers to call it interest-based advertising.[64] There are obviously privacy concerns with this mode of advertising but there are also concerns of fairness in pricing as behavioral targeting makes differential pricing possible, for example by offering discounts to loyal customers [27].

The information about our search behavior can also be used to personalize the search results themselves, a topic we will discuss in Section 6.4. This could lead to improved quality of search and further lock-in of users to a specific search engine thus increasing the market share of that engine. Ultimately, search engines may charge users for software that will provide additional personalized services.

There is an ongoing conflict for a search engine between the goals of delivering high-quality results to users and maximizing the profit from advertising. As the barriers to entry in the web search space are very high, mainly due to high infrastructure costs that need to scale to the size of the growing web, the competition to dominate the web search engine market is only between few players led by Google, Yahoo, and Microsoft. This narrow competition and the effort expended by search engines to lock-in users to their service through additional services such as e-mail, make the resolution of the conflict even more uncertain. Still, search engines need to be wary, as when the quality of search falls below a threshold then users will defect to another search engine [184]. Bhargava and Feng [80] looked at this problem in the context market demand as a function of the quality of the search technology and the bias caused by sponsored search advertising (also known as *paid placement*, when ads are shown side-by-side with the free organic results returned by the search engine for a given query; Section 6.2). Increasing the quality increases demand, while increasing the bias decreases demand. A search engine must find the equilibrium point between users' demand for quality and advertisers' demand for bias. In the context of sponsored search, the bias can be viewed as the number of advertising slots, that is, the number of sponsored results, allocated by a search engine when displaying the search results. This has an effect on the quality of the search engine, as increasing the bias will decrease the quality of search as perceived by its users, which in turn will cause users to defect to another search engine and thus reduce the demand for advertising. Feng *et al.* [214] conducted simulation experiments which showed that when the willingness of advertisers to pay for an ad is positively correlated with the relevance of the ad to the query terms it is associated with, there is a maximum number of advertising slots beyond which the expected revenue of the search engine from sponsored search will decrease.

4.3 SEARCH ENGINE WARS, IS THE DUST SETTLING?

And then there were three: Google (www.google.com), Yahoo (www.yahoo.com), and Microsoft's rebranded search engine, Bing (www.bing.com). The search engine wars have heated up in the last quarter of 2003 with a string of acquisitions

[64]Google Ad Preferences, Interest-based advertising: How it works. www.google.com/ads/preferences/html/about.html.

leaving only three players to fight for domination of the search space. Fast forward to the beginning of 2010 (and the foreseeable future) and Google is still the most popular search engine with the lion's share of users, but Microsoft and Yahoo are fighting back. Since July 2009 Yahoo and Microsoft have joined forces in a 10-year deal in which Microsoft will power Yahoo's search engine and Yahoo will drive the search engine advertising sales for both companies.[65]

As we will see, the competitors in this game cannot be more different from each other.

4.3.1 Competitor Number One: Google

Google is the epitome of search engine technology and its name is synonymous with efficient high-quality search. According to Word Spy, the word google has been elevated to a verb synonymous with searching for information on the Web.[66] For example, if you are going on a date, "googling" the prospective partner means using the search engine to find more about this person. Up until Google became a public company, it had been the darling of the search engines, but it seems that the honeymoon period is now over. As a business, its growth since its inception in September 1998 has been outstanding, and it had remained a private company until its IPO (Initial Public Offering) in August 2004.[67] Google's IPO was not without controversy, as most of the shares were issued through a Dutch auction mechanism. The way this type of auction works is that investors bid for a number of shares at the price they are willing to pay, and then the price is set by considering the highest bids that add up to the number of shares allocated and setting the share price at the lowest price of these winning bids[68]; there is even a web site fully dedicated to discussion and news regarding the IPO (www.google-ipo.com).

There is some worry about the power that Google is amassing, as it is evident that it is currently the dominant player in the search space. Most of its revenue streams are coming from advertising, and as a profitable company it must first consider its paying customers in order to further increase its income. Its acquisitions of the internet ad-serving company DoubleClick (www.doubleclick.com) in 2008, and the mobile advertising company AdMob (www.admob.com) in 2009, show Google's determination to dominate search engine advertising in all its forms.

As an early user of Google, when it was still in the beta stage as an unknown new search engine developed by two graduate students in Stanford, it is now hard for me to imagine searching the Web without it. As web users we should enjoy quality searching yet be aware that there are pitfalls that can endanger this quality if search becomes monopolized by any company. At the

[65]Microsoft, Yahoo! Change Search Landscape, July 2009. www.choicevalueinnovation.com/thedeal.

[66]WordSpy on the verb google. www.wordspy.com/words/google.asp.

[67]Google Inc. prices initial public offering of class a common stock. www.google.com/press/pressrel/ipo.html.

[68]Q&A-How the Google float will work. http://news.bbc.co.uk/1/hi/business/3559050.stm.

moment Archie Searcher is primarily concerned with satisfying his information needs by finding relevant web pages, and current search technology, with Google leading the pack, is not letting him down.

4.3.2 Competitor Number Two: Yahoo

Our second competitor Yahoo is a veteran dot-com company that was founded by two different graduate students from Stanford at the earlier date of February 1994. For a long time, Yahoo's directory listing of web sites provided the main entry point for web surfers seeking to find useful sites. If Google is synonymous with search, then Yahoo is synonymous with the dot-com boom and is probably the best-known brand on the Web.

As opposed to being a search engine, Yahoo started off as a directory, allowing its visitors to browse web pages according to an intuitive and useful set of categories. Its directory is maintained manually by a team of editors who determine which web pages will be included in a category according to a set of internal criteria; most of the included sites are suggested by users and then evaluated by the editors for inclusion in the directory.[69] Yahoo's main revenue streams are from advertising and its partnerships with e-commerce vendors.

Up until 2003, Yahoo did not have its own search capabilities and was using Google to power its search. But its acquisitions of the major search provider Inktomi in March 2003, and of the paid placement search engine Overture in July 2003, which in turn acquired the web search engines AlltheWeb (www.alltheweb.com) and AltaVista (www.altavista.com) in April 2003, has dramatically changed this situation. After these takeovers, Yahoo's CEO said that "owning the algorithmic search technology would allow Yahoo to be more innovative and creative about the search-related services it will provide."[70] Indeed, much of the Web's search technology is now split between Yahoo and Google, and the battle between these giants is far from over as each player will do its best to capitalize on its search technology and market reach. An important milestone is Yahoo rolling out its own integrated search engine in the beginning of 2004.[71]

Yahoo has continued to innovate in its search provision in a bid to compete with Google. As an example, its tool SearchScan warns users about spammy sites and sites which may contain potentially harmful spyware or viruses, and its tool Search Assist offers users suggestions and related concepts to help completing, expanding or modifying query terms.[72]

4.3.3 Competitor Number Three: Bing

The third player, Microsoft, is synonymous with PC software. We have already seen how Microsoft has come to dominate the browser market when it decided

[69]How to suggest your site. http://docs.yahoo.com/info/suggest/suggest.html.

[70]Yahoo! CEO: Usage Up "Dramatically," by P. Parker, January 2003. www.clickz.com/1565351.

[71]Yahoo bids farewell to Google search, by J. Hu and S. Olsen, CNET News.com, February 2004. http://news.zdnet.co.uk/internet/ecommerce/0,39020372,39146616,00.htm.

[72]Introducing the New Yahoo! Search, October 2007. http://tools.search.yahoo.com/newsearch.

to enter into competition with Netscape, using its immense power through its control of the desktop. It is now evident that Microsoft is investing heavily in web search technology in order to boost Bing, which is their web search engine that is now also powering search on the MSN portal. As of late 2004, MSN was still using Yahoo's search technology through its subsidiaries, Inktomi (now integrated with Yahoo search), for powering its search service, and Overture for managing its paid listings. Moreover, until the beginning of 2004 MSN Search was using LookSmart, which is a smaller player in this game, for its directory services.[73]

As an indication of their commitment to search, Microsoft first overhauled the site search on its corporate web site, with the main goals of increasing the relevance of its search results and standardizing the search experience across Microsoft.com. Part of Microsoft's interest in search is related to the development of its Windows operating system in which it intends to bind search localized to the PC with web search, by linking to Bing's search services.

Microsoft's short-term goal in the web search arena, at the time, was to replace Inktomi's search technology with its own.[74] As a first step, in mid-2003, it unleashed MSNBot, which is a prototype web crawler developed by MSN Search, which builds a global index of web pages and web sites that is being used as the underlying database for Microsoft's proprietary web search engine. A web crawler is a software program that traverses web pages, downloads them for indexing, and follows (or harvests) the hyperlinks that are referenced on the downloaded pages. (A web crawler will typically start from a multitude of web pages and aims to cover as much of the indexable web as possible; we will discuss web crawlers in detail in Section 4.6.)

From the second half of 2004, MSN Search has been offering a preview of its proprietary web search engine on its Sandbox site, where some of its prototype technologies are put on display.[75] In November 2004 MSN released the beta version of its search engine, supported by an index of over 5 billion web pages.[76] In February 2005, MSN Search was officially released through their main search site.[77] There was more to come from MSN Search as they added new features to their engine.

MSN Search was rebranded to Live search in late 2006 and at this stage, was separated from the MSN portal. As a further rebranding effort, Microsoft unveiled Bing search (www.bing.com) in May 2009, as a replacement to Live search. Bing is being marketed as a decision engine (www.decisionengine.com),

[73]MSN drops LookSmart, by G.R. Notess, January 2004. www.searchengineshowdown.com/newsarchive/000762.shtml.

[74]Microsoft.com revamps search, by S. Olsen, July 2003. http://news.com.com/2100-1032_3-5058462.html.

[75]MSN Search gets new look; Microsoft gets new search engine, by D. Sullivan, July 2004. www.searchenginewatch.com/searchday/article.php/3376041.

[76]Microsoft unveils its new search engine-At last, by C. Sherman, November 2004. http://searchenginewatch.com/searchday/article.php/3434261.

[77]MSN Search officially switches to its own technology, by D. Sullivan, February 2005. http://searchenginewatch.com/searchday/article.php/3466721.

indicating that Microsoft would like to move beyond search by being more user-centric and helping people make better decisions. Microsoft has also integrated its shopping engine into Bing, providing surfers with more incentives to use its search engine through its cash-back program (www.bing.com/cashback), which offers users money back when they make purchases through the site.

4.3.4 Other Competitors

Behind the scenes lurks the computer giant IBM that has been involved in search engine technology since the early days of the Web. IBM's CLEVER search engine, which never saw the light of day [131], has been very influential in the development of methods that exploit the linkage between web sites to improve the quality of search results. One can never discount IBM even as a latecomer into this race, and its WebFountain project [271] has been described by its senior vice president of research as "Google on steroids."[78]

Two smaller search services to look out for are Ask Jeeves or simply Ask (www.ask.com) and Cuil (www.cuil.com), but we should not discount new players entering the battle with new search technologies such as those described in later chapters. Ask is a search service that, in addition to search, uses natural language technology to provide answers to queries formulated as questions or keywords. Its search is powered by the search engine Teoma, which they acquired in September 2001, and rebranded into the Ask search engine early in 2006. On the other hand, Cuil is a relatively new search engine that went live in mid-2008 with a massive index of 120 billion web pages. It had teething problems as its servers crashed on the day it was launched and there was also some criticism about the relevance of its results.[79] Cuil is also entering the social search arena, by analyzing real-time web data from microblogging (see Section 9.5.5) and social networks sites (see Section 9.1.5) to display relevant data as soon as it appears or is being discussed.[80]

The search engine wars, much like the portal wars,[81] are a battle to attract users to their sites, where various services are offered. From the search engine revenue point of view, these services have so far been mostly related to advertising. The winners in this game will provide search for the whole planet.

Of course, by the time this book goes to print the search engine battle field will not look exactly the same as it is now during the middle of 2010, but at the moment it seems that the conflict may be prolonged, and hopefully one from which the end user will benefit with even higher quality search technology.

[78]IBM's path from invention to income, by L. DiCarlo, June 2003. www.forbes.com/2003/08/07/cx_ld_0807ibm.html.

[79]Cuil shows us how not to launch a search engine, by R. Needleman, July 2008. http://news.cnet.com/cuil-shows-us-how-not-to-launch-a-search-engine.

[80]Launching Streaming Results, by Abhishek & Ankit, September 2009. www.cuil.com/info/blog/2009/09/25/launching-streaming-results.

[81]Business: The company file portal wars, November 1988. http://news.bbc.co.uk/1/hi/business/the_company_file/220942.stm.

4.4 STATISTICS FROM STUDIES OF SEARCH ENGINE QUERY LOGS

What are the most popular search terms on the Web? And, how do users' queries relate to the events and moods of the people at any given moment? Such questions and others relating to web searchers' habits can be gleaned from search engine logs that record every query that we issue. Google's Zeitgeist page[82] records search trends and patterns through the usage of its engine on a daily basis and summarized over longer periods. (According to the Oxford dictionary, zeitgeist is the German word for "time-spirit" more often translated as "spirit of the age"; it refers to the defining spirit or mood of a particular period of history.)

The trends are based on many billions of Google searches that were conducted during the year, from all over the world. You can find out who were the most popular people in that year, what were the most popular brands, and other information such as the top news stories for the year.

With billions of searches per day to contend with, which amounts to tens of thousands of searches every second, Google is able to get a very clear picture of what web searchers are looking for (see Section 2.1.2 for more detail on search engine usage statistics).

4.4.1 Search Engine Query Logs

The query log of a search engine records various bits of information for each query issued. First, an anonymous user code is assigned to the query, and this code is used to identify the web address of the user (cookies may be used to track users' queries over time). Second, the time and date of the query are recorded. Third, the query terms as submitted by the user are recorded and lastly, the pages viewed by the user and their rank in the search result listing are recorded. The format of the log data allows the determination of query sessions, where a search session is a sequence of consecutive queries made by a single user within a small time window.

Apart from term popularity, other useful statistics that can be measured from query log data are the most popular topics related to the queries, average number of terms per query, average number of queries per session, average number of result pages viewed per query, and the use of advanced search features. Table 4.1 summarizes some of the results found from the query logs of AltaVista (1998) [608], Excite (2001) [625], AlltheWeb (2002) [333], and the metasearch engines Vivisimo (2004)—which has been rebranded as Clusty [386]—and Dogpile (2005) [335]. As can be seen, web queries contain very few terms; most query sessions contain only one to two queries, users only view between one to two screens of results, and in most cases, the terms are just typed into the query box without the use of any advanced query syntax. (Similar conclusions were obtains from an analysis of an MSN Search query log from 2006 [700].)

[82]Google Zeitgeist-Search patterns, trends, and surprises according to Google. www.google.com/press/zeitgeist.html.

TABLE 4.1 Summary of analysis of search engine logs.

Statistic	AltaVista	AlltheWeb	Excite	Clusty	Dogpile
Average terms per query	2.35	2.30	2.60	3.13	2.79
Average queries per session	2.02	2.80	2.30	3.62	2.85
Average result pages viewed	1.39	1.55	1.70	1.07	1.67
Usage of advanced features	20.4%	1.0%	10.0%	23.3%	9.8%

It is interesting that the main conclusions from query logs seem to transcend language. Analysis that was carried out on a query log of Naver, which is the leading search engine in Korea, came up with similar results [531]. One difference is that sequences of simple nouns in Korean can either be separated with delimiters or put together into a compound noun. Thus, the average number of terms in a Naver query was 2.03 counting the simple nouns in a query but only 1.13 when considering compound nouns inputs. Another study carried out on a query log of Timway (www.timway.com), which is a web portal and directory designed to search for web sites in Hong Kong, showed similar patterns for searches using Chinese characters [135]. As with Korean searches, there is a language effect, since Chinese is a character-based rather than term-based language. It was found that the average number of characters per query is 3.38, which is larger than the number of terms in English-based queries, as shown in Table 4.1. There are significantly less Chinese characters than English terms and this is reflected by the fact that 50 of the characters account for a quarter of all the characters in the log, which is much higher than in the English logs; for example, in the Dogpile log the 100 most frequent terms account for less than a fifth of all the terms in the log data [335].

More recent statistics from 2009 provides some evidence that searches are getting longer.[83] In particular, since 2008, queries with an average of five or more terms have increased by about 8%, while queries having an average length of one to four terms have decreased by about 2%. A possible explanation of this, assuming this trend continues, is that as the Web gets bigger and users become more experienced, searchers are better able to express their information needs.

Temporal analysis of query logs shows that users spend more time interacting with search engines during the day than during the night (520, 699). Moreover, if we analyze the query traffic across a week we see a marked decline on Fridays and a peak in traffic over the weekend [66]. This analysis was done over an AOL log of searches in the United States, so we would expect the peaks to move according to the culture of the searchers.

When doing a topical analysis of the categories users are searching on, there may also be cultural differences but overall, categories relating to our lifestyle such as Entertainment, Shopping, Computing, Places, News, Health, and Adult

[83] Longer search queries becoming more popular. http://www.hitwise.com/us/press-center/press-releases/google-searches-mar-09.

are the most popular (66, 53, 530). Combining topical and temporal analysis reveals that some categories differ in popularity according to the time of day or day of week, and that there are pronounced seasonal effects over longer periods for some categories, notably Holidays. It is interesting to note that many queries are misspelled, and many queries are just URLs when users wish to reach a web site through the search engine rather than typing it into the browser's address bar.

A line of research emanating from long-term query logs to learn about the world we live in, was described by Richardson [565]. The idea is to look at how individual user queries evolve over time and relate to other queries. A correlation between, say a query such as "coffee" and a reference query such as "tea," will tell us if users who are interested in the main query are also likely to be interested in the reference query. Another useful measurement is looking at how the popularity of queries changes over time, and how users' interests change over time. Tracking queries over a long period may contain valuable information which could be useful for scientific research.

The availability of search engine logs is essential for researchers who are studying patterns of web searchers. In most cases, such data sets are not released publicly due to privacy concerns and a data asset license agreement is attached to their use.

On August 4, 2006 AOL released a log file containing details of 200 million queries from over 650,000 of its users in the United States within a three-month period, intended for research purposes.[84] Despite users being anonymized by a unique number, the query terms in the log were very revealing, and at times containing personally identifying data such as a social security number. On August 7, AOL removed the logs from public access due to their violation of privacy, but in the meanwhile the logs were mirrored on several sites on the Web from where they could be downloaded. AOL apologized for releasing the data and fired the researcher who released the logs and his supervisor. A month later AOL decided to create the new post of chief privacy officer. The personal search histories of the AOL users caused a flurry in the media and even inspired a theatrical production called *User 927*.

The release of this log has inspired research on anonymizing query logs [488], and is still being analyzed by researchers despite the controversy surrounding it.

4.4.2 Search Engine Query Syntax

What is the added value of using advanced query syntax? Jansen [328] has been considering the impact of using advanced search options on the top ten results returned from a search engine. He considered the Boolean operators "AND" and "OR" with their intuitive meanings, phrase matching by surrounding the keywords in the phrase with double quotes, and the plus operator "+", where

[84]AOL search data scandal. http://en.wikipedia.org/wiki/AOL_search_data_scandal.

a "+" in front of a keyword such as "chess" means that you insist that each result web page must include the term "chess." The outcome was that overall, approximately 6.6 out of the first ten results returned from a search engine using no advanced query syntax, also appear in the top ten results when advanced syntax is being used. So Archie's choice to specify his query simply as a list of keywords has been vindicated, as advanced syntax will not have much impact on his ability to find the information he seeks.

The explanation for this outcome is in the way search engines operate in determining relevance of web pages. For most search engines, the query "computer chess" is the same as "computer AND chess," so adding the "AND" operators between keywords does not make any difference. Also, many search engines interpret a keyword such as "chess" as being equivalent to "+chess," so if you type in a keyword you are actually insisting that it be included in all results on the hit list. Now, what about the use of "OR," say in the query "computer OR chess"? Most search engines will rank a web page containing both keywords higher than a page containing only one of the keywords, so pages answering the query "computer chess" will be ranked higher than any pages appearing in the separate queries with just "computer" or just "chess."

Regarding phrase matching, the query "computer chess" insists that all web pages returned contain exactly that phrase. This will exclude web pages that contain "computer" and "chess" that are not right next to each other as a phrase. In general, search engines consider how near query terms are to each other on the pages returned. So for the query "computer chess," which does not include phrase matching, search engines assign higher ranks to pages having the keywords "computer" and "chess" closer to each other. This type of ranking rule is called *proximity matching*. For example, if the query is "computer chess" pages that have the phrase "computer chess" will rank higher than pages that only have the phrase "computer programs that play chess" where the keywords "computer" and "chess" are further away from each other.

Another point to make is that the order in which the keywords were typed into the search engine makes a difference. So, the query "computer chess" is different from the query "chess computer," in the sense that search engines will take the keyword order into account in the final ranking, preferring web pages that maintain the order of the terms as in the query. All the above statements are not 100% accurate, since each search engine has its own quirks, and also, apart from the content of pages, there are other ways in which search engines measure relevance, for instance through link analysis, which may override the expected behavior I have just outlined.

That is not to say that all advanced syntax is useless. There are other operators that search engines provide such as the minus operator "-," where a "-" in front of a keyword such as "bridge" excludes web pages containing the term "bridge" from the results list. Other useful features are restricting the date of results so that, for example, only web pages that were updated during the last year are returned, and restricting the search engine's result to a specified web site, which is often useful when you are surfing within a specific web site.

4.4.3 The Most Popular Search Keywords

Table 4.2 shows the top five keywords found in the query logs, from the above-mentioned studies, excluding extremely common words such as "of," "and," and "the" which are called *stop words*. The frequent occurrence of the term "applet" stands out as anomalous (an applet is a small program running on a web browser). It turns out that most of the queries containing this term were submitted to the search engine by a software program rather than a human user.

Research in which the author of this book is involved in [457], has been looking into the association between surfing behavior and user queries. Suppose Archie submits a query to a search engine and then clicks on one of the result links presented to him. In this case, we would like to know how many more links Archie is likely to follow. It turns out that on an average, users only follow 1.65 additional links. So, although web searchers' queries are often underspecified, searchers still wish to have high-quality results at their fingertips and follow these up with as little navigation as possible.

To see what other people are searching for, search engines provide us with a buzz index, presenting to us information such as the most popular searches for the period, the top news stories, and more generally, which topics people are interested in on the Web.[85] This may be a mere curiosity but I can well imagine that those addicted to web searching and surfing are very interested in knowing what is popular at this moment.

Popularity of search terms and trends can also be put to more serious uses. One example is that of detecting flu activity within a region [254]. Millions of users are searching weekly for health-related information and the frequency of flu-related queries is highly correlated with the number of people having influenza-like symptoms. Although a person searching for "flu" may not actually be ill, the search patterns within a region provide collective evidence that helps estimate the severity of flu in a particular region. To test the idea, the researchers processed hundreds of billions of past queries to Google within a 5-year time window to generate models that monitor flu outbreaks. It was shown that the models generated from Google searches have a high correlation with models generated from traditional data collection methods.

TABLE 4.2 Top five keywords from search engine logs.

AltaVista	AlltheWeb	Excite	Clusty	Dogpile
Sex	Free	Free	Free	Free
Applet	Sex	Sex	Download	Girls
Porno	Download	Pictures	New	Sex
mp3	Software	New	2004	Nude
Chat	UK	Nude	Software	Lyrics

[85]Google Trends. www.google.com/trends; Yahoo Buzz. http://buzz.yahoo.com/; MSN a-list. http://a-list.msn.com/; Ask IQ. http://sp.ask.com/en/docs/iq/iq.shtml.

Another use of the data from Google Trends (www.google.com/trends) is to measure present economic activity in given industries [147]. So for example, the volume of queries of a particular car brand during the second week of the month may be useful in predicting the sales of that brand by the end of the month. To explain how the prediction works, note that queries are classified into a small number of categories; so, for example, car-related queries would belong to the automotive category. For a given query composed of one or more search terms, its *query index* is a number that represents the relative volume of that query in a given region at a particular point in time. Plotting the query index over time gives a time series from which trends can be detected and predictions made, using time series forecasting models [449]. This approach to short-term economic prediction in economic time series was found to be useful in several areas including car sales, home sales, retail sales, and travel behavior. Moreover, the researchers concluded that relevant Google Trends variables tend to outperform models that exclude these predictors.

4.5 ARCHITECTURE OF A SEARCH ENGINE

If you were to build a search engine, what components would you need and how would you connect them together? You could consult Sergey Brin and Larry Page's seminal paper "The anatomy of a large-scale hypertextual web search engine" published in April 1998, before Google was incorporated later that year [105]. I will present you with a simplified answer, which is given in the architecture diagram shown in Fig. 4.5. The main components of a search engine are the crawler, indexer, search index, query engine, and search interface.

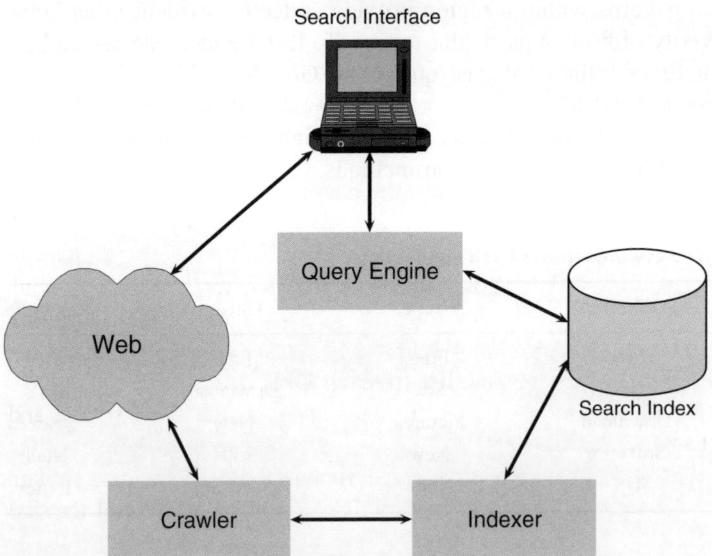

Figure 4.5 Simplified search engine architecture.

As I have already mentioned, a *web crawler* is a software program that traverses web pages, downloads them for indexing, and follows the hyperlinks that are referenced on the downloaded pages; web crawlers will be discussed in detail in the next section. As a matter of terminology, a web crawler is also known as a *spider*, a *wanderer* or a *software robot*. The second component is the *indexer* which is responsible for creating the search index from the web pages it receives from the crawler.

4.5.1 The Search Index

The *search index* is a data repository containing all the information the search engine needs to match and retrieve web pages. The type of data structure used to organize the index is known as an *inverted file*. It is very much like an index at the back of a book. It contains all the words appearing in the web pages crawled, listed in alphabetical order (this is called the *index file*), and for each word it has a list of references to the web pages in which the word appears (this is called the *posting list*). In 1998 Brin and Page reported the Google search index to contain 14 million words, so currently it must be much larger than that, although clearly very much smaller than the reported number of web pages covered, which is currently over 600 billion. (Google reported that after discarding words that appear less than 200 times, there are about 13.6 million unique words in Google's search index.[86])

Consider the entry for "chess" in the search index. Attached to the entry is the posting list of all web pages that contain the word "chess"; for example, the entry for "chess" could be

```
chess → [www.chess.co.uk, www.uschess.org,
            www.chessclub.com, ...]
```

Often, more information is stored for each entry in the index such as the number of documents in the posting list for the entry, that is, the number of web pages that contain the keyword, and for each individual entry in the posting file we may also store the number of occurrences of the keyword in the web page and the position of each occurrence within the page. This type of information is useful for determining content relevance.

The search index will also store information pertaining to hyperlinks in a separate *link database*, which allows the search engine to perform hyperlink analysis, which is used as part of the ranking process of web pages. The link database can also be organized as an inverted file in such a way that its index file is populated by URLs and the posting list for each URL entry, called the *source* URL, contains all the *destination* URLs forming links between these source and destination URLs. The link database for the Web can be used to reconstruct the structure of the web and to have good coverage, its index file will have to contain billions of entries. When we include the posting lists in the calculation of the size

[86] All Our N-gram are Belong to You, by A. Franz and T. Brants, August 2006. http://googleresearch.blogspot.com/2006/08/all-our-n-gram-are-belong-to-you.html.

of the link database, then the total number of entries in the database will be an order of magnitude higher. Compression of the link database is thus an important issue for search engines, who need to perform efficient hyperlink analysis. Randall *et al.* [556] have developed compression techniques for the link database, which take advantage of the structure of the Web. Their techniques are based on the observations that most web pages tend to link to other pages on the same web site, and many web pages on the same web site tend to link to a common set of pages. Combing these observations with well-known compression methods, they have managed to reduce the space requirements to six bits per hyperlink.

The text which is attached to a hyperlink, called *link (or anchor) text*, that is clicked on by users following the link, is considered to be part of the web page it references. So when a word such as "chess" appears in some link text, then the posting list for that word will contain an entry for the destination URL of the link.

4.5.2 The Query Engine

The *query engine* is the algorithmic heart of the search engine. The inner working of a commercial query engine is a well-guarded secret, since search engines are rightly paranoid, fearing web sites who wish to increase their ranking by unscrupulously taking advantage of the algorithms the search engine uses to rank result pages. Search engines view such manipulation as spam, since it has dire effects on the quality of the results presented to the user. (Spam is normally associated with unsolicited e-mail also known as *junk e-mail*, although the word spam originally derives from spiced ham and refers to a canned meat product.) It is not straightforward to distinguish between search engine spam and organic search engine optimization, where a good and healthy design of web pages leads them to be visible on the top results of search engines for queries related to the pages; we will elaborate on the inner workings of a search engine-ranking algorithm in Chapter 5. Suffice to say at this stage that some of the issues regarding search engine spamming will have to be settled in court.

The query engine provides the interface between the search index, the user, and the Web. The query engine processes a user query in two steps. In the first step, the query engine retrieves from the search index information about potentially relevant web pages that match the keywords in the user query, and in the second step a ranking of the results is produced, from the most relevant downwards. The ranking algorithm combines content relevance of web pages (see Section 5.1), and other relevance measures of web pages based on link analysis (see Section 5.2) and popularity (see Section 5.3). Deciding how to rank web pages revolves upon our understanding of the concept of what is "relevant" for a user, given a query. The problem with relevance is that what is relevant for one user may not be relevant to another. In a nutshell, relevance is, to a large degree, personal and depends on the context and task the user has in mind. Search engines take a very pragmatic view of relevance and continuously tweak and improve their ranking algorithms by examining how surfers search the Web; for example, by studying recent query logs. Of course, there is also the issue of personalization and once search engines encroach into this territory, which I believe is inevitable, the competition for relevance will move into a higher gear (see Section 6.4).

4.5.3 The Search Interface

Once the query is processed, the query engine sends the results list to the *search interface*, which displays the results on the user's screen. The user interface provides the look and feel of the search engine, allowing the user to submit queries, browse the results list, and click on chosen web pages for further browsing. From the usability point of view, it is important that users can distinguish between sponsored links, which are ads, and organic results, which are ranked by the query engine. While most of the web search engines have decided to move away from the web portal look toward the simpler, cleaner look pioneered by Google, several of them, notably Yahoo and MSN, maintain the portal look of their home page, offering their users a variety of services in the hope of converting them to customers, independently of their use of the core search services.

4.6 CRAWLING THE WEB

Google's web crawlers scour the Web covering over a trillion web pages in a continuous spidering effort. Periodically, Google updates its search index,[87] which as of late 2009 was distributed across more than 500,000 servers in several clusters and as of mid-2008, was geographically dispersed in 36 data centers (see Section 4.7 for more details).

Google stores dozens of copies of its search index across its clusters and during the Google dance, which is the period of time between the start and end of the index update, some of the servers will inevitably have an old version of the index, and thus search results will vary depending on the servers from which results are retrieved. Normally, the Google dance takes a few days, and this period is considered to be the best time for web sites to update the content of their web pages. As soon as the dance is finished, Google starts a new crawl in full swing, and if the new crawl does not harvest the updated web pages, webmasters will have to wait for another month before Google will have a fresh copy of their site. The Google dance period is also the time when Google introduces tweaks to its query engine, so webmasters are eager to find out the up-to-date ranking of their site in order to optimize it before the next dance.[88]

Google and other search engines are continuously crawling the Web and as of 2008, Google was already reprocessing the web graph on a daily basis.[89] Despite the more frequent updates that occur these days, webmasters and search

[87]Google dance-The index update of the Google search engine, M. Sobek. http://dance.efactory.de.

[88]GDS: The Google Dance Syndrome, Parts 1 and 2, by D. Sullivan, July 2003. www.clickz.com/search/opt/article.php/2228391 and www.clickz.com/search/opt/article.php/2228411.

[89]We knew the web was big ..., by J. Alpert and N. Hajaj, July 2008. http://googleblog.blogspot.com/2008/07/we-knew-the-web-was-big.html.

engine optimizers still report on major changes that occur as a result of the Google dance when it is detected.

Web crawlers surf the Web collecting web pages, which are passed on to the indexer for updating the search index. If the Web was static and none of its content ever changed, a search engine would only have to crawl the Web once. But as we know, the Web is continuously evolving with new pages appearing and old ones either changing or disappearing altogether. Due to the size of the Web and its growth, search engines are involved in an uphill struggle to cover as much as the Web as they can, and as I have pointed out, coverage is of prime importance to search engines as a prerequisite to quality and relevance.

4.6.1 Crawling Algorithms

The basic algorithm of a crawler works as follows [528] (Fig. 4.6): the crawler starts from a list of seed URLs to visit. The seed set must not only contain at least one URL from the largest strongly connected component of the web graph, so as to be able to reach as many web pages as possible, but it must also contain URLs from other parts of the Web to cover pages not reachable from the core. A good seed set can be obtained from a directory such as Yahoo or the Open Directory, while established search engines base their seed set on the URLs already in their search index. The list of URLs used by the crawler is dynamic; once a page is visited, it is removed from the list and after the links on a page being processed

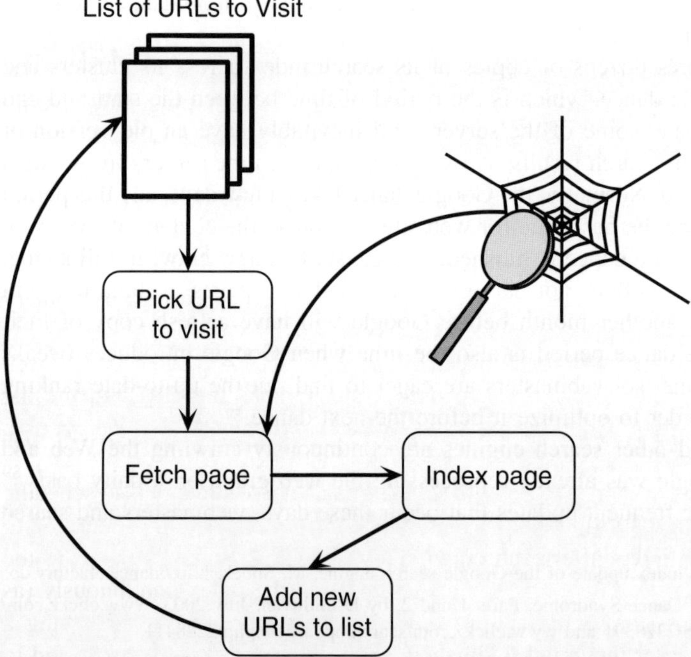

Figure 4.6 Basic crawler algorithm.

are identified, they are added to the list of remaining URLs to visit. The process normally terminates after a certain number of web pages have been indexed or a certain time has elapsed. In some cases where the goal of the crawl is clear, for example to crawl a list of pages whose date in the search index has expired, the crawl is terminated when the spider's mission is completed.

A crawler has to resolve several problems in order to carry out its job efficiently. One important issue is that of detecting duplicate web pages having different URLs (web page addresses). This can be done by mapping each URL to a compact string representing the content on the page, and comparing the content string of each new URL to existing ones [491]. Another important issue is the problem of which web pages to visit first.

A related problem is the quality of the web pages fetched. First, there is the issue of syntax: a crawler will have problems indexing a page that has errors such as misspecified URLs. Then there is the issue of dynamic HTML pages, having embedded scripts that can modify not only the look of a web page but also its contents, depending on the events occurring in the browser when the page is being viewed. A crawler will find dynamic HTML pages hard to interpret and therefore, may ignore them. There are other issues related to nonstandard page formats that crawlers have trouble in understanding, which is why web designers encourage using standard HTML as much as possible and being conscious of the fact that crawler-unfriendly web pages may not get indexed by search engines.

In a *breadth-first* crawl, URLs are picked from the list in the order in which they were put onto the list; in computer science terminology such an order is called *First-In-First-Out or FIFO*. Other metrics used to guide the crawl may rely on the link structure of pages, for example URLs having more hyperlinks pointing to them may be prioritized, which gives more importance to popular pages. Another metric may be guided by the domain; for example a URL ending in "`.com`" may deemed to be more important than other URLs in the list. Najork and Wiener [492] have demonstrated that when using link metrics to evaluate the quality of a page, the breadth-first strategy is very competitive, efficient, and discovers high-quality pages early in the crawl.

A breed of crawlers focusing their attention on a particular topic are called *focused crawlers*. In their simplest form, focused crawlers are driven by a query (i.e., a list of keywords) and the decision, which URL to pick from the list, is based on the textual similarity between the query and the content of the web page addressed by the URL. So a focused crawler ranks the URLs in the list and chooses the highest ranking to crawl first; this strategy is also known as a *best-first* strategy.

Yet another problem is to do with scheduling. A naive strategy is to schedule a new crawl of the Web immediately after the current crawl is finished, and to update the search index after each crawl. This type of arrangement leads to the commotion related to the Google dance, so updating the index continuously (as Google and other search engines are most likely doing) rather than having a complete update after the crawl is finished, should dampen the effects related to the index update.

4.6.2 Refreshing Web Pages

Another difficult problem is how often a crawler should refresh its pages. The simplest approach is to revisit all pages at the same frequency, independently of how the page changes and a more sophisticated approach is to revisit pages that change more often, more frequently. In practice, search engines will crawl sites with highly dynamic content such as news sites and e-commerce sites much more often than sites which change infrequently. Fetterly *et al.* [220] have shown that although most web pages do not undergo much change, larger web pages tend to change more often and to a larger extent than smaller ones. It was also shown that change is more frequent and extensive for pages whose top-level domain is `.com` or `.net`, than for pages from other domains such as `.edu` and `.gov`. It also turns out that past change to a web page is a good indicator of future change, which is encouraging for prediction purposes.

4.6.3 The Robots Exclusion Protocol

Crawlers need to be polite. By this, we mean that they should spread their visits to a particular web site over a period of time, since bombarding a web site with HTTP requests (the protocol for requesting a web page from a site) within short intervals will slow down the web site for human users. Web sites that wish to exclude crawlers from indexing some of their web pages can indicate this preference through the robots exclusion protocol.[90] This is done by keeping a text file called `robots.txt` in the root directory of the web site. For example, the following text indicates that all crawlers should not visit any URLs starting with "/docs" or "/logs". The "*" indicates that the exclusion pertains to all crawlers. If for some reason a web site only wishes to exclude Googlebot (the name of Google's crawler) or Slurp (the name of Yahoo's crawler) from these URLs, then the "*" is replaced by Googlebot or Slurp. A list of active web crawlers is kept in a database at www.robotstxt.org/wc/active.html.

```
User-agent: *
Disallow: /docs
Disallow: /logs
```

A curiosity observed by Greg Notess of Search Engine Showdown during mid-2003, was that Google was indexing the robots.txt files.[91] Whether this is intentional or is a mistake is not known.

The `robots.txt` file can also be used to publish URLs through the sitemaps directive. Sitemaps (www.sitemaps.org) is an XML protocol that allows webmasters to inform search engines about web pages in their site that are available for crawling [595]; see also Section 6.2.1. Sitemaps also includes additional metadata for each URL, including the date the page was last modified,

[90] A standard for robot exclusion. www.robotstxt.org/wc/norobots.html.

[91] Indexing robots.txt files, by G.R. Notess, July 2003. www.searchengineshowdown.com/newsarchive/000686.shtml.

how frequent the page is likely to change, and the relative priority of the page within the site.

Sitemaps are a relatively easy way for webmasters to publish the URLs in their sites and as of 2009, approximately 35 million web sites publish sitemaps including several billion URLs. For example, Amazon.com's sitemaps includes around 20 million URLs. As another example, media sites can make good use of sitemaps to publish daily news, as does CNN.com, which publishes daily news in Sitemaps of 200 to 400 URLs that change multiple times each day.

Web crawlers can incorporate sitemaps into their schedule to complement their discovery of web pages. Detecting sitemaps through the `robots.txt` file, and downloading them is inexpensive. On the other hand, relying solely on sitemaps is not enough, as they are not reliable enough and some are spammy. Nonetheless they can beneficially be integrated into the discovery process and URL ordering policy of a search engine's crawler.

4.6.4 Spider Traps

"Spider traps" are scripts embedded in URLs that can dynamically generate a large number of URLs referring to the same page. One type of spider trap is a dynamic URL, which is a web address that contains a question mark allowing a query to be embedded in the URL. For example, if you enter the URL www.google.com/search?q = dynamic+urls, into your browser, then it will display a results page from Google for the query "dynamic urls." When a crawler encounters such a spider trap that generates a web page with a large number of URLs, the spider will add all these links to its list of pages to visit and essentially get stuck in an unintended loop, consuming its computational resources. A well-known example of a spider trap is a dynamic URL that generates a web page with a calendar full of links for each date, all pointing to the same URL.

4.7 WHAT DOES IT TAKE TO DELIVER A GLOBAL SEARCH SERVICE?

How does a web search engine deliver an efficient and high-quality service to millions of surfers, hitting its servers billions of times a day, and on top of this maintain a fresh index in an environment that is in continuous flux? Well Google can do it, and in an article published in IEEE Micro several of Google's engineers revealed some of the ingredients of their system [58].

In 2003, Google's computer cluster combined over 15,000 standard PCs, running in-house developed fault-tolerant software. As of late 2009 this number increased to about 500,000 which is indicator of Google's tremendous growth in computing power and its ability to index and store billions of web pages and an enormous amount of multimedia such as YouTube videos. A standard Google server has 16 GB of RAM and 2 TB of disk space.[92]

[92]Advice from Google on large distributed systems, by G. Linden, October 2009. http://glinden.blogspot.com/2009/10/advice-from-google-on-large-distributed.html.

This architecture is much cheaper than using high performance servers and also much more efficient according to Google's engineers. Reliability of the system is attained at the software level by replicating services across many machines and automatically detecting and handling failures. With that many PCs, energy efficiency is another key factor, as power consumption and cooling are critical for this scale of operation.

How is a Google query served? To provide capacity for the massive query traffic, Google's service consists of several clusters distributed worldwide. Each cluster has thousands of PCs, the distribution protecting Google from catastrophic failures. (As of mid-2008, Google's servers were distributed world wide in 36 data centers.[93])

When a query is issued, a cluster is chosen to serve the query according to geographic proximity and once chosen, the query is processed locally on that cluster. Query execution consists of two main phases.

In the first phase, index servers consult an inverted index to match each keyword in the query to a list of web pages. The set of relevant pages for the query is determined by intersecting these lists, one for each keyword, and then computing the score of each relevant page in order to determine its rank. The result that is returned at this stage is a list of document identifiers.

In the second phase, the list of document identifiers is used to compile the results page that is delivered to the user's browser. This is handled by document servers and involves computing the title, URL, and summary of each relevant web page. To complete the execution, the spell checking and ad-serving systems are consulted.

Both phases are highly parallel, as the data, which comprises many petabytes in size (a petabype is equal to 1000 TB and a terabyte is equal to 1000 GB), is distributed across multiple servers. Overall, Google stores dozens of copies of its search index across its clusters. If part of a cluster is down for some reason, it will use machines from another cluster to keep the service operational, at the cost of reducing the overall capacity of the system. One of the axioms of Google's service is that it must be continuous and efficient at all times.

Updates to the index are done separately offline and the clusters are then updated one at a time; see Section 4.6, where we described the Google dance, which is the name coined for the time when its index is in the process of being updated.

Operating many thousands of PCs incurs significant administration and maintenance costs, but these are manageable due to the small number of applications running on each one of them. Additional costs are incurred for special cooling, which is needed for the clusters, due to the high level of power consumption.

The central design principles of Google's architecture are purchasing the CPUs with the best price-to-performance ratio, exploiting massive parallelism by distribution and replication, and using highly reliable and scalable software for all the applications, all of which is developed in-house.

[93]Where Are All The Google Data Centers?, by E. Schonfeld, April 2008. www.techcrunch.com/2008/04/11/where-are-all-the-google-data-centers.

Google's distributed architecture is based on three components: the Google File System (GFS) [251], the MapReduce algorithm [181], and the BigTable database system [134].

GFS is a very large, highly used, distributed, and fault-tolerant file system that is designed to work with Google's applications. GFS supports clusters, where each cluster has a single master and multiple chunkservers, and is accessed by multiple clients. Files are divided into chunks of fixed size (64 MB), and the chunkservers store chunks on local disks. For reliability, each chunk is replicated on multiple chunkservers. Metadata is maintained by the master, who controls the system-wide activities by communicating to the chunkservers. There is no caching of file data on the chunkservers or the clients. The master's involvement in reads and writes is minimal so as to avoid bottlenecks. It is expected that the traffic is dominated by reads and appends as opposed to writes that overwrite existing data, making consistency-checking easier.

MapReduce is a programming model borrowed from functional programming for processing large data sets on a distributed file system such as GFS. A computation is specified in term of *map* and *reduce* functions and the computation is automatically distributed across clusters. The computation can be carried out in parallel as the order of individual map and reduce operations does not effect the output, and although new data is created, existing data is not overwritten. The map operation takes a collection of key/value pairs and produces one or more intermediate key/value outputs for each input pair. The reduce operation combines the intermediate key/value pairs to produce a single output value for each key. For example, the input to map could be a URL (key) and document text (value). The intermediate output from map could be pairs of word (key) and occurrence (value), which would be one for each word, so in this case, the map splits the document into words and returns a one for each occurrence. Reduce will then combine the values from the pairs for each word and return a pair for each word with its count in the document. More than 10,000 MapReduce programs have been implemented in Google, and an average of 100,000 MapReduce jobs are executed daily, processing more than 20 PB of data per day [181].

Hadoop (http://hadoop.apache.org) is an open-source distributed file system for very large data sets, inspired by GFS and MaReduce [373]. Yahoo has been a large contributor to Hadoop and has been using it in their applications. Cloudera (www.cloudera.com) is a start-up centered on support and consulting services for enterprise users of Hadoop. It has its own distribution of Hadoop, making it easy for users to install and deploy the software. It has also released a graphical browser-based interface to Hadoop allowing easier management of clusters.

BigTable [134] is a distributed storage system designed by Google to scale reliably for very large data sets, with petabytes of data served over thousands of machines. BigTable is used widely in Google applications including web indexing, Google Earth, Google Finance, and Google Analytics.

Data in a BigTable is organized along three dimensions: row keys, column keys, and time stamps, which taken together uniquely identify a cell. A particular kind of BigTable is a webtable, where row keys are URLs, column keys are features of web pages, and the cells are page contents. Rows with consecutive keys are organized into tablets. For example, in a webtable all the rows from the same domain may form a tablet. Columns are grouped into column families. For example, "anchor" may be a family and each single anchor will be qualified by the name of its referring site, and the cell value will be the anchor text. Time stamps allow stating different versions of the same data.

BigTable uses GFS to store its data, and can be used with MapReduce to run large-scale parallel computations on tables. BigTable clusters, that is, a set of processes that run the BigTable software, have been in production at Google since mid-2005 and have taken about 7 years to design and develop. As of late 2006, there were more than 60 projects in Google using BigTable [134]. An open-source version of BigTable, called HBase, has been implemented over Hadoop [688]. Another open-source distributed database storage, modeled after BigTable, is Hypertable (www.hypertable.org); Hypertable is used by the Chinese search engine Baidu.

The BigTable concept arose from the need to store large amounts of distributed data in a wide table format with a large number of columns and sparsely populated rows, that is, where most fields are null, and where the schema, that is, the use of columns, may evolve over time [688]; see also Ref. 419. Moreover, due to the large number of columns, keyword search is the most appropriate when querying a wide table. This is the reason BigTable was designed and implemented in-house rather than over a traditional relational database management system.

CHAPTER SUMMARY

- A typical web search is keyword-based, without the use of advanced syntax. In addition to the organic results, query results often contain distinguishable sponsored links. For each result, the search engine displays dynamic summaries which highlight query terms and other information such as the URL of the result, its size, and possibly its category. The user may also have access to a cached copy of the result, and may be able to view similar pages.
- Search engines are the current information gatekeepers of the Web since to a large extent, we view the Web through the search engine's lens. There is a growing voice supporting the regulation of search engines, due to possible commercial bias of their indexes. This also involves a proposal for search engines to disclose their algorithms, although this is unlikely to happen in practice, as webmasters are constantly trying to use such knowledge to manipulate search engines' ranking to their advantage.
- The three main contenders in the current search engine wars are Google, Yahoo, and Bing. The first player Google, has raised the bar on search quality and dominated the search space in the last few years. The second player, Yahoo, is the veteran dot-com company that has boosted its search capabilities with a string of search engine technology acquisitions, and continues to provide many internet-related services apart from search.

The third player, Bing, which is Microsoft's search arm, is committed to continue developing its proprietary search technology and use Microsoft's control of the desktop to gain control of the search space.

- Statistics from studies of search engine query logs reveal that the average number of terms per query is just over two, the average number of queries per session is also about two, the average number of result pages scanned is between one and two, and in most cases, users do not use any advanced query syntax. Search engines keep track of popular queries to follow search patterns and trends.
- The architecture of a search engine includes a crawler, indexer, search index, query engine, and search interface. The crawler is a software program that traverses the Web by following links and downloading web pages that are sent to the indexer, which creates the search index. The search index is organized as an inverted-file data structure, which can be likened to a book's index. Information about hyperlinks is stored in a link database, giving quick access to a web page's outlinks through its URL. The query engine processes the query by first retrieving information about relevant web pages from the search and then combining this information to provide a ranked list of result pages. The search interface is responsible for displaying the results on the user's browser.
- Crawling the Web is an immense task, which is central to the function of a search engine. In order to continuously crawl billions of pages, a web crawler must efficiently resolve problems such as dealing with different page formats, detecting duplicate pages, choosing the links to follow next during its crawl, and deciding how often to refresh the pages it has visited. The robots exclusion protocol is an important mechanism by which web sites can exclude crawlers from indexing specified web pages.
- Delivering a 24/7 global web search service capable of answering billions of queries per day is an awesome task. It requires large-scale distributed computing power, replication of the indexes, and highly reliable and scalable software.
- Google's distributed architecture is based on three components: the Google File System (GFS), the MapReduce algorithm, and the BigTable database system. GFS is a very large, highly used, distributed, and fault-tolerant file system, that is designed to work with Google's applications. MapReduce is a programming model for processing large data sets on a distributed file system. BigTable is a distributed file system designed to scale to very large data sets.

EXERCISES

4.1. **[Discuss]**. Write an update on the state of play in the search engine wars, backing it up with facts you have collected from recent events reported in the online technology news.

4.2. [Miniproject]. Due to the dynamic nature of the Web, where new pages are being added, old ones removed, and current ones modified, the ranked list of a search engine's results for a given query will not be stable over time. Moreover, different search engines will, in general, return different lists of results for the same query.

The objective of this exercise is to determine the stability of a search engine's ranking algorithm over time, and to compare the ranking algorithms of different search engines.

Choose two queries, one which is very topical and the other which is not, and submit these queries to Google, Yahoo, and Bing twice a day, during the morning and evening, at approximately the same times, for the duration of a week. For each query and search engine, record the ranked list of the top ten results.

Report how each search engine's ranking changes over time and compare the rankings of the two search engines during the time period. Suggest, with appropriate justification, methods for comparing the two sets of search results (51, 52).

4.3. [Miniproject]. Save a log of your search queries for the duration of a week; see Ref. 520.

For each search, record (i) the search engine used, (ii) the keywords used in the search, (iii) any advanced syntax used, (iv) the time of the search, (v) whether the search was a reformulation of the previous query, (vi) the number of search results inspected, and (vii) the time when the search session was finished.

Analyze the results and summarize your findings.

4.4. [Explore]. Evaluate the user interface of the search engines, Yippy (www.yippy.com formerly clusty) and Carrot (www.carrot-search.com), and compare them to a standard web search engine interface such as that of Google, Yahoo, or Bing.

Have a look at the alternative search engine visual interface of quintura(www.quintura.com), and discuss their special features in relation to the standard search engine interface.

What is your wish list of features for the "ideal" search engine user interface?

4.5. [Miniproject]. Focused crawlers restrict the web pages they fetch to those that are relevant to a particular topic. Let us call a focused crawler, *simple*, if it only fetches pages, where the anchor text of the link leading to the page contains a specified keyword.

For example, a simple focused crawler could fetch only pages reached from links, whose anchor text contains the keyword "car." This is a straightforward way of building an index containing pages about cars.

Implement a simple focused crawler to operate on a small web site of your choice. Starting with the home page of the site as the sole seed URL, crawl the site several times with different specified keywords to guide each crawl.

For each fetched page, the crawler should store the URL of the page, its title if it has one, and the links on the page.

Compare the page sets that have been fetched as a result of the crawls, discussing the effectiveness of simple focused crawling.

CHAPTER 5

HOW DOES A SEARCH ENGINE WORK

> "Every once in a while a revolutionary product comes along that changes everything. One is very fortunate if you get to work on just one of these in your career."
>
> — Steve Jobs, Cofounder of Apple

IN THIS chapter, the nuts and bolts of how a search engine works and is evaluated are described. We detail how content relevance of web pages is measured, how the link structure of the web is used to measure the authority of web pages (emphasis is given to the explanation of Google's PageRank), and how popularity measures can be used to improve the quality of search.

CHAPTER OBJECTIVES

- Discuss the issue of the relevance of a search result to a query, and how we might measure this relevance.
- Explain how the indexer processes web pages before adding words and updating their posting lists in the inverted index.
- Explain how search engines process stop words, and discuss the issues related to stemming words.
- Introduce the notion of term frequency (TF) as a measure of content relevance.
- Discuss the activity of search engine optimization (SEO) and the problem of search engine spam.
- Introduce Luhn's argument that the words that best discriminate between documents are in the mid-frequency range.

An Introduction to Search Engines and Web Navigation, by Mark Levene

- Introduce Zipf's law regarding the frequency of occurrences of words in texts.
- Introduce the notion of inverse document frequency (IDF) as a measure of content relevance.
- Explain how TF–IDF (term frequency–inverse document frequency) is computed for a web page with respect to a query.
- Explain how caching popular queries can speed up the delivery of search results.
- Point out the potential usefulness of phrase matching and synonym detection.
- Point out how link text, URL analysis, and the date a web page was last updated can help search engines to detect the relevance of a page.
- Explain how the HTML structure of a web page can be taken into account by the ranking algorithm, by assigning different weights to words according to their surrounding HTML tag.
- Point out that spell checking query terms has become a standard feature of search engines, and describe how query logs can help with spelling suggestions.
- Discuss the proliferation of non-English queries on the web and the problems that search engines need to address to support non-English querying.
- Explain the bias of search engines toward finding home pages of web sites.
- Describe how query suggestions and related searches and concepts are derived to help users specify and refine queries.
- Motivate the use of link analysis as a method for measuring the importance of web pages.
- Highlight two different uses of links, as referential and informational.
- Show how, in the ranking of web pages for a given query, link analysis metrics can be combined with content relevance.
- Illustrate through a small case study the commercial implications of a major search engine using a link analysis metric such as PageRank to measure the importance of a site.
- Give a detailed explanation of the PageRank metric and show how it can be computed.
- Present the formal statement of the PageRank of a web page.
- Point out that the PageRank can be computed online while a crawler is spidering the web.
- Describe how PageRank can be approximated using a Monte Carlo computation, and point out that as in the online method the computation can be updated continuously during a web crawl.

- Explain the HITS (hyperlink-induced topic search) hubs and authorities link analysis algorithm for scoring web pages with respect to a query.
- Explain the SALSA (stochastic approach for link-structure analysis algorithm) for scoring web pages, which combines PageRank's random surfer model with the HITS algorithm.
- Indicate that in some cases a simple count of inlinks to a web page can be a useful metric.
- Point out that PageRank is biased against new pages and how this problem may be resolved by promoting the PageRank of a small fraction of new pages.
- Mention that despite the bias, search engines will direct users to sites with low PageRank when the queries come from the long tail.
- Explain the strategy of maximizing the PageRank of a new page added to a web community.
- Show how links in weblogs can influence, and, in some cases, manipulate PageRank values.
- Highlight the problem of link spam and how it can be combatted.
- Discuss citation analysis as the precursor of link analysis.
- Explain how co-citation works and its application in finding similar or related web pages.
- Present Google Scholar, a special purpose search engine that indexes scholarly articles and books that are available on the Web and provides citation counts for them.
- Explain Direct Hit's popularity metric and the problems in making it effective.
- Trace the roots of the popularity metric to the technique of document space modification.
- Describe how query logs can be used to improve a search engine's ranking algorithm.
- Explain how machine learning can be effective for learning to rank search engine results.
- Introduce BrowseRank, a page ranking method based on real user browsing behavior.
- Present different ways of evaluating the quality of search engines.
- Discuss how eye tracking studies can be used to discover and quantify how users view search results, and highlight the significant result that searchers' behavior exhibits an F-shaped scan patten.
- Discuss the issues of using test collections, which include relevance assessments on a predefined set of topics, in order to evaluate search engines.
- Present a method for inferring the ranking algorithm of a search engine.

5.1 CONTENT RELEVANCE

Prior to web search engines coming on the scene, there were information storage and retrieval systems that were mainly used in institutions such as libraries to index and retrieve document collections. A classical treatment of IR by van Rijsbergen from 1979 can be found on the Web [655], and the IR book that has been the most influential in terms of measuring content relevance by Salton (the leading authority on IR of his time) and McGill from 1983 is now out of print [583].

The issue of "relevance" has haunted the IR community for decades. As it was mentioned earlier, relevance is a relative concept and depends not only on the query but also on the user and the context in which a query is issued. As search engines do not normally have much information on hand about the user other than the query, the context does not currently have much influence on the ranking process. It is conceivable that search engines currently take into account information such as geographic location and time of day, but utilizing further user context such as search preferences and history of previous searches is a massive operation involving regular data collection from each user on an individual basis. It is likely that search engines technology is moving in the direction of personalizing search results to increase relevance, but there are still many issues to resolve including technical, logistic, and privacy related issues, some of which are discussed in Section 6.4.

So, how do we measure relevance of a web page to a query? One way to measure relevance is to present web pages (documents) to the searcher, say Archie, and simply ask him to assess how relevant these pages are to the query. In the simple scenario, all Archie has do is to judge documents as being relevant or nonrelevant (this is called *binary relevance assessment*). In a more complex scenario, Archie has to grade documents, for example, on a scale of one to five, according to how relevant the documents are (this is called *nonbinary relevance assessment*).

From the search engine's point of view such a solution is far from satisfactory. First, there is the problem of in what order to present the initial set of documents to users, and second users are often reluctant to provide feedback and their query sessions are typically short. Over 50% are less than 15 mins long and over 25% are less than 5 mins [332]. So, we need a more pragmatic approach to computing relevance with respect to a query.

5.1.1 Processing Web Pages

Archie has just submitted the query "computer backgammon" to his favorite search engine. As a first step to determining, which web pages have content that is relevant to the query, the query engine could pick up from the inverted file all the web pages that have at least one occurrence of both the keywords "computer" and "backgammon."

Before we dig deeper to see what the query engine does with the web pages that match all the keywords in the query, let us discuss the way in which a web page (document) is processed by the indexer before entries for these keywords are added to the inverted file. The first step is to parse the page into words. To determine word boundaries, the occurrence of a space is often not enough; punctuation marks, special symbols, and specific syntax such as HTML tags needs to be taken into account. Nowadays, indexers have to deal with a variety of popular file formats such as plain old text, HTML, PDF, MS Word, Postscript, and dynamic HTML pages written in a scripting language, for example, JavaScript. Once we have split the page into words we need to determine which words to get rid of. Do we index numbers, or words that contain numbers or special characters? For example, submitting the query "1:0" to Google will return, amongst others, web pages about football matches with that result.

Most web search engines try and index as much as possible, so, for example, strings of numbers and characters are often catalog numbers, which users may find useful when they are e-shopping. Some words are so frequent that they appear in almost all documents, for example, "of," "an," "a," "to," and "the". You could probably find a list of such stop words somewhere on the web but I was somewhat unsuccessful in my search.[94]

Most web search engines actually index stop words to take care of queries such as "to be or not to be," but they normally exclude them from queries unless they are specified in a phrase such as "in a bottle" or the user forces them to be included with a plus, such as "+in +a bottle." This is done for efficiency reasons, for example, during late 2004 Google reported that it has found about 7.39 billion pages containing the stop word "a," and Yahoo reported that it has found about 2.18 billion such pages.

Stemming is a technique for removing the suffixes of a word to expose its root form known as its stem. The Porter stemmer[95] is the most widely publicized in the IR literature. The idea is that a word such as computer is replaced by comput, as are its variants computation, computers, computing, and computed. Stemming reduces variations of common words to a single stem thus reducing the size of the vocabulary included in the index. The flip side of the coin is that the size of the posting lists are increased. A partial stemmer is often used, which focuses only on plurals and the most common suffixes such as ED and ING.

The effect of stemming is an increase in the number of documents retrieved for a given keyword due to the increase in the posting list for that keyword, and thus the recall (number of relevant documents retrieved divided by the total number of relevant documents) of the system is also increased. This means that the results list returned by the query engine will be much larger, but it does not necessarily imply that the results list will contain a higher proportion of relevant pages, that is, the precision of the system may in fact decrease.

In general, stemming may not improve the relevance of the first page of results returned by the query engine, and since users do not view much more than this first set of results, it is not clear whether stemming will improve the

[94]A portion of a stop word list, Table 2.1, van Rijsbergen's book on Information Retrieval. www.dcs.gla.ac.uk/Keith/Chapter.2/Table_2.1.html.

[95]Porter stemming algorithm. www.tartarus.org/~martin/PorterStemmer.

overall quality of a web search engine. This is the reason why in large corpora such as the web full stemming is often not used, although there may still be a strong case for partial stemming.

For this reason AltaVista (now powered by Yahoo's integrated search engine) did not originally support stemming at all. Until late 2003 Google did not support stemming, but then it started to use partial stemming, which includes singular and plural forms; the full extent to which stemming occurs in Google has not been disclosed.[96] Yahoo also supports some form of partial stemming, but again the details have not been disclosed.

Another feature called *truncation* allows users to query just a portion of a word; for example, the keyword "comp*" will find web pages with keywords beginning with "comp" such as company, computer, and compare. As with stemming, this feature will increase recall but not necessarily precision, so it is not surprising that only one major web search engine, namely, AltaVista, is known to have supported truncation.

One further issue worth mentioning is that before inserting the word into the index, the indexer may wish to convert all words to lower case to reduce the size of the word index. On the other hand, in some circumstances we may wish to retain the original so as to be able to discriminate, for example, between "Explorer" (a shorthand for Microsoft Internet Explorer) and "explorer." Google and Yahoo do not distinguish between upper and lower case letters; however, AltaVista did, when the keywords were surrounded by double quotes.

5.1.2 Interpreting the Query

Remember that when Archie submitted the query "computer backgammon," the query engine fetched the web pages that have at least one occurrence of both the keywords "computer" and "backgammon." This can be done by finding the common web page addresses in the posting lists for the entries "computer" and "backgammon," found in the index of the inverted file, that is, the intersection between these two lists is computed. As discussed in Section 4.4, the search engine is interpreting the query as "computer AND backgammon," which is why it is assuming that the user is interested only in web pages having both the keywords in the query. It is of prime importance for web search to narrow down the set of candidate web pages as quickly as possible, since users expect subsecond response times to their queries. For this reason, a looser interpretation of the query as "computer OR backgammon," which would result in far more results, has to be stated explicitly by the user.

5.1.3 Term Frequency

The now standard way for computing the baseline content relevance is called *TF–IDF* (term frequency–inverse document frequency). For a given document, its TF is computed by counting the number of occurrences of the word in the

[96]The basics of Google search, Word variations (stemming). www.google.com/help/basics.html.

document; just imagine that all the words in the document are put into a bag and shaken up so that all occurrences of "computer" and "backgammon" can be lifted out and counted separately.

The computation of TF should take into account the length of a document, since otherwise longer documents will be favored as they are more likely to have more occurrences of any keyword. The simplest way to normalize TF is to divide it by the length of the document, that is, the number of words in the bag. Other normalization methods exist such as dividing by the byte size of the document, dividing by the number of occurrences of the most frequent word in the document, or dividing by the deviation of the document's length from the average length document in the corpus.

TF is based on the observation that the frequency of occurrence of a term in a document is a useful indication of whether this term is meaningful in the context of the document. So, web pages about backgammon should have a high TF for the keyword "backgammon," and, moreover, if the page is about computer backgammon, the combined TF values for "computer" and "backgammon" should be high.

Being visible to a search engine has strong implications for web sites in terms of the number of hits they will receive, so there is a temptation for webmasters to repeat the keywords they perceive the page to be about in order to increase its search engine ranking. As long as the text on a web page is designed to get a clear message across, then such design practices should be encouraged, but taking it to an extreme could result in the page being labeled as spam. A working definition of content spam is a portion of a web page designed to deceive search engines in order to improve the ranking of the page without adding any relevant information to the user browsing the page.

Techniques used by search engine spammers include keyword stuffing, hidden text, tiny text, redirects, page swapping, duplicate pages, doorway pages, and cloaking [644].

- Keyword stuffing involves numerous repetition of keywords without improving the content. This can be made invisible to the user browsing the page by hiding the text between tags, using a color which is not visible to the user or making the text very small, possibly placing it atthe bottom of the page.
- A redirect is a web page that sends the user to a different page after a short period, which is in fact the page the spammer wants the user to see.
- Page swapping is simply changing the content of the page once the page is indexed, but this involves synchronization with the search engine crawling schedule, which is quite difficult.
- Duplicate pages involve the creation of many web pages, which are very similar, to make sure that the web site as a whole appears high on the search engine ranking.
- Doorway pages are an extreme variation of keyword stuffing, purely for obtaining a high ranking, and since doorway pages often do not make

sense, cloaking is used. This means that the spammed version of the page is presented to the crawler, while the web page presented to the user is a different page altogether.

What is common to all these spamming techniques is that it raises the TF of the spammed page without adding any relevant content to the page.

A very high TF value for a non-stop word is suspicious in any case and can indicate one of two problems. First, it could be due to a very short document, where in the extreme case we have a single word document. Second, it could be spam, for example, if the same word is repeated too often, say over 50% of the time, the document will generally not make sense. These sort of anomalies can be detected by search engines and dealt with, by biasing against pages containing words with an abnormally high TF.

Search engine optimization (SEO) is the activity of designing pages in a web site so that they rank highly on search engines for targeted queries. There is much sound advice that an SEO firm can give to a web site owner, but it seems that there are a few SEO firms out there encouraging web sites' owners to create spam pages in an attempt to unfairly manipulate the ranking of their sites. The problem has become important enough for Google to address it directly by giving advice to webmasters on how to distinguish between spam and ham (ham is the opposite of spam).[97] Google's message is simple: if you try and spam us as a means of increasing your chances of improving your ranking, you will increase your chances of being dropped altogether from the index.

Luhn, who is considered the "father of information retrieval," pioneered the use of automatic methods in IR, that we now take for granted. He advocated using the frequency of a word as a measure of its significance in a document [444]. Luhn argued that words in a document that are either very frequent or very infrequent are not useful for discriminating the document from other documents in the corpus.

We have already mentioned stop words that occur frequently in almost all documents and thus do not help in discriminating one document from another, which is why they are normally removed from queries. The Web is very diverse in terms of its coverage of topics, so apart from stop words, such as "the" and "of," no other words are normally excluded, but in a more restricted corpus, for instance on games, the word "games" and its variants would probably appear in most documents and therefore would not provide any discriminative power.

Luhn also argued that very infrequent words that only appear rarely, say once or twice, in a document do not convey much meaning. This is harder to justify than the absence of meaning for very frequent words and is, to some degree, in contrast to IDF (inverse document frequency) commonly used for measuring content relevance, and explained below. (However, note that IDF refers to the number of documents containing a word rather than the number of occurrence of a word in a document.)

[97]Google information for webmasters, Search engine optimizers. www.google.com/webmasters/seo.html.

For example, consider a very infrequent term such as "labsheet10." If you type the query "labsheet10" into Google or Yahoo you will get in return a URL containing the SQL lab exercise for the 10th lab in my database management course (the last time I submitted this query was early 2010). The term "labsheet10" on its own does not convey any meaning and I could have called it "last-labsheet" without any loss of information. Looking up "labsheet" in the Oxford dictionary will not return any results, so the term "labsheet10" is not a very literate description of the lab sheet, although arguably it is excellent for discrimination purposes, which is why IDF is widely used by search engines. Sequences of numbers and characters such as part numbers are good examples of low-frequency terms that do not have any linguistic meaning but are very useful for product searching, since their IDF is high.

One way to measure the significance of terms and provide some justification for Luhn's argument has been advocated by Losee [439]. Losee suggested looking at phrases, say of two terms, rather than individual words and then to test their statistical dependence on each other. Using more technical language, the dependence between two terms is measured through their mutual information for a given corpus. It turns out that the very low-frequency terms (as well as the very high-frequency terms) have higher mutual information than the mid-frequency terms. So, terms in the mid-frequency range are less influenced by neighboring terms and are thus more discriminative on their own.

Another aspect of text that is often referred to is called *Zipf's law*, named after the Harvard linguistic professor George Kingsley Zipf (1902–1950), who discovered that the frequency of occurrence of words in a text corpus follows a regular pattern.[98] What Zipf observed is that if you take a text, say a book or in our case a large collection of web pages, count the number of occurrences of each word in the text, and rank them from the most frequent to the least frequent, then the frequency of any word is, to a good approximation, inversely proportional to its rank. So, the most frequent word in English, "the," is roughly twice as frequent as the second most common word and 10 times more frequent than the 10th common word. Zipf's law can be rephrased as stating that the product of the rank of a word and its frequency is approximately constant across the corpus. Zipfian distributions, technically known as *power laws* (see Section 9.6), are abundant in nature and also occur in the analysis of the structure and usage of the Web. Luhn used Zipf's law as a baseline distribution for providing the cutoff points for very frequent and rare words, leaving the most significant words between these two cutoff points.

5.1.4 Inverse Document Frequency

We now turn to the IDF, which is a measure of content relevance that is higher for terms that occur less frequently in the corpus. In its raw form we compute the IDF of a keyword by dividing the total number of documents in the corpus by the number of documents in which the term appears.

[98]Zipf's law, Resource maintained by W. Li. http://www.nslij-genetics.org/wli/zipf.

Strictly speaking, there is a small technical problem if the term does not appear in any documents, but this is easily overcome if we add a small constant to both the numerator and denominator when computing the raw IDF of a term.

The intuitive justification for the IDF measure is that low-frequency terms having higher IDF are better at narrowing down the set of relevant documents that the user is interested in given the query. To complete the computation of the IDF, we take the logarithm (to the base 2) of its raw form, in order to dampen its effect, so doubling the size of the corpus only adds one to the IDF values rather than doubling it; that is, IDF = log(total number of documents/number of documents containing the term).

From an information-theoretic point of view, the IDF of a term tells us how many bits we need in order to represent the term, or using information-theoretic jargon the IDF of a term is its *self-information*. Thus, keywords with greater IDF or self-information convey more information as measured in units of bits.

An interesting explanation of the significance of IDF was given by Church and Gale [150]. They found that the overall frequencies of words such as "somewhat" and "boycott" were about the same in the corpus they were looking at, but that the IDF of "somewhat" was lower than that of "boycott"; that is, both keywords appear about the same number of times in the corpus but "somewhat" appears in more documents than "boycott." The researchers also observed that interesting words such as "boycott" appear more frequently within a document, than one would be expected by pure chance (i.e., with the aid of a Poisson distribution [208]), while less interesting words such as "somewhat" are more likely to appear in a document according to a process governed by pure chance. This observation was substantiated by showing that the variance of the TF of interesting keywords was larger than would be expected from a process of pure chance, while the variance of the TF of less interesting words did not substantially deviate from that of a pure chance process.

IDF is not as easy to spam as TF, since, unlike TF, its computation is based upon global knowledge relating to the Web; that is, in how many documents, in the Web as a whole, does a word appear. So, spammers that add to their web pages words that have high IDF, that is, words which are rare on the web, will obviously gain a high ranking for these words. But since, as we have discussed above, these rare words do not convey much meaning and web searchers are unlikely to use them as query terms unless they actually wish to view the spammed pages, the spammers would not have gained much for their effort.

5.1.5 Computing Keyword TF–IDF Values

The TF–IDF values are computed for each keyword in the query and each web page that contains at least one occurrence of that keyword. For any keyword, such as "backgammon," we obtain a list of all the web pages that contain "backgammon" from the posting list for the entry "backgammon" in the inverted file. On the other hand, the IDF, which is common to all occurrences of "backgammon," is obtained from the index entry for "backgammon."

Once we have the TF and IDF values for each keyword and every web page in which it appears, we compute the TF–IDF value for a keyword in a web page by multiplying the TF value for the keyword in the page by its IDF value.

We can then sum up the TF–IDF values of all the keywords in the query for each web page in which all the keywords appear at least once to obtain the final TF–IDF values, which the query engine then uses to rank the web pages. Note that we rank only web pages that include all the keywords, since this is the default interpretation of search engines; this could be relaxed to include web pages that have at least one occurrence of any keyword with the query "computer OR backgammon."

Let us examine Archie's query "computer backgammon" in more detail. To compute the TF–IDF for a given keyword, say "backgammon," we compute the TF for each web page that has at least one occurrence of "backgammon," and multiply this by its IDF value. The TF value is obtained from the posting list of the inverted file entry for "backgammon," while the IDF value is obtained from the inverted file index entry for "backgammon."

Consider a web page such as the WWW Backgammon Page (www.gammoned.com/wwwbg/backgammon) inspected a while ago. The TF value for "backgammon" in this page was calculated as its term frequency divided by the length of the page, which is this case was $53/1837 = 0.0289$, as there were 53 occurrences of "backgammon" on the page out of a total of 1837 words. The IDF value for "backgammon" in the web at the time was about log(3 billion/578,000) = 12.3416, since Google reported 578,00 hits for "backgammon," and at that time Google indexed about 3 billion web pages. Finally, the TF–IDF value for "backgammon" is obtained by multiplying the TF value by the IDF value, obtaining $0.0289 \times 12.3416 = 0.3567$.

Similarly, the TF value for "computer" in the WWW Backgammon Page at the time was $8/1837 = 0.0044$ (since there were eight occurrences of "computer" in the page out of a total of 1837 words), and the IDF of "computer" in the web was log(3 billion/92.1 million) = 5.0256 (since Google reported 92.1 million hits for "computer" at the time), obtaining $0.0044 \times 5.0256 = 0.0221$ for the TF–IDF value for "computer".

Once we have the TF–IDF values for "backgammon" and "computer" for a given web page, such as the WWW Backgammon Page, we add these scores together to obtain the TF–IDF value for the page given the query, which in this case is $0.3567 + 0.0221 = 0.3788$.

Looking at another backgammon web page inspected at the same time as the preceding web page, its TF for "backgammon" was $12/252 = 0.0476$, and for "computer" was $3/252 = 0.0119$. So, the TF–IDF value for "backgammon" for this page was $0.0476 \times 12.3416 = 0.5875$, and the TF–IDF for "computer" for this page was $0.0119 \times 5.0256 = 0.0598$. Finally, the total TF–IDF value for the page is $0.5875 + 0.0598 = 0.6473$.

So, judging by the TF–IDF of these two pages, the second page would rank higher than the first page.

The detailed computation of the TF–IDF values for documents is rather involved, so web search engines have to find methods to efficiently carry out this task. One observation that is useful is that users generally only view just over one screen of results implying that a search engine may not need to fetch the full posting lists of the keywords indexed. To be able to implement this, the posting lists of web pages can be sorted according to TF so that web pages with higher TF appear first allowing the query engine to ignore entries with very low TF. (Recall that TF is normalized relative to the size of the document.)

5.1.6 Caching Queries

Another way in which search engines can reduce their computations is by caching queries. Caching a query simply means storing precomputed results of the query on the search engine's servers, so that these results can be accessed directly without further computation when the query is issued. Candidates queries for caching are popular single terms such as "yahoo" or "ikea" and phrases such as "jennifer lopez" or "harry potter." Popular queries are issued by numerous web searchers on a daily basis, so caching them will benefit the search engine, with the proviso that the precomputed results will need to be refreshed on a regular basis. There is also a case to be made for user side caching of queries; that is, caching frequent queries made by an individual searcher on their local machine [684]. Queries such as "IDF information retrieval" will not be common on a global basis, but I have issued many similar queries when doing the research for this book. Local caching can be implemented only through software installed on the user machine; such a facility could presumably be added to the search engine toolbar utility.

5.1.7 Phrase Matching

When a query such as "computer backgammon" is issued, the search engine will attach a higher weight to web pages having the exact phrase "computer backgammon". In general, the query engine will prefer matches where the distance between the keywords is small, so the match "computer backgammon", where the distance between the query terms is one, is considered better than the match "computer plays backgammon", where the distance between the query terms is two. The query engine can deduce the distance between the keywords from the position of each matched term within the web page, which is stored in the entry for the page in the posting list. The exact weights that a search engine attaches to these factors is a well kept secret.

5.1.8 Synonyms

Being able to detect synonyms can be a useful feature. For a keyword such as "facts" a search engine could recognize that it is synonymous with "information" and match web pages that contain either keyword. This could be achieved by using a thesaurus to expanding the query, so that the query "facts" would be rewritten as "facts OR information."

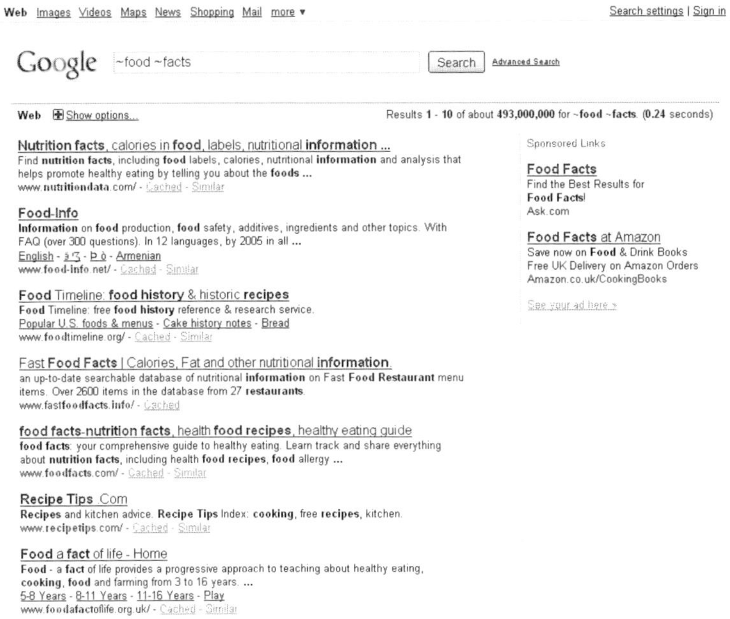

Figure 5.1 Results from "~food ~facts" Google.

The main problem with expanding queries as the default behavior is, foremost, the additional number of results generated for the query, increasing recall but not necessarily precision. This may also give rise to errors, since the expanded query may be further removed from the user's intended meaning of the query. Opening the filter by adding synonyms will also have an effect on the efficiency of retrieval, so it makes sense to have this feature user driven.

Google has introduced the tilde operator "~," where a "~" in front of a keyword such as "facts" indicates that you would also like to search for synonyms of "facts."[99] The results for the query "~food ~facts" submitted to Google during January 2010 are shown in Fig. 5.1.

5.1.9 Link Text

There are few other tricks that a search engine can use to increase its detection of content relevance. One technique pioneered by Google is to include the link text (also known as *anchor text*) with the web page that is referenced by the link.

For example, on my home page I have a link to the home page of the department, whose link text is "Department of Computer Science and Information Systems". This link text is then associated with the home page of the Department. This behavior of current web search engines should encourage web designers to put meaningful text on links, rather than something benign such as "click here."

[99] Search Features, Choosing Keywords, Synonym Search. www.google.com/intl/en/help/features.html.

The link text may be weighted by some measure of the strength of the link, such as the PageRank of the referencing page (see Section 5.2) to discourage spammers from creating bogus links to a page to increase its ranking through link text.

5.1.10 URL Analysis

Search engines also carefully analyze the URL of a web page for any keywords that would help identify the site. This is especially true for company names, for example, the home page of the Sun Newspaper (www.thesun.co.uk) was the first hit on Google, Yahoo, and Bing as of early 2010 for the query "sun". When the same query was issued to Google during late 2003, the home page of Sun Microsystems (www.sun.com) was the first hit for this query, and the first site that I could find that was actually about the sun (www.nineplanets.org/sol.html) was ranked 18th on the results list. (At the time to get information about "the sun" in the top ten hits I had to issue the query "'the sun'" using phrase matching.) Close behind the newspaper, as of early 2010, are Wikipedia's entry for the solar system sun, and Sun Microsystems home page. To get the nine planets web site you will have to work a bit harder now, for example, by adding the keyword "planets" to the query.

It is not exactly clear how words that appear in URLs are weighted into the ranking algorithm, but it is one of the many factors taken into account.

5.1.11 Date Last Updated

Another interesting issue worth mentioning is that the date at which a web page was last updated could also be taken into account when ranking web pages. This is especially important for news pages, where topicality often overrides other content relevance considerations. Web search engines let users restrict the search according to the time the pages were last updated; for example, restricting the results to be at most six months old.

The Internet Archive, mentioned in Section 2.1, contained about 150 billion web pages as of early 2010. It is a partial archive of the web, which started up in 1996, allowing historical access to web pages by specifying a URL to the Wayback machine.[100] The Internet Archive provides a subscription service, called *Archive-It* (www.archive-it.org), that allows institutions to build, preserve, browse, and search born-digital collections made accessible through the Web.

5.1.12 HTML Structure Weighting

Most web pages are written in HTML, which allows some structuring of a document according to various tags enabling authors to highlight text (e.g., bold, italic, and underlining), to specify a title for the page, to specify paragraph headings, to add link text, and other formatting information. HTML also allows authors to specify meta-information, which is not visible to a user browsing the page, but is

[100]The Wayback machine. www.archive.org/web/web.php.

detected by crawlers. Meta-information normally consists of a short description of what the page is about, and a set of keywords relevant to the page's content. Meta tags are very open to spamming, which is the reason that most search engines' crawlers ignore their contents.[101] Meta tags can also be used to tell a search engine crawler not to index the page, but this just duplicates information contained in the robots.txt file.

The idea of taking the HTML structure of a page into account for ranking purposes is most probably utilized by all web search engines, but the exact details of the weighting scheme used is kept as a trade secret. Weighting words according to the tags that they appear in is based on the assumption that the tagging is meaningful. For example, highlighting a keyword or putting it in a high level heading will normally indicate that it is more important than nontagged keywords.

An ingenious method of learning the weights to attach to various tags through the use of genetic algorithms [472] was described by Kim and Zhang [372]. Their technique assumes a test corpus and a set of queries for which the relevance of pages to the queries has already been assessed, so that different weighting schemes can be compared with respect to the queries and the underlying corpus. Genetic algorithms are based on the Darwinian principle of the survival of the fittest. In this case the algorithm has a population, where each individual in the population is a possible weighting scheme, and its fitness is evaluated against the test corpus by measuring the ranking it produces relative to the ideal ranking for the test queries. The high fitness schemes are selected for survival, and then crossed over and mutated in order to introduce new weighting schemes for the next generation. This is repeated for a number of generations, until finally the fittest weighting scheme is chosen for the search engine's ranking algorithm to use.

As many of the members of Google's and Yahoo's research teams have a strong background in machine learning,[102] it is not inconceivable that they use a similar technique to adjust their weighting scheme of HTML tags.

5.1.13 Spell Checking

Spell checking terms in queries is now a standard feature of web search engines. Roughly 10–15% of search engine queries contain a spelling mistake [165]. According to Rappoport from SearchTools (www.searchtools.com), analysis of query logs and testing indicate that spell checkers can provide useful suggestions for up to 70% of the errors [558].

An interesting web page[103] showing numerous misspellings for the query "britney spears" submitted to Google within a three-month period illustrates the

[101]How to use HTML meta tags, March 2007. www.searchenginewatch.com/webmasters/article.php/2167931.

[102]Papers written by Googlers (http://labs.google.com/papers.html) and Yahoo! Research Labs (http://research.yahoo.com/).

[103]Misspellings detected by Google for the query "britney spears". www.google.com/jobs/britney.html.

scale of the problem and its potential use. The most common misspelling was "brittany spears" submitted by over 40,000 different users, and one of the rare misspellings was "brittanyh spears", submitted by just two users over that period. In total 592 misspellings are shown, all of which were corrected by Google's spell checker, suggesting the correct spelling to the user. It is important that search engine spell checkers base their suggestions on the content of the inverted file index, so that words that do not appear in the index are not presented to users.

Two properties of query logs that can help with spelling suggestions are that correct spellings tend to be more frequent than misspellings, and that the easier a misspelling is to correct the more frequent it is [165]. (By easier it is normally meant that the edit distance between the misspelt and correct spelt versions is smaller.) Thus, a method for spelling corrections can use the search engine query logs to replace a possible mistake with a suggestion from the query log that is close to the original query in edit distance and more frequent than it. This process can be iterated if the proposed suggestion is still a possible mistake. Additional evidence for a spelling correction suggestion can be found in the search engine results for the query [138]. Here, the terms in the titles, URLs, and snippets of the search results that are close to the misspelt query terms can be used in suggestions. Moreover, the more frequent these terms are the more likely they are to be suggested.

5.1.14 Non-English Queries

As of 2009, less than 30% of Internet users were English speaking, and therefore it is important for search engines to support non-English queries.[104] Various problems that arise with non-English queries are dealing with different morphologies, handling diacritics (e.g., Polish and Greek), encoding texts in non-Latin scripts (especially Asian languages), transliteration of queries in non-Latin scripts, dealing with compound words (e.g., Dutch and German), text segmentation (e.g., Chinese), and investigating user behavior when using non-English search engines through query log analysis [409, 410].

Evaluation of the support for the non-English languages, Russian, French, Hungarian and Hebrew, has shown that the major search engines fall short of fully supporting these languages [50]. Despite this, the major search engines are still very popular in these countries and the users, who may not be aware of the engine's shortcomings, will have a lesser user experience than they could have.

Support for non-English querying is bound to improve over time with growing user demand. As was reported in Section 2.1.2, as of 2009, there were several non-English speaking countries, namely, China, Korea, and Russia, where the major search engines (Google, Yahoo, and Bing) do not have a dominant market share, and thus there is local incentive to support a wider range of language-specific features.

[104]Internet World Stats, Internet world users by language. www.internetworldstats.com/stats7.htm.

5.1.15 Home Page Detection

Search engines are great at finding home pages. Type in a name be it of a person or a company and you will get their home pages on the top ranks of the results list. If you try a common name such as "'john smith'" you will get approximately 4.5 million hits from Google, while for a less common name such as "'mark levene'" you get about 50 thousand hits and from these many of the hits are pages related to two academics having this name.[105] Company names are easier; it is actually a challenge to find a company name query, where the company's web site is not the first hit, unless several companies have a similar name.

There are various query-independent features that explain why search engines are so good at finding home pages. Although link analysis discussed in the next section contributes to this, it was found that link text and URL analysis were the two main features in the ranking algorithm that consistently improve home page finding [652].

This bias of search engines toward the discovery of home pages is one of the reasons that users are generally content with search engine results. To get highly relevant matches for more specific documents, more than the average number of keywords issued are needed in the input query. As an example, the web has changed many of the working habits of academic researchers. If I need to find a known recent article, then the title, or part of the title, and some of the authors' names are normally sufficient to locate the article. Such searches are called *known item searches*; as long as you know its there and you have enough keywords to differentiate it from other items, you can find it through the choice of keywords used in the query.

5.1.16 Related Searches and Query Suggestions

The major search engines provide query suggestions with autocompletion to users as they type in a query, and present related searches to users in order to help them refine queries.[106] Query suggestions are most likely mined from search engine query logs and are ordered by a combination of factors, including popularity, alphabetical order, and length from shortest to longest.

Yahoo's search assist tool[107] combines two query refinement tools: suggestions and related concepts. Suggestions are mined from search engine query logs and related concepts are derived from an analysis of the top search results and concepts derived from query logs as described below in some more detail (about 15 related concepts are associated with a query).

A longitudinal study of the use of these tools revealed that more than a third of users engage with query suggestions with autocompletions, while less than about 6% make use of the related concepts, which are only available

[105]The queries "'john smith'" and "'mark levene'" were issued to Google early in 2010.

[106]Predictive Search Query Suggestions, by B. Slawski, May 2009, www.seobythesea.com/?p=1375; How Search Engines May Decide Upon and Optimize Query Suggestions, by B. Slawski, July 2009, www.seobythesea.com/?p=2409.

[107]Introducing Search Assist, October 2007, http://tools.search.yahoo.com/newsearch/searchassist

after the search is completed [32]. Related concepts are derived in the following manner [33]:

1. A concept dictionary is built offline from concept-rich sources such as query logs, web sites, and entity name feeds.
2. A term vector is precomputed for each web page when the search engine indexes crawled web pages; the term vector contains co-occurrences of terms appearing in the concept dictionary and in indexed web pages.
3. The terms in the term vectors of the top-*n* retrieved results for the user query are weighted, and the top-*m* terms with the highest weights are retained in a result set term vector.
4. Similar phrases are generated from the terms in the result set term vector with the aid of a large search engine query log.
5. The result set term vector and the generated similar phrases are then compared to the original query terms via the vector similarity measure, which is then used to rank the terms and similar phrases to produce a list of related concepts.

5.2 LINK-BASED METRICS

What differentiates the Web from a mere collection of documents is its hypertextual nature. The hyperlinks that are embedded in web pages allow us to surf the web by following the links that transport us from one page to another. What is the meaning of these links, and how can a search engine use the linkage information to improve its quality?

A common assumption about the meaning of a hyperlink is that a link from page `A` to `B` is a recommendation or endorsement of page `B` by the author of page `A` [294]. It is common for web pages to have links to related and useful resources, in fact my home page has many of these. One objective of the links on my home page is to help me navigate to the resources that I frequently use, and another is to direct others to information I think they may find useful. The links, by virtue of being there, are waiting to be clicked upon, and the link text is providing some hint of what is on the other side of the links.

Google, for example, interprets a link from page `A` to page `B` as a vote by the author of page `A` for page `B`,[108] so the more votes a pages has the more authoritative or important it is deemed to be. A link from `A` to `B` can also be viewed as a citation, in the sense used by information scientists who analyze citations to articles in order to measure their influence, where the more links pointing to `B` the more influential `B` is. All these interpretations are variations of the same theme implying that placing a link on a web page is encouraging surfers to click on it.

A simple importance metric of a page is a measure that is relative to the number of links pointing to the page, that is, relative to the number of votes it

[108]Our search: Google technology. www.google.com/corporate/tech.html

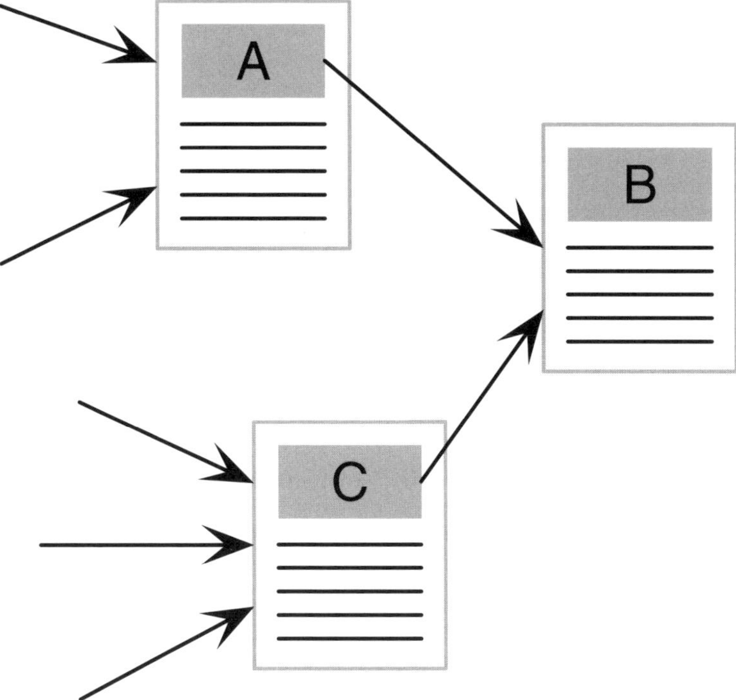

Figure 5.2 Web pages both A and B have a link to C.

has received. In Fig. 5.2, page B has two links pointing to it, which according to this simple measure would make it more important than a page, say D, which only has one link pointing to it. But such a simple measure would not take into account the quality of the recommendations, that is, of the source pages of the links. It may actually happen that the source of the link to D, say E, is much more important than A and C; that is, E received many more votes than A and C put together, and so D is actually more important than B.

To solve this problem, Google's PageRank metric, discussed below, also takes into account the quality of the source page recommendations; that is, how many votes did these pages get. So, a page is more important if more important pages link to it; that is, a vote from a more important page counts more than a vote from a less important page. The way I have described the importance of a page, based on the level of recommendations it receives, can be computed from the structure of the hypertext and is thus independent of any user query.

5.2.1 Referential and Informational Links

There are two fundamentally different uses of links. The first use is referential and the second use is informational. A referential link can be navigational as in "clicking on this link will get you back to the home page of the site" or "clicking on this link will take you to this other web site," and it can have some dynamics attached to it as in "clicking on this link will add this item to your shopping basket" or "clicking on this link will download a PDF file." An informational link relates the content of the source (page A) to the destination (page B) as in "clicking on this link will explain this concept," or "clicking on this link will give you more details," or "clicking on this link will lead you to related information."

For informational links it can be assumed that if A has a link to B, then the content of B is likely to be similar to the content of A. This is called *topic locality* and has been verified experimentally by examining the similarity of the contents of the source and destination pages of many links [175]. Topic locality is also possible for navigational links, but often links are unrelated such as an ad that pops up out of the blue saying "click here and you will win a big prize." For this reason search engines make an effort to relate sponsored ads to the user's query.

5.2.2 Combining Link Analysis with Content Relevance

Now, to briefly answer the second question, how is link analysis used to improve the quality of search, assume we have a query such as "computer backgammon" and that the query engine has produced a list of results ranked by content relevance. Also, assume that we are using PageRank as the link analysis metric to measure the quality of a web page. The PageRank is precomputed for each web page and stored in the link database ready to be merged into the query results before the final ranking is presented to the user. The way in which Google combines the PageRank with its content relevance measures such as TF–IDF is one of its well kept secrets. The simplest way to factor the PageRank value into the query is to multiply the PageRank of a page with its TF–IDF value for the query to obtain a relevance score for the page to be used in the final ranking of the results.

A more subtle way to incorporate the PageRank into the computation of the relevance of a page is to have some weighting scheme, which determines the importance of the PageRank value versus the TF–IDF value. As with HTML tag weighting, the weighting scheme may be computed with the aid of machine learning techniques and may even vary for different web sites.

5.2.3 Are Links the Currency of the Web?

The case of SearchKing against Google illustrates how links may become the currency of the web, and that there is a growing "black market," where links are sold to web sites in order to increase their PageRank [666]. The reason for this is that if search becomes monopolized, as discussed in Section 4.2, a web site whose livelihood depends on a high ranking and is competing in an open market will be willing to spend hard cash in order to increase its visibility. This implies that apart from increasing the values of its content, a web site must increase the value of its incoming links, which translates to increasing its PageRank, with the aim of being highly ranked for Google searches.

In spring of 2002, Bob Massa, the founder of SearchKing, discovered that his site has a very high PageRank. The PageRank of a site can be viewed on the Google toolbar, with the PageRank display option, on a range from 0 to 10. It is believed that the scale of the displayed PageRank is logarithmic with a base of about 10, so moving from one PageRank value on the toolbar to a higher one means that the actual PageRank is 10 times higher.[109]

At the same time, Massa became aware of the potential revenue for his company from selling links from his site or other sites with high PageRank values. In August 2002, he launched the "PR Ad Network" with the idea of selling text ads put on sites with high PageRank containing a link to the customer's site and charging monthly rates according to the PageRank of the site on which the ad was placed. This way the customer's PageRank is increased and as a result their Google ranking and their visibility. By being a web links broker Massa put a financial value on PageRank, and the expected reaction from Google followed penalizing Massa by dropping SearchKing's PageRank to a low value and thus nullifying the premise on which his ad network was founded.

The next move by Massa was to sue Google in October 2002 for dropping his PageRank value, resulting in a drop in value of SearchKing's business. Google filed a reply arguing that PageRank "is solely an expression of Google's view or opinion of the importance of a particular web page" and that Google lowered SearchKing's PageRank because it "had engaged in behavior that would lower the quality of Google's search results and that was designed to manipulate the integrity of those search results." Google also claimed that SearchKing "admitted that Google had the right to take action in response, including changing Google's opinion of the importance of the SearchKing site by changing the PageRank assigned to that site."[110] The suit against Google was dismissed in May 2003 on the grounds that the Google's PageRank formula constitutes opinions protected by the First Amendment.[111] Despite the dismissal of the law suit, the sale of links by SEO firms will continue, and search engines will fight back whenever they feel that their results are being unfairly manipulated.

Daniel Brandt who hosts a site called *Google-Watch*, mentioned earlier, questions the validity of PageRank. For starters he demands that Google stops reporting PageRank values from its toolbar in order to de-emphasize its importance. Brandt's view is that PageRank is the most important part of Google's ranking algorithm and that its search engine does not give content analysis its due significance in ranking query results.[112]

To counter these claims, Chris Beasley has set up a web site to watch over Google-Watch (www.google-watch-watch.org) and put the record straight. He

[109]Google's PageRank Explained and how to make the most of it, by P. Craven. www.webworkshop.net/pagerank.html.

[110]Google-Opoly: The game no one but Google can play, The strange Google lawsuit over its page-ranking monopoly, by D. Lithwick, January 2003. http://slate.com/id/2077875.

[111]Judge dismisses suit against Google, by S. Olsen, CNET News.com, May 2003. http://news.com.com/2100-1032_3-1011740.html.

[112]PageRank: Google's original sin, by D. Brandt, August 2002. www.google-watch.org/pagerank.html.

claims that PageRank is a mirror of the public's opinion on every web page and is thus an objective ranking measure.

Although PageRank has received a lot of press as the feature distinguishing Google from other search engines and a main ingredient in its success, an important fact to remember is that PageRank is only one of many factors that Google uses to determine the rank of a web page, many of which were explained in the section of content relevance. Google's success in engineering a search engine that produces high-quality results, despite the heterogeneous nature of the web, its massive size, and the terse and underspecified makeup of user queries, is quite a feat. Google has raised the quality of search to higher levels than ever before, and has thus effectively raised our expectations as consumers of web searches.

5.2.4 PageRank Explained

PageRank has an intuitive meaning in terms of a random surfer navigating through the Web by clicking on a randomly chosen link each time he browses a web page. The PageRank of a web page reflects the chance of the surfer arriving at the page. Thus the random surfer is continuously following links executing a random walk on the Web. Whenever the surfer has a choice between n outgoing links to click on he will choose any one of them with probability $1/n$; in the special case when there are only two links to choose from, he can toss an unbiased coin in order to make a decision.

The process the random surfer is going through can be modeled as a Markov chain, which we are familiar with from Section 3.4. The states of the Markov chains are the web pages and the transition probabilities are uniformly random according to how many outgoing links a web page has.

A simple web site illustrating PageRank is shown in Fig. 5.3. The random surfer starting at page `B` has four choices, so with probability of 1/4 he will choose one of them, say `C`. Page `C` has only one outgoing link to `E`, so he must move to that page. From `E` there are two outlinks, one back to `C` and the other to `D`. Our random surfer continues on his mission ad infinitum. But, what does he do when reaching page `A`? This page, which does not have any outlink, is said to be *dangling*. The random surfer is at a dead end when arriving at such a page.

The solution is to add *teleportation* to the model. According to the Oxford Dictionary of Philosophy, teleportation, or teletransportation, is a fictional mode of change of place in which a person "dematerializes" at one place, and emerges at another. In our case, the surfer at a dangling node can execute a random jump, teleporting himself to another page in the web. As before, the probability of arriving at any other page is uniformly random. In terms of the Markov chain model, we can imagine that dangling pages have outlinks to all other pages, which are followed with equal transition probability, so that the surfer does not get stuck in his travels.

There is another problem to solve called a *rank sink*, which is illustrated in Fig. 5.4. Suppose that the random surfer somehow arrives at page `A`. From there he must follow the link to `B`, then the link to `C`, and finally the link back to `A`. Our surfer is stuck again, this time in a loop he cannot escape from. He continues

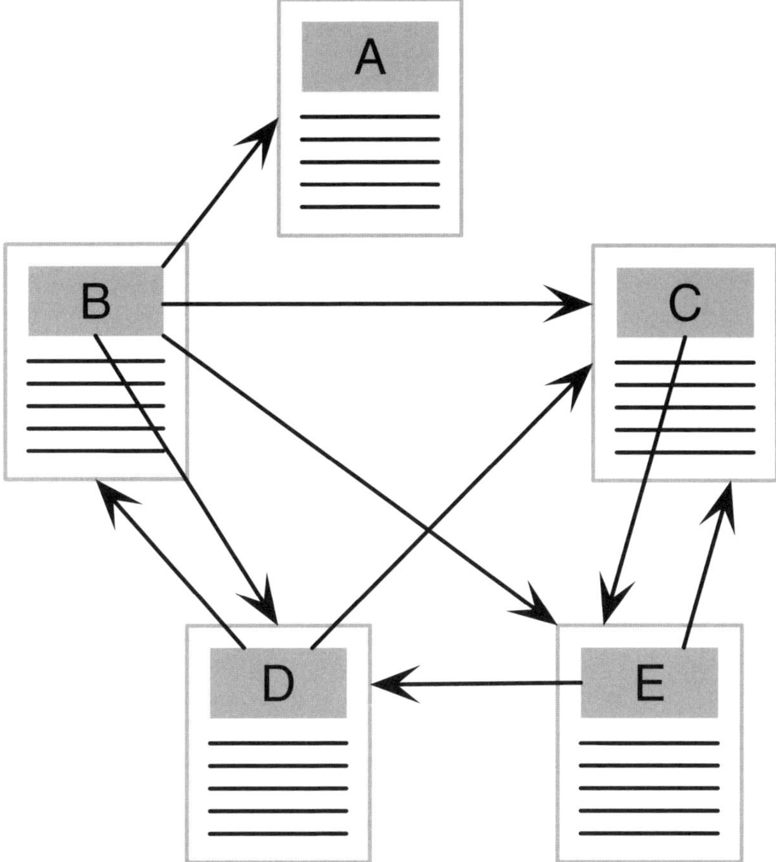

Figure 5.3 Example web site to illustrate PageRank.

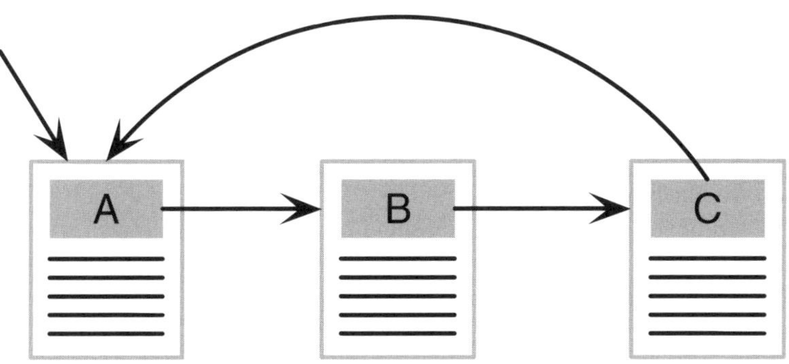

Figure 5.4 Example of a rank sink.

to revisit the pages in the loop forever with no chance of breaking out of this trap. The effect this has on the PageRank is that pages in the loop accumulate their PageRank value by virtue of the surfer repeating his visits to them forever, but they never distribute it outside the loop.

Yet again teleportation helps us to get out of this quandary. The solution that Google's founders Brin and Page suggest is to occasionally allow the random surfer to teleport himself to any other web page [522]. This is a way of modeling the situation when the surfer "gets bored" and decides to jump to a random page, from where he restarts his navigation session. To implement this behavior, Brin and Page suggest to set a teleportation probability, T, whose default value is set to 0.15 [105]. So, wherever the surfer is, the chance that he be teleported to a random page on the web, chosen uniformly at random, is T, and the chance that he follows an outlink present in the web page he is browsing is $1 - T$.

This ingenious method solves both the problems of dangling pages and rank sinks, and from a statistical modeling point of view the resulting Markov chain is well defined. Using the theory of Markov chains it can be shown that, if the surfer follows links for long enough, with teleportation happening randomly as I have described, the PageRank of a web page is the long-run probability that the surfer will visit that page.

In other words, the PageRank of a web page is the proportion of time a random surfer is expected to visit that page during a very long navigation session. The beauty of this idea is that the PageRank can be precomputed offline for each web page, and then incorporated into the query engine's ranking formula at no additional cost. What is even more amazing is its usefulness as a query-independent measure of the importance of a web page, although we do not know the exact details of how Google factors this fascinating indicator into their ranking algorithm.

You may have wondered why the teleportation probability is set by default to 0.15. Well there is a good reason. Let us call the complement of the teleportation probability, in this case 0.85, the *walk* probability of the surfer. It turns out that the chance of hitting a web page during the random walk of the surfer used to explain PageRank, where the probabilities followed are according to the Markov chain induced by the walk, converges to the PageRank value of that page at a rate given by the walk probability, which is 0.85 in this case. So, the number of iterations for convergence can be determined within a small tolerance level by raising 0.85 to the appropriate power, causing it to be close enough to zero. Thus, with $T = 0.15$, to attain a tolerance of less than one over a million, less than 100 iterations are needed.

What do we mean by number of iterations? The Markov chain modeling the random surfer's probabilities can be represented by a matrix with many billions of rows and the same number of columns; the exact number in billions comes from the approximate number of web pages in Google's index. Now, to compute the PageRank of these billions of web pages, we need to multiply this enormous matrix by itself, repetitively, until its entries converge to the PageRank values.

This method is known as the *power method* and the number of multiplications until convergence is the number of iterations we have referred to earlier.

From a linear algebraic perspective, the power method is a way of solving a system of equations, in this case with many billions of equations to solve. This is undoubtedly the world's largest matrix computation.[113] Wow, but even 100 iterations seem a lot when dealing with such a huge matrix. The reason the computation is feasible is that the matrix is sparse, that is, most of its entries are empty. This is due to the fact that the average number of links outgoing from a web page is between seven and eight, which is very much less than the billions of rows and columns.

It is interesting to note that a fair amount of detail on how the PageRank may be computed can be found in Google's patent "Method for node ranking in a linked database," whose inventor is Lawrence Page and assignee is Stanford University[114]. Note that as the walk probability of the surfer approaches one and the teleportation probability approaches zero, the number of iterations needed to compute the PageRank dramatically increases. For example, setting the walk probability to 0.99 instead of to 0.85 with a similar level of tolerance would require over 1300 iterations. So, the choice of 0.85 for the walk probability is a very sensible one [403].

Another justification for choosing the walk probability to be 0.85 is related to the stability of PageRank. Imagine that we make some small change to the web graph by adding or removing some hyperlinks. How much will the PageRank values change as a result of this perturbation of the web graph? It turns out that if the walk probability is too close to one, then small changes in the link structure of the web graph may cause large change to the PageRank values. However, when the choice of walk probability is 0.85, which is not too close to one, PageRank values are stable and thus insensitive to small changes.

According to computer science researchers from Stanford University, due to the sheer size of the Web, computing the PageRank values can take Google several days. These researchers have found ways to speed up the computation of PageRank by a factor of two or higher, which is significant given the scale that Google has to deal with [359].

We have computed the PageRank values for the simple example graph structure shown in Fig. 5.3, using the notation PR(`W`) for the PageRank of page `W`. They are PR(`A`) = 0.0688, PR(`B`) = 0.1276, PR(`C`) = 0.2880, PR(`D`) = 0.2021, and PR(`E`) = 0.3136. The PageRank computation converged after 24 iterations, when the teleportation probability was set to 0.15. It can be seen that, in this example, `E` has the highest PageRank and `A` has the lowest PageRank.

The formal statement of the PageRank of a page W is given in Equation 5.1. As the equation is recursive, to compute the PageRank of W, we must compute the PageRanks of all pages, $W_1, W_2, \ldots, W_n$, that have a link to W. $O(W_i)$ is the number of outlinks from a page W_i, T is the teleportation probability, and N is the number of pages in the web graph.

[113]The world's largest matrix computation by C. Moler, Matlab News and Notes, October 2002. www.mathworks.com/company/newsletters/news_notes/clevescorner/oct02_cleve.html.

[114]Method for node ranking in a linked database, United States Patent 6,285,999, Inventor L. Page, September 2001. http://patft.uspto.gov/netacgi/nph-Parser?patentnumber=6285999.

We note that the computation of PageRank values, based on iterating the equations for all web pages such as W, as defined in Equation 5.1, will converge for any assignment of initial PageRank values to web pages whose sum is 1. For example, we could set the initial values of all pages to be $1/N$. If we prefer the PageRank to be a number between 1 and N rather than a number between 0 and 1, we could replace T/N in Equation 5.1 with T, and set the initial values of pages to be 1. (To get a feel of the PageRank computation you should set up the equations for the graph structure shown in Fig. 5.3 according to Equation 5.1, then iterate them, treating the equals sign as an assignment operation, and finally check your result against the solution given above.)

PageRank:

$$PR(\mathrm{W}) = \frac{T}{N} + (1 - T)\left(\frac{PR(\mathrm{W}_1)}{O(\mathrm{W}_1)} + \frac{PR(\mathrm{W}_2)}{O(\mathrm{W}_2)} + \cdots + \frac{PR(\mathrm{W}_n)}{O(\mathrm{W}_n)}\right) \tag{5.1}$$

5.2.5 Online Computation of PageRank

Researchers from the French National Institute (INRIA) and a start-up company called *Xyleme* (www.xyleme.com), which is providing content solutions based on XML (www.w3.org/XML) and database technologies, have developed an alternative way to compute PageRank values online, while the crawler is traversing the web and harvesting web pages [1].

The idea is that every web page is given an initial value or "cash," and when a web page is visited it distributes its current "cash" to the pages it links to thus reducing its "cash" to zero. Thereafter, the "cash" stored at a page goes up whenever a page that links to it is crawled and it goes down to zero whenever it is visited by the crawler. The "credit history" of a page is the total "cash flow" through the page from the start of the crawl, and is proportional to the importance of the page.

What the researchers managed to show is that the importance metric, as measured by the "credit history," is in fact equivalent to the PageRank, assuming that the crawl is long enough. An interesting consequence of this online approach is that different crawling strategies may be pursued. Two possible strategies are random crawling following links according to the random surfer model, where outlinks are chosen uniformly at random, and focused crawling, where the link leading to the page with the highest cash is chosen. The greedy focused crawling strategy was shown to converge faster for important pages, which are given priority in this scheme.

5.2.6 Monte Carlo Methods in PageRank Computation

Monte Carlo methods are a class of computational algorithms that attempt to solve problems by carrying out a large number of random simulations over the sample space. Monte Carlo methods are useful for approximating problems whose sample space is very large, for example, in evaluating complex integrals.

The computation of PageRank can also be accomplished through a Monte Carlo computation as suggested by Avrachenkov *et al.* [41]; see also Fogaras *et al.* [227] for a similar idea in the context of computing a personalized version of PageRank discussed in Section 6.4.5. Rather than a random surfer executing one long random walk, he/she can follow many sampled random walks. Each sampled random walk starts at a web page chosen uniformly at random. Then, at each step, the walk is terminated with the teleportation probability or else, as before, the random surfer follows an outgoing link to the next page with uniform probabilities of outgoing links. In the special case, when a dangling page is reached, the next page is chosen uniformly at random from all web pages. When the walk is terminated, the random surfer is teleported to a web page chosen uniformly at random and a new sampled random walk is started at this page. The PageRank of a web page is computed as the number of times the random walk ended at that page divided by the total number of sampled random walks made. Rather than starting each sampled random walk from an arbitrary page, we can start the random walk a fixed number of times from each web page. This method is simpler for the random surfer and the approximation of PageRank can still be performed in the same way. A further refinement is to stop the sampled walk at dangling pages, and to count all the visits to all pages on the walk rather than just the last one by factoring into the PageRank computations the teleportation probability at each step.

Experiments with the Monte Carlo method have shown that only a few samples are needed from each web page and for pages with a high PageRank only one sample is sufficient for a reasonable approximation. There are several potential advantages of the Monte Carlo method. The first is that the sampled random walks can be computed in parallel, which will result in a substantial speedup. The second is that the PageRank can be updated continuously during a web crawl rather than being recomputed from scratch periodically at the end of a crawling cycle. Using this method could alleviate some of the problems related to the changes in PageRank as a result of the Google dance described in Section 4.6.

5.2.7 Hyperlink-Induced Topic Search

Web pages with high PageRank are considered authoritative, since many other pages point to them, as shown in Fig. 5.5. Another type of useful web page is a resource page, known as a *hub*, which has many outgoing links to informative pages, as shown in Fig. 5.6. Kleinberg [378] developed an ingenious method called *HITS (hyperlink-induced topic search)*, based on the idea that a good authority is pointed to by good hubs, and a good hub points to good authorities.

The first step in the implementation of HITS as a search method is to collect a *root set* of web pages for a given input query of say the top 200 hits from a search engine for the query. The root set is then expanded to the *base set* by adding all the pages pointed to by at least one page in the root set, and all the pages that point to at least one page in the root set, limiting this number to say 50, for each page in the root set (Fig. 5.7). To complete the preprocessing step,

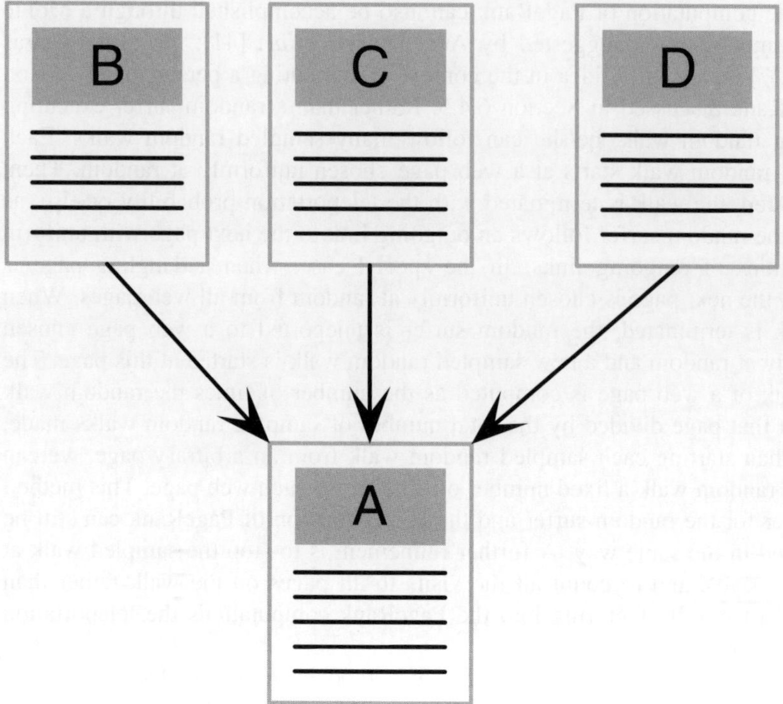

Figure 5.5 Page A is an authority.

links between pages within the same web site are removed from the base set, since these are often navigational rather than informational. The resulting set of pages in the base set is called a *focused subgraph*.

HITS uses this subgraph to determine the hubs and authorities for the input query; it typically contains between 1000 and 5000 pages. The algorithm then recalculates two computations several times, one for hubs and the other for authorities, in order to obtain a hub and authority weight for each page in the focused subgraph. Starting from an initial set of weights, at each step, the hub score of a page is the sum of the weights of the authorities it points to, and the authority score of a page is the sum of the weights of the hubs that point to it. The HITS algorithm normally converges within 20 or so steps. As with the computation of PageRank, the focused subgraph can be expressed as a matrix, and the HITS computation can be expressed via matrix multiplication. Linear algebra shows us that the hub and authority weights must eventually converge.

The formal statement of the HITS algorithm is given by the two equations in Equation 5.2, which define the two operations for updating the hub and authority weights of web pages. $A(p)$ and $A(q)$ represent the authority weights for pages p and q, $H(p)$ and $H(q)$ represent the hub weights for these pages, and F is the focused subgraph.

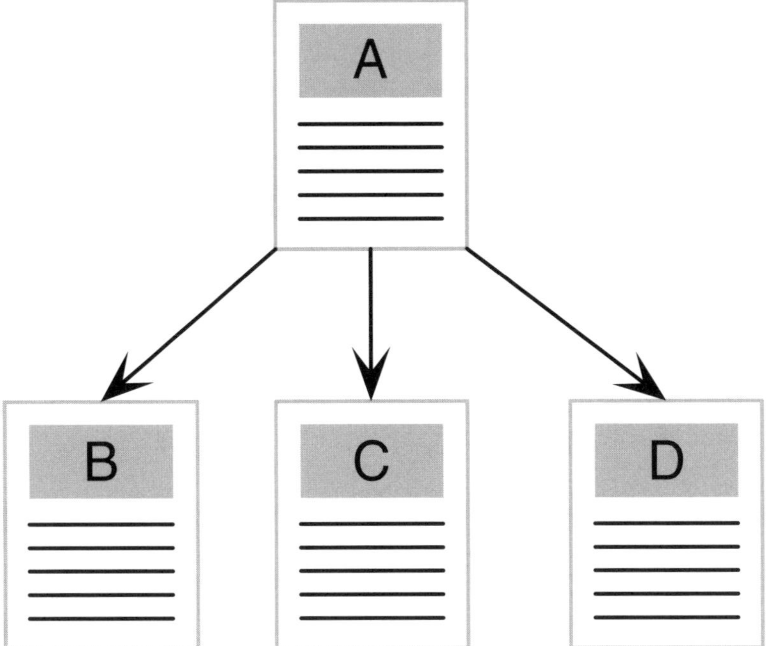

Figure 5.6 Page A is a hub.

HITS:

$$A(p) = \sum_{q:q \to p \text{ in } F} H(q) \qquad H(p) = \sum_{q:p \to q \text{ in } F} A(q) \tag{5.2}$$

The results from HITS are encouraging. For example, for the query "search engines," it returns the major web search engines as authorities. As far as we know, a variant of HITS has to date been deployed only in a single commercial search engine, namely Teoma (www.teoma.com), whose founders from Rutgers University devised an efficient approximation of the algorithm [176]. The lack of wide use of the HITS algorithm is probably due to the lack of a general efficient implementation, since unlike PageRank the hub and authority scores are computed at query time rather than offline. Another factor influencing the lack of deployment of HITS may be due to IBM holding a patent on the algorithm, as Kleinberg was working in IBM at the time.

Another problem with HITS, called *topic drift*, is the problem that pages in the focused subgraph that were added as a result of expanding the root set may be on a different topic from the query, and as a result the hubs and authorities may also be on a different topic. Topic drift can be dealt with to a large degree by taking into account the link text, when adding pages to the root set.

Apart from ranking the hub and authority search results, HITS can be used in the following ways: (i) to find related pages by setting the root set to contain a single page, and up to 200 pages that point to it, (ii) to help categorize web

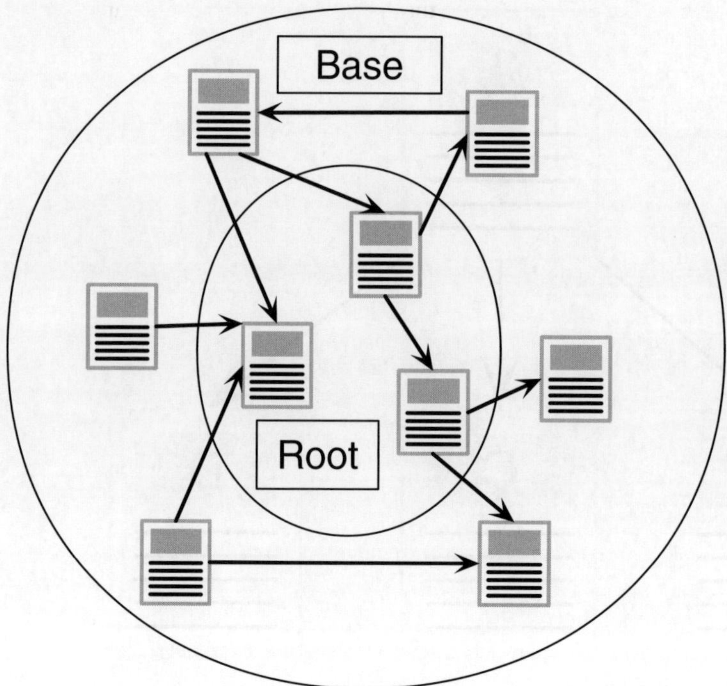

Figure 5.7 The base set for the HITS technique.

pages by starting with a root set of pages having a known category, (iii) to find web communities defined as densely linked focused subgraphs, and (iv) to study citation patterns between documents [130].

5.2.8 Stochastic Approach for Link-Structure Analysis

Lempel and Moran [414] proposed a method, called *SALSA (stochastic approach for link-structure analysis)*, which combines the random surfer model of PageRank with the mutually reinforcing nature of the HITS hub and authorities. The preprocessing stage of SALSA is the same as that of HITS; that is, a focused subgraph is created.

In HITS, each hub score is computed by summing up the authority weights it points to, and each authority score is computed by summing up the hub weights that point to it. SALSA modifies the computation so that each hub distributes its weight equally among the authorities it points to, and each authority distributes it weight equally among all the hubs pointing to it.

In terms of the random surfer model, the surfer performs two random walks on the focused subgraph: a hub walk and an authority walk. To explain these, it is convenient to take two copies of each page in the focused graph, so that each page has two separate roles as a hub page and as an authority page. Hub pages have (forward) links to the authority pages they point to, and authority pages have (backward) links to the hub pages that point to them; such a graph having two distinct sets of nodes is called a *bipartite graph*.

The hub random walk starts from a hub node and ends at a hub node. An outlink is selected uniformly at random from the hub start node and the chosen link is followed to the authority node at the other side of the link. Then, one of the inlinks to the authority node is selected uniformly at random and the chosen link is followed backwards to the end hub page at the other side of the link. Similarly, the authority random walk starts from an authority node and ends at an authority node. An inlink is selected uniformly at random to the authority start node and the chosen link is followed backwards to the hub node at the other side of the link. Then, one of the outlinks of the hub node is selected uniformly at random and the chosen link is followed to the end authority page at the other side of the link. Initial hub and authority pages are chosen from each connected component of the bipartite hubs and authorities graph, and the random surfer then performs hub and authority random walks ad infinitum on the graph. This results in two well-defined Markov chains on the bipartite graph constructed from the focused subgraph, one from hub pages to hub pages and the other from authority pages to authority pages. For a given web page in the focused subgraph, the SALSA hub score of this page is long-run probability that a hub walk will visit the page, and correspondingly the SALSA authority score for this page is the long-run probability that an authority walk will visit the page.

The formal statement of the SALSA algorithm is given by the two equations in Equation 5.3, which define the two operations for updating the SALSA hub and authority weights of web pages. As in HITS, $A(p)$ and $A(q)$ represent the authority weights for pages p and q, $H(p)$ and $H(q)$ represent the hub weights for these pages, and F is the focused subgraph. Moreover, $O(q)$ is the number of outlinks from q, while $I(q)$ is the number of inlinks to q.

SALSA:

$$A(p) = \sum_{q:q \rightarrow p \text{ in } F} \frac{H(q)}{O(q)} \qquad H(p) = \sum_{q:p \rightarrow q \text{ in } F} \frac{A(q)}{I(q)} \tag{5.3}$$

A tightly knit community (TKC) is a small but highly interconnected set of web pages. In such cases, where every web page in the community is connected to almost every other web page in the community, HITS will assign them all artificially high hub and authority values as they each mutually reinforce the others. TKC is a type of link farm set up by web spammers trying to artificially boost their link-based ranking; see Section 5.2.13 for a discussion on link spam. SALSA is less susceptible to the TKC effect as its computation of the weight of a page combines the overall popularity of the community the page belongs to with its popularity within the community [95].

Arguably the evaluation of link-based algorithms lies in their effectiveness in ranking web search results. In particular, for ranking purposes, we are interested normally in the authority scores, which are a form of endorsement or popularity of a page. Experiments to evaluate the effectiveness of link-based algorithms were carried out by Najork [489] on a large web graph and a substantial number of query results, some of which were labeled by human judges for relevance. Looking at the authority scores of link-based metrics in isolation, SALSA was the overall winner, followed by HITS, and then by PageRank and inlink count having comparable performance. When combining the link-based metrics with a content relevance method that includes link text, SALSA was only marginally better than the others that have comparable performance. It is worth noting that adding a link-based metric to content relevance is a substantial improvement on using content relevance in isolation. Link-based features are especially good for general queries, which produce a large set of results. For very general queries, link-based metrics are very competitive even in isolation, and SALSA was, again, the most effective.

As a result of these experiments it seems worthwhile to investigate how to efficiently implement SALSA for use in a web search engine. A method pursued by Najork and Craswell [490] samples the neighboring links in the base set to obtain a much more compact focused subgraph that can be stored offline and consulted online during query answering. In the online phase, the compact focused subgraph is retrieved for each query result in turn, and the authority scores that are both in the focused subgraph and the entire query results set are summed to obtain an authority score for this query result. This method performs well although the computed scores are not mathematically equivalent to the original SALSA authority scores.

5.2.9 Counting Incoming Links

We have seen several different ways of measuring the quality of a web page in PageRank, HITS, and SALSA. Another metric, which is much simpler, is simply a count of the number of incoming links to a page.

Researchers from AT&T Labs set up an experiment to compare several metrics including PageRank and HITS against the judgment of human experts [29]. Their results confirm that indeed PageRank and HITS do a very good job at identifying high-quality pages, but a surprising outcome was that the simple link count metric performs just as well as the other two on the data sets they used for testing. Another surprise was that a simple count of the number of pages in a web site is almost as good a predictor of quality as the other methods.

They noted that large-scale experiments on a wide range of topics need to be carried out to verify or refute their results. Also, the data sets used in these experiments, which were constructed by starting with the pages in the relevant topic directories in Yahoo, guaranteed that the neighborhood formed by following the links from and to these pages was also likely to be relevant. Data sets constructed from search engine results are likely to contain noisier neighborhoods, and so the simple link counting metric may not be as accurate as the more sophisticated link analysis techniques such as PageRank and HITS.

Further support on the value of counting inlinks was demonstrated by Fortunato *et al.* [229], who discovered a correlation, that is, a linear relationship, between the PageRank of a page and its number of inlinks, especially when this number is large. They also showed that the cause for this is the weak correlation that is exhibited between the number of inlinks of neighboring web pages on the other end of the inlinks to a page.

5.2.10 The Bias of PageRank against New Pages

The older a web a page the more likely it is to have more inlinks and as a consequence its PageRank is more likely to be higher. (This property of older web pages having a "first mover advantage" is discussed in Section 9.6.4 in the context of the evolution of the Web.) This bias of PageRank, also known as *Googlearchy*, has a direct effect on the popularity of a web page in terms of the traffic, that is, number of clicks, it receives from users. So, new, yet high-quality, web pages and sites will find it hard to gain visibility quickly, although it is of course possible as sites such as Facebook and Google have shown when they were newcomers.

An idea suggested by Pandey *et al.* [524] is to promote the PageRank (or the scores of other link-based metrics used) of a small fraction of new web pages in order to promote their visibility. The promoted pages are chosen randomly from a pool of new pages; the pool can be narrowed down by selecting only pages that satisfy certain criteria related to how low their current visibility is and/or their intrinsic quality. Extensive simulations have shown that a random selection of about 10% of the pages from the pool leads to higher quality search results.

In an empirical study conducted by Fortunato *et al.* [230], the authors discovered that search engines have an egalitarian effect by directing more traffic than expected to less popular sites. The explanation for this is revealed when looking at the actual queries that users submit. It is known that query popularity is long tailed [415], that is, follows a power-law distribution, as discussed in Section 9.6. This implies that few queries are very popular, but most queries, comprising the long tail, are rare. In addition, most queries in the long tail have many fewer relevant results than more general and popular queries. Taking this into account, many of the results from the long tail are unlikely to have a high PageRank or a large number of inlinks. Moreover, high-quality new web pages will have a higher chance of being relevant to more specific tail queries, thus giving them some visibility. Of course, for the popular queries, the bias will still be present and the method suggested in Ref. [524] is applicable for promoting new pages.

5.2.11 PageRank within a Community

We define a web community to be a set of web pages that are related in some way; for example, they may be on the same topic or a cohesive part of a web site. A webmaster who has created a new page within a web community may be tempted to try and artificially increase the PageRank of this page using link spam methods described in Section 5.2.13. If the webmaster is honest he/she may consider the effect on the PageRank of the community when adding outlinks from the new page. The worst case is having no outlinks from the page, when it becomes a dangling page. It was shown in Refs [82, 40] that this option leads to a considerable loss of PageRank within the community when pages from within the community link to this page. The intuitive explanation for this is that this page consumes a portion of the PageRank of all the pages linking to it and, due to teleportation, only redistributes a negligible portion of its PageRank back to the community. Thus, apart from causing a loss of PageRank to the pages linking to it, on an average, dangling nodes will also have a very low PageRank themselves. Assuming that the pages in the community can reach each other by following a small number of links, then the optimal strategy of the webmaster, in terms of maximizing its PageRank, is to create a single outlink from the new web page to another page in the community [40]. Such a policy is also likely to increase the PageRank of all members of the community.

5.2.12 Influence of Weblogs on PageRank

A weblog, most commonly referred to as a *blog*, is a frequently updated web site made up of entries arranged in reverse chronological order from the newest entry to the oldest.[115] Blogs are often personal self-published diaries written in an informal nature, although they could also be used as a collaboration tool within a company or in any other context, where groups wish to communicate with each other. Blogs are managed by social software [641], allowing bloggers to publish their diary in a simple way by filling in a form they set up, and publishing it with a single mouse click; blogs will be described in more detail in Section 9.5 in the context of social networks.

Here, we are interested in the way in which blogs link to other blogs and web pages. Most blogs are generous in their use of links and include a blogroll, which is a list of permanent links to other blogs and web sites that the author chooses to be linked to. This is where link analysis is related to blogging. Since blogs are a rich source of links and Google is crawling blogs, it follows that blogs are having an effect on PageRank and therefore on Google's ranking.

One way in which bloggers can manipulate the PageRank is by setting off, what has become known as a *Google bomb*.[116] The first known Google bomb was dropped by Adam Mathes, who asked fellow bloggers to add a link to his friend's web site with the anchor text "talentless hack." Once there are enough links in the direction set by the bomb, the PageRank of that site will grow, and a query with the anchor text entered into the search box will result in a high rank of that web site for this query, which in this case is "talentless hack."

This can be viewed as a weakness in Google's ranking algorithm, in the sense that it is impossible to discriminate between genuine informational or navigational links and bogus ones, solely authored with the intent of increasing the ranking of the destination web site. If Google could detect such links it would,

[115]Final version of weblog definition, by J. Walker, June 2003. http://jilltxt.net/archives/blog_theorising/final_version_of_weblog_definition.html.

[116]Google Time Bomb, will Weblogs ruin Google's search engine?, by J. Hiler, March 2002. http://www.slate.com/id/2063699.

in a similar way it dealt with SearchKing, tweak the PageRank of the offender. But, in the case of bloggers' links, it is practically impossible to track the source of the bomb. One way Google can combat such bombs is by biasing the PageRank against links that emanate from blogs, or at least to decay their significance with time, but it would be a nontrivial and computationally intensive exercise to follow-up all these blogs and links. Maybe this is one of the reasons why in February 2003, Google bought the company Pyra Labs who through their site, www.blogger.com, have distributed their blogging software to millions of users.[117]

5.2.13 Link Spam

Google bombing is related to the issue of link spam [275], when a web site obtains additional incoming links, which were put in place with the sole intention of improving the PageRank of the site; these additional links do not improve the user's surfing experience.

One technique used by some SEO firms is to set up link farms and web rings, where web sites exchange reciprocal links to increase their PageRank. A typical link farm consists of n boosting pages, all linking to the target page whose rank is to be artificially increased. Often, a link farm consists of a network of web sites densely connected to each other and with one or more boosting pages in each site in the farm [274]. To complete the link farm, several "normal" pages from outside the farm link into the web farm, thus distributing their PageRank to the farm which in turn boosts the PageRank of the target page. Presumably, Google could detect such link farms by inspecting the linkage patterns from, to, and within web sites, although this is by no means a simple computational task. Moreover, if such practices become rampant they will become harder to police, and with the increase in the size of the Web it will be difficult, if not impossible, to detect the increase in PageRank due to links in blogs or the sale of links from high ranking sites.

Google is not the only search engine that has to fight link spam, but due to the high profile of PageRank and its current number one status it is definitely the most vulnerable. The publicity arising from such cases will continue to be reported and debated in the technology news and search engine forums.

One way search engines try to control link spam is through the HTML attribute value rel = "nofollow", which instructs search engines to ignore the link and its anchor text. In particular, Google will not use the link or its anchor text for the purpose of PageRank computations. As an example, Wikipedia links are generally nofollow to discourage editors from creating link spam with the objective of boosting the PageRank of sites being linked to. The nofollow attribute value may also be used when links are paid for (disclosure of paid links is strongly encouraged by the search engines) or to prevent a site from distributing its PageRank to untrusted sites (for example, though comments in blogs). Search

[117]Fame or misfortune beckons for weblogs?, by G. Turnbull, February 2003. http://news.bbc.co.uk/1/hi/sci/tech/2775249.stm.

engine optimizers have been using the nofollow attribute to affect the distribution of PageRank within a web site and from one web site to another; this controversial practice is known as PageRank *sculpting*.

There is merit in trying to recognize link spam automatically. A technique using decision trees was devised by Davison [174], who defined 75 features for comparing the source and destination web pages of a link, which could indicate that it is nepotistic, that is, that it was not included on its merit to enhance the user experience, implying that it might be spam. Some of the features are the source and destination pages have a certain percentage of overlap, their page titles are identical, they share some percentage of their outgoing links, or the source is an SEO company.

Some SEO companies generate a large number of spam pages automatically, which exist solely to increase search engine ranking and are completely useless for human visitors. Such pages may be detected by statistical techniques that measure the variance of these pages from human generated ones [219].

As much of the link spam aims to boost PageRank, some methods to combat such spam have looked at the way PageRank is distributed through outlinks. One suggestion is to use a variant of PageRank, called *TrustRank* [276], to detect pages that are likely to be propagating link spam.

In the original definition of PageRank, when teleporting himself, the random surfer can end up at any other page with equal probability. However, in the personalized version of PageRank (described in more detail in Section 6.4.5) once the surfer is teleported, we can bias the probability of jumping to another web page according to some preference [287]. To compute TrustRank, we bias the teleportation to a set of trusted and reputable seed pages, identified and weighted by human experts; the weight of all other pages is set to zero, so the random surfer is not teleported to any of these pages. TrustRank is then computed in the same way as PageRank, biasing its distribution toward web pages that are linked directly or indirectly from the trusted seed set.

Another way of detecting link spam is to investigate where the PageRank is coming from. In particular, for a given web page, we would like to find the set of supporting pages whose contribution to the PageRank of this page is significant. Now, as the PageRank for the whole web follows a power-law distribution [662] (see Section 9.6), it follows that the PageRanks of an honest set of supporters should approximate a power-law distribution. So, SpamRank suggested by Benczúr *et al.* [73] penalizes web pages whose supporting pages do not approximate a power law. For example, a web page that receives its PageRank solely from a large number of pages whose PageRank is low is suspicious, as is a web page where the PageRank of its supporting pages all come from a narrow range of values.

Looking at the supporting pages can also help detect link farms [703]. In the case when a small set of supporters contribute to make up most of the PageRank of a target web page, this may be an indication of a link farm. In particular, when the contribution is efficient in the sense that the structure of the link farm maximizes its possible contribution to the PageRank of the target page, this is further evidence of a link farm. Several heuristics are also suggested as metrics for the likelihood of a link farm such as when (i) the PageRank of the target is much larger than the PageRank of its set of supporters, (ii) the number of links between the supports of the target is minimized in the attempt to maximize the PageRank of the target, and (iii) the ratio of the indegree of the target and the average indegree of the supporters is high.

It is also useful to be able to use as training data web pages, which were labeled by human experts with their likelihood of being spam pages. Thus, in a similar way to TrustRank, we could start from a seed set of weighted spam pages from the training data (i.e., pages that are not trusted) and propagate their values using the PageRank algorithm to form an Anti-TrustRank [393]. We could then make further use of the Anti-TrustRank and classify a target page as likely to be spam if a large contribution to its PageRank comes for pages that have been labeled as likely to be spam or have a high Anti-TrustRank [30].

5.2.14 Citation Analysis

Bibliometrics [681] involves the study of the structure and process of scholarly communication. It offers quantitative measures and statistical analysis to describe patterns within the publications in a given field. Citation analysis, which is a major area in bibliometrics, studies the relationships between authors and publications when authors cite others in their work. Citation is to bibliometrics what link analysis is to web search, and so it comes as no surprise that the foundations of link analysis can be found in the citation analysis literature.

Eugene Garfield was one of the pioneers of citation analysis from the mid-1950s. He invented the impact factor[118] in the 1960s and founded the ISI, the Institute for Scientific Information, that publishes journal citation reports that are widely used to measure the quality of research and are extremely influential in the funding of scientists and research organizations. The impact factor of a journal is determined by dividing the number of current year citations to articles appearing in the journal during previous two years, by the number of articles published in the journal during previous two years. The impact factor of a journal can be interpreted as the average number of citations an average article will receive per annum in the two years following its publication.

There has been quite a bit of controversy regarding the use of the impact factor to determine the quality of research output [5]. It has been pointed out that comparing between journals in disparate fields is meaningless as, for example, mathematicians rarely cite many articles, while in the natural sciences an article may contain dozens of references. It is argued that the impact factor should not be used to evaluate individual scientists or research groups, since it does not represent the citation rate of individual articles.

For a typical journal, 15% of the articles account for about 50% of the citations, and 50% of the articles account for 90% of the citations, so it is unfair to assign the same score to all articles in a journal. Also, it may not be the case that an author's most cited article appears in the journal with the highest impact

[118]Essays/Papers on Impact Factor, by E. Garfield, www.garfield.library.upenn.edu/impactfactor.html.

factor, so impact factors are only a meaningful measure for the average article. There is also a problem of which articles to count for citation purposes, since, for example, review articles have a much higher citation volume than other types, and the calculation of the impact factor does not always recognize this.

Raw citation counts of articles are the equivalent of inlink counts of web pages. As we have seen a more sophisticated metric such as PageRank may better capture the notion of quality than simply counting the number of inlinks. To this end we can form a citation network of authors (or units such as research groups or journals), with links between authors representing citations. As with web pages, we can view the citation network as a Markov chain, and the importance or influence of a unit as the long-run probability that it will be cited. Interestingly, in the mid- to late 1970s researchers have already considered this notion of influence [248], but this idea never seemed to be a threat to the dominance of the impact factor as a citation metric, whose computation is much simpler and easier to understand, although it lacks the sophistication and robustness of a metric such as PageRank.

Two papers that are cited in the same publication are said to be co-cited. In the context of the Web, if two web pages are pointed to by a third page they are co-cited. We can build a co-citation network of documents, whose links represent the found co-citations and are annotated with the frequency of co-citation; normally, a link is included in the co-citation network only if the co-citation frequency of the link is above some threshold. Co-citation measures the relationship or association strength between two documents. Once the co-citation network is formed, clustering techniques can be used to separate out different areas of research, where the centers of the clusters consist of the highly co-cited documents in the area common to the clustered documents.

Co-citation analysis was pioneered in the early 1970s by Henry Small, then the director of research at ISI and later its chief scientist [611]. One of the applications of co-citation in the context of the Web is that of finding related or similar pages [182], a feature that is often available on search engines' results pages. A visualization of related web pages as shown by Google can be viewed with TouchGraph's Google browser (www.touchgraph.com/TGGoogleBrowser.html); see Fig. 5.8 for the web pages similar to Yahoo from late 2009.

Google Scholar, released by Google in late 2004, is a special purpose search engine that indexes scholarly articles and books that are available on the Web and counts the number of scholarly citations to them. For each article found, Google Scholar provides a link to the publisher's site where the article is stored, and an additional link to a public, open-access, version if one can be located. Google Scholar is freely accessible for querying as part of Google's provisions, rather than being subscription based as are the major citation databases, Elsevier's Scopus and Thompson Reuters' Web of Science.

There have been several comparisons of these three resources in the context of citation analysis [48] and an ongoing debate on the utility of Google Scholar as a source for citation analysis.

Google Scholar has an impressive coverage of many resources and it provides support for publishers and libraries on how to help Google identify and

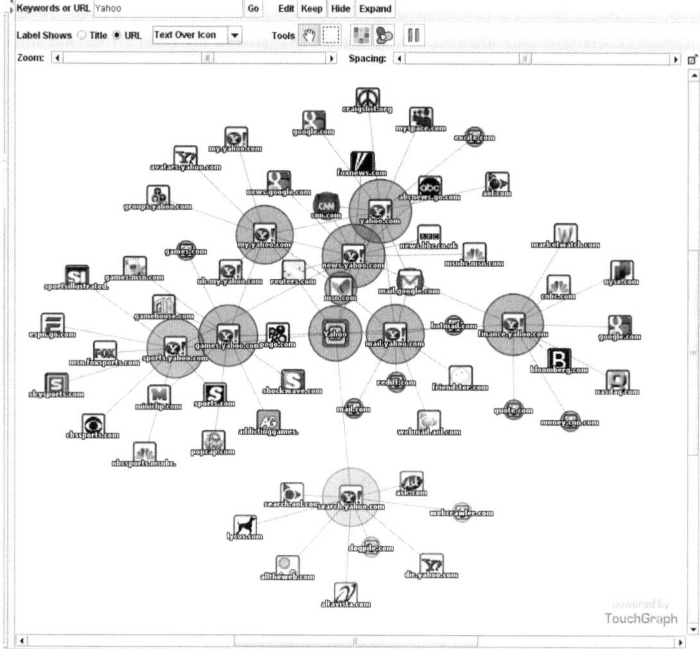

Figure 5.8 Web pages related to Yahoo.

index their publications. Despite this, its coverage of scholarly resources is not complete as it is based on automated crawling technology. However, its geographic and language coverage is impressive compared to the subscription-based citation databases. Google Scholar is also easy to search and is freely accessible, which probably makes it the most widely used resource for academics and practitioners searching for articles.

Jacsó [325] claims that most of the weaknesses of Google Scholar are to do with software issues and its inability to fully understand the various fields used in the citation information. This is, generally speaking, an information extraction problem that will no doubt improve over time; see Section 7.4.12 for a brief introduction to information extraction.

There is also a problem that each citation database covers resources that the others do not and therefore citation analysis is not consistent across the databases [285]. Moreover, Google Scholar contains citations to nonscholarly sources, although, looking at the big picture, this is unlikely to have a big effect on the citation metrics. One could argue that the different databases complement each other, especially as the coverage of each is uneven across different fields of study.

5.2.15 The Wide Ranging Interest in PageRank

The topic of PageRank has received a fair amount of attention due to its immense innovation in successfully factoring link analysis into web search engines, and due to the meteoric rise of Google, the favourite search engine of the day. PageRank has and is being covered in the business and technology press as part of Google's success story and the controversy that it is generating by attempts to manipulate it. Computer and information scientists are researching the effects of PageRank on search technology and proposing further innovations to improve its utility in ranking web pages. Mathematicians are looking at PageRank from a linear algebra point of view, and statisticians are investigating PageRank as a result of a stochastic process. PageRank has also generated interest from social scientists who are interested in the social and economic issues related to web links, and PageRank has infiltrated into popular science with various articles explaining its inner working to a wider audience. Finally, the SEO companies are writing about PageRank in an attempt to advise their customers how to improve their search engine ranking.

5.3 POPULARITY-BASED METRICS

After attaining a bachelor's degree in mechanical engineering, Gary Culliss went on to work as a patent agent. He then entered Harvard Law School in 1995 with the intention of returning to patent law on graduation. Having the idea that search should be user controlled, based on the popularity or number of hits to a web page, he created a prototype search engine with the help of a computer programmer from MIT, which he called *Direct Hit*.

In order to get off the ground, in 1998 the Direct Hit team entered its idea to the MIT $50K entrepreneurship competition, and won the first prize. Within a short time of receiving the prize he secured venture capital funding of $1.4 million, and gracefully gave the prize money back to be distributed amongst the other finalists.[119] After building the Direct Hit brand, the company went public at the end of 1999 and in January 2000 was acquired by Ask Jeeves—the question answering search engine, which is discussed later in Section 6.5—for around $500 million. A true success story from the internet boom days.

To complete the history, Direct Hit survived until February 2002, when it was merged with Teoma (www.teoma.com), which is another search engine that was bought by Ask Jeeves in September 2001.

5.3.1 Direct Hit's Popularity Metric

The Direct Hit technology is based on information obtained from the query log of a search engine [167]. The basic idea is to factor users' opinions, as represented in the query log, into the ranking algorithm of the search engine. The query log records the details of user visits to web pages, known as *clickthroughs*, whenever the user clicks on links within the search engine's results page. The details can include the duration of the visit (which can be computed only if the user returns

[119]A hit director, by N. Knapp, Harvard law Bulletin, Class Notes, Fall 2000. www.law.harvard.edu/alumni/bulletin/2000/fall/classnotes_culliss.html.

to the search engine's results page), the position of the page in the ranking of the query results, and the keywords used in the query. Aggregating these indicators over many users we obtain a popularity metric, which can be factored into the search engine's algorithm, in order to boost the ranking of web pages that have high clickthroughs.

Popularity is a form of collaborative filtering, which is a technology that uses the preferences of a community of users to recommend items to individual users. (This technology in the context of social networks is elaborated in Section 9.4.) In contrast to many collaborative filtering systems that rely on users rating items, for example, on a three level scale of bad, good, and very good, popularity-based metrics are implicit rather than being explicit, as they are computed from users' usage of the system. Although popularity metrics can be spammed, for example, by excessive clicking on chosen sites to increase their score, such spamming may be detected by putting a threshold on the allowed number of clicks, from any user, that can influence the popularity of a site. It is also possible for the search engine to use cookies to identify its user base, which makes popularity spam detection easier, and can also be used for personalization purposes. In any case, as with all web search engine logistics, there is a scalability problem to overcome, if the search engine is to cope with a potential user base of billions rather than millions.

Using a popularity metric has some problems attached to it, which need to be addressed. One issue is that popularity is to some degree self-reinforcing. If a certain web page is the most popular, say for the query "shoes," then it will appear in the top-ranking page for that query. As we know, users are unlikely to inspect more than a single page of query results, so the popular pages are more likely to remain more popular than other pages, which are also relevant to the query. Of course, popularity should not be the only metric to score a web page, content relevance and link analysis should be factored in too. The crucial issue is how to weight the various metrics relative to each other; in this case, it is the problem of how much weight popularity should have in the ranking algorithm. One way to deal with this problem is to make popularity dependent on age, so that the popularity of a page is dampened with age. This means that for a page, say on shoes, to maintain a high ranking, its popularity must increase in time to balance the decay with age.

Another problem is that a popularity metric will, by virtue of its nature, only be statistically significant for a relatively small number of queries that are popular. This is not necessarily a disadvantage of using a popularity-based metric, but it implies that some caution needs to be taken so that the sample of clickthroughs is large enough before recommending web pages to other users.

Keeping a tab on user queries and the web pages they visit will work best for short queries, as for longer queries with more terms the number of term combinations explodes at a very fast rate. Luckily, as we have observed in Section 4.4, the average number of terms in a typical query is between two and three, so the storage of popularity data is feasible on a large scale. This also means that the search engine can precompute popular queries for efficiency purposes, although these query results need to be refreshed regularly.

Interestingly, no current search engine is marketing itself as using popularity-based metrics, although there is no doubt that such metrics are already being used by search engines to improve users' search experience.

5.3.2 Document Space Modification

The roots of the Direct Hit approach can be traced to the SMART retrieval system, initially developed by Gerard Salton and his collaborators at Cornell University during the early 1970s. Their idea was to boost the ranking of relevant documents using a technique they called *document space modification*. The technique relies on user judgments, associating queries with relevant documents; in the context of the Web, 30 years on, the user judgments are obtained from the traces of clickthroughs left in the query log file of the web pages that users inspected for a given query. For each user judgment that has been voiced, the relevant document (visited web page) is transformed by boosting the weights of the query keywords for this document. So for subsequent queries, popular documents for the keywords in the query will be ranked higher than before due to the increased content relevance score for these documents, resulting from higher weights for the query keywords. Salton and his coresearchers tested the document transformation technique on their system and reported significant improvements in retrieval performance [101].

A modern day version of this idea was implemented by Kemp and Ramamohanarao [366] using search engine referral data from a server log. Their results were also positive showing that document transformation is a viable technique for improving the performance of web search engines.

5.3.3 Using Query Log Data to Improve Search

Another use of query log data to improve a search engine's ranking algorithm is advocated by Schaale *et al.*, who have developed an algorithm they call *Vox Populi* (voice of the people) [592]. The idea is to incorporate the relative importance (or weight) of the keywords from user queries into the search engine ranking process. The weights of keywords are learnt from the query log of a search engine according to their popularity, taking into account the co-occurrences of keywords in queries. So, for example, the researchers found that in queries containing the keywords "free mp3 downloads," the importance of "mp3" outweighs the importance of "downloads" which outweighs the importance of "free."

A clustering technique to find related queries and web pages from clickthrough search engine log data has been implemented in order to experiment with methods for offering users of the Lycos search engine suggestions of related queries to the ones they submitted [65]. The underlying idea of the suggestion mechanism is that two different queries that induced users to follow a link to web pages with overlapping content are related, and two different web pages that were browsed by users as a result of overlapping queries are also related. Although the viability of this technique was demonstrated, it is not clear if Lycos is actually using this algorithm.

Research conducted by Joachims [345] has been looking at ways in which machine learning techniques can be used to improve the ranking of query results, utilizing clickthrough log data to train the search engine. Clickthrough data conveys relative relevance judgments; for example, if the user clicked on the result whose rank was 3, but not on the first two query results, we can deduce that the user prefers result 3 to results 1 and 2. The problem of learning an optimal ranking for a given query can then be couched in terms of learning a preference relation on the documents in the corpus. The algorithm learns the weights of features of the search engine's ranking algorithm (such as HTML tag weights and the weight of PageRank in the combined relevance score), so that the search engine's result list be as close as possible to users preferences, as measured from the clickthrough log data.

5.3.4 Learning to Rank

Machine learning can provide a general framework for learning to rank search engine results [436]. In this framework, the input may be a query log with click data, or it may be a benchmark data set consisting of queries and documents together with human relevance judgments on which documents are relevant to each query. The advantage of using a query log as opposed to a benchmark data set is the availability of very large query logs from search engines, but benchmarks are very useful for comparing the performance of different learning algorithms. Learning to rank attempts to find the optimal weights of features used in a search engine's ranking algorithm so that more relevant document are ranked higher than less relevant ones. To achieve this each document can be represented as a vector of features such as TF, IDF, HTML tag weights, PageRank or some other link-based metric, and the popularity of the document as measured by the number of clicks it attained over a period. The weights of the features are tuned for the full data set and are thus query independent.

Learning to rank algorithms can be grouped into three approaches: the pointwise approach, the pairwise approach, and the listwise approach. In the pointwise approach, a degree of relevance is output for each document, and the documents are ordered according to their relevance. One problem with the pointwise approach is that it does not naturally consider the relative ordering among the documents that are relevant for a given query nor does it take into account the position of a document in this ranked list. Another problem is that the number of relevant documents varies largely for different queries, which may adversely affect the learning algorithm. In the pairwise approach, for each pair of documents a preference is output from which an ordering on the documents is deduced. The pairwise approach has the advantage over the pointwise approach in that it can model the relative order between documents. However, the number or pairs per query can be very skewed, which can have a considerable impact on the learning algorithm in that it will be dominated by queries having a large number of document pairs. In order to tackle this problem, normalization per query by the number of pairs associated with the query can be introduced into the learning algorithm. In the listwise approach, which generalizes the pairwise approach, a total order on two or more documents is output. The listwise approach is more natural than the other two approaches in modeling the position of a document in a ranked list, and, moreover, all the documents for a given query are grouped into a single list so it can better distinguish between queries compared to the other two approaches. Its main problem relative to the pointwise and pairwise approaches is that it is more complex to train.

The first learning to rank algorithm that has been deployed in a commercial search engine is RankNet [118], which was used by Microsoft as part of their ranking algorithm.[120] RankNet is pairwise learning algorithm, where, given two documents associated with a training query, a target probability that the first document is preferred to the second is constructed based on the relevance scores attached to the documents. The learning is accomplished on a two-layer neural network with a modified backpropagation algorithm using gradient descent [561].

Richardson *et al.* [567] applied the RankNet algorithm for combining query-independent, that is, static, ranking features rather than just using PageRank for query-independent ranking. The static features used for each web page were PageRank, popularity (i.e., the number of visitors to the page over a period collected from logs of search toolbar users or clickthroughs from query logs), anchor text and inlink metrics (such as number of unique words in anchor text and number of inlinks), on-page and URL metrics (such as the frequency of the most common term and the number of words in the body of the page), and averages of other features over all pages in the domain of the page. The results show that combining many features significantly outperforms PageRank on its own, and that even individual features such as on-page features and popularity outperform PageRank. This evidence suggests that although PageRank is an important static metric for ranking web pages, other metrics, for example, based on user popularity, maybe just as or even more useful than PageRank.

5.3.5 BrowseRank

In reality, the random surfer assumption of PageRank is not an accurate reflection of real user traffic, as some links are more popular than others. Surprisingly, PageRank is positively correlated with web site traffic [93]; however, the correlation is quite weak for the most popular portion of the Web [464]. Meiss *et al.* [464] observed from a large data set that 54% of page requests are a result of direct navigation; that is, typing a URL into the address bar, or clicking on a bookmark or an entry in the user's history, rather than following a link from another web page. Direct navigation can be viewed as teleportation, and thus arguably the teleportation constant of PageRank should be closer to 0.54 than to the standard default setting of the teleportation to 0.15. In the definition of PageRank in Section 5.2.4, when teleporting himself, the random surfer can end up at any other page with equal probability, that is, teleportation is uniform. To cater for nonuniform teleportation, the personalized version of PageRank,

[120]Local, Relevance, and Japan!, by Ken Moss, June 2005. www.bing.com/community/blogs/search/archive/2005/06/21/431288.aspx.

described in more detail in Section 6.4.5, allows biasing the probability of the surfer teleporting himself to another web page according to some nonuniform preference [287]. A further observation by Meiss *et al.* [464] is that actual user traffic does not conform to uniform teleportation, and is biased toward popular web sites.

The failure of PageRank to model real user browsing behavior has led researchers to consider page ranking models based on popularity. BrowseRank proposed by Liu *et al.* [437] is one such attempt that has caught the attention of the technology press as Microsoft's answer to PageRank.[121]

PageRank is computed from the web graph, while BrowseRank is computed from the browsing graph, which consists of pages and links from the web graph and their associated statistics. The browsing graph can be constructed from the data generated from search engine toolbars installed on users' browsers, from search engine log data, and from web server log files. The browsing data will normally be segmented into sessions, where each session consists of a sequence of web pages (also known as a *trail*) with a time stamp when each page was viewed. From the session data, the browsing graph can be constructed where each page is tagged with its number of hits and the average time users stayed on the page, and each link is tagged with the number of clicks on the link. The number of hits on a page can be divided into two categories according to how a page was reached, either (i) by direct navigation or (ii) by clicking on a link. The statistics pertaining to direct navigation allow us to construct a teleportation vector and those pertaining to clicks allow us to compute transition probabilities from one page to another in such a way that both are biased toward users' actual behavior. The additional information about users' staying time when viewing pages allows us to model the users' behavior as a variant of the traditional Markov chain, called a *continuous Markov chain* [577]. In this continuous Markov model, our random surfer Archie is now *biased*; he starts his journey from a web page according to the biased teleportation vector and follows links according to the biased transition probabilities of links. When arriving at a new page, Archie stays on the page according to a distribution governed by the average staying time recorded for the page and then moves to the next page according to the biased transition probability of links. As in the PageRank model Archie gets bored after a while, with probability equal to the teleportation probability, and instead of following a link he is teleported to another page according to the biased teleportation vector. Archie's journey continues ad infinitum. In similarity with PageRank, the proportion of time that Archie is expected to visit a page after surfing in this biased manner for a long time is the BrowseRank of the page.

Experimental results with BrowseRank [437] confirm that BrowseRank is a useful metric that can improve the performance of a search engine. Moreover, BrowseRank is competitive with TrustRank (see Section 5.2.13), which is based on PageRank, for fighting link spam, in the sense that it is not easy to artificially manipulate the BrowseRank of a web page.

[121]Microsoft tries to one-up Google PageRank, by Stephen Shankland, July 2008. http://news.cnet.com/8301-1023_3-9999038-93.html.

5.4 EVALUATING SEARCH ENGINES

One way to evaluate search engines is by the level of their use, simply let the users vote with their feet. In that case, as of early 2010, Google was the current favorite (see Section 2.1), and many would argue that it is also technically the best that the web has to offer at this time (although Yahoo and Bing are also competing for the top place in the search engine wars; see Section 4.3).

5.4.1 Search Engine Awards

In the movie industry, we all look toward the Oscars as a measure of popularity and quality, so it will not surprise you that there are webby awards (www.webbyawards.com), which are given out yearly to the best of the Web in a variety of categories. The webby awards have been handed out since 1997 and are selected by members of the International Academy of Digital Arts and Sciences (www.iadas.net), which was formed in 1998 to "to help drive the creative, technical, and professional progress of the Internet and evolving forms of interactive media." Along side the webby awards, there are the people's choice awards determined by popular online choice.

Google has done well in the awards winning several awards for technical achievement, best practices, and navigation/structure of its web site. It has also won awards for its Google Maps and Google Earth services. Yahoo has also done well over the years excelling particularly in its provision of different services through its properties. For example, Yahoo properties such as Flickr, Delicious and Yahoo Answers have all won awards. Google has not won a webby award in 2007, 2008, and 2009, probably indicating that it has matured as a company and is concentrating mostly on provision of search in its different facets.

The well-established search engine portal, Search Engine Watch (http://searchenginewatch.com), founded by Danny Sullivan in mid 1997, also hands out awards, as voted by its members, recognizing "outstanding achievements in web searching" in various categories, the most notable one being "outstanding search service." As expected, Google has won this award four times in a row since 2000, but in 2005 Yahoo finally won the award.[122] There has been a hiatus in the awards since Danny Sullivan left Search Engine Watch and founded Search Engine Land (http://searchengineland.com). However, the Search Engine Watch awards have resumed in 2009 (http://searchenginewatch.com/sew-awards), with Yahoo winning the award for the search engine with the most relevant results.

5.4.2 Evaluation Metrics

Popularity of a search engine is not necessarily a measure of technical quality. What we really want to measure is *relevance*, that is, given a query, will the

[122]5th Annual Search Engine Watch Awards, By Danny Sullivan, March 2005, Search Engine Land. http://searchenginewatch.com/3494141.

search engine return the most relevant results, and are these relevant results highly ranked. I have already introduced the concepts of *precision* and *recall* in Section 5.1. To refresh your memory, precision measures the ratio of the number of retrieved results that are relevant and the total number of retrieved results, while recall measures the ratio of number of retrieved results that are relevant and the total number of relevant results.

Given that most users inspect only the first page of query results, measuring the top-n precision, where n is the number of results that fit in a results page, may be more meaningful than measuring general precision and recall. In the case of top ten precision, we measure the number of relevant results within the 10 most highly ranked results returned by the search engine.

We could also average the precision scores by summing the precision scores after each relevant document is returned starting from the top-ranked one, and then dividing by the number of relevant documents retrieved to get an average. If we compute the average precision for several queries and then take the average (or mean) of these, we obtain the *mean average precision* (MAP) measure.

A method of combining the precision and recall is often used, known as the *F-score*. It is computed by taking the harmonic mean of the precision and recall values, which is a weighted average of the precision and recall. This is done by dividing twice the product of the precision and recall values by the sum of the precision and recall values. Note that the highest value of the F-score is one and its lowest value is zero.

In Section 5.1, it was also mentioned that search engine coverage is another important measure and that it is related to recall. This may be one of the reasons for the search engine size wars, where search engines have been proudly reporting the number of web pages they index, and how much larger their index is than the opposition's.

For question answering systems (see Section 6.5), we often use a different metric for evaluation, for the case when the query is a known answer search; that is, when we expect one answer to be returned. In this case, we find the first position in the results list that gives the correct answer to the query and note its reciprocal rank. For example, if the second result gives the correct answer then the reciprocal rank is 1/2, and if it is the eighth result that gives the correct answer then it is 1/8. We note the reciprocal rank for all the test queries, and return the average of these as the *mean reciprocal rank* (MRR) measure. The higher the value of this metric, the better the system.

The *discounted cumulative gain* (DCG) [337] is a measure of the effectiveness of a search engine that accumulates the relevance of documents, or their *gain*, based on their rank in the returned list of documents for a given query, and applies a discounting factor to each document so that the lower the rank the heavier the discount. DCG is based on two assumptions (i) that highly relevant documents are more useful than less relevant ones and (ii) that the lower ranked results are less useful as they are less likely to be examined.

Assume that each result returned has a graded relevance score; for example, this could be a value between 0 and 9 (if it is a binary grading then there are only two grades, 0 and 1). The cumulative gain at rank n is the sum of the scores of the first n documents returned by the search engine. In order to discount the gains, we divide each score by a function that increases with the rank of the document; a commonly used discount function is the logarithm, so that a document at rank i is divided by $\log(i+1)$. So, the DCG at rank n sums the n discounted gains at ranks 1 to n. For example, if $n = 3$ and the top three documents have grades of $1, 0, 1$, then the DCG at rank 3, $1/\log(2) + (0/\log(3) = 0) + 1/\log(4) = 1.50$, assuming the logarithm is taken to the base of 2.

The normalized discounted cumulative gain (NDCG) is computed by dividing the DCG at rank n by the ideal DCG at rank n, obtained by ordering the results according to their grades and then computing the DCG. So, in our example to compute the ideal DCG, we swap the grades of the second and third documents obtaining $1/\log(2) + 1/\log(3) + (0/\log(4) = 0) = 1.63$. The NDCG is then $1.5/1.63 = 0.92$. Note that the NDCG is always less or equal to one, assuming there is at least one relevant result.

Other metrics can be computed by inspecting a search engine's query log to find out what users are actually doing and how long it takes them to do it. Moreover, from the clickthrough data in the log, we can see at which rank in the results page are users clicking, how many pages they inspect, and other statistics as detailed in Section 4.4. For example, if users normally click on the first result on the page, that may indicate that the first result is relevant most of the time, while if users normally click on a result in the middle of the page, it may indicate that the most relevant results are not the most highly ranked.

5.4.3 Performance Measures

There are other measures to consider. Performance is always crucial. A search engine should assume that you are surfing the web from a relatively slow internet connection and still deliver a subsecond response time. This also implies that the results page should be lightweight without any slow loading multimedia. The user interface should be simple, clear, easy to use, uncluttered, and visually appealing. Closer studies with users including questionnaires can gauge user satisfaction, although user studies can only be carried out with a limited number of surfers, and are normally very time consuming and demand much human effort to carry out properly. It is also interesting to evaluate the number of interface actions, such as mouse clicks and keyboard entries, as a measure of the difficulty of completing a search task. Fast delivery of the search results is only one side of the coin, the other side from the user's perspective is how efficiently can the information seeking process be carried out to completion.

To get an independent assessment a search engine may commission a test of their system from a company such as VeriTest (www.veritest.com). Both AltaVista, in May 2000, and Google, in September 2000, commissioned reports from eTesting Labs (formerly known as ZDLabs), which was acquired by VeriTest in 2002. Although the AltaVista test was far from being conclusive, the overall winner was AltaVista, with AlltheWeb in second place and Google in a humble third place. The Google test showed Google as a clear winner, with AlltheWeb in second place and AltaVista down to fifth place, out of six tested engines. These tests recorded a substantial improvement in Google's search quality in 2000, as the methodology used was much the same in both tests. Each test was composed of five subtests: natural language queries, simple one-word queries, simple multiword queries, complex multiword queries, and home page finding. In each subtest five queries were performed, each in a chosen category, and the top ten results were recorded for each query and then scored according to their relevance to the query. The queries were finally weighted according to web usage, where the weight assigned to simple word queries was 30%, to natural language queries 10%, and to the remaining types 20% each.

Google also employs human quality raters from around the world to evaluate its search engine. Training is carried out through manuals[123] and videos. Part of the evaluation is concerned with spam, so that when it is detected Google may take manual action to fix the problem; for example, when a site appeared high for a search query it is not relevant for.

A recent suggestion in collaboration with researchers from Microsoft is to use an online game, they call *Page Hunt*, to help tune search engine results [445]. Page Hunt is a game where players are presented with a web page and are asked to find a query that will get the web page into its top few search engine results. Players earn bonus points for successful queries according to their rank. A pilot study revealed that some pages are easy to find (27% of pages have 100% findability, that is, for these it is easy to find a query that gets the page into the top five results), while others are not (26% of pages have 0% findability). It was found that as the length of the URL of the pages increases, it becomes harder to find queries. Results from the game can also be used to find query modifications that increase the findability of web pages.

5.4.4 Eye Tracking Studies

A tool for discovering and quantifying how users view search results is eye tracking [438]. A joint study by search marketing firm Enquiro and Did-it in collaboration with eye tracking firm, Eyetools, was conducted in 2005 with 50 people using Google in five distinct scenarios. A main result from the study was that searchers' behavior exhibits an F-shaped scan patten, known as the *golden triangle*, as shown by the heatmap in Fig. 5.9. A heatmap in this context is an aggregate representation showing the areas that users fixated on when viewing search results. The heatmap can be viewed as a probability map, which tells us what content on the results page users are most likely to see. The specific F-pattern demonstrates how searchers scan the first three to four results that are expected to be the most relevant to the query submitted. Moreover, the scan is done linearly, in a top down manner, oriented toward the top left-hand corner of the page. It is interesting to note that there is a smaller F-pattern for the sponsored listing appearing on the right-hand of the results page, with a much smaller chance of a user actually inspecting any of the ads.

[123]The Google Quality Raters Handbook, by Barry Schwartz, March 2008. http://searchengineland.com/the-google-quality-raters-handbook-13575.

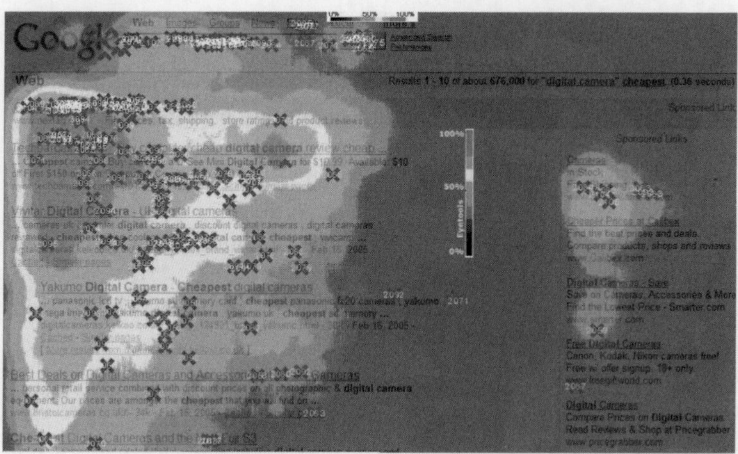

Figure 5.9 Heatmap of Google's golden triangle. (Source: Enquiro Develops Google's Golden Triangle, 2005 eye tracking research study from Enquiro. www.enquiro.com/enquiro-develops-googles-golden-triangle.php.)

A scan path is the path that the eyes follow when looking at a results page. Scan paths illustrate very effectively how users navigate the page. Analysis of the scan paths of search results indicate that most often if the top few results are not relevant then the user does not scan additional results. It was also shown that although the top two search results were viewed approximately equally, users were still more likely to click on the first result even when the first two results were swapped. Thus the position of a result can influence user behavior. The low number of results that users inspect is an indication that users tend to reformulate queries fairly quickly if they do not find what they are looking for in the top results. An eye tracking study comparing users' behavior when using Google and Yahoo showed no significant differences between the two search engines [438].

A question is whether the F-pattern carries over to other cultures. A study was conducted with 50 Chinese students in 2007, using the popular Chinese search engine, Baidu, and the Chinese version of Google, which is much less popular than Baidu in China.[124] Surprisingly, the Chinese heatmap does not exhibit the typical F-pattern, although it still has the typical upper left orientation and a preference to scan the first search result. The horizontal scanning in the Chinese search engine was much more spread out and the interaction with the search engine lasted much longer. There were also differences between the way people used Baidu and Google China. In Google China, users found what they were looking for in literally half the time than on Baidu. In Google China, users do not scan beyond the fourth result, while in Baidu users scan right to the bottom of the page. So, why do the Chinese prefer Baidu to Google? As we have already mentioned in Section 2.1.2, it may be the preference for a local home

[124]Chinese Eye Tracking Study: Baidu Vs Google, by Gord Hotchkiss, June 2007. http://searchengineland.com/chinese-eye-tracking-study-baidu-vs-google-11477.

grown product with a better Chinese search experience, but it may also be due to its very popular MP3 search facility.

5.4.5 Test Collections

Various test collections exist, the best known are the ones prepared for the yearly Text REtrieval Conference (TREC) competitions, mentioned in Section 2.6. The commercial search engines do not participate in this competition, but it is still possible to evaluate them on test collections without their cooperation. The last large-scale evaluation we know of was carried out late in 1999 by Hawking *et al.* [289]. They included 20 search engines in their study and over 50 topics with human compiled relevance assessments. The relevance assessments were carried out by asking human judges to assess which pages are relevant to each topic, from a pool of pages compiled from the combination of pages returned by all the search engines for the topic. Six judges were employed for this purpose and a relevance assessment tool was used to assist them in their task. The results showed that the large web search engines of the time were, as expected, the leaders of the pack.

TREC distinguishes between a *topic*, which is a statement of a user information need, and a *query*, which is the sequence of words presented to the search engine as input. A topic generally consists of a title, a description, and narrative text. This allows a wide range of queries to be constructed for each topic in order to test the search engines, and avoids participants from tuning their search engine to specific queries, since the exact queries are not known in advance.

To evaluate web search engines, we need large test collections of well over a million documents, and therefore it is not practical to get humans to assess each web page in such a collection. The web track test collections are normally obtained from focused crawls that are made available to the participants to search over. The way the TREC relevance judgments are constructed for a given test, without assessing each page in the collection, is as follows. First, a number of topics are fixed for the test. These could be mined from available query logs, so that they represent real users' information needs, or suggested by human assessors. Once the topics are fixed, each search engine participating in the competition submits the 100 top-ranked web pages for each of the topics. These are then combined and put into a pool for assessment. Assuming 50 participants and 50 topics with some duplication of pages in the submissions, the pool is still likely to contain over 100,000 pages. Documents that are not in the pool for a given topic are assumed to be irrelevant to that topic. All the documents in the pool are then assessed by human judges as being relevant or irrelevant to the topic under consideration [665]. The participating search engines can then be evaluated using these relevance assessments.

In order to save human effort in assessing documents, and bypass the problem of human disagreement of which pages are really relevant, several researches led by Ian Soboroff [617] have suggested to randomly choose a small set of documents from the pool, and tag these random documents as the relevant ones. Although, in general, the performance of the search engines, when documents are randomly assessed, correlates with the performance, when using humanly assessed documents, the best systems performed much worst in the random setting than in the human setting. An explanation for this phenomenon is that the random method evaluates the search engines based on popularity and not on relevance [38]. The point is that, overall, documents that are considered by several systems to be relevant are more likely to be chosen as relevant, than other documents retrieved only by a small minority. But, the best search engines distinguish themselves from others by catching the relevant documents that others do not. Human assessors are more likely to spot the documents that distinguish the better systems from the average ones, but random choice does not discriminate between them.

Another method for automating the evaluation of web search engines builds on the fact that web pages in humanly constructed directories such as Yahoo and the Open Directory are manually assessed for relevance within a category. A large set of query document pairs are constructed as follows. The queries are mined from search engine logs and the matching documents are mined from the Open Directory. To ensure that the results are not biased toward any particular search engine, each matching document from the Open Directory is chosen so that only queries that are an exact match with the title of the document from the directory are chosen. The queries, all of which are known item searches, are then submitted to the web search engines being evaluated, and the rank at which the document is returned is recorded. The MRR where the matching document was found, over all the test queries, is the score of the search engine. The technique was tested on a 12 MB query log from AOL Search, resulting in 41,000 query document pairs. Out of these, three random samples of 500, 1000, and 2000 were chosen for the test. Four web search engines were evaluated, and a clear winner emerged; unfortunately, the researchers did not reveal the identities of the search engines tested [148].

5.4.6 Inferring Ranking Algorithms

Although search engines do not reveal their ranking algorithms, what can we learn about the way a search engine works from the query results it produces? Moreover, although the algorithms used by search engines are in most cases proprietary, we would still like to know what is the magic formula that the search engine uses in order to determine whether a web page is relevant or not. Back in 1998, Pringle *et al.* [545] set out to infer the inner working of various popular search engines of the day, using decision trees, which are widely used in machine learning.

A decision tree is a way of classifying information [575], in our case information from search engines, according to a set of attributes. The researchers measured the search engines according to nine attributes, concerning the number of times a keyword appeared in a particular part of the document (in the URL, in the title, in the first heading tag, in a meta-tag, or in the whole document), the length of the various parts of the document (the title, the first heading tag, or the whole document), and whether the document was a relevant example or not. The technique they used to infer a decision tree was from training data they collected from the web about each search engine under consideration. As training data, they choose answers to single word queries, where the queries were collected from a public search engine log. The pages that were returned as answers were considered as positive (relevant) examples, and pages which were not returned as answers were considered as negative (not relevant) examples.

The result showed that the most important attribute is the number of keyword matches, that is, the TF. The other attributes varied from one search engine to another, for example, some penalize long documents, some ignore meta tags, and some put more stress on the title and headings in a page. It would be very interesting to repeat this experiment on the current leaders in search, with a much wider set of attributes that reflect the various components that have been introduced in this chapter to measure web page relevance

CHAPTER SUMMARY

- The indexer must preprocess web pages before the information is put in the inverted file. This involves, amongst other things, splitting the page into words, detecting meta-information such as HTML tags, detecting stop words that are often omitted from queries, and stemming of words.
- TF–IDF is the baseline method for computing content relevance. For a given keyword, it involves computing the number of occurrences of the keyword in a page (its TF value), and multiplying this by the logarithm of the total number of pages in the Web divided by the number of pages containing the keyword (its IDF value). For each page under consideration, the TF–IDF value is computed for each keyword in the user query, and then these values are summed up to give a content relevance score for the page.
- TF is vulnerable to search engine spammers, using various methods to artificially boost the number of occurrences of chosen keywords in their web pages. The activity of SEO is concerned with designing web sites that will rank highly on search engines for targeted queries. Search engines are concerned with SEO firms that, rather than giving sound advice, are encouraging web sites to create spam.
- Search engines augment TF–IDF with further analyses to improve relevance scoring, such as phrase matching, detection of synonyms, analysis of link text, URL analysis, taking into account the date a web page was last updated, judicious weighting of text according to its HTML structure, spell checking, dealing with non-English queries, home page detection, and helping users formulate and refine their queries.
- Link-based metrics take into account the hypertextual nature of the Web, where a hyperlink from one page to another can be viewed as a recommendation to follow the link. Metrics such as the PageRank can be combined with TF–IDF, simply by multiplying the two scores together. Using link

analysis to score web pages has commercial implications, since there is fierce competition to be ranked highly on the major search engines. In Google's case, spammers create link spam in an attempt to artificially increase their PageRank values, and thus unfairly increase their search engine ranking, while Google will fight back when such spam is detected.

- Links created in weblogs pointing to other weblogs, which appear in the blogroll, have an effect on the PageRank. In some cases, when enough weblogs have created a link to a certain web page, these are able to manipulate the PageRank, and thus effect Google's ranking for certain queries. This type of manipulation of the PageRank is known as a *Google bomb*.
- PageRank can be explained using the random surfer model, a process which involves a surfer following links, chosen uniformly at random from the web page he/she is browsing, and occasionally getting bored and being teleported to another random page on the Web. The PageRank can also be stated as a system of equations, one for each web page. An important problem that has been keeping researchers busy is that of speeding up the computation of PageRank, which demands the solution of a system of many billions of equations. It is also possible to compute and update the PageRank, online, while crawling the Web, or via a Monte Carlo. PageRank is biased toward older pages that have more inlinks rather than newer ones, which have not had time to acquire sufficient inlinks to boost their PageRank. Despite this, search engines address this imbalance for long tail queries, when users search for less popular pages.
- An alternative link-based metric is HITS, which is computed on a query by query basis, rather than being query independent as the PageRank is. HITS is based on the idea that a good authority (a page with many inlinks) is pointed to by good hubs, and a good hub (a page with many outlinks) points to good authorities. Using this mutually reinforcing relationship between hubs and authorities, HITS computes a hub score and an authority score for each page in the focused subgraph, constructed from the top 200 or so pages returned by the search engine for the query.
- Another alternative link-based metric is SALSA, which combines PageRank's random surfer model with the HITS algorithm. SALSA is less susceptible to the TKC effect, where in a densely connected community of web pages each of the web pages reinforces the other to attain high hub and authority scores, since its computation takes into consideration the popularity of the community a page is in together with its popularity within the community. SALSA can be efficiently implemented within a search engine by approximating its scores via an offline sampling method.
- Other link-based metrics include a simple count of inlinks, and metrics such as co-citation from the area of citation analysis, looking at how authors cite others in their writings. Google Scholar is a special purpose search engine that counts citations of scholarly works that appear on the web.

- Popularity-based metrics boost the ranking of web pages that have high clickthroughs, as measured from query logs. Popularity can be self-reinforcing, since in any case users tend to select highly ranked pages. To deal with this problem it is possible to dampen popularity with age. Ranking by popularity has its roots in document space modification, a technique from the 1970s, whose central idea is to boost query keywords in documents, so that in subsequent queries the popular documents would be ranked higher.
- Learning to rank search results attempts to learn the optimal weights of search features from an input consisting of queries and the links clicked on from the result sets of these queries, in order to improve the ranking algorithm of a search engine. Experiments with learning to rank algorithms, where PageRank is just one of the features, suggests that although a link-based metric such as PageRank is important for ranking web pages, other metrics, say based on user popularity, may be just or even more important than PageRank.
- While PageRank is computed from the web graph, BrowseRank is computed from the browsing graph containing pages and links from the web graph that users followed together with their associated statistics. The random surfer model on the browsing graph is a biased random walk according to a distribution governed by the behavior of previous surfers. Experimental results with BrowseRank confirm that it is a useful metric that can improve the performance of a search engine.
- Search engines can be evaluated in different ways. One way is simply to let users vote for their favorite search engine. Another, based on the relevance of the returned results, is to use metrics such as precision and recall. Eye tracking studies are useful in determining how users scan search results and what spatial areas of the results users fixate upon when viewing the results. Test collections such as those prepared for the TREC can be used in conjunction with these metrics, since the collections include relevance assessments. Measuring the performance of a search engine in terms of response time and the ability of users to successfully complete their information seeking process is also important.
- Ranking algorithms can be inferred using machine learning methods, such as decision trees, that learn the features that are used by a particular search engine.

EXERCISES

5.1. (Explore). What guidelines would you give to a webmaster to improve or maintain their search engine ranking of his or her web site, without creating pages a search engine might consider as spam?

Find out about Google's, Yahoo's, and Bing's advice to webmasters, and comment on these with reference to the guidelines you have proposed.

5.2. (Discuss). There is some controversy regarding the "visibility" of web sites on search engines, taking into account the fact that most users only view between 10 to 20 search results.

The ranking algorithms of web search engines favor the construction of tightly knit web communities that are specifically designed to maximize the ranking of the participating web sites. Gori and Witten [265] call this process the *bubble of web visibility*, where the "bubble" has been created as a result of the escalating battle between the search engines, who frown on such activity, and the artificial web communities, who reinforce it.

Comment on this view of the search engine space, and how the issue of "visibility" can be addressed.

5.3. (Explore). Choose a language other than English, and investigate its support by one of the major search engines. Is there a local web search engine for the language you have chosen? If there is one, how does it compare with the major search engine for queries in the language you have chosen?

Now choose a set of queries in English and translate them to the language you have chosen. How do the English search results on the major search engine compare with the non-English results of the local web search engine?

5.4. (Explore). PageRank's random surfer model assumes the user is navigating the web by randomly clicking on a new link each time a new page is being browsed. This model is a very useful simplification of the real process, where the user may interact with other available navigation tools. Since the back button is the most popular browser tool, it is natural to extend the random surfer model to allow "back steps" by clicking on the back button [458, 636, 262].

Extend the PageRank to take into account the effect of the back button, and present the formal statement of your extension.

5.5. (Explore). The PageRank tends to favor older web pages, since they have had time to accumulate inlinks, while newer pages will typically have few inlinks and thus a low PageRank. To remedy this situation, the age and freshness of web pages can be taken into account in the ranking process [44, 75, 692].

Find out how the age and freshness of web pages can be traced, and then suggest a modification to PageRank that is sensitive to these time parameters.

5.6. (Explore). An interesting suggestion to combat link spam is to truncate the computation of PageRank by reducing the importance of pages at a short distance from the page whose rank is being computed [63].

How could you modify the PageRank to operationalize this idea, and how would such a truncated PageRank help in the fight against link spam?

5.7. (Explore). The random surfer model of PageRank assumes that the user will choose to click on outgoing links with equal probabilities. In reality, users' choice of which link to follow may be biased by the relative popularity of the links.

A natural extension of PageRank can take into account the popularity of web pages, as measured from the usage patterns that can be extracted from web and query log files [521].

Suggest an extension of PageRank that takes into account the popularity of links and web pages. Using a weblog file from a small web site, compare the ranking of its pages using the original PageRank formulation and your extension.

5.8. (Explore). Experiment with Google Suggest (www.google.com/webhp?complete=1&hl=en), which predicts query terms as they are typed into the search box. This feature uses log data about the overall popularity of various queries to rank the refinements it offers.

Evaluate this feature as a popularity-based metric, and suggest how it could possibly be directly factored into the ranking of search results in order to improve their relevance.

CHAPTER **6**

DIFFERENT TYPES OF SEARCH ENGINES

"We look at our users' interests, without our users we don't have business."
— Jerry Yang, Cofounder of Yahoo

THERE ARE different types of search engines serving different purposes. We look at web directories, search engine advertising, metasearch engines, personalization of search, question answering engines, image search, and special purpose search engines. All of these variations play an important part in the search engine landscape with the aim of satisfying the diverse needs of users and the commercial objectives of the competing search engines.

CHAPTER OBJECTIVES

- Introduce the notion of a web directory as providing a service, which is complementary to that provided by a standard search engine.
- Explain how a web directory categorizes pages and the problems encountered in keeping the directory up to date.
- Explain how search engine advertising works and how it generates revenues for search engines.
- Show how webmasters can help search engines index their pages with paid inclusions and Sitemaps.
- Discuss banner ads as a form of search engine advertising.
- Explain the notion of sponsored search and how organic and sponsored search engine results must be clearly identified.
- Introduce behavioral targeting, where information is collected about users in order to increase the effectiveness of the advertising.
- Discuss user behavior in terms of the clickthough rate of an ad, the bounce rate of an ad, ad fatigue, users' preference for organic links over sponsored

An Introduction to Search Engines and Web Navigation, by Mark Levene

links, repeat visits to advertisers' web sites, and whether a query has commercial intent.

- Explain the trade-off between the bias created by using as much screen real estate as possible to display sponsored results and the demand from users for a quality search service.
- Describe the bidding process used in sponsored search auctions and explain why the generalized second auction mechanism was chosen by the major search engines.
- Introduce two ways of ranking the bids in an auction: rank by bid, where the winner of an auction is determined solely by the bid price and rank by revenue, where the winner is determined by a combination of the bid price and the quality score.
- Describe how sponsored search auctions are managed online and in real time taking into account advertisers' budgets.
- Introduce pay per action (PPA) as an alternative to pay per click (PPC), whereby the advertiser is charged only when a specified action such as a purchase or download takes place.
- Discuss forms of advertising fraud, especially click fraud, and ways search engines can combat the fraud.
- Introduce the notion of a metasearch engine and explain how it works.
- Discuss the problems metasearch engines have in delivering a competitive and high quality search service, and potential solutions.
- Explain how search results can be clustered and how they can alternatively be classified.
- Motivate the importance of personalizing search engine results.
- Indicate how personalization can be integrated into a search engine and raise the critical issues of privacy and scalability.
- Introduce the notion of relevance feedback as a technique for the machine to learn which documents are more relevant to a user.
- Introduce personalized PageRank as a method of personalizing the PageRank to individual users.
- Explain the technology behind annotation-based question answering systems.
- Indicate how factual queries can be answered by a knowledge intensive approach.
- Explain the ideas behind open domain question answering, with the Web as its corpus.
- Motivate the need for image search on the Web.
- Explain how current search engines use textual cues to implement image search, and the potential of content-based approaches.

- Introduce VisualRank as a method inspired by PageRank to rank images according to content-based similarity.
- Introduce CAPTCHA as a visual method to tell computers and humans apart.
- Motivate the need for special purpose search engines through examples.
- Review selected special purpose search engines.

6.1 DIRECTORIES AND CATEGORIZATION OF WEB CONTENT

Yahoo is one of the first massive successes of the Internet boom, and is probably still the number one brand on the Web. It started off as a guide to the Web, which was manually compiled by its two founders Filo and Yang while studying for their PhD degrees at Stanford. During late 1994, before Yahoo was incorporated, there were only 10,000 web sites but finding information was already a problem, as at that time search engine technology was still in its infancy. By late 1994, there were over 100,000 visitors a day to the Yahoo web site, making it one most popular sites on the Web. Back then, the number of web sites was doubling every three months, so the scale of the operation of maintaining the Yahoo directory was already well beyond the capabilities of its two founders. In March 1995 Yahoo was incorporated, obtaining $2 million venture capital funding, and in April 1996, Yahoo was able to go public with a highly successful IPO. Yahoo now integrates search over its directory with general web search, allowing its users to have access to both manually catalogued and automatically spidered web pages.

The directory is organized by subject matter, the top level containing categories such as Arts and Humanities, Business and Economy, Computers and the Internet, Education, Government, Health, News and Media, Recreation and Sports, Science, Society and Culture, and so on. The natural hierarchical structure of the directory allows users easy navigation through and across its categories. The directory is not strictly hierarchical, as it has many cross-references between categories from different parts of the hierarchy. For example, the subcategory Musicals under the Theater category, has a reference to the Movies and Film subcategory, which comes under Entertainment.

The decision whether to include a site in the directory is made by human editors, who monitor the quality of submitted pages before inclusion. Sites can be suggested by any user, but to speed up the inclusion process Yahoo charges a fee.[125] Yahoo's past directory services competitor, Looksmart, had a similar procedure, while the Open Directory, which is a nonprofit organization, relies on volunteers to act as the directory editors. It is not known exactly how many full-time editors Yahoo employs, but the number is likely to be about 100 at any

[125]How to Suggest Your Site. http://docs.yahoo.com/info/suggest/submit.html.

given time. On the other hand, the Open Directory has reported, at the beginning of 2010, to have over 84,500 part-time editors, which is quite amazing. In terms of size, Yahoo's directory had, as of 1999, over 150,000 categories populated by several million web pages [399] (I could not find a more recent statistic on Yahoo's directory), the Open Directory had, as reported on their home page at the beginning of 2010, over 590,000 categories populated by over 4.5 million web pages, and, Looksmart's directory had, as of mid-2002, over 300,000 categories populated by over 3 million web pages.[126]

Web directories provide an important alternative to search engines, especially for novice surfers, as the directory structure makes it is easy to find relevant information provided when an appropriate category for the search query can be found. The fundamental drawback of directories is their lack of coverage. The Web now contains roughly 600 billion accessible pages, so current directories cover only a very small portion of the accessible web. Moreover, manually maintained directories cannot keep up with the dynamics of the Web, and so in the long run their contents will not be as fresh as they should be. But all is not lost for web directories as the categories themselves are extremely valuable. Knowing the category of a web page that a user clicked on is very indicative of the user's interests, and may be used to recommend to the user similar pages from the same or a related category. To solve the problem of how to automatically associate a web page with a category we need to make use of machine learning techniques for automatic categorization of web pages, as discussed in Section 3.2, where we introduced the naive Bayes classifier, which has often proved to be as effective as more complex classification methods.

Web directories are in a very good position to undertake the task of classifying web pages as they can use their existing directory as a high-quality training set for the classifier. They may also use their experience in manual classification to tweak the classifier, and thus improve its accuracy. Moreover, they can make use of query log data through the document transformation technique, discussed in Section 5.3, in order to improve the description of a web page, which in turn will provide higher quality input to the classifier.

Much of the world's commercial search engine technology is now in Yahoo's hand, as it now owns AlltheWeb, AltaVista, Inktomi, and Overture. As mentioned above, in addition to searches over its directory, Yahoo provides its users with general web search. Until February 2004 it was using Google to power its web search service[127], when it rolled out its own proprietary search engine (http://search.yahoo.com), thus consolidating and enhancing the search technologies it has acquired.

[126]Looksmart Search. http://investor.shareholder.com/looksmart/releasedetail.cfm?releaseid=81889. In the meanwhile, Looksmart has evolved from providing directory services to a search advertising network. http://www.looksmart.com/about-us

[127]Yahoo! Birth of a new machine, by C. Sherman, February 2004. http://searchenginewatch.com/searchday/article.php/3314171

6.2 SEARCH ENGINE ADVERTISING

If search engines did not have to generate any revenue, for example, if they were funded by the taxpayer, then their result lists would be completely free or organic, generated by the algorithms described in Chapter 5. In the early days of search engines this was indeed the situation, although the funding was from venture capital, who believed in the potential of search engines to generate profits. During the height of the Internet boom, a dot-com such as a search engine could go public with the promise of making money and, in this way, the venture capitalists, funding the operation, made a return on their investment. Long gone are the days where a search engine's interface was free of advertising. Commercial search engines such as Google, Yahoo, and Bing need to generate revenue streams in order to stay in business, and as it turns out advertising is their main source of income. Search engines such as Google are trying hard to infiltrate the enterprise search market, with some success, but the revenues from selling their technology are not as lucrative and forthcoming as those from advertising, and the competition from content management systems providing integrated solutions is tough. Although web search engines are in a good position to earn a share of the enterprise site search market, we have already seen in Section 2.7 that there are differences between web search and site search that may prove to be distracting to a web search engine, from the product development point of view. With their global audience reach and e-commerce profits growing, search engines are in an ideal position to deliver advertising on a massive scale.

6.2.1 Paid Inclusion

One way for search engines to make some money is to charge webmasters for speeding up the process of their site being included or listed in the search index. This revenue generating method is called *paid inclusion*. In the case of a directory such as Yahoo, depending on the service chosen, the payment may cover the privilege of being included in the directory listing.

Paid inclusion does not affect the ranking of the site within query results, but ensures that the site will be listed within a few days rather than within a few weeks, which is the typical time it might take a crawler to reach the site without any prompting. So paid inclusion is a quick way of getting a site onto the organic results of a search engine, and having the search engine's crawler visit the site on a regular basis to check for updates.[128]

The only major search engine that was offering paid inclusion as of 2009 was Yahoo, with its Search Submit services, but the future of this service is uncertain.[129] One reason that the other search engines are reluctant to provide paid inclusion is that many webmasters felt that it provides an unfair advantage

[128]Buying your way in: Search engine advertising chart, by D. Sullivan, May 2003. www.searchenginewatch.com/webmasters/article.php/2167941.

[129]Rest in Peace, Yahoo! Paid Inclusion, by J. McCarthy, December 2009. www.adotas.com/2009/12/rest-in-peace-yahoo-paid-inclusion.

to those web sites that could afford to pay for the service, and in any case the regular crawling of web sites is a core activity of a search engine regardless of who owns the site. It was also argued that paid inclusion makes it harder for users to trust search engine results as it may effect the integrity of organic search results. (It should be noted that both Microsoft and Ask Jeeves provided paid inclusion services, which were discontinued in 2004.)

An XML [259] protocol, called Sitemaps (www.sitemaps.org), allows webmasters to inform search engines about web pages that are available for crawling and to include additional metadata for each web page such as when the page was last updated, how often the web page is updated and the relative priority of the page within the site. The Sitemaps protocol was originally introduced by Google in mid-2005, and is now supported by all major search engines as a free service. Using Sitemaps can assist the search engines' crawlers but does not guarantee inclusion of these pages in their indices, nor does it have any effect on the ranking of these pages had they been discovered by a crawler without the aid of Sitemaps.

6.2.2 Banner Ads

In the early days of search engine advertising, prior to the paid placement mechanism described in Section 6.2.3, search engines relied on banner advertising. Displaying banner ads on a search engine's home page is problematic as they are unlikely to be related to the topic of search a user is interested in, and present a dilemma to the search engine, which should be encouraging users to use the search engine rather than stay on the search engine's home page [211]. Banner ads are now more commonly associated with web portals and are often sold through advertising networks that display the ads on multiple web sites for a share of the ad revenue. Banner ads are priced by the number of impressions displayed; this method of payment is called *pay per impression* (PPM) also known as *cost per impression* (CPM) (211, 331). (The M in PPM and CPM stands for Roman numeral of 1000.)

Banner ads suffer from the phenomenon of "banner-blindness," where users often ignore banner ads that are displayed on web sites. This may explain why the clickthrough rates (CTRs) of banner ads have decreased over time and are reportedly less than 1% [319]. An eye-tracking experiment revealed that only about 50% of the ads are actually seen by users, and only about 10% of users can recall the brand name a day later [319]. In this experiment the users were navigating the Web with a specific goal in mind. However, in another experiment [523] it was shown that when users are surfing aimlessly they are more likely to notice banner ads than in a goal directed session.

6.2.3 Sponsored Search and Paid Placement

A far more effective and profitable form of advertising for search engines, pioneered by GoTo.com (that was renamed to Overture in 2001 and acquired by Yahoo in 2003), is called *paid placement* also known as *sponsored search* [211].

In this scheme the search engine separates its query results list into two parts: (i) an organic list, which contains the free unbiased results, displayed according to the search engine's ranking algorithm, and (ii) a sponsored list, which is paid for by advertising managed with the aid of an online auction mechanism described in Section 6.2.7. This method of payment is called *pay per click* (PPC), also known as *cost per click* (CPC), since payment is made by the advertiser each time a user clicks on the link in the sponsored listing.

In most cases the organic and sponsored lists are kept separate but an alternative model is to interleave the organic and sponsored results within a single listing. (Most notably the metasearch engine Dogpile (www.dogpile.com) combines its organic and sponsored lists [334].)

The links in the sponsored list are ranked according to the product of the highest bid for the keywords associated with the query and the *quality score*. The quality score is determined by a weighted combination of the CTR of the ad, its quality as determined by the relevancy of the keywords bid to the actual query, and the quality of the landing page behind the sponsored link. Although the weights of the quality features have not been disclosed by the search engines running the online auctions, the CTR is the major factor in the formula for computing the quality score.

In the context of CTRs it is worth mentioning that query popularity gives rise to a long tail, more formally known as a *power law distribution*, which is discussed in Section 9.6. A distribution is long tailed when a few data items (in this case queries) are very popular and most of the items, comprising the long tail, are rare. Silverstein *et al.* [608] found in their analysis that 63.7% of queries occurred only once, 16.2% occurred twice and 6.5% occurred thrice (totaling 86.4%), which is consistent with the size of the long tail reported in other studies of search logs such as Ref. 415. This phenomenon has enabled small advertisers to show their presence by bidding for rare queries, which are related to the products they are trying to sell [400].

Overture's listing was founded on the paid placement model, so it displayed as many sponsored results as it had to answer a query, before displaying any organic results, which were delivered by another search engine; see Fig. 6.1 noting that each sponsored result is clearly marked as such at the end of the entry in the list. (The Overture listing was eventually phased out by Yahoo after they rebranded Overture's services and transformed them into their current search engine marketing platform.)

The main web search engines display sponsored links on a results page in three possible places: above the organic list, below the organic list, and in a separate, reduced width, area on the right-hand side of the organic results. See Figs 6.2, 6.3, and 6.4, for sponsored links on Google, Yahoo, and (Microsoft's) Bing, respectively, highlighted by surrounding rectangles. Both Yahoo and Bing display additional sponsored links below the organic results, while as of early 2010 Google did not. All search engines have a heading above or besides the sponsored links to demarcate them from the organic results. We observe that the ads above and below the organic list come in horizontal blocks, while the ones on the side come in vertical blocks and are known as *skyscraper ads*. It is worth

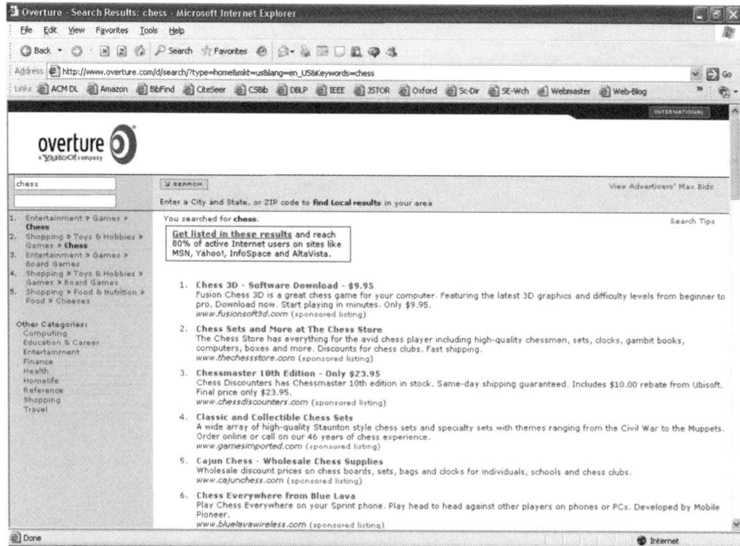

Figure 6.1 Query "chess" submitted to Overture. (Source: Reproduced with permission of Yahoo! Inc. (www.overture.com). © 2010 by Yahoo! Inc., OVERTURE, and the OVERTURE logo are registered trademarks of Yahoo! Inc.)

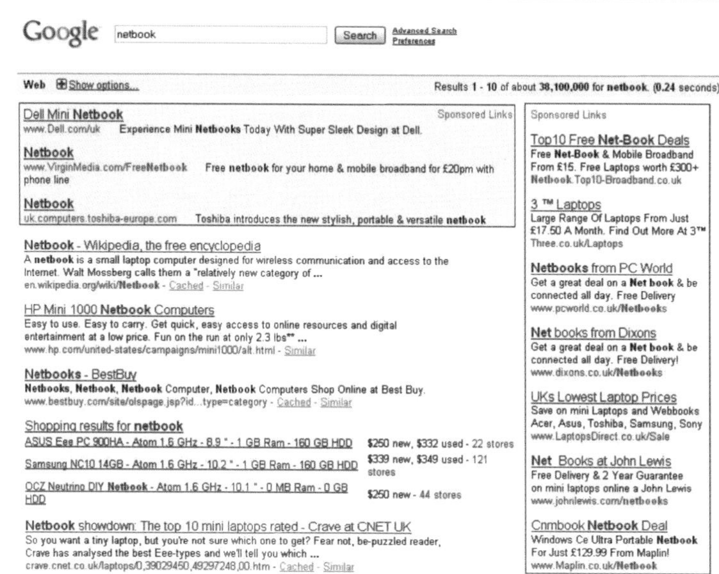

Figure 6.2 Query "netbook" submitted to Google.

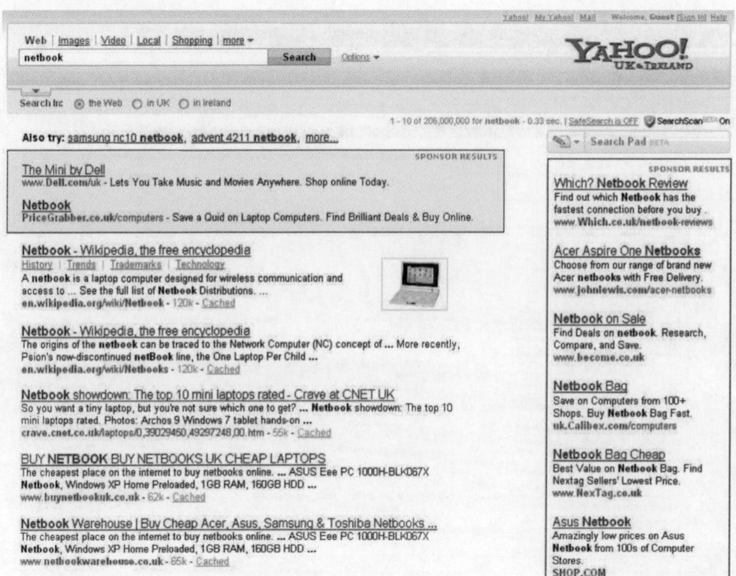

Figure 6.3 Query "netbook" submitted to Yahoo. (Source: Reproduced with permission of Yahoo! Inc. (http://search.yahoo.com). © 2010 by Yahoo! Inc., YAHOO!, and the YAHOO! logo are registered trademarks of Yahoo! Inc.)

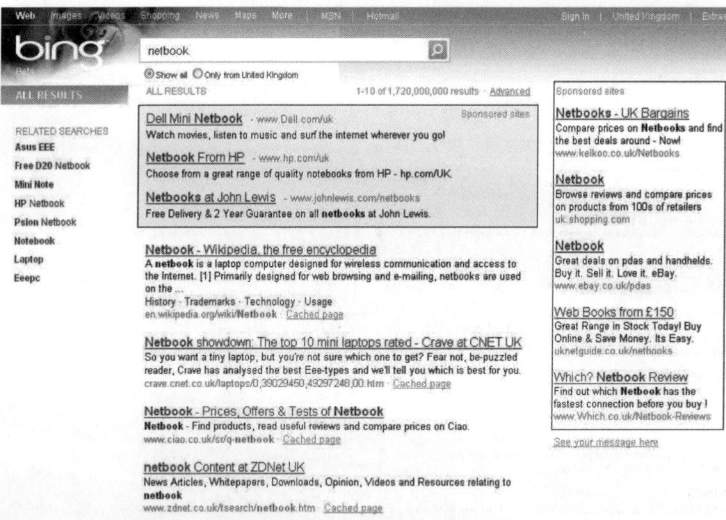

Figure 6.4 Query "netbook" submitted to Bing.

noting that the sponsored ads are geographically sensitive to the country from the search emanates, in this case from the United Kingdom.

As we have seen search engines clearly mark results that are paid for, to distinguish them from organic results output from their ranking algorithm. This keeps them in line with a warning issued by the US Federal Trade Commission

(FTC) to search engine companies, that they should "clearly and conspicuously disclose" that certain query results are paid for by web sites in order to have a higher placement in the ranked results.[130] The FTC also urged search engine companies to provide clear descriptions of their paid inclusion and paid placement programs, and their impact on search results, so that consumers would be in a better position to use this knowledge when choosing which search engine to use. All commercial search engines we know of, now, clearly distinguish between organic results and sponsored results or links. This is good news for users, many of whom may be unaware of paid placement.

6.2.4 Behavioral Targeting

The next logical step in sponsored search is that of *behavioral* targeting, or as Google calls it, interest-based advertising.[131] Behavioral targeting is a form of advertising where information is collected about users' searching (queries) and browsing (page views) habits, and then analyzed in order to deliver personalized ads in order to increase the advertising effectiveness. For example, suppose that based on a user's past searches that have been recorded by the search engine, it is found that this consumer is interested in science fiction. Then, when the user is searching for book stores, a behavioral targeting algorithm will, for example, deliver an ad recommending to the consumer the latest science fiction book in an advertiser's store. What behavioral targeting tries to do with users' data is to narrow down their interests to a set of categories or subcategories such as a general interest in antiques, a specific outdoor recreation, a particular car brand, or a holiday in a given location.

Contextual targeting is a weaker form of advertising based only on the current search, without any previous knowledge of the user's behavior. In our book store example, a contextual ad will only recommend the advertiser's book store, as the information about the genre the consumer is interested in not known to the algorithm. As can be seen in Figs 6.2, 6.3, and 6.4, web search engines are deploying contextual advertising by optimizing the relevance of the ads to the query. Apart from query terms, contextual advertising takes into account other features such as geographical (i.e., where is the consumer), temporal (when is the consumer query issued), and popularity (i.e., how many consumers issued the query in past).

Behavioral targeting is deemed to be successful if it increases the CTRs of targeted ads. An empirical study by Yang *et al.* [685] of a large commercial search engine log, which tracked users' clicks with cookies, suggests that behavioral targeting is effective. First they found that users who click on the same ads are much more similar than users who clicks on different ads. They then segmented users with the aid of a clustering algorithm according to the queries they clicked on, and found that the CTRs can be significantly improved by targeting ads

[130]FTC warns search engine companies, by R.W. Wiggins, July 2002, Information Today, Inc., NewsBreaks. http://newsbreaks.infotoday.com/nbreader.asp?ArticleID=17140.

[131]Google Ad Preferences. www.google.com/ads/preferences/html/about.html.

to users within segments. Another important observation was that short-term (one day) behavioral targeting was more effective than long-term (seven days) targeting.

Alreck and Settle [27] surveyed over 1000 adults from the United States through a questionnaire about their attitudes to behavioral targeting from an e-commerce perspective. Overall there was considerable awareness of the respondents that they are being tracked. They showed concern about this intrusion into their privacy but this did not, in general, inhibit them from online shopping.

As part of the US FTC endeavor to understand the online marketplace and consumers' privacy concerns, they have issued in early 2009, some self-regulatory principles for online behavior advertising.[132] The four proposed principles are: (i) maintaining transparency about data collection and its use in advertising, and allowing users to choose whether their information should be collected, (ii) data collected should be secure and retained only for as long as is necessary, (iii) data should only be used for the purposes it was originally intended to be used, and (iv) sensitive data should only be collected with user consent.

6.2.5 User Behavior

Before we describe the mechanism of sponsored search auctions we look into several aspects of user click behavior relating to sponsored search. The *click-through* rate (CTR)or an ad can be estimated by dividing the number of clicks on the ad divided by the number of impressions it had within a given time period; this is called the *maximum likelihood estimate*. However, because the CTR for most ads is generally low due to the long tail of query popularity, the variance of such an estimate is quite high. This motivates using a feature-based approach to supplement the CTR estimate. In particular, logistic regression [18] can be used, providing an estimate between zero and one (which can be viewed as a probability) based on a weighted sum of the features used. Richardson *et al.* [566] considered the baseline prediction to be the average CTR of ads from a data set used to train the model. They then considered several features, which were tested as to whether they improve the performance of the baseline prediction. Significant improvements came from several features: (i) the CTR of other ads sharing the same query terms, (ii) the quality of the ad (measured within several broad categories, that is, its relevance to the query, the quality of the landing page behind the sponsored link, its reputation, its appearance, and its ability to capture the attention of users), (iii) how varied are the query terms associated with an ad (note that, in general, a single ad will be associated with several query terms), and (iv) external data sources such as the numbers of hits on a web search engine and the popularity of the query in a sizeable search engine log. It was also shown that the feature-based method is useful for up to about 100 clicks on an ad after which the simple maximum likelihood estimate is sufficient.

One limitation of the CTR is that is does not capture users' satisfaction once they arrive at the landing page after clicking on an ad. The *bounce rate*

[132]FTC Staff revises online behavioral advertising principles, February 2009. www.ftc.gov/opa/2009/02/behavad.shtm.

[598] of an ad measures the fraction of users that click on an ad and immediately move on to another task, that is, they bounce from the advertiser's site. How immediate they bounce from the site is measured by a threshold, which typically ranges from 5 to 60 secs. It turns out that ads with a very low bounce rate have a very high CTR. Moreover, low bounce rates coincide with high-quality ads based on the expected user satisfaction as judged by experts. It also turns out that the mean bounce rate for advertisers that follow Google's quality guidelines is over 25% less than the bounce rate of advertisers that do not follow the guidelines. Another interesting observation is that navigational queries such as company names and commercial keywords such as "books" and "flights" have low bounce rates, while entertainment keywords such as "games" and "chat" have higher bounce rates. In general, the more popular keywords have lower bounce rates, possibly because the competition leads to higher quality advertising. Even in the absence of a substantial amount of clickthrough data the bounce rate can be estimated, using a machine learning technique such as one based on logistic regression, from features extracted from the query terms bid, the ad text displayed on the search engine, and the landing page of the ad. In summary, high bounce rates can be useful in identifying ad quality problems but the bounce rate alone does not suggest how to fix the problems.

Another aspect that has an effect on users' experience is that of *ad fatigue*, where users get tired of repeatedly seeing the same ads [4] or seeing irrelevant ads [432]. As a result of ad fatigue users are less likely to click on any ad at all. In order to tackle this problem the search engine needs on the one hand to optimize the number of times and the rank at which an ad is displayed [4], and possibly also the positioning and colors of the ads. On the other hand, it has been suggested to tax irrelevant ads in order to compensate for the revenue loss caused by their low quality [432].

An important line of research is to investigate the factors that influence users' selection of sponsored links as opposed to organic links. Jansen *et al.* [330] looked at this problem for e-commerce searching tasks for information from three categories about (i) a class of products, (ii) a specific product, and (iii) a product in a specific geographical location. They found that for more than 80% of the time users prefer organic results to sponsored results, and most of the time they will inspect the organic list before the sponsored one. Generally, there was a bias against sponsored links and users rated sponsored links as having lower relevance than organic ones. In fact, relevance was their main evaluation criterion of sponsored links. Although users prefer the organic list, over 70% of users viewed both listings, but less than 40% actually click on a sponsored link. As of 2009, the CTRs for sponsored links were estimated to be between 15% and 30%, and these vary dramatically by market segment; presumably for e-commerce queries the CTRs are higher [334].

A navigational query is one whose intent is to locate a single web site. A study by Microsoft's Atlas Institute (www.atlassolutions.com) [109] found that over 70% of clicks on sponsored search links are navigational, noting that Jansen *et al.* [329] found that about 10% of all queries on web search engines are navigational. In the context of this study a sponsored search click was categorized as navigational when it was a repeat visit to a web site, implying prior knowledge of the advertiser, or if the query was a branded keyword search, that is, where the query contained terms associated with the advertiser's name or web site address. In these cases the reason for conversion, assuming a purchase was made after the click, is probably not the sponsored link, since the user was already actively looking for the advertiser's site. One implication of this finding is that advertising across several channels to raise awareness of a product or brand may be worthwhile, as it is not necessarily the last click that leads to the conversion. Another implication is that if the user can find the web site without the sponsored link, for example, if the web site is at the top of the organic list, then the sponsored search advertising may not be so effective.

Another important factor in the user behavior is whether the query has commercial intent, that is, the intention of buying a product or a service. For example, terms such as *cheap*, *sale*, and *download* probably indicate commercial intent while terms such as *school*, *news*, and *weather* do not. An analysis by Ashkan and Clarke [36] found that queries having terms with commercial intent were better predictors of clicks on sponsored ads than queries with no commercial intent, where the queries we judged as commercial or not by human annotators.

6.2.6 The Trade-Off between Bias and Demand

As most users only view one page of query results, the number of displayed paid results has a strong effect on what users will view and thus creates a bias that will, overall, decrease the demand for the search engine. From the screenshots showing how the major search engines display ads, their strategy stands out as one way to decrease the bias by displaying the paid results only on the side rather than in the middle of the web page, but this has the effect of narrowing the organic part of the screen. There is a trade-off between bias and demand, and this influences the revenue model, as the number of customers is closely related to the demand, that is, the user base of the search engine, which is measured by the search engine's CTR. So a search engine has to maximize its user-based revenues as measured by the CTR (the demand) and maximize its profits by increasing the size and visibility of the paid listing (the bias). The question is what is the optimal balance between the demand and bias, that maximizes the search engine's revenues from paid placement advertising.

As discussed in Section 4.2, in the context of the conflict search engines have between delivering high-quality search results and maximizing their profit, we reiterate that the search engine with the better technology has an advantage in the competition for paid placement customers, and thus can choose the bias level that maintains its overall higher quality service. Bhargava and Feng [80] looked at this problem in the context of market demand as a function of the quality of the search technology and the bias caused by sponsored search advertising, and developed a model where increasing the quality increases demand, while increasing the bias decreases demand. They showed that a search engine must find the equilibrium point between users' demand for quality and advertisers' demand for bias, as increasing the bias beyond this point will cause users to defect to another search engine and thus will have the effect of reducing the demand for advertising. Feng *et al.* [214] conducted simulation experiments, which showed that when the willingness of advertisers to pay for an ad is positively correlated with the relevance of the ad to the query terms the ad is associated with, there is a maximum number of advertising slots beyond which the expected revenue of the search engine from sponsored search will decrease.

In this context, it is worth noting that Overture's business model was founded on paid placement. The question that begs an answer is, why was Overture so successful, given that it did not position itself as a search engine in the way that, say, Google does? There are several possible reasons for this. Overture pioneered the PPC paid placement scheme providing a good match with sites wishing to advertise on the Web. It successfully partnered with many other search providers, which guaranteed advertisers a wide audience. The PPC scheme is based on a sound model, allowing customers to measure their return on investment (ROI), and adjust their bids accordingly. The takeover of Overture by Yahoo has strengthened the paid placement market as Yahoo controls a sizeable slice of the web search market.

When Yahoo acquired Overture it also inherited its patented paid placement technology, which it has been vigorously protecting through the courts.[133] In April 2002 Overture filed a lawsuit against Google for infringement of their patented bid for placement process. The lawsuit was eventually settled in August 2004, between Yahoo, the parent company of Overture, and Google, who agreed to license the technology.[134]

An interesting model that may be viable for a high-quality search engine is to charge users for a premium service with no bias in its results, that is, no paid listing or any other form of advertising, and to provide a basic version, which is free but has a paid placement bias. Such a model may give rise to a difficult dilemma for the search engine, if enough users join the premium service to make paid placement less attractive to customers due the lower audience reach of its advertising.

6.2.7 Sponsored Search Auctions

We now describe in some detail the keyword bidding process as implemented by all the major web search engines [201]. The model is based on the Google AdWords paid placement model that was originally developed by Overture. (As a parenthetical remark we note that Overture was acquired by Yahoo in 2003, and in 2009 Yahoo struck a deal with Microsoft (www.choicevalueinnovation.com/thedeal), where Microsoft will power Yahoo's search and also its advertising online auction and delivery technology through its AdCenter platform (http://advertising.microsoft.com).) The competition for sponsored search advertising is very fierce as it has become a multibillion dollar industry. In this context

[133]Overture to a patent war?, by S. Olsen, Cnet News.com, July 2003. http://news.cnet.com/2100-1024_3-1027084.html.

[134]Google, Yahoo settle patent and share disputes, by C. Sherman, August, 2004. http://searchenginewatch.com/searchday/article.php/3392421

it is worth mentioning that the revenue from sponsored search is not limited to the major search engines that control the advertising software. In order to increase their profit they are partnering with smaller search engines to manage their sponsored listings as a third party in a revenue sharing scheme. Taking this a step further web site publishers can join the Google AdSense (www.google.com/adsense) program to display on their web site ads that are relevant to the content of their site, and earn a share of the advertising revenue.[135]

As an advertiser your first step is to choose the keywords and phrases for which you wish to have a high search engine ranking. It is recommended you to choose a range of search terms from a wide range of terms you consider to be relevant. The search engines provide advertisers with tools for helping them to select the appropriate keywords and estimate the CTRs and the CPC. For example, Google provides tools for finding keywords that are relevant to the web site you are advertising[136] and for estimating how many clicks these keywords generate and their cost within a daily budget.[137]

Once you have chosen the keywords and phrases then you will need to write a title and description (T&D) for each one, which will appear on the paid listing when your site is displayed on the search engine's results. It is important to note that the search engine will review the keywords you choose and the T&D for relevance to your site, to ensure that there is a close match between these and the content on your site. Another point to make is that when you appear on the organic listing (as opposed to the sponsored listing) the T&D is automatically created from the web page by the search engine's summarization software. The next step is to participate in the online auction for keywords by putting in a bid for these terms. There may be a reserve price on the terms you bid for, forcing you to bid above this minimal price. When putting in your bid you do not have knowledge of the level of other bids, but as we discussed above you can decide on your bid with the help of the tools provided by the search engines, taking into account the price you are willing to pay. If you are already advertising on the search engine you will have reports on your past performance so that you can calculate your ROI, which will most likely effect your bid price.

In a sponsored search auction there are several slots to be won according to the number of sponsored links displayed for the search terms, which could be up to about 10 for popular queries as we have seen above in Fig. 6.2. What this means is that even if you do not win the top slot, you may still obtain one of the lower slots.

When the auction mechanism is a generalized first price (GFP) auction, the price you pay for each click on your ad is a function of the price that you bid on; we will make this more precise below in the context of the deployed auction mechanism. Originally Overture employed a GFP, where the winning bids were

[135]Yahoo and Microsoft have similar advertising programs: Yahoo Publisher Network, http://publisher.
yahoo.com; Microsoft AdCenter Publisher, https://advertising.microsoft.com/publisher.

[136]Google Search-based keyword tool. www.google.com/sktool.

[137]Google AdWords Traffic Estimator. https://adwords.google.com/select/TrafficEstimatorSandbox.

ranked by the bid prices posted and the winner paid the bid price; this ranking mechanism is known as *rank by bid*.

A known problem with GFP is that of a bidding war, where bidders will keep on changing their bids in response to other bidders' behavior. For example, suppose there are two bidders: One, who is willing to up to £1 and Two who is willing to pay up to £2. Now assume that One bids £1, then Two will increase the bid by 1p to £1.01 and win the auction. One will then reduce his bid to the reserve price, say £0.01, lowering his costs and getting the second position. Then, Two can win the auction by increasing the bid by 1p to £0.02, and thereafter the bids will increase incrementally until One bids £1, and the cycle will repeat itself.

This problem does not arise in the generalized second price (GSP) auction [201], where the payment is a function of the bid below yours, that is, if your bid was the top bid then the price you pay for a click is a function of the price of the second top bid. So in the above bidding wars example, we see that if One bids £1 then Two will win the auction at that price by bidding £1.01, while One will get the second position at the reserve price. It can be shown in GSP that a stable assignment of bids arises when advertisers will bid the least amount they can in order to retain their slot, as long as this price is not more than what they are willing to pay; this is known as a *locally envy-free equilibrium* [201]. In 2004, following Google AdWords, which started in 2002 and adopted GSP, Overture switched to GSP, while still ranking by bid at the time.

In AdWords, the winner determined by the *ad rank*, which is the product of the bid price and the *quality score* of the advertisement; this ranking mechanism is known as *rank by revenue*. The quality score of an ad is determined by three factors in decreasing order of importance: (i) its CTR, (ii) its relevancy, that is, how relevant are the keywords bid for to the T&D of the ad and to a user's search query, and (iii) the quality of the landing page.[138] Google's guidelines regarding the quality of the landing page emphasize: (i) relevant and original content, (ii) transparency into the nature of the business, and (iii) navigability to the product advertised.

The price the winner of the ad auction pays is the ad rank of the bid below it divided by the quality score of the winner, so the higher your quality score the less you pay. Although rank by revenue is more complex than rank by bid, it is based on the assumption that if the price is driven solely by the bids, then the quality of ads will not be maintained and thus the clickthough rates will decrease. This in turn will have an impact both on the revenue of the search engine and potential conversions for the advertisers. In 2007 Yahoo switched to a rank by revenue method. Until 2006 Microsoft was using Yahoo's sponsored advertising platform. AdCenter, which is Microsoft's own platform, now delivers their sponsored search advertising, and as a result of the deal between Microsoft and Yahoo, will be powering Yahoo's sponsored search. It employs a GSP auction and a similar rank by revenue mechanism for selling sponsored links.

[138]Introduction to ad auction by Hal Varian. http://adwords.blogspot.com/2009/03/introduction-to-ad-auction.html.

Another issue for advertisers is to decide what they are willing to pay for a keyword. As an example, suppose that your bid for "book" was the second, and as a result your T&D will appear second when users type in "book" or "books" or common misspellings of the word. Bids are fluid, so if someone outbid you for that keyword your ranking will drop unless you increase your bid. One useful bidding strategy is "gap bidding," when you find a gap between two bids, say the second and third places, and then place a bid for the minimum amount above the third bid. So, if the second bid for book is 20p and the third bid is 10p, you can obtain the third place by bidding 11p.

A rational strategy for determining the amount you should bid for the keywords is based on the "conversion rate" (*CR*), which is the percentage of visitors to your site that convert to paying customers. This means that if out of 100 visitors to your site you make one sale, your *CR* is 1. Now assume your profit per sale is £x, then on every 100 visitors you make $CR \times £x$, and so to get a return on your investment this amount should be at least 100 time your bid, which is what you are willing to pay for 100 clicks. So, if your *CR* is 1 and your bid was 11p, you will need to make a profit of more than £11 per unit sale to justify your participation in a PPC scheme. The ROI will probably effect your bidding strategy, to place higher bids for more specific terms, since the clickthough rates for these will be lower but the CRs may be higher. The search engines managing the listings have deals with other search services they call affiliate partners, so that your site may also be advertised in the partners paid listing and increase the exposure of your ads.

At any given time bids for a multitude of keywords and phrases will be in place, although they are continuously changing as advertisers see fit to update them. The actual auction mechanism runs in real time by the ad servers, which rank the bids online in response to a user query, taking into account advertisers' daily budgets. As the major search engines such as Google have to deal with many thousands of queries per second this is a daunting computational task. This problem can be paraphrased algorithmically as an online matching optimization problem, where for every user query advertisers are matched to slots, in such a way that the objective is to maximize the search engine's daily revenue from a given set of advertisers who have placed bids on various keywords and have daily budgets that cannot be exceeded.

As a simple example that shows why we should take into account daily budgets, assume we have two advertisers, One and Two, with the same daily budgets and that there are two keywords to bid on. Further assume that Two has placed bids on both keywords but One had placed a slightly lower bid only on the first keyword. Moreover, the situation is such that there is only one slot to fill for each keywords and Two has won the auction for both of them. A naive algorithm would allocate the slot to Two for both keywords, but once Two's budget runs out the slot for the second keyword cannot be filled anymore, which may lead to loss of revenue to the search engine depending on the frequencies and CTRs of the keywords.

To solve the problem Abrams *et al.* [3] employ linear programming, which is an optimization method that maximizes a linear objective function subject to a set of linear inequality constraints. Abrams assumes that query frequencies are known, as this has an effect on the number of times an ad can be displayed. As we have discussed above the distribution of queries has a long tail [415], which makes it easier to forecast queries in the head at the expense of queries in the tail. Now suppose that the query frequencies are unknown, and that the ratio of a bid to the overall budget is small. A greedy algorithm would simply allocate an incoming query to the advertiser with the highest bid. It was shown by Mehta *et al.* [463] that a much better solution is to allocate the query to the advertiser that maximizes the product of the bid and a function of the fraction of the budget that has already been spent, which they call a trade-off revealing linear program.

6.2.8 Pay per Action

PPC allows an ad network such as a search engine to manage large-scale and very profitable advertising that funnels traffic to advertisers. Still it has several drawbacks. The biggest problem, discussed in Section 6.2.9, is that of click fraud, which has become a major headache for the search engines. Another problem is related to the bounce rate discussed above, where search terms may lead to clicks but users do not perform any activity on the advertiser's site. Yet another issue is that of the long tail of queries, where for small advertisers the ROI may not justify the expense of bidding for broad terms, while the narrow terms in the long tail may not get enough clicks to accurately estimate the ROI from PPC advertising.

The pay per action (PPA) model, also known as cost per action (CPA), goes beyond the PPC and PPM models by only charging the advertiser for a more concrete action from the user than just a click or an ad impression [448]. An action may involve the purchase of an item, downloading a file, filling in a form, signing up for a newsletter, or any other trackable action that the advertiser is willing to pay for. A major difference between PPC and PPA or PPM from a logistic point of view is that, while the ad network (i.e., the search engine in this case) can measure the clicks and ad impressions taking place on the search results page, conversions take place on the advertisers' sites and are thus not directly measurable by the ad network.

In order to track conversions, ad networks will normally require the advertiser to place a small script in the web page that is triggered after the action is carried out, as in Google's conversion tracking feature.[139] When a user clicks on an ad, a cookie is inserted on the user's computer. Then, if the user reaches the conversion web page, the inserted script causes the user's browser to send the cookie back to the ad network and a match can be made between the ad and the conversion. This mechanism of inserting a script is not foolproof and involves a level of trust between the advertiser and the ad network. Sophisticated advertisers may be able to manipulate the script to misreport the number of conversions [16]. Although PPA is more resistant to fraud with than PPC we will see in Section 6.2.9 below that it is not immune to fraudulent behavior.

[139] Google AdWords help, Conversion Tracking. http://adwords.google.com/support/aw/bin/topic.py?hl=en&topic=16344.

Another unique issue for the PPA model is the timing of events. An ad impression takes place on a user's browser once a decision has been made to display the ad, and a clickthough happens shortly after the impression or not at all depending on the user's decision whether to click on the ad or not. On the other hand an action, such as a purchase, may take place some time after the user clicked on the ad. This is the reason a cookie is needed to record the user's click and its ID matched later when the conversion page is reached. Moreover, as part of specifying the action the advertiser would also have to specify the maximum time after the ad was clicked for a conversion to be counted.

6.2.9 Click Fraud and Other Forms of Advertising Fraud

As search engine advertising has become such a lucrative business so has advertising fraud. Thus it is important to understand the types of fraud that are possible and to develop ways to effectively combat them. We distinguish between online advertising fraud [171], which is a type of internet crime, and advertising spam, which has no benefit for the user and may even be deceptive, as is e-mail spam [695], but is not necessarily fraudulent. Here we concentrate on fraud, while acknowledging that advertising spam, which may cause malicious software (malware) to be installed on your computer when clicked on, has also become a serious problem [200].

In banner advertising the advertisers can be victims, when the ad networks overcharge them for false impressions [200]. One method is displaying the ads on web sites, known as *banner farms*, which are fully populated by ads but with no real content. Another is stacking ads one on top of another or displaying very small ads which are hardly visible.

A common type of advertising fraud, known as *click fraud*, is the practice of clicking on a sponsored link with the sole purpose of forcing the advertiser to pay for the click in a PPC advertising scheme. This is naturally a major concern to the search engines serving the ads, who closely monitor the click patterns on sponsored links for any irregularity.

We note that according to Kourosh Gharachorloo from Google's Ad Traffic Quality Team, less than 10% of clicks are fraudulent [250]. One source of nonfraudulent clicks is to do with the problem of counting duplicate clicks. For example, a user may click on an ad and as a result visit the landing page behind the sponsored link. If the user subsequently reloads the landing page into the browser the referrer URL will be counted as the original one, which is the search engine from which the ad was served, and thus counted an extra time. One solution to this problem is to use a feature called *auto-tagging*, which is provided by AdWords and attaches a unique ID to the URL of each landing page, thus allowing reloaded pages to be spotted and not counted more than once.

Two sources of click fraud are *advertiser competitor clicking* and *publisher click inflation* [171]. In advertiser competitor clicking, a malicious advertiser clicks on a competitor's ad with the purpose of causing the competitor as much expense as possible with no ROI. As a result this could allow the malicious advertiser to obtain the competitor's keywords at a lower price if the defrauded advertiser reduced his PPC budget to compensate for his loss.

Publisher click inflation occurs in third-party programmes such as AdSense, where ads are displayed on third-party web sites (the publishers) and when clicked on the publishers earn a share of the profit. Here a publisher has a monetary incentive to increase the number of clicks on his site; so by simply generating as many clicks as possible on the ads on his site the publisher will generate a steady revenue stream for himself.

The fraudulent clicks can be generated either by humans or software robots. Humans are harder to manage than software robots, but in economies where human labor is cheap hiring human clickers is viable. Such attacks are harder to uncover when the humans are using multiple machines and multiple IP addresses and cookies. However, the pattern resulting from the same human's repeated return to the same site and clicking on ads, is easy to detect. To make manual clicking harder to detect and trace, some fraudsters route the clicks through HTTP proxies, which can obscure the source of the clicks. On the downside, from the fraudster's point of view, ad networks may view clicks coming from HTTP proxies as dubious and count them as invalid.

Clicks generated by software robots, called *clickbots*, are designed with the sole purpose of defrauding the ad networks. Clickbots are more predictable than humans, but are easier to manage and can generate a large number of clicks at a low cost. A case study of an attack on Google's advertising network by a software robot, known as Clickbot.A, occurred in 2006 from a robot consisting of a network of 100,000 machines from multiple IP addresses [171]. Clickbot.A acted as a publisher and made use of "doorway sites" that contained ads that were automatically clicked on by the software. Although coming from multiple IP addresses the IPs used exhibited a strong correlation with e-mail spam blacklists, which helped in their detection.

Another form of automated click fraud is the technique of forced browser clicks, which tampers with the JavaScript code snippets that publishers need to add to their web pages in order to display the ads [242]. The fraudster creates a "badvertisement," which rewrites the genuine script and performs automatic clickthroughs on ads hosted on the fraudster's web site when a web page from the site is loaded into a user's browser. The users will not be aware of this behind the scenes activity as the ads will be invisible to them.

Ad networks apply some prevention measures, which involve careful screening of publishers before they are allowed to join the network, and devising more secure and reliable scripts for publishers in PPC schemes and advertisers in PPA schemes to add to their web pages.

Detecting fraudulent behavior is an ongoing concern for search engines managing their advertising networks. We assume that the advertising networks are not initiating fraud themselves, as it would be detrimental to their business if uncovered. In this respect, government agencies such as the FTC have an important role to play in monitoring the behavior of ad networks.

There have been several suggestions to detect click fraud that identify anomalies in the stream of click data. As a baseline, estimating the true CTRs

[322] of ads is obviously useful in detecting anomalous patterns that may arise as a result of fraud. Another technique that has been proposed involves detecting duplicate clicks within a time window using the IP address of the user and the information stored in cookies [468]. (Note that if the IP address comes from an internet service provider (ISP) and is dynamic, it is still in a known range.) When the cookies may not be reliable or available it is still possible to detect fraud from correlations between IPs and publishers that may be present in a clickstream and uncovered by scanning the publisher and IP pairs in the stream [469].

Although PPA advertising schemes eliminates click fraud it is not immune to fraudulent behavior. As discussed in Section 6.2.8 PPA relies on accurate tracking of conversions as specified by the actions that should take place on the advertiser's site for conversions to be counted. The obvious motivation for underreporting CRs is that an advertiser will thus reduce their advertising costs. If the advertiser is intent on maintaining the same budget he can increase his bid for the slot and win a higher rank and/or bid on more keywords to attract more traffic to his site [16]. Of course this strategy may backfire since advertisers that underreport their conversions will cause their quality score to decrease and as a result this will have an effect on the placement of their ads.

6.3 METASEARCH

A metasearch engine combines results from several search engines and presents one ranked list to the user through a common interface [466]. No search engine is perfect, and each individual search engine may perform better than the others in some circumstances; so in principal a metasearch engine may actually exceed the quality of the individual search engines it aggregates. The whole may be better than the sum of its parts, but the reality is much harsher than this. Metasearch engines are at the mercy of the search engines they wish to query, and some have banned metasearch engines from "free riding" on top of them, arguing that the additional internet traffic slows down their service. This has led some metasearch engines to negotiate a commercial arrangement with the major search engines, which usually involves delivering paid placement advertising from the search engine on the metasearch engine's site.[140]

The problem of metasearch is known as the *rank fusion* or the *rank aggregation* problem, where the metasearch engine submits a query to multiple search engines, and then has to combine the individual ranked lists returned into a single ranked list, which is presented to the user. One of the problems that a metasearch engine has to solve, when fusing results, is that of detecting and removing duplicate web pages that are returned by several search engines. For example, the URLs www.bbk.ac.uk and www.bbk.ac.uk/index.html are actually the same and should be detected as such. Users may or may not be aware that they are using a metasearch engine, since from the user's perspective the interaction is essentially

[140]Google added to Go2Net's MetaCrawler and Dogpile metasearch services, Google press release, January 2000. www.google.com/press/pressrel/pressrelease12.html

the same as with a standard search engine. Some metasearch engines let the users choose which search engines they wish to fuse, giving them more control. A metasearch engine has the advantage of being lightweight, since there is no need for crawling and large-scale indexing. One implication is that a metasearch engine may even be able to reside on the user's machine, which increases the scope for personalization of the search results. Another important potential of metasearch is the ability to aggregate information from databases residing in the deep web, that are normally hidden from web crawlers and web search engines.

Metasearch engines often have only sparse information about the relevance of web pages returned for a search engine query. In many cases all that the metasearch has to go with is a ranked ordering of the returned results, and a summary of each of the web pages included in the results. Despite this, some metasearch engines rely on relevance scores to fuse the results, which means that they need to infer the scores in some way, while other metasearch engines fuse the results based solely on the ranked results obtained from the search engines queried. Another dimension on which metasearch fuse algorithms differ, is whether they require training data or not, to learn about the search engines they are querying.

A metasearch engine, which uses relevance scores, can store a representative of each search engine, giving an indication of the contents of the search engine's index. The index of representatives could be built as the meta-engine is queried, so that it is compact and represents user queries rather than the full set of keywords in the underlying search engine's index. The meta-index enables a standard normalization of relevance scores across all the search engines deployed. In order to get the relevance information about the web pages returned, the metasearch engine can simply download these pages before merging the results, but this will, obviously, slow down the response time for the query.

When merging the results, it is useful to weight each search engine answer by the perceived quality of the answer. This is where training can kick in, so that a search engine can be assessed on its previous performance; see Section 5.4 for the methods of search engine evaluation.

6.3.1 Fusion Algorithms

To fuse results that rely on relevance information, the relevance of a web page is taken to be the sum of its relevance scores according to each of the individual search engines. It has been shown that weighting each web page score by the number of search engines that returned the page improves the performance of the fusion algorithm [411].

Experiments have indicated that fusion algorithms, which rely only the search engines ranking, called *rank aggregation algorithms*, can perform as well or even better than ones that use relevance scores [562].

Two such algorithms are based on voting systems.[141] In our case, the search engines are the voters and the web pages the candidates; in real elections there are

[141]Making sense out of consensus, by D. Mackenzie, SIAM News, 2000. www.siam.org/news/news.php?id=674

many voters and only few candidates, but in the case of metasearch the situation is reversed.

In the *Borda count* each voter ranks the candidates. Assuming there a n of them, then the top candidate receives n points, the second candidate $(n - 1)$ points, and the last candidate 1 point. The vote tally is computed by adding up the scores of all the candidates. If one search engine ranks web pages A, B, and C in that order and a second search engine ranks the pages in the order C, A, and B, then the score of A is 5, the score of B is 3 and the score of C is 4.

In the *Condorcet count* the winner is the candidate that defeats or ties with all the others in a head-to-head election. A is ahead of B according to both voters and thus defeats B, and A is ahead of C according to the first voter but behind C according to the second voter and thus A and C are tied. B and C are also tied, as each is ahead of each other once. Overall A is the Condorcet winner and B and C are tied for second place. We may then prefer C above B as C has suffered fewer defeats than B.

Initial experiments with these algorithms have shown that Condorcet fuse works best [479], followed by Borda fuse, which is competitive with fusing using relevance information [37]. If we weight each search engine according to its performance, then the quality of these algorithms is further improved. The Borda fuse has an advantage over the Condorcet fuse, in that it is much easier to implement. What is impressive about these methods is that they do not need to know the content relevance of web pages. The ranking output by the search engine and its overall quality seem to be sufficient for merging the results. Another fusion algorithm that has been suggested, relying solely on the rankings utilizes a variation of Kleinberg's HITS algorithm introduced in Section 5.2, called *weighted* HITS [412]. The idea is to view the search engines as the hubs for the query and the web pages as authorities for the query. In addition, each link from a hub to an authority is weighted by the Borda count of the page. The fused ranking is taken to be the ranking of the authorities, once the weighted HITS algorithm has converged. Initial experiments show that this relatively simple algorithm is competitive with state-of-the-art mestasearch engines.

6.3.2 Operational Metasearch Engines

There are many operational metasearch engines,[142] some of which we now review.

- Dogpile (www.dogpile.com) is commercially popular, and has been available since 1996. It was founded by research attorney Aaron Flin and was acquired by Go2Net in 1999. Subsequently, Go2Net was acquired by InfoSpace in 2000. It partners with web search engines Google, Yahoo, and Ask Jeeves to provide paid placement advertising, and with vertical

[142]Metacrawlers and metasearch engines, by C. Sherman, June 2003. http://searchenginewatch.com/links/article.php/2156241.

search services to provide news, image, audio, and video search facilities.[143] Dogpile's query results can be viewed either by relevance or by search engine.

- MetaCrawler (www.metacrawler.com) has been around since 1995, coming out of an academic project from Washington University, and to our knowledge was the first metasearch engine to be utilized on a commercial basis on the Web. It demonstrated that metasearch is viable, scalable, and adaptive to new web search technologies appearing and old ones disappearing [601]. Before it was licensed to Go2Net in 1996, it was handling almost 100,000 queries per day according to Erik Selberg, its original developer. In July of 2000, both MetaCrawler and DogPile, managed by Go2Net, were each handling over 2 million queries per day.[144]
- SavvySearch (www.savvysearch.com, now redirected to www.search.com), has also been around since 1995 and came out of an academic project at Colorado State University. Its core algorithm is based on a method of assessing which search engines will be effective for a query. This is done using a meta-index, which stores previous interactions it had with each search engine. Two types of events are recorded for each search engine: no results, when for a given query the engine did not return any results, and a page view when a user follows a link to a result suggested by the engine. Search engines are penalized if the average number of results for a query falls below a threshold or when the average response time is above a threshold. This scoring mechanism is very coarse and does not work for queries which are new or have been submitted very few times [311]. It was acquired by CNET in 1999.
- ProFusion is the third metasearch engine to have been around since 1995, this time coming out of an academic project at the University of Kansas. ProFusion assigns weights to search engines according to a confidence factor obtained by evaluating the engines through a training process from a number queries submitted to the search engines. ProFusion classifies queries according to a fixed number of categories, each having a fixed set of terms associated with it. Some of the categories used are science and engineering, computer science, travel, business and finance, recreation and entertainment, art, music, food, and so on. Each search engine that is considered by ProFusion is rated against the categories, and this rating is used when a query is submitted in order to associate the engine with one or more categories. The merging process uses relevance scores returned from the search engines, when these are available, and the confidence factor of the search engine is weighted into the ranking [245]. It was acquired by Intelliseek in 2000, which was acquired by BuzzMetrics in 2006, and is no longer in operation.

[143]Dogpile enhances search results, by C. Shermen, November 2004. http://blog.searchenginewatch.com/blog/041110-124938.

[144]Online CV of Erik Selberg. www.selberg.org/~speed/papers/jobs/vitae.pdf

You can well imagine that during these acquisitions a lot of money changed hands in the metasearch space, which is still a very active one, with revenues mainly coming from paid placement advertising.

- Inquirus, developed at the NEC Research Institute (now rebranded as NEC Laboratories America), is another metasearch engine coming out of a research project. It avoids the difficulty of merging the results from several search engines by downloading all the web pages returned for a query and scoring each of them with respect to the query according to its relevance. Downloading pages in such a way can slow down the search considerably and requires optimization such as presenting the user with results as they are processed, rather than processing the full set of results before returning an answer. Inquirus considers a collection of possible information need categories that the user can select from, in order to focus the search. Examples of categories are current events, research papers, home pages, product reviews, and so on. For each information need, Inquirus has an associated list of resources and a set of query modification rules to transform the query into a more specific one given the information need category [258].
- Kartoo, which closed down in January 2010, was different from other metasearch engines in that it provided a visual user interface. It was thought provoking and worth a try as an alternative way to view query results.
- Vivisimo (www.vivisimo.com) is a latecomer into the metasearch arena but has the distinctive feature of clustering results on the fly.[145] During late 2004, Vivisimo launched Clusty (www.clusty.com) as a separate repackaged web search engine, based on the same clustering technology but with a different, more focused look. As with most of the meatsearch engines, it also came out of an academic project, this time from Carnegie Mellon University. It first appeared on the Web in 2000, and has emerged as a leader in the search results clustering business. Clusty was acquired by Yippy (www.yippy.com) in May 2010.

Figure 6.5 shows the Clusty user interface for the query "chess"; the Vivisimo user interface is very similar. It consists of a two-frame window. On the left-hand side Clusty shows the generated clusters, and on the right-hand side the main results list is displayed much in the same way as web search engines do. The user can click on any cluster name to view its contents. Some of the named, top level, clusters for this query are Play Chess, Downloads, Board Game, History, Chess Club, Chess Strategy, and Internet Chess. The clusters themselves have subclusters, so beneath "Play Chess" we have Free Chess and Kids, and these subclusters are further divided.

Vivisimo creates it clusters dynamically, when the query results are returned from the search engines and being merged. The clustering algorithm uses the URLs, titles, and summaries attached to each search engine result to measure the similarity between web pages; it does not download the full document for

[145]Power searching with Vivisimo, by C. Sherman, July 2003. www.searchenginewatch.com/searchday/article.php/2226841.

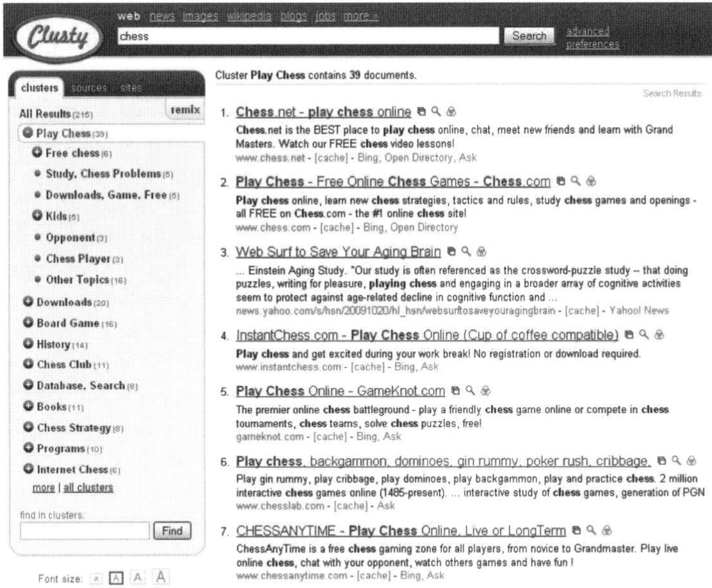

Figure 6.5 Query "chess" submitted to Clusty.

inspection as does Inquirus. The clustering algorithm is hierarchical so clusters are organized in a familiar tree structure, allowing the user to drill down the hierarchy to inspect subclusters.

6.3.3 Clustering Search Results

Cluster analysis is an important technique used in data mining and exploratory data analysis to group similar data items together [326]. Clustering algorithms do not require the assumptions that are often made when using statistical methods. At the heart of any clustering algorithm is the *similarity matrix*, establishing how similar one item is to another. In the case of web pages, similarity is normally measured by the amount of textual overlap. An *agglomerative* hierarchical clustering algorithm starts, in the context of web search, by putting each web page into an individual cluster. During the next step the algorithm merges the most similar pair of clusters into a bigger a cluster, at this stage containing two web pages. This process of merging the most similar clusters continues until we end up with a single cluster at the root of the hierarchy containing all the web pages returned. At any level of the hierarchy, the cluster names, which are either single-word or multiword phrases, are determined by the textual overlap of the web pages in the cluster. The ranking within the clusters is done by fusing the results within each cluster, separately. As Vivisimo has not published its clustering algorithm our description is only a conjecture of how it actually works; in any case as with many algorithms implemented in commercial systems, the devil is in the details. Although Vivisimo is a metasearch engine its clustering algorithm could also be extremely useful as an interface to a standard search engine.

Grouper is an experimental clustering interface to a search engine, which was developed by researchers from the University of Washington within the same research group that developed MetaCrawler [693]. It was developed earlier than Vivisimo and is based on a novel and fast clustering algorithm called *suffix tree clustering* (STC). The idea is to treat a document as an ordered sequence of words rather than a collection of words, allowing the matching of phrases, in addition to single words. The algorithm first forms base clusters of documents sharing a common phrase, and these are scored according to the number of documents in the cluster and the length of common phrases. As a further step, STC combines base clusters that have a high overlap in their documents set into final clusters, noting that a document may appear in more than one base cluster, and thus in more than one final cluster. This is done to reduce the proliferation of clusters, which are very similar. The clustering engine based on STC works well when presented with snippets of text such as summaries, rather than with full documents, which is consistent with Vivisimo's performance.

Carrot (www.carrot-search.com) is an open source search results clustering engine, which has a novel method of discovering clusters by first assigning labels to the clusters. To discover meaningful cluster labels a method known as *singular value decomposition* (*SVD*) [261] is used. (See also Section 9.4.10 on the use of SVD in the context of collaborative filtering.) Given a matrix, M, SVD factorizes the matrix into three parts, U, Σ, and V such that M is equal to the product of U, Σ, and the transpose of V. When M is a term-document matrix, that is, each row in M corresponds to a term, each column to a document (or a web page), and a term-document entry holds the number of terms in the document, then the columns in U are the discovered term factors and the rows in V are the discovered document factors. (Note that, since the search engine employs metasearch, instead of documents we only have the snippets from the search engine results, which provide summaries of the full documents.)

The matrix Σ is a diagonal matrix with the diagonal entries corresponding to the singular values in order of magnitude and the nondiagonal entries being zero. Often a good approximation of the original matrix M is to consider only the first K singular values and to set the rest of the singular values to zero. In this way we reduce the dimensionality of the matrix, while still obtaining a good approximation of the original one.

The term factors output from the SVD of M correspond to abstract topics, each representing a cluster [517]. The labels of clusters are frequent phrases, that is, the sequences of words that appear frequently in the search result snippets. To assign a label to a cluster we find the most similar cluster to the label, where similarity is computed between the two vectors by multiplying the values in the two vectors term by term and summing the result. To form the clusters themselves, we find for each snippet (representing a document), the label whose similarity is larger than some threshold.

In summary, the goals of clustering search engine results are [126]:

1. Fast topic/subtopic retrieval: Cluster labels allow the user to quickly identify the topic/subtopic they are interested in, while in a conventional search

interface the topics are mixed according to the search engine ranking algorithm.

2. Topic exploration: Cluster labels provide users with a high-level view of the topics pertaining to their query that are easily explored when the results are clustered.
3. Alleviating information overlook: Users tend to view only the first results page output by a conventional search engine and thus may overlook potentially relevant results, which may be more visible with an interface that supports clustering.

6.3.4 Classifying Search Results

In classification, as opposed to clustering, the categories are fixed beforehand according to a web searchers ontology. The ontology could be based on categories from the Yahoo directory or the Open directory, which contains a very large number of categories and subcategories. In most cases a collection of 20–40 top-level categories, such as those shown in Table 6.1, will be sufficient to satisfy searchers' information needs. The class URL captures situations when the user types in the URL of a web site they wish to visit; this covers many navigational queries for which search engines are very good at answering. "Misspelling" covers misspelt queries detected by the search engine (see Section 5.1.13s), while "Other" covers any query that does not fall into any of the other categories.

A simple example to motivate classification of search results is a query such as "jaguar". This query could conceivably be in either the "Auto" or the "Nature" categories. Typing this query into a conventional search engine will produce a ranking, which is independent of the topic. So, the search engine's rank ordered list will mix the topics, making it harder for users to find the result they are looking for, despite the fact that they will most likely know which topic they are interested in.

TABLE 6.1 Possible top-level classes.

Adult	Nature
Art	News
Auto	Organizations
Business	People
Computing	Places
Entertainment	Science
Finance and economy	Shopping
Food and drink	Society and community
Games	Travel
Health	URL
Holidays	Misspelling
Home and garden	Other

The advantage that a classification-based approach has over a clustering-based one is that the searchers' ontology used is well-established and corresponds to a natural grouping of web pages that is easy to navigate. The downside of classification is that a high-quality classifier needs to be trained offline. For this a sufficient amount of training data is required and an algorithm that minimizes the false positives, that is, the number of results that are incorrectly classified and put into the wrong class, is required. In general, this is a difficult machine learning problem, but tackling it can pay dividends by enhancing the usability of search engines. Clustering has the advantage that it is done on the fly and the grouping depends only on the result set that is returned. The labeling of clusters is of significant importance to the interface, in terms of the navigability of the result set. In classification, this problem does not arise as the class labels are well-understood by most users.

Radovanović and Ivanović [550] propose using the web pages in the Open Directory to train the classifier. In their implementation of a classification-based metasearch engine they call CatS, 11 out of the 16 top levels of the Open Directory as well as a selection of the second-level categories were chosen as training data for the classifier. Figure 6.6 shows the CatS user interface for the query "chess". It uses the well-known metaphor of a folder, in similarity to interfaces of clustering-based search engines. Chen and Dumais [136] implemented a category-based interface and conducted a user study with 18 subjects, concluding that a classification-based search interface can lead to quicker search times and fewer page views than a conventional list-based search engine interface.

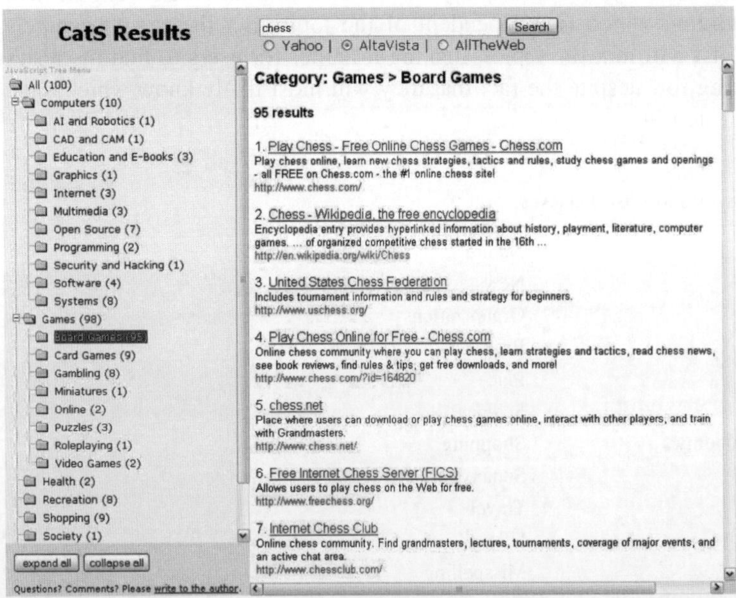

Figure 6.6 Query "chess" submitted to CatS.

A web page classifier can be constructed from summaries of web pages in order to focus on the main topic of the page and reduce some of the noise such as from a navigation bar and ads [606]. On the other hand, full web page classification takes into account the HTML structure [547], where using information derived from HTML tags can boost a classifier's performance. For example, taking into account tags that indicate title, headings, metadata, and main text, it is beneficial to weight these elements to tune the classifier. The link structure of the web page can also be used to improve the classifier by extracting features such as link text and titles from web pages that link to or are linked by the web page being classified. The URL of a web page can also be useful in classifying it. In fact, it was shown that even the URL on its own provides good classification results through a judicious analysis of the components of a URL [62].

Classifying search engine queries [67] is a challenging task that can be useful in order to understand the user's intent in terms of the need behind the query (navigational, informational, or transactional, see Section 2.5), and its topic in terms of 20 plus top-level categories as those shown in Table 6.1.

A classifier for determining query intent was manually devised by Jansen *et al.* [329] and shown to be sufficiently accurate when tested on 400 manually classified queries from a large query log. Applying this classifier to the large query log of over 1.5 million queries they found that more than 80% of web queries are informational and about 10% each are either navigational or transactional.

A support vector machine (SVM) classifier for determining a query's topic was constructed by Zhu *et al.* [705] from about 18,000 manually classified queries from a large query log. As the queries are very short, we take a prior step to building the classifier by enriching each query with keywords from the top-n summary snippets from the search engine results for that query; $n = 10$ was empirically chosen. Applying this classifier to the large query log of about 15 million queries and getting 30 users to assess the classification quality of 470 random queries each, spread across the topics, it was concluded that its F-score (see Section [5.4.2]) is about 75% [53], which is sufficiently accurate.

In order to facilitate a classification-based search engine, the classifier returns a score for a *snippet enriched query* indicating its probability of belonging to the class. (Here we may enrich the query with the single result for which we wish to test class membership, or with several results when we wish to test the prior membership of a query in a class.) A threshold will also be set on the score, so that only if it is above the score for any given class, we will consider the snippet enriched query to be a member of that class.

Thus, we consider a search result to be a member of a given class if the score of the query enriched with the snippet of this result is above the threshold for this class. In this way we can classify all the search results into classes, where a result can be a member of more than one class if its score is above the threshold for these classes; in the case when the score is below the threshold for all classes we can consider its class to be "Other". Results within a class are ranked by their conventional search engine ranking relative to each other.

There remains the additional problem of ranking the classes. There are several features that can be used for this purpose. The first feature is the search engine rank of the top result in a class [704]; this is probably better than using the average rank, since users normally only look at the first few search engine results in any case. A second feature is the average classification score of the results in the class, a third one is the size of the class, and a final feature is the score of the query enriched with the top-n search engine results, which gives us a prior probability on membership in any given class.

We cannot omit to mention Northern Light (www.northernlight.com), which was one of the leading search engines in the late 1990s. Its unique defining feature was its classification system based on custom search folders used to organize and refine the results into a hierarchy. The categorization process of the results works by classifying documents according to predefined attributes such as subject, type, source, region, and language. Northern Light was introduced in 1997 and shutdown its operations in 2002. It was relaunched in 2003 to compete in the enterprise search market.

6.4 PERSONALIZATION

A major deficiency of current search tools is their lack of adaptation to the user's preferences. Current generation search engines operate according to the algorithms we have explained in previous sections. Although the quality of search has improved dramatically in the last few years and as a result user satisfaction has risen, search engines fall short of understanding an individual user's need and, accordingly, ranking the results for that individual. We believe that to further improve the quality of search results, next generation search engines must adapt to the user's personal needs.

Search engines collect a huge amount of data from user queries. This together with the use of cookies to identify returning users, and utilities such as the search toolbar, which are installed on users' browsers, put search engines in an excellent position to provide each user with a personalized search interface tailored to the individual needs of that user. The first ingredient, that is, the collection of personal search data, is already present, and search engines such as Google have been hard at work to gain our trust so that they can collect this personal data without raising too many privacy concerns. We benefit by getting more powerful tools and the search engine benefits from the increased internet traffic through their site.

We have already seen in Section 5.3, when we discussed popularity-based metrics, that query log data can be factored into the ranking of search results. The popularity-based approach can be taken a step further by considering each user and their search habits. As part of their technology, the now defunct search engine Direct Hit (discussed in Section 5.3), looked into personalized search as a specialization of their popularity metric. Some degree of personalization can be achieved by using the popularity metric to narrow down users' searches according to demographic information such as age, gender, and geographic location, or even more specifically, according to the users' individual interests and preferences. In order to get initial personal data into the search index, the search engine can solicit information from anonymous searchers. When surfers use the search engine, cookies can be used to store their past interaction with the search service, and the inference mechanism can then personalize their query results. For example, if a searcher can be identified as a man, a query such as "shoes" may be narrowed down to "men shoes". As another example, men searching on the topic of "flowers" may show more interest in online floral services, presumably to send flowers to their dear ones, while women may be more interested in information on growing flowers, presumably for home gardening.

Two approaches to search engine personalization based on search engine log data may be useful. In a click-based approach [192], the user's query and click pairs are used for personalization. The idea is simple. When a user repeats queries over time, he or she will prefer certain pages, that is, those that were more frequently clicked. The downside of this approach is that if a search engine presents the same old pages to the user each time a query is repeated it does not encourage the user to discover new pages. On the other hand, this type of historical information may be quite useful to the user. This approach can be refined by using content similarity to include similar queries and web pages in the personalized results.

In a topic-based approach [628], a topical ontology is used to identify a user's interests. The ontology should include general topics that are of interest to web surfers such as the top-level topics from the Open Directory. Then a classification technique, such as naive Bayes, needs to be chosen in order to be able to classify the queries that users submit and the pages that they visit; see Section 6.3.4 for a discussion on the classification of search results. The next step is to identify the user's preferences based on their searches, and finally these preferences can be used to personalize their results, for example, by ranking them according to the learned preferences.

Care needs to be taken in the choice of which approach to use, since short-term interests may be inconsistent with long-term ones. For example, when issuing a navigational query a user wishes to find a web site, independently of any topical interests. Moreover, taking a long-term approach may introduce noise due to off-topic queries that were submitted and irrelevant web pages that were clicked on along the way.

A dynamic and adaptive approach to personalization must be capable of monitoring the users' activity over time and to infer their interests and preferences as their behavior changes over time. To implement dynamic user profiles, machine learning techniques, such as Bayesian or neural networks, provide a sound basis for improving the machine's understanding of the human behind the machine. I believe that personalization is the "next big thing" for search engines, in their quest to improve the quality of results, and that dynamic profiling of users is already on the horizon. I expect that we will soon see personalization tools emerging from various research labs. It is hard to predict exactly when personalization will become the norm, as issues such as privacy and scalability, discussed in Section 6.4.3, need to be resolved, but it may be rolled out to users gradually.

6.4.1 Personalization versus Customization

It is important to distinguish between personalization and customization of the user interface. Customization involves the layout of the user interface, for example the color scheme to be used, the content displayed on the personalized web page and various other settings. A study of 60 search services published in July 2003 in the online journal First Monday, has revealed that most of the features offered are related to e-mail, business and financial information, entertainment listings, sports, news headlines, and various information tools such as a local weather report and a personal horoscope [369]. At the time of the study, which was in May 2001, only 13% of the services included some personalization features, and My Yahoo (http://my.yahoo.com) had the most extensive list of features; as far as I know the situation has not changed much as of early 2010. All the personalization features offered are based on a static user profile. Information such as the user's address, age, sex, occupation, and topics of interest are recorded and used for personalization purposes. The user can change these parameters at a later date, but otherwise their value will remain constant. The problems with the static approach are that the profile is, generally, incomplete, becomes stale after a certain period of time, and does not take into account the user's continuous interaction with the system. Moreover, users are reluctant to provide the system with profile information.

6.4.2 Personalized Results Tool

At the Department of Computer Science, Birkbeck, University of London, we have been developing an adaptive personalization tool, which reranks search engine results according to the user's preferences. These include the search terms they have previously entered, the web pages they have been browsing and the categories they have been inspecting. Although this tool is just an experimental prototype it highlights the issues that need to be addressed in the implementation of personalization.

The Personalized Results Tool (PResTo!) is implemented as a plug-in to the browser rather than being server based [364]. This is a unique feature that bypasses some of the privacy and security issues, which are becoming increasingly important to users, since in the case of PResTo!, the ownership of the software and the personal data generated from searches are in the user's hands. A client-side approach is also more efficient for the search engine, since it does not have to manage the user profiles, and thus scalability will not be an issue. A downside of the client-side approach from the users' point of view is that the profile is less portable, but a partial solution to this problem may be to store the profile on a local trusted server, which would enable remote access. A downside from the search engines' point of view is that a client-side approach can, in principle, be used to personalize results from any search engine that the user interacts with, using a single profile applicable to all searching. More importantly, not having access to the user profile is contrary to their aim of using personalization as a means of locking users into their search services and being able to provide them with additional personalized services. A compromise between client- and server-based personalization, which is amenable to both parties, will have to be found.

Personalization proceeds as follows: suppose that the user issues a query to his or her favorite search engine. The personalization plug-in detects this and sends the query results, which have been returned to the user's browser, to the personalization engine (on the user's machine), which then reranks the results according to the user's profile and makes its recommendations to the user in a separate window within the browser, alongside the results returned by the search engine.

As a simple example of PResTo! in action, the keyword "salsa" may be associated with "recipes" or "dancing", or alternatively with "music" or some other aspect of "salsa". A search engine ranking its results for the query "salsa" without personalization, will not have access to the user's profile, and as a consequence will rank web pages about "salsa" only according to its internal criteria. Now suppose that the user had previously searched for "recipes" and "dancing", then PResTo! will filter web pages relating to "recipes" or "dancing" to the top of the search engine's results list. This can be seen in the left-hand side window, generated by the PResTo! prototype when the query "salsa" is typed into Google, shown in Fig. 6.7. The numbers in parentheses appearing after the titles of results, show the position where the pages were originally ranked by Google.

Adaptive personalization tools need to change in time, as the user's preferences change. So, if the user suddenly becomes interested in "music" and less in "dancing" or "recipes" the system should recognize this shift of interest.

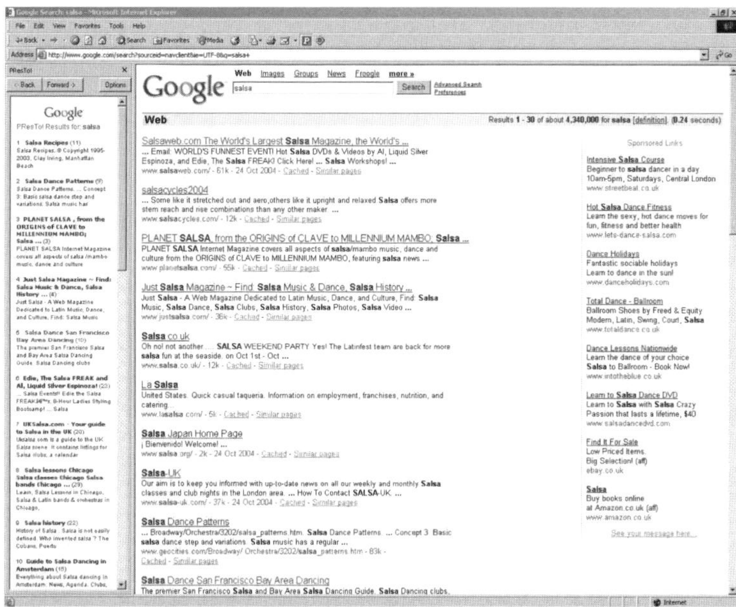

Figure 6.7 The right-hand window, generated by PResTo! when the query "salsa" is typed into Google.

6.4.3 Privacy and Scalability

Whenever personalization is discussed there are two issues, that we have already mentioned in Section 6.4.2, which are raised. The first is privacy, and the second is scalability.

Privacy will always be an issue, and it is therefore essential that all search engines have a clear and upfront privacy policy. Without gaining our trust and showing us the clear benefits of using a tool, which tracks our cyber-movements, any server-based personalization tool is doomed to failure. A related issue to privacy is spam. The problem of being bombarded with information we may consider as junk is a serious one, so much so, that users will not sign up to any tool that, although useful, may increase the spam coming in their direction. As part of the privacy policy, users will want to be assured that their information remains private, and is not circulated around the Net just to bounce back in the form of unwanted spam. Another related issue is targeted advertising. Through paid placement schemes, which are query sensitive, search engines are already delivering targeted ads that are relevant to user queries. Taking this a step further toward personalized advertising may not be popular with users for a variety of reasons that I will not go into here. In any case it makes it necessary for search engines to have a clear privacy policy covering these issues.

Scalability is another problem that search engines getting into the personalization business should consider. If the service is managed through the search engine's servers, then an already stressed system will become even more loaded. Storing hundreds of millions of user profiles and updating them on the fly may not be viable, but a partial solution may be to shift some of the processing and data storage to the user's machine. This may also be a very good mechanism for the search engine to lock surfers into using their search service, by providing users with proprietary software that sits on their desktop.

6.4.4 Relevance Feedback

Personalization is closely related to *relevance feedback*, a technique that was initiated by Rocchio within the SMART retrieval system during the mid-1960s and the early 1970s [573]. The idea behind relevance feedback is simple. When a user such as Archie is presented with a results page for a query, we give him the opportunity to mark each document in the results as being relevant or not. This can be done by having two radio buttons next to each ranked document, one for specifying the document as being relevant and the other for specifying it as nonrelevant. Once Archie has marked the documents of his choice, the important noncommon terms or keywords present in the relevant documents are used to reweight the keywords in the original query, and expand the query with new terms. The effect of reformulating the original query is to "move" the query toward the relevant documents and away from the nonrelevant ones. As a result we expect the reformulated query to retrieve more relevant documents and less nonrelevant ones, thus moving closer toward satisfying the user's information need. The relevance feedback process can be repeated for a specified number of times or until the user does not mark any more documents in the results page, that is, until no more feedback is given.

There are many variations of relevance feedback according to how many documents to include in the process, how many keywords to include in the expanded query, and what weights to attach to these keywords. Ide's "Dec-Hi" method, originally tested in the late 1960s and the early 1970s, within the SMART retrieval system [321], includes all marked relevant documents but only the highest ranked marked nonrelevant one. The "Dec-Hi" method has proven to be useful over the years in several relevance feedback experiments.

An interesting variation, called *pseudorelevance feedback*, assumes that the top-ranked documents are marked as relevant, and thus does not need any user feedback as such. Pseudorelevance feedback is also called *blind feedback*, since once the query is submitted, no additional input from the user is needed. Blind feedback has produced mixed results, due to some of the top-ranked results actually being nonrelevant. It has been shown that when the precision is high for the top-ranked documents, blind feedback provides consistent improvements in the quality of the retrieved documents [474]. It should be noted that blind feedback is not personalized, since the user is not involved in the feedback loop.

Another way to look at relevance feedback is as a classification process, whereby the retrieval system attempts to improve its ability to discriminate between relevant and nonrelevant documents for an individual user and an initial query. When Archie marks a document as being relevant or nonrelevant, he is acting as a teacher by providing the system with training data, used to tune the classifier.

Fast forward over 30 years ahead from the initial SMART retrieval experiments to the beginning of 21st century, where web search engines receive hundreds of millions hits a day and must respond to each search in less than a second. Relevance feedback as formulated by Rocchio and his followers, done on a single query basis with explicit user input, is not feasible. Modern users would not be willing to invest the effort to give feedback, and the additional burden on the search engine's servers would be overwhelming. The way forward is to collect implicit user feedback from the users' clickstream data. When Archie clicks on a link from the results page and browses the web page displayed for a given time period, he is providing feedback to the system that the page is relevant to his information need. This information can then be used to personalize Archie's queries through a special purpose tool such as PResTo!

Spink *et al.* [624] have examined a large query log of the Excite search engine from 1997, one of their aims being to investigate the use of relevance feedback by its users. At the time the Excite search had a "more like this" button next to each query result, so that when the user clicked on it, thus marking the result web page as relevant, the system would initiate a relevance feedback process with this information. The researchers found that under 5% of the logged transactions came from relevance feedback; so, only few users used the relevance feedback facility. They also measured the success rate from relevance feedback to be 63%, where a success was counted if the user quit searching after the relevance feedback. They concluded that relevance feedback on the Web merits further investigation.

6.4.5 Personalized PageRank

In Section 5.2 I have already mentioned that a group of researchers from Stanford have developed new algorithms that can significantly speed up the PageRank computation. These improved algorithms are particularly important when the PageRank values are personalized to the interests of an individual user, or biased toward a particular topic such as sports or business. The optimization step is of prime importance because each personalized PageRank vector will need to be computed separately, and for web search companies such as Google, scalability of their operation is a crucial ongoing concern.

Recall that in the original definition of the PageRank, when the random surfer teleports himself, he can end up at any web page with equal probability. In the personalized version, once the surfer is teleported, we bias the probability of jumping to any other web page according to some preference [287]. In the extreme case, when teleported, the surfer could always (i.e., with probability one) jump to his home page, or some other favorite page. We refer to this special case of personalized PageRank when the surfer is always teleported to a single page, as the *individual* PageRank for that page. A more realistic preference may be to jump to a page that the user has bookmarked or to a page from the user's history list, with the probability being proportional to the number of times the user visited the page in the past. An interesting fact is that personalization of PageRank had already been suggested in 1998 by the founders of Google, but at that time they could not foresee an efficient and scalable computation of personalized PageRank vectors. There are several problems in realizing personalized PageRank vectors. First, data has to be collected for each individual user, secondly, a personalized PageRank vector has to be efficiently computed for each user, and thirdly, the personalized PageRank has to be factored into user queries at the time the queries are submitted.

An important result, called the *linearity theorem* [340], simplifies the computation of personalized PageRank vectors. It states that any personalized PageRank vector can be expressed as a linear combination of individual PageRank vectors. In particular, one application of this is that the global PageRank vector can be expressed as the average of the linear combination of all possible individual PageRank vectors, one for each page in the Web. This can simplify the computation of personalized PageRank vectors by precomputing individual PageRank vectors and then combining them on demand, depending on the preferred web pages in a personalization instance.

As we have seen in Section 5.2.6, we can compute PageRank via a Monte Carlo simulation that samples many random walks from each web page. The PageRank of a given page is then computed as the proportion of random walks that end at that page. Looking at it from a personalized perspective we can compute individual PageRank vectors by looking only at the samples that start at the single web page being personalized, as suggested by Fogaras *et al.* [227]. The individual PageRank vectors can then be combined in an arbitrary way, according to the linearity theorem, to obtain the required personalized PageRank vector.

An interesting variation of PageRank is *topic sensitive*. This version of PageRank is biased according to some representative set of topics, based on categories chosen, say, from the Open Directory [286]. These could be biased toward the topics that the user prefers to explore, so if, for example, a user prefers sports over world news, this preference would translate to a higher probability of jumping to sports pages than to world news pages. A related approach, biasing the PageRank toward specific queries, is called *query-dependent* PageRank [564]. Its motivation was to solve the topic drift problem of PageRank, when a site with a high PageRank may be ranked higher than a site which is more relevant to the query. For example, for the query "computer chess", a site having a link from an advertiser with a high PageRank may be ranked higher than a site having links from other "computer chess" sites, despite the latter being more relevant to "computer chess" as judged by its incoming links. Query-dependent PageRank is computed on a query basis, by adjusting the random surfer model so that only pages that are relevant to the query are followed. The relevance of a page to the query is then factored into the PageRank calculation. In order to make query-dependent PageRank practical, it has to be computed offline for a selection of query terms. The query terms selected could be topic-based as in topic-sensitive PageRank, they could be popularity-based by looking at query logs, or they could include a selected subset of the words in the search index.

Another variation of PageRank, called *BlockRank*, computes local PageRank values on a host basis, and then weights these local PageRank values according to the global importance of the host [359]. BlockRank takes advantage of the fact that a majority of links (over 80% according to the researchers) are within domains rather than between them, and domains such as stanford.edu, typically contain a number of hosts.

BlockRank could be used to create personalized PageRank vectors at the web host level rather than the web page level, so for example, a user may prefer to jump to a sports site rather than to a general news site. The other attraction of BlockRank is that it can speed up the computation of PageRank by up to 300%.[146]

Three members of the PageRank group at Stanford were quick to realize the importance to Google of their research on speeding up the PageRank computation and its personalization, which led them to set up a stealth start-up, called Kaltix, in June 2003. The next thing that happened was that Google acquired Kaltix in September 2003.[147] This move by Google is a strong indication that personalization is high up on their agenda, and that they view PageRank as a suitable vehicle for personalizing query results. As the competition between the

[146]Researchers develop techniques for computing Google-style Web rankings up to five times faster, by D. Hart, National Science Foundation. www.nsf.gov/od/lpa/news/03/pr0356.htm.

[147]Google Acquires Kaltix Corp. www.google.com/press/pressrel/kaltix.html.

major search engines stiffens, Google has taken the research into its labs for dissection and further development.[148]

6.4.6 Outride's Personalized Search

In fact, a couple of years earlier, in September 2001, Google acquired the assets of another company specializing in personalization of search, called Outride, which was a spin-off from Xerox Palo Alto Research Center (PARC).[149] The acquisition of Outride was strategic, with Google making a claim on the intellectual property that it considered valuable within the personalization of search area.[150] Luckily, in September 2002, the founders of Outride published a research paper in the Communications of the ACM, one of the leading computing magazines, revealing some of the ideas behind the technology they were developing [542]. Together with the intellectual property from Kaltix, these acquisitions put Google in a strong position to lead the way to personalization.

Link analysis based on the evaluation of the authority of web sites is biased against relevance, as determined by individual users. For example, when you submit the query "java" to Google, you get many pages on the programming language Java, rather than the place in Indonesia or the well-known coffee from Java. Popularity or usage-based ranking adds to the link-based approach, by capturing the flavor of the day and how relevance is changing over time for the user base of the search engine. In both these approaches, relevance is measured for the population of users and not for the individual user. Outride set out to build a model of the user, based on the context of the activity of the user, and individual user characteristics such as prior knowledge and history of search.

The Outride system set out to integrate these features into the user interface as follows. Once Archie submits his query, its context is determined and the query is augmented with related terms. After it is processed, it is individualized, based on demographic information and the past user history. A feature called "Have Seen, Have Not Seen" allows the user to distinguish between old and new information. The Outride user interface is integrated into the browser as a side bar that can be opened and closed much like the favorites and history lists. According to the authors of the research paper, searches were faster and easier to complete using Outride. It remains to see what Google will do with this thought-provoking technology. Jeff Heer, who is acquainted with Outride's former employees, said in his weblog that "Their technology was quite impressive, building off a number of PARC innovations, but they were in the right place at the wrong time".[151]

It is worth mentioning that Google has released a tool enabling users to search the Web from any application within the Windows operating system.[152]

[148] Searching for the personal touch, by S. Olsen, August 2003. http://news.cnet.com/2100-1024_3-5061873.html

[149] Google acquires technology assets of Outride Inc. www.google.com/press/pressrel/outride.html.

[150] Google may get personal, by D. Sullivan, October 2001. www.searchenginewatch.com/sereport/article.php/2164251.

[151] Search (and destroy), by Jeff Heer, July 2003. http://jheer.org/blog/archives/000006.html

[152] Google Desktop, Sidebar with gadgets. http://desktop.google.com.

In releasing this desktop search tool, Google has taken a step toward integrating search within a broader context than the user's browser, and paving the way toward a personalized search tool. Another significant feature of the tool is that its query results can be displayed in a separate window rather than in the user's browser; it also allows the user to customize the tool to search within specific web sites.[153]

In December 2009, Google launched a personalized search service that delivers customized search results to each user based on his or her history of web searches and resulting page views.[154] If the user is signed into Google and has enabled a feature called *web history*, then this information is used for personalization. Otherwise, when the user is not signed in or web history is disabled, personalization is based on the user's past history stored in a cookie. Up to 180 days of search activity is stored in the cookie including the searches and clicked results. Personalization is based on reranking the original Google results according to previous searches and clicks, possibly constructing a personalized PageRank for each user as described in Section 6.4.5 and building on OutRide's personalization algorithms.

6.5 QUESTION ANSWERING (Q&A) ON THE WEB

Ask Jeeves' original mission, as set out in 1996, when it was founded, was to provide natural language question answering on the Web.[155] Its founders, venture capitalist Garrett Gruener and technologist David Warthen, came up with the idea of using P.G. Wodehouse's butler character "Jeeves" as their public face, conveying quality of service together with friendliness and integrity. This branding has been very successful, as the Ask Jeeves logo is clearly memorable in searchers' minds. There was a price to pay for the use of the Jeeves character, since they were eventually sued early in 2000 by the owners of the copyright to Wodehouse's novels, and we assume that there was an amicable out of court settlement. In 2006, Jeeves retired from his services at the search engine Ask Jeeves, which was rebranded simply as Ask (www.ask.com). In 2009, Jeeves has come out of retirement to revitalize the brand on the UK site and on askjeeves.com.[156]

[153]Google tests desktop search, by S. Olsen, November 2003, Cnet News.com. http://news.com.com/2100-1032_3-5103902.html?tag=nefd_top.

[154]Personalized Search for everyone, by B. Horling and M. Kulick, December 2009. http://googleblog.blogspot.com/2009/12/personalized-search-for-everyone.html.

[155]Happy birthday, Ask Jeeves!, by C. Sherman, April 2003. http://searchenginewatch.com/searchday/article.php/2177081.

[156]I say ... Jeeves is back! Due to popular demand, Ask Jeeves returns to the UK, with more answers than ever before, by N. Kelly, April 2009. http://sp.uk.ask.com/en/docs/about/press2009/release.shtml?id=pr2009_2004.

6.5.1 Natural Language Annotations

Natural language processing solutions are still very much in the research labs, especially when dealing with an open domain such as the Web. In the Q&A space Ask Jeeves has progressively moved away from an editorially driven knowledge base used to derive answers to user queries, to being able to answer queries directly by tapping into existing structured information resources (i.e., databases compiled by human editors) or by mining information from web pages, which are unstructured information sources.

The editorially driven approach, which is still of interest, is to build and maintain a humanly edited knowledge base containing questions that users are likely to ask, based on query logs of web searchers, in the hope of matching a searcher's question with an existing template that will link to an answer from the knowledge base. As already mentioned, such a knowledge base is maintained by humans rather than being automated, so its coverage in comparison to a crawler-based search engine such as Google, Yahoo, or Bing is very low. We are talking about a knowledge base of a few million entries compared to a search engine index containing billions of web pages. Interestingly enough, at the end of 1999, Ask Jeeves were sued by Boris Katz and Patrick Winston from the MIT Artificial Intelligence Laboratory, for infringement of two natural language patents issued in 1994 and 1995 on generating and utilizing natural language annotations to facilitate text retrieval.[157] The natural language annotations correspond to the former Ask Jeeves question templates, that pointed to answers from the knowledge base. The case was successfully settled before the trial, presumably through some licensing agreement.

The Artificial Intelligence Lab maintains its own natural language question answering system called START, which can be found at http://start.csail.mit.edu. START was the first Q&A system to become available on the Web, as it has been operating since the end of 1993. It is based on the idea of natural language annotations, which are sentences and phrases in computer analyzable form that point to relevant documents [362]. Thus, a question such as "who is the president of the usa?" matches an annotation in the knowledge base yielding the correct answer at this moment in time, and pointing to the source of the answer. START taps into a wealth of online resources on the Web by employing annotations that point to specific databases that are most likely to contain the answer. So, for example, if the question is about movies, START retrieves possible answers from the Internet Movie Database (www.imdb.com). To annotate a substantial portion of the information on the Web, much more than a handful of annotators will be required. One suggestion is to enlist millions of web users to help out in a collaborative effort through a simple tool that would allow users to contribute to the knowledge base by annotating web pages they stumble upon.

[157]Winston, Katz sue Ask Jeeves, January 2000. http://www-tech.mit.edu/V119/N66/66winston.66n.html.

Ask Jeeves' Q&A technology is based on extracting answers to questions through a combination of natural language processing and Teoma's algorithmic technology. (As mentioned in Section 4.3.4 Teoma has been subsequently rebranded into the Ask search engine.) On the one hand, "smart answers" extracts information from structured data sources, while the newer "web answers" attempts to find answers directly from web pages. This approach signifies a move by Ask Jeeves toward open Q&A, described briefly in the Section 6.5.3.[158]

Ask Jeeves had an immensely successful IPO in 1999 and by early 2000, it was in the top 25 most popular destinations of web surfers. It nearly collapsed after the Internet bubble burst, but has picked up the pieces, mainly through paid placement advertising and its acquisition, in March 2004, of Interactive Search Holding, whose web properties included Excite.[159] As noted in Section 2.1, as of 2009, it handled about 4% of web searches, which is a respectable share for a niche player, in a very competitive yet lucrative market.

Originally Ask Jeeves was a metasearch engine as it did not own proprietary search engine technology. Eventually it transformed itself by acquiring the search engine Teoma in September 2001 for under $4 million, which seems like a bargain compared to the $500 million price tag for acquiring Direct Hit in January 2000. In July 2005 it was acquired by the e-commerce conglomerate IAC/InterActiveCorp for a price tag of $1.85 billion.

If Ask Jeeves can compute the answer to a question with confidence, it will present the answer. So when you type the query "who is the prime minister of the uk?" into the search box at www.ask.com the answer will appear at the top of the search results page, stating that, as of early 2010, "The Chief of State of the United Kingdom is Queen Elizabeth II, and the Head of State is Prime Minister James Gordon Brown" (Fig. 6.8).

In any case, the question to Ask Jeeves is also fired as a query to its underlying search engine, Teoma, and the search results are integrated into the results page presented to the user. Below the answer to the question, you will find a list of sponsored links, if there are any for the particular query, and below these the organic results from Teoma will be displayed.

Other search engines are now also providing a limited question answering facility. Typical queries to Google such as "weather in london" or "time in london" produce the desired answer above the organic results.

For a standard query Ask Jeeves behaves much the same as any other search engine, as can be seen when you type the query "computer chess" into its search box. First some sponsored links are displayed, following these the first batch of organic web results is displayed, and at the bottom of the screen additional sponsored links are shown.

[158]Ask Jeeves serves up new features, by C. Sherman, May 2005. http://searchenginewatch.com/searchday/article.php/3507871

[159]Ask Jeeves, and ye shall receive, by L. Carrel, March 2004. www.smartmoney.com/onedaywonder/index.cfm?story=20040304.

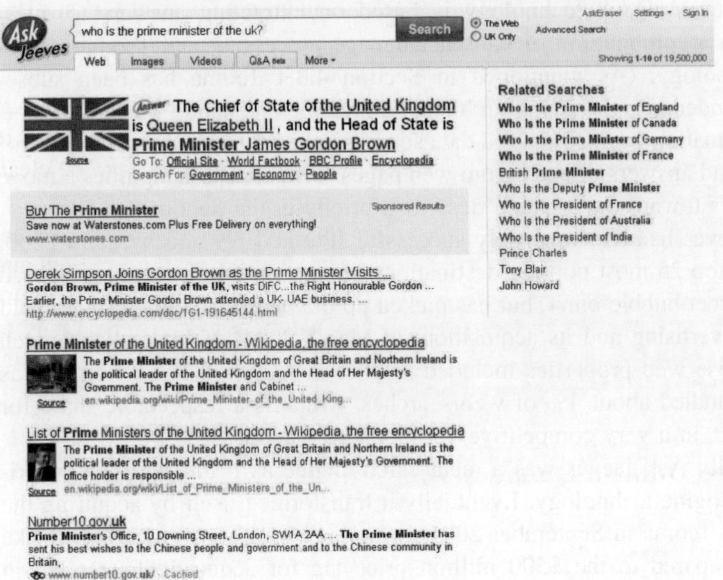

Figure 6.8 Question "who is the prime minister of the uk?" submitted to Ask Jeeves. (Source: Reproduced with permission of © IAC Search & Media, Inc. 2009, all rights reserved (uk.ask.com). ASK.COM, ASK JEEVES, the ASK logo, the ASK JEEVES logo, and other trademarks appearing on the ASK and ASK JEEVES web sites are property of IAC Search & Media and/or its licensors.)

Ask Jeeves' user interface has a look and feel that is similar to that of other search engines. In addition, related searches are displayed on the right-hand side of the results page, where users can refine their search or explore related topics. These refinements use clustering technology based on Teoma's variant of the HITS algorithm, and may well incorporate information from query logs as utilized by the popularity search engine Direct Hit.

6.5.2 Factual Queries

Wolfram Alpha (www.wolframalpha.com), released to the public in mid-2009, aims to make knowledge computable and accessible [640]. The data that is used by the knowledge engine is domain specific and structured, rather than open web crawled data, and is curated, that is, collected under the supervision of one or more experts. The knowledge engine accepts natural language as input but will also accept a mathematical formula that it will then attempt to solve. It is implemented in Mathematica, which is the flagship product of Wolfram Research, and has capabilities in many domains, with the data coming from different sources.

Its goal is to provide definitive answers to factual queries. So, for the query "who is the prime minister of the uk?" it will present a template with the answer and various related facts, as can be seen in Fig. 6.9, as of early 2010. (Examples of Wolfram Alpha in action in many domains, including many scientific and arts subject domains, can be found at www.wolframalpha.com/examples.) Bing has teamed up with Wolfram Alpha to enrich its search results in select areas across nutrition, health, and advanced mathematics.[160]

One criticism of Wolfram Alpha is that it is a black box in comparison to the major search engines, where the primary source of information is made clear, and so its results are hard to verify.

Google squared (www.google.com/squared) is a tool that collects facts from the open web and presents them in a tabular format, with a row for each fact and a column for each attribute derived by the tool. It is not in direct competition with Wolfram Alpha as its data sources are not curated and its function is to compile information into a structured table rather than to provide a computational knowledge engine that can derive and display information in different forms.

6.5.3 Open Domain Question Answering

Question answering is not new, for example in Salton and McGill's now classical 1983 text on information retrieval, they cover Q&A concentrating on the natural language aspects. The Web as a corpus for Q&A, is an open domain without any subject boundaries. The main problem here is that although the Web is a tremendous resource of information, the quality of documents is extremely variable, it is often out of date, and not always factual. Despite this shortcoming the Web has a huge asset, which is data redundancy. If you ask a question such as "what is the capital of the uk?", assuming we can extract relevant phrases from web pages, then by a simple voting system we expect the correct answer to emerge as the majority answer.

Some prototype Q&A systems, which are now surfacing out of research labs, are attempting to tackle the open domain question answering on the Web using this voting technique. This approach, which builds on the fact that in a huge corpus such as the open web, the correct answer is likely to be stated many times, in multiple ways, and in multiple documents, and is known as the *redundancy-based method* [429].

One system based on this method is Microsoft's AskMSR [104], which may be deployed in a future Microsoft product. AskMSR avoids sophisticated natural language processing in favor of simple phrase analysis with question template matching, and the use of a search engine to retrieve snippets that may contain the answer. AskMSR first parses the input question to generate a series of queries to a backend search engine (they have used Google for this purpose), based on specific question templates and keyword matches. The problem of transforming the input question into a set of search engine queries that are likely to return results containing the answer, is a difficult problem, and machine learning techniques are currently being enlisted to solve this task [17]. The queries output are then submitted to the search engine, and the answers returned are ranked according

[160]Bing teams up with Wolfram Alpha, November 2009. http://news.bbc.co.uk/1/hi/technology/8356217.stm

WolframAlpha computational knowledge engine

who is the prime minister of the uk?

Input interpretation:

United Kingdom	prime minister

Result:

Gordon Brown

Basic information:

official position	Prime minister
start date	27 June 2007 (2 years 4 months 14 days ago)

Sequence: More

June 2007 to present	Gordon Brown
May 1997 to June 2007 (10 years 1 month)	Tony Blair
November 1990 to May 1997 (6 years 5 months)	John Major (Conservative)
May 1979 to November 1990 (11 years 6 months)	Margaret Thatcher (Conservative)

Related leaders:

queen	Elizabeth II

Personal information:

full name	James Gordon Brown
date of birth	20 February 1951 (age: 58 years)
place of birth	Glasgow, Glasgow City, United Kingdom

Timeline:

Gordon Brown

1940 1960 1980 2000

Computed by: Wolfram *Mathematica* Source information » Download as: PDF | Live *Mathematica*

Figure 6.9 Query "who is the prime minister of the uk?" submitted to Wolfram Alpha. (Source: Reproduced with permission from © Wolfram Alpha LLC—A Wolfram Research Company (www.wolframalpha.com).)

to how likely they are to contain the answer, which is a combination of how well they match an answer template, and the number of snippets from the web pages in which the answer occurs. This approach is proving to be successful, although at the moment it mainly deals with factual questions such as "who is the president of the usa?" rather than more complex question such as "is the usa out of recession?", which would involve advanced reasoning.

Named entity recognition, which is a subtask of information extraction (see Section 7.4.12), is useful in Q&A systems to pinpoint answers in text snippets [656]. The goal of named entity extraction is to locate and classify small units of text into predefined categories such as names of people, organizations, and locations. In the context of Q&A, named entities are natural candidate answers to questions. As an example, for the question, "who is the prime minister of the uk?", the named entity recognizer will determine that the answer should be a person. Using this information it is possible to filter out all snippets that do not have a person entity in them. The redundancy-based method can then be used to find the majority answer as the most likely one.

Mulder is another experimental Q&A interface to a search engine, which was developed by researchers from the University of Washington within the same research group that developed MetaCrawler and Grouper [398]. Mulder uses more sophisticated natural language parsing than AskMSR by modifying existing natural language processing tools, and using many other heuristics including a voting procedure to rank candidate answers. Mulder also uses Google as its backend search engine, to which it submits queries that it believes will contain an answer to the question at hand. Mulder was evaluated against Ask Jeeves for Q&A tasks and against Google as a baseline comparison. The results showed that, overall, Mulder outperformed Ask Jeeves, which was due to Ask Jeeves' method, at the time, being based on human edited annotations of a relatively small number of web pages, rather than being fully automated and using a web search engine as its corpus, in the way that Mulder and AskMSR do. It is not surprising that Mulder also outperforms Google on Q&A tasks, which again is as we would expect, since Google was not designed as a Q&A system.

6.5.4 Semantic Headers

In 2003 a colleague of mine, Boris Galitsky, wrote a book on natural language question answering, which emphasizes a semantic approach based on logic programming, rather than a template-based approach as Ask Jeeves had employed in the past [240]. The *semantic header* approach, as Boris calls it, represents potential answers to questions through relationships between objects that are relevant to the domain under consideration. So, for example in an e-commerce domain the objects may be of type product, customer, vendor, order, shopping basket, and so on, and the relationships between the objects may be of type purchase (between customer and product), and payment (between customer and vendor). The semantic header approach is designed to work in closed domains such as e-commerce, tax, law, or medicine, rather than in an open domain such as the Web as a whole. This makes the task of building the semantic headers feasible, so that the number of potential answers the system has to cater for is of the order of tens of thousands (this number was specifically discovered to be useful in financial domains). The technique of building the knowledge base of semantic headers is done in cooperation with domain experts, and is improved on a regular basis from feedback obtained by inspecting log data of customers using the service. In this sense the system is semiautomatic, much in the same way the Ask Jeeves service used to be, but it requires substantial human effort to maintain the knowledge base and keep it up to date. The payback from the semantic header approach is that it is potentially more accurate and less prone to error, than the syntactic natural language approach, which has no "understanding" of the domain. Boris' approach is very much in the spirit of rule-based expert systems, which are still a very important topic in artificial intelligence. The tax advisor answering system he developed was deployed in a commercial setting in 2000 on the CBS Market Watch site, which publishes business news and information. An analysis of the system showed that over 95% of the customers and quality assurance staff agreed that the advisor was a preferred method for nonprofessional users accessing the information.

6.6 IMAGE SEARCH

Web image search is important, since there is a substantial amount of visual information in web pages that users may wish to find. In some cases an image may act as a discriminator for a text-based search, for example if you are looking for a company and all you can remember is that their logo has an image of a chess piece. In other cases the result of the search could be an image, for example, if you wish to view an image of Senate House in London. Some of the images in this book were obtained from the public web through a judicious search process, but none of the searches involved *content-based retrieval*, using features contained in the images.

Several applications of image search are [368] filtering offensive and illegal material (such material is not always easy to detect by the text in web pages), travel and tourism (images and maps of places we are planning to visit), education and training (images to illustrate ideas), entertainment (for fun), e-commerce (we wish to see what we plan to buy), design (such as building plans), history and art (we wish to view artifacts or paintings), fashion (we wish to see what is trendy), and domain-specific image retrieval (such as trademarks, fingerprints, and stamps).

Compared to text-based web search, content-based image search is very much still in the research labs. In addition to image search, there are the issues pertaining to searching general multimedia content, whatever it may be, and the specific problems that need to be addressed for each specific type of media.

Searching and retrieving 3D models [237] is a challenging problem. It involves finding shape representations of objects that allow similarity between objects to be detected. Querying 3D models can involve text, but also a sketch of the model to be matched, for example a skeleton of a car can be drawn and the system will return car-like objects from the repository. A demonstration of a 3D search engine, under development by the Princeton Shape Retrieval and Analysis Group, can be found at http://shape.cs.princeton.edu/search.html.

Searching audio content [228] is an area that is developing in parallel to speech recognition. However, audio information retrieval is much wider in its scope than speech recognition. An important application of audio retrieval is being able to recognize, compare, and classify music objects on the Web. One concrete application of audio search, commercialized by Shazam Entertainment (www.shazam.com), is the recognition of songs via mobile phones [668]. The user dials in to the service, and then points the phone at the source of the music for a period of about 10–15 secs. Within several additional seconds the service will identify the track from a database containing over 8 million fingerprints of tracks (as of 2009), using music recognition software developed by Avery Wang, while he was a PhD student in Electrical Engineering at Stanford University.

Searching video content [139] is a natural extension of web image and audio retrieval, as more video is becoming available on the Web. Video is richer in content that other multimedia as it includes images and audio. One challenge specific to video retrieval is being able to detect an image over a sequence of frames, which satisfies a *motion query* such as "a person moving in a specific direction".

The current approach to audio and video search taken by the major search engines is mainly text based. Google (http://video.google.com) indexes the closed-captions hidden in the video signal of TV broadcasts to provide a search tool for TV programs. In addition, Google searches for YouTube videos and other videos found by its crawlers. Yahoo (http://video.search.yahoo.com) and Microsoft Bing (http://video.bing.com) provide comparable search facilities, which include video content available on the Web, while Singingfish (http://video.aol.com), which has been acquired by AOL, is a dedicated multimedia search engine using a text-based approach for both video and audio.

We now concentrate on image search. Although text-based web search engines are designed to find relevant web pages, they do not have in-built capabilities to find images within these pages. To remedy this situation the major web search engines now provide image search as a separate service.

In the context of the Web, image search, is the problem of finding relevant images contained in web pages. To answer a query, an image search engine can use the textual cues within the page containing the image, and the content embedded in the image itself. The grand challenge of image search is to be able to reliably retrieve images by content (580, 172). Below we will discuss how this can be done, but first we will see how text-based image search is carried out by the major search engines.

6.6.1 Text-Based Image Search

Google (http://images.google.com), Yahoo (http://images.yahoo.com), and Microsoft Bing (http://images.bing.com) provide image search as part of their service, while Picsearch (www.picsearch.com) is an independent image search engine, managed from Stockholm, which is devoted to video, image, and audio retrieval. As of early 2010, Picsearch was providing access to more than 3 billion pictures, and the main web search engines with their powerful crawling mechanisms will be indexing a much larger number.

In all these image search engines the query is specified textually; no visual input, such as the user providing an example image, is possible. At this time (early 2010), apart from using available textual information as described below, image search engines are already using some low-level features from the image's content in the search process; see Sections 6.6.2 and 6.6.3.

How can images be ranked using textual information? When the search engine's crawler downloads HTML web pages, it also downloads the images it contains, which are specified within the IMG tag. Together with the image, the crawler extracts the image filename, the text describing the image from the ALT field, the title of the image, the URL of the web page containing the image, and any text surrounding the IMG tag [643]. The keywords obtained from these snippets of text are then stored in the image index, and used to search for the image utilizing the standard TF–IDF text retrieval method.

Link-based metrics (see Section 5.2), which are independent of the image content, can be used to enhance the image retrieval algorithm, in a way similar to the PageRank and HITS (hub and authorities) algorithms used for web page search. In this context, a page is said to link to the image if either (i) the image is contained in the page, (ii) the image is the source of a link to the page, or (iii) the page has a link pointing to the image.

Using a variation of HITS, it is possible to detect *image containers*, defined as pages containing high-quality images, and *image hubs*, defined as pages pointing to good image containers.

The results from such link analysis can be included in the image retrieval algorithm, by factoring in the score of the page the image is contained in, and also the scores of pages linking to the page it is contained in. In particular, if an image is part of an image container or pointed to by an image hub, its score will be higher. This algorithm has been implemented in an experimental image search engine called PicASHOW [416].

We urge the reader to try out some image search queries. It is interesting to note that, for many queries, there is very little overlap between the first few results returned by the three search engines, which probably indicates that there are substantial differences in the images they each store, and that the algorithms they use to rank the images may be quite different.

6.6.2 Content-Based Image Search

Apart from the standard textual query, a user may specify an image as input to the search engine. Often it is hard to find an image, which is similar to the one we are searching, so the initial query may be textual. An interesting visual alternative, apart from presenting an image, that is provided by some image search engines is to enable users to sketch the main feature of the image they are looking for, or to provide a representative icon [424]. After the initial results are returned the user may wish to refine their query through relevance feedback, as described below.

When an image is added to the search engine's index, the image is segmented into smaller regions that are homogeneous according to some criterion. Low-level features, notably, color, shape, and texture, are extracted from the image and stored in the index. As the number of dimensions of the feature vectors may be high, dimension reduction techniques, such as clustering, will often be employed before the features are stored. In practice the information stored about the image is only a partial description of the objects represented in it. Moreover, low-level features cannot describe high-level ones such as the object being a car, a person, or a holiday beach. Worse still is the fact that humans tend to interpret images in terms of high-level semantic features. This, most challenging, problem is called the *semantic gap* [249]. One way to address the semantic gap is to add textual annotations to images, but in the context of web search this is not a scalable solution. We have already discussed how current search engines use textual cues in web image search; these textual cues provide a form of high-level annotation. Organizing images by categories in a directory structure, in a similar manner to a web directory, is another method to help users identify images through semantic concepts; but as with web page directories, this is also not a scalable proposition. However, a well-built image directory could provide many example images a user could use to initiate a content-based image search.

To illustrate the retrieval process, assume that the query is specified as an image. This input image is segmented and its features are extracted. Then an index lookup is carried out to find the images most similar to the input, in particular, its k nearest neighbors are found and ranked by similarity. These are presented to the user, who can then refine the query through relevance feedback.

In an attempt to find a suitable similarity measure, researchers have borrowed ideas from the psychological theory of similarity assessment [586]. One common assumption is that similarity is a positive and a monotonically nondecreasing function satisfying certain distance axioms, but a different, probabilistic approach to similarity, is also possible.

The idea behind relevance feedback, introduced in Section 6.4, is that the user, say Archie, can refine his initial query as follows, after the image retrieval system returns to him a ranked list of result images, as answers to his initial query. Archie then inspects the returned images and marks some of them as "relevant" (positive examples of what he wants to see, i.e., more like this) and others as "not relevant" (negative examples of what he does not want to see, i.e., less like this). The system responds to this feedback by adjusting the query in the direction of his feedback. The adjustment involves modifying the weights of features in the original query and expanding the query with new features from the marked images. The weights of features from positive examples are increased and the weights of features from negative examples are decreased. The adjusted query is then reissued to the image search engine, and the expected outcome is that the new set of result images have "moved" in the direction of what Archie wants to see, that is, more of the images are relevant and less are irrelevant. The process of relevance feedback can be iterated several times until Archie is satisfied with the results or until the set of results has stabilized. Relevance feedback is especially important in the context of image search [697], as often the best way to formulate a query is by giving the system example images of what you want to see, in addition or without a textual query.

Relevance feedback can also be collaborative, in the sense that it can be stored in a log file and then aggregated across many users. The idea here is to adjust the feature weights of all users with similar queries, thus sharing feedback between different users. Experiments with iFind [141], a content-based image search engine developed at Microsoft Research China, have shown that this form of collective relevance feedback is effective in improving the precision of the image search engine.

A variation, called *pseudorelevance feedback*, can be used to improve query results based only on textual cues and without any user interaction. This is how it works. Archie submits the query to the image search engine as before, and an initial set of result images is returned. Now, instead of returning these to Archie, the system reranks the initial results using a text-based search engine, as follows.

First we consider the web pages that contain the initial results and build a vector for each page that stores the TF–IDF values of each word in the page, after omitting stop words and possibly stemming the remaining words; we call these vectors, the *image vectors* for the query. The original query is then submitted to a text-based search engine, which returns an alternative set of result pages. At this stage, we construct a single *text vector*, storing the TF–IDF values of all the words in the results, by considering all the text-based results together as if they were present in a single page. (We note that in this scheme it is possible to give higher weight to words appearing in higher ranked pages.)

The reranking of the initial results is now carried out by computing the similarity between each image vector and the text vector, and ranking them from highest to lowest similarity. One measure of similarity that can be computed between the two vectors is the dot product of the vectors. This is called *vector similarity* and is computed by multiplying the TF–IDF values in the two vectors word by word and summing up the results; if desired these could be normalized to output a similarity measure between 0 and 1.

Experiments using pseudorelevance feedback to rerank results [431] from Google's image search have shown substantial increases in precision of the image search system.

6.6.3 VisualRank

Jing and Baluja from Google [344] have proposed to build a content-based similarity graph of images and to compute a VisualRank for each image inspired by the PageRank computation for web pages.

The way this is done is as follows. First, local features for each image as computed using Lowe's scale-invariant feature transform (SIFT) algorithm [440]. The idea is to compute local descriptors for the image that are relatively stable under different transformations to the image such as scaling, rotation, or noise. The output of SIFT is a set of keypoint descriptors for the image describing all the features of a keypoint, where a keypoint is a local point in the image that is identified as distinct. The similarity between two images is defined as the number of keypoints they have in common, divided by the average number of keypoints in the two images.

VisualRank is then computed on the image similarity graph with some important differences to the PageRank computation. The edges in the graph, called *visual links*, are weighted by the similarity between the images on the two sides of the edge, that is, the graph is weighted. Moreover, unlike web links, visual links are symmetric, that is, the image similarity graph is undirected. As in PageRank we have a teleportation factor, and the VisualRank vector can also be personalized (see Section 6.4.5), for example, by biasing it to the top-m image results from an image search engine. The VisualRank of the graph can then be computed by the power method (see Section 5.2.4) or some optimization thereof.

Computing VisualRank for all the Web is computationally prohibitive as it would involve generating a similarity graph for billions of images. A practical approach, which was used to compare VisualRank to the ranking generated by Google's image search, is to make the VisualRank query dependent. This is done by fixing the query and extracting the top-n images, say 1000, from an image search engine for this query, and reranking the results according to VisualRank. Jing and Baluja did exactly this for 2000 popular product queries such as "ipod", "Xbox", and "Picasso". Figure 6.10 from [344] shows the similarity graph generated from the top 1000 search results for "Mona-Lisa"; the largest two images in the center have the highest VisualRank.

A user study of the performance of VisualRank as compared to Google Images, showed that VisualRank can significantly reduce the number of irrelevant images in search results and increase the number of clicks from the top-20 ranked images.

The method of VisualRank could also be extended to the domains of audio and video search.

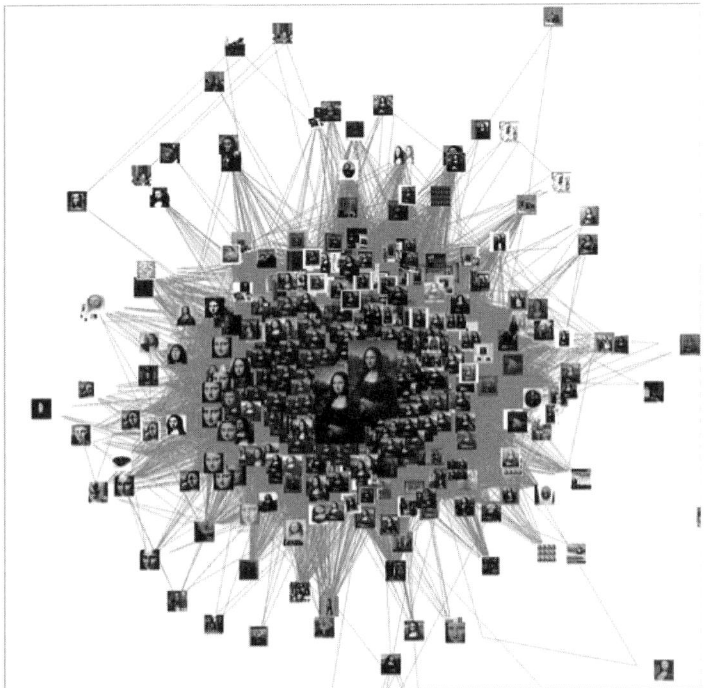

Figure 6.10 Similarity graph generated from the top 1000 search results of "Mona-Lisa".

6.6.4 CAPTCHA and reCAPTCHA

CAPTCHA stands for completely automated public Turing test to tell computers and humans apart [663]. It usually involves a computer asking a user to perform a task that will differentiate a human from an automated program. A common type of CAPTCHA is a distorted text image that needs to be typed in, but it could also be image-based requiring the user to either to identify an object in an image, to answer questions about the image, or to find the odd one out of several images [172]. Ahn *et al.* [664] estimate that more than 100 million CAPTCHAs are answered by humans every day and suggest making use of this effort to help machines read scanned text and thus complement optical character recognition (OCR), which cannot recognize about 20% of words in older faded prints.

The suggested method, called reCAPTCHA, presents a scanned text from a newspaper or book, which OCR software cannot read, and asks the user to decipher it. When multiple users decipher the text in the same way, the text is accepted, and when multiple users reject the text, it is deemed unreadable. As of late 2008, the system could transcribe 4 million words per day. This is a very good example of how "human computation" can be harnessed to help solve problems that are difficult for computers to solve.

The company reCAPTHA (http://recaptcha.net), which grew out a project of the School of Computer Science at Carnegie Mellon University, was acquired by Google in September 2009.[161]

6.6.5 Image Search for Finding Location-Based Information

A novel application of image search in mobile computing, developed in the MIT Computer Science and Artificial Intelligence Laboratory, is the use of photographic images to specify a location [690]. The scenario is that of a user taking a picture of a landmark with his or her mobile phone, and sending it as a query over the mobile web to an image search engine, which will find relevant location-based information and return it to the user.

A more detailed description of the process, after an image has been sent, is as follows: (i) the most similar images to the snapshot are retrieved from a content-based image search engine, restricted to a chosen geographic region, (ii) relevant keywords are extracted from the web pages containing these images and are submitted to a web image search engine as a query, which will return the highest ranking images for the query, and (iii) content-based image retrieval is used to choose the most similar images to the snapshot, and finally the web pages these images are contained in are returned to the user.

In step (i) the content-based image search engine has a relatively small index, covering only few images of each landmark, within the region the user is expected to be in; this is done for efficiency purposes. To get accuracy we need step (ii), leveraging the power of web image search engines, so that the quality

[161] Teaching computers to read: Google has acquired reCAPTCHA, by Louis von Ahn, September 2009. http://googleblog.blogspot.com/2009/09/teaching-computers-to-read-google.html.

of the final results returned to the user is ensured. Step (iii) is needed in order to get a small number of focused results back to the user.

6.7 SPECIAL PURPOSE SEARCH ENGINES

Web search engines are at our finger tips, serving hundreds of millions of surfers on a daily basis, and their quality is continuously on the increase. They are excellent in finding relevant home pages and answering known-item queries, accounting for a large proportion of web queries. But when it comes to specialized information, web search engines often fail miserably. We should not see this as a deficiency of these tools, as they are not endowed with domain-specific knowledge. There is an ever increasing number of search engines covering specialized domains and targeting specific audiences that may benefit from a search engine with deeper knowledge.[162]

Amazon.com (www.amazon.com), one of the defining brands of the Web, can be viewed as a specialized search engine for finding books. Much of its database is visible to web search engines, so much of its book catalogue is searchable directly through web search engines. Another example is the Internet Movie Database (www.imdb.com), which has been in existence since 1990, was acquired by Amazon.com in 1998, and as of late 2009, visited by 57 million surfers every month.[163]

A web search engine cannot crawl information that is buried inside a database unless it is made visible through crawlable web pages. There is also a limitation in terms of the resource that a web search engine has, so information that can only be found deep inside a web site is often not crawled. Even if search engines could overcome these problems, there will be a need for special purpose search, where focused domain knowledge replaces breadth of coverage. This does not exclude web search engines from branching out. Yahoo, which is a service provider in addition to being a search engine, provides financial, news, and shopping information, apart from standard web search. Google and Bing are not far behind and provide a similar variety of search services that complement web search, although they do not as of 2010 provide the wide range of personalized services that Yahoo does.

One good example of web search engines leveraging their technology is news search. A standard web search engine cannot keep up with the pace of change in news, and to get up-to-date information, it needs to have access to the relevant daily news feeds and to process and aggregate them on a continuous basis with special software. All major search engines now provide a special purpose news search facility, again with Google leading the way (http://news.google.com). The information for Google's news search is culled from over 4500 sources and

[162]Specialty search engines, by D. Sullivan, February 2002. www.searchenginewatch.com/links/article.php/2156351.

[163]IMDb Turns 19. Yes, 19. Older Than The Web Browser, by M.G. Siegler, October 2009. http://www.techcrunch.com/2009/10/17/imdb-turns-19-yes-19-older-than-the-web-browser.

is a completely automated process with query results ranked by relevance or by date and time.[164] In an interview conducted in 2003, Google news creator Krishna Bharat, discussed the popular tool that is now visited by millions of unique surfers every month.[165] The news tool aggregates over 100,000 articles a day, which would make the editing process impossible for a human within the strict publishing time constraints. Google news detects commonality between the articles it processes to detect when they are talking about the same event, and in ranking them it takes the reputation of the source into account.

The special purpose search engines mentioned in this section are far from an exhaustive list; we urge the readers, through web searches, to find search engines covering their favorite topics. We strongly encourage you to query a search engine with keywords such as "specialty search engines" to evaluate for yourselves what is out there. There are also many specialty search engines, which point to databases that are part of the deep, hidden, or invisible web, not directly accessible to search engines [607].

There are many professional search engines, which you may find useful. For example, FindLaw (www.findlaw.com), which has been around since 1995, specializes in legal resources on the Web. It is organized in a directory structure outlining the many resources it covers. As another example, HealthFinder (www.healthfinder.gov) is a US federal web site, that can be used for finding government and nonprofit health and human services information on the Web. Its information is collated from over 1500 health-related web sites, and also has Spanish and kids versions.

A valuable academic resource is CiteSeer (now known as CiteSeer^X, http://citeseerx.ist.psu.edu), which is a scientific digital library containing a repository of over 1.47 million downloadable documents and 28.5 million citations (as of early 2010), with many features including summaries, citations, related documents, and links to the authors' home pages. If you are searching for scientific papers, mainly in the computer science area, this is a good point to start from.

DBLP (Digital Bibliography and Library Project, www.informatik.uni-trier.de/~ley/db), provides bibliographic information on major computer science journals and proceedings. It has indexed over 1.3 million articles (as of early 2010), with links to electronic versions provided by the publishers. It is a valuable resource to the computer science community, which I have personally got a lot of mileage from.

Started in 1991, the arXiv.org e-Print archive (http://arxiv.org) is much more than a searchable archive of electronic research papers in various scientific fields, especially in physics. It allows authors instant prereview dissemination of material, so that other members of the community can download the articles and read them while they may be under peer review for a more formal publication

[164] About Google News. http://news.google.com/intl/en_us/about_google_news.html.

[165] Google news Creator watches portal quiet critics with 'best news' webby, by S.D. Kramer, September 2003. www.ojr.org/ojr/kramer/1064449044.php.

such as a journal. It has already proved to be an invaluable resource of information to scientists all over the world; in 2002 alone there were over 20 million downloads of documents from the archive.[166] On an average, each article has been downloaded 300 times during the period from 1996 to 2002, and some have been downloaded tens of thousands of times. In 2001, I started putting several of my papers on the archive and was very surprised at the positive response, when I received some e-mails from fellow researchers commenting on the work and suggesting related articles. The archive is more a collaborative tool than a search engine, and the major search engines crawl its content on a regular basis, making most of the documents on the archive searchable and easy to locate.

Online dictionaries and encyclopedias can also be viewed as specialty search engines, although in these cases it is the quality proprietary content, which is often subscription based, that motivates the search rather than the gathering of specialized information, which is out there on the Web for all to find. The online, collaboratively edited, free encyclopedia, Wikipedia (http://en.wikipedia.org), containing about 3.15 million articles in English (as of early 2010), is a notable exception; see Section 9.10.7 for a discussion on Wikipedia and how it works.

During 2004, I was trying to teach Tamara and Joseph, then aged 9 and 8, how to use the Web, with the intention of introducing them to search engines. Although I am a web expert and a regular user of search engines, I was not sure how to proceed. At first I went to Google's home page and asked Tamara and Joseph what information they would like to search for. Their first inclination was to view sites related to the brands they favor, so we typed a brand name into Google, and as expected we got a page full of relevant results, from which they could choose from. Without my help they found it hard to evaluate the Google summaries, and there was always the possibility that, left to their own devices, they would view an irrelevant site and thereafter "get lost in hyperspace." Flashing ads with titles such as "win a big prize" are especially attractive to kids, and apart from being misleading they are very distractive. There is also the natural worry of a parent that they may view an adult site or some other unsuitable information.

Then, they remembered that they needed to find some information for school, Tamara wanted to know about "electrical circuits" and Joseph about "barn owls". We did some searches but it was hard to find web pages that would help them with their projects, by blindly querying a web search engine. My conclusion was that good old encyclopedias (or maybe online versions of these) would best answer such an information need.

Still, children can enjoy surfing the Web and find both entertaining and educational material, without it replacing more focused material that can be found in books, some of which may also be online. It did not take me long to come the conclusion that kids need to interact with a special purpose search engine, whether it be for entertainment or educational purposes. I discovered three such

[166] Can peer review be better focused?, by P. Ginsparg, March 2003. http://arxiv.org/blurb/pg02pr.html.

resources, Yahoo Kids (http://kids.yahoo.com), Ask Kids (www.ajkids.com) and KidsClick (www.kidsclick.org), which are good starting points to enable kids to search with less supervision. The common theme between all these kids search portals is that they combine within the search facility, suitable material chosen by humans according to some topic structure. There are many other search tools for kids, [167] http://searchenginewatch.com/links/article.php/2156191. but I believe that this space is still open to newcomers. It would be nice to see government getting involved in an initiative in this direction.

Search engines are expanding into *local search*, which allows users to restrict their search to a geographic location.[168] A big part in the impetus for local search is the opportunity of search engines to work with Yellow Pages publishers, in order to sell paid placement search to local businesses. For example, if you are looking for local book shops or restaurants you could find them by querying a search engine with location details. This could be done in the office or at home, from a laptop or a desktop, or while on the move, from a mobile device.

We mention that Google (http://local.google.com) and Yahoo (http://local.yahoo.com) have already released their own local search services, combining search, Yellow Pages, and map information. Some of the other search engines have been partnering with local search providers such as Citysearch (www.citysearch.com), which has been providing local search in the United States since 1996. Another player in the local search market is Yelp (www.yelp.com), which specializes in reviews and recommendations of local services that are provided by its users, which form an online local community.

The high entry cost into the search market is enough to deter established firms, let alone start-ups and nonprofit organizations wishing to provide users with a novel search service. At the end of the day, it is all about innovation. Who would have thought that in less than 10 years, from late 1998, Google would rise from a virtually unknown search engine project to a world leader in the field. It is still possible to develop a proprietary search engine in the research labs, since as we have seen, much of the basic technology is common knowledge. Still, to get a search service off the ground will take much time and effort, well beyond "internet time" deadlines. You could invest in search tools but this will cost you dearly, and you will not find it easy to find robust, scalable search tools that you could then modify and extend to suit the needs of your development.

Would it not be nice if there was an open source search engine we could get our hands on. This is exactly what Nutch (www.nutch.org) has set out to do.[169] Nutch builds on the open source search software, Lucene (http://lucene.apache.org), to provide an open source web search engine with unbiased and trusted results, that is both cost effective and world class [123]. Nutch's aim is that its software will be able to crawl billions of web pages per month, maintain a search index of these pages, search that index up to 1000 times per second,

[167]Kids search engines, by D. Sullivan, January 2002.

[168]Local Search Series. http://searchenginewatch.com/searchday/article.php/3111631.

[169]Project searches for open-source niche, by S. Olsen, CNET News.com, August 2003. http://news.com.com/2100-1032_3-5064913.html.

provide very high-quality search results, incorporate PageRank-like link analysis into its algorithm, and operate at minimal cost. If this project is successful it could lead to many more innovations in search on a much wider scale than is currently possible.

Despite the domination of the search engine space by a few players, we will continue to see innovations from newcomers. As an example, Kosmix (www.kosmix.com) is a topic exploration engine that concentrates on informational queries rather than navigational ones (see Section 2.5) [554]. It aims to explore the Web with the aid of a categorization engine that builds a topic page for each topic it knows about containing information from various web sites including social network sites and deep web sources (see Section 2.1.1). Its taxonomy is hierarchical and consists of millions of topics reflecting ISA (for example, London ISA city) and other relationships types. New topics are being added to the taxonomy on an ongoing basis. The categorization engine matches the closest topics in the taxonomy to users' queries, in order to compile the answer page. Kosmix was founded in 2005 by Venky Harinarayan and Anand Rajaraman, who were cofounders of Junglee, the first shopping search engine, which was acquired by Amazon.com in 1998.

CHAPTER SUMMARY

- A directory allows users to locate web pages by navigating through categories rather than using a search box and scanning through results. The maintenance of a web directory is very costly in terms of the human effort involved, and its size is only a fraction of that of a web search engine's index.
- One way search engines generate revenue is through paid inclusion and paid placement schemes. Paid inclusion guarantees the inclusion of a site in the search engine's index and regular crawling of the site so that the index record for the site is up to date. This can be supplemented by a Sitemap, which informs search engines about the web pages in a site and includes additional metadata about the pages.
- Paid placement is a form of advertising, where sites bid for the rank at which their ad will appear in the sponsored results list. The sponsored results are clearly demarcated from the organic, that is, free list of results. Behavioral targeting is a method to increase the CTR of ads by delivering personalized ads to users based on information collected about the user, and contextual advertising is a weaker form of advertising using only the current search to personalize the advertising. Being able to understand and predict user behavior can help search engines increase the effectiveness of sponsored search advertising. Some of the factors of interest in this respect are the CTR, the bounce rate, ad fatigue, when and why do users view the sponsored results, and commercial intent.

- In paid placement, payment is made on a PPC basis or on a PPA basis. Major search engines employ a GSP auction to sell advertising on their sponsored search listings and rank the bids either by bid or by revenue. When ranking sponsored search results in real time, the budgets of the advertisers are important in deciding what final ranking will be displayed. Click fraud is of major concern to search engines and come in two flavors: competitor clicking and click inflation. Clickbots and forced browser clicks automate click fraud, forcing ad networks to apply preventive measures when possible, and to develop methods to detect and tackle these problems.
- Metasearch is a method of combining results from several search engines and presenting a single ranked list to the user. Metasearch engines are lightweight, as they do not have their own index, but their information about the relevance of web pages is often not much more than the ranking of the results, and the summaries of the pages returned. Several fusion algorithms were introduced, and some operational metasearch engines were discussed. Metasearch engines that dynamically cluster results were explained.
- Grouping search results can be used to improve users' interaction with search results. Two methods for grouping are clustering, where the grouping is decided at run time when the search results arrive, and classification when the categories are fixed beforehand according to a web searcher's ontology.
- Personalization is an important feature that is gradually being introduced into search engines. In order to personalize results the search engine must have knowledge of its users preferences. This can be done by users explicitly specifying their preferences, or implicitly through collection of data about the users from the log of their searches. Privacy and scalability of personalization are two issues that need to be addressed in order to make personalization viable. The relatedness of relevance feedback to personalization is discussed, and it was shown how PageRank can be personalized.
- Question answering allows users to pose natural language queries to a search engine. Annotations of answers to likely or popular questions can be stored in a knowledge base, and then retrieved in reply to users questions. Maintenance of such a knowledge base is a human intensive operation, that is arguably not scalable to the Web as a whole. Tools for providing definitive answers to factual queries and collecting facts from the Web are being developed and incorporated into search engine technology. Open domain question answering, with the Web as a corpus, is an alternative that may be viable as the research carried out in this area matures.
- Image search is an important type of search, when the results of a query involve visual information. The main search engines provide an image search service by ranking the resulting images mainly by the text that surrounds them in the web pages they are embedded in. Content-based search is still an unsolved problem, although prototypes that utilize features of an image such as color, texture, and shape are emerging. The technique of

relevance feedback can help users implicitly specify features of the images they require, by allowing them to mark positive and negative example images from an initial results list. A content-based similarity measure can be used to build a similarity graph of images, and a ranking method, called VisualRank, inspired by PageRank, can be applied to rank the images. This method may also be applied to audio and video search.

- Special purpose search engines have specific domain knowledge in their area of expertise, and may access the information from a tailor-made database, which may not be accessible to a web search engine. There are many special purpose search engines on the Web that are regularly used and maintained, some of which are provided as a separate service by the major search engines.

EXERCISES

6.1. **(Explore)**. Gimpsy (www.gimpsy.com) is directory service that lists web sites that help you carry out an online activity or perform a specific task.

Gimpsy's directory is unlike that of the Open Directory or Yahoo's directory, which organize sites according to their subject matter. In Gimpsy, web sites are categorized in terms of what you can do on the site. For example you can submit to Gimpsy queries such as "buy computer books" or "open bank account", which would not be understood by a conventional search engine.

Evaluate the service provided by Gimpsy, in comparison to conventional directory services such as the Open Directory or Yahoo's directory.

6.2. **(Discuss)**. Pay per click (PPC) is a lucrative revenue stream for search engines from users clicking on ads in the form of sponsored links, which are displayed as a result of a user query.

Do you think there are any benefits of this form of advertising, apart from generating revenue for the search engines [268]?

One could argue that fraudulent clicks still generate revenue for the search engines. In this light, explain why click fraud is a huge threat to the search engine advertising business.

6.3. **(Miniproject)**. Using only the information in the URL of a web page, implement a naive Bayes classifier to classify web pages into a selection of several of the top levels of the Open directory (www.dmoz.org); cf. [62]. Discuss the features from the URL that you have selected to use and specify which prove to be the most effective.

Include the title of a web page in your classifier and reevaluate the classifier.

6.4. **(Miniproject)**. Implement a classifier for user intent when a query is submitted to a web search engine [329]. (We remind you that user intent can be classified into three categories: navigational, informational, and transactional as described in Section 2.5.) For evaluation purposes choose 100 or so queries and label them with one of the above categories specifying the intent of each query.

Modify your algorithm to classify whether a query has commercial intent or not.

6.5. **(Discuss)**. Web data is only one type of information we interact with. Other types of information include e-mail, instant messaging, and other types of documents and images that are stored on the desktop.

Stuff I've Seen (SIS) [194] is a personal information storage and retrieval tool that indexes all information that the user has interacted with or previously "seen." It provides a unified index for all this information, made accessible through a search engine, whose user interface allows viewing and sorting the information according to several attributes.

Discuss the potential usefulness of such a personal tool, and how you think that search across different applications on the desktop, including web search, can be integrated.

6.6. **(Miniproject)**. Adaptive hypertext is form of personalization that utilizes a models of its users, in order to adapt the behavior of web-based systems to the knowledge, interests, tasks, and goals of its users [112].

One form of adaptive hypertext is *adaptive navigation support*, whose aim is to develop techniques that help users choose which link to click on, whenever they are browsing a web page.

Suggest several methods for adaptive navigation support and how they could be implemented.

6.7. **(Discuss)**. Suggest simple and efficient ways in which web image search engines, based solely on textual cues, can be improved by including a selected number of image features, and using relevance feedback without requiring an excessive amount of explicit user interaction (486, 401, 697).

6.8. **(Explore)**. Experiment with Google's "define" feature (www.google.com/help/features.html), which gathers definitions of words or phrases from various online resources [434].

How do you think definition type questions can be answered [304]?

CHAPTER 7

NAVIGATING THE WEB

"It's impossible to move, to live, to operate at any level without leaving traces, bits, seemingly meaningless fragments of personal information."

— William Gibson, Writer

NAVIGATION TOOLS assist users in their surfing tasks. Some are built-in to the browser or provided though plugins, and others are delivered through web sites in order to help users locate information local to the sites. Various techniques have been developed to analyze the navigability and usability of web sites, including web data mining methods, which are concerned with the content, structure, and usage of web sites. Visualization is also important as a means of improving usability by aiding web analytics, and in providing visual user interfaces that can help users surf the Web.

CHAPTER OBJECTIVES

- Describe the frustration that users experience when surfing the Web.
- Describe some issues related to web site usability that, if addressed, could reduce user frustration when surfing.
- Discuss the basic browser navigation tools, including the link marker and tabbed browsing.
- Explain how the back and forward buttons work.
- Present results from studies on how surfers use the available browser navigation tools.
- Point out the use of search engine toolbars as a way to search the Web directly from the browser taskbar.
- Discuss the utility of the bookmarks tool, how clustering and categorization technologies can be used to organize bookmarks into folders, and point out ways in which bookmarks may be managed.

An Introduction to Search Engines and Web Navigation, by Mark Levene

- Discuss the history list and indicate how it can be integrated with other browser tools.
- Point out that web pages can be identified by their URL, by their title, or by a thumbnail image of the page.
- Introduce breadcrumb navigation as a way to help users orient themselves within web sites.
- Introduce quicklinks for navigational queries, which are additional links displayed beneath a search result, that act as shortcuts to help users navigate within the site that the result links to.
- Give a brief review of orientation tools in hypertext, and point to the Hypercard programming environment as being influential in the design of web browsers.
- Introduce the potential gain link-based metric for measuring the utility of a page as a starting point for navigation.
- Discuss several structural metrics that can help analyze the topology of a web site and evaluate different user navigation strategies.
- Present techniques that can be used to understand and improve the navigability of a web site.
- Introduce the concept of web data mining and its three perspectives: content, structure, and usage mining.
- Present common metrics for measuring the success of a web site, namely the hit rate and the conversion rate.
- Explain the concept of web analytics and its objectives.
- Introduce content and commerce e-metrics.
- Introduce web analytics tools and weblog file analysis tools.
- Discuss how a user may be identified from weblog files.
- Introduce the rules of thumb used to identify user sessions from weblog files.
- Show how Markov chains can be used to model user navigation within web sites, and how, using this model, frequent trails can be mined.
- Point out some of the applications of web usage mining.
- Introduce information extraction as a collection of methods for extracting structured information from unstructured or semistructured web sources.
- Introduce the Best Trail algorithm for supporting user navigation within web sites by suggesting relevant trails for users to follow, given an input query.
- Suggest three alternative interfaces for user interaction with trails.
- Illustrate different methods for visualizing user trails.
- Illustrate different methods for visualizing web site structure.

- Mention visual search engines as providing an alternative way of presenting search results to users.
- Motivate social data analysis as a novel way of combining visual data analysis with social interaction.
- Introduce web usage mining of user trails through physical spaces.
- Describe the museum experience recorder as a possible device to capture user navigation within a physical space, and transport the trails followed to a virtual web space.
- Introduce reality mining as the process of collecting real-world data from sensors and making inferences from the data about human social behavior.

7.1 FRUSTRATION IN WEB BROWSING AND NAVIGATION

The *browser* is the software component, which requests and displays web pages for the user to inspect. Although there are many different browsers that have been developed, the most popular browser that users employ is Microsoft's Internet Explorer, while the second in popularity is Mozilla Firefox, which can also be used on platforms other than Microsoft Windows such as Linux or Mac OS; see Section 3.5 for some details on the browser wars.

It should not be too hard to convince you how important standards are for the smooth operation of the web. It is highly annoying when a web page does not display properly either due the browser not supporting some basic web standard or because the web page designer did not adhere to a standard.

7.1.1 HTML and Web Site Design

Most web pages use the HTML file format [501], although there are a wide variety of other file formats such as TXT (simple unmarked text), PDF, JSP (Java script), PHP (PHP: hypertext preprocessor scripting language; this acronym is recursive, i.e., it humorously refers to itself), Flash, and graphics formats such as JPEG (joint photographic experts group); see www.wotsit.org for details on many other file formats.

HTML allows web site designers to create web pages containing text, graphics, and hyperlinks (normally referred to simply as links), which are suitable for being displayed in a web browser. With HTML a web site designer can structure web pages, in analogy to a word processor being used to stylize and edit documents.

7.1.2 Hyperlinks and Surfing

The hyperlinks that are embedded in web pages can be clicked on by users, causing the referred web page to display in the browser window. The activity of clicking on links and browsing pages is called *navigation*, better known as *surfing*. We have already seen in Chapter 3 that web surfers often "get lost in hyperspace" and experience a feeling of frustration and disorientation as a result of not finding the information they are looking for.

What is the origin of the term *surfing the web* (or "surfing the internet", or even cooler, "surfing the net")? Some claim that the term derives from "channel surfing" when television viewers click on the remote control moving from one channel to another, sometimes randomly, without settling down to watch any particular program. Channel surfing may be due to boredom, lack of attention span, or simply due to not finding any interesting program to view. An argument against this claim, is that web surfing is most often not a random process. A surfer has a choice of links to click on, and the decision of which link to follow is often made with the help of contextual cues such as snippets of text surrounding the link, and with the surfer having a particular goal in mind. A different more sporting metaphor for web surfing, as opposed to being a couch potato, is that of being on a surfboard riding the waves. Once on an information wave, the surfer strives to stay on the wave as long as possible.

A study at the University of Maryland has shown that between a third and a half of our time on the computer is spent on frustrating experiences [408]. And guess what, web navigation is the largest cause of user frustration. Less experienced surfers suffer more frustration than experienced users, which probably means that novice users need more training. Despite this, much of the frustration is due to badly designed web pages, and user interfaces that are unpredictable.

The most frustrating experiences are due to: (i) dropped connections, (ii) long download times of web pages, (iii) web pages that are not found, giving rise to the infamous 404 error, and (iv) pop-up ads.

7.1.3 Web Site Design and Usability

It is well known that download times can be improved by designing web pages using standard HTML, and minimizing the use of graphics and scripting. But beyond that, the problem of sluggish internet connections, which are not continuous and tend to drop from time to time, is due to the fact that we are still moving out of the stone age (or more poignantly the modem age) of the web. Relatively fast and reliable broadband connections are now available and affordable in many countries, but despite this we still suffer these types of frustrations.

The 404 error—web page not found—will persist as long as links are not fully maintained, and search engine indexes are not completely fresh. This problem can be partially solved by software that detects stale links, but will probably not go away due to the enormous scale of the problem. It is worth mentioning that in databases the problem of links pointing to information that does not exist is called the *referential integrity problem*, and the maintenance of referential integrity is one of the postulates of relational databases.

Pop-up ads can be very annoying to say the least, which is why many users are installing software on their browser that blocks pop-ups. Other forms of advertising such as banner ads, that mimic error messages or familiar interfaces, can be very deceptive, causing the user additional frustration, for example, when clicking on an "ok" button and being diverted to a web page they did not intend to browse.

Web designers can improve the quality of their web sites by keeping in mind the usability problems that users may encounter when visiting the site. From the user side, awareness of the pitfalls and limitations of the web on the one hand, and knowledge of the tools that can assist users during navigation on the other hand will help reduce some of the frustration.

7.2 NAVIGATION TOOLS

Surfer Sue, who is a typical web searcher and surfer, gets lost in hyperspace like the rest of us. In order to improve her surfing skills she is keen to learn about the navigation tools she might utilize to improve her surfing skills.

7.2.1 The Basic Browser Tools

Clicking on the *home button* on the standard browser toolbar will take Surfer Sue to the web page that she has designated as her home page. Her home page is often a good starting point for a navigation session, and the home button saves her from typing the URL into the location (or address) bar on the browser.

A simple orientation tool is the *link marker*, which acts as a signpost to tell the user what links can be immediately followed, and what links have recently been traversed. In the context of HTML, link marking is achieved by highlighting *link text* (or anchor text) in blue and underlining it. The link text should give an accurate yet concise description of the page at the other side of the link. Gone are the days when web designers authored link text such as *click here*, which is normally meaningless as it does not convey any information to the user. When a user clicks on a link its color changes from blue to purple to indicate that the link was recently visited. It will change back to blue if the link is not revisited after a certain time period.

Although marking links in this way has become a web standard, many web designers override this behavior by using different colors, with and without underlining, and by changing the font or background color instead of highlighting. The argument for nonstandard link marking is that the current standard reduces the readability of the text, since it stands out more than it should [510]. There is an even more radical proposal of displaying the links on demand only, so that by default no links are visible to the user browsing a web page. In this way when Surfer Sue is reading a web page, she will not be distracted by the links unless she wishes to see them.

Among other simple browser tools that help is the ability to open a web page on the other side of a link in a new browser window. Of course too many open windows can cause disorientation but often two to three open browser windows can save the user some clicks. A related feature, called *tabbed browsing*, allows the user to open several web pages in the same window by loading them in tabs within the same browser window. The user can then easily switch between the tabs by clicking on the desired one; see Exercise 7.4. When the user rolls the mouse over a link it would be useful to have a small pop-up with a summary of the web page pointed to by the link, so the user can decide if the page is relevant before clicking on it. The summary may contain information such as the title of the page, the author, a short description of the page, the language the page is written in, and the time and date last visited [675]. Moreover, when the user clicks on a link the browser may warn the user of any issues related to the security of the site such as malware, viruses, or phishing scams.

7.2.2 The Back and Forward Buttons

The back and forward buttons are the basic navigation tools on the standard browser toolbar; see top arrow in Fig. 7.1. The mechanism underlying the back button is *stack-based*. What this means is that each time a user clicks on a link, the address of the web page loaded into the browser, that is, its URL is added to the top of the stack. As an analogy consider books stacked on your desk. You start with no books on your desk and each time you add a book to the top of the stack. When you remove a book from the stack, that is, hit the back button, the book that was beneath it is exposed and becomes the top of the stack. The removed book, which was previously on the top of the stack, is no longer part of the stack but can be put back onto the stack if need be, that is, by hitting the forward button. Let us look at a simple example of how the back button works,

$$\text{Home} \rightarrow \text{Research} \rightarrow \text{Web Technologies} \Leftarrow \text{Research} \Leftarrow \text{Home} \rightarrow \text{Staff}$$

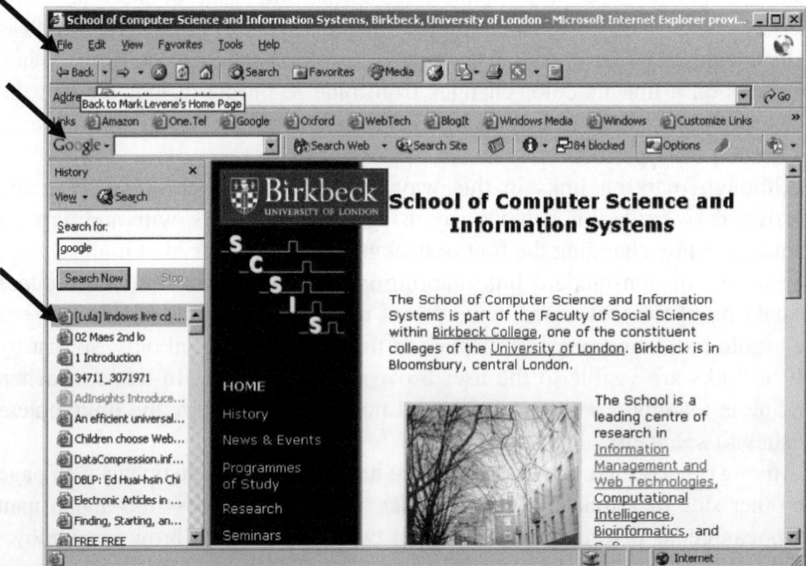

Figure 7.1 Navigation tools built-in to the browser.

where "$\rightarrow$" is a click on a link and "$\Leftarrow$" is a click on the back button. In the final state the stack contains two URLs: Staff is on the top of the stack and beneath it is Home. If you press on the back button the Home page will appear in the browser, and the stack will contain only the one URL, Home. Clicking on the forward button will cause the Staff page to be reloaded into the browser. The stack-based behavior of the back button means that temporal sequence of the user's clicks is lost. So, the fact that the Research page was browsed before the user hit the back button, is lost, since Research was popped off the stack and the Staff page was then visited. The user has access to the temporal, or historical, sequence of clicks through the history list, discussed below. Although the stack-based behavior may seem awkward when the user is navigating back and forth and choosing different alternatives each time, it is simple and efficient.

Studies conducted with web users have shown that the back button is the most popular browser tool used to get to a web page (just over 40%), after clicking on links (just over 50%) [155]. In this context a study of the browsing activities of 17 Computer Science staff and graduate students using Netscape Navigator over a 119-day period from early October 1999 to late June 2000 was carried out by researchers at the University of Canterbury in Christchurch, New Zealand.

The *revisitation rate* for a user is the ratio of the number of web pages visited by the user more than once and the number of distinct web pages visited over a period of time. It expresses the percentage of web pages the user visited more than once over the time period. The average revisitation rate reported from the study was just over 80%, meaning that four out of five pages that we visit have been previously seen by us. Users also tend to have one to two pages that they revisit far more often than others; these could be for example, their home page and the home page of their favorite search engine.

7.2.3 Search Engine Toolbars

As more users are turning to search engines as a means of initiating their surfing activities, toolbars provided by search engines have become very popular and useful; see middle arrow in Fig. 7.1 pointing to the Google toolbar I have downloaded and installed on my browser. Such a toolbar allows surfers to submit a query to the search engine directly from any page they are browsing, either by typing in the query in the toolbar's search box or by selecting text on the web page with the mouse.

To make searching easier, toolbars include features such as restricting the search to the site of the web page being browsed, doing special purpose searches such as image search or video search, highlighting the query terms on the page, and the ability find the next occurrence of a query term in the page by clicking on the term on the toolbar.

Google's toolbar has the option of displaying the PageRank of the page being browsed on a scale of 0–10, although Google may monitor the pages being browsed when this feature is turned on. This feature has been used by many webmasters to watch the PageRank of their site, and monitor how it changes as a result of various marketing campaigns. (See Section 5.2 for a detailed discussion on the possibility of links becoming the currency of the web.)

Toolbars provide other useful features such as pop-up blocking, bookmarking, and the ability to translate the web page being browsed. The toolbar is also a vehicle for the search engine to promote other services such as news, shopping, and specialized search tools.

There are many search toolbars available at the moment, so that Surfer Sue can use her favorite search engine with greater ease and flexibility. The downside is that, with the search box sitting nicely on the browser's taskbar, we are unlikely to use other search tools and thus we become less exposed to choice [507].

7.2.4 The Bookmarks Tool

The *bookmarks* tool (also known as the *favorites list* or the *hot list*) is a standard browser tool. It allows surfers to create shortcuts in the form of links to web pages they wish to return to on demand. The bookmarks can be viewed on a pop-up menu or, alternatively, in a side window within the browser by clicking on the favorites button on the standard toolbar. The title of a bookmarked page is displayed as the default reminder for the page, but an alternative description of the page can be entered by the user. Clicking on the bookmark will cause the web page to be immediately loaded into the browser. The pages in the favorites list can also be grouped into folders for ease of use. A special folder, which Internet Explorer calls "Links", stores the bookmarks displayed as icons on the links bar, that can readily be clicked on. When browsing a web page its URL can be dragged to the links bar and an icon will be created on the bar for immediate use.

Bookmarks provide a useful memory aid that can speed the information seeking process, but their organization is a challenging task [2]. On an average the size of the favorites list tends to grow over time, since, for most users, the rate of addition of bookmarks to the list far outweighs the rate of deletion from the list. This monotonic growth implies that, over time, users will experience problems in organizing their bookmarks list and managing its size. For example, when the list gets large, the pop-up menu of bookmarks is very cumbersome to handle. Personally, I either remove bookmarks when the pop-up menu is longer than I can manage (over 20 or so bookmarks), or at least put the less used bookmarks at the bottom of the list. A simple mechanism to enhance the usability of bookmarks would be to put the most recently added bookmarks at the top of the list. A more complex mechanism would involve utilizing adaptive technology, as mentioned in Section 3.2. The idea is that the browser should filter the most popular and relevant bookmarks to the top of the list, without the need for user intervention. Popularity is obtained by measuring usage conditioned by recency, while relevance can be obtained, for example, via classification that determines the categories that are of most interest to the user.

A study of how surfers use bookmarks, was carried out by researchers at the Concorida University in Montreal, Quebec, through an online survey given to web users, who were customers of an ISP in a major North American city [642]. The researchers obtained 1440 usable responses revealing that about 32% of respondents had 1–10 bookmarks, 44% had 11–50 bookmarks, and about 24% had more than 51. They found that the size of the favorites list is strongly affected by the amount of use and experience of user. In addition, they found that bookmark usage negatively affects reliance on search and positively affects the perceived ease of finding information on the web. Regarding the structure of their bookmarks, 44% of users organize their favorites into category folders, and out of these most of them (60.4%) use 1–4 categories, 19.9% use 5–9 categories, and 19.6% had 10–19 categories. The results suggest that surfers that categorize their bookmarks make less use of search engines to find information.

Bookmarks could potentially be automatically clustered into folders using a clustering algorithm similar to the one Vivisimo uses (see Section 6.3), where similarity between web pages can be measured by the amount of textual overlap between them. If the number of folders is fixed, at say, k, the well-known *k means* clustering algorithm can be used to group together similar bookmarked pages. To get the algorithm to work we need (i) a representation of a web page, such as the vector of the TF–IDF values of the keywords appearing in the page, and (ii) a similarity measure between two web pages such as the dot product between their TF–IDF vectors, which is obtained by multiplying the TF–IDF values of the corresponding keywords in the two vectors, and summing up the results. The k means is based on the idea of finding a *centroid* of a cluster of pages, which in our case would be computed as the average vector representation of all the web pages in the cluster. The algorithm first selects an initial partition of the bookmarks into k clusters; it is not important how this is done, for example, the user can provide the initial clusters. The algorithm then repeats the following two steps until the values of the centroids do not change by much: (i) compute the centroids of all the clusters and (ii) assign each web page to the cluster with the most similar centroid. The idea underlying the algorithm is that the pages are redistributed to the clusters at each iteration of the two steps until the clusters become stable. There are several issues that need to be resolved to make the algorithm work in practice; some important ones are what should the number of clusters, k, be, what is the best similarity measure to use, and how to generate meaningful labels for the clusters.

Jung and Jo [351] have been using bookmarks as an indication of users interests and preferences. They assume that the bookmarks are categorized according to a known taxonomy such as that used by Yahoo or the Open Directory. They use Bayesian networks to infer the degree of user interest in a category, based on the assumptions that the degree of interest is proportional to the number of times the category is found in the favorites list, and that a category influences the users interests to a larger degree if it is more specific, that is, found lower in the hierarchy. So, an interest in the Basketball subcategory is more specific than a general interest in the Sports category. Regarding bookmarks, the more popular a bookmark is with the user, that is, the more times it is revisited, the more influential it is on the user's preferences. Taking both the interest in a category and the popularity of bookmarks into account, the most preferred categories can be extracted.

Organizing bookmarks into category folders can be useful. This can be done manually by the user with the standard browser favorites list tool, but an automatic classification scheme could be potentially very useful, using for example, the Yahoo or Open Directory categories as a reference taxonomy. Researchers from IIT, Bombay have been using clustering algorithms to discover a personalized category structure for each user, by clustering similar bookmarked pages together [129]. This facility for managing the pages that users visit has been implemented within a more general browsing assistant, whose aim is to organize not only the favorites list but also the history list, into a set of coherent topics that may be shared by different users within a community [133].

Another proposal is to automatically archive web pages that were visited, that is, bookmark them, according to the number of visits to the page, and to integrate link analysis such as PageRank to evaluate the importance of the visited pages [639]. Moreover, these dynamically created bookmarks can be clustered according to the web sites they belong to, so that landmark pages within the site can be displayed to the user, where landmark pages are ones that are prominent within a web site. A formulae for discovering landmark nodes in the web graph, based on the number of pages that can be reached from a given page or that can reach the page when following at most two links, is simple and easy to compute [484]. Once the landmark pages are known, the context of the page that the user is currently browsing can be displayed by its relationship to nearby landmark pages. In addition to landmarks, it is useful to display to the user resources that point to the sites that the user has visited.

There have been several start-up companies that have made it their business to manage user bookmarks. You can find a listing of bookmark managers on Yahoo or the Open Directory, both of which have a subcategory devoted to bookmarks. Most of these bookmark tools are server based; once you register with the provider of the service you will be able to store your bookmarks on their server, and they will provide you with a set of features allowing you to add and remove bookmarks, to search for them, to put them in folders, and to share them with other users of the tool. The facility to share bookmarks is an important collaborative aspect that could lead to the formation of communities of like-minded surfers. One of the most known bookmark managers was Backflip (www.backflip.com), which was a start-up company that was one of the causalities of the economic meltdown during the first year of the new millennium. Diigo (digest of internet information, groups and other stuff, www.diigo.com) launched in mid-2006, is a more recent bookmarking tool that allows users to archive bookmarks, add them to topic folders, tag and annotate them, and share them with others. Diigo can be viewed as a social tagging and bookmarking site, as discussed in Section 9.8.

A *bookmarklet* is a special kind of bookmark, which instead of providing a shortcut to a web page as does a standard bookmark, contains a small program written in JavaScript, a scripting language for writing interactive web pages [506]. When a bookmarklet is clicked upon, the JavaScript code is executed on the current page being browsed, to perform some useful function, such as highlighting all occurrences of a word in the page, opening the previously browsed page in a separate window, searching the web from any page or back-tracking two pages back (i.e., the same as pressing the back button twice); see www.bookmarklets.com for many example boomarklets. This mechanism provides a simple and clever way to augment the browser's functionality. To create a bookmarklet you simply need to create a web page that includes a link with the JavaScript of the bookmarklet in the HTML tag instead of a URL. As with any standard bookmark, the link to the bookmarklet can be added to the links bar or to the favorites list.

7.2.5 The History List

Another important standard browser tool is the *history list*. The history list contains the links of all the web pages you have visited up to a limited number of days according to your preference. The bottom arrow in Fig. 7.1 points to the history list, which is displayed in a separate side window within the browser, when the user clicks on the history button on the standard browser toolbar; the bookmarks can also be displayed in this side window by clicking on the favorites button on the standard toolbar. The history list can be viewed sequentially according to the time browsed or some other criteria such as the most visited page. Current browsers also provide a search facility over the history list. The history list is displayed linearly, although in practice web pages act as branching points, for example, users often start navigating from a home page of a site and take different routes according to their information need.

Figure 7.2 shows a screenshot of the GroupLab Internet Explorer History System developed at the University of Calgary,[170] which integrates the browser tools that help users to return to previously browsed web pages [353]. In this integrated system a bookmark is distinguished from a web page that was visited but not explicitly bookmarked, by displaying its thumbnail as "dog-eared." Moreover, pages that are more popular are distinguished by adding a vertical colored band to their thumbnail, whose size increases as the page is visited more often.

This integration makes sense, as it transpires from user studies that most surfers use the favorites and history lists much less frequently than the they use the back button, despite the limitations of the stack-based semantics of the back button. The idea is to merge the favorites and the history lists using different representations of web pages, and to alter the back and forward buttons to work according to a temporal-based model allowing the user to move up and down the merged list. Pressing the back button (respectively, the forward button) will cause the previous page (respectively, the next page), in terms of recency of access, to be highlighted on the list and loaded into the browser.

7.2.6 Identifying Web Pages

Web pages can be identified by users in three ways: by their URL, by their title, or by a thumbnail image of the page.

[170]Grouplab Internet Explorer History System. www.cpsc.ucalgary.ca/grouplab/software/IEHistory.

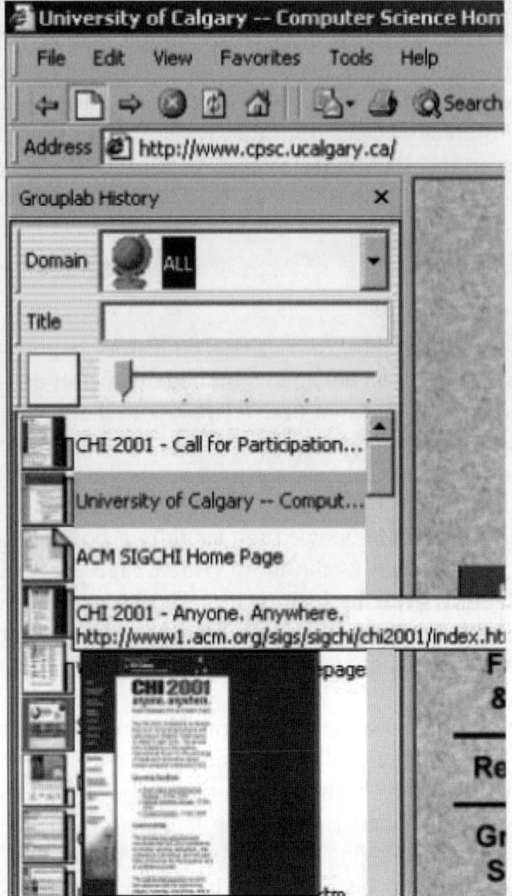

Figure 7.2 GroupLab Internet Explorer History System.

A thumbnail of a web page is a small image of the web page allowing the user to preview a miniature representation of the page without it filling the browser window; we note that several search engines now use thumbnail images to allow users to preview a web page.

The representation of web pages can also make a difference to usability, since the different representations of pages can complement each other [354]. Titles and URLs are not always informative, for example, they may be too long or giving a meaningless description of the site; so, in these cases thumbnails may help. Often the colors or layout of the site are sufficient to reveal its identity, and in other cases, any legible text that stands out may provide the needed clues to identify the page.

In the integrated tool, mentioned above, bookmarks are distinguished from ordinary pages that were visited by having their thumbnails dog-eared. Each thumbnail has a vertical bar attached to it, where the height of the bar is proportional to its popularity, that is, the number of times it was visited. A search filter can be applied to the list as with the standard history list. In addition, a slider is provided so that moving it to the right filters out unpopular pages leaving only popular pages and bookmarks. Moving the slider completely to the right displays only the bookmarks, thus transforming the history list into a favorites list.

An insightful comment by Marc Andreessen, one of the founders of Netscape, in an interview for Wired News in February 2003, was

> If I had to do it over again, I'd probably show some sort of graphical representation of a tree, so you could see what path you're travelling on and could backtrack. I'd also include thumbnail renderings on the tree to show where you'd been.

7.2.7 Breadcrumb Navigation

Just as in the fairy tale, where Hansel and Gretel drop the breadcrumb trail to find their way home through the forest, a virtual *breadcrumb trail* can be created to help users navigate within web sites.[171] Breadcrumb trails provide information as to where the user is in the site, and allows the user to "jump" to any previous page in the trail without using any of the browser navigation tools such as the back button. An example of a breadcrumb trail is

Home > *Research* > Seminars

The last page on the trail represents the page that the user is currently browsing, which is why it is not marked as a link. Breadcrumb trails are provided by the web site rather than being a tool within the browser, and the above trail is depicted in the conventional manner using the standard way a browser displays links, although no standard for breadcrumbs exists as yet.

Location breadcrumbs convey the position of the page within the web site hierarchy, starting from the first page in the breadcrumb trail. These trails are static and do not change when a user arrives at a page through a different path. For example, web directories such as Yahoo use location breadcrumbs to describe the current category being browsed. On the other hand, *path breadcrumbs* show the pages a user has visited to reach the current page being browsed, and are thus more general. These trails are dynamic and depend on the navigation history of the user through the site. Most sites that utilize breadcrumbs use location breadcrumbs as they are easier to implement, but path breadcrumbs are becoming more common.

Two studies conducted in 2003 have shown that in the presence of breadcrumb trails surfers use the back button less frequently, and the results also suggest that surfers who use breadcrumb trails are more likely to choose a hierarchical model as representing the structure of the web site.[172]

[171]Location, path & attribute breadcrumbs, by K. Instone. http://keith.instone.org/breadcrumbs/.

[172]Breadcrumb navigation: An exploratory study of usage, by B. Lida, S. Hull and K. Pilcher, Usability News, Volume 5, 2003, http://www.surl.org/usabilitynews/51/breadcrumb.asp and Breadcrumb navigation: Further investigation of usage, by B.L. Rogers and B. Chaparro, Usability News, Volume 5, 2003. http://www.surl.org/usabilitynews/52/breadcrumb.asp.

One of the advocates of breadcrumb trails is the web usability guru Jakob Nielsen, who has positioned them in the navigation bar at the top of each web page of his web site www.useit.com. The general idea of breadcrumbs can be refined by using a sidebar to highlight links, which provide navigation options to the visitor from the current page they are browsing. The research web site of Sun Microsystems makes use of such a navigation sidebar as can be seen, for example, on the left-hand side of the web page http://research.sun.com/awards. Taking this idea a step further would be to provide the user with dynamic personalized recommendations, but we leave the discussion of this to Section 9.4, when we introduce collaborative filtering, which is a technology that Amazon.com has been successfully using for some time.

7.2.8 Quicklinks

A navigational query is one where the user's intention is to find a specific web page, often the home page of a web site (see Section 2.5). Navigational queries often include part of the URL of the site and the search engine displays the matching web site as the top result. When the intention is navigational the user is likely to navigate from this page to find information deeper in the site. To help users navigate the site in such situations search engines display up to eight links below the first result that act as shortcuts so that the user can directly jump to one of these eight web pages within the site. Yahoo call them quicklinks, Google call them sitelinks, while Bing calls them deeplinks; we will refer to them as *quicklinks* [132]. As an example, the quicklinks displayed for the query "Birkbeck" are shown in Fig. 7.3.

The problem that arises is how to select quicklinks for a web site [132]. Two sources of data that can be used to tackle the problem are (i) search engine logs recording user queries and their clicks on search results, and (ii) trails users followed that were recorded from search engine toolbar usage.

Using (i) quicklinks could be selected simply as the top web pages from the site that users clicked on from the search engines results page, and using (ii) quicklinks could be selected as the most visited web pages that users navigated to while surfing. A third method for selecting quicklinks is to take the top-n, say for $n = 8$, ranked pages according to PageRank computed from the weighted

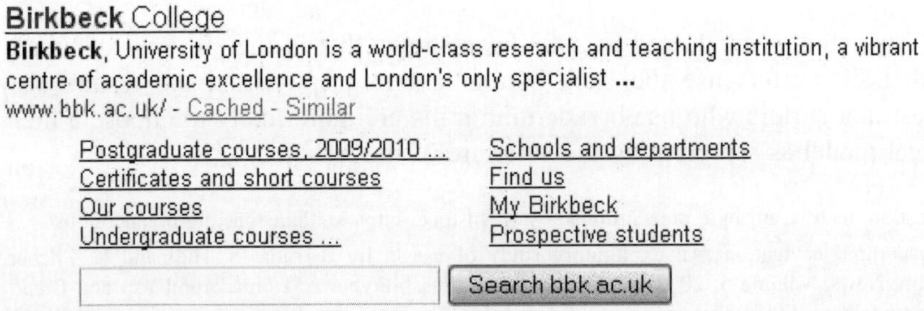

Birkbeck College
Birkbeck, University of London is a world-class research and teaching institution, a vibrant centre of academic excellence and London's only specialist **...**
www.bbk.ac.uk/ - Cached - Similar

Postgraduate courses, 2009/2010 ... | Schools and departments
Certificates and short courses | Find us
Our courses | My Birkbeck
Undergraduate courses ... | Prospective students

Search bbk.ac.uk

Figure 7.3 Google sitelinks for query "Birkbeck".

browsing graph constructed from the user trails collected from toolbar usage. A more sophisticated method, which was shown to be more effective by Chakarbarti *et al.* [132] is described as follows. First, a noticeability function is introduced for quicklinks, which measures the likelihood of a user to click on a quicklink; this can be taken as the number of clicks that the link received when presented on the search engine's results page, counted from the search engine query log. Then, quicklinks are selected by a greedy algorithm that maximizes the expected benefit to the user, taking into account the noticeability of web pages encountered by the user when navigating the browsing graph constructed from toolbar usage data, starting from the home page of the web site the user requested with the navigational query. The benefit of quicklinks relative to a trail being followed could be inversely related to the number of clicks or amount of time it takes to get to the quicklink from the home page.

7.2.9 Hypertext Orientation Tools

Hypertext can be loosely defined as nonsequential writing, organized as a network of nodes and links much like the web. As such hypertext provides a high-level model, and, in this context, the web can be viewed as an inspired implementation of the general features of hypertext. Although the web can be considered as a hypertext, its nonhomogeneous nature means that in reality it is composed of a multitude of smaller hypertexts. There was a surge in research on hypertext during the late 1980s, the two highlights being the first dedicated hypertext conference and the release of Apple's Hypercard software package, both in 1987.

Many of the currently available navigation tools derive their origin from the orientation tools designed for navigators of the early pre-web hypertext systems. An influential paper, written by Mark Bernstein in 1998 [79], described many of the orientation tools that are used today in the context of web navigation. *Maps* (or *overview diagrams*) give readers a more global context by displaying to them links, which are at a distance of one or more hops from the current location of the user. In the context of the web, current sites often provide a *site map* to give visitors an overview of the contents of the site; site maps and their visualization will be discussed in more detail in Section 7.6.

Apart from bookmarks, which are personal to an individual, Bernstein mentions thumb tabs, which are authored links to landmark nodes in the hypertext made visible to all readers. (In the hypertext literature surfers are often referred to as *readers*.) In the modern web, thumb tabs are often provided by the navigation sidebar mentioned above. Margin notes are often useful in reading paper documents, so the ability to add notes to web pages should be useful, but are not supported by current web browsers. Another orientation tool, which Bernstein calls *crumbs*, is the ability to leave a small marker on a web page indicating that it has been visited. In current browsers the link color changes after a link has been clicked on, but when browsing a web page there is no additional indication on the browsed page that it has been visited and when, although this information can be found in the history list.

7.2.10 Hypercard Programming Environment

In a seminal paper on hypertext navigation, published in 1990, Nielsen describes a small hypertext reporting on the events during the first hypertext conference in 1987 [502]. Nielsen's hypertext was implemented in *Hypercard*, originally released by Apple in 1987 and shipped as free software with the Macintosh, but as it became very popular, Apple started charging for it. Hypercard was built as a graphic programming environment, with a programming language called Hypertalk, which is very easy to learn and use. Apple no longer sells or supports Hypercard, and the URL, www.apple.com/hypercard, is currently redirected to the Wikipedia article on this topic.

The elementary building block in Hypercard is a *card*, and a collection of cards is called a *stack*. In terms of hypertext support, cards may contain not only text and graphics but also links, called *buttons* in the Hypercard terminology.

A button can implement a simple link, so that when it is pressed it takes the user to another card, but, in general, a button can compute any Hypertalk program. I was personally interested in Hypercard in the late 1980s, when it came on the Macintosh I was using, and playing around with it at the time, fueled my emerging interest in hypertext. I am still the proud owner of book on Hypercard written by Wolfgang Kitza in 1988, which is an English translation of the German version published in 1987 [375]. According to John Sculley, former CEO of Apple, Hypercard was one of the missed opportunities of Apple to apply its user interface to the Internet, but this is just hindsight.[173]

Bill Atkinson, the genius behind the Hypercard software, said that had he realized at the time that instead of sitting on one machine, cards and stacks could be linked together on different machines through the Internet, he would have created the first web browser.[174] There still exists a thriving Hypercard user group (iHug, www.ihug.org), whose members would like to see the product maintained and upgraded for the benefit of its many users worldwide.[175]

A standard page in Nielsen's hypertext, which was implemented in Hypercard, is shown in Fig. 7.4. In his design, he recognized the navigation problem as being one of the central usability problems that should be addressed. He included back and forward buttons, where the back button was stack-based and the forward button took the user to the next page according to the hypertext narrative. Also, present was a link to the front cover (the home page) and to a history list which included, for each visited page, the time since the page was last visited. All pages were time-stamped so that users could see the accumulated time they spent reading a page, and check-marks or footprints highlighted places that were already visited.

[173]Riding the next technology wave by D. Kawamoto, CNET News.com, October, 2003. http://news.com.com/2008-7351-5085423.html?tag=nefd_gutspro.

[174]HyperCard: What could have been, by L. Kahney, CNET News.com, August 2002. www.wired.com/news/mac/0,2125,54370,00.html.

[175]HyperCard forgotten, but not gone, by L. Kahney, Wired News, August 2002. www.wired.com/news/mac/0,2125,54365,00.html.

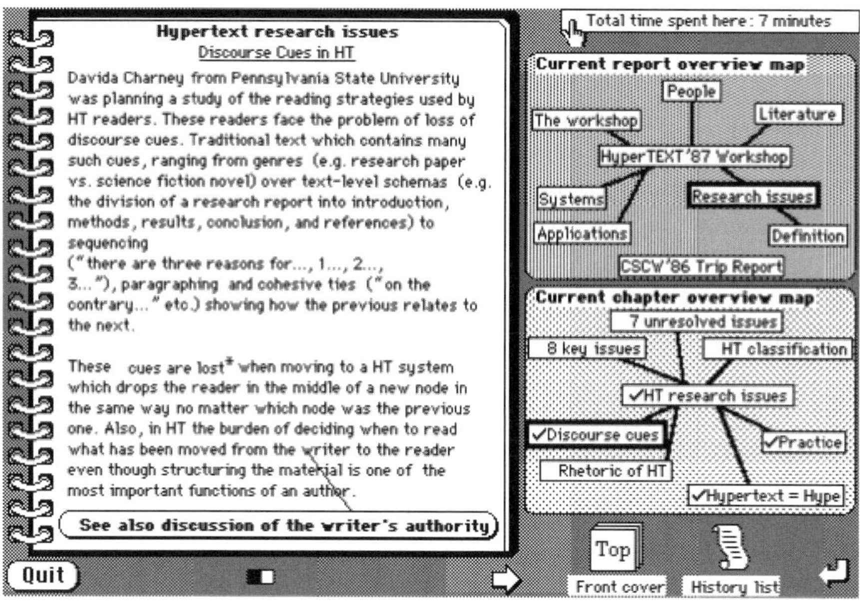

Figure 7.4 Nielsen's hypertext implemented in Apple's Hypercard. (Source: Two Basic Hypertext Presentation Models, Card Model, Copyright J. Nielsen. http://www.useit.com/alertbox/hypertextmodels.html.)

In addition, individual users could add annotations to pages. Nielsen had two levels of overview diagrams as can be seen on the right-hand side of Fig. 7.4. A global diagram on the top, which is a simplified site map, and a local one on the bottom showing the neighborhood relative to the page the user is currently at. Although this hypertext was authored well over a decade ago, the orientation tools it incorporated are comparable, and in some sense more advanced, than the ones provided in current web browsers.

7.3 NAVIGATIONAL METRICS

PageRank measures the sense in which a web site (or a web page) is recommended and how authoritative it is, but this does *not* necessarily imply that this site (or page) is a good starting point for navigation. Resource pages or hubs, having many links to informative pages, are normally a good place to start navigation on a particular topic. Also home pages, which are a special kind of hub, are good starting points, and as far as we know, search engines' ranking algorithms attach a higher weight to home pages. Despite this, search engines do *not* yet employ a general mechanism that takes into consideration the navigation potential of web pages. A question to ask is, are there some general criteria that a web page should satisfy in order to be considered as a good starting point for navigation?

- First, it should be *relevant* to the information seeking goals of the surfer, since we would normally prefer to start from pages that have a high ranking on the search engine's results list.
- Secondly, it should be *central*, in the sense that its distance (in terms of number of clicks) to other web pages should be minimal.
- Thirdly, it should be able to reach a maximum of other web pages, that is, it should be well connected.

By inspecting the fragment of a web site, shown in Fig. 7.5, it seems that both Mark and the WebTech pages are "good" starting points to navigate within this fragment, while the pages Kevin and WebDyn are not.

7.3.1 The Potential Gain

In our research group at the Department of Computer Science and Information Systems at Birkbeck, University of London, we have proposed a metric, which we call the *potential gain* of a web page, which captures the notions of centrality and connectivity. Once the user query is known, its relevance can be factored into the query score for ranking purposes, in a similar way that PageRank values can be combined with page relevance values. In this case, the combined value captures the notions of navigational utility and relevance within a single value. Our initial investigation of the potential gain was motivated by the desire to provide high-quality starting points for the automated navigation algorithm we have been developing, as described in Section 7.5; but we believe that this notion has wider applicability within the general context of search and navigation tools.

The computation of the potential gain of a page is based on the observation that on the one hand there is a gain for Surfer Sue when she discovers relevant

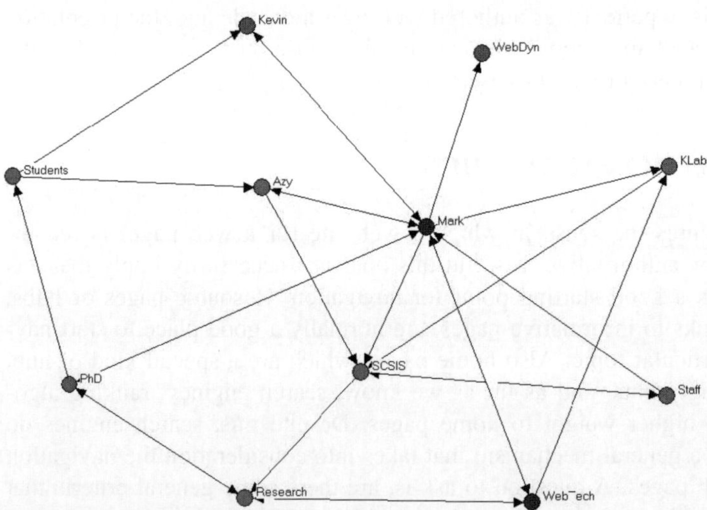

Figure 7.5 Example web site.

information, but on the other hand, each click comes at a cost, which can be measured, for example, by the time spent surfing and the mental effort exercised.

Thus the utility of surfing diminishes with the distance from the starting point, and this can be taken into account, for example, by making the gain inversely proportional to the number of clicks from the starting point. So, following the first link could count for one unit of gain, following the second link will add half a unit to the gain, following the third link will add a third of a unit to the gain, and so on. In this way the utility of following a trail of length three is, $1 + 1/2 + 1/3$, and the potential gain of a starting point is computed by adding up the utility of all possible trails from that point, up to a given maximum depth.

The potential gain values for the pages in the example fragment, shown in Fig. 7.5 are listed in Table 7.1. Our guess that Mark and WebTech have high potential gain is vindicated, and it turns out that PhD also has a high value, due to its outlink to Mark and its inlink from Research, which also has a relatively high potential gain. WebDyn obviously has a low potential gain but surprisingly also KLab, due to the fact that it only links to SCSIS, whose potential gain is relatively low. The potential gain of Kevin is determined by its outlink to Mark, and thus is higher than we anticipated.

The notion of centrality is also important in the physical world, for example, when deciding where to place an emergency service, such as a fire engine station. An established definition of a central node (i.e., position in the network), from the theory of graphs, is one that minimizes the sum of distances to other nodes in the network. In the context of the Web, or on a smaller scale of a web site, it may be that some pages are not reachable from others by following links; so in these cases we must set the distance to a constant, normally the number of pages in the web site. We shall return to the notion of centrality in Section 9.2, when we introduce social network analysis.

TABLE 7.1 Potential gain values for the example web site fragment.

Web Page	Potential Gain
Mark	0.2000
PhD	0.1354
WebTech	0.1209
Staff	0.1025
Azy	0.1025
Research	0.0958
Kevin	0.0748
SCSIS	0.0741
Students	0.0663
KLab	0.0277
WebDyn	0.0001

7.3.2 Structural Analysis of a Web Site

A set of tools that aid the construction of maps by performing structural analysis of a graph's topology, such as the topology of a web site, was described in the early 1990s by Rivlin *et al.* [572]. One such tool is finding an hierarchical structure that can be imposed on a web site, where its root is chosen to be a central node, whose distance to other nodes is relatively small. Another tool creates semantic clusters within the web site by identifying the strongly connected components (SCCs) of the underlying graph, where a subset of the graph is an SCC if all nodes in the subset are reachable from each other.

Two global metrics that can be used to measure the complexity of a web site are the *compactness* and *stratum*. Compactness reflects the degree to which a network is connected, where values close to zero indicate sparse linkage and values close to one indicate dense linkage. Stratum reflects the degree of linearity in a network, indicated by the extent to which certain nodes must be browsed before others. Stratum values close to zero imply that the network has very little hierarchy, while values close to one imply that the network is very linear. The difference between the compactness of a stratum is highlighted by looking at two networks, the first having a single path, say

$$\text{Home} \rightarrow \text{Research} \rightarrow \text{Seminars} \rightarrow \text{Autumn}$$

and the second, obtained by adding to this path a link from Autumn to Home. The stratum of the first network is one, while that of the second is zero. On the other hand, the compactness of the first is just under a half, while that of the second exactly a half, which is not such a big change compared to the change in stratum. It is interesting to note that these metrics are based upon concepts of status and contrastatus, defined in the late 1950s in the context of social networks by the father of graph theory, Frank Harary [282].

The stratum and compactness can also be computed for an individual user by considering the trail, that is, the sequence of web pages that the user has followed within a navigation session. The trail can be extracted from the history list of that user, or with the aid of a cookie stored on the user's machine. From this information, the fragment of the web site visited by the user can be constructed, where each link is weighted by the number of times the link was clicked on during the session.

An experiment carried out in the Department of Reading and Language Arts at Oakland University asked a group of students to respond to a set of information seeking tasks within a specified web site that provided two buttons, one for moving to the next page and the other to the previous page, and a main table of contents for the site [462].

The results revealed that the most effective user navigation strategy consisted of shallow hierarchical navigation, with repeated visits to central pages, measured by low stratum but high compactness of these users' trails. On the other hand, the users who were less successful in completing their tasks, were, overall, following a linear sequence with little revisits to previous pages, measured by high stratum but low compactness of their trails.

7.3.3 Measuring the Usability of Web Sites

Can these metrics be used in some way to improve the organization of web sites? There is no simple answer to this, as a web site is a complex network and it is impossible to foresee all the ways in which it may be used. Designing for usability, which happens to be the name of Nielsen's best selling book [504], is an essential ingredient. Usability does not end once the site is built. Continuous monitoring of how the site is used, which is the essence of web data mining, is a daily routine of many webmasters; but what actions should be taken to improve the site, as a result of this monitoring? Often controlled usability testing is recommended, but this is expensive and may not capture the real scale of usage of the web site.

One solution proposed by the User Interface Group at Xerox Parc is to simulate users navigation on the web site, with specific information seeking goals [146]. The user model is based on the notion of *information scent*, developed in the context of the theory of information foraging.

In its original form, as devised in the 1970s, foraging theory explains the choices made by animals when foraging for food in term of maximizing the "benefit per unit cost." Peter Pirolli and Stuart Card from Xerox Parc have been using foraging theory to understand how users surf the web.[176] In the context of information foraging the benefit is the attainment of relevant information, and the cost is the time spent to find the information. Users surfing the web pick up proximal cues, such as snippets of text, in order to assess distant content, which is only revealed after following one or more links. The *scent of information* is the perception of the value and cost obtained from these proximal cues representing distant content.

The model developed to predict the information scent employs a technique, called *web user flow by information scent*, which simulates a number of agents navigating through a web site. Using this technique the agents have information needs described by a simple textual descriptions such as "research groups in the computer science department" and, as in the foraging model, the scent at a given page is evaluated by comparing the user's need with the information scent associated with linked pages. The navigation decisions based on the information scent are probabilistic in nature, so more agents follow higher scented links. Agents stop surfing when they either find a target page or have expended a given amount of effort.

The BloodHound project at Xerox builds on the above technique to automatically infer the usability of a site. The last bit of terminology we introduce is that of the *information scent absorption rate*, which measures how easily users can achieve their goals and provides a numerical indicator of the chance of success. Preliminary experiments with a service built on these algorithms, have shown that BloodHound correlates with real user data. It remains to be seen whether Xerox will attempt to commercialize this product.

[176]Surf like a bushman by R. Chalmers, New Scientist, November 2000. http://www2.parc.com/istl/members/pirolli/pirolli_files/NewScientist_pirolli.html.

A mathematical approach to measuring the average cost of navigating through a web site was proposed by the well-known statistician David Aldous [24]. We simplify the model by assuming that the user starts navigating from the home page and stops at some web page within the site. To further simplify matters let us assume that the path chosen by the user is always the shortest path. The cost of traversing the path is taken to be the number of links on the path. Alternatively, we could measure the cost of the path in terms of the sizes of the web pages along the path, measuring the amount of data transfer to the browser when following the path.

The average cost of navigation is taken to be the sum over all web pages P in the site, the cost of the path from the home page to P, multiplied by the popularity of P, where the popularity of a page, P, is its frequency of access as obtained from the web site's log files; the frequency is normalized to be a number between 0 and 1. So, when reorganizing a web site, the average cost of navigation is the quantity that should be minimized.

One can now turn to a well-known result from information theory dating back to 1948, when its originator Claude Shannon showed amongst other things that the average cost of information cannot be lower than its entropy [603]. This is important since it puts a lower bound on the cost of navigation.

A tool developed in the School of Computer Science at Carleton University, optimizes the performance of a web site by reducing the average cost of navigation through the addition of *hotlinks*, where a hotlink is a link that acts as a shortcut to its destination page [170]. The optimization process works by adding hotlinks to popular pages in such a way that the average navigation cost is locally minimized at each step, and where there is a constraint on the number of hotlinks that can be added to any page.

7.4 WEB DATA MINING

Data mining is concerned with finding useful and interesting patterns in large data sets. Often the term *data mining* is accompanied by the phrase "knowledge discovery" as an indication of the intent to convert raw data or information into knowledge, which is more meaningful, compact, and understandable. In web data mining the data source is the Web. We can view web mining from three perspectives depending on the data that is being scrutinized [385].

7.4.1 Three Perspectives on Data Mining

- *Content mining* deals with the information contained in web documents. Web pages may contain diverse types of data such as text, images, audio, and video. Text mining has been the most widely looked at, and, as we have seen, a search engine's success is to a large degree dependent on its ability to extract textual knowledge from web pages. Text classification is a well-developed subdiscipline of data mining that is steadily becoming more important with the growing demand to be able to automatically classify web pages into categories [547]. Such text classification can, for example, augment the work of human web directory editors and indicate the categories that surfers are interested in. There is also growing interest in image retrieval and classification [172]; although search engines provide an image search facility, it is still mainly based on the textual captions and surrounding text rather than on an analysis of the images themselves (see Section 6.6). Another component of content mining is *information extraction*, which is concerned with the automatic extraction of structured information from unstructured or semistructured sources such as web pages [587] (see Section 7.4.12).

- *Structure mining* is concerned with link analysis as presented in Section 5.2, and with the analysis of the structure of individual documents as carried out by search engines; see Section 5.1.
- *Usage mining* attempts to discover patterns in web data, as collected from web server log data, a proxy server log, or the user's browser. The web server, which is the computer program managing users' requests to browse web pages, records the information relating to the request in a log file. There is a common format for the log data (see httpd.apache.org/docs/logs.html), which is supported by most analysis tools. For each web page it includes information such as the web address of the agent making the request, the time and date of the request, the volume of data transferred, the web address of the referrer (where the request came from), the query if the request came from a search engine, and the content of the cookie sent or received, if any. The agent making a request may be a human wishing to view a web page, but it also may be a crawler wishing to download a page for a search engine or some other application such as business intelligence gathering. There is an issue for weblog analysis tools to detect whether the request came from a human or a robot, since including these in the analysis, say of potential customers to an e-commerce web site, will distort the access distribution.

As we have already touched upon content and structure mining, we will concentrate mainly on web usage mining, and at the end of the section introduce information extraction in Section 7.4.12.

7.4.2 Measuring the Success of a Web Site

From the early days of the Web the most common metric for measuring the "success" of a web site was the number of visitors to the site, known as the site's *hit rate* or *traffic*. During the height of the dot-com boom share prices of young start-ups were often linked to visitor traffic through their web sites.[177] One of the reasons for this was that most of these dot-coms had no revenue or hard assets to be measured by, and after all web surfing is all about user clicks. The problem with this metric is that a raw measure such as the hit rate of a web site is often a weak indicator of sales levels or company growth.

[177]Stock valuation traffic drives internet stock price, by B. Buell, Stanford Business August 2000. www.gsb.stanford.edu/community/bmag/sbsm0008/faculty_research_stockvalue.html.

It really depends on the type of business, for a example, for a firm selling networking services to other businesses, the hit rate is not the most crucial factor driving its revenues. On the other hand,ISPs will attach a high value to the number of visitors to their home page, since advertising on their site depends on the number of "eyeballs" they can attract. E-commerce sites are somewhere in between these two extremes, as they need a large number of potential online customers. But what is most important for e-commerce sites is not the hit rate but the *conversion rate*, that is, how many of the visitors are converted into paying customers. In general, performance of a web site may be measured by looking at the number of visitors that actually complete an application (such as filling in a registration form or downloading a demo program), view some relevant content, click on a sponsored ad, stay on the site for a certain period of time, or as mentioned above, purchase a product.

A metric related to the conversion rate is the *batting average* of an item, which may be downloaded or purchased [19]. Assuming that such items have a description page, then the batting average is the proportion of times that visitors to the description page of the item, also acquired it.

The batting average is different from the popularity of the item, which is just the number of times it was acquired, that is, downloaded or purchased. The dynamics of the batting average and the popularity of an item are quite different. The popularity of an item will never decrease when the description page of the item gets more hits, which could happen when a link to the description of the item is put on the home page of the site. On the other hand, the batting average can fluctuate, when more users hit the description page depending on whether the new population of visitors to the description page of the item are likely to acquire the item or not.

In general, the popularity of an item is relatively stable while the batting average of an item is more turbulent. An interesting observation is that the batting average of an item may be related to an external event. As an example, the appearance of an external link to an item from another web site will often cause the batting average to fluctuate. For example, suppose that the description page of some software was mentioned in a review on the home page of a popular portal. This will probably cause the batting average of the item to fluctuate within a short period of the appearance of the review. Now depending on the population of users visiting the description page of the item, its batting average may fluctuate in either direction within a short period of readers being exposed to the review of the item.

There is another crucial issue to deal with, which is how do we count the number of visitors to a web site. First there is the problem of identifying nonhuman visitors such as web crawlers, but there is also the problem of identifying users revisiting the site within a short period, so as not to recount these revisits. Moreover, not being able to distinguish between different types of visitors is a problem, and the lack of information regarding the profile of a user may lead to a skewed count. For example, we may only wish to count visitors to the site that are over a certain age, or more generally, take into account their demographics, which in most cases are unknown to the web site.

7.4.3 Web Analytics

Web analytics is concerned with the conversion of web data into meaningful reports and charts. At the heart of web analytics are *e-metrics*, which measure the level of "success" of a web site [631]. The aim of web analytics is to inject statistical precision into the analysis of surfers through a web site, and to provide actionable metrics that allow the web site owner to track the changes in visitor behavior as a result of changes made to the web site. From a business perspective, the conversion rate is the crucial metric, and this is affected by the conversion process from the time a visitor enters the site to the time the visitor exists. Metaphors such as "stickiness," "slipperiness," and "leakage" are useful when trying to understand the how well the site is achieving its goals: (i) "stickiness" is a measure of how long users stay on the site, (ii) "slipperiness" is a measure of how quickly users exit the site (this is equivalent to low stickiness), while (iii) "leakage" is a measure of the drop out rate of users from the site once they have entered the site.

In general, a web site owner wishes surfers to stay longer on the site and view more content; so a high "stickiness" value is desirable. Once a user has finished viewing the content, for example, filled her shopping basket and entered the checkout, the web site owner wishes to get her to successfully exit the site (i.e., to make a purchase) as quickly as possible; in this case a high "slipperiness" value is desirable. The fewer steps there are in the conversion process the less leakage there is likely to be. To be able to measure leakage it is important to know users' paths through the site and their exit point. For a given page, the leakage is the proportion of times a visit to that page was the last page in the visit, that is, how often the page was the exit point from the site.

The average conversion rate for offline, bricks-and-mortar companies is 50%; their biggest problem is to get customers into the shop. For online companies, the average conversion rate is between 2% and 4%; this is proof that the hit rate on its own is not a good measure of the success of the site.[178]

7.4.4 E-Metrics

Ultimately, commercial web data mining tools must go beyond the standard usage statistics and track actionable e-metrics, which measure the success of the web site and indicate corrective action if needed, as discussed above. There are two general types of metric worth analyzing and tracking: *content metrics* and *commerce metrics* [203]. Content metrics are about the quality of the pages in the site; tracking these can help improve the number of pages viewed by each visitor. On the other hand, commerce metrics are about the conversion of visitors to customers; tracking these can help increase sales.

The data needed to calculate the content metrics include page views (clicks), visitor sessions (all the page views within a user session, that is, the trail a surfer follows within the site), length of visitor session, number of unique visitors, number of repeat visitors, top entry pages to the site, and top exit pages from the

[178] Ignore marketing and increase your revenues?, in Conversion rate marketing newsletter, December 2000. www.grokdotcom.com/closingrate.htm.

site. To calculate commerce metrics, sales information, and marketing and web site maintenance expenses are needed.

Let us look at some specific e-metrics. First, we list some content metrics. The *take rate* is the proportion of visitors that complete some activity such as signing up for a newsletter or downloading some content, and the *repeat visitor rate* is the proportion of repeat visitors. We may categorize visitors as "heavy" if they view more than 10 pages in a session, "committed" if that stay on the site more than 20 min, and "rejecting" if they view only a single page in a session. Given this categorization we can define metrics that measure the proportion of "heavy", "committed," and "rejecting" visitors.

We now list some commerce metrics. The *conversion rate* is the proportion of visitors that make a purchase. The *repeat order rate* is the proportion of orders from existing customers. The *cost per order* is the ratio of the marketing and other expenses and the number of orders. The *cost per visit* is the ratio of the expenses and the number of visits. These are just a few of the e-metrics that can be derived from the log data, to give you a flavor of the power of web analytics.

7.4.5 Web Analytics Tools

Web analytics can be performed by analyzing server weblog files, as discussed in Section 7.4.6. Two problems with using log files for the data analysis are browser caching and outsourcing. The problem of browser caching is that the browser has a private cache that stores copies of web pages we have visited, which can be served from the cache when revisited. This behavior is quite common when users click on the back or forward buttons on the browser to reload a web page they have just visited. When the pages are served from the cache they are not logged, thus impinging on the accuracy of log file analysis. The problem of outsourcing occurs when the servers and thus the log files are local, but the web site wishes to outsource the web analytics.

To address these problems a small piece of code, normally in JavaScript, is added to each web page that needs to be tracked. Each time the page is visited the code is responsible for sending the information about the visit back to the web analytics tool. The page tag also ensures that the page is reloaded, that is, that the cache is busted, rather than a cached copy being served. This is often done by the code generating a random number that is added to the URL, so that the browser thinks that a new page is being requested.

The page tagging service also manages the process of assigning cookies to visitors. As discussed in Section 7.4.7, cookies are a more reliable method of identifying visitors than the IP address of the computer requesting a page; but often browsers are configured to block cookies, especially if they come from a third party, which may well be the case when the web analytics is outsourced. Page tagging is very flexible in terms of what information it can collect and does not necessitate access to the local web servers, but each and every page that needs to be tracked has to be tagged, and there is the added complexity of maintaining the code in the tags, and moreover, the code execution may effect the download speed of the tagged pages.

A free web analytics tool, which has become very popular is Google Analytics (www.google.com/analytics) [153]. It allows webmasters to track visits to their sites through a series of reports, including a map overlay showing the geographic location of the visitors. The dashboard, allows users of the tool to get an overview of the available reports, and by zooming into specific reports to get more detailed statistics and visualizations of the data. Web analytics tools are particularly useful for identifying good and poorly performing web pages in terms of the site's objectives, and for tracking and optimizing online advertising campaigns. (A comparable free tool is Yahoo Web Analytics, http://web.analytics.yahoo.com.)

For a list of weblog analyzers and web analytics software, open source and proprietary, see the Wikipedia entry at http://en.wikipedia.org/wiki/List_of_web_analytics_software.

7.4.6 Weblog File Analyzers

There exist many weblog file analyzers that provide standard usage statistics such as the number of hits, the average numbers of hits per time period, the popular pages on the site, who is visiting the site, what keywords are users searching for to get to your site, and what content is being downloaded.

One of the popular analyzers, which is also open source, is called Analog (www.analog.cx). It was developed by Stephen Turner, who was the CTO (Chief Technology Officer) of a web analytics company, which provides more sophisticated analyses such as tracking visitor behavior when navigating through the site, reporting on search engine keyword performance, and measuring the effectiveness of online ad campaigns.

It is easy enough to download and use Analog, so I collected server log data of hits to my personal web site, whose home page is www.dcs.bbk.ac.uk/~mark, for the period from late September to mid-November 2003 and let Analog do the data mining for me.

As an example of Analog's output, in Fig. 7.6 you will see the most popular pages on my site during that period, and in Fig. 7.7 you will see the most popular keywords that led surfers to hit my site. The most popular page on my site was my home page generating 3229 requests during the period, and the tenth most popular page was my heuristic games page generating 363 requests during the period. All pages generating less then 363 requests were aggregated into "other" in the pie chart. We observe that the top-10 pages generated over 50% of total page requests during the period. The most popular keyword shown is "database" generating 339 requests during the period, and the 10th most popular keyword was "data" generating 117 requests during the period. All keywords generating less then 117 requests were aggregated into "other" in the pie chart. We note that the top 10 keywords generated about 27.5% of the total keyword requests for the period. These sorts of statistics, where the number of requests for the top 10 in a category generate a substantial portion of the overall number of requests, are typical in weblogs analysis.

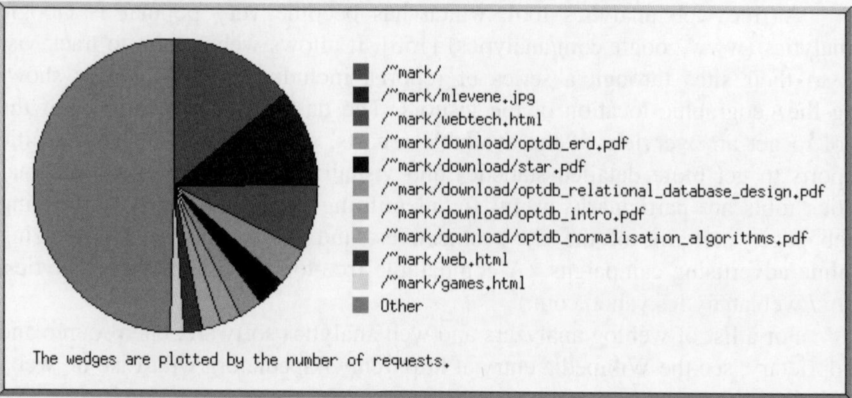

Figure 7.6 Pie chart showing the page request to my site.

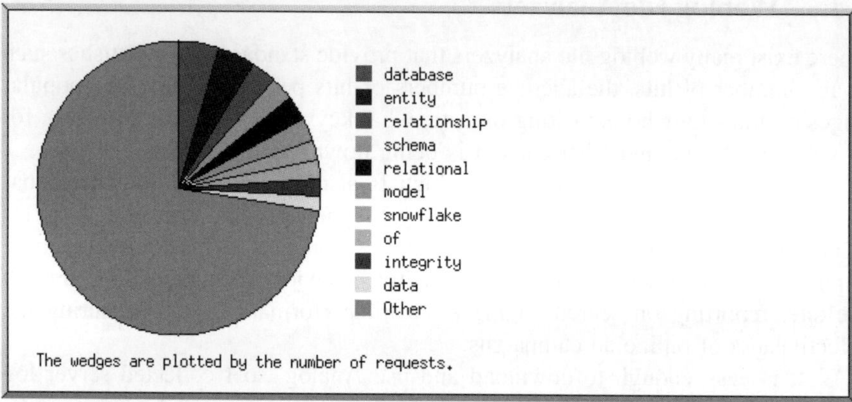

Figure 7.7 Pie chart showing the keywords that led to referrals to my site.

7.4.7 Identifying the Surfer

There are three rules of thumb used for identification of the surfer from a weblog file.

- The standard way is to identify a user by the host name or IP address recorded in the log file. The IP address is a number uniquely identifying a computer within the subnetwork it resides in. The host name is the address of a server on the Internet, obtained from the DNS (domain name system) service, which translates IP addresses to domain names. (It is quite amazing that a single computer can be identified within the Internet, which is such a huge global network.) This form of identification is not always reliable as IP addresses are often generated dynamically when users, for example, log on to their ISP, and even if the IP address is assigned to a single computer (as is the computer in my office at work), several people may use this computer, for example if it is in a computer laboratory.

- The second way to identify users is through a cookie placed on their machine. This method is reliable but the user may remove it at any time, and there are privacy and security issues to consider.
- The third and most definite way is through user login to the site, but in this case the user must be registered on the site. In general, users will register only if there is some compelling incentive to do so, for example, when a user is a customer.

Owing to these considerations, in many if not most cases, visitors will have to be identified by IP address, which is the weakest form.

7.4.8 Sessionizing

It is often beneficial to consider the trails that surfers follow through the site. In order to do so we must be able to identify a user session, from the entry point to the site to the exit point. Identifying the sessions is not a simple task; so, as before, there are some rules of thumb to follow [622].

- *Time-oriented* sessionizing considers either the total duration of the session, normally no more that 30 min per session, or the browsing time of individual pages, normally no more than 10 min per page. Sessionizing by total duration is the most common and robust method, while single page stay is good for short sessions.
- *Navigation-oriented* sessioning is based on the movement of the user through the site. The referrer-based method looks at the referrer field in the weblog (the web address or URL from where the request to the current page came from) and tries to match the page having this address to the previous page in the session. The problem with this method is that the referrer is often undefined, so in this case we may consider the two pages to be in the same session, if the requests were made within a small time interval, say 10 secs of each other.

The link-based method considers the topology of the web site being navigated and checks that two consecutive page views are connected by a link from the first page to the second. Navigation-oriented methods are good for short sessions, and when time stamps are unreliable.

7.4.9 Supplementary Analyses

Ron Kohavi, who was the director of data mining and personalization at Amazon.com, and Rajesh Parekh, who was a senior data mining engineer at Blue Martini Software, recommend some supplementary analyses that they have found to be useful in practice for e-commerce web sites [380].

- First they emphasize the importance of detecting hits by web crawlers and filtering these out.

- They then stress that collecting simple statistics such as a bar chart showing the average, minimum, maximum, and the number of null and nonnull values for an attribute can be extremely useful; for example, a bar chart showing the breakdown of customers by age.
- Another important issue is the analysis of errors that may have prevented visitors from completing a task. For example, a login box, where an e-mail should be typed in, may be confused for a search box leading to frustrated users trying to search for information and receiving an error message such as "invalid e-mail".
- We have already introduced the conversion rate as the most important metric for an e-commerce web site. Knowing the intermediate steps to conversion, called the *microconversions*, can reveal why visitors abandon the site prior to conversion. As an example, it may be that a large percentage abandon the site after adding items to their shopping cart, and a further substantial percentage abandon the site after initiating the checkout process, but prior to concluding a purchase. Further investigation may reveal how to improve the process to increase the conversion rate.
- We have already mentioned the analysis of keywords that caused surfers to visit the site from a search engine. In an e-commerce site, a local site search facility will allow visitors to search for products within the site. An analysis of unsuccessful searches such as ones with no results or too many results, may imply that corrective action needs to be taken.
- The design of hub pages such as the home page can have an effect on the conversion rate. For example, if it turns out that the link to the "cooking" page leads to higher sales, then this link could be given a more prominent position on the home page.
- Recommending to users other items such as books, music, or movies is another important feature that an e-commerce site can provide; we will discuss how recommender systems work in Section 9.4.
- In addition, identifying types of customers, such as customers who are currently low spenders but are likely to migrate to being heavy spenders, is a challenging problem for an e-commerce site.
- Lastly, geographical analysis of the visitor base can be helpful in understanding the customer's needs. An interesting observation is that customers who are further away from a bricks-and-mortar store tend to spend more online.

7.4.10 Markov Chain Model of Web Site Navigation

During the mid-1990s I had started working in earnest on the navigation problem in hypertext, and it eventually became apparent that in order to reason about a hypertext network the size of the web, we would need to consider a probabilistic model. The Markov chain emerged as the natural model due its relative simplicity and flexibility, and the fact that it is well understood, as described in Chapter 3.

A simple example of a Markov chain modeling user navigation through a web site, repeated from Section 3.4, is shown in Fig. 7.8. Such a Markov chain model depicting the usage of a web site can be built from web server log data, recording the activities of visitors to the site over a time period. The transition probability on each link in the chain is computed by counting the number of user clickthroughs from the source page of the link to its destination, that is, the probability records the frequency with which users followed the link.

So, for example, users navigating from Mark's home page chose the link to the Department's home page (SCSIS) 70% of the time, while the link to the Teaching home page was chosen only 30% of the time. Suppose that the surfer chose to move to the Department's home page. From that page, 55% of the time, users chose to click on the link leading to the Staff home page, and 45% of the time, they chose to click on the link leading to the Research home page.

The statistics used to construct the Markov chain probabilities can be collated on an individual basis for each visitor for personalization purposes, but they can also be aggregated over a group of users having something in common, in order to obtain a more general picture of the navigation patterns of the site's visitors. As we will see there are several applications of the model, and the granularity of the user base to be considered depends, to a large degree, on the application in hand.

Together with a colleague, Jóse Borges, from the University of Porto, then a PhD student, I set out to apply the Markov chain model to the web usage mining task. The problem we were confronted with was: given that we have access to server log data over a period of time, how can we build a faithful representation of the usage of the web site, and then find the preferred trails of users through the site.

The first step in the process was to sessionize the log data, so that each session is represented by a trail, that is, a sequence of web pages, followed by

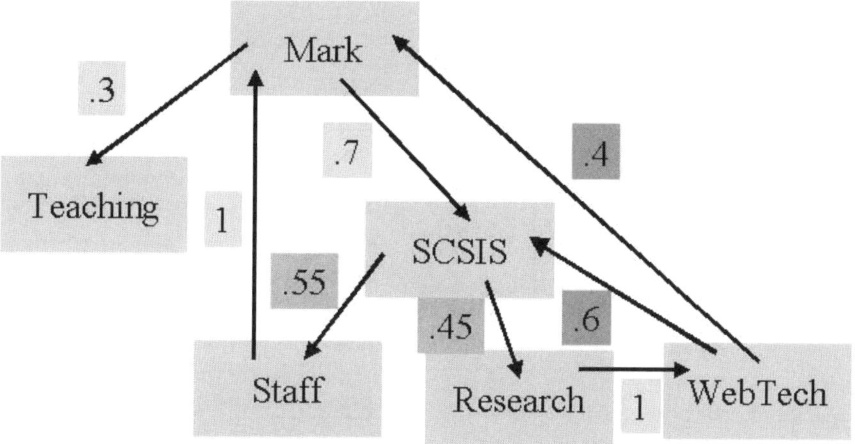

Figure 7.8 Markov chain example.

a visitor of the web site at a particular time. An important point to make is that the more log data that is available the more reliable the statistics, and that depending on the circumstance, the statistics of the site may change over time. So, for example, when a particular product is on special offer, the usage statistics for the link leading to the product web page will have a burst of activity during the discount period, increasing the transition probability of the link.

Once we have at our disposal the trails users followed, we can build the Markov chain by counting the number of transitions in trails from one page to another. We compute the initial probability of a web page as the frequency that the web page was the first in a session. For simplicity let us assume that all visitors start their navigation session from the home page of the site. The resulting Markov chain for our example is shown in Fig. 7.8, where the home page of the site is labeled Mark.

The next step in the process is to run a data mining algorithm on the resulting Markov chain to find the frequent trails that were followed through the site. These are the navigation behavior patterns we are interested in. A frequent trail is any trail from the home page, whose probability is greater than or equal to some threshold above zero but not greater than one.

Recalling that the probability of a trail is obtained by multiplying the transition probabilities of following the links in the trail, with a threshold of 0.3, we have in our example four frequent trails, as shown in Fig. 7.9. An important aspect of our algorithm is that it is scalable, since its running time is, on an average, proportional to the number of web pages represented in the Markov chain. This is implied by the fact that, for a given threshold, the number of patterns increases linearly with the number of web pages in the site being mined. It should be noted that decreasing the threshold increases the number of patterns, and this will eventually cause a combinatorial explosion in the number of

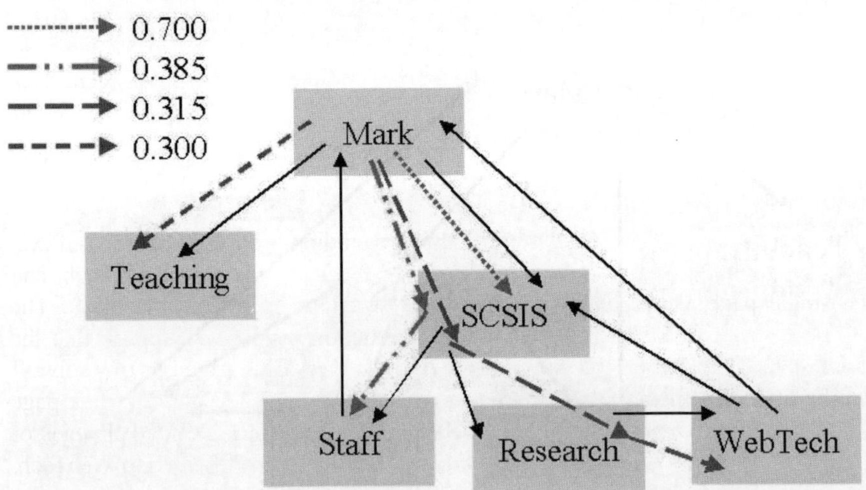

Figure 7.9 Frequent trails.

returned patterns. This is due to the fact that each time a web page has a choice of two or more links, the number of trails passing through that page doubles or more, leading to a huge number of combinations.

Our method for mining frequent usage patterns was presented by Jóse Borges in 1999 at the first workshop on web data mining, WEBKDD'99 [90]. The WEBKDD workshop has become a regular event as part of the yearly Knowledge Discovery and Data Mining (KDD) Conference offerings, and since then the number of events, which are relevant to web data mining, have proliferated.

Our initial model has several drawbacks, which we have subsequently addressed. The first one is do to with the history depth taken into account in the model. To illustrate the point, suppose that the visitor has just added an item to their shopping cart and they have the choice of either continuing to the checkout or doing something else. We can inspect the transitions from the shopping cart and see what percentage proceeded to the checkout. Now suppose that this percentage is small, the next step is to find out what users did prior to adding an item to the shopping cart. Although the user sessions may contain the answer, the (first-order) Markov model we have described does not. In the first-order model we ignore the history, and only look at decisions made when browsing the current page. It may be that visitors browsing the discounted books section earlier in their navigation session were much more likely to reach the checkout than visitors who did not. To be able to infer this information from the sessionized log data, we need to move from a first-order Markov model to a higher-order Markov model. This can be done within our model by adapting a technique known as *dynamic Markov modeling*, which records a variable history depth of users' activity depending on whether there is sufficient evidence that the browsing of a previous page will have an effect on the transition from the current page [422]. We note that the first-order model is more stable over time than higher-order models, and in practice, when a higher-order model is needed, a history depth of one to two give sufficiently accurate patterns.

It is worth mentioning that since the late 1990s there have been many proposals of algorithms for web mining frequent patterns. An early paper by Schechter *et al.* [594] highlights an approach complimentary to ours. The proposed usage mining algorithm records the variable user history by utilizing a data structure called a *suffix tree*. Consider the user trail

$$\text{Mark} \rightarrow \text{SCSIS} \rightarrow \text{Research} \rightarrow \text{WebTech}$$

The algorithm constructs the suffix tree by adding the trail and all its suffixes (i.e., the subtrails SCSIS → Research → WebTech, Research → Webtech, and the single page WebTech) to the tree data structure as traversable paths. The resulting suffix tree can then be used for prediction purposes. Suppose that the user has navigated from the Research page to the WebTech page. As this subtrail can be traversed in the suffix tree, a prediction can be made that the next page the user will browse will be either SCSIS or Mark depending on frequencies of the routes taken previously by users when navigating from Research to WebTech.

To evaluate the prediction accuracy of the model [94], such as the suffix tree one, the data should be split into a training set and test set (a standard ratio is 70/30). Then the suffix tree is constructed from 70% of the trail data and the remaining 30% are used for testing. A more elaborate testing method is called *cross validation*, where the data set is divided into k, with $k > 2$, random parts, and then $k - 1$ parts are used for training and the remaining part for testing; this is repeated for all possible choices of $k - 1$ parts for training.

Scoring the test data can be done in several ways. We assume that our prediction method is that of *maximum likelihood*, that is, we predict that the user will follow the link with the highest frequency. Two popular metrics are *hit and miss* (HM) and *mean absolute error* (MAE).

In the HM method a successful prediction of the next page the user will visit, that is, a hit, is counted as a 1, and a failure to predict the next page, that is, a miss, is counted as a 0. The HM score is the ratio of hits to the number of predictions made.

To compute the MAE, the possible next pages the user could visit are ranked from the most frequent (rank 1) to the least frequent (the last rank). The absolute error in prediction is the rank of the link to the page the user visited minus 1. So, for example, if there are three possible pages to visit and the highest ranked was actually visited by the user then the absolute error is 0, if the second highest was the one the user visited then the absolute error is 1, and if the lowest ranked was the one the user visited then the absolute error is 2. The MAE is the average absolute error over all predictions made.

Another drawback of our original algorithm is the lack of control over the number and length of frequent trails returned for a given threshold. On the one hand, if we increase the threshold we get fewer trails, but these trails become short and may be less interesting. On the other hand, if we reduce the threshold we get longer trails, but there may be too many of them. We tackled this problem by utilizing two rules of thumb. The first one, which we have called the *inverse fisheye heuristic* [92], reduces the threshold dynamically as we explore more trails, in order to obtain a manageable set of longer trails. The second one, which we have called the *fine-grained heuristic* [91], explores the frequent trails on a one-to-one basis stopping the exploration process when the sum of the probabilities of the remaining trails falls below a second threshold.

Another issue currently being looked at is incorporating content mining into the equation, the point being that users navigate within a web site by inspecting the content they are browsing, and considering what activity they ought to do next given their information seeking goals. For example, knowing the category of a book a user is inspecting may help in recommending similar books to the user. Another example from e-commerce [116] is combining the content and usage data to figure out the intention of the visitor, whether it is to *browse*, *search*, or *buy*?

7.4.11 Applications of Web Usage Mining

Apart from e-commerce there are other important applications of web usage mining. One such application is prefetching and caching of web pages in order to increase the site's performance, by reducing the latency in serving web pages to visitors. The idea is, that by having a guess at the web pages that will be hit upon, the web server can give faster access to these page by fetching them before they are requested, and putting them into a cache server supporting fast access. The guesses of which pages are likely to be hit are based upon the frequency of usage as reported by our usage mining tools.

The desire for an accurate prediction method has been occupying scientists for many centuries. A well-known quote by Niels Bohr, the famous Nobel laureate in physics, summarizes the problem:

> Prediction is very difficult, especially if it's about the future.

Although the future may be inherently unpredictable, we can still measure the degree of predictability of our algorithms. In the context of web mining, we can make use of cross validation with maximum likelihood prediction, as described in Section 7.4.10, with a server log file as our input data to be divided into k random parts. We build the Markov chain from the training data ($k - 1$ parts) and test its validity on the remaining part, called the *test set*. Then, we try to predict the next page access within each session in the test set, and use the HM or the MAE metrics evaluate the predictions. A more accurate model of the data will result in less prediction errors.

Information theorists have been looking into the prediction problem, since the inception of information theory in the late 1940s. They have shown that in the case when the underlying model is Markovian, there exist algorithms called *universal predictors* [212], which given enough data, will minimize the average prediction error no matter what the underlying order of the Markov chain is, that is, the predictor does not need to know how much history is required to make an accurate prediction [582]. In the context of web usage data, this implies that if the underlying model of the log data is Markovian, then given enough data our technique can, in principle, be used to minimize the number of prediction errors.

Another application is that of an *adaptive web site* [539], which is modified automatically according to how users access the site. The idea is to automatically generate hub pages in the site, which contains links on specific topics that were of interest to the users visiting the site.

In Section 4.3 we have already mentioned IBM's WebFountain [271], which is a scalable text analytics data mining platform, with the broad aims of detecting trends, patterns, and relationships over the web. Up until now web search engines have had a monopoly on any analytics on a web-wide scale, but their ability to do any sophisticated data mining involving massive aggregation of data has been minimal. One service offered by WebFountain is the ability to track a company's reputation over the web. This would involve ongoing analysis of many data sources from web pages and weblogs to news and mailing lists. WebFountain has the capacity to store and analyze billions of documents, and is set up so that it can crawl as much as the web as possible every week. When its crawlers visit a web page, its semantic annotators tag the document making it more machine understandable. An annotator can recognize, for example, geographic locations, proper names, weights and measurements, or adult content. WebFountain is an open architecture that will allow new data miners to be plugged into its system, with the potential of deploying search and navigation technologies under one umbrella.

7.4.12 Information Extraction

Information extraction on the web can be defined as the automatic extraction of structured information from unstructured or semistructured web sources. Structured information is traditionally organized in relational databases, where the data comes in the form of tables of records, with each record containing a fixed number of fields populated with data items corresponding to the attributes of its table. So the process of information extraction can be viewed as the process of populating a relational database using a program, called an *extractor* or a *wrapper*, whose input comes from a web source, for example HTML web pages in a web site.

A notable application of web information extraction is the comparison shopping service [667], such as Shopping.com (www.shopping.com), which extracts information from many e-commerce web sites to find products and their prices. As many web surfers use comparison shopping services, a simpler technology than wrappers, called *data feeding*, has also been deployed. Data feeding allows e-commerce vendors to provide their product information in a structured format such as really simple syndication (RSS) (see Section 9.10 for a discussion of RSS in the context of Web 2.0). This simplifies the task of the comparison shopping sites and allows them to reduce errors and receive more information regarding the product apart from price, such as the shipping cost and discounts that may apply. Data feeding can also be beneficial to the vendors as it ensures their presence in the comparison shopping sites. Most established comparison shopping sites make use of both data feeding and wrapping, to ensure that they have the widest amount of information available for any product.

Entity and relationship structures are the most common extracted structures but also adjectives describing entities (see Section 9.9 for a discussion of opinion mining, which is another name for this type of extraction) and more complex structures such as lists and tables are needed in various applications [587]. Entities are typically noun phrases having one or more tokens. The most common types of entities are named entities like people and organization names, locations, and temporal information. Relationships are defined over two or more entities via a predicate such as "is employee of" between an employee name and a company name or "is price of" between a price tag and a product name.

Textual information extraction involves five subtasks [461]: (i) segmentation determines the starting and terminating boundaries within a text snippet that fills a field, (ii) classification determines which is the correct field for a text segment, (iii) association or relationship extraction determines which fields belong together in the same record, (iv) normalization puts the extracted text in a standard format, and (v) deduplication removes redundant information to avoid duplicate records in the database.

An information extraction system may be hand-coded, where humans define the rules or regular expressions for performing the extraction. This approach is neither generalizable nor scalable to a large number different sites and document types, but is potentially very accurate. Automatic machine learning methods are generally scalable but less accurate. There are two main types of machine learning methods employed in information extraction: rule-based and statistical [587].

Rule-based systems contain rules of the form $Pattern \rightarrow Action$. A Pattern could be a regular expression defined over features of tokens in the text, and an action indicates how the text is to be tagged. In many cases rules can be automatically learnt from labeled examples in the text; this is also known as *wrapper induction*.

The most common statistical methods treat the unstructured text as a sequence of tokens and the extraction problem as one of assigning appropriate labels to the tokens. A state-of-the-art method for labeling tokens is conditional random fields (CRFs). Simply stated, a CRF [635] is a conditional distribution with an associated graphical structure that specifies the dependencies among its random variables. The objective of the learning method is to maximize the conditional likelihood of the output labels assigned to tokens given the input sequence of tokens.

KnowItAll (www.cs.washington.edu/research/knowitall) [207] is an open information extraction system, which as opposed to a traditional information extraction system is autonomous, domain-independent, and scalable to the web. KnowItAll uses a general model of binary relationship patterns that can be used to bootstrap the system. In this model, part of speech (POS) tagging can be used to instantiate relationships, for example, for a relationship of the form <X Verb Y>, where X and Y are entities. Moreover, statistical information from web search engines can be used to attach probabilities to relationships, so for example the probability of <London capital of England> should be much higher than <X capital of England> for any other X.

The extraction problem is treated as a sequence labeling problem, and makes use of CRFs to find the most likely labels. This method has no *a priori* bound on the number of entities and relationship types extracted and has been shown to be highly scalable.

Tasks in which open information extraction can be useful due its scale are question answering (see Section 6.5), opinion mining (see Section 9.9), and fact finding.

7.5 THE BEST TRAIL ALGORITHM

A paper that has influenced my thoughts about web navigation is "Effective view navigation" by George Furnas [238]. I will now summarize some of the important ideas in the paper with some commentary.

7.5.1 Effective View Navigation

Issues of navigation within the topology of the Web can be explored in terms of a *viewing graph*, which is a small subset of the web that the user is currently navigating in. Furnas defines *navigability* as the property of being able to find the shortest path to a target page from the page currently being browsed, by making decisions based solely on local information visible at the current page. We note that trails that surfers follow are often *not* the shortest, especially if there are many possible routes to choose from. The idea of finding information based on local decisions is related to following the "scent of information" (see Section 7.3). Furnas quantifies the "scent" at a given web page through the notion of "residue," which essentially helps users to decide the outlink to follow in order to achieve their goal. The definition of navigability implies that at each page in the viewing graph, sufficient information must be available to guide the user to the correct target page via the shortest route. Moreover, the information available at each page must be "small", meaning that in practice there is a manageable set of outlinks on the page for the user to inspect prior to deciding which one to follow. Under this definition of navigability, navigation on the Web is, in general, not effective, due to the fact that local information at web pages is limited. Two ways of improving navigation on the web include organization of information into classification hierarchies, and the ability to make local decisions through similarity-based measures between nodes of close proximity. Examples of classification hierarchies are Yahoo Directory and the Open Directory, and an example of a similarity-based measure, is the similarity of link text to a user query.

7.5.2 Web Usage Mining for Personalization

Frequent patterns obtained from usage mining algorithms could be useful in the context of personalization, for example in recommending relevant links to users during a surfing session [477]. One idea already mentioned in the previous section, is to recommend links to users navigating on a frequent trail according to the transition probabilities of subsequent links that they had previously followed. One problem with this approach is that it ignores the specific goal that the surfer has in mind at that particular moment. Assuming that Surfer Sue's goal can be expressed in terms of a search engine query, we could use content mining to assess whether the content of any of the pages that can be reached by a click on a link is relevant to Sue's goal, and use this information to provide a more accurate recommendation. Another possibility is to use collaborative filtering, introduced in Section 9.4, which attempts to find what like-minded users have done in a similar situation, and then recommend their actions to Sue. In any case to be able to provide a sensible recommendation for Sue the system must have some indication of her surfing goal, and must also have access to the content of the web pages she is, or could be, browsing.

7.5.3 Developing a Trail Engine

During 1999, together with Nadav Zin and Richard Wheeldon, who were PhD students of mine at the time, we were considering the problem of how to provide online navigational support for surfers. Although search engines are good at suggesting relevant web pages to users, their recommendations in the form of a results list ignore the topology of the web site each result is situated in, and thus ignore the context within which the user is navigating in. We found that although many researchers and web practitioners were describing web surfing activity in terms of paths or trails that users follow, little support was given within navigation tools to suggest and assist users in finding relevant trails. The idea we came up with was that of a trail engine, as briefly discussed in Section 3.3. The user submits her query to the trail engine in the same way it is input to a search engine, but instead of returning a list of relevant pages, the trail engine returns a list of relevant trails. In order to be able to implement this idea we needed to solve quite a few technical problems and to devise an efficient trail building algorithm, which we have called the *Best Trail* algorithm.

One problem is that although we know how to score web pages given a query, it is not so clear how trails are to be scored. In order to make progress, we turn to the interpretation of the probability attached to a link as measuring the strength of the relevance of following that link with respect to a specific surfer's goal. The simplest way a surfer can express a goal is through a query submitted to a search engine.

As we have seen in Section 3.4, once the search engine has scored the pages, the transition probabilities of the Markov chain can be computed as proportionate to the score of pages, as shown in Fig. 7.10. In this figure, the numbers in parentheses near the titles of pages represent the search engine's scores of the pages in the web site, as opposed to the probabilities assigned to links. Also, note that Research and WebTech have been lumped together, since the surfer has only one navigation choice from Research, which is to go to Webtech. We then apply a decay factor to the value of following the link from Research to WebTech, justified by the observation that pages that are further away take more effort to get to, and are thus "worth" less to the user. So, given the Markov chain construction, our solution for finding high scoring trails is for the machine

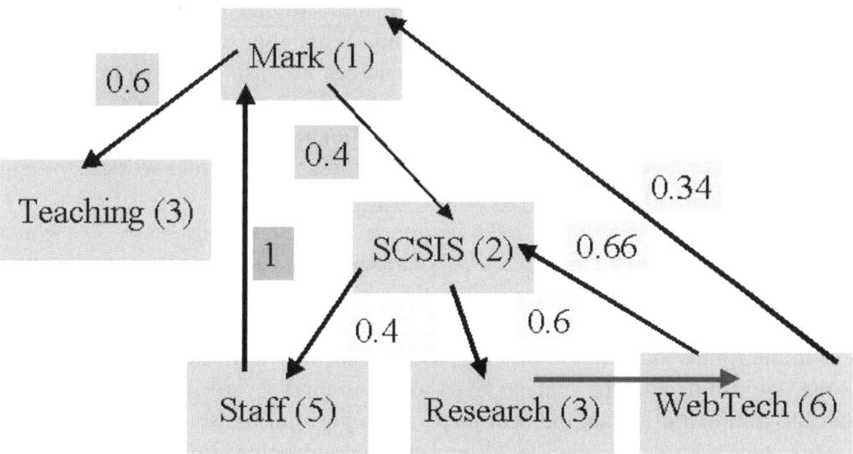

Figure 7.10 Markov chain constructed from search engine scores.

to dynamically search for trails, mimicking user navigation according to the "residue" implied by the transition probabilities.

We have found that we can improve the precision of the "residue" implied by probabilities by considering the full trail that the machine followed from the starting point to reach the current page, and then scoring this trail by applying a decay factor to the score of each page that was followed, which reduces the influence of pages as the machine is further away from the starting point. To achieve this we add up the scores of all the pages on the trail leading to the current page, and decay the score of each page by a larger amount the further it is down the trail. We then adjust the score of the current page by the score of the trail leading to this page and adjust the transition probabilities from the page accordingly.

The next problem we were faced with was that although we knew how a search engine efficiently computes the result list for a query, we were not sure how this could be done for trails, especially as the number of potential trails can very quickly become unmanageable, since their number multiplies every time we click on a link and face a new choice of outlinks. Our way of tackling the additional complexity that computing trails entail is to use the Best Trail algorithm, which is the core algorithm of the navigation system we have developed within our research group at Birkbeck University of London [679].

To demonstrate the working of the Best Trail algorithm, consider the Markov chain shown earlier, where the probabilities were constructed from the scores of the search engine attached to the individual web pages, given the user query. The algorithm takes as input K web pages from which to start the navigation from, and a number M that tells the algorithm how many times to repeat the navigation process. The starting points are selected on the basis of their search engine ranking for the user query, taking into account their potential gain (see Section 7.3).

The Best Trail algorithm is probabilistic and so the M different runs may result in different outputs. The output from the algorithm is the set of K best scoring trails, one for each of the K starting points. From the computational point of view, the algorithm is what is known in the artificial intelligence literature as a *probabilistic best first search* algorithm. What this means is that at each step the algorithm weighs all the possible choices and using a random device it probabilistically chooses a link to follow, favoring links that appear to be better. I believe that this type of algorithm has additional application in agent-based systems, for example in games, where agents navigate in virtual worlds, to help guide these agents through the environment they reside in.

The algorithm maintains a *navigation tree*, as shown in Fig. 7.11, which keeps track of the trails that were already explored. At each step it expands a link chosen probabilistically in proportion to the score of the trail emanating from the starting point and ending at the page reached when following that link. The numbers in the figure indicate the order in which the links were expanded according to the algorithm, and the leaf nodes, shown as circles, are the destinations of possible trail extensions at the next step. The algorithm has two separate phases, the first being an *exploration stage* and the second being a *convergence stage*. During the exploration stage the algorithm's choice of which link to expand is

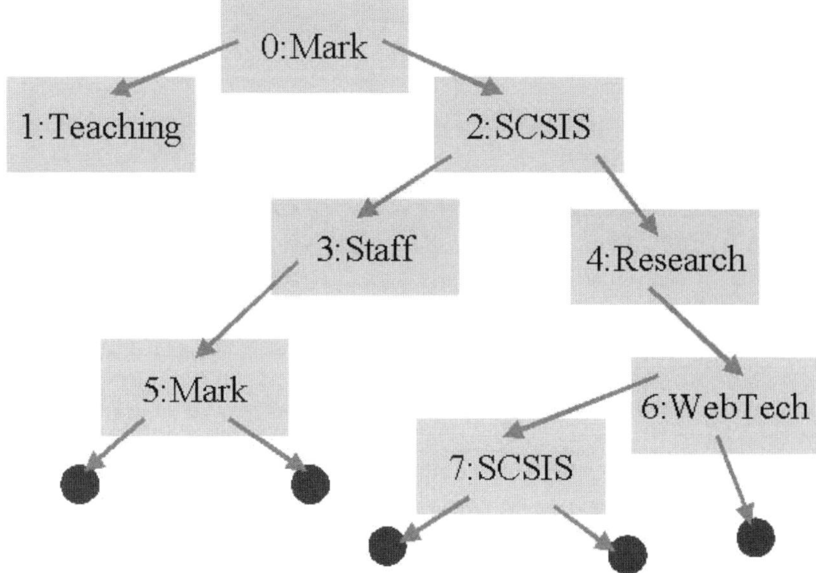

Figure 7.11 A navigation tree.

purely proportional to the score of the trail ending at the destination page of the link. On the other hand, during the convergence stage trails with higher scores gets their scores boosted, so that the probabilistic choice is biased toward these higher scoring trails rather than being proportional to their score. At each iteration of the convergence stage, the bias toward higher scoring trails is increased, so that after a few iterations the "best trail" emerges as the winner [423].

The Best Trail algorithm is at the heart of the navigation engine we have developed, and architecturally it sits on top of a conventional search engine that scores the individual pages that are needed to construct the preferred trails. The navigation system works as follows: first the user types in a query as in a conventional search engine, the system then responds by presenting to the user relevant trails, and the user can then interact with the trails by choosing a web page to browse.

We have developed three alternative user interfaces for the user to interact with, and demonstrate these over our example web site.

- In *trail search* we display the trails as a linear sequence, in the tradition of a conventional search engine, as shown in Fig. 7.12.
- In *nav-search* we display the recommended trails as a navigation tree in the window within a frame on the left-hand side of the display, as shown in Fig. 7.13. The user can interact with the navigation tree by selecting any web page on one of the trails, which will then be displayed in the browser window. Putting the cursor over a link in the navigation tree will cause a small window to pop-up displaying a dynamic query-specific summary of the destination web page.

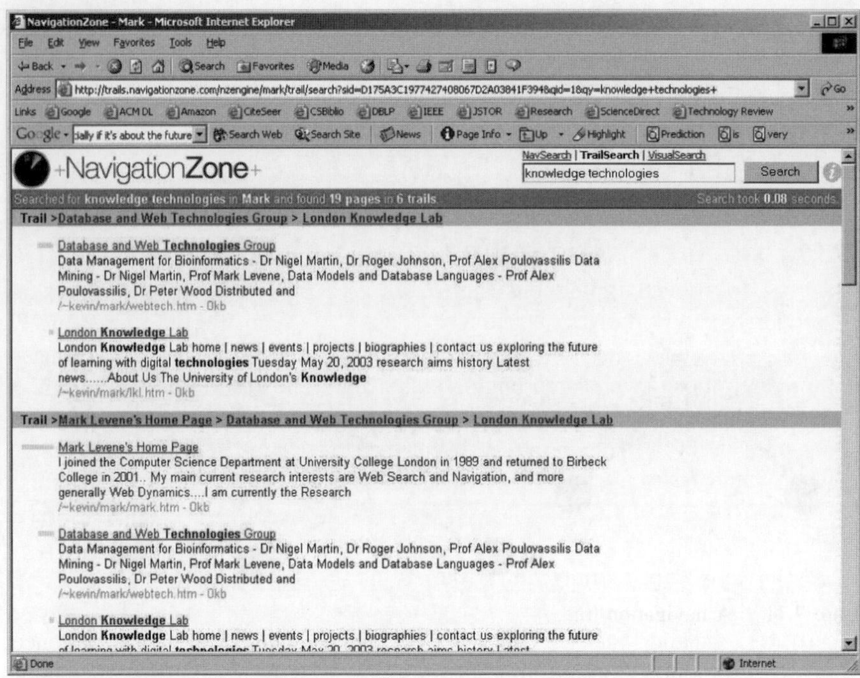

Figure 7.12 Trail search for the query "knowledge technologies".

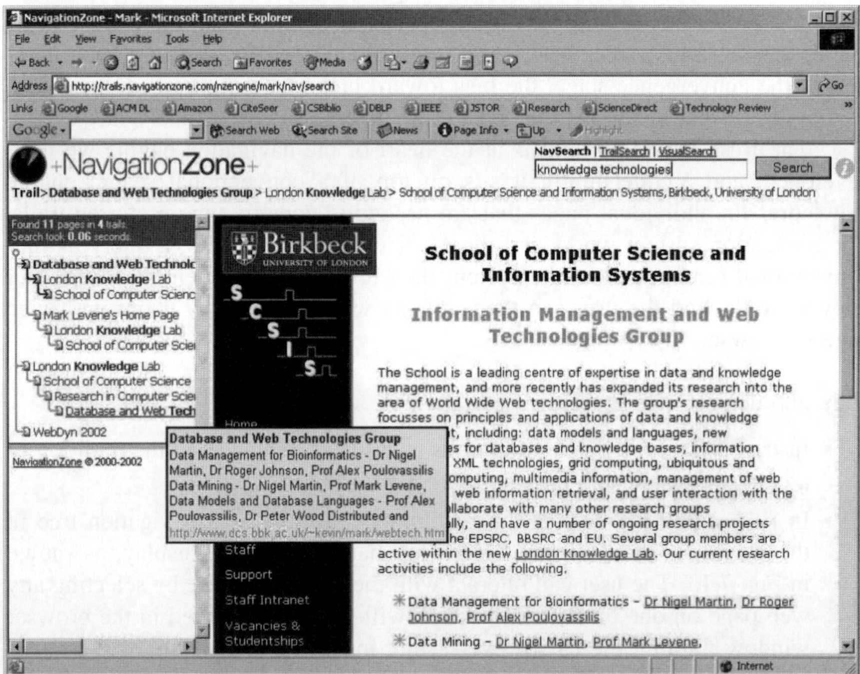

Figure 7.13 Nav-search for the query "knowledge technologies".

- The third interface is *visual search*, which displays the returned trails visually in the form of a graph showing how the web pages in the trails connect to each other, as suggested in Fig. 7.14. I believe that such visual interfaces have value in showing the user the context in which they are navigating, providing query-specific maps for the user to interact with.

More research is needed to ascertain the most appropriate interface from the user's point of view, given the task being carried out.

To summarize, the mechanisms of the user interface provide the user with guidance and context throughout a navigation session. The user interface can be embodied within a web site as a navigation mechanism complementing or replacing a web site search engine. Issues of scalability of a navigation engine are similar to those of a search engine as discussed in Section 4.7, and without access to a large pool of machine resources, it would not be feasible to manage an operational web-wide navigation engine. One way around the resources problem would be to use metasearch (see Section 6.3) to gain access to search engine results that could then be fed into the navigation engine. What we have demonstrated in our experiments with the Best Trail algorithm is the feasibility of automatically constructing relevant trails that can be presented to the user as an effective navigation aid to help users find an appropriate answer their query.

To test whether our navigation system enhances users' search experience, we have carried out a thorough usability study [456]. Our results show the potential of navigational assistance in search tools, since overall, users of the navigation system employed fewer clicks and took less time in completing their tasks than those using a conventional search engine. One reason for these positive results may be that users of the navigation system did not have to click on the back

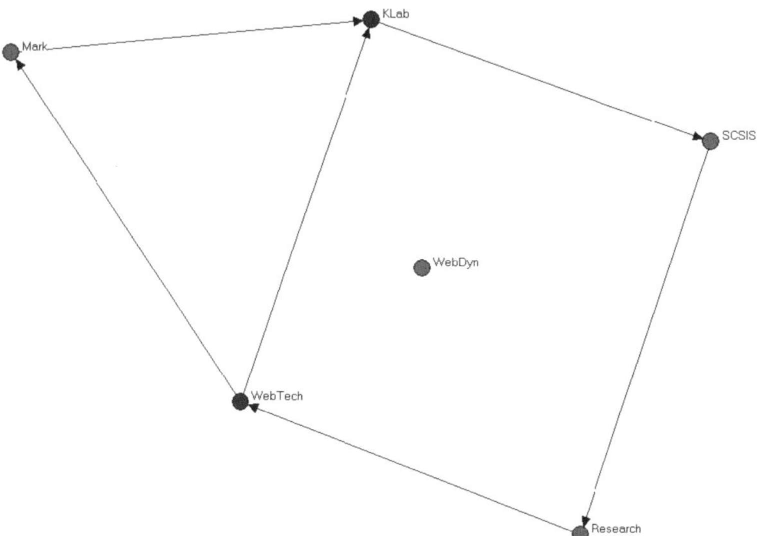

Figure 7.14 Visual search for the query "knowledge technologies".

button as much as users of a conventional search engine, but instead could use the navigation tree for this purpose.

The quicklinks feature (see Section 7.2.8) is one way of incorporating trails into search results, by showing users' links to strategic pages within a site, which could potentially aid their navigation.

Another proposal by Pandit and Olsten [525] is that of navigation-aided retrieval. In order to combine navigation with retrieval in this model, in addition to conventional search engine scores that rank web pages according to their relevance to the query, scores are computed for the likelihood of navigating from a relevant anchor page along a link to a destination page, based on the notion of information scent as described in Section 7.3.3. For each link from a relevant anchor page to a destination web page, the search engine score of the anchor page is multiplied by the information scent of the destination pages, and these combined link scores are summed over all links from the anchor page to obtain a navigational score for this page. Pages can then be ranked according to their navigational score, and further navigational assistance can be given to the user once they take action and choose a link to follow. This method can be generalized to compute navigational scores for all pages reachable from an anchor page rather than just pages reached by following a single link. In this way trails can be scored according to the utility of reaching the final page on a trail, which is consistent with the assumption that this final page is the one the user is interested in reaching.

7.6 VISUALIZATION THAT AIDS NAVIGATION

Usability of navigation tools is crucial for the success of the Web. There are two areas were visualization can make a difference in the context of web navigation. The first is in visualization of web site structure and web usage data to aid web analytics, and the second is in visual user interfaces that can help users surf the Web [202].

Even for medium web sites the amount of usage data can quickly accumulate, making the interpretation of the statistics coming out of conventional log data analysis tools difficult. Visualization has the potential to make it easier to interpret large amounts of data, and spot patterns and anomalies that may be present in the data [620].

7.6.1 How to Visualize Navigation Patterns

As a motivating example, consider the WebCanvas visualization tool of navigation patterns on a web site, developed in the Information and Computer Science Department at the University of California, Irvine, in collaboration with Microsoft Research [122]. The researchers applied a clustering technique to group similar trails followed by users, according to the categories of pages they browsed at www.msnbc.com during a 24 hours period.

A trail such as

$$\text{news} \rightarrow \text{health} \rightarrow \text{business} \rightarrow \text{business}$$

indicates that the user started their navigation at a news page then moved to a health page and finally browsed two business pages.

In the actual visualization, several clusters are displayed in a window as a matrix plot, with each cluster being displayed in a cell. Each cell contains several rows corresponding to the trails in the cluster, and each trail can only belong to one cluster. The intention is to show the behavior of a random sample of users in each cluster, so that the display can fit into a single window on a screen. Each page request in a trail is represented by a square and the color (or shade) of each square represents the category of the page browsed.

For example, one cluster may represent users interested in the weather, a second cluster may represent users that did not go beyond the front page of the site, a third cluster may represent users interested in sports, while a fourth cluster could represent users interested in tech news. The composition of mixed clusters, where users browsed through more than one category, is also interesting, for example to detect categories that are more likely to co-occur. Innovative visualizations ideas such as WebCanvas, which combine a data mining method such as clustering with a visual element, are at the heart of pattern discovery.

7.6.2 Overview Diagrams and Web Site Maps

Visualizing web site structure is important for orienting users within a web site. We have already mentioned maps and overview diagrams as giving surfers a better context of where things are in the web site, and their position relative to other pages.

One type of overview diagram, which shows you where you are and where you can go to, is WebBrain (www.webbrain.com), which is a visual interface to the Open Directory. Its interface is shown in Fig. 7.15 in contrast to the standard web directory interface as shown in Fig. 7.16.

At the granularity of a web site there are several ways to present the map of a site, to give visitors an overview of the contents of the site. A popular organization of a web map is hierarchical, as shown in Fig. 7.17 originally from www.dynamicdiagrams.com, but large sites often organize their link set according to some categorization allowing the user to drill down, and "semantically navigate" within well-defined categories and subcategories. As an example, see www.google.com/about.html for an overview of a site and www.google.com/sitemap.html for a more detailed view of the site. Maintaining such a site map of categories can be time intensive in terms of the human effort needed to keep it up to date, and is not necessarily effective when the user is already lost in hyperspace and trying to orient themselves. Supplementing manual categorization with automated machine learning techniques may be a step forward, but such methods are yet to be deployed in practice.

A graphical display, which is faithful to the web site structure, is also possible as in our example web site shown in Fig. 7.5. An innovative way of

Figure 7.15 The WebBrain user interface.

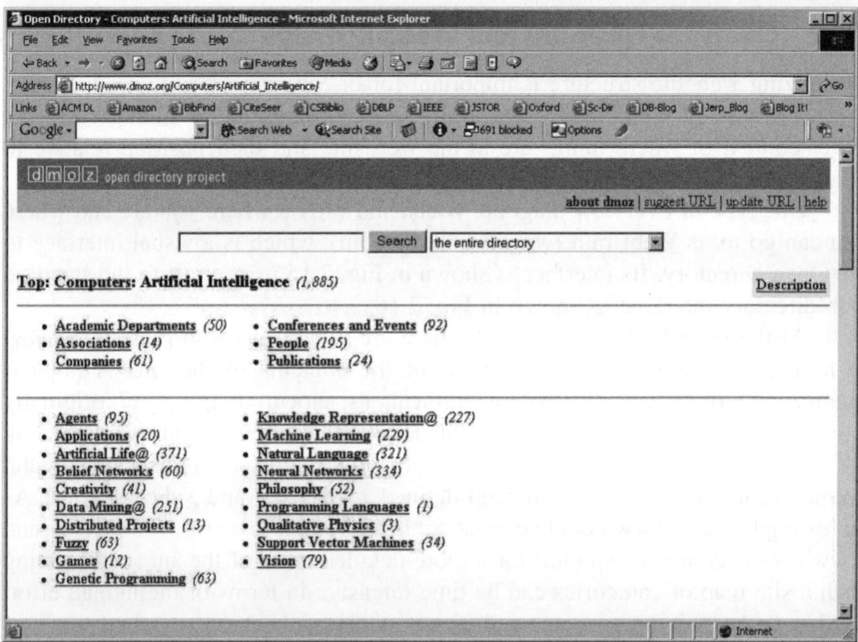

Figure 7.16 Open Directory home page.

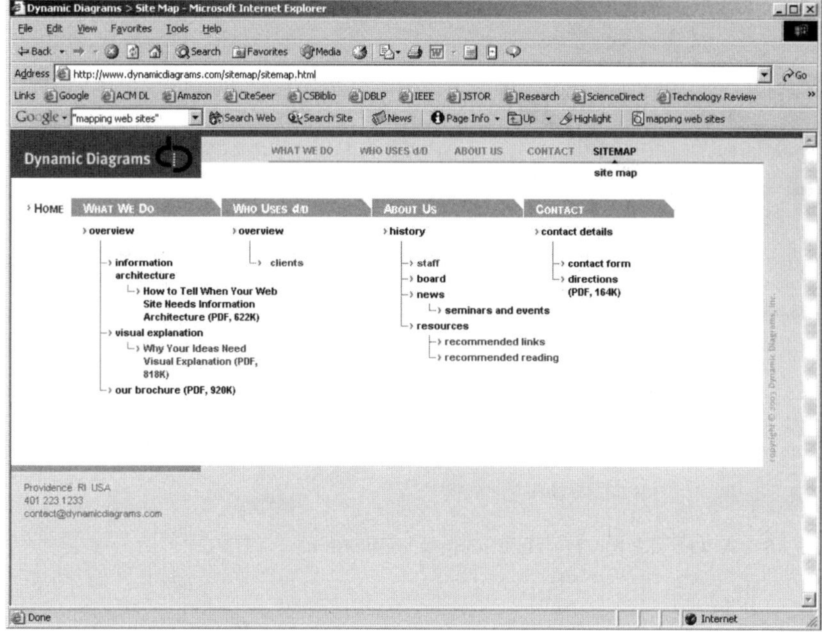

Figure 7.17 Hierarchical site map.

visualizing a web site in 3D, which highlights both the hierarchical structure and the interplay between various levels of the site is shown in Fig. 7.18 as suggested by Kahn *et al.* [355]. An interesting suggestion of Jacob Nielsen, as a standard browser feature, is to support a visualization feature that creates a site map in the browser on-the-fly.[179] Of course Nielsen is only joking, and this is his way of stating the importance of providing web site maps.

Site maps are static and provide a global view, with the user having to navigate through the map to locate the part of the web site they wish to surf. One tool that we have developed within our research group at Birkbeck, University of London, to provide a more dynamic view of the site is the query-specific map. As an example, if you are browsing the Department's web site and your query is "web technologies", a graphical map generated on-the-fly from the web site will display the trails related to the query in a graphical format (see Fig. 7.19). This type of projected site map narrows down the region within the web site that the user should navigate through.

7.6.3 Fisheye Views

How can we navigate visually within a relatively large information space? One way of viewing the space is though a wide-angle lens that shows local objects in

[179]Site map usability, Jacob Nielsen's Alertbox, January 2002. www.useit.com/alertbox/20020106.html.

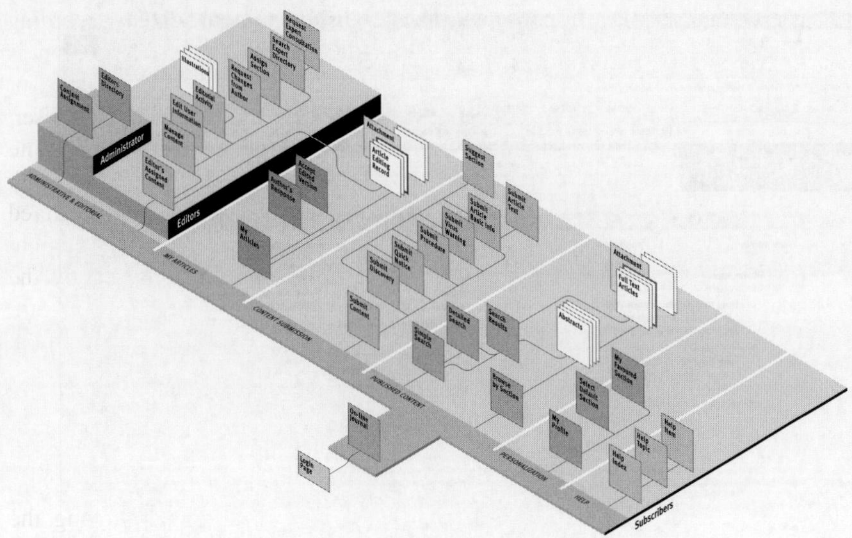

Figure 7.18 A web site for an online journal application.

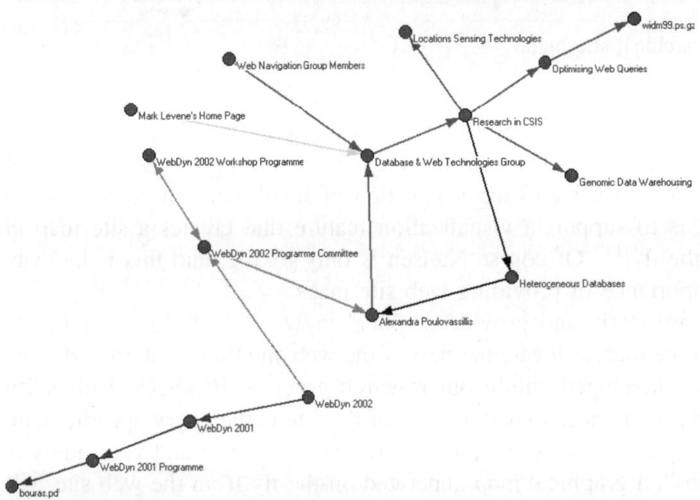

Figure 7.19 Query-specific site map.

great detail while still showing a global view in lesser detail, as one gets further away from the center of activity. Such a view where the local context, within which the user is navigating, is the point of focus and context, giving the user a more global view of the hypertext, and becoming distorted and less clear as one moves away from the point of focus, is called a *fisheye view*. In order to display a web site map as a fisheye view, we can choose the home page to be the focal point of the display. If we allow users to interact with the map, then the focal point can be changed by the movement of a mouse.

The value of a web page within the display is calculated according to its *degree-of-interest*, which decreases as the page under consideration is further away from the focal page of the display [645]. An ambitious kind of site map, based on the fisheye concept is provided by the hyperbolic browser, which allows the user to dynamically focus on different parts of a web site by using a novel visualization technique based on hyperbolic geometry [402]. Inxight (www.inxight.com), which was spun off Xerox PARC in 1997, offered a visualization tool based on the hyperbolic browser, called *StarTree*. Inxight survived the economic downturn of the dot-com bust and was bought by the enterprise software company, Business Objects, in 2007, which was in turn acquired by the multinational software development and consulting corporation, SAP AG, in 2008.

7.6.4 Visualizing Trails within a Web Site

In Section 7.3, we have already introduced the idea of surfers following the "scent of information," that is, picking up the proximal cues, such as text snippets surrounding links and graphics, representing distant content. Visualization of trails that were followed by users, combined with information scent predictions of the trails that satisfy their information seeking goals, can help expose where the strongest scent in the site is and whether the predicted and actual paths match [143].

Often when we look inside a book or a catalogue we riffle through its pages to get a feeling of its content and relevance. This process is known as *rapid serial visual presentation* (RSVP) [621]. In the context of navigation, the outlinks in a web page being browsed can be presented visually using RSVP, as well as a backtracking mechanism to view the trail the user followed to a arrive at the page being browsed. This technique is especially useful for browsing on small screen devices such as mobile phones and personal digital assistants (PDAs). Suppose you are browsing a web page as shown in Fig. 7.20 from [177]. This page can be seen on the display but there is no space on the screen to show the possible destination pages that we can go to next, or to view the trail we have followed to reach the current page. Thus we must trade space for time, and RSVP can be used to examine the destination pages one by one in rapid succession, or to trace the trail we have followed.

VISVIP is a tool that provides a visualization of the trails that users followed within a web site [166]. It is part of a more general set of tools called the NIST Web Metrics Testbed (http://zing.ncsl.nist.gov/WebTools) designed to test and evaluate the usability of web sites. VISVIP overlays the users trails over a visualization of the web site as shown in Fig. 7.21, where each page in the site has a short label attached to it, and its color (or shade) reflects the page type (for example, HTML, image, audio, or video). Users' paths are shown as smoothed curves through the pages in the web site, with arrowheads used to indicate the direction of flow. The time users spent browsing a page is indicated by a dotted vertical bar coming out of the page being inspected, and the height of the line

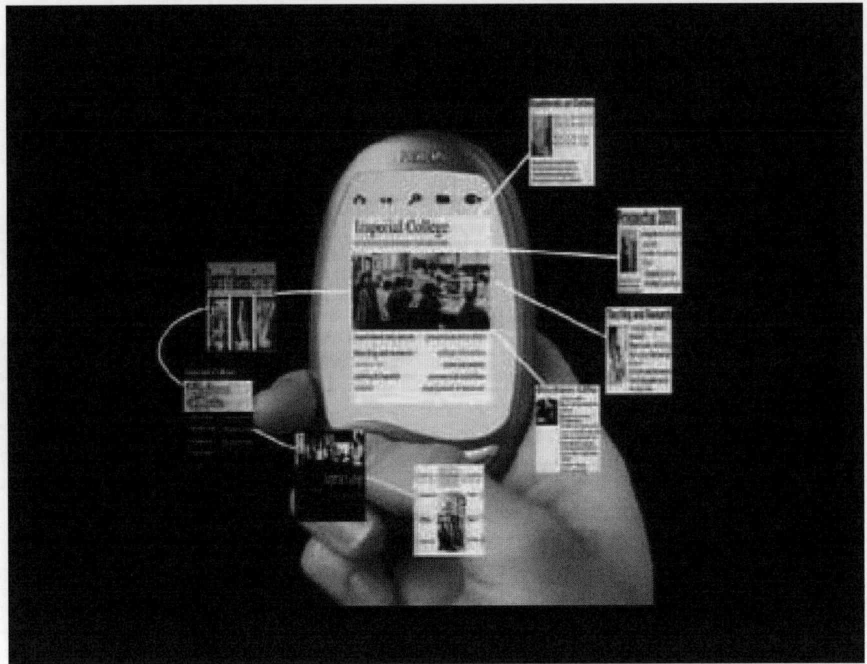

Figure 7.20 RSVP browser on a small screen.

is proportional to the amount of time spent. It is apparent that the page at the bottom left-hand side of the figure is the one that users' spent most time at.

Another interesting visualization of web site usage, with emphasis on the changing structure of the site, was devised by Ben Fry from the MIT Media Laboratory. Anemone is a visualization based on the metaphor of a branching and growing organism, giving the appearance of a sea anemone as can be see in Figs 7.22 and 7.23. Branches appear in the visual representation as data is read from the server log file, and a page is visited for the first time. Usage data allows the structure of the web site to be created on-the-fly rather than being predetermined by knowledge of the topology of the site. To counteract growth, branches not visited, slowly decay away and are eventually removed from the system. Movement rules govern the distance between neighboring pages so that there is as little overlap as possible between branches. Each time a page is revisited the node representing it gets slightly thicker, so that heavily visited pages stand out.

7.6.5 Visual Search Engines

Visualization can also be used in the context of search to help users find information in a graphical way [571], while providing context. Two representatives of this breed of visual search engine are Carrot (www.carrot-search.com) and Kartoo (now defunct), both employing metasearch to query the web. What these

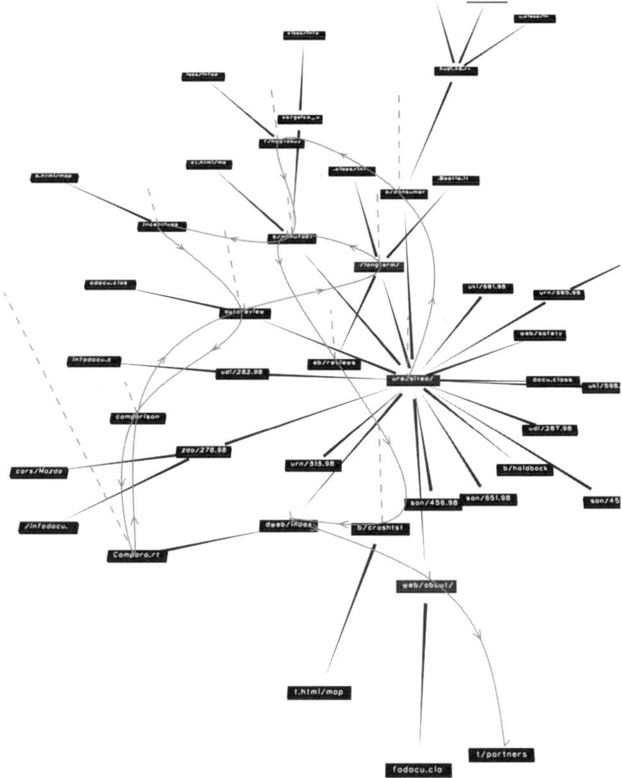

Figure 7.21 VISVIP visualization of user trails laid over the web site. (Source: Gallery of VISVIP Pix, Figure 7.3. www.itl.nist.gov/iaui/vvrg/cugini/webmet/visvip/pix/fig3.gif.)

search engines do is build a topic map [632], using some underlying clustering algorithm, as does Clusty, now Yippy (www.yippy.com), which was discussed in Section 6.3.2 and Carrot, which was discussed in Section 6.3.3. The topic map visualizations created for the query "beatles" by Carrot and Kartoo, respectively, can be seen in Figs 7.24 and 7.25.

7.6.6 Social Data Analysis

Visual analysis of data is a powerful method for turning data into knowledge. Social data analysis combines visual data analysis with social interaction to support collaborative discovery of meaningful patterns or nuggets in data. Collaborative visualization [293] facilitates social data analysis by enabling data sharing, discussion, graphical annotation, and social navigation as an integral part of visual data exploration and analysis.

Several web sites have sprung up to support social data analysis by allowing users to upload data sets, create interactive visualizations, and discuss them online. One of these sites is Many Eyes (http://manyeyes.alphaworks.ibm.com)

Figure 7.22 Sea anemones in an aquarium. (Source: Sea anemones at the aquarium in Bristol Zoo, Bristol, England, taken by Adrian Pingstone in August 2003. http://en.wikipedia.org/wiki/Image:Anemone.bristol.750pix.jpg.)

Figure 7.23 Anemone web site usage visualization. (Source: Mapping how people use a website, Ben Fry's anemone visualization. Mappa Mundi Magazine, Map of the month, June 2001. http://mappa.mundi.net/maps/maps_022.)

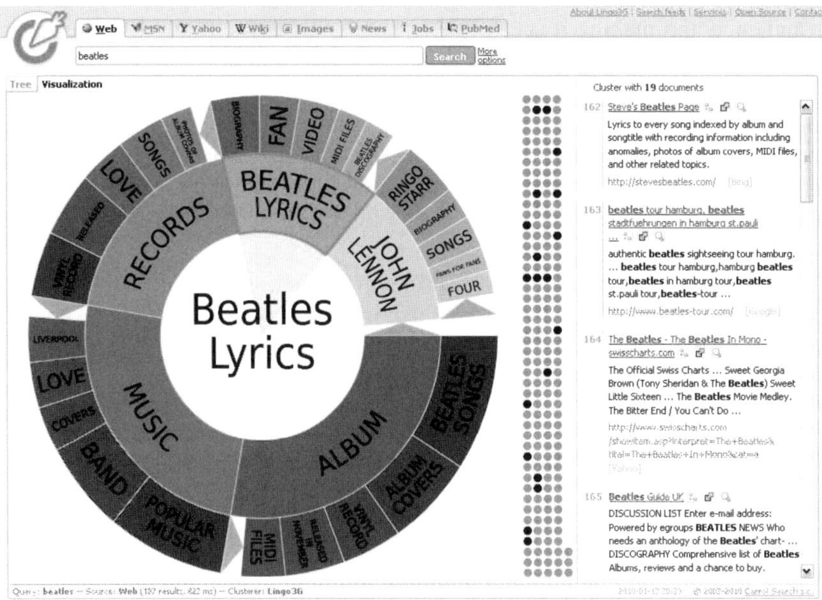

Figure 7.24 Carrot's topic map for the query "beatles".

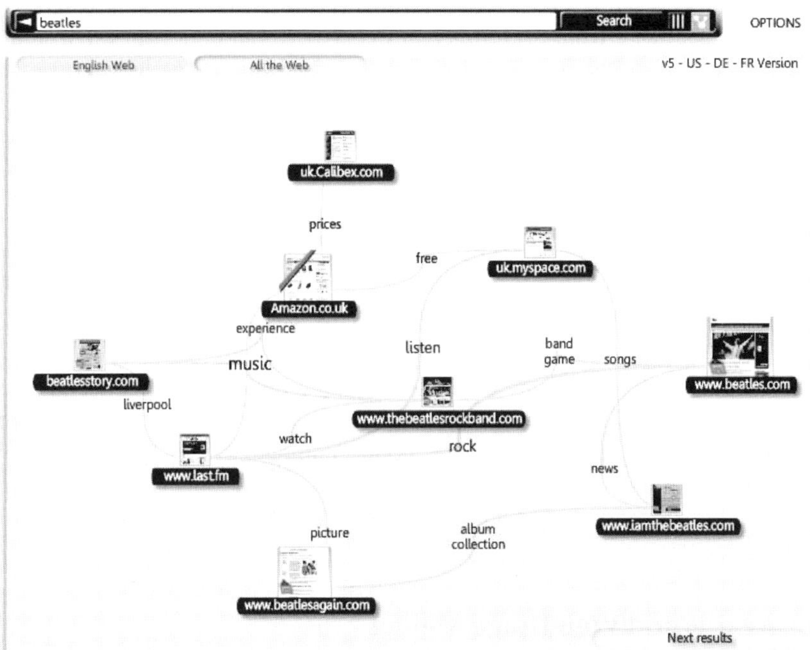

Figure 7.25 Kartoo's topic map for the query "beatles".

[661], launched in 2007. The challenges facing such a site are scaling up to a large audience and making it accessible to nonexpert users. Many Eyes supports a wide range of visualizations divided into several categories, according to the exploration task the user wishes to carry out on the data: (i) see relationships among data points, for example, using a scatter plot; (ii) compare a set of values, for example, using a bar chart; (iii) track rises and falls over time, for example, using a line graph, (iv) see the parts of a whole, for example, using a pie chart; (v) analyze a text, for example, using a tag cloud (see Section 9.8.7); or (vi) see the world, by overlaying data values on a map.

While Many Eyes is a research project, another social data analysis site, Swivel (www.swivel.com) [224], launched in 2006, is a commercial venture. Swivel provides support for generating simple visualizations, in particular, line graphs, scatter plots, bar charts, and pie charts.

7.6.7 Mapping Cyberspace

The issue of mapping cyberspace is one concerning researchers from a variety of disciplines involving, computer scientists, sociologists, geographers, and cartographers [189]. (The term *cyberspace* is a general term used to refer to a virtual space, such as the Internet, residing within a computer or a network of computers.) To map the Web, a spatial model must be formulated, and although it is large in a physical sense, since it is spread out all over the world, it differs from a geographical map in several ways. In cyberspace the notion of distance in the traditional sense is nonexistent. Remotely distant physical sites may be just a few clicks away from each other in cyberspace, and one can often jump from one web site to another by a single click, for example with the aid of a search engine. We leave it to the reader to explore this fascinating area further and browse through the cybermaps that can be found on the Web, for example using image search.

7.7 NAVIGATION IN VIRTUAL AND PHYSICAL SPACES

As computing is becoming ubiquitous, users will be carrying wearable devices that can record a digital trail of their navigation sessions through physical spaces such as buildings. More than any other device, the mobile phone has become an integral part of our lives, enabling "anytime and anywhere" communication not only between people, but also between mobile computing devices. The ability to detect the location of a user carrying a mobile phone or any other mobile computer is a technology that promises to make the web location aware; we will take up on this issue in Chapter 8 when we discuss the mobile web.

7.7.1 Real-World Web Usage Mining

Web usage mining, as I have described it, attempts to find patterns in web data collected from server logs of users surfing through the virtual space, we call the Web. Now imagine that surfer Sue is navigating through a physical space such as a museum, and that the trail that she is following during her visit is recorded on a web server that has a communication link with her mobile device. Within a museum the communication link could be established through a wireless network using Wi-Fi (Wireless Fidelity, www.wi-fi.org) or Bluetooth technology (www.bluetooth.com). If this is the case, then we have created a bridge between the physical world and cyberspace, and we can adapt and modify web usage mining techniques to discover navigation patterns in physical trails.

As with web usage mining, real-world usage mining, can be used by, say a museum, to figure out how visitors are navigating through an exhibition space, and also to personalize users' visits by recording their individual experiences of the exhibition. Figure 7.26 shows how the trail of a visitor to a museum exhibition may be embedded on a map showing the topology of the physical space. By keeping a hypertextual record of the visit, such as the one shown in Fig. 7.26, where the exhibition space becomes a web site, the visitor can continue navigating through the exhibition within the virtual space of the museum web site. There is benefit to the museum, as the dialogue with their visitors extends beyond the confines of the museum space, and, in addition, usage mining techniques can enable them to gain a better understanding of how people negotiate the space, which may help improve various aspects of the space such as access, layout, and provision of navigational aids. There is also benefit for visitors, who can augment their experiences at the physical museum, with new experiences at the

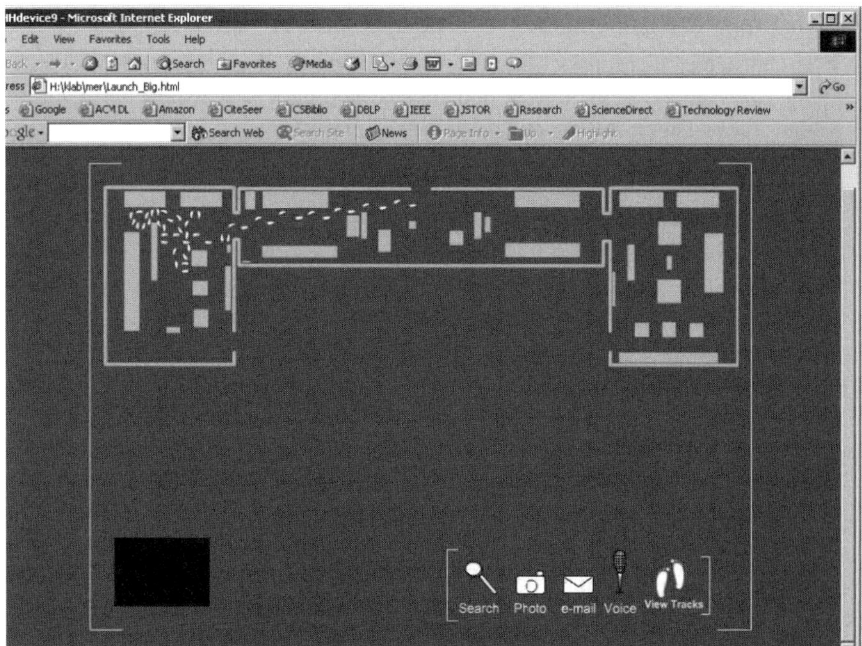

Figure 7.26 The trail of a visitor to a museum.

museum's web site, personalized through usage mining techniques that take into account the trails they had followed while at the museum.

Research along these lines to predict a visitor's next location in a museum was carried out by Bohnert *et al.* [87]. They propose a collaborative model, taking into account both the time users spent viewing an exhibit as an indication of user interest, and a first-order Markov model of probabilities of users moving from one exhibit to another as a measure of popularity of trails through the museum. Experimental results showed that predictions based on the Markov model are superior to those based on the time viewing model, but that a hybrid model, combining both, is significantly more accurate than the individual models.

7.7.2 The Museum Experience Recorder

We now briefly describe a possible wearable device, which we call the *museum experience recorder*, which allows the transporting of navigation experiences within a physical space into a virtual space such as the Web. We will avoid implementation details in our description, but stress that it is within the remit of current technology. The experience recorder is a small, lightweight wearable computing device, the size of a badge, which has the following computing capabilities:

1. It can monitor the orientation of a user in the exhibition and embed the user's trail through the exhibition on top of the exhibit map, with temporal information relating to the times the user spent at various landmarks.
2. It can detect landmarks within the navigation session, for example, where the user views an exhibit. When such a landmark is detected the recorder can interact with it. The interaction may involve:
   (a) downloading an image of the exhibit, or a hyperlink to the image;
   (b) downloading a hyperlink to content about the exhibit such as text, or, more generally hypermedia;
   (c) taking a picture (or a video) of the user viewing the exhibit, or a hyperlink to such a picture; and
   (d) recording the user's voice when instructed to do so.

The experience recorder works together with a wireless network, embedded in the architecture of the museum. After a navigation session, the log data created by the experience recorder is postprocessed into a record of the trail followed by the visitor, and is embedded on a map of the physical space that was navigated. The trail record is made available to the visitor as a web site and is augmented with links to relevant content. The process of visiting the museum is then augmented with a virtual record of the visitor's experiences, and finally the loop is closed when the museum is revisited. This can be viewed as a learning process, which we call *navigational learning* [541].

Although we have described this technology with the context of a museum, it could be used for recording any real-world navigation experience. In fact, current smartphone technology could support all the functionalities of the experience recorder, and is arguably the most practical means of implementing it [551].

7.7.3 Navigating in the Real World

Models of spatial cognition describe the representations of processes that relate to location-based behavior such as navigation from one place to another [284]. Spatial behavior involves place recognition, direction orientation, and cognitive maps, which are mental representations of space involving topological information. Navigation can be enhanced by the use of various tools such as maps providing topological information, landmarks that are memorable places, trails in analogy to footprints through the space, and direction finding and orientation tools such as the compass.

The activity of user navigation within a hypertext such as the Web can be compared to the activity of *wayfinding* through a physical space, where wayfinding is defined as the process used to orient and navigate oneself within a space. The overall goal of wayfinding is to transport oneself from one place to another within the space [370]. Both activities, in a virtual space and a physical one, include user tasks such as being aware of one's current location, planning a route to follow, and executing the plan. Research into wayfinding in physical spaces is based upon the assumption of the existence of cognitive maps encoding the user's knowledge about the space being navigated through. Such spatial knowledge can be classified into the representations of place, route, and survey knowledge, which concerns the spatial layout of the salient places.

Reality mining pertains to the collection of real-world data from sensors and the inferences made from the data about human social behavior. Cell phone sensor data collected on a large scale is an example, where social patterns such as proximity and interaction between people, daily and weekly routines, can be deduced from the data [197].

When longitudinal data is available, that is, data that is collected over a period of time, then structure in the daily routines of individuals can be analyzed and can be used to predict subsequent behavior and to cluster individuals into groups with similar behavior. One way to model a person's daily routine is in terms of the locations he/she inhabits at any time during the day. Assume that the set of locations is fixed and that we have N of them; for example, home, work, and other locations that the person may visit during a day. Also assume that we take hourly measurements, to obtain a matrix with one 24-item vector per location for any given day, with a binary value in the vector positions for each hour. So, for example, for the home vector on a given day we may have ones for hours 1–7 and 19–24, and zeros for the other hours; the vector values will vary from day to day according to the user's activities on that day. We can now combine the N location vectors for each day to obtain *daily behavior vectors*, each having $N \times 24$ dimensions. Using *principal component analysis* (PCA) [346] we can obtain eigenvectors (which are called *eigenbehaviors* in Ref. [198]) ranked by the total amount of variance they account for in the data. The top few eigenbehaviors will account for most of the variance in an individual's behavior, and can be used for further analysis. For example, the first eigenbehavior may correspond to a typical week day routine, while the second eigenbehavior may correspond to a typical weekend routine.

Experiments with eigenbehaviors have shown that they are effective for finding structure in individual's routines, and, moreover, can also be used to model aggregate behavior within communities in a social network based on the affiliation of individuals, and to find similar individuals within these communities.

Mining user trails in a physical space to learn significant locations and in order to predict users' movement is also possible from longitudinal reality mining data sets. A Markov chain model, similar to the one we have proposed for modeling navigation within web sites, was suggested by Ashbrook and Starner [35]. To make the prediction meaningful only significant locations were used, where a significant location is one where a user spends a meaningful amount of time. When movement is monitored with GPS technology, a reasonable method is to consider a location to be significant when a signal is lost, that is, when a building is entered.

In a more general setting, reality mining data may be collected from several sources of wireless data such as cell phones, GPS, Wi-Fi, and Bluetooth. We use the term *reality analytics* to convey collection, measurement, and reporting of reality mining data to discover and predict movement in a physical space. Reality analytics is concerned with four dimensions of activity: *spatial* (where are the users), *temporal* (when are they there), *social* (with whom are they), and *context* (what is the context of their activity). The operators of wireless services can use the knowledge obtained from reality analytics to provide better and more targeted services to their customers. An architecture for a navigation engine to support reality analytics is shown in Fig. 7.27. We are developing a prototype navigation engine within our research group at Birkbeck University of London, with the aim of providing an efficient platform for the querying, mining, and visualizing very large data sets [529].

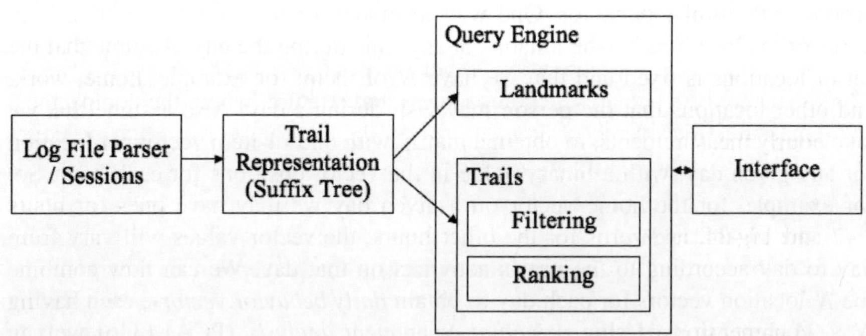

Figure 7.27 Navigation engine architecture.

CHAPTER SUMMARY

- Users suffer from frustration when surfing the Web, more so novices than experienced users. Some of the causes of this frustration are to do with slow and unreliable internet connections, bad web site design, and confusing and annoying forms of advertising such as pop-up ads.
- Browsers support various navigation tools. The link marker is one of the basic tools that tells users which links can be followed and which links have been recently clicked on. The back button is probably the most used navigation tool to get a web page, which reinforces the evidence that four out of five of the pages we view have been seen before. Search engine toolbars allow users to submit queries directly from any page they are browsing, which is one reason why they have become very popular.
- Other prominent tools are the bookmarks and the history list. There have been various suggestions to improve the bookmarks tool, for instance by automatically clustering bookmarked pages into folders. It has also been proposed to integrate the history list, the bookmarks and the back and forward buttons into a single revisitation tool.
- Breadcrumb trails are a useful navigation tool within web sites. These can be static, that is, they do not change according to the path that the user arrived at a given page, or dynamic, that is, showing how the user arrived at the page. A study has shown that in the presence of breadcrumb trails surfers use the back button less frequently.
- Quicklinks provide users with up to eight links below the first result of a navigational query, in order to help users navigate within the site of the result by directly jumping to one of these eight pages. Search engine logs and toolbar user trail data can be used as input to an algorithm that selects the quicklinks to display.
- Many of the browser navigation tools originate from the orientation tools designed for hypertext in the pre-web days. The Hypercard programming environment, from the late 1980s, supported many of the features of modern day browsers, and is still used today by a group of enthusiasts.
- The potential gain is a link-based metric, capturing the notions of centrality and connectedness, which is designed to measure the utility of a web page as a starting point for navigation. Other metrics that can be used to analyze the structure of a site are the compactness and stratum, where the compactness measures the degree of connectivity of the site, and the stratum measures the degree of linearity in the site.
- Measuring the usability of a web site may help to suggest improvements to the organization of the site. One idea, based on foraging theory, is to make use of the scent of information, which is the perception of the value and cost obtained from proximal cues within web pages representing distant content, in order to try and ascertain whether users are achieving their goals. Another measure of the navigability in a web site is the average cost

of navigation, that is, how long does it take to a reach a destination web page from the home page.

- Web data mining can be viewed from three perspectives: content mining, structure mining, and usage mining. Weblog data can be collected from web servers in a standard format, and used to discover patterns in users' navigation behavior.
- The hit rate and conversion rate are e-metrics used to measure the "success" of a web site. The hit rate is simply the number of visits to the site, which is a measure of popularity, while the conversion rate measures the number of visitors that were converted into customers.
- Web analytics is concerned with the use of e-metrics to provide meaningful reports and charts that allow webmasters to track the usage of their site and measure the "success" of the site with respect to its objectives. "Stickiness" is a measure of how long users stay on the site, "slipperiness" is a measure of how quickly users leave the site, and "leakage" is a measure of the drop out rate from the site.
- Web analytics tools often require tagging of web pages with snippets of JavaScript code. This solves the problem that when cached pages are displayed they are not recorded in the server log file. Moreover, it allows outsourcing the web analytics in situations when the web servers and thus the log files are local. Search engines provide web analytics tools to their customers that allow tracking and optimizing online advertising campaigns.
- Weblog analyzers provide standard usage statistics for a web site over a period of time. Identifying the user from log data can be done by IP address (the standard way), through cookies that have been placed on the user's machine, or by user login information. In order to identify users' trails their sessions must be identified from the log data. Time-oriented sessionizing places a time limit on the total duration of a session, or a maximum time interval between any two page views. Navigation-oriented sessionizing considers the links that were followed within the web site.
- A Markov chain can be used to model the navigation patterns of users through a web site. An efficient algorithm operating on a Markov chain, constructed from sessionized log data, can find the frequent trails that users follow in the web site. The basic, first-order model ignores the navigation history and assumes that decisions of where to go to next are based only the current page being viewed. This first-order model has been refined into a higher-order Markov model, to take into account the navigation history of a user prior to viewing a given page. Another important issue is that of combing content and usage mining, in order to have better knowledge of the user's intent.
- Web usage mining has applications in e-commerce, prefetching, and caching web pages, in the construction of adaptive web sites, and more generally in trend detection and reputation tracking, when web data across several web sites is available.

- Information extraction is the process of extracting structured information from unstructured or semistructured web sources. Entity and relationship structures are most commonly extracted. Typical entity extraction are named entities such as people, organizations, and location names. The two main machine learning methods employed in information extraction are rule-based and statistical. Open information extraction attempts to extract information from the Web in an autonomous, domain-independent, and scalable manner.
- The Best Trail algorithm semiautomates user navigation by suggesting relevant trails to the user, given an input query. It is a probabilistic algorithm that builds trails by traversing the Markov chain model of the site, where the probabilities are interpreted in terms of the relevance, to the user, of following a link. The algorithm scores trails according to the paths the algorithm follows by applying a decay factor to the score of pages, which decreases with the distance from the starting point. Trails can be displayed to the user as a linear sequence, as a navigation tree, or in the form of a graph.
- Visualizing the structure of a web site can help users orient themselves within the site; overview diagrams, web site maps, and fisheye views are examples of such visualization. Visualization of the navigation patterns of users through a web site can supplement web usage mining. Trails can also be visualized using techniques such as RSVP, which provide an alternative browsing mechanism. Visualization can also be used by search engines as an alternative user interface.
- Social data analysis combines visual data analysis with social interaction to support collaborative discovery of meaningful patterns and insights from the data. Collaborative visualization enables data sharing, discussion, graphical annotation, and social navigation as part of visual exploration in a social context.
- The ubiquity of mobile devices and the ability to detect their location gives rise to real-world data mining. Mining navigation patterns of users through a physical space such as a museum can be used to create a bridge between physical and virtual spaces, by keeping a hypertextual record of the trails that emerge, and applying web mining techniques to this record. The museum experience recorder is a possible device to capture user navigation within a physical space, which can be postprocessed into a web site to be explored by the user.
- Reality mining includes the processes involving the collection of data from sensors and the inferences about human behavior made from this data over a period of time. Structure in daily routines can be analyzed from longitudinal data and used to predict subsequent behavior.

EXERCISES

7.1. **(Mini-project)**. Topic detection and tracking (TDT) [26] is an emerging area, whose aim is to analyze a continuous stream of text from a newswire or a newsfeed, breaking it into individual stories, monitoring the stories for new events, and grouping related stories together.

TDT is narrower than topic-based categorization in that it is event-based. It is concerned with topics that start at some point in time, develop according to the events that follow, and become obsolete a some later time point.

TDT is focused on the following five tasks: (i) story segmentation, (ii) first story detection, (iii) clustering stories as they arrive, (iv) tracking a story as it develops, and (v) deciding whether two stories are topically linked.

Give an example of each of the five TDT tasks, using two topical news stories that have recently appeared in a newsfeed, by tracking the stories over a short period of time.

Using your example suggest techniques that may be used to tackle the five TDT tasks.

7.2. **(Explore)**. A document stream is a set of documents organized by topic, whose arrival is temporally ordered. Examples of document streams are e-mail, online discussion forums, weblogs, and news articles.

Suppose we are tracking an online discussion forum on a single topic. Typically the activity generated on the topic will change over time, and, moreover, there may be bursts of discussion activity triggered by some external event. Identifying bursty activity in such a stream corresponds to detecting high-frequency spikes of certain words or phrases used to describe the topic being tracked [377].

Choose a conversation topic from your e-mail, and track the topic within as long an interval as you can using a set of characteristic keywords for the topic.

Suggest a method for automating the detection of bursts within a stream.

7.3. **(Miniproject)**. Summarize the salient features of the common weblog file format (httpd.apache.org/docs/logs.html) using examples from a recent log file you have access to.

Suggest how to analyze the referrals from search engines, including tracking pay per click campaigns.

Use the log file at your disposal to illustrate the analysis.

7.4. **(Explore)**. Tabbed browsing is a browser feature that allows you to open several web pages in the same window and switch between them by clicking on the tabs; see www.mozilla.org/firefox/tabbed-browsing.html, for tabbed browsing in the Firefox web browser.

Discuss tabbed browsing as a navigation tool in the context of getting lost in hyperspace.

Live bookmarks is another feature implemented in Firefox that allows you to bookmark headlines of newsfeeds published on web sites; see www.mozilla.com/firefox/livebookmarks.html. The format used to publish the newsfeeds is called RSS (really simple syndication); see http://blogs.law.harvard.edu/tech/rss. A live bookmark is different from an ordinary, static bookmark, in that it always displays the latest headlines from the newsfeed as they are published by the web site bookmarked.

Comment on the usefulness of live bookmarks, and how you might add functionality to this feature.

7.5. **(Explore)**. Web usage mining can be used for personalization by tracking visitors on an individual basis, and grouping similar visitors together to make recommendations [477].

Assuming that the log data has already been divided into sessions, first suggest a method for clustering these sessions. Then, treating the resulting clusters as aggregate user profiles, suggest a method for recommending a ranked set of pages to a user navigating the web site, from which he or she can choose the next page to be viewed.

7.6. **(Discuss)**. Users express their information needs both by querying search engines and by navigating the Web by following links. In predicting which link users will click on, users' past behavior, based on the keywords in the pages they visit, has shown to be a good predictor of future behavior [84].

Discuss the differences in querying and navigation in terms of predicting users' behavior and how the two modalities can be combined to form a more accurate predictor.

7.7. **(Explore)**. Treemap visualization is a method for displaying hierarchical data in terms of nested rectangles, and has been suggested as a method of displaying clustered or classified results [149].

Explore this concept in the context of displaying web analytics data.

7.8. **(Miniproject)**. Web search engines are being used in unexpected and novel ways, due their function as "universal knowledge sources."

One application of mobile and wearable computing is to provide support for older people that need help in carrying out activities of daily living such as "making a cup of tea" [540]. A prerequisite for this application is building statistical models that capture the probabilities of certain objects being involved in a given activity. For example, when making tea, we may expect to see a tea bag 60% of the time, and sugar only 40% of the time.

Suggest how a web search engine can be used to discover the probability of an object occurring in an activity, where the object and activity are each described by a short phrase. Use your suggestion to compute several such conditional probabilities of your choice.

CHAPTER 8

THE MOBILE WEB

"The world has arrived at an age of cheap complex devices of great reliability; and something is bound to come of it."

— Vannevar Bush, Electrical Engineer and Science Administrator

THE MOBILE web is the extension of the stationary web to mobile phones, PDAs, and other mobile and handheld computing devices. The limitations of such devices in terms of screen size, computing power, bandwidth, energy capacity, and the lack of traditional input devices forces us to reassess and tailor the search and navigation technologies we have presented to face the new challenges posed. With the ubiquity of the mobile phone, it is inevitable that the mobile and stationary web will eventually become inseparable. Meanwhile, mobile devices such as phones provide additional impetus for developing technologies such as voice, touch screen, and pen input interfaces, and web services such as personalization and location awareness.

CHAPTER OBJECTIVES

- Introduce the mobile web as an extension of the (stationary) web, and the challenges that it entails in terms of user interaction.
- Discuss markup language support for mobile devices.
- Discuss the i-mode mobile service as a leader in the delivery of wireless internet services.
- Present mobile commerce (m-commerce) as the mobile counterpart of e-commerce.
- Present two case studies of mobile services: the delivery of personalized news and learning resources to mobile devices.
- Discuss mobile web browsers, and the trend to support a media-rich mobile web browsing experience.
- Introduce the problems in mobile information seeking on mobile devices.

An Introduction to Search Engines and Web Navigation, by Mark Levene

- Discuss different methods of text entry on mobile devices, including predictive text.
- Introduce voice recognition on mobile devices and its potential as an input modality.
- Discuss information presentation on mobile devices, including summarization.
- Introduce the navigation problem in mobile portals, and the click-distance as a measure of user navigation effort.
- Introduce a method for reducing the click-distance based on machine learning techniques, whereby the structure of a mobile portal becomes adaptive and personalized.
- Introduce the issues of searching on mobile devices.
- Discuss the problem of mobile search interfaces.
- Present solutions for supporting mobile web search.
- Describe a solution to mobile search, which involves offline searching of information stored on the mobile device.
- Indicate how mobile search can be carried out as a background activity on a desktop PC, and transferred to the mobile device once the search is completed, to be browsed in an offline mode.
- Describe a technique for improving mobile web search utilizing query logs.
- Indicate how mobile search can be personalized.
- Discuss the issues related to location-aware mobile search.

8.1 THE PARADIGM OF MOBILE COMPUTING

Mobile and wearable computing devices, have been miniaturized to the degree that we can carry them around with us at all times, and they also have the ability to interact with other computing devices, some of which are embedded in the environment. While the Web is an informational, navigational, and transactional tool, mobile devices, such as mobile phones and personal digital assistants (PDAs), add to it the dimension of being a ubiquitous and pervasive social communication tool.

Mobile computing supports the paradigm of "anywhere, anytime access" whereby users can have continuous access to computing and web resources at all times and wherever they may be. The *mobile web* is a natural extension of the (stationary) Web and as such poses new problems and challenges, especially due to the fact that the development of software tools to support user interaction with these devices is lagging far behind the innovations in hardware.

The limitations of mobile devices in terms of screen size, computing power, bandwidth, energy capacity, and the lack of traditional input devices such as keyboard and mouse, mean that alternative input modalities such as pen, voice, and touch screens will become the norm for such devices. As a consequence innovative software solutions such as voice recognition, handwriting recognition, predictive text systems, and novel user interfaces will be necessary.

Users of mobile devices are often on the move and do *not* have the attention span or the time that users have when sitting in front of their desktop or laptop. Thus, information needs that do *not* require complex and lengthy navigation such as browsing news headlines, addresses, and train schedules, can readily be supported on mobile devices. Other information needs, which involve more navigation such as information gathering on a particular topic are poorly suited for mobile devices [602].

Location aware services, which focus the application delivered to users to their physical location, can play an important role in narrowing down the information needs of mobile users. For example, technologies such as GPS and wireless networks can assist users in physical navigation, such as helping them to find a local restaurant serving their favorite cuisine. The time dimension can also play a part in the delivery of mobile services in order to further narrow down the user's information needs; in the local restaurant example, the time of day will obviously have an effect on the information provided.

8.1.1 Wireless Markup Language

To support the delivery of web services to mobile devices, a standard and open wireless protocol such as WAP (wireless application protocol, which is part of the open mobile alliance, www.openmobilealliance.org) is needed [560]. WAP supports the wireless markup language (WML), which allows developers to deliver web pages to mobile devices. When designing content for mobile devices it is convenient to think in terms of a deck of cards rather than in terms of pages, with a single card representing a screen full of information on a device. Often, a standard web page will be represented by linking several cards together. WML has eventually evolved into extensible hypertext markup language (XHTML), which is a W3C (World Wide Web Consortium, www.w3c.org) standard, set to replace HTML. XHTML is based on XML, which is the language behind the semantic web vision of machine-understandable information, and in doing so enforces compatibility with standard web browsers. Moreover, XHTML is suitable for mobile devices, since it separates the contents of a web page (or a deck of cards) from its display format, making it easier to implement wrappers to display standard web pages on mobile devices. (A *wrapper* is a program that converts between different formats so that they can be displayed on different interfaces.)

Another, possibly more compelling, reason for adopting XHTML as the standard markup language is the convergence, to XHTML, of various variants of HTML used for mobile devices. One such variant is compact hypertext markup language (cHTML), which is a subset of standard HTML, designed specifically for mobile devices, and is being used as the markup language for the i-mode wireless internet service. The success of cHTML has been notable in Japan, with easy access to more than 95,000 web sites as of late 2009. Moreover, Jindal et al. [342] found that over 90% of cHTML pages are in Japanese, while only about 6% are in English.

8.1.2 The i-mode Service

Japan's NTT DoCoMo *i-mode* mobile phone service (www.nttdocomo.com/services/imode) is one of the most notable successes of the mobile web. It was first offered in February 1999 and has grown at an extremely rapid pace to a volume of about 50 million subscribers in Japan as of late 2009.[180] In Europe i-mode has been far less successful, partly due to the uptake of the mobile web being much slower in Europe and also due to i-mode being a closed system that requires proprietary software to be installed in the handsets and web sites to be specifically designed for the service.[181]

The huge difference between the numbers of early mobile web users in Japan and Europe is typical of the East–West divide, in this aspect of mobile phone usage. Data from 2001, showed Japan and Korea leading the field, with 72.5% and 59.1%, respectively, of mobile phone users subscribing to mobile web services, and the USA and Europe trailing behind with less than 8% of mobile users subscribing to mobile web services (in Canada and Finland the uptake at that time was 13.8% and 16.5%, respectively) [324].

Eventually, the West has been catching up in mobile internet uptake. According to Cisco (www.cisco.com) [151], global mobile traffic will double every year until 2013, increasing 66 times between 2008 and 2013. By that time it is predicted that 80% of mobile traffic will be driven by high-end mobile devices with fast internet connections. Moreover, Western Europe will have the most mobile video traffic of all regions by 2013. (It is interesting to note that a smartphone such as the iPhone or the BlackBerry generates as much traffic as 30 basic-feature mobile phones, while a laptop generates as much traffic as 450 basic-feature mobile phones.) Also by 2013, Western Europe will account for about 28% of all mobile internet traffic, while Japan will account for about 7.5% of the traffic. In comparison, in 2009 Western Europe accounted for about 30% of the mobile traffic, while Japan accounted for about 16.5% of the traffic.

i-mode provides a variety of wireless internet services. E-mail is the most popular service, where statistics from 2004 show that subscribers receive on an average 10 e-mail messages a day, which is equivalent to 750 Japanese characters. According to Japanese survey results, e-mail from mobile devices has a positive effect on social interaction with friends, as e-mails are mainly exchanged between close friends and family, while on a PC e-mail is mainly used for business purposes. Other services include information such as weather, news, train schedules, city maps, and direct web browsing of i-mode compatible content. i-mode allows mobile commerce transactions such as online banking, ticket reservation, and finding a restaurant. i-mode also supports Java-based applications, extending i-mode to dynamic applications such as games, with rich animation capabilities and user interaction [391].

Jeffrey Lee Funk [236] has been investigating the reasons for the huge early success of the mobile web in Japan as opposed to the West. It appears

[180]NTT DoCoMo Subscriber Growth. www.nttdocomo.com/companyinfo/subscriber.html.

[181]Forerunner of mobile Internet, i-mode is fading in Europe, by Kevin J. O'Brien, July 2007. www.nytimes.com/2007/07/17/business/worldbusiness/17iht-imode.5.6701270.html.

that using the mobile web is more appropriate for young people to whom the portability aspect of mobile devices outweighs the problems associated with their size, computing power, and bandwidth. This has been less disruptive for Japanese service providers than for their Western counterparts, who have traditionally been more focused on business users rather than on young people, to which the mobile web is initially more appropriate and attractive. As a result of the emphasis on young users, new market concepts and technologies that form the basis for the mobile internet have evolved. The popularity of entertainment in Japan's mobile internet use has led to new firms becoming market leaders in providing services such as ring tones, screen savers, photos, short videos, horoscopes, games, and other entertainment related content.

Apart from entertainment, personalized information services have been very popular in the Japanese mobile internet market. Examples of such services are personalized news, sports and weather services, train/bus timetables, and personal banking facilities, which can be accessed through bookmarked URLs, thus saving the user interaction time.

An interesting trend has been the popularity of e-mail magazine portals, where a personalized web page is created for the user and its URL is delivered through e-mail. These portals specialize in particular topics to which users subscribe, and relies on "viral marketing" to promote their services by including links, in each e-mail magazine, to key places on the provider's web site. Opt-in e-mail mobile services have been very successful in Japan for advertising and sending users discount coupons, which can, for example, be redeemed directly in shops via short-range infrared communication technologies present in new generation mobile devices.

Mobile shopping in Japan is a market which, back in 2002, exceeded US$20 million a month in sales. Popular mobile shopping items include CDs, DVDs, concert and train tickets, games software, fashion and accessories, as opposed to the (stationary) Web, where travel, computers, and books dominate the shopping market. As with mobile content services, most purchases are made through opt-in e-mail, and the top-ranked products are the popular ones.

Location-aware services have not yet realized their potential, especially outside Japan. To a large degree this is due to the fact that mobile phone companies have given priority to voice and short message service (SMS) traffic over mobile internet traffic, since their profit margins and market are much larger for these. There is also the issue of location detection (geolocation) technology, which can be network-based or can make use of GPS. Network-based geolocation can be done by sensing the distance from the nearest base station antenna, but is only accurate if the density of antennas is large enough. On the other hand, assisted GPS [187] offers superior accuracy, by making use of a GPS receiver embedded in the phone and the network's ability to process the information, but there is an additional cost of putting GPS technology into phones and setting up the network to calculate the geolocation information. In addition, to supply location-aware services a sufficiently large information base of destinations such as restaurants, hotels, and bars, having large coverage, needs to be put in place, and this requires partnerships between the information providers and the mobile phone companies.

The way in which the mobile web has evolved in Japan has important implications for Western mobile service providers. So far they have focused on enabling technologies, rather than on finding the groups of users who will use the mobile web. Another factor in Europe is the success of SMS, since in the past, service providers had not wished mobile web services to effect revenues from SMS.

8.2 MOBILE WEB SERVICES

People carrying mobile devices have special requirements; their information needs often necessitating immediate, compact, and personalized answers, with minimal interaction. To cater to these needs many search services and portals provide a mobile version of their offerings, and there are other portals that specialize in mobile services. There are also services that take into account the geographical location of the mobile device requesting the service, called *location-based services* (LBSs). Applications of LBSs include mobile guides, intelligent transport systems, location-based gaming, and assistive technology to aid people with health problems [557].

8.2.1 M-Commerce

Mobile commerce (m-commerce) [459], the descendent of e-commerce for the wireless web, may yet turn to be a "killer application," as a new generation of web-enabled mobile devices hits the street.

To benefit from m-commerce, devices need access to some basic mobile services that will most probably come prepackaged with the device's operating system. These include e-mail, messaging, web browsing, a voice interface, and location sensing capability. (The user will often have a choice of service provider for some of these services, but many users will be satisfied with the prepacked services.) Once these services are in place the user will be able to interact with other connected users and surf the wireless web.

Mobile portals provide their users with various services, and, in general, the flavor of these services is the same as in standard web portal services. Information services include news, sports, stock quotes, weather, travel, entertainment, yellow pages, hotels, restaurants, and other web directory services; some of these services will be location aware. Shopping and booking facilities need to be personalized and navigation efficient. Electronic tickets (e-tickets) enable bookings to be more efficient by saving time and paperwork; e-tickets can be used, for example, to book flights, trains, cinema, theater, and opera shows. Other portal services that can be delivered to a mobile device include online banking, gaming, and stock trading. Mobile portals need not be commercial and may deliver services pertaining to, for example, e-government, local authority, or e-learning.

Portals may also specialize in one of the above services such as the provision of maps and directions. This particular type of personal navigation service is important in the areas of travel and tourism, for users wanting to know where they are, where a service or site they are looking for is, and how to get there. In fact, the three major search engines, as well as MapQuest (owned by AOL, http://wireless.mapquest.com), provide mobile mapping and direction finding services.

Going beyond personal navigation, location-based services can have a social element. One such application is the ability to see in real time where your family and friends are at any given time and allowing you to quickly send a message to them. Several products building on the idea of sharing your location are Google Latitude (www.google.com/latitude), Yahoo's fire eagle (http://fireeagle.yahoo.net), and Loopt (www.loopt.com). These applications raise some major privacy concerns as the location information is made known to a third party that must be trusted. The front page heading on my local newspaper reporting on the launch of Google Latitude on February 5, 2009 read, "Google puts spy in your pocket".[182] In this context it is important for users of location-based services to know when an application can detect your location, how it uses it, and who it may share this information with [657].

Mozilla Geode (https://wiki.mozilla.org/Labs/Geode) is a Firefox add-on, which lets you share your location with another application. When an application requests your location a notification bar lets you know this and allows you to specify whether you are willing to share your exact location, the neighborhood you are in, the city you are in, or no information at all. Geode is designed to support the W3C Geolocation API Specification (http://dev.w3.org/geo/api/spec-source.html), which defines a high-level interface that provides web sites with optional access to the geographical location information of a hosting device.

We now look at two brief case studies of information delivery to mobile devices. The first one is the delivery of personalized news to mobile devices and the second is the delivery of learning resources.

8.2.2 Delivery of Personalized News

News is a popular domain for evaluation of personalized and mobile applications, since there is a high demand for this service from web users (mobile and static), and also there are many sources of online news feeds allowing experimentation. In many mobile services, including news delivery, reducing both the data transmission and user interaction to a minimum is necessary, as the service is costed on the basis of these measures. Owing to the limitations of mobile devices and the fact that mobile users are "on the move," there is a reluctance from mobile users to give *explicit* feedback by rating items, and thus a system using *implicit* feedback to learn about users interests is preferable.

Examples of implicit feedback are the rank of the item clicked on, the time spent reading the item, the number of pages viewed, and the amount of scrolling performed. Once the system records the implicit feedback, it can detect the preferences according to the content that the user has read. Each news story

[182]Google puts spy in your pocket, London Metro, February 5, 2009.

(or part of a news story) read can be broken down into its keywords, and a profile of the user's interests can be constructed. The profile can be used to ascertain the news categories the user prefers to browse through. For the news domain there is a well-defined categorization of stories that is used by most service providers, making it easier to pinpoint user preferences. At the top level we have categories such as headlines, top stories, world, local, politics, business, sports, entertainment, technology, science, health, and weather, and each one of these categories is broken down to subcategories at a lower level.

The Daily Learner is an adaptive and personalized news agent that has web and Palm PDA interfaces. It is based on a client/server architecture, in which the server periodically downloads and stores news feeds in a database and, in addition, stores and updates the user models when the user is logged on to the system [85]. We concentrate on its news delivery service to wireless PDA devices, which uses implicit user feedback to personalize the service. The main menu of the Daily Learner interface for Palm PDAs, is shown on the left-hand side of Fig. 8.1 from Ref. 85, and a headlines screen is shown on the right-hand side; the thumbs-up icon indicates that the story is highly recommended to the user. Apart from being able to browse the stories presented in a category, there is a keyword search facility for stories, which are ranked according to the user's preferences as recorded in her profile.

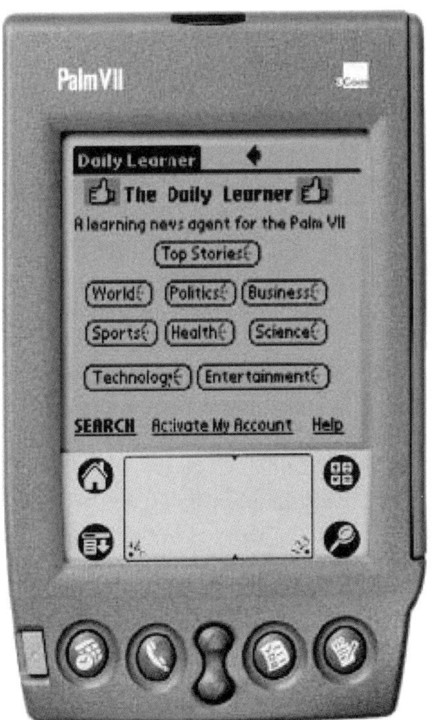

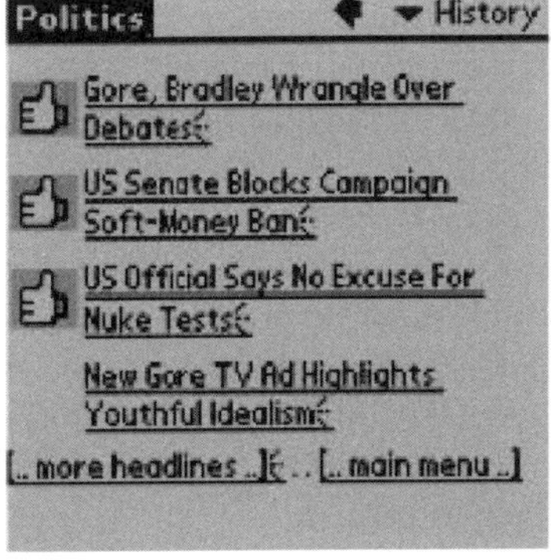

Figure 8.1 The Daily Learner adaptive news agent.

The user model is learnt as follows. When the user clicks on a headline, requesting the first paragraph of the story, its is labeled as *interesting*. Its score is initially less than one, and is increased as the user requests additional paragraphs from the story. A maximal score of one is attained, when the story is downloaded in its entirety. A story that is skipped is labeled as *uninteresting*, and its score is decremented by a constant.

The learning is separated into short-term and long-term user models. The short-term model includes only the most recent information, so it is very adaptive to the user's changing interests. Such a model is useful within a session, or for tracking how a story, viewed in a recent session, evolves. For this purpose the nearest-neighbor (NN) classification algorithm is used. The algorithm stores, in its memory, the recently presented news items and their labels (interesting or uninteresting). In order to label a new item it uses a similarity measure between stories, based on the TF–IDF of words in these stories. The most similar story, in its memory, to the new story is called the *nearest neighbor*, and the label of the nearest neighbor is assigned to the new story. (It is possible to consider the k-nearest neighbors and take a weighted average of these as being the nearest neighbor.) The NN algorithm is well-known in classification as being simple and effective, and we will encounter it again when describing collaborative filtering in Section 9.4. It also has the advantage that it only needs a single story in its memory to be able to classify a new story. To be effective, the nearest neighbor must be closer than a minimum threshold to the new story, or else it is labeled uninteresting. Moreover, it should not be closer than a maximum threshold to the story, otherwise it is labeled *known*. The score of a known story, that is, one that the user is most probably aware of, is reduced to a very small score so that it will not be presented as interesting.

The long-term model bases its decisions on stories collected over a longer period of time, and for many news categories. The features for each category are the most frequently occurring words as measured by their TF–IDF values. (TF refers to the frequency of a word in a single story, and IDF refers to the inverse story frequency of a word across all stories.) To classify a new story the long-term model uses the naive Bayes (NB) classifier explained in Section 3.2. NB assumes that the probability of features appearing in a new story are statistically independent, assuming that the story belongs to a given class (interesting or uninteresting). The NB classifier will then label a story interesting, if the probability of the story being interesting exceeds its probability of being uninteresting by a given threshold.

To decide if a new story is of interest, the Daily Learner first uses the short-term model, and then, if this cannot be used because the story is not close enough to the stories in its memory, the long-term model is deployed. The interesting stories presented to the user are ranked according to their score. An evaluation of the Daily Learner from a user's perspective revealed that the average display rank of selected stories was 4.2, while, when the personalization was turned off it increased to 6.4. The implication of this difference was that 86.7% of the selected stories were on the top two selected screens (each screen had four headlines), while when the personalization was turned off, this was true only for 68.7%. It was also found that when the personalization was present, users returned to the site 60% more often and read over 40% more content.

WebClipping2 is another adaptive personalized news delivery service to Palm PDAs [127]. It also uses a NB classifier to rate news stories that are likely to be of interest to users based on their profile.

When users subscribe to the system they must provide a list of topics they are interested in, to allow the generation of an initial profile consisting of keywords for these topics from a precompiled database with preset probabilities. Subsequently, user behavior is monitored, and each time the user reads a story the profile is adjusted by increasing or decreasing the weights of its keywords, according to how much the user is interested in the story. Interest is measured implicitly by the total reading time of the story divided by the average reading time it would take to read the story, where the average reading time of one line of text is user specific. WebClipping2 also allows explicit feedback by allowing users to rate stories on a scale of 1–4, and the feedback is taken into account when given. The NB classifier is used to classify new stories, based on the information in the user profile. A story is considered as interesting if its probability of being interesting exceeds its probability of being uninteresting by a given threshold. Interesting stories are then presented to the user.

Evaluation of the system was carried out with a small number of users. When users were allowed to build their own profiles, they expressed satisfaction with the system after using it for only one to two days. To test how well the profile adapts to changing user preferences, some users began using the system with a profile of interests, which is opposite to their actual interests. In this case it took 8–10 days before the profile had adapted enough for the users to be satisfied with the news stories presented to them. In a third experiment some users were given a neutral profile, where all interests had the same weight. In this case it took a few days before the profile adapted sufficiently. It was noted that if a keyword in a subject of interest appears in an unrelated story this will have a negative effect on the classification.

8.2.3 Delivery of Learning Resources

The potential of using mobile devices in education cannot be understated [178]. There is great potential within a wireless classroom, where learners can interact with mobile devices as part of their classroom activity, within a campus context, where mobile devices can be used for communication with and between students, and in a more general context, when learners are on the move and learning materials such as lectures or training modules can be delivered to their mobile devices. An example of a large Europe-based project in this area is MOBilearn (www.mobilearn.org), whose aim was to look at the use of mobile devices in the context of informal, problem-based, and workplace learning.

Much of the e-learning material has been designed for desktops or laptops assuming standard input and output interfaces and fast internet connections; so novel ways of interacting with learning objects on mobile handheld devices need to be developed. Knowledge Sea [113] is one such interface, which was designed

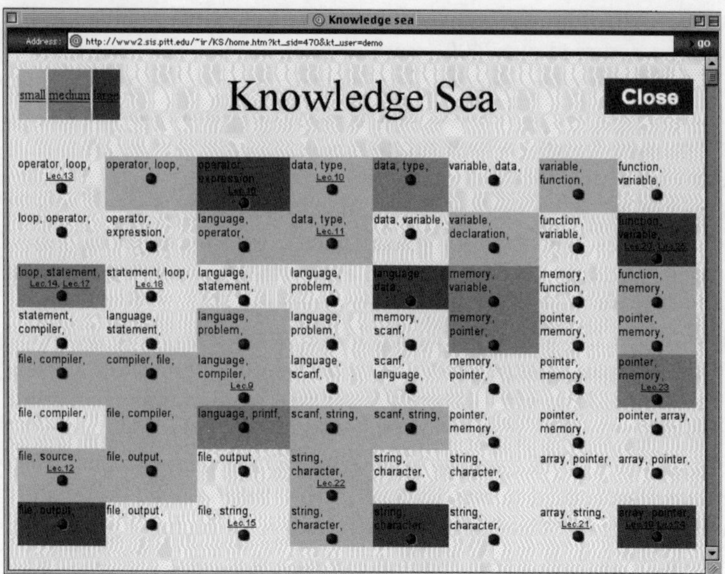

Figure 8.2 A map in the Knowledge Sea system. (Source: Knowledge Sea, Teaching and Learning Research Lab, School of Information Sciences, University of Pittsburgh (http://www2.sis.pitt.edu/~taler/KnowledgeSea.html)).

to allow access to multiple learning resources on mobile devices, and is based on a self-organizing neural network that automatically builds a concept map of learning objects. The concept map is two-dimensional, as shown in Fig. 8.2, where each cell in the map groups together a set of learning resources on a topic. Moreover, cells with semantically related resources are close to each other on the map. To help the user locate material each cell displays a set of keywords. The color (or shade) of the cell indicates the "depth" of the sea, that is, the number of resources in the cell, while the colored dot on the cell can be clicked upon to obtain a list of links to these resources. The Knowledge Sea prototype was designed to support a course on the C programming language, to enable students to navigate from lectures to relevant tutorial pages collected from different sites, and to be able to navigate between these pages. An evaluation of the system on a desktop platform revealed that better students rated the system higher. This is consistent with other evidence that offering students with less knowledge, a rich set of navigation possibilities, is not such a good idea, while it works well for students with a higher level of knowledge.

8.3 MOBILE DEVICE INTERFACES

8.3.1 Mobile Web Browsers

Several browsers are competing in the mobile web market [298]. This is due to increasing wireless traffic, much higher bandwidths of mobile internet connections, and larger uptake of smartphones equipped with dedicated mobile operating systems such as iPhone (www.apple.com/iphone), BlackBerry (www.blackberry.com), Palm (www.palm.com), and other multiplatform mobile operating systems such as Windows Mobile (www.microsoft.com/windowsmobile), Android (www.android.com), and Symbian (www.symbian.org), all of which have advanced mobile computing capabilities.

Users of smartphones expect to have access to full web capabilities, while those using "dumb" phones will only be able to access a limited range of services depending on the actual phone. There is a distinction here between browsers that directly render requested web pages and browsers that render a transcoded version of the web pages, which are funneled through a proxy server that compresses the web pages for faster display on smartphones or for limited display on dumber phones.

There are several competing browsers in this market that render HTML web pages by wrapping the content onto the mobile device, and are compatible with the XHTML standard for mobile devices. Typically these browsers also support JavaScript, Ajax (see Section 9.10), and a range of multimedia formats to give its user base a comprehensive web experience.

We briefly mention some of the popular mobile browsers that are available on the market. Opera Mobile (www.opera.com/mobile) supports a full web browsing experience, with over 30 million users as of late 2009.[183] Skyfire (www.skyfire.com) supports a media-rich web browsing experience with full flash and streaming video, and it seems that other mobile browsers will have to follow suit with comparative multimedia provision. Skyfire has been very popular on the Windows Mobile platform due its wide range of built-in features as in desktop browsers, and its speed attained by using server transcoding for fast rendering of web pages. NetFront (www.access-company.com/products/mobile_solutions/netfrontmobile/browser) is a competitive mobile browser having a worldwide user base, reported to be installed in over 800 million devices as of mid-2009. NetFront is also the browser on some propriety mobile devices such as Amazon's Kindle (www.amazon.com/kindle), a wireless tool for reading books. Fennec (mobile Firefox, https://wiki.mozilla.org/Fennec) is Mozilla's contribution to the mobile browsers war, while Safari (www.apple.com/iphone/iphone-3gs/safari.html) is Apple's propriety browser that comes with the iPhone. Some browsers use a separate rendering engine, for example, Safari, Android, and Palm make use of the open source web browser rendering engine, WebKit (www.webkit.org), as the display engine of their browsers.

Microsoft has developed a version of their Internet Explorer (IE) browser for its Windows Mobile platform. The advantage that Microsoft always have is that their products are compatible with their windows software, so their long-term prospects for capturing a large portion of the market are always good. Windows mobile and the other operating systems for mobile devices provide opportunities for other vendors to develop software that will run on their platforms.

[183] State of the Mobile Web, by J.S. von Tetzchner, August 2009. www.opera.com/smw/2009/08.

8.3.2 Information Seeking on Mobile Devices

Owing to the limitations of mobile devices, the navigation problem on the mobile web is even more acute than on the (stationary) Web. As we have already seen, the two strategies that users employ to find information are search and navigation. To improve the performance of information seeking on mobile devices we aim to *reduce* the following factors:

1. the amount of text that users need to input, by providing predictive text support and alternative input modes such as voice and pen input;
2. the amount of information displayed on the screen, by providing summaries of textual information and reducing the amount graphics and images;
3. the number of clicks the user needs to employ to find information, through personalization software that predicts the user's destination;
4. the amount of information presented to the user, through personalization software that narrows down the information presented to that relevant to the user's interests; and
5. the amount of information that needs to be delivered to the device, by techniques such as local caching (i.e., storing relevant information on the mobile device so that it may be accessed without downloading it from the Web).

Input of text to mobile devices is problematic due to the lack of a keyboard, or the presence of a keyboard of limited size, or having a small number of buttons to interact with. Mobile phones normally have the limited 12-key keypad, while PDAs, may not have a keyboard at all, and even when they do it is much harder to use than a standard keyboard, due to its small size. Touch screen keypads such as the iPhone's, which render a virtual keyboard, are designed for usability but still have similar size problems.

Pen and voice input modes are alternatives for mobile devices, requiring handwriting and speech recognition technologies. On Palm devices, the Graffiti writing software can be used for pen input, or alternatively the user can tap into an on-screen keyboard, which is available on PDAs. Voice input is also possible, for example, to input commands such as launching an application or looking up a contact.[184] Another method of voice input is through voice spelling [425]. In this mode of input a user enters characters one-by-one, so to input "d" the user would utter, say "dog". The advantage of voice spelling is that it reduces the error-rate, but this comes at the expense of throughput. It may also be possible to combine several input modes to obtain better accuracy and faster throughput rate.

8.3.3 Text Entry on Mobile Devices

Owing to the ubiquity of mobile phones, several text entry methods have been developed specifically for the 12-key keypad, shown in Fig. 8.3.

[184]Voice command. www.microsoft.com/windowsmobile/products/voicecommand/default.mspx.

Figure 8.3 Standard mobile phone 12-key keypad.

The most common technique is *multitap*, where a letter is entered by repeatedly pressing a key until the desired letter appear. For example, to get to type "a" you press the 2-key once, to get "b" you press the same key twice, and to get "c" you press it thrice.

An improvement on multitap, called *lesstap* [537], rearranges the letters within each button according to their frequency in the language used. So, for example, the letters "d", "e" and "f" on the 3-key are rearranged to "e", "d" and "f", since in English "e" is more frequent than "d". This is a simple enhancement of multitap to improve text entry speed.

To overcome the ambiguity when selecting a letter, Patel et al. [535] suggested a a *two-thumb chording* method, that is, a method based on concurrent presses on multiple keys. Keys 2–9 are used as character keys, while the other keys are used as chording keys for disambiguation. By pressing on a character key alone the first character will be displayed, so pressing on the 2-key will result in "a" being displayed. To get "b" both the 2-key and the *-key should be pressed simultaneously, and to get "c" both the 2-key and the 0-key need to be pressed. This model is quite natural given the common use of thumbs in text entry using mini-keyboards on smartphones, and is competitive with the other methods in terms of the typing rates on 12-key keypads.

To type in a word using the *T9 predictive text* method, you press the number key only once per letter, and the software guesses the word you want to input as the most likely word for that input sequence.[185] Just in case it is not the word you require, the software lists all the alternatives, one-by-one, in order of their likelihood. For example, suppose you press the 2-key followed by the 6-key. The software would detect two possibilities "an" or "am", and presents the most likely. If this is not what you want, the software will present to you the second

[185]How to type on your phone. http://www.t9.com/us/learn.

TABLE 8.1 KSPC for different mobile phone text entry methods.

Method	KSPC
Mulitap	2.0342
Lesstap	1.5266
Two-thumb chording	1.6000
T9	1.0072
Letterwise	1.1500

alternative for the sequence you entered. T9 predictive text is a dictionary-based disambiguation method, as it uses a database for storing the possible words and their likelihood.

One problem with the T9 approach is that the database cannot cover all possible words that are used, for example names and text messaging abbreviations. Although a facility to add words to the dictionary would be useful, T9 cannot deal with words it does not store, and in these cases an alternative entry mode such as multitap must be used. Another shortcoming of T9 is that its memory requirements are large compared to other techniques requiring very little storage.

To overcome these problems, a technique developed by Eatoni (www.eatoni.com), called *letterwise* [447], uses the frequencies of prefixes in the language to guess the next letter input. In this context a prefix is the sequence of letters preceding the current entry. Although the performance of letterwise improves with the length of the prefix, prefixes of at most three have given sufficiently accurate results. As in T9, if the prediction is wrong the user can press a key to get the next most likely prediction.

A useful metric for evaluating text entry is keystrokes per character (KSPC), defined as the average number of keystrokes required to input a single character [446]. The baseline of KSPC is taken to be one, which is the number of keystrokes on a standard QWERTY keyboard without any prediction techniques and assuming no input errors. KSPC values for the methods we have introduced are shown in Table 8.1. The impressive result for T9 is obtained on the assumption that the user only enters dictionary words; for nondictionary words the performance of T9 degrades below that of the alternative text entry method used.

8.3.4 Voice Recognition for Mobile Devices

Modern mobile phones can support applications that require accurate and robust speaker-independent speech recognition [157]. As an example, Google provides an application that uses voice recognition to connect users to local businesses (www.google.com/goog411).

Speech recognition is technologically more demanding than text entry methods (see Section 8.3.3) but is potentially very powerful as a complementary input modality. One such system being developed is Parakeet [658], which augments speech recognition within a touch screen mobile device. Errors in the recognition process are ultimately unavoidable so allowing users to correct any errors using a different modality, such as a touch screen, enhances usability. In addition to a touch screen, which displays alternatives to the best hypothesis of the system for the user to choose from, a software keyboard with predictive text capabilities allows the user to make corrections to the input.

Google has released a voice activated search that includes web and local search, which automatically detects the location of the phone (www.google.com/mobile/google-mobile-app). A similar mobile phone feature is provided by the Microsoft subsidiary, Tellme, providing a voice recognition application that activates web and local searches (www.tellme.com/you).

8.3.5 Presenting Information on a Mobile Device

Owing to the limited screen real-estate on mobile devices, the information presented to the user must be condensed and focused. Just rendering search engine results on the screen of a PDA or even worse on the screen of a mobile phone will be insufficient, since users will only see a small portion of the results displayed on a screen of a desktop PC. A conventional solution is to present to the user a cut down version of the results display, containing the title and a short summary of each result. (When using a smartphone such as the iPhone, the user may opt for a full desktop web experience, although the user satisfaction will very much depend on the capabilities and interface of the device.) Alternatively, replacing or augmenting each title of a search result with a set of key-phrases extracted from the document can enhance usability [350].

Creating and presenting concise and relevant summaries of web pages is an important issue for web search engines, that becomes much more critical when the user's device is mobile. In the context of mobile devices a summarizer must be used not only to present search results but also at the browser level when users are inspecting web pages.

One way to bypass the summarization issue is to partition web pages into meaningful fragments of content such as paragraphs, lists, images, and sidebars, and provide a two-level hierarchy for their display. At the top level, a thumbnail view of the fragments is presented and at the lower level any fragment in the view can be selected to obtain a detailed presentation of the chosen fragment's content [140]. Figure 8.4 shows screenshots of the thumbnail view of a web page (a) and a detailed view of a fragment (b) as displayed by SmartView presented in [470], developed in Microsoft Research, which is a browser feature that performs content and layout analysis for handheld devices.

The Power Browser project [120] in the Stanford University Digital Libraries Lab, has also been looking at ways to ease and speed up browsing on handheld devices. Its web page summarization method divides the page into fragments, as above, but its display strategy is different. The fragments in a page are organized in a hierarchy, so for example, if the fragment is a list, then all its elements are nested within the list. The display method, called *accordion summarization*, has three progressive modes; see Fig. 8.5.

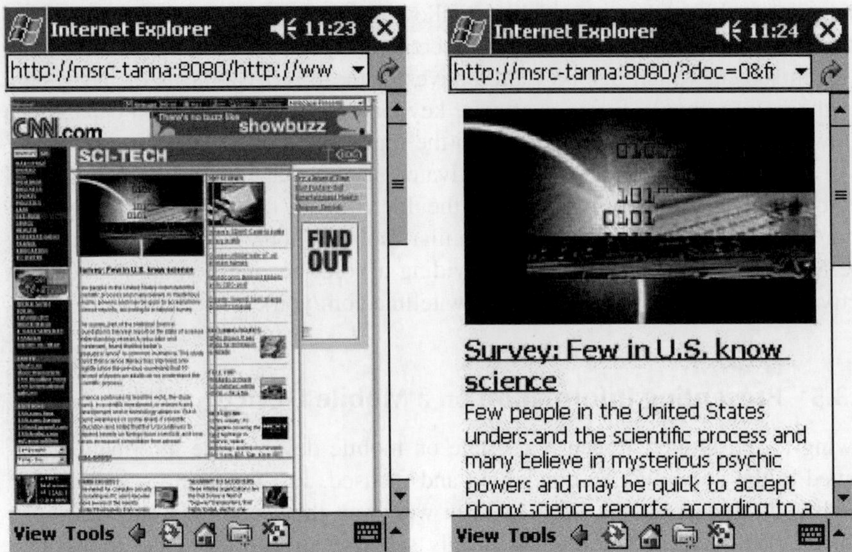

Figure 8.4 A web page thumbnail overview (a) and a detailed view of a selected segment (b) as presented by SmartView.

- In the first mode, the first line of the fragment is displayed, indicated by a fully colored circle on the left margin of the line.
- In the second mode, at most three lines of the fragment are displayed, indicated by a half colored circle on the left margin of the first line.
- In the third mode, all the lines of the fragment are displayed, indicated by an empty circle on the left margin of the first line.

In addition to these modes of displaying the content, "+" and "−" signs on the left margin indicated that nested fragments can be opened or closed, thus controlling the display of the structure of the fragment.

Accordion summarization allows the user to drill down the structure of a web page and to discover its relevant parts in a gradual manner. To improve browsing, if the user inputs keywords, then instead of displaying the first line of the fragment, the first line where one of the keyword appears is displayed, and, in addition, all occurrences of keywords in the displayed part of the fragment are highlighted on the screen.

Experiments with this method compared to one that renders web pages on handheld devices in as faithful a way as possible, showed that accordion summarization results in a substantial improvement in browsing speed and input effort. This technique may also be applicable to conventional mobile phones, although on mobile phones summaries have to be very concise as typically a user will only be able view very few sentences (up to three).

To reduce the latency of web content delivery to mobile devices, data can be fetched on demand [137]. In this scenario, users can decide if they need to see more content according to the relevance of the information they have already

Figure 8.5 Accordion page summary on Power Browser. (Source: Power Browser, Stanford Digital Libraries Technologies. http://diglib.stanford.edu:8091/testbed/~doc2/PowerBrowsing/desc.html.)

seen. Structural information regarding a web page is delivered first, to be followed by fetching fragments of the page on demand.

It is also possible to apply a more sophisticated summarizer, which extracts significant sentences using the TF–IDF scoring method described in Section 5.1. We assume that the IDF of the corpus is known, and that the TF of words in the page being summarized is computed online, when the page is requested and downloaded.

Once this information is available, the sentences in the page are ranked according to the aggregate TF–IDF of their constituent words, and the highest ranked sentences are chosen for inclusion in the summary according to the number of sentences required. We note that if the user has input some keywords, then the summary can be biased toward these keywords. It is also possible to use other criteria to bias the ranking of sentences, such as their position in the page; for example, in news stories the first sentences are normally the most important [451].

For handheld devices and especially mobile phones, summaries must be very compact as the physical limitations of mobile devices are very noticeable. Understanding the structure of web pages, most of which are HTML, can be used to categorize individual sentences into the four classes of image, text, link, or other (for example a list or a table) [21]. Contiguous blocks of homogenous content according to the above classes can be merged together, and importance can be detected by visual cues such as title, heading level, font size, and font type (bold, italics, or underlined).

As a further step, text is summarized by selecting the most important sentences according to TF–IDF (as described above), or natural language processing involving the identification of semantically related words that tend to co-occur (for example, the relationship between "student" and "class" in sentences containing the two words).

Figure 8.6 shows a summary of a web page related to US congressional documents and debates using this technique, where "[Navi]" indicates an entry for navigation links as opposed to "[Links]", which indicates an entry for informational links. On the other hand, "[Story]" indicates a summary of textual content, while "[Image]" indicates that the content has an embedded image in it. More detailed content, such as the display of images, can be obtained by clicking on links embedded in the summary.

An intuitive way to segment a web page is to divide the page into visual regions, typically, top (header), down (footer), left (navigation bar), right (links menu), and center (main content), based on the page layout (home pages of news sites are good examples of this type of layout) [387].

A more refined model segments a web page into blocks and uses both spatial features such as position and size, and content features such as length of text and image size, to gauge the importance of a block in a page [619]. Moreover, the importance of a block is measured according to four levels: (i) noisy information such as advertising or decoration, (ii) useful information that is not relevant to the topic of the page such as navigation links, (iii) relevant information to the

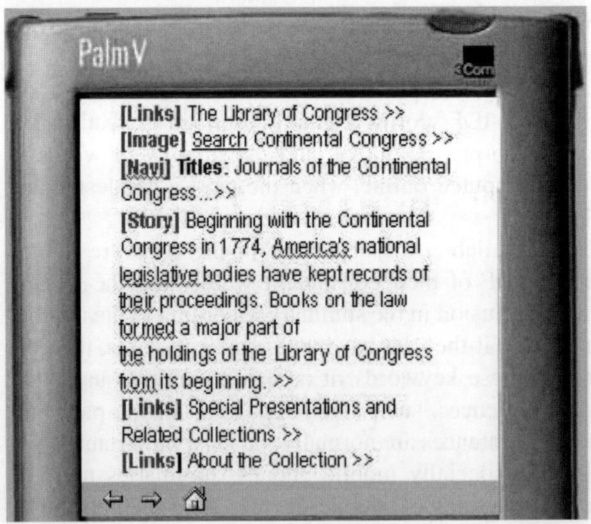

Figure 8.6 Example summary generated by BCL Technologies (www.bcltechnologies.com) summarizer.

topic of the page but not the most important such as related topics, and (iv) the most important part of the page such as titles, section headings, and the main content.

Using labeled web pages as examples, machine learning techniques can be used to determine the importance level of blocks in a web page. Apart from an application in summarization of web pages, block importance can also be used by search engines to improve the analysis of page relevance.

Recent work on automatic classification of images according to the function they serve on web pages can be used to prioritize the transmission of multimedia content to PDAs and mobile devices [312]. For example in news sites, commercial images acting as advertisements can be given low priority, while story images associated with the main topic of the page could be given high priority.

8.4 THE NAVIGATION PROBLEM IN MOBILE PORTALS

For mobile internet use, with their limitations in terms of size, computing power, and input capability, we have already seen that usability is a real problem. In the context of mobile searching, the "traditional" way, which is carried out through textual query input and scrolling through the list of returned results, may prove to be too time consuming as, on mobile devices, text is hard to input and excessive scrolling may degrade performance. Despite this, we will see that there are innovative ways of easing textual input and scrolling, thus enabling efficient search on mobile devices.

An alternative method to the search box and results list way of locating information, is by navigating through a categorized directory structure, as described in Section 4.1. In the context of the Web as a whole, there are serious scalability issues for directories, but in a more restricted domain, browsing through a directory structure combined with a search engine facility is a very powerful information seeking tool.

It may be that a mobile user looking for an information service, for example related to travel, or wishing to carry out a transactional service, for example downloading software, would prefer to do so within a directory-based mobile portal, as long as the portal's structure is transparent to the user.

8.4.1 Click-Distance

It may still overburden the user to navigate through lengthy menus of options and suboptions in order to locate the service they wish to use. The navigation problem in mobile portals is thus the situation, where due to the menu-driven nature of mobile portals, users spend a significant fraction of time navigating to the content they wish to browse. Navigation actions include menu selections (to select an item the user clicks on a specific menu option) and scrolling (the user scrolls up or down the menu options).

Thus the navigation effort needed to access a service can be modeled by the *click-distance* to that item, that is, the number of selections and scrolls necessary to access the service. If the click-distance to the service is too large, the user is likely to give up before reaching the service.

This observation has been experimentally verified in the context of navigating within web portals, which are often organized as a hierarchy of links [694]. The depth of the hierarchy is its number of levels, and its breadth is the number of menu selections on any given menu in the hierarchy. In these experiments, it was shown that the access time of an item is proportional to the depth of the hierarchy traversed, probably due to the limited span of short-term memory, and concluded that a good web page design should, as far as possible, minimize depth and increase breadth.

In mobile portals, this design advice is problematic due to the small screen size of devices. A solution to this navigation problem is even more acute, since the accepted task time for mobile users is at most 30 secs corresponding to at most 10–12 clicks, and in many portals the click-distance is in excess of 16 clicks. Moreover, the number of mobile portals is increasing and more mobile devices, such as smartphones, are internet enabled.

8.4.2 Adaptive Mobile Portals

Tackling the navigation problem on mobile devices amounts to reducing the click-distance to the desired information or service, and the way to achieve this is by *adaptive* and *personalized* software that uses machine learning techniques [615]. More specifically, we briefly explore an algorithm, which adapts the structure of a mobile portal to the needs of each individual user by adding personalized shortcuts to the portal according to an individual's profile. Tracking accesses to individual menu items provides the basis for building user profiles, and all menu accesses are stored in a *hit table*, which provides a historical record of the user's activity.

By collecting the user's past clicks on menu items, conditional probabilities can be computed for each menu item. For example, the entertainment menu item may have several options including music, TV, cinema, and dining. The conditional probability of the user accessing the cinema option, given that she is currently at the entertainment option, is the number of times she accessed the cinema option from the entertainment option. In cases when the hit table is sparse for a given menu item, since it has not been much visited by the user, a default conditional probability could be used. This default may assume that the probabilities of accessing menu options are equal, or it may use aggregate usage statistics of other users accessing the menu item, favoring options that were clicked on more often.

The conditional probabilities can be extended to more than one level down the hierarchy, so, for example, the conditional probability of accessing the movie times option (which is an option of the cinema menu item), given that the user is currently at the entertainment menu (two levels above), is the conditional probability that the user accesses the cinema option from the entertainment menu multiplied by the conditional probability that the user accesses the movie option from the cinema menu. The idea behind this personalization technique is to *promote* the most likely items that a user may access lower down the portal hierarchy, to higher level positions within the portal menu structure. (We note that promotion to a high-level menu can be viewed as the insertion of a hotlink into that menu.)

A typical user navigation session within the predefined menu options leads to a click-distance of 19, as shown in Fig. 8.7. Now suppose that the user regularly navigates from the entertainment option to the local cinema entry, whose click-distance is 19. Since the content the user is interested in is too far away, the local cinema entry could be promoted to the entertainment menu, as shown in Fig. 8.8. The limited menu size within mobile portals (considering the limitations of the devices that will access the portal) must be taken into account when promoting items, so the technique only considers the most likely k options as candidates for promotion.

Even if no promotion occurs, a simple menu adaption method could reorder options within a single level according to their access probabilities. As the technique is adaptive, the user's preferences may change over time, and promoted items may eventually be demoted to lower levels. Moreover, in some cases, when promoting an item, it may be better to copy the item rather than move it from its current menu. Another issue is that speed of personalization must be controlled, to avoid users becoming disoriented by rapid promotions from deep inside the hierarchy.

Trials of this personalization algorithm on European WAP portals, have shown that it reduces the click-distance by up to 50%, and due to the ease

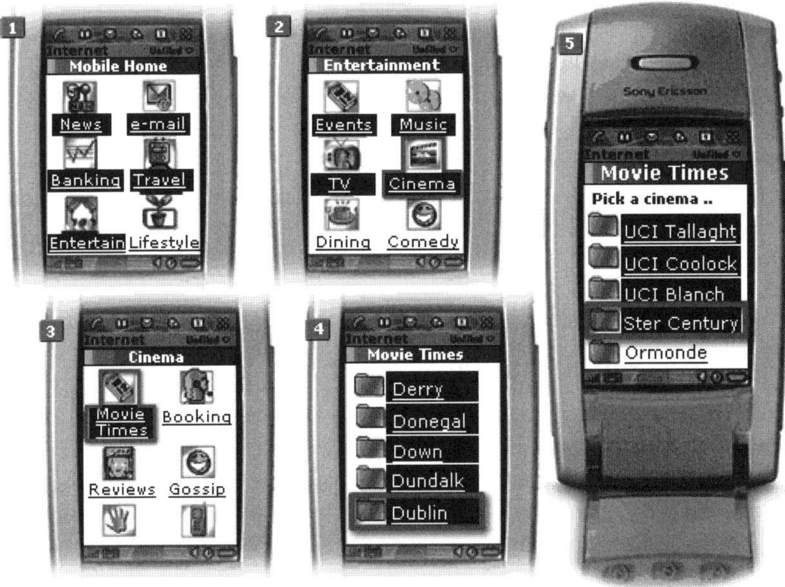

Figure 8.7 A typical navigation session in a mobile portal. (Source: ChangingWorlds advanced personalization technology. www.changingworlds.com.)

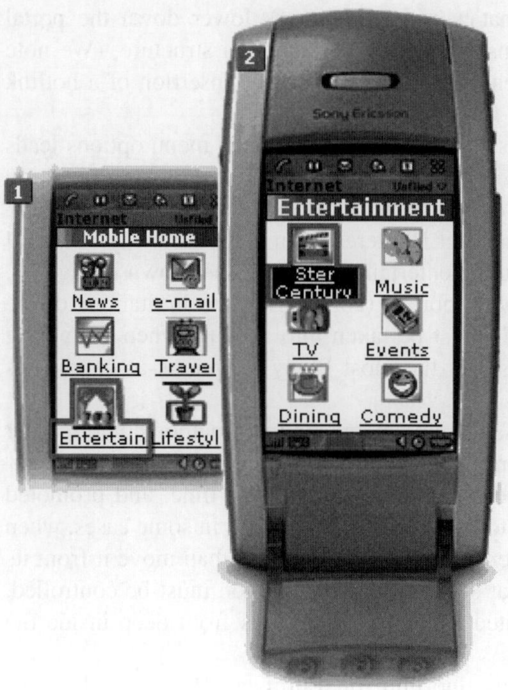

Figure 8.8 The portal menu after personalization. (Source: ChangingWorlds advanced personalization technology. www.changingworlds.com.)

of navigation, there is more than 20% increase in airtime (i.e., the amount of time users are navigating within the portal). That is, users are spending more time browsing more content and the portal's hit rate increases. Although click-distance has proven to be a useful measure, other metrics such as viewing time, time of day, recency of access, and content similarity between source and destination, may be used to construct the conditional probability. In addition, location awareness of the service would strongly enhance its personalization capabilities.

8.4.3 Adaptive Web Navigation

A similar approach is to develop an adaptive algorithm to improve web navigation for mobile devices by adding shortcut links to web pages, thus allowing the user to reach a destination page as quickly as possible [31]. The shortcuts that are created employ a predictive model of usage statistics, based on the navigation history of users modeled in terms of a Markov chain. For example, if we often to follow the three links

$$\text{entertainment} \rightarrow \text{cinema} \rightarrow \text{movie times} \rightarrow \text{local cinema}$$

to get to the local cinema entry from the entertainment menu, it may be appropriate to add a direct link

$$\text{entertainment} \rightarrow \text{local cinema}$$

thus saving the user two clicks to get to the local cinema entry. The goal of inserting shortcut is thus to minimize the expected number of links users have to follow to reach their destination.

For each trail a user might follow to the destination page from a given source, the probability of reaching the destination can be computed from a Markov model of the user's navigation patterns, or, if the data is sparse, by clustering similar users together and aggregating their navigation statistics. The expected savings of the shortcut for a given trail is thus the product of the probability of the trail and the reduction in the number of links to be followed to the destination using the shortcut (two in the above example). The overall expected savings is the sum over the expected savings of all trails that can be followed to reach the destination. For example, if there are two possible trails the first having probability 0.6 and saving three clicks and the second having probability 0.4 and saving two clicks, then the expected savings of the shortcut is $(0.6 \times 3) + (0.4 \times 2) = 2.6$. As in the previous algorithm, we choose to add the top k shortcuts, in order to maximize the savings in the number of clicks the user has to follow to reach the destination.

8.5 MOBILE SEARCH

Searching (rather than navigating) on mobile devices such as phones, raises several issues that must be resolved before users can gain benefit from such a service. We have already mentioned the importance of the mode of entry of a query (including the use of predictive text entry methods), the problem of rendering web pages on small devices, and how to tackle the problem of presenting concise and informative summaries of web pages.

An important issue in mobile search is how to display the results on the browser of a mobile device; see Fig. 8.9, captured from dotMobi, http://mtld.mobi/emulator.php for an example of the limited display of search results on a mobile phone with a WAP browser as opposed to a smartphone whose display would provide a much richer web experience. A related issue, which we have already touched upon is the ability to render web pages on mobile devices. There is some debate on whether web pages should be designed separately for desktop use and mobile use, but there is wide agreement that XHTML should be the standard markup language for both these type of devices, and in fact XHTML has been recommended by W3C as a general replacement for HTML.

Two other important issues for mobile search are *personalization*, which, due to the limitations and mode of use (i.e., the user is "on the go"), is probably more critical than on desktop devices, and *location awareness*, which is an important parameter of mobile search that can be viewed as a form of personalization.

Figure 8.9 Web search on a standard mobile phone. (Source: Screenshot of the Yospace smartphone emulator. www.yospace.com/index.php/spe_main.html.)

8.5.1 Mobile Search Interfaces

The standard search engine interface does not work well for mobile devices, where scrolling (both horizontal and vertical) and excessive clicking can be viewed as a luxury, mainly due to the small screen size and limited computing power and bandwidth. We have seen novel summarization techniques for web pages displayed on mobile devices but this does not solve the problem of presenting search results that are already summarized.

Usability experiments with different search interfaces on mobile devices [348], have shown that mobile phone WAP search interfaces result in very poor performance. Users searching on WAP-enabled mobile phones took almost twice as long, on an average, to find what they were looking for or to give up, than it took users of a conventional desktop search interface. Also, WAP users were almost 60% less successful in completing the allocated tasks than desktop users. Users of PDAs were only 14% less successful than desktop users, and it took them only 20% longer to complete their searches.

As in other studies of how people use search engines, users of mobile devices normally only issue a single query during a session and rarely view more than two results pages. This implies that, due to the limited screen size, mobile device users view at most one half of the search results that desktop users would normally view. On both WAP and PDA interfaces users spend twice as long on failed tasks than on successful ones, and when the task is completed successfully it is done quickly (within 2–3 mins), and with few clicks and page scrolls. It appears that one reason for unsuccessful searches on mobile devices is that navigating a web site selected from the search results, that is not designed for mobile use, is difficult and frustrating.

An interesting mobile search interface in this context, called WebTwig [347], is shown in Fig. 8.10. WebTwig is based on an outline-style interaction, presenting the search results within a fixed hierarchical category tree that can be expanded and contracted by the user to expose subcategories.

FaThumb [361] is a novel approach to browsing large data sets on a mobile phone that combines search and navigation. It is designed for a 12-key keypad mobile phone but could also be used on a smartphone. Navigation with FaThumb is hierarchical, where each attribute of the data, for example, the category of a business, its location, its rating or its opening hours, is organized as a facet (or dimension) that can be browsed. The user interacts with the interface through the keypad, which activates one of nine zones, each displaying a facet; on a smartphone the system could be designed for touch screen interaction. Pressing on a number zooms the display into the associated zone. The user can also apply text filters to narrow down the items in a facet. FaThumb was tested on a regional Yellow Pages data set with encouraging results. The attribute metadata about businesses, that is part of the Yellow Pages, proved to be very useful in the context of mobile geographical searching.

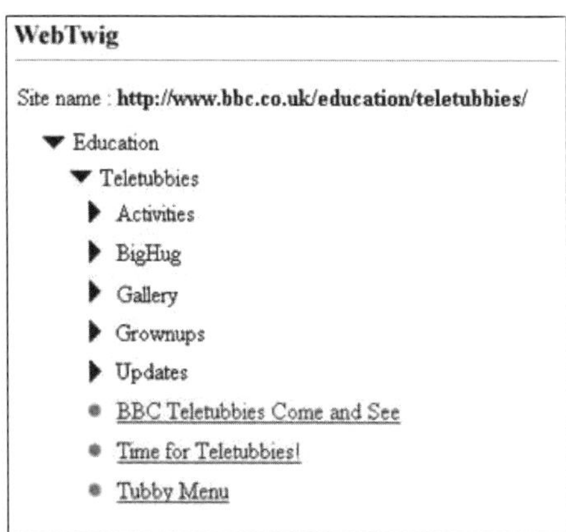

Figure 8.10 Screenshot of WebTwig prototype interface. (Source: WebTwig screenshot. www.cs.waikato.ac.nz/oldcontent/mattj/screenshots.html.)

8.5.2 Search Engine Support for Mobile Devices

The major search engines provide support for mobile devices, and this will grow with the increase in usage of the mobile web. Google (www.google.com/mobile) provides search interfaces to support a range of mobile devices, and other services including location-based applications such as Google maps. Yahoo provides similar services (http://mobile.yahoo.com) as does Microsoft (http://mobile.msn.com). As mentioned in Section 6.7, all the major search engines provide local (geographic) search for both mobile and desktop computers. Local search is combined with mapping applications, and is central to the search engines' strategy in terms of getting local businesses to advertise with them.

As the use of the mobile web is increasing and with it mobile commerce, there are larger incentives for the major search engines to invest resources in providing better mobile device interfaces and a larger number of mobile applications.

A mobile search engine, called WithAir, has been developed specifically to search i-mode content [363]. The WithAir system is based on four important design concepts:

1. Keyword input to mobile phones is simplified using a predictive text method that uses the popularity of keywords from the search engine log.
2. Search results output is simplified by presenting users with one or two words to describe each result.
3. Focused crawling is used to index i-mode content, distinguishing i-mode content pages from general web pages.
4. Regional information searching is provided by classifying i-mode pages according to geographical location, allowing users to find, for example, local restaurants and hotels.

A disadvantage of the WithAir search engine is that it only covers i-mode-specific content, which is a small fraction of the totality of web pages that are relevant to the query. For many queries such an approach is limited, but it may be possible to apply the concepts of WithAir to a much larger web index as provided by the web search engines.

Nokia (www.nokia.com) have been looking into mobile phone searching as an alternative, for certain queries, to portal navigation by clicking on links [579]. Common search functions such as news, weather, financial information, train time tables, and other information that is *a priori* known as important, does *not* need search engine capability as it can be provided through a menu-based mobile portal. Other queries, which are not known in advance yet require quick, possibly location-sensitive, answers may be best dealt with by a mobile search engine. Two types of location-aware searches that are specific to mobile users are:

- Real-time searching for nearby objects. In this type of location-aware search, the user may be looking for a restaurant or a cash point (ATM) while driving or walking, so the query must be easy and quick to input and the result speedy and accurate.

- Predefined search for objects that the user may pass by. In this type of location-aware search the user may be interested in buying an item, and would like to be made aware of its price when passing by a shop that is selling it. Predefined search can be viewed as a kind of reminder. For example, if the user needs to go to the bank, then she would like to be made aware that there is one in the vicinity.

For such location-aware searches to become popular, the criteria defining the query must be easy for the user to specify, and for the system to accurately evaluate. As keyword search is generally hard for mobile users, due to the input limitations of mobile phones, predictive text for fast input and hotlinks to popular searches may provide suitable solutions.

It is worth mentioning Avantgo, which was acquired by Sybase in 2002 and ceased it operations in 2009.[186] Its software allowed users having mobile devices to download a large variety of web sites to their devices, including news, weather, sports, stock quotes, and maps. To use Avantgo no wireless connection was necessary, as the information was downloaded to the mobile device by synchronization of the device with a desktop PC. Once the information was downloaded to the device the user could browse through the web pages offline. The Avantgo offline model was very popular, but with mobile users having faster, cheaper, and more reliable internet connections the service was no longer cutting edge.

An interesting idea to speed up searches on PDAs, implemented in IBM's Pirate Search,[187] is to store a compacted portion of the search index on the mobile device itself, so that searching can be carried out offline. A typical user search involves the input of a query, browsing through the results list, and then selecting the entry that the user wishes to inspect in more detail. The knowledge acquisition phase is initiated online through an internet connected computing device, for example a desktop, and once completed downloaded to the PDA.

8.5.3 Focused Mobile Search

In many cases when up-to-date information is not urgently needed, offline searching, with periodic online sessions to update the local information, can be effective. In other real-time scenarios, when the information is needed "now," say when requiring a list of nearby restaurants which are open at this moment, or needing a train timetable of departures in the next half hour, offline searching may not be of any use. Focused search within specific user-defined topics is a type of task that can be well supported by an offline search engine such as Palm Pirate, since

[186] AvantGo Is Going Away, by Jennifer Johnson, June 2009. http://palmtops.about.com/b/2009/06/17/avantgo-is-going-away.htm.

[187] Pirate search, Palm information retrieval application for textual search, IBM, Haifa, Information Retrieval group. http://www.alphaworks.ibm.com/tech/piratesearch.

it will not require a large index in order to cover high-quality pages focused on the topic.

We now describe the approach to implement focused search, which was taken by researchers at IBM Haifa [34]. Once the topic is defined, the information stored for the topic will include a topic-specific lexicon, a small number (of the order of 100) of authoritative and hub web pages for the topic, whose text is stored on the device in its entirety, and a relatively larger number (of the order of thousands) of links, for which only the anchor text is stored on the device. In addition, an index supporting keyword search for this information is stored on the device.

In order to define a topic such "main course recipes" or "Java programming language" the user gives a small set of queries related to the topic, and a small set of *seed* URLs used to find quality pages related to the topic. Once this is done an iterative process is executed on a server to find a *core* set of relevant pages for the topic. The core set is the set of pages fully stored on the mobile device, together with its larger set of embedded links. The lexicon and index are constructed from the core set, and are also stored on the mobile device. Several topics may be stored on a device, and these can be periodically updated when the user is able to connect the PDA to the server.

Initially the core set contains the seed set. It is then evolved as follows, with one further iteration for each query that the user has defined for the topic. At the beginning of each iteration the current query is submitted to one or more web search engines, and the set of top-ranked pages returned, called the *root* set, is expanded to include neighboring pages that can reach and be reached from these pages; this set is called the *candidate* set. Then, the pages currently in the core set are added to the candidate set. The candidate set is then ranked using a weighted variation of the HITS algorithm (see Section 5.2), where links are weighted according to the similarity of their anchor text with the query, taking into account the similarity of a page's text with the query, and the ranks of their source and destination points from the previous iteration. Finally, the top ranking pages from the candidate set, according to the weighted version of HITS, form the new core set, where the maximal size of the core set is a parameter of the algorithm. After completing all the iterations, one per query, the training is completed and the core set can be downloaded to the PDA, and searched over locally.

One way to view the core set is as a minidirectory on a user-defined topic. It is also possible to augment the topic information on the PDA, with pages taken from categories of a web directory such as the Yahoo Directory or the Open Directory, chosen by the user according to her interests [160].

8.5.4 Laid Back Mobile Search

Another possible scenario for mobile search is a "laid back" mode, where the search is carried out as a background activity, while the user is otherwise engaged [349].

One way to implement this idea is to carry out the search on a desktop PC, as follows. First the user specifies a set of queries on the handheld device, and when the device is connected to a PC, the PC records the queries and executes them on a web search engine. The web pages returned from the search engine are stored on the PC and copied to the handheld device, when it is reconnected to the PC. In this way the user can browse through the results offline, at her leisure. This is similar to the popular service of browsing news offline on a handheld device, as provided by Avantgo. Such a relaxed approach is, of course, viable only for certain types of queries, when the user is not demanding an immediate response.

8.5.5 Mobile Query Log Analysis

In accordance with a standard web information seeking task, a mobile searching task typically involves a query phase and a navigation phase to explore search results, and both these phases can be iterated (when the user refines her query) before a search session is finished. As in web usage mining, search sessions can be reconstructed from the log file of a search engine (or from the log of a web proxy sitting in-between the mobile network and the Web), and these sessions can then be analyzed.

As with query log analysis from the standard web search interface, analyzing the query logs from a mobile search interface can reveal behavioral user patterns [357].

While the average number of terms per query on a desktop or laptop (PC) is approaching 3, on a mobile device it is closer to 2.5, and while the number of characters per query on a PC is about 19, on a mobile device it is between 16 and 17 [360]. Interestingly, on a smartphone such as the iPhone the statistics are more similar to those of a PC rather than to those of dumber mobile phones. So it seems that smartphones are addressing the usability issues relating to text entry on mobile devices head on. In fact, although the average text entry rates (measured in words per minute or wpm) on iPhones (about 30 wpm) are less than those on standard PC keyboards (about 40 wpm), they are much higher than mobile phone entry rates on 12-key keypads using multitap (less than 10 wpm) or T9 (up to 20 wpm) [195]. It also transpires that the content that people are looking for on iPhones and PCs are similar, while on standard mobile phones the content is significantly different and less diverse.

Kamvar and Baluja proposed to use query logs for query suggestions on mobile phones in order to make query entry more efficient [358]. A comparison between query suggestions from logs and standard mobile phone text entry showed that query suggestions do not save time, but they do cut down the key presses by about one half. Users rated their workload as reduced with query suggestions and expressed a higher level of enjoyment from the experience. All users who were shown suggestions accepted at least one of them, and if a suggestion was shown three times but not accepted it is a strong indication that the suggestion is not the user's intended query and can thus be replaced in the suggestion list.

Further examination of mobile log data reveals that queries that refer users to similar web pages are topically related. In order to cluster queries together, suppose that we have K different clusters of queries. With each query appearing in the log data we can associate the URLs that users clicked on as a result of issuing that query. Thus for each query, we have counts of the number of times each URL was inspected by users issuing the query. Now, the full set of URLs can be clustered into K groups using a similarity measure between URLs, say using the TF–IDF of terms in the pages they refer to, in order to compare their content. Finally, we can use the counts of URLs associated with each query, to find the most likely cluster a query belongs to, and the queries in a cluster of URLs can then be used to describe the topic of the cluster they belong to. Now, the URLs for a given query will belong to several topics, and these topics can be ranked according to their total co-occurrence counts with the query. This is very useful for mobile search, as results can be aggregated by topic and the user can browse the topics before looking at the resulting URLs.

This technique for improving mobile web search was implemented at Bell Labs in a system called Hyponym [39]. As an example, consider the query "picasso", which may be grouped according to different museums that exhibit his or related art. Moreover, if the search is location aware and the user is in New York, then only museums in the New York area would be relevant. As this technique is based on the analysis of search engine log data, it can be viewed as a recommendation system. The data in the log will not have the coverage of web pages that a traditional search engine has, and it will only cover queries that were previously issued by users. In the case when the user issues a query that has not been issued before or has not been issued by a sufficient number of users, the mobile search engine will return traditional search results. In the other case when the query has been issued previously, and its results have been analyzed and clustered, a mixture of recommendations and traditional search results will be presented to the user. It is important to present the user with some new results, in addition to the analyzed results, so that the system can continue to train and adapt when these new results are clicked on.

8.5.6 Personalization of Mobile Search

Personalization is as important for mobile search as it is for mobile navigation. Assuming that the query has been issued and processed, only few results can be displayed on the screen of the mobile device. While, on a desktop we typically examine one screen of results, normally the top-10 ranked URLs, on a mobile device a screen of results can vary from, say four on a PDA, to two on a standard mobile phone. So, it is critical that the displayed results are highly relevant to the goal that the user is seeking to achieve.

To build a profile of each user's search activities over time, machine learning techniques that modify the profile over time according to the user's change in preferences, can be used. Users' search activities include clicking on a query result, browsing the web page at the end of the link, and iterating this process by choosing a different result or reformulation of the query. These activities can be recorded through a proxy between the search service and the mobile device, or through software installed on the mobile device; note that in either case the limitations of mobile devices in terms of bandwidth, energy capacity, and computing power need to be taken into account.

Once the user's profile has been learnt the personalization engine can reorder the results returned by the search engine according to the user's interests. Suppose the user is looking for "french food", and that the search engine returns four results ordered from 1 to 4. The user then clicks on results 2 and 3, so, in order to train the classifier, the personalization engine uses these results (2 and 3) as positive examples and the remaining results (1 and 4) as negative examples. In this case, the machine learning technique has to classify results as either being relevant or not relevant to the user's query, and the examples are used to build the individual's profile. For efficiency, when learning the profile, the personalization engine may work on a summary of the pages viewed, as presented by the search engine, rather than on the web pages themselves. With this technique the user's profile is revised each time a user issues a query and inspects the results, and so it adapts to change. Once the classifier is built it can classify new results, and the personalization engine can reorder them so that relevant ones are presented first.

An experimental front end to Google, called Toogle [581], implements a personalization engine as above, in the tradition of relevance feedback, where the learning occurs on the fly for a single-user query session. This personalization technique will probably work best by storing personal profiles that persist over multiple user sessions, as, in general, personalized search algorithms targeted at desktop computers do.

8.5.7 Location-Aware Mobile Search

Geographic information retrieval introduces another dimension into search, with the aim of making searches location aware, and thus returning results that are personalized and more relevant [454]. As we have already mentioned, technologies such as GPS and wireless networks can detect the location of a mobile user, providing additional parameters for search engines to narrow down their results. An alternative, less automatic mode, is for users to specify their location as part of the query, which is useful, for example, if the user is planning a trip to New York and looking for hotels, rather than being in New York and looking for hotels.

A prerequisite for a geographic search engine to be able to match a location in a query to a web page, is the ability to determine the geographic properties of the web page. Tagging web pages with geographic information involves the processes of geoparsing and geocoding. Geoparsing is the process of finding geographic contexts such as place names, addresses, and phone numbers, and geocoding involves assigning geographic coordinates to the found contexts. In addition, the whois directory service (www.internic.net/whois.html), provides publicly available information about who is responsible for the domain name and where it is located. Of course, this is not a completely reliable source of geographic information, since the domain may be registered in a different location to where the web site is hosted, but using the whois database together with the top-level country codes (for example, uk or fr), and a thesaurus of geographical names (see www.getty.edu/research/conducting_research/vocabularies/tgn), has been shown to give a success rate of over 80% in locating the correct geographic location of the URLs of web pages [671]. It is also possible to do some reverse engineering given an IP address using nslookup to attempt to find the host name.[188]

The ranking of geographical search results should take into account the location, in addition to the content, so that web pages whose locations are closer are ranked higher. A notable problem is that distance is relative to the mode of transport we are using, and the time we allocate to get to the location. One way to resolve this issue is to allow the user to tune the search results by telling the search engine whether the results should be closer or further way, and whether to give higher or lower weights to distances in relation to content. Depending on the query the search engine may be able to tell if it is *global* or *local* [267]. For example, finding a restaurant is normally a local query, while finding a recipe is normally a global query. On the other hand, depending on the user's context, whether she is on the move using a mobile device, at work using a desktop, or at home using a laptop, the importance of location to the query may be different.

Search engine log files can inform us about the extent to which users already include geographic location in queries. An analysis of an Excite query log from 2001 revealed that 18.6% of the queries had geographic terms, and 14.8% had a place name. Moreover, the average length of a geographic query is 3.3 terms, which is about 25% higher than the average length of 2.6 for all queries [585].

Analysis of a large AOL query log from 2006 found that about 13% of the queries were geographical, although these do not include nongeographical queries that have a geographical term such as the query "Paris Hilton", which commonly refers to the celebrity with that name rather than the Hilton hotel in Paris [241]. The queries from the AOL log come from a web search engine and not from a local (geographic) search engine, and thus underestimates the volume of geographical queries. Many users deploy search tools such as Google maps (http://maps.google.com), Yahoo maps (http://maps.yahoo.com), or Bing maps (www.bing.com/maps) for geographical querying, as these services include details about local businesses and directions as to how to get there.

Typical geographic queries locate a regional section of a service or business. For example, we may wish to find a local branch of a shop rather than their online store, or the location of a local library. Another type of geographic query

[188]How do I find the geographical location of a host, given its IP address?, by Uri Raz. www.private.org.il/IP2geo.html.

involves local information such as news, weather, or local events. Tourism is another significant source of geographic queries, where, in this case, searchers typically require information related to places, which are not their main place of residence.

We mention, *dynamic bookmarks* proposed by researchers in the Mobile Computing Group at IBM [196], as an interesting modification of the standard bookmarks tool, where bookmarked pages may vary from location to location. As opposed to storing the URL of the bookmarked page, a dynamic bookmark is associated with a name and a set of attributes such as the type of service required, for example, a supermarket, and the location-based capabilities of the service such as a nearest store locator.

CHAPTER SUMMARY

- The mobile web is a natural extension of the (stationary) web, supporting the "anywhere, anytime access" computing paradigm. Mobile devices have limitations in terms of their screen size, computing power, bandwidth, energy capacity and they necessitate the use of different interaction modalities to those used with desktop computers. The information needs of mobile web users are also different, and are often dependent on the time and location of the users.
- There have been several proposals for a wireless markup language that are converging to XHTML, which is set to replace HTML. Mobile web browsers have to provide a solution to the problem of rendering web pages on small screens.
- NTT DoCoMo's i-mode mobile phone service has had a huge uptake in Japan (over 50 million users as of late 2009). i-mode provides a variety of internet services such as e-mail, weather, news, sports, train schedules, city maps, and web browsing of i-mode content. It also supports mobile commerce transactions such as online banking and ticket reservation. The way in which the mobile internet has evolved in Japan has important implications for Western mobile service providers.
- Mobile commerce (m-commerce) is the extension of e-commerce to mobile devices. Mobile portals can provide mobile users having internet-enabled devices with a variety of services, similar to web portals, although some of these services will be location aware.
- Delivery of personalized news to mobile devices is a popular application. Owing to the limitations of mobile devices, it is preferable to learn the user's interests through implicit feedback. The categorization and ranking of stories according to the user's preferences is desirable, and it is important that new stories, which are not too close to ones the user has already viewed, be presented to the user. Delivery of learning resources to mobile devices is a challenging problem, and novel ways of interacting with learning objects

such as concept maps, that take into consideration the limitations of the device, are needed.

- Information seeking on mobile devices can be improved by reducing the following form factors: the amount of text input, the number of clicks needed to find information, and the amount of information that needs to be delivered to the device. Pen and voice input modes are alternative entry methods for text, requiring handwriting and speech recognition technologies. Text entry techniques such as multitap, lesstap, two-thumb chording, T9, letterwise, and other predictive text methods, save users time when using a mobile phone keypad. To present information succinctly on a mobile device summarization can be employed. Another method is to partition web pages into logical units and display these separately.
- To deal with the navigation problem in mobile portals the click-distance, which is a measure of the user's navigation effort in terms of the number of clicks needed to access the desired service, should be reduced to a minimum. This can be done through personalized and adaptive software, which adds shortcuts to services that the user is more interested in and thus more likely to access.
- Mobile search presents both the problems of text entry and the concise display of search results. Owing to serious usability problems, there is also the dilemma of whether mobile search should cover all web pages or only a subset of web page especially designed for mobile use.
- In some cases when the user does not urgently require up-to-date information, the information needed from the Web could be found on a PC, and the results downloaded to the mobile device, so that searching and browsing can be carried out in an offline mode.
- Mobile query logs can be used for query suggestions on mobile phones in order to assist the user during query entry. Query logs can also be used to improve mobile search by using a clustering technique that groups queries together by considering a similarity measure on the result web pages that were browsed by users after issuing these queries. This technique is useful in the context of a mobile device, as the grouped queries can be used to describe the topic of a cluster, thus enabling users to browse topics before inspecting the query result web pages.
- Mobile search can also be personalized by using machine learning techniques that build a user profile over time by recording the user's search activities. Once the profile is learnt search results can be reranked according to the user's interests.
- Another important issue for mobile search is location awareness, when the answers to a query must be location sensitive. In order to process geographic queries a search engine must be able to determine location-based information that is associated with a web page. In addition, the ranking of

query results should be influenced by the location of the device, so that web pages about closer locations are ranked higher.

EXERCISES

8.1. **(Discuss)**. Comment on the statement that adaptation and personalization are critical to the success of mobile web applications. (Use a brief case study to illustrate your points.)

8.2. **(Miniproject)**. Tourism is big business in which the mobile web has a natural role to play [222, 627].

Suggest ways in which mobile adaptive personalization technologies, and location awareness, could be used in this context.

Use web search engines to find out whether and how mobile technology is being commercially deployed in tourism. What queries did you use in your research?

8.3. **(Miniproject)**. Television is still the most popular medium for content delivery, and with digital TV already being deployed in countries such as the United Kingdom, there is the ability to personalize program viewing through an explicit or implicit dialogue with the user.

The Web is a rich informational and transactional resource, and its content is complementary to TV content. While TV programs are expensive to produce and are mainly video-based, web content is relatively cheap to produce and is mainly textual. Thus, an interesting direction that is being pursued is to augment content from the one medium with the other [706].

News, in the broad sense, including local news, sports, finance, weather, technology, and so on, is very popular both on TV and on the Web, and is thus a natural test bed for the possible convergence of the two types of media. Moreover, news is a key application for mobile users, and thus providing users with access to both the latest web and TV news could prove to be very popular.

Design a news delivery system for a mobile device that combines content from the Web and from TV, with emphasis on personalization and ease of use.

8.4. **(Miniproject)**. Location-aware search ranks query results taking into account the geographic properties of web pages and their implied distance from the user's location. An important scenario for location-aware retrieval is when the user is in a confined space such as a building or a shopping mall [125].

In this case, in order to be able to find close objects, a geographical model of the space needs to be defined, giving a description of the objects, and specifying their geometric properties and coordinates.

Devise an algorithm for confined spaces that takes as input the user's location and a user query, and outputs a list of nearby objects which are relevant to the query.

Modify your algorithm to take into account the orientation of the user, which is measured as a compass reading pointing to the direction he or she is facing.

8.5. **(Explore)**. Personal (real-world) navigation guides using technologies such as GPS, usually guide the user along a route by presenting maps, and giving audio and text instructions along the way on a turn-by-turn basis.

It has been observed that using landmarks to help users orient themselves along a route can be very effective [264].

Suggest how the use of landmarks could be incorporated into a guide containing predefined routes, in the context of pedestrian navigation.

8.6. **(Discuss)**. Geocaching is a location-based activity played throughout the world, which involves locating hidden containers, called *geocaches*, using a GPS device [511]. The locations of the geocaches are found on a geocaching web site, the largest one being www.geocaching.com, where players' can also share their experiences.

Discuss geocaching as being both a location-based experience as well as a social experience.

CHAPTER 9

SOCIAL NETWORKS

"The internet is becoming the town square for the global village of tomorrow."
— Bill Gates, Cofounder of Microsoft

SOCIAL NETWORKS bring another dimension to the Web by considering the links between people and emerging communities, in addition to the links between web pages. Social network analysis is having a major impact on search and navigation technologies in ways which were hard to predict a few years ago. Technologies such as peer-to-peer networks, collaborative filtering, and weblogs (known as *blogs*) are examples of social software, utilizing the way in which web users interact with each other and with the web in order to add value to existing information seeking methods.

CHAPTER OBJECTIVES

- Introduce the concept of a social network.
- Describe Milgram's small-world experiment and a recent counterpart experiment using e-mail, rather than post, to forward messages.
- Introduce the concepts of a collaboration graph and the Erdös number.
- Show how social networks can be extracted from the Web.
- Give an account of some of the social network start-ups.
- Introduce the basic terminology used in social network analysis.
- Show how web communities can be identified.
- Introduce the three different types of peer-to-peer (P2P) networks: centralized, decentralized, and hybrid.
- Describe the method of distributed hash files to locate content in P2P networks.
- Introduce the BitTorrent file distribution system.
- Introduce JXTA P2P search.

An Introduction to Search Engines and Web Navigation, by Mark Levene

- Discuss incentives in P2P systems to deal with the free riding problem.
- Explain how collaborative filtering (CF) works.
- Describe user-, item-, and model-based CF algorithms.
- Explain how content-based recommendation works.
- Discuss the evaluation and scalability of CF systems.
- Present a case study of CF.
- Describe the Netflix prize.
- Present some CF systems.
- Introduce the concept of weblogs (known as blogs).
- Describe blogspace and how it is studied.
- Introduce the real-time web and microblogging.
- Introduce the notions of a power-law distribution and a scale-free network.
- Discuss how power-law distributions can be detected.
- Point out the ubiquity of power-law distributions on the Internet.
- Introduce an empirical law of web surfing and a comparative law of voting.
- Explain how the Web may have evolved through a combination of growth and preferential attachment, and provide alternative explanations to the evolution of the Web.
- Introduce the concept of a small-world network.
- Discuss the vulnerability and robustness of scale-free networks.
- Discuss the notion of social navigation.
- Introduce the concept of a social search engine.
- Discuss navigation strategies within social and P2P networks.
- Discuss navigation strategies within small-world networks.
- Introduce the notions of social tagging and bookmarking.
- Describe Flickr for sharing photos, YouTube for broadcasting yourself, and Delicious for web page social bookmarking.
- Explain what a folksonomy is.
- Describe tag clouds as a method to visualize text and the importance of words within the text.
- Explain how tags can assist users in social searching and browsing.
- Discuss whether tagging is efficient.
- Point out the usefulness of clustering and classifying tags.
- Introduce opinion mining and sentiment analysis from user-generated content.
- Describe the three important opinion mining tasks on texts: feature-based mining, sentiment classification, and comparative sentence and relation extraction.

- Introduce Web 2.0 and collective intelligence as a paradigm in which users can take an active role in shaping the Web.
- Discuss Ajax (asynchronous JavaScript and XML), RSS, open APIs (application programming interfaces), mashups, and widgets, as influential Web 2.0 technologies.
- Explain the software as a service (SaaS) model for remote hosting of software, and delivery to customers on demand through the Internet.
- Examine the central Web 2.0 concept of collective intelligence.
- Discuss algorithms for enabling collective intelligence.
- Describe the world's largest encyclopedia, Wikipedia, and how it works.
- Describe the world's largest online trading community, eBay, and how it works.

9.1 WHAT IS A SOCIAL NETWORK?

The Web is a network of documents, and documents are part of web sites, all of which are interwoven together by links. The Web is the largest man-made complex network, created in a decentralized manner without a single guiding hand. In a social network, the links are between people rather than web pages. A network of acquaintances is an example of a social network. It contains direct links to our closest acquaintances, which would be our friends and the people we work with. Indirect links can then be found to the friends of our friends, and so on. Other examples of social networks are business relationships, sibling and spouse relationships in extended families, and collaboration networks between academics or film actors.

How do social networks relate to the Web? Although from a technological point of view the Web is an information network, it provides an electronic communication medium between people who can transform real-world social networks into virtual ones. One view is that computer networks are inherently social, allowing people and organizations to make connections [676]. Computer networks allow wide ranging interactions that are not possible amongst small, densely knit, bounded neighborhood groups. Web sites transcend physical boundaries, as does e-mail, enabling multiple local communities to form larger online communities.

There are many interesting sociological questions regarding how the Web, and more generally the Internet, is changing our social fabric. In the context of this book, it suffices to say that a debate is going on whether the changes are positive or negative. The positive impact of the Internet on community ties is evident both for physically close relationships and for far ones. E-mail is a good example of this: we use e-mail at work to communicate between colleagues at the same physical location, and at home to communicate between friends and relatives, who may be living far away from us. The virtual relationships often have a reinforcing element on the face-to-face ones, as we are probably more likely to go out for lunch with a colleague we have an e-mail correspondence with. There is also a "dark" side to computer networks as one encounters antisocial behavior such as junk e-mail (spam), viruses, and offensive web sites. Interestingly, online and offline communities have been formed to counter such distasteful behavior, by trying to encourage new legislation (for example, antispam laws), and in other ways, by means of developing special-purpose software (for example, child-safe filtering software) and secure protocols.

9.1.1 Milgram's Small-World Experiment

Social networks reflect the shift from studying individuals toward structural analysis of larger units. The unit of analysis is the relation among two people (or actors or agents) representing, for example, collaboration, friendship, or the flow of information in an organization. A milestone in social network analysis is Milgram's small-world experiment, which we now describe.

It happens to most of us once in a while: you meet someone at a party or a dinner and discover that there is a seemingly unlikely mutual acquaintance, then you both say "isn't it a small world" [243]. Stanley Milgram, a renowned professor of sociology, described the small-world problem as follows: if you choose two people, say A and B, at random, how long is the shortest chain of acquaintances between them? If A is a friend of B then the length of the chain is one, otherwise if A is a friend of C and C is a friend of B then the length of the chain is two, and so on for longer chains.

Professor Milgram carried out his well-known small-world experiment in 1967. He randomly selected a number of "starters," who were given some information about a "target" person. The starters' task was to send a folder by mail to someone they knew on a first name basis, whom they believed would be more likely either to know the target or to know someone who would know the target. The information the starters were told about the target was supposed to help them and the people they sent the folder to, to select the next person in order to get closer to the target. In his original experiment Milgram selected 296 starters, of which 217 (73%) actually participated, and 64 of the started chains (29%) reached the intended target. The average chain length of the completed chains was found to be six; hence, the famous hypothesis that any two people are connected by "six degrees of separation." Milgram and other researchers have carried out additional small experiments with similar results.

Because of the low rate of successful chains, some doubt has been raised regarding the six degrees of separation hypothesis [379]. In addition, there is some evidence that chains spanning different social classes are longer. Despite this, it seems that people are generally comfortable with the hypothesis, one explanation being that it gives us a sense of security about the world, and another that we have a poor intuitive understanding of coincidences.

A recent small-world experiment was carried out by Dodds *et al.* [188], where the messages were passed from one person to the next via e-mail rather than by post. Over 24,000 participants, the starters, were randomly allocated one of 18 target persons situated in 13 countries. In order to reach the target they started a chain by forwarding the original message to an acquaintance whom they thought was in some way "closer" to the target. Recipients of the message were then asked to follow the same instructions until, at the end of the chain, the message would reach the intended target. Over 61,000 emails were sent in 166 countries, and only 384 of the original 24,000 messages reached their target.

Chains do not rely heavily on close friends, which makes sense, as close friends tend to know each other, but acquaintances often know people you do not know. Successful chains typically involved professional ties rather than friendship or family connections. The two main reasons for choosing the next person in a chain were (i) geographic proximity to the target and (ii) similarity of occupation. Geography dominated in the early stages of a chain, while after the third step occupation was the most important.

In this study the presence of hubs, that is, highly connected individuals, was not an important factor in getting the message through to the target. The fact that a person had many acquaintances was rarely the reason for choosing this person as the next in the chain. Moreover, in this study there was no evidence of a "prominent" person, that was chosen as an intermediate messenger in many chains. The low chain completion rate (i.e., 384) can be attributed to random failure, that is, unwillingness to participate or lack of interest or incentive. The study confirms the "six degrees of separation" in social networks. Successful chains averaged just over four emails, and taking into account the unsuccessful chains, it is estimated that the degree of separation is between 5 and 7 hops, depending on the geographic distance from the source to the target. It was concluded that small differences in either participation rates or chain lengths can have a dramatic influence on the number of completed chains.

9.1.2 Collaboration Graphs

Scientific research is very much a collaborative enterprise, and this collaboration can be described via a social network between researchers, which we call the *Erdös collaboration graph*. Paul Erdös (1913–1996) was an incredibly prolific Hungarian mathematician, who published over 1500 scientific papers, collaborating with many other researchers in many areas. The collaboration graph of Erdös can be described through the concept of *Erdös numbers*. The Erdös number of Erdös himself is 0, those who coauthored a paper with Erdös have Erdös number 1, those who coauthored a paper with someone having Erdös number 1 but not with Erdös himself have Erdös number 2, and so on. The Erdös number of someone who has no coauthorship chain leading back to Erdös is infinite. (I have Erdös number 3 as I have collaborated with Fenner who has collaborated with Bollobás who has collaborated with Erdös.) There are 509 researchers with Erdös number 1, and at the beginning of 2004 there were 6984 researchers with Erdös number 2; see www.oakland.edu/enp for online information on Erdös numbers. Analysis of the Erdös collaboration graph of researchers having Erdös numbers 0 or 1 reveals that the there are, on an average, four degrees of separation between the researchers, and adding the researchers with Erdös number 2 increases the degrees of separation to five [60].

The same concept can be applied to movie actors, football players, and any other group of people.[189] The Oracle of Bacon is one such web site (http://oracleofbacon.org), assigning Bacon numbers to movie actors who have been together in a movie, where Bacon number 0 is reserved for the Hollywood actor Kevin Bacon. It is based on a game whose object is to start with a movie actor or actress, and find the smallest chain of actors connecting him or her to Kevin Bacon; two actors are linked if they have been together in a movie. For example, Alfred Hitchcock has a Bacon number 3.

9.1.3 Instant Messaging Social Network

Instant messaging (IM) has the potential to support social networking search. Suppose you need some information, then you might try and contact your friends on your "buddy list". If you do not get an answer you may wish to ask the friends of your friends, taking advantage of the potential of social networking. This can be done by adding functionality to an IM system, as is done in the small-world instant messaging (SWIM) prototype [701]. SWIM adds two functions to IM. The first is the ability to maintain a user profile including expertise, interests, and keywords mined from the user's home page and bookmarks. The second is social network search, carried out by a referral agent, initially, broadcasting the query to all people in the user's buddy list. The referral agent in a buddy's SWIM searches its own profile to try and find a match. If it cannot find a match it forwards the query to the people on its buddy list, and so on, until either a match is found or a predefined path length is exceeded. If a match is found, the user is put in touch with the closest person who may know the answer to the query.

The process of finding a match is based on two criteria: the *proximity* of the person to the user who initiated the query (the closer the person, in terms of number of hops from the user, the more relevant the match is) and the *similarity* of the profile of the person to the user (both the query and the profile are represented as weighted keyword vectors, and similarity is computed as in the TF–IDF computation of a document being relevant to a query). To maximize efficiency and minimize network congestion, control is needed over how far the query will travel, and a threshold is set, beyond which matches are not considered. It is also possible to add an economic dimension to the model to take into account people's willingness to answer a query and the compensation they may receive. Privacy is built into the system, so that there are limitations on who can be searched on a buddy list, and what information can be passed on.

9.1.4 The Social Web

One way of extracting social networks from the Web is through users' home pages [7]. The information on home pages is a rich source of information about

[189] Groups, graphs, and Erdös numbers, by I. Peterson. Science News Online, June 2004. www.sciencenews.org/articles/20040612/mathtrek.asp.

a person's interests, friends, and colleagues. The text on a home page can be mined to discover co-occurrences of text fragments (such as organization names, people's names, and noun phrases) that appear on other home pages, indicating common interests. Incoming links from other users' home pages and outgoing links to others' home pages may also indicate social relationships. Finally, if we have access to mailing lists, these can be used to find community structure that may not be present on home pages.

Let us call the home pages in a web site and the links between them the site's *social web*; when home pages are linked across web sites, we may consider a wider reaching social web. Figure 9.1 shows the Stanford University social web analyzed in Ref. 7, where nodes represent home pages and the edges represent links between them (the directionality of the links is ignored). In the Stanford social web, there are just over nine degrees of separation, so it still qualifies as a small world. About 30% of home pages are connected to each other, either by having inlinks or outlinks from and to other users, and over 50% of the links are reciprocated. As in the Web (of pages), whose links obey a power-law distribution (see Section 9.6), most users in the social web (of people) have one to two links (either outlinks or inlinks) with a very small but significant proportion having many links.

In order to predict if one user is linked to another, the similarity of the pair is measured according to how many items they have in common. Items include shared fragments of text, links to and from each other, and being on the same

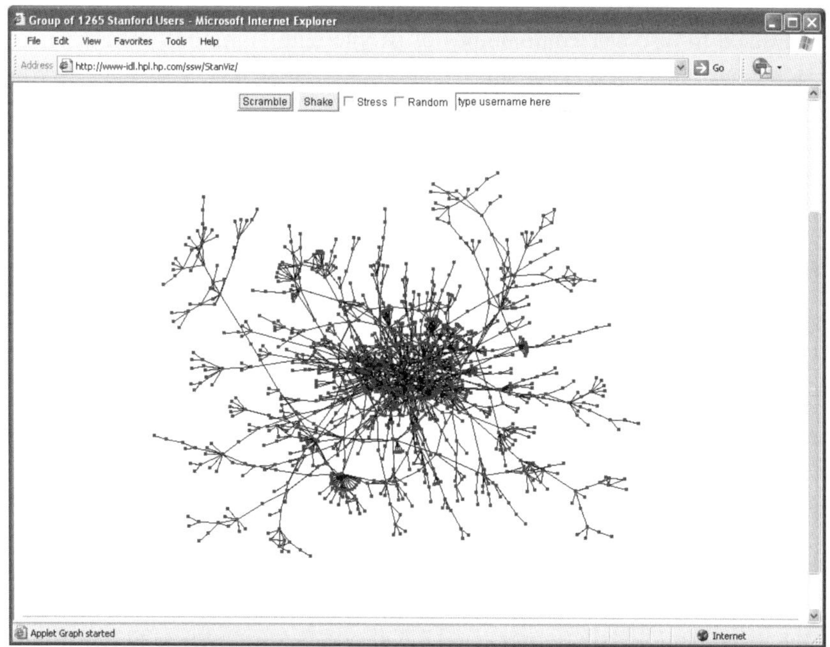

Figure 9.1 Stanford University social web.

mailing list. Shared items are weighted so that when there are less users that share the item the similarity is stronger.

The similarity measure can be used to cluster the users into communities with common interests. Smaller groups are more likely to be tightly knit, as the items they share tend to be unique to the community. The density of the community, which is the ratio of the number of links between users in the community and the maximum number of links possible (i.e., $N(N-1)/2$ for a community of size N where links are undirectional), is an indicator of how tightly knit the community is. One way to distinguish between a "community" and a random collection of links is to check if the density is above a certain threshold. The threshold should be above the density that would result from a network, known as a *random graph* [88], in which each link out of the possible $N(N-1)/2$ is present with a fixed probability p.

Users' e-mail contacts may be considered a good indicator of their social network [168]. Names of peoples can be extracted from e-mail and their presence on web pages can be discovered; these people constitute the seed set of the following network formation algorithm. A social network is formed starting with the creation of links between the people, whose names were mined from an input set of e-mail messages, and the people who own the web pages that mention these people. A larger network containing "friends of friends" can then be formed by using the same procedure to find web presence of the new people added to the network, and so on, for several hops from the seed set. In addition to name extraction, the system extracts keywords from home pages describing the expertise of the their owners. The resulting social network is one where a link indicates that a person is mentioned on others' home page. The network can be further utilized to discover communities of people with common interests.

Home page detection is a nontrivial exercise as there are, in general, several people with the same name, so knowledge of the name is not sufficient for accurate home page retrieval. In order to build a good classifier for home page detection, several strategies can be combined: (i) a keyword profile of the person can be constructed from e-mail and web pages mentioning the person; (ii) web searches can be performed to extract relevant web pages using the most common form of the person's name, restricting the search to the domain indicated by their e-mail, for example, a query may be "Mark Levene site:dcs.bbk.ac.uk"; and (iii) the URL of a web page can help determine if it is a home page, since most of these will contain some form of the person's name. Once a home page is found the user's personal web site can be crawled to enlarge their profile.

9.1.5 Social Network Start-Ups

In 2003, there was a surge in social networking start-ups, which was to some degree reminiscent of the internet boom of the mid-1990s, although at a lower scale [223]. It took some time for social networking to become a mainstream web application [97], but with the founding of Myspace and Facebook the number of social network users grew exponentially to reach well over a billion users worldwide as of 2010. Apart from the open services there are many niche social networks that cater for narrower audiences. It is also easy to initiate new social networks with technology such as that provided by Ning (www.ning.com), which is an online platform for creating and hosting social networks on any common theme; as of early 2010 Ning had more than 1.9 million networks created and 40 million members.

As in the early days of web search, despite the astonishing growth of social networks, it is not yet clear how social networks will make a profit [653]. The main efforts in this direction revolve around advertising and marketing but there are several hurdles to overcome (as of early 2010) before this becomes a reality.

People using a search engine are focused on a goal and when this coincides with advertising content, users will take notice of it. Most social network users are involved in chat and posting and receiving messages so are not as focused as search engine users and pay very little attention to advertising. In search, advertising is related to query terms, but in social networks the content that users are browsing is unpredictable and often does not match well with the advertisers' requirements in terms of matching content. Behavioral targeting (see Subsection 6.2.4) attempts to match ads to a user profile based on age, location, and other personal data. So, for example, in the context of a social network, an advertiser can use the information about what your friends like or have bought to target ads. The problem that needs to be addressed here is users' privacy. If their information is to be shared, users should have the option to opt in and opt out at any time rather than their personal data being automatically used and shared.

It is claimed that social networks can help discover valuable information locked up in the relationships a business has, and allow the business to find the person who has the critical information when it is needed. Often the contact information is known only to individuals or small groups in a company. Social network software can track who is talking with whom, and has many applications from forming new friendships through access to friends of your friends, and discovering useful business contacts, to the analysis of terrorist organizations and viral epidemics. We mention several typical social network start-ups.

- Friendster (www.friendster.com) is a social networking site, where people sign up and identify friends who are also part of the network. They can then browse the profiles of their friends (containing their interests and demographics) and, in the initial design, only those of the friends of their friends up to four degrees away. Friendster's social network was initially used for dating, although people who are not looking for dates were also encouraged to join under the natural assumption that the larger the network the more value it has. Apart from the profile, members can post public testimonials about each other. In mid-2005, Friendster claimed to have amassed over 17 million members. In Friendster, friendships are binary, someone is either a friend or not, and the level of friendship is not indicated. In reality public and private articulations of friendship are not the same, and, since the weight of a friendship is not articulated, trust is not guaranteed [96]. There are other issues in maintaining a social network such as Friendster:

(i) most profiles are rarely updated; (ii) people tend to remove old friends rather than adding new ones, which impinges on the growth of the network; and (iii) some users create fake personas, and, although many users like these Fakesters, the question arises whether any of the profiles on such a network are "real." The presence of Fakesters has created some tension between the company, who disapproves of such profiles, and the users, who enjoy searching for them.

As Friendster's membership numbers surged, it was plagued with technical difficulties in coping with the scale of the operation, limitations of the initial design, and the lack of new features to compete with the newer social network sites such as Myspace. This led to a decline in its English speaking membership, but to compensate for this Friendster has become very popular in other countries. Most of its 110 million members (about 90%), as of early 2010, were from Asia.

- Myspace (www.myspace.com) was founded in 2003 as a competitor to Friendster. One of the features that made it stand out was the ability of users to customize their profile pages. It also attracted many bands to show off their music and thus attracted a young membership. It was acquired by News Corporation in 2005 for $580 million. It operates mainly on revenues generated from advertising as do other social networking sites. Myspace became the most popular social network in the United States in June 2006, only to be overtaken by Facebook in April 2008. In August 2006, the 100 millionth member joined the network. Its membership as of early 2010 was in excess of 200 million.
- Facebook (www.facebook.com) is Myspace's main competitor as of 2010. It started off as social networking site for college students and has been the fastest growing social network. As of early 2010, it has over 350 million users. It is hard to pinpoint why Facebook has become so successful but it is probably a combination of the following factors: the network effect ("success breeds success"), good timing, usability, flexibility, and allowing third party applications to interact with it.

  Three other popular social networks in this space are Orkut (www.orkut.com) developed by a Google employee which is very popular in Brazil, India, and Pakistan and had over 67 million users as of 2007; Hi5 (www.hi5.com), which is particularly popular in Latin America, had over 50 million members as of early 2010; and Bebo (www.bebo.com), which was acquired by AOL in 2008, had more than 40 million users at that time.
- Linkedin (www.linkedin.com) is a social networking site that aims to connect professionals and businesses. It can be viewed as a business network of professionals who want to find a job, a suitable employee, or a business partner. People joining can receive referrals through the network of contacts they are connected to, up to four degrees away, about topics they make themselves available for, such as potential jobs or business partnerships. Linkedin claimed to have over 2.8 million users as of mid-2005, and

since then its membership has soared, so that as of early 2010 Linkdin had over 55 million users.

- Visible Path has developed a social network tool that mines contact lists and customers relationship management (CRM) applications within a company in order to evaluate the strength of relationships with people outside the company. The tool runs on a server and communicates with software installed on each employee's PC. The PC software monitors the employees' communications, and sends data back to the server, where it is analyzed and a social network is constructed that all employees can search. It is different from the other companies we have mentioned in that its network is closed; that is, it is only available to empolyees within the company, and its analysis is solely based on the internal resources of the company. It was acquired in 2008 by Hoover's (www.hoovers.com), a company that offers business information through a database that it maintains about 32 million organizations (as of early 2010).
- Dodgeball is an interesting social networking start-up, which is a bit like Friendster but for the mobile phone space. The service uses text messaging to connect friends, and friends of friends, who happen to be in the same vicinity up to 10 blocks away. When users wish their location to be known they "log in" by sending a text message to a central server and in return they receive a message with the location of any of their friends or friends of friends, who have logged on and are close by. Dodgeball had over 15,000 users by March 2005,[190] and at that time the service was available in 22 cities in the United States. It was acquired by Google in May 2005, shut down in March 2009, and replaced by the location aware mobile application, Google Latitude (www.google.com/latitude), which is available in many languages and countries; see Section 8.2.1 for a discussion on mobile commerce.

As usual, there are also privacy issues with social network software, especially as you entrust the network with information not only about yourself but also about the friends you identify. There is also the problem that people who register may not be willing to share their best contacts. This does not rule out discovering the network by looking at corporate information buried in emails and other documents, although more research needs to be carried out to establish the quality of the resulting networks.

There are two ways in which social networks can be more open. One is by enabling people to share their profiles and relations across networks. The friend of a friend (FOAF) project (www.foaf-project.org) enables this sort of sharing by providing a machine readable ontology capable of describing people, their networks, and relations with other people and objects. Another is providing a standard for third party developers so that they can embed applications into the profile pages of their users across social networks.

[190]MoSoSos Not So So-So, by D. Terdiman, Wired News, March 2005. www.wired.com/news/culture/0,1284,66813,00.html.

OpenSocial (www.opensocial.org) developed by Google defines a common application programming interface (API) for doing this.

9.2 SOCIAL NETWORK ANALYSIS

Social network analysis [597] is concerned with metrics that measure the characteristics of the relationships between the people participating in the network. We will give a brief overview of these metrics with emphasis on introducing the terminology commonly used in social network analysis [244].

Consider the collaboration graph shown in Fig. 9.2, where the nodes (or actors or agents) represent researchers and the bidirectional edges represent collaborations. The network was visualized using Netdraw (www.analytictech.com/netdraw/netdraw.htm), which is a free program for visualizing social networks.

9.2.1 Social Network Terminology

In social network analysis, an edge is often called a *relation*. Relations typically differ in strength, for example, some collaborations are stronger than others, and the strength of a relation may be measured by a weight. Note that the edges in the graph are undirected in the sense that if person A collaborates with person B, then the reverse is also true, that is, the relation is symmetric. Not all social networks are symmetric, for example, the flow of information in an organization is typically directed from the top of the hierarchy downward.

Ties connect (or link) pairs of actors via one or more relations. For example, two people might collaborate, be friends, and one might be the manager of the other. The tie between a pair describes the aggregate of all the relations they maintain. The strength of a tie can be described by a weight, which may depend on the relations maintained by its pair. The weight may denote, for example, a distance,

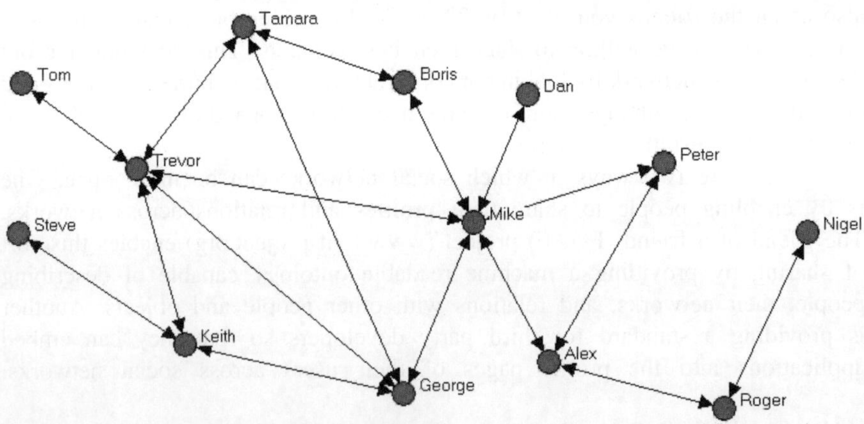

Figure 9.2 Example of a collaboration graph.

a frequency, a probability, or a rate of flow. So, for example, in Fig. 9.2, we could annotate the ties with the number of joint articles the two people have written.

A tie that connects two people who would otherwise be several steps away from each other in the network is called a *local bridge*; a local bridge of degree k is a tie between two people, whose removal causes the shortest distance between the two people to be at least k. In our example, the local bridge between Mike and Peter is of degree 2, while the local bridge between Tamara and Boris is of degree 3. Normally, if we do not specify k, it is assumed that the local bridge is of degree greater than 2. A *global bridge* (or simply a bridge) is a tie that, if removed, will disconnect the network. In Fig. 9.2, the ties between Alex and Roger, Tom and Trevor, Steve and Keith, Dan and Mike, and Roger and Nigel are examples of (global) bridges.

A *triangle* (or a transitive triple or a triad) is a subset of three people in the network such that each has a tie to the other two, as between Mike, Peter, and Alex in Fig. 9.2. When two people, say A and B, are part of only few, if any, triangles, then a tie between A and B is referred to as a *weak tie*; so a bridge between A and B is the weakest form of a tie. On the other hand, if A and B are part of many triangles, then the a tie between A and B is said to be a *strong tie*.

The shortest path between two actors is called a *geodesic*, and the length of a geodesic is the *distance* between its endpoints [115]. The average distance among the actors in Fig. 9.2 is 2.52564.

The longest geodesic between any two actors in the network is called its *diameter*. The diameter of the network in Fig. 9.2 is 6, which is the length of the geodesic between Steve and Nigel.

The *degree* of an actor is the number of actors he/she has a tie with, that is, the number of neighboring actors; in a directed network, we distinguish between the indegree and the outdegree of an actor. The *degree distribution* of the network gives for each i, varying from 1 to the maximum degree of the network, the number of actors having degree i. Table 9.1 shows the degree distribution of our example collaboration graph.

The *clustering coefficient* of an actor is the ratio of the number of ties between his or her neighbors to the maximum possible number of ties between his or her neighbors, obtaining a number between 0 and 1. (For an actor having

TABLE 9.1 Degree distribution for the network in Fig. 9.2.

Degree	Number of Actors
1	4
2	3
3	3
4	1
5	1
6	1

n neighbors, the maximum number of ties between them is $n(n-1)/2$.) Note that the clustering coefficient is high if there are many triangles between an actor and his or her neighbors. The average clustering coefficient of the network in Fig. 9.2 is 0.2256.

The *density* of the network is the proportion of ties it has; that is, for a network with n actors, it is the number of ties divided by $n(n-1)/2$, assuming that loops are not counted, and, in a undirected network, assuming that the arcs from A to B and from B to A are considered as a single tie. The density of the network in Fig. 9.2 is 0.2179, as its has 17 ties and 13 actors.

9.2.2 The Strength of Weak Ties

A cornerstone in social network analysis was the investigation of the "strength of weak ties" by Granovetter [266]. Removal of strong ties from the network does not have much effect on the number of degrees of separation between any two people in the network. For example, removal of one edge in a triangle will increase the distance between these two people from one to two. On the other hand, removal of a weak tie, will cause two people to be far apart, or in the worst case, when the weak tie is a bridge, the two people will become disconnected. For this reason, weak ties are often more important than strong ties. They provide "shortcuts" between people, where, if broken, the communication between these people would be very difficult.

It is known that people often find new jobs through personal contacts. In the scenario of job hunting it is the weak ties, that is, the people we do not know so well, that are the most valuable source of information. They are more likely, than strong ties, to introduce us to someone we do not know directly, or to provide us with a new piece of information. The contacts that our strong ties have are most likely to be known to us, as is the information they possess. Weak ties thus provide "shortcuts" to more distant people, that we would find harder to get in touch with. People who occupy either side of a bridge, especially if the disconnected components are dense (in this case the bridge is called a *structural hole*), are in a very good position to act as mediators between the two components.

9.2.3 Centrality

Centrality is an important network characteristic. Apart from its significance in understanding social networks, the concept of centrality has implications in the design of computer networks such as P2P networks discussed in Section 9.3 [390], and in the location of facilities such as hospitals, fire stations, and shopping centers. Figure 9.3 shows a simple collaboration graph, looking very much like a kite, that we will use to illustrate the concept of centrality in social networks; the network was visualized using Pajek (http://pajek.imfm.si/doku.php).

The three main measures of actor centrality are *degree centrality*, *closeness centrality*, and *betweenness centrality*, already studied by Freeman in the late 1970s [233].

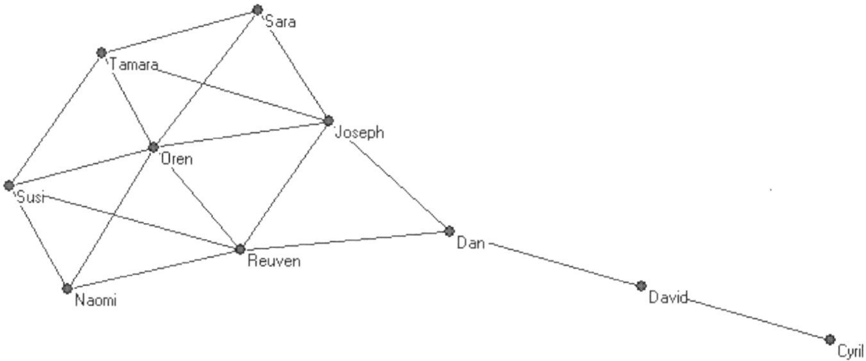

Figure 9.3 Example to illustrate centrality in social networks.

- A *star* (or a wheel), which has one central point and a number of connections, is the simplest topology with one obvious center and several satellites. In our example, the subgraph comprising five actors Oren, Tamara, Susi, Reuven and Joseph, with Oren in the center, is a star of five actors. This motivates a simple way to measure the centrality of an actor by the ratio of its degree to the maximum possible degree centrality. (The maximum degree centrality of an actor in a network with n actors is $n - 1$, which occurs in the star of n actors.) In our example, Oren has the highest degree centrality of 0.6667.
- The closeness centrality of an actor is defined as the reciprocal of the sum of distances of all geodesics to other actors in the network; that is, the larger the distance, the smaller the closeness. The relative closeness centrality is the ratio of the closeness centrality to the reciprocal of the minimum possible sum of distances, which is $1/(n - 1)$ for a network with n actors. In our example, Joseph and Reuven have the highest relative closeness centrality of 0.6429.
- Betweenness centrality of an actor measures the extent to which the actor falls between other actors on the geodesic connecting them. An actor with high betweenness is located on the communication paths of information flowing through the network. The betweenness proportion of an actor A for two other actors B and C is the proportion of geodesics between B and C that pass through A. The betweenness centrality of an actor is the ratio of the sum of the betweenness proportions of the actor, for all pairs of actors in the network, to the maximum possible betweenness centrality. In our example, Dan has the highest betweenness centrality of 0.3889.

We note that in all centrality measures the maximum possible centrality value is achieved only by the central actor in a star. The network with the lowest overall centrality value is the complete graph, where all actors are connected to all other actors. Actors who have the lowest centrality in the network are regarded as *peripheral*.

The centrality measures we introduced are for individual actors. A centrality measure for the network as a whole, called *centralization*, can be defined as the ratio of the sum of differences between the centrality scores of actors and the most central actor to the maximum possible sum of differences. (The maximum will occur in a star with the appropriate number of actors, which is the most central network.) In our example the centralization for the network, using relative closeness centrality, is 0.27037.

In addition to centrality, we can include link analysis measures such as PageRank and HITS in order to identify hubs and authorities in the network. (In undirected networks, we do not distinguish between hubs and authorities.) The degree, PageRank, HITS, closeness, and betweenness centrality scores for the actors of the network in Fig. 9.2 is shown in Table 9.2; on all metrics, Mike scores highest.

9.2.4 Web Communities

Clustering techniques such as hierarchical clustering and k-means are often used to partition a network. *Clustering* is a partition of the actors in the network such that the actors in each partition all share or have the same connection patterns. Each cluster induces a *block*, where a block is the subset of the network having all the existing relations between actors in the cluster. The actors who belong to a block are determined through the notion of *structural equivalence* of actors, determined by the extent to which they have the same neighborhood. The process of clustering according to structural equivalence is known as *blockmodeling* [59]. In general, blockmodeling identifies clusters of actors that share structural characteristics defined in terms of the existing relations between actors in the network.

TABLE 9.2 Metrics for actors in the network of Fig. 9.2.

Actor	Name	Degree	PageRank	HITS	Closeness	Betweenness
1	Steve	1	0.0363	0.0262	0.2927	0.0000
2	Trevor	5	0.1353	0.1539	0.5455	0.3182
3	Boris	2	0.0574	0.0744	0.4138	0.0303
4	Roger	2	0.0741	0.0211	0.3429	0.1667
5	*Mike*	6	*0.1619*	*0.1596*	*0.6000*	*0.6288*
6	George	4	0.1048	0.1443	0.5217	0.1515
7	Keith	3	0.0874	0.0921	0.4000	0.1667
8	Nigel	1	0.0430	0.0060	0.2609	0.0000
9	Tamara	3	0.0809	0.1058	0.4000	0.0379
10	Alex	3	0.0916	0.0684	0.4615	0.0303
11	Dan	1	0.0345	0.0443	0.3871	0.0000
12	Tom	1	0.0342	0.0437	0.3636	0.0000
13	Peter	2	0.0604	0.0637	0.4286	0.0000

A *web community* can be defined as a collection of web pages that are focused on a particular topic or theme. Although a web community is characterized by the pages it contains, it can be viewed as a social network between the owners of these pages.

It is possible to employ clustering methods to identify web communities by analyzing the similarity of textual content of web pages, but due to the size of the Web and its decentralized and complex nature, such analysis is difficult to carry out on a large scale. On the other hand, methods that employ link analysis based on the structure of the Web graph have the potential of efficiently discovering communities, with minimal textual information.

A useful definition of a community in terms of the structure of the network is a set of nodes (actors), say C, such that for all nodes (actors) in C there are at least as many links (ties) with other nodes (actors) in C, than there are with nodes (actors) outside C [226].

A procedure for forming a community works as follows. It starts from a set of *seed* pages on the topic of interest, say from an existing category within a web directory. It then carries out a fixed-depth crawl from the seed set and adds the pages with the most links to the existing community, defined at this stage by the seed set. This procedure is iterated several times adding pages to the seed set as long as the definition of community is satisfied. Once a community is formed, textual features, consisting of words and word pairs, can be extracted from its pages to describe the community.

Another method of detecting communities utilizes the distinction between hub and authority web pages. The assumption is that a community contains dense patterns of links from hubs to authorities [549]. To formalize this, the notion of *bipartite graph* is utilized; a bipartite graph is a network, whose node set is partitioned into two nonoverlapping sets, in this case one set contains hubs and the other authorities such that its links only connect nodes from one set with those in the other. A *core* of a community is a complete bipartite subgraph of the community, where each hub has links to all the authorities in the subgraph. Using this definition of core, a technique called *trawling* enumerates all the cores in the web graph (as output from a large web crawl) of up to, say, 20 pages. Trawling through a large crawl, from 1997, of over 40 million web pages yielded 130,000 3×3 cores. To form communities, the cores can be expanded into larger subgraphs by providing them as input to the HITS hubs and authorities algorithm.

Yet another method for finding communities is based on the notion of betweenness centrality, applied to edges rather than nodes. Assume we have a social network such as the web graph or an e-mail network, where the betweenness of an edge (a pair of vertices) is the number of geodesics that pass through the pair [649]. The idea for detecting communities is that tightly knit communities will either be isolated or connected to other communities by a few edges having high betweenness. Identification of communities works as follows: (i) calculate the betweenness of all edges; (ii) remove the edge with the highest betweenness; (iii) recalculate the betweenness of the remaining edges; and (iv) repeat the process until some stopping criterion is satisfied, and then return the connected components of the network as the communities.

The identification process can stop when the components of the network cannot be meaningfully further subdivided. A component of five or less actors cannot be meaningfully further separated; the smallest separable component contains six actors organized in two triangles connected by a single edge. For components of six or larger, consider edges connecting a leaf node of degree one to the rest of the component. It is clear that this edge should not be removed since, although peripheral, the leaf node should still be considered as part of the community. Moreover, this edge must have the highest betweenness, which in the case of a leaf is $N - 1$, for a component of size N, as it has a geodesic to all other nodes in the network (assuming the network is undirected). The second heuristic stopping criterion for components of size at least six is, therefore, that the highest betweenness of any edge is at most $N - 1$.

An alternative stopping criterion is simply to remove edges until none remain in the network and to keep track of the components of the network at each step, where the removal of an edge with the highest betweenness increases their number [255]. This induces a hierarchical structure of communities according to the sequence of edge removals. At the coarsest level, there is a single community (assuming the network is connected) and at finest level each actor is a community of its own.

This method has been used successfully to detect communities from e-mail networks (two actors are connected if one sent an e-mail to the other), collaboration networks (two actors are connected if they did some joint scientific work), and other social networks.

9.2.5 Pajek: Large Network Analysis Software

Pajek, meaning spider in Slovenian, is a comprehensive software package for large network analysis that is free for noncommercial use [61]. It supports *statistics* both global (such as the number of nodes, edges, and components) and local (such as degree, centrality indices, hubs, and authorities), and *decomposition* into subnetworks that can be further analyzed, for example, by clustering techniques. Pajek also provides network visualization tools, using techniques such as force-directed methods [99].

9.3 PEER-TO-PEER NETWORKS

A peer-to-peer (P2P) network can be viewed as a social network between computers that communicate over the Internet [515].

In a client/server architecture, a few computers act as dedicated servers and the rest as clients. For example, a web server deals with http requests to a company web site, an e-mail server deals with the management of e-mail exchange, and a database server deals with retrieval and update of database records. The client/server model delineates between the tasks of the client and the server. For example, once an http request is made and the page is served to the browser, the browser is responsible for rendering the page on the user's monitor and for any further user interaction with the information on the local computer. In the client/server model, the client is often idle and may have unused storage capacity, while the server may be overburdened due to its limited capacity. The P2P architecture aims to make use of the computing power present in the clients by breaking down the distinction between clients and servers.

In a P2P network, the distinction between clients and servers is blurred, and the computers in the network may act as both a client and a server, according to what is most appropriate for the system given the task to be performed. In principle, such an architecture helps to distribute the load between the computers in the network and make use of the collective computational power available at a lower cost and higher efficiency. The challenge of P2P computing is to build large and scalable networks.

P2P has become very popular for file sharing among internet users and is very successful as an internet telephony model. In fact, a study on internet traffic showed that P2P applications generate the most internet traffic in all world regions and that the BitTorrent file sharing protocol (see Section 9.3.5) is by far the most used.[191]

9.3.1 Centralized P2P Networks

Recall the star network, which has one central node connected to all the other nodes in the network. This is like the client/server model, with the central node being the server and the satellite nodes being the clients. In order for a client to find information in this type of network, the client needs to first contact the server who will then refer this client to another client having the information needed, and finally the two clients can talk to each other in order to exchange the information. This is the simplest P2P architecture, which is very close to a client/server model; the highest profile example of this type of centralized network is Napster (www.napster.com).

Napster was designed as a centralized P2P network for music swapping. In order to join Napster, a user registered and downloaded software to his or her computer. Napster's central server stored information about music files of members currently connected to the network, which was automatically updated as users logged on and off the network. When a member issued a search for a song, the central server provided information to the member, who could then establish a direct connection with another member's computer having the song. The downloading of the song then took place between the two members, and did not involve the central computer; this was the P2P element of Napster.

This model of file sharing is very powerful, provided the system has many members, since it makes it easy to find files a user may want (the more members the more files are shared, the more likely it is to find a file) and the burden of computation (download time) is between the members swapping files, rather than

[191] Internet Study 2008/2009. www.ipoque.com/resources/internet-studies/internet-study-2008_2009.

between the members and the central server. In mid-2001, Napster hit the headlines when it was forced to close down for copyright infringement, due to action taken by the RIAA (recording industry association of america). Subsequently, it reopened as a subscription-based service, but it remains to be seen if it can regain its peak popularity of over 36 million users.

9.3.2 Decentralized P2P Networks

Gnutella[192] was designed as a decentralized P2P network for file sharing. As opposed to Napster, it does not have any central server. Gnutella is an open and decentralized group membership and search protocol. To use Gnutella, you need to download or develop software that adheres to its protocol. To join the network a new node, also known as a *peer*, connects to an available known host, which then forwards the new user's information to other Gnutella peers creating a *neighborhood* of peers that the new node will be connected to. Once joined to the network, a peer can perform the tasks of both a server and a client. A study of the Gnutella network from November 2000 to June 2001 showed that 40% of the peers leave the network in less than 4 hours, while only 25% of the peers remains connected to the network for more than 24 hours [569].

The communication between peers in Gnutella happens by a peer broadcasting a message to its neighbors, then these neighbors broadcast the message to their neighbors (i.e., to the neighbors of the neighbors of the peer initiating the original message), and so on. To prevent messages being broadcast indefinitely throughout the network, Gnutella tags messages with a *time-to-live* (TTL) number. The TTL of a new query is typically seven, and it is decremented by one each time the message is passed to a neighboring peer. A message with a TTL of zero is not broadcast any further, and thus every message is timed-out in this way. The aforementioned study also showed that 95% of any two peers could exchange messages in at most seven hops.

When a peer responds to a message, it backpropagates the response to the peer from which it received the message, then this peer further backpropagates the message to the peer it received the message from, and so on, until the response propagates back to the peer that initiated the original message. To prevent indefinite backpropagation, due to loops in the network, each peer has a limited memory of the messages that have passed through the peer.

There are several types of messages in Gnutella: (i) a *ping*, asking "are you there?"; (ii) a *pong*, which is a reply to ping saying, "yes, I am here"; (iii) a *query*, stating "I am searching for this file"; (iv) a *query response*, which is a reply to a query message including the information needed to download the requested file to be propagated backwards along the path of the original query message; (v) *get*, which requests for the file returned from a query, by connecting to the peer that has the file and then downloading the file; and (vi) *push*, intended for peers located behind a firewall, which asks the peer having the file to initiate a connection to the requesting peer and then to upload the file to that peer.

[192]Gnutella Protocol Specification. http://wiki.limewire.org/index.php?title=GDF.

To summarize, searching for a file in Gnutella works as follows. A peer sends a query message to the neighboring peers it is connected to. The neighbors that receive the query broadcast it to their neighbors using the same protocol, noting where the query came from and decrementing the TTL by one. This process continues until the TTL is zero. On receiving the query, if the peer has a file that matches the query, it sends an answer back to the peer from which it received the query, and continuing in this manner the answer backpropagates to the peer that originated the query. This peer can then get the file from the peer having the file, or the file can be pushed to the peer. The Gnutella search algorithm is essentially a breadth-first-search (BFS) of the network. This type of search is very efficient from the point of view of finding the closest peer with the required file. However, because the search is essentially exhaustive to the depth specified by the TTL (i.e., all the peers are visited), it is computationally expensive and thus may consume excessive network and processing resources. Peers with low bandwidth can easily become bottlenecks in the network.

Several alternative search algorithms have been proposed for P2P networks [696]. One idea is for a peer to store a profile of its most recent queries together with the neighbors from which a successful query response was received. It can then estimate, for a new query, which of its neighboring peers is more likely to find a match for the query, by ranking them according to the similarity of the present query to previous queries and the number of successful responses it received during the past for these queries. Another idea is to simply rank each neighboring peer according to the number of successful responses that were received from this neighbor in the past several queries.

A problem that arises in decentralized P2P networks is that of *free riding*, where peers download files from others but either do not share any files or do not provide any content that others may desire to download. This is especially a problem for Gnutella, where peers only have local information, and thus they cannot detect free riding peers beyond their neighbors.

A study of Gnutella based on sampling messages over a 24 hours period in August 2000 showed that nearly 70% of peers do not share files and nearly 50% of successful query responses are received from the top 1% of sharing peers [15]. Moreover, over 60% of peers never provided a query response although, in theory, they had files to share. During this 24 hours period, the number of peers sharing files was above 33,000. A more recent study in 2005 has, overall, confirmed these results, and moreover has shown that free riding has significantly increased since the first study [318].

Given the significant amount of free riding, there is a danger that the few peers providing successful query responses will become saturated. Another problem with the decentralized approach is that with the growth of the network, a large part of it will be unaccessible to queries, and thus beyond the search horizon of peers, according to the value of the TTL. Despite this situation, Gnutella has been very successful, especially since the demise of Napster.

Limewire (www.limewire.com) is the most popular P2P client using the Gnutella network and the BitTorrent protocol (see Section 9.3.5). As of early

2010, it had over 70 million unique monthly users and millions of active users at any given moment.

9.3.3 Hybrid P2P Networks

A hybrid approach between the centralized (for example, Napster) and decentralized (for example, Gnutella) P2P architectures was taken by the proprietary file sharing application Kazaa (www.kazaa.com), using the concept of *super-peers* (also known as *ultrapeers* in an enhancement of Gnutella) [428]. There are two types of peers in Kazaa, regular-peers and super-peers. Every regular-peer connects to a super-peer and the super-peers are connected to each other. In this two-level architecture, regular-peers act as clients of the super-peers and the super-peers acts as both clients and servers. The super-peers are elected by the Kazaa Media Desktop software, the main criterion being that super-peers have broadband capabilities; peers can opt out of being a super-node through the software interface. The Kazaa protocol is similar to that of Gnutella with the difference that regular-peers communicate with the network through super-peers, and super-peers communicate with each other and with the regular-peers that are connected to them. Lists of active super-nodes are frequently exchanged and updated by Kazaa peers. Super-peers store information about the files that are available at the regular-peers that are connected to them, so that queries can be answered by the super-peers prior to the file transfer taking place. As in other P2P models, once a query is answered the file that is found is transferred directly between the peer requesting the file and the peer having it.

A study of the Kazaa network [413] showed that sharing is concentrated around a small minority of popular items. It was observed that 65% of all downloads go to 20% of the most popular files, implying that caching could be effective to reduce the traffic in the network. Moreover, 60% of the traffic is generated by files larger than 700MB (movies and games). Internet traffic is increasingly being dominated by file sharing applications such as Kazaa rather than by standard search and navigation web interaction activities.

Kazaa was by far the most popular file sharing P2P application in 2003, although other P2P applications have since overtaken it. In early 2003, it had 3.2 million downloads per week, with over 3.5 million users connected to the network at any given time. Apart from music there are an increasing number of software applications and videos being shared. Kazza faced several copyright infringement lawsuits, but due to its decentralized nature it is not so easy to pinpoint the sources of violation as it was with the centralized Napster architecture. Following a series of high profile legal battles, Kazaa eventually became a legal download music service in 2006.[193] Unauthorized modifications of the original application are still available on the Web, but the Kazaa network is now largely defunct.

There are challenging legal issues that still need to be resolved, but in any case it is clear that the public demand for P2P file sharing will continue to

[193] Kazaa site becomes legal service, by , July 2006. http://news.bbc.co.uk/1/hi/technology/5220406.stm.

flourish, and newer technologies such as BitTorrent, discussed in Section 9.3.5, will be widely deployed.

There are also serious issues concerning privacy and security when using file sharing applications. A study of the Kazaa network, carried out in 2003, showed that users are unintentionally sharing confidential files such as e-mail and financial data [263]. These and other related problems can be reduced, by improving the user interface so as to make users aware of what files they are sharing, and providing clearly demarcated default folders for file sharing.

9.3.4 Distributed Hash Tables

Distributed hash tables (DHTs) provide a method for locating content in a P2P system [570]. A hash table is a dictionary containing key, value pairs, where the keys are mapped onto values using a hash function. In a DHT, the pairs are distributed among the nodes in the P2P system, and can be queried by any node in the system. For example, if a node wishes to find a node having a "P2P tutorial", then this key is mapped by the hash function to a numeric value, say 1212. The next step is to find a short path to a target node that has the object with content 1212; often nodes are assigned ranges, so 1212 must be within the target node's range. DHT routing algorithms differ in the way they locate a path from the source node to the target. The important property of a DHT topology is that for a given key and node, either the node is responsible for the value of the hash function mapped to it by the key or it has a link to a node which is closer to the target node in terms of a distance measure defined over the key space. Using such a greedy algorithm, the target node can be found. When a node leaves the system, its range needs to be redistributed among the remaining nodes.

The largest deployed P2P DHT network with several million concurrent users as of 2010, is called *KAD*, which is based on Kademlia [460]. Kademlia implements a tree-based routing topology making use of the exclusive-or binary operation as the distance metric.

9.3.5 BitTorrent File Distribution

BitTorrent is a file distribution system that takes advantage of the situation when multiple users are downloading the same file at the same time, by having them upload pieces of the files to each other [156]. The idea is to redistribute the upload cost to the users downloading the file, making affordable the concurrent download of the file by many users, thus encouraging users to share files. It routinely enables sharing of files of hundreds of megabytes in size to hundreds of simultaneous peers.

The decision to use BitTorrent is made by the peer sharing a file. Suppose several peers are downloading the same file. BitTorrent helps them connect to each other by making the information about the other peers available to the others. A peer having the complete file, known as the *seed*, must be connected to the network. In order to keep track of what part of the file peers have, BitTorrent divides the file into fixed size pieces, typically 0.25MB. Once connected, each peer reports to the other peers what pieces it has. The peers then continuously download pieces from other peers having these pieces, until they have the whole file. Each peer is responsible for attempting to maximize its own download rate. This is done by a peer uploading pieces of the file to other peers that reciprocate by uploading to them pieces they need. Using this strategy peers get better download rates. We note that none of the downloaders can complete, until the seed has uploaded every part of the file. Finally, it is considered polite to leave the BitTorrent client uploading for a while after a peer has completed the download.

9.3.6 JXTA P2P Search

As we have noted earlier, web search engines are not able to index the hidden web residing in online databases, which are invisible to web crawlers. P2P networks have the potential to make available such content through distributed search protocols.

JXTA search in P2P networks is part of Sun's JXTA (https://jxta.dev.java.net) open source protocols and applications that allow any devices connected to the network to communicate and collaborate in a P2P manner. In particular it is a suite of protocols to facilitate searching a decentralized P2P network [670]. The architecture of a JXTA network is similar to that of Kazaa, with regular- and super-peers (in JXTA super-peers are called *hubs*). JXTA search is based on the Infrasearch engine, which was powered by Gnutella.

Peers in a JXTA network can be both information providers and consumers. JXTA's query routing protocol consists of three components: registration, request, and response; all components are expressed in XML syntax. The providers (i.e., the servers) register a description of the queries they are willing to answer for the consumers (i.e., the clients). Consumers, who are the users of the system, request information by querying the network, and responses are returned from providers who can answer the queries through the P2P network protocol. Because JXTA search supports arbitrary XML, it is extensible and can be integrated with emerging standards. In particular, JXTA could lend itself to consumer web searching, for example, to provide a search engine interface to hidden web information.

9.3.7 Incentives in P2P Systems

The problem of free riding, where users download files but do not contribute to the community by uploading in return, is one of the main problems in P2P systems. When there are a very large number of anonymous users and most of the transactions between users occur only once, it is not surprising that cooperation is not the norm. Thus the design of incentives in P2P systems to encourage cooperative behavior is important [43]. Three types of incentive are reputation, currency, and barter.

Reputation is an effective way to facilitate reputation in P2P systems. Contributing users who upload files obtain a good reputation, while those who do not posses a bad reputation. Good peers are rewarded by the system by gaining priority and higher bandwidth when downloading. Reputation can also be used, in conjunction with other techniques, to measure trust and detect malicious peers. Currency is similar to reputation, in that "good" peers earn currency by contributing to the system, which they can spend to obtain resources such as increased download amounts and bandwidth.

BitTorent has incentives built into its protocol, as peers have to cooperate when downloading a large file. When a large file is being downloaded there will be multiple interactions between the interacting peers, which allow cooperation through direct reciprocity. Each peer must upload in order to download, which is where the bartering comes in.

9.4 COLLABORATIVE FILTERING

9.4.1 Amazon.com

Amazon.com (www.amazon.com), founded in July 1995 by Jeff Bezos, was one of the first widely used e-commerce web sites. Known as the biggest online bookshop, Amazon also sells other items such as music, videos, software, and electronics. Amazon has also been able to leverage its popularity and robust e-commerce software to act as a third party for other booksellers.

Amazon.com has become a household name through its convenient, friendly, streamlined, efficient, and trustworthy online shopping process, starting from viewing a book to getting through the checkout, and following up orders until the actual books finally arrive in the post. It has become one of the best known brands on the Web and continues to be one of its greatest successes. According to Kohavi, Data Mining and Personlization director at Amazon.com, they had 41 million active customers as of 2004.[194]

Two subsidiaries of Amazon that specialize in search and navigation technologies are Alexa (www.alexa.com) and A9 (www.a9.com). Alexa.com, which started up in April 1996 and was bought by Amazon in April 1999, is best known for its toolbar that, once installed, collects information about the sites you are surfing through, and shares this information with other toolbar users. On the other hand, A9, which started up in October 2003, concentrates on search and personalization technologies for e-commerce use. A novel search facility provided by A9 returns quotes from pages in books that match the user's query. This feature of being able to search inside a book is also available to users viewing book details on Amazon.com, for the books that have already been scanned by the company.

Amazon have also ventured into the gadget arena with the Amazon Kindle wireless reading device,[195] for reading and downloading e-books and other digital media, including online free content that can be viewed wirelessly. Although attempts to commercialize a platform for e-books have come and gone, Amazon

[194]Front line internet analytics at Amazon.com, by R. Kohavi and M. Round. Emetrics Summit 2004-Web Analytics Summit, Santa Barbara, June 2004. http://ai.stanford.edu/~ronnyk/emetricsAmazon.pdf.

[195]Kindle Wireless Reading Device, www.amazon.com/Kindle-Amazons-Wireless-Reading-Generation/dp/B00154JDAI.

are committed to making it a success with a large, growing number of titles being made available for the Kindle at a competitive price [64].

Part of the success of Amazon.com is the innovative use of technology to enhance the user experience. It has been a pioneer in mass scale use of personalization and CF, delivered to its millions of customers, all of which are online. A quote from Jeff Besoz, founder and CEO of Amazon.com, in an interview for Business Week during March 1999 is appropriate:

> "Today we add a little bit of value from personalization and discovery. Once you've ordered once or twice, we start to recommend products using a technology we use called *collaborative filtering*. The site will say, 'Welcome Rob,' and 'Click here for your personal recommendations.' Actually, now it works pretty darn well, but it's going to work even better in the future. And that notion of being able to help people to discover exactly what they're looking for saves them time and improves their lives. That's going to become, over the next 10 years, a bigger and bigger factor of the value proposition. *We have 6.2 million customers, we should have 6.2 million stores*. There should be the optimum store for each and every customer."

9.4.2 Collaborative Filtering Explained

What is CF? In a nutshell it is recommendation by "word of mouth" [568]. The following definition of "word of mouth advertising" can be found in the Oxford dictionary:

> "The process in which the purchaser of a product or service tells friends, family, neighbors, and associates about its virtues, especially when this happens in advance of media advertising."

So, how does CF work in practice. As an example, suppose that I read a book, I like it, and recommend it to my friends. Those of my friends who have a similar taste in books to mine may decide to read the book and then recommend it to their friends. This is CF at work, through the power of social networking.

In an e-commerce site, this process may be automated as follows [590]. When I buy a book, this in itself is an implicit recommendation, but the site could ask me for an explicit rating of the book, say on a scale of 1 to 10. When my friend logs onto the site, the CF system will be able to deduce that his taste in books is similar to mine, since we have purchased similar items in the past. The system will also notice that he has not yet bought the book that I have rated highly, and then recommend this book to my friend. This is the essence of collaborative filtering. In practice, the system will collect as many recommendations as it can and score them according to their overall popularity before presenting the top recommendations to the user. We will look at this type of CF algorithm and variations of it in more detail below.

CF has applications also in e-learning in order to recommend content to teachers and students, and, in general, it can be used in web navigation to recommend links to like-minded surfers (see Section 9.7).

TABLE 9.3 A user–item rating matrix.

	Item				
User	Data Mining	Search Engines	Databases	XML	...
Alex	1		5	4	...
George	2	3	4		...
Mark	4	5		2	...
Peter			4	5	...

9.4.3 User-Based Collaborative Filtering

Consider the user–item matrix shown in Table 9.3. Each row represents a user, and each column represents an item. A number in the ith row and jth column is the rating that user i assigned to item j; an empty cell indicates that the user did *not* rate that item. The ellipsis $(\cdots)$ at the end of each row indicates that we have shown only a small fraction of the items. In a typical e-commerce scenario, a user would normally rate (or purchase) only a few products, say 30, out of the millions that may be available, so that the user–item matrix is very *sparse*.

This sparsity problem has a negative effect on recommendation systems, since there may not be enough data for the system to make a reliable prediction. In order to find like-minded users, that is, users with similar tastes, there needs to be sufficient overlap in their buying habits (in case of an e-commerce site) or page views (in case of an e-learning or e-content site), for the system to have a statistically significant assessment of their similarity. Another related problem is the *first-rater* problem, when an item has not been rated yet, questioning how can it be recommended. An e-commerce site may still want to promote items having no rating, and in this case a *content-based* approach is necessary.

The ratings for an item can be collected *explicitly* or *implicitly*. Explicit rating demands the user to give feedback to the system on the quality of the item, it is normally a number between 1 and 10, low numbers providing negative feedback and high number providing positive feedback. Implicit feedback is collected without any special user intervention; the system observes the user behavior and constructs a rating for the item based on the information it has. The best indicator of positive feedback in an e-commerce setting is when users buy the item; in other settings, such as e-learning, the amount of time users spend and/or the number of mouse operations they carry out when viewing the content is normally used to measure their interest in the content.

A CF algorithm takes the user–item matrix as input and produces user recommendations for the *active user* as output. For each user, an item vector is constructed, where 0 implies that the item is unrated. For example, the item vector for Alex is $<1, 0, 5, 4>$, for George it is $<2, 3, 4, 0>$, for Mark it is $<4, 5, 0, 2>$, and for Peter it is $<0, 0, 4, 5>$. Assume that Alex is the active user.

One measure of similarity that can be computed between the two vectors is the dot product of the vectors. This is called *vector similarity* and is computed by multiplying the ratings in the two vectors item by item and summing up the results. (The result may be normalized so that it is a number between 0 and 1.) For example, the vector similarity between Alex and Peter is 40, between Alex and George it is 22 and between Alex and Mark it is 12.

Another measure of similarity between two rows in the user–item matrix is to compute the Pearson correlation between them, taking into account only the overlapping nonzero items; that is, items that were rated by both users. (You can find the definition of correlation in any standard book on statistics or online at MathWorld (http://mathworld.wolfram.com).) Correlation measures only linear relationships between users, giving a number between -1 and 1; more complex nonlinear relationships cannot be measured with this method.

Both these similarity measures suffer from problems related to the sparsity of the user–item matrix. First, the similarity may be based on a few observations and therefore may not be accurate. In the extreme case of only two items in common, the Pearson correlation will always return either 1 or -1. The second problem is the case when there is no overlap in the users nonzero rated items. In this case, both approaches cannot detect any similarity and a content-based approach must be used instead.

The users who have positive similarity to the active user are called its *neighbors*. In the next step of the CF process, the predicted score for the active user on an item he or she has not rated is computed using the *k-nearest neighbors* to the active users; that is, the k users who are most similar to the active user. More specifically, the predicated score is computed by adding to the active user's average score the weighted average of the deviation of the k-nearest neighbors from their average weighting; the weighting of each neighbor is given according to his or her similarity to the active user.

The predicted rating for search engines for Alex is computed as follows. The nearest neighbors to Alex who have rated search engines are George and Mark. George's average rating is 3 and Mark's is 3.33. The deviation of George's average rating from his score for search engines is zero, while the deviation from Mark's score is $5 - 3.33 = 1.67$. Weighting this deviation by Mark's similarity and dividing by the sum of similarities of the nearest neighbors, $22 + 12 = 34$, we get $1.67(12/34) = 0.59$. Finally, adding Alex's average, we get the prediction of $3.33 + 0.59 = 3.92$ for the item search engines.

We note that when the ratings are binary, that is, 0 for no rating and 1 for a positive rating, then the average rating of rated items is always 1, and so the deviation of a rated item from the average will always be 0. In this case, the predicted rating for an item the active user did not see will always be 1, independent of the weighting of its neighbors, as long as there is at least one other user having positive similarity to the active user.

To summarize, the user-based CF method has the following steps [296]:

1. users rate items either explicitly or implicitly;
2. similarity between like-minded users is computed;
3. predications are made for items that the active user has not rated, and the nearest neighbors ratings are used for scoring the recommendations.

The formal statement of the prediction made by user-based CF for the rating of a new item by the active user is presented in Equation 9.1, where

1. $p_{a,i}$ is the prediction for the active user, a, for item, i;
2. k is the number of nearest neighbors of a used for prediction;
3. $w_{a,u}$ is the similarity between a and a neighbor, u of a;
4. $r_{u,i}$ is the rating that user u gave to item i, and $\overline{r}_a$ is the average rating of a.

User-Based CF:

$$p_{a,i} = \overline{r}_a + \frac{\sum_{u=1}^{k}(r_{u,i} - \overline{r}_u)w_{a,u}}{\sum_{u=1}^{k} w_{a,u}} \tag{9.1}$$

9.4.4 Item-Based Collaborative Filtering

Item-to-item recommendation systems try to match similar items that have been co-rated by different users, rather than similar users or customers that have overlapping interests in terms of their rated items [591]. With regards to the user–item matrix, item-to-item CF looks at column similarity rather than row similarity, and, as in user-based methods, vector similarity can be used. For the matrix shown in Table 9.3, the vector similarity between data mining and search engines is 26, between data mining and databases it is 13, and between data mining and XML it is 12.

In order to predict a rating, $p_{a,i}$, for the active user, a, for an item i, all items, say j, that are similar to i, and were rated by a, are taken into account. For each such j, the similarity between items i and j, denoted by $s_{i,j}$, is computed and then weighted by the rating, $r_{a,j}$, that a gave to j. These values are summed and normalized to give the prediction.

The formal statement for the prediction made by item-based CF for the rating of a new item by the active user is presented in Equation 9.2.

Item-Based CF:

$$p_{a,i} = \frac{\sum_{j \text{ rated by } a} s_{i,j} r_{a,j}}{\sum_{j \text{ rated by } a} s_{i,j}} \tag{9.2}$$

In item-to-item algorithms, the number of items to be recommended is often limited by a constant, say n, so that only the top-n predicted ratings of items similar to the items rated by the active user are returned [183]. Experiments comparing the item-to-item algorithm to the user-based algorithm, described above, have shown consistently that the item-to-item algorithm is not only much faster but also produces better quality predictions.

The predicted rating for data mining for Peter is computed as follows. The normalized weighting of the similarity between data mining and databases is $13/(13 + 12 = 25) = 0.52$, and between data mining and XML is $12/25 = 0.48$. Adding up these weights multiplied by Peter's ratings gives a predicted rating of $0.52 \times 4 + 0.48 \times 5 = 4.48$ for data mining.

9.4.5 Model-Based Collaborative Filtering

Apart from the algorithms we have presented there have been several other proposals, notably methods, which use machine learning techniques to build a statistical model of the user–item matrix that is then used to make predictions [102]. One such technique trains a neural network for each user, which learns to predict the user rating for a new item [371]. Another technique builds *association rules* [430] such as

> "90% of users who like items i and j also like item k, 30% of all users like all these items."

The rules are generally of the form $X \Rightarrow Y$, where X is a set of items and Y is another item, as in user-based algorithms. In this case, the rule is $\{i, j\} \Rightarrow \{k\}$. The 30% in the rule refers to its *support*; that is, out of all the users in the user–item matrix, 30% like all three items (this includes the items in both X and Y). The 90% refers to the *confidence* of the rule; that is, it is the proportion of users who like all three items (this includes the items in either X or Y) out of the proportion of users who like only i and j (this includes only the items in X).

For prediction purposes, we are interested in rules such that all the items in the left-hand side of these rules were rated by the active user but the item on their right-hand side was not. Setting the support and confidence to the minimum desired levels, the rules can be ranked according to their confidence, for those whose support is above the desired minimum.

Yet another technique uses the naive Bayes classifier, introduced in Section 3.2 [476]. The basic idea is as follows, with the user–item matrix being the input. For the purpose of this algorithm, we consider items to be rated as "liked" or "disliked," or to be unrated. The problem is to compute the probability that an item will be liked or disliked by the active user given ratings of other users.

The naive Bayes assumption states, in this case, that the probability that a user (other than the active user) likes an item, given that the active user likes an item, is independent of the probability that yet another user likes an item given that the active user likes an item. This allows us to asses the probability that an item is liked by the active user, given other user ratings, as being proportional to the product of the probabilities of each user liking an item given that the active user likes an item.

It remains to compute the probability that a user, say j, likes an item given that the active user likes an item. This probability measures the similarity between user j and the active user. For this we make use only of the items that both j and active user have rated. Suppose that there are n items, which both user j and the active user rated, and out of these the active user liked m items. Moreover, suppose that k out of the m item were also liked by user j. Then the probability that j will like an item given that the active user likes an item is k/m. Thus the estimation of the probability that the active user will like an item, say i, that user j has liked but the active user has not rated is also k/m. Multiplying all these probabilities together for all other users that like item i gives us an estimate of the probability that the active user will like i. Preliminary experiments with this method have shown it to be more accurate than the standard user-based algorithm.

9.4.6 Content-Based Recommendation Systems

In order to deal with the sparsity problem (where few if any users have rated any items that the active user has rated) and the first-rater problem (where no users have rated an item), a content-based approach to recommendation needs to be deployed. Content-based approaches are not collaborative, since they involve only the active user and the items they interact with.

For content-based systems to work, the system must be able to build a profile of the user's interests, which can be done explicitly or implicitly; see Section 6.4 for more details on the user profile. The user's interests include the categories he/she prefers in relation to the application; for example, does the user prefer fiction to nonfiction books, and pop music to classical music. Once the system has a user profile, it can check similarity of the item (or content) a user is viewing to the profile, and according to the degree of similarity create a rating for the item (or content). This is much like the search process, where, in this case, the profile acts as a query and the items presented to the user acts as the query results. The higher the item is rated, the higher is its ranking when presented to the user.

Content-based and CF systems can be combined as follows, assuming we wish to make a prediction for item i, and that we are measuring the similarity between the active user and another user, say j. The item vectors for the active user and user j are normally sparse, so we make use of content-based filtering to fill in *pseudoratings* for items that were rated by one but not the other user, ensuring that the range of pseudoratings is the same as for other user ratings.

After this stage, both vectors have a larger overlap, alleviating the sparsity problem of CF methods. The content-based predictions can be weighted according to the number of ratings the user had, since its accuracy depends on this number. The algorithm can now continue much as before, making a prediction for item i using the k-nearest neighbor method [465].

Another aspect of CF algorithms is that of serendipity, defined in the Oxford dictionary as

> "The occurrence and development of events by chance in a happy or beneficial way."

Although users like to get recommendations that they are familiar with, they also like to see novel recommendations that they did not expect but are interesting to them. It is especially pleasing to get a recommendation of something that I do not know and was not already aware of.

CF has an advantage over content-based method in this respect, since the recommendations are not based on the content but rather on how it is rated. This factor can be boosted by giving preference to similar but "nontypical" users, and by not always recommending the most popular items. For example, every customer of an online supermarket will buy the standard items such as milk and apples, so there is not much point in recommending these items.

A notable content-based recommender system for music is Pandora (www.pandora.com), founded by Tim Westergen in 2000 on the back of the music genome project. The way it works is that each song is represented by a vector of up to about 400 features, called *genes*, each assigned a number between 1 and 5 in half integer increments. For example, there are genes for the instrument type, for the music style, and for the type of lyrics. The song vectors are constructed by experts, each song taking about 20–30 mins to construct. As of mid-2006, the music genome library contained over 400,000 songs from 20,000 contemporary artists. In addition, according to the FAQ on Pandora's site, about 15,000 new song vectors are added to the library every month. When a user listens to a song, a list of similar songs can be constructed using a similarity measure such as standard vector similarity. Content-based recommender systems inevitably have the effect of reinforcing what the user listens to rather than being serendipitious as are CF systems. However, one advantage of Pandora's approach is that its listeners have access to music in the long tail, as the experts can construct vectors for less popular songs, for example, very new songs of musicians that may not be known or old songs that have fell out of fashion. On the other hand, this approach does not scale to the degree that, say, CF does due to the time consuming human effort in constructing the song vectors. In order to tune its recommendations, Pandora also collects user ratings to allow its algorithms to adjust the feature weights and personalize future suggestions. Another interesting content-based approach that is proving to be competitive is to analyze the signal waveform of songs and to make automated recommendations based on musical similarity [450].

9.4.7 Evaluation of Collaborative Filtering Systems

The evaluation of CF systems is a crucial matter, as is the choice of data set to test the predictions discussed in Ref. 297. Once we have a data set, the standard technique is to withhold the rating we wish to predict, then to execute the CF algorithm on the modified data set, and finally to compare the predictions with the original ratings. The most common metric used to measure the distance between the predicted and true ratings is the *mean absolute error* (MAE). This is simply the sum of the absolute values of the differences between the predicted and true ratings divided by the number of predictions made.

The MAE is less appropriate when we wish the accuracy of the top rated items to be higher than the low rated items, or when we are only interested in a binary rating; that is, is the item "good" or is it "bad?"

The advantages of MAE are that it is simple to compute and its properties have been well studied. A related measure, the root mean squared error, which puts more emphasis on large errors, is mentioned in Subsection 9.4.10. Other metrics such as precision (the ratio of relevant recommended items to all recommended items) and recall (the ratio of relevant recommended items to all relevant items), which were studied in Section 5.4 in the context of evaluating search engine results, can also be used. In this context, a relevant item could be an item with true rating 4 or 5, for a rating scale of 1–5. As is the case with search engines, recall, in its pure sense, is hard to measure since it demands global knowledge of the relevant items, and users typically only examine a page of recommendations (or search results). Moreover, as with search engines, measuring the top-n precision is an appropriate measure.

9.4.8 Scalability of Collaborative Filtering Systems

In order for CF systems to deal with millions of users and items, they must be scalable, that is, sublinear or constant time in the size of the user–item matrix, since recommendations must be generated in real time for every user individually.

To do this, recommendation process can be broken up into two separate stages, as is done in Amazon.com's recommendation system [433].

- In the first stage, the user–item matrix is preprocessed offline into an item-to-item matrix. This offline stage, which is computationally intensive, calculates a similarity measure between co-rated items as in item-to-item recommendation systems. The computation, although extremely time intensive, is manageable since the user–item matrix is sparse. However, it can be made more efficient for very popular items by sampling users who have rated these items. It is also possible to discard users with very few rated items, and to discard extremely popular or unpopular items.
- In the second stage, the recommendations uses the item-to-item matrix output from the first stage to deliver recommendations for the active user in real time, via a computation, which is independent of the size of the original user–item matrix, and depends only on the number of items the active user has rated.

To provide recommendations, the most similar items to the ones that have been rated by the active user can be found from the item-to-item matrix, and once predicted ratings for new items are computed, these items can be ranked. To compute the prediction for an item, say i, not rated by the active user, the similarity between item i and each of the items that the active user has rated is computed from the item-to-item matrix and these are then summed and weighted as described above (Eq. 9.2).

9.4.9 A Case Study of Amazon.co.uk

We now provide a short case study of Amazon.co.uk (the UK subsidiary of Amazon.com). When you enter the site, assuming that you are a customer and have identified yourself on the machine you are using, a cookie on the machine allows Amazon to identify you. You are then greeted with "Hello `Your Name`, we have *recommendations* for you." If you click on the recommendations you get a web page with a list of items related to the items that you have purchased or are on your wish list. The wish list is provided by the system so that you can save links to books that you may buy in the future. Amazon makes use of a star system for rating books and providing reviews that others can read, and you are encouraged to give the system feedback in order to improve your recommendations and to get more information on why the recommendation was made. (Note that the user interface will be enhanced over time, but, overall, I expect the functionality to be similar.)

When you view a book you get a list of other books headed by the now famous slogan:

"Customers who bought this item also bought ..."

In addition, you are offered to buy related books under the heading "Frequently bought together," encouraged to explore similar items, to look inside the book if it has been scanned, and to read customer reviews.

9.4.10 The Netflix Prize

Netflix (www.netflix.com), founded in 1997 by Reed Hastings, is a mail video rental service in the United States, also offering online streaming of movies and TV episodes to its customers. It went public in 2002, announced its billionth DVD delivery early in 2007, and its second billionth DVD delivery two years later. As of early 2010, its rental collection included over 100,000 tiles, its subscription base was over 11 million, and it distributed about 2.2 million DVDs a day to its customers.

Netflix has developed an internal recommender system, called *Cinematch* [74], using an item-based CF algorithm. By 2007, Netflix had collected about 2 billion ratings from over 10 million customers on over 85,000 titles since 1998, with 2 million new ratings being added to its system on a daily basis. Cinematch makes hundreds of millions of predictions a day and retrains its system about once a week. About 60% of all movies that users add to their queue (which is the prioritized list of movies a user wishes to view) come from recommendations.[196]

In October 2006, Netflix released a large data set and a challenge to the data mining community to beat its system by a predefined margin. The accuracy of Cinematch is measured by the *root mean squared error* (RMSE), which is the square root of the average of the sum of squares of the differences between the true and predicted ratings. The grand prize of $1 million would be awarded to the team that would improve on the RMSE of Cinematch by 10%. As long as the grand prize was not achieved, a progress prize of $50,000 would be awarded to the team with the best result so far, which would have to beat the previous result by at least 1%.

The released data set contains over 100 million ratings (including their dates) from over 480,000 randomly chosen subscribers on nearly 18,000 movies. Each rating is on an integer scale between 1 and 5. Over 3 million of the most recent ratings from the same set of subscribers have been withheld as the

[196]The Cinematch System: Operation, Scale Coverage, Accuracy Impact, Video presentation by Jim Bennett of Netflix, September 2006. http://blog.recommenders06.com/wp-content/uploads/2006/09/1jimbennett.wmv.

qualifying set of the competition. Each competing team would have to submit predictions for all the ratings in the qualifying set. The RMSE for these is computed for a fixed half of the qualifying set, known as the *quiz* subset, and posted on the leaderboard. According to the rules, the RMSE of the other half of the qualifying set, known as the *test* subset, is not reported but is used by Netflix to determine the prize winners if any. In addition, Netflix identified a *probe* subset, which contains 1.4 million records with the ratings attached, that could be used by teams for testing their algorithms before submitting their results. The quiz, test, and probe sets have all been chosen with the same statistical random sampling process.

By mid-2007, over 20,000 teams had registered for the competition from over 150 countries, and 2000 teams had submitted over 13,000 prediction sets. The first progress prize was awarded in 2007 to the team KorBell consisting of three researchers from AT&T for improving on the RMSE of Cinematch by 8.43%. The second progress was awarded in 2008 to the team BellKor in BigChaos, which was a joint team consisting of the KorBell team members and another team, BigChaos, whose members are from an Austrian recommender systems consulting firm. They improved on the RMSE of Cinematch by 9.44%. Finally, the grand prize was awarded in 2009 to the team BellKor's Pragmatic Chaos (www.research.att.com/~volinsky/netflix/bpc.html), which added a third team, Pragmatic Theory, consisting of two computer engineers from Canada, to the BellKor in BigChaos team. BellKor's Pragmatic Chaos improved on the RMSE of Cinematch by 10.06% and were awarded $1 million dollars for their efforts.[197]

The last minute finish of the competition was quite dramatic as another team, The Ensemble (www.the-ensemble.com), was in a head to head competition with BellKor's Pragmatic Chaos. Very close to the finish, BellKor's Pragmatic Chaos submitted an entry with an improvement of 10.09% as measured from the "quiz" subset, and just a few minutes before the closing time of the competition The Ensemble submitted a new entry with an improvement of 10.10% as measured from the "quiz" subset. The final result as measured from the "test" subset was a tie with both teams showing an improvement of 10.06%, as shown in Fig. 9.4 As BellKor's Pragmatic Chaos was the earlier one they were awarded the prize. Netlfix has donated the full data set to the research community, and it can be found in UCI machine learning repository, at http://archive.ics.uci.edu/ml/datasets/Netflix+Prize.

The Netflix prize has stimulated researchers and practitioners to innovate, cooperate, and share ideas. As a side effect, many of the important algorithms used in CF have become accessible to a wider audience rather than just the academic community, and, in addition, a high-quality data set has been made public allowing new algorithms to be objectively tested against the existing ones.

There are several innovations of the winning entry that we will briefly mention. One important lesson that was learnt is that the most successful submissions resulted from combining several prediction models into a single model through

[197]Grand Prize awarded to team BellKor's Pragmatic Chaos, by prizemaster, September 2009. www.netflixprize.com/community/viewtopic.php?id=1537.

NETFLIX

Netflix Prize COMPLETED

Home | Rules | Leaderboard | Update | Download

Leaderboard

Showing Test Score. Click here to show quiz score

Display top 20 leaders.

Rank	Team Name	Best Test Score	% Improvement	Best Submit Time
Grand Prize - RMSE = 0.8567 - Winning Team: BellKor's Pragmatic Chaos				
1	BellKor's Pragmatic Chaos	0.8567	10.06	2009-07-26 18:18:28
2	The Ensemble	0.8567	10.06	2009-07-26 18:38:22
3	Grand Prize Team	0.8582	9.90	2009-07-10 21:24:40
4	Opera Solutions and Vandelay United	0.8588	9.84	2009-07-10 01:12:31
5	Vandelay Industries !	0.8591	9.81	2009-07-10 00:32:20
6	PragmaticTheory	0.8594	9.77	2009-06-24 12:06:56
7	BellKor in BigChaos	0.8601	9.70	2009-05-13 08:14:09
8	Dace_	0.8612	9.59	2009-07-24 17:18:43
9	Feeds2	0.8622	9.48	2009-07-12 13:11:51
10	BigChaos	0.8623	9.47	2009-04-07 12:33:59
11	Opera Solutions	0.8623	9.47	2009-07-24 00:34:07
12	BellKor	0.8624	9.46	2009-07-26 17:19:11
Progress Prize 2008 - RMSE = 0.8627 - Winning Team: BellKor in BigChaos				
13	xiangliang	0.8642	9.27	2009-07-15 14:53:22
14	Gravity	0.8643	9.26	2009-04-22 18:31:32
15	Ces	0.8651	9.18	2009-06-21 19:24:53
16	Invisible Ideas	0.8653	9.15	2009-07-15 15:53:04
17	Just a guy in a garage	0.8662	9.06	2009-05-24 10:02:54
18	J Dennis Su	0.8666	9.02	2009-03-07 17:16:17
19	Craig Carmichael	0.8666	9.02	2009-07-25 16:00:54
20	acmehill	0.8668	9.00	2009-03-21 16:20:50
Progress Prize 2007 - RMSE = 0.8723 - Winning Team: KorBell				
Cinematch score - RMSE = 0.9525				

There are currently 51051 contestants on 41305 teams from 186 different countries.
We have received 44014 valid submissions from 5169 different teams; 0 submissions in the last 24 hours.

Questions about interpreting the leaderboard? Please read this.

FAQ | Forum | Netflix Home

© 1997-2009 Netflix, Inc. All rights reserved.

Figure 9.4 Netflix prize final leaderboard.[198]

a process known as *blending* or *ensemble* learning [543]. One of the simplest yet successful blending strategies is to combine the models in the ensemble in a linear fashion. Thus the objective in this case is to learn the optimal weights of the models in the ensemble such that the weighted linear combination of different models best fits the solution. This can be solved using linear regression or the more complex ridge regression, also known as *regularization* (536, 637), which introduces a penalty term into the regression process to avoid overfitting. The winning Netflix prize entry was the result of blending over 100 different predictive models.

The traditional nearest-neighbor approach to CF, as exemplified in Equations 9.1 and 9.2, compute a weighted average of ratings using a similarity measure between users, or, respectively, items. Bell and Koren, from the winning Netflix prize team, question this traditional approach in that the similarity measures that have been used are somewhat arbitrary and do not take into account interactions among neighbors. For example, the movies in

[198]Source, Netflix, Inc., Netflix Prize, Leaderboard. www.netflixprize.com/leaderboard.

the Lord of the Ring Trilogy are strongly correlated and therefore should not be counted more than once. To resolve these problems a machine learning approach was suggested that replaces the weighted average by a weighted sum (71, 70, 383). The weights are interpolated as a least squares minimization problem of the sum of squares of the differences between the true and predicted weighted nearest-neighbor ratings as given in the training data. This method can be viewed as a linear regression problem and, as with blending, regularization can be deployed to avoid overfitting. It is important to note that this scheme of learning the weights is not based on any similarity measure.

Another approach to CF that has proved to be a major component in the winning teams methods is the use of latent factor models (71, 637, 69, 72, 638). Latent factor models attempt to explain users ratings by the discovery of a number, K, say 50, of factors.

The most common factor method used is known as *singular value decomposition (SVD)* [261]. Given a matrix, M, SVD factorizes the matrix into three parts, U, Σ, and V such that M is equal to the product of U, Σ, and the transpose of V. When M is a user–movie matrix, that is, each row in M corresponds to a user and each column to an item, then the rows in U are the discovered user factors and the rows in V are the discovered movie factors. The matrix Σ is a diagonal matrix with the diagonal entries corresponding to the singular values in order of magnitude and the nondiagonal entries being zero. Often, a good approximation of the original matrix M is to consider only the first K singular values and to set the rest of them to zero. This is exactly what is done in CF and has the effect of reducing the complexity of the SVD computation.

Matrices of movie ratings are sparse, since most users rate only a few movies. The basis for the successful SVD methods used in the Netflix prize was popularized by Simon Funk (whose real name is Brandyn Webb), when in late 2006 he posted, on his blog, the code and explanation of how it works.[199] One method is to replace the missing entries with zeros or possibly with an average rating, and then compute the SVD using a conventional method. What Simon Funk proposed, and was basically taken up by other researchers (71, 637, 69, 72, 638), is to view the problem as one of machine learning. Each prediction can be written as an unknown value in an equation, where the objective is to minimize the sum of squares of the true and predicted user–movie ratings, with a regularization term to avoid overfitting. This form of optimization, known as *ridge regression*, serves as the basis of many of methods used in the Netflix prize to fit parameter values to a model. In fact, it is also possible to combine the neighborhood and latent factor method by plugging the SVD predictions directly into the nearest-neighbor algorithm, where estimates of user ratings are needed, resulting in a neighborhood aware factorization scheme (71, 383).

The Netflix prize data set also includes the dates when the ratings were made. It turns out that this information was instrumental in achieving the 10% improvement over Cinematch to win the grand prize (384, 72). Modeling temporal

[199]Netflix Update: Try This at Home, by Simon Funk, December 2006. http://sifter.org/~simon/journal/20061211.html.

effects to account for how users' ratings change with time can improve prediction accuracy. For example, the popularity of a movie could be affected by external events such as an advertising campaign when it is released. Moreover, some movies age better than others skewing up or down over time. Another example is when users taste changes over time. There is also the case of users who rate many movies at one time, some of which they may have seen a long time ago. Of course, the ratings they give to such movies may be different than the rating they assign to movies they have recently seen. Temporal effects can be incorporated into both neighborhood and latent factor models by parameterizing the variables by time.

9.4.11 Some Other Collaborative Filtering Systems

MovieLens (http://movielens.umn.edu) is a movie recommendations system, which uses the nearest-neighbor CF algorithm. It was developed by the researchers who developed GroupLens [382], an early CF system for Usenet news. (The Usenet discussion service was acquired by Google in February 2001; see http://groups.google.com.) A screenshot of the MovieLens recommendation system is shown in Fig. 9.5. As can be seen, it has a star rating system, with increments of half a star, and the ability to save a movie on a wish list. John Reidl and Joe Konstan, from the Department of Computer Science and Engineering at the University of Minnesota, have commercialized the collaborative filtering method behind GroupLens, by founding Net Perceptions in 1996, which eventually became a victim of the dot-com bubble.[200]

Predictions for you	Your Ratings	Movie Information	Wish List
★★★★½	Not seen	**About a Boy (2002)** DVD, VHS, info | imdb Comedy, Drama	☑
★★★★½	Not seen Not seen 0.5 stars 1.0 stars 1.5 stars 2.0 stars 2.5 stars 3.0 stars 3.5 stars 4.0 stars 4.5 stars 5.0 stars	**Chicago (2002)** info | imdb Comedy, Crime, Drama, Musical	☑
★★★★½		**And Your Mother Too (Y Tu Mamá También) (2001)** DVD, VHS, info | imdb Comedy, Drama, Romance	☐
★★★★½		**Monsoon Wedding (2001)** DVD, VHS, info | imdb Comedy, Romance	☐
★★★★½		**Talk to Her (Hable con Ella) (2002)** info | imdb Comedy, Drama, Romance	☐

Figure 9.5 The user interface of MovieLens. (Source: MovieLens, The MovieLens Tour. http://movielens.umn.edu/html/tour/movies.html.)

[200]David Cotriss Where are they now: Net Perceptions, by D. Cotriss, The Industry Standard, September 2008. www.thestandard.com/news/2008/09/03/where-are-they-now-netperceptions.

PocketLens [471] is a spin-off from GroupLens, implementing CF for mobile users. It is designed to run in a P2P environment, where users can share their ratings with their neighboring peers and update their ratings using an item-to-item CF algorithm. The up-to-date item vector of each user, that is, the row in the user–item matrix pertaining to the user, is sufficiently compact so that it can be stored on a PDA.

It is worth mentioning Ringo [604], an early system for recommending music, that used the Pearson correlation to compute the similarity between users, and also employed an item-to-item algorithm as an alternative to a user-based collaborative filtering algorithm. Pattie Maes, from the MIT Media Lab, commercialized the CF method behind Ringo, by founding Firefly in 1995. Firefly was acquired by Microsoft in April 1998 and was eventually shut down in August 1999.

Music is still high on the list of applications of CF. As an example, the prominent music site CDNow (www.cdnow.com) has teamed up with Amazon.com since the end of 2002, and uses Amazon's e-commerce platform, including its CF recommendation system. An interesting use of CF is done at Last.Fm (www.last.fm), an online music station using recommendation technology for discovering new music based on the user's musical taste, and for sharing musical tastes between users.

CF is an example of a technology that has already been successfully deployed within big e-commerce web sites [593]. Since, on the one hand, the Web is becoming more personalized, and, on the other hand, it is becoming more collaborative, technologies such as CF have been accepted as an integral part of any web recommendation system, and will continue to be improved by researchers and practitioners.

9.5 WEBLOGS (BLOGS)

A *weblog*, pronounced as "web log" or even "we blog" and commonly referred to as a *blog*, is a frequently updated web site made up of entries arranged in reverse chronological order from the newest entry to the oldest [574]. Blogs can be viewed as a personal form of journalism published by, often dedicated, individuals, who in many cases are not affiliated to any organization. Some of the bloggers are professional journalists maintaining blogs that have established a large readership, but most of the bloggers are ordinary people with small audiences. Blogs can be about technology, politics, or any other topic, personal or public. News related blogs provide links to and commentary on breaking or current stories, and personal blogs may take the form of a diary describing the blogger's daily life. Another use of blogs is as an online research tool that tracks a particular line of research as it develops.

In fact, the possibilities are only limited by the blog format. As an example of the diversity of blogs, I have used a blog as a bulletin board for a course I teach (using the Moveable Type web publishing system, www.moveabletype.org), and blogs such as MetaFilter (www.metafilter.com) and Slashdot (www.slashdot.org)

cater for a community, where members can post links and a short description of the link, and other members can comment on and discuss these links.

It is very easy to set up a blog and publish it on the Web. Several companies such as Blogger (www.blogger.com), purchased by Google in February 2003, DiaryLand (www.diaryland.com), and LiveJournal (www.livejournal.com) maintain weblog publishing tools that allow registered users to publish their blog almost instantly after they have typed in their entry. Publishing a blog entry is very simple, all you need to do is fill in a form on which you specify links and highlight text, with minimal use of HTML syntax, or even simpler through a familiar word processing user interface.

The ability of a blog to portray a personal view of an event, often incompatible with that of the traditional media, is quite compelling. In some cases, blogs can give "on the scene" information before it reaches the media. For example, it is now common for bloggers attending technology conferences to create real-time blogs as the event is happening, giving up-to-date information to their readers. As there is no editorial stage in writing a blog, there is no delay in getting it out. Personal accounts from disaster areas and war zones through blogs are another form of news from an individual's perspective.

9.5.1 Blogrolling

The "power" of blogs is in their links to other blogs and sites, and the activity of linking is known as *blogrolling*. Links are the means by which the ideas in a blog are spread throughout the Web. They are also a way for bloggers to collaborate with each other, by acknowledging mutual contributions to a debate or news commentary. Now that search engines regularly index many of the blogs, linking between blogs is even more influence bearing. As we have already seen, link analysis mechanisms, such as Google's PageRank attach higher relevance to sites, have more incoming links, so blogs have the "power" to influence the ranking of sites on search engines (see Google bombing in Section 5.2). In order to keep links from becoming stale, they use absolute addresses that will always work regardless of the address of the web page you are linking from. The term *permalinks* is used for such links emphasizing their permanence.

9.5.2 Blogspace

The space of weblogs, known as *blogspace*, is a social network between the authors of blogs, which arises from the links between their blogs [482]. Blogs cluster together naturally as related blogs tend to link to each other. The most well-established cluster of blogs, known as the *A-list*, is a cluster of some of the early very popular blogs. These blogs have persisted over time, but cannot be distinguished through a particular style, so it seems that writing an interesting blog over a period of time increases its chance of being read; I leave it to the reader to identify the A-list [152].

There also exist special-purpose search engines for blogs notably Technorati (www.technorati.com), making the space of blogs searchable and tracking the most linked blogs within subject categories over a short period, thus reinforcing their popularity. As of mid-2005, there were over 11 million blogs according to Technorati, and they were tracking over 110 million blogs as of mid-2008.[201]

As all blog entries have a date attached to them, they provide an ideal source for studying the temporal evolution of blogspace, the network induced by the links between blogs. Blogs are also interesting in that, at any given time, some topics are discussed and debated more intensely than others, and after a fierce period of debate their topicality fades away and they cease to be the topic of the day. Such intense activity during a time interval is known as *bursty*; see Exercise 7.2.

A study of the evolution of about 25,000 blogs was carried out during the second half of 2002 [395]. It revealed that there was a rapid expansion period in blogspace around the end of 2001, when its largest connected component grew from 3% to around 20% in 2002. The study also discovered increased bursty activity in blogspace toward the end of 2001, that continued in 2002. The increase in the number of bursts is not explained by the expansion of blogspace alone. There seems to be a correlation between the transition behavior in the structure of blogspace and the behavior of bloggers at the time. It may be that the increased availability of easy-to-use blogging software, and as a result the increase in the number of bloggers and the general interest in the blogging phenomenon, contributed to the transition.

9.5.3 Blogs for Testing Machine Learning Algorithms

Blogs serve as an ideal test bed for new machine learning algorithms, due to their availability for crawling, their regular format, and their rich linking structure. BlogPulse (www.blogpulse.com) publishes daily lists of key phrases, key people, and top links mined from a large collection of active blogs, which are archived and refreshed on a daily basis [257]. An inverted file over these blogs makes them searchable through phrases, links, dates, and URLs. In order to detect trends in search results, they are plotted over time as *trend graphs*. These are created by iterating search results over a time period within a specified range and binning the count of the number of results into time buckets, which are by default one day buckets. The points in a trend graph can be normalized as the relative percentage of hits for a query at each point. An example of the use of trend graphs is trends of products mentioned in blogs, and their relationship to sales trends. In Fig. 9.6, we show trend graphs for the keywords "google" and "yahoo", which was created in 2004 using BlogPulse's Trend Search tool.

9.5.4 Spreading Ideas via Blogs

Blogs are a means of spreading ideas (or *memes*) throughout the Web by the use of links, which are an electronic form of "word of mouth" for propagating information. A study of about 40,000 blogs investigated how ideas spread though

[201]Technorati's State of Blogosphere. http://technorati.com/state-of-the-blogosphere.

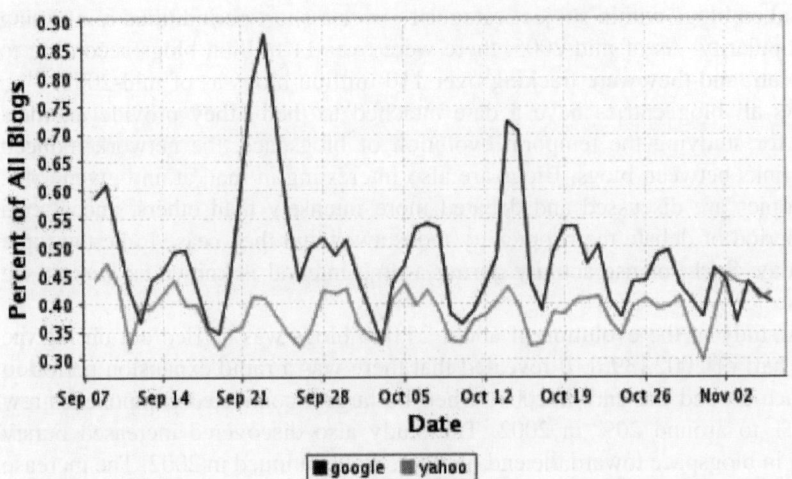

Figure 9.6 Trend graph for keywords: "google" and "yahoo". (Source: The Nielsen Company, BlogPulse, Trend Search tool, www.blogpulse.com/trend; data extracted in 2004.)

blogspace [13]. To characterize patterns of spreading information, triples are used storing (i) the URL of the idea, (ii) the URL of the blog spreading the idea, and (iii) the date of the citation of the URL of the idea in the blog spreading the idea. For each idea (represented by a URL), a vector, ordered by day, is created and normalized. Each element of the vector contains the number of citations to the URL on the given day. To measure the different profiles of ideas spreading, k-means clustering is applied to the resulting vectors of ideas. It was found that most ideas have a short peak and then a decay period which may be fast or slow, and only a few ideas have sustained interest.

To find the blogs that are instrumental in spreading ideas, a ranking algorithm can take into account the time at which an idea is cited, and attach higher weight to more recent citations. In addition, popular blogs having more incoming links will also be influential, and can be discovered by their high PageRank.

9.5.5 The Real-Time Web and Microblogging

The real-time web is a snapshot of the Web as it is evolving. Tapping on to the real-time Web will enable search engines to query information as it is received. For example, news, blogs, social networks, and sites that provide up-to-date reviews and recommendations are part of the real-time web. An analogy to the real-time web in the "real world" is getting current traffic information whilst driving. In the web context, we may want to know people's opinion of a show that they saw last night, or whether there is a current discount on a phone we want to purchase. The ranking of real-time search results must take into account the freshness of the results as a significant component in determining their relevance to the user.

Several real-time search engines have started up in 2009 and we expect fierce competition in this area as the main web search engines incorporate real-time information into their results.[202]

On an individual basis, users may wish to get real-time updates from their friends and share real-time information with them. A service which collates such content is called a *social aggregator* [273]. An example of such an aggregator is FriendFeed (http://friendfeed.com), which can aggregate information from social networks, video, photo, and blogging services that your friends are sharing, and present the information as a customized real-time feed. Users can comment on the feeds and converse about them.

Microblogging is a form of blogging where a single entry is very short, typically a text fragment of less than 200 characters, a single photo, or a short video snippet. It has a wide number of uses such as keeping in touch with friends and family on a regular basis, reporting real-time news, marketing, giving feedback to students, relaying information during emergencies and public relations.

Twitter (www.twitter.com) is a popular microblogging service that allows users to post short messages ("tweets") of up to 140 characters; the average number of words in a tweet is nearly 16 [336]. Other users can subscribe to another member's tweets and are known as *followers*. A member can restrict who is allowed to follow his or her tweets or allow them to be open, which is the default. Twitter also has a tagging system (see Section 9.8) in the form of hashtags (http://twitter.pbwiki.com/Hashtags), which are words prefixed by the # symbol. Twitter also supports geolocated tweets, allowing users, through an API, to add a location to messages.

Twitter was founded in 2006 inspired by the idea of using the SMS service for sending messages to a group. By early 2009, Twitter had over 7 million members with a steep growth rate of about 1400% from early 2008.[203]

A Pew Internet report, based on a daily tracking survey of a sample of 2253 American adult internet users during about a month from mid-August to mid-September 2009, found that about 19% of these users use Twitter or another service to share updates about themselves, or to see updates of others [231]. Web users who were members of social network sites were more likely to use Twitter than people who did not use social networks. Moreover, mobile internet users are also more likely to use Twitter allowing them to stay in touch at all times.

Twitter users can be divided into three typical groups [392]. Members of the first group (information sources) has a much larger number of followers than they are following. Many of these are online broadcasters such as radio stations, and media companies generating news. The second group (friends) reciprocate in their relationships and follow their followers. This type of behavior is typical in online social networks. The third group (information seekers) follow a much larger number of users than are following them, possibly in the hope that they

[202]Who rules real-time search? A look at 11 contenders. by K.M. Cutler, June 2009. http://venturebeat.com/2009/06/20/who-rules-real-time-search-a-look-at-9-contenders.

[203]Twitter's Tweet Smell Of Success, by M. McGiboney, March 2009. http://blog.nielsen.com/nielsenwire/online_mobile/twitters-tweet-smell-of-success.

will be followed and get clickthroughs to their site; this type of behavior is known as *follower spam*.

The main user intentions on Twitter are [339] (i) chatting about daily routine, (ii) conversation using the @ sign to send a message directly to another user although it can still be seen by others, (iii) sharing information and web addresses, and (iv) reporting some news.

Twitter is a powerful "word of mouth" marketing tool as people share their thoughts and sentiments toward products [336]. The information on Twitter about brands has an effect both on corporations and individuals. Roughly 19% mention an organization or product brand, and 20% of those express a sentiment concerning that brand, some of which could be viewed as customer feedback. The other 80% may be seeking or giving information on brands, which potentially makes it a useful advertising medium. Twitter may also be a good way to explore and track trends in the marketplace, as the information that flows though it is up-to-date.

Aardvark (www.vark.com), acquired by Google in February 2010, is a mobile social search service that enables its users to ask their social network a question in real-time via the Web, an e-mail, an instant message, or Twitter. Aardvark searches through the user's social network to establish if there is an expert that can answer the question, and it normally takes a few minutes for an answer to be received. Aardvark is especially useful for recommendations and suggestions, for example, of a book, a movie, or a restaurant.

ChaCha (www.chacha.com) is another mobile search service that answers questions in real-time by phoning a special number or sending a text message. Rather than using your social network as does Aardvark, ChaCha employs a team of "guides" who answer questions within a few minutes of receiving the question. After receiving an answer, you can follow up on the question by replying to the answer. Both ChaCha and Aardvark include brand advertising within the Q&A process.

9.6 POWER-LAW DISTRIBUTIONS IN THE WEB

The Web viewed as a network may at first seem to be a random graph, where each link appears with some fixed probability, but this is far from the truth. In fact, there are many regularities present in the web graph, some local and some global, that distinguish it from a random network and provide insight into how the Web is evolving and how users surf through its content.

The statistical notion of a *distribution* is the standard way of characterizing the probabilities of different values of properties such as height or wealth in a given population of entities, for example, people. The most common distribution is the *normal distribution* (also known as the *Gaussian distribution*) [208], characterized by its bell curve shape, whose tails decay at a fast, exponential rate. The height of people is normally distributed, since most grown-up people's height does not vary that much from the average height of about 5 feet 10 inches (1.78 m); we do not find anyone twice as tall or half as tall than the average. (Enter the query "5 feet 10 inches in meters" and let Google do the conversion.) On the other hand, the distribution of wealth is not normally distributed, rather it is an example of a *power-law distribution*. In a power-law distribution, the probability of an entity having value x is proportional to $1/x^{\alpha}$, where the exponent α is positive. Pareto, an early twentieth century Italian economist, observed that most people are not wealthy but there is a small, yet significant, number of very wealthy people. Through empirical evidence he showed that the distribution of wealth within a country is a power law with exponent between 2 and 3. This is the root of the widely quoted 80/20 rule, which roughly holds in many situations. In the case of economics, it states that about 80% of the wealth is held by roughly 20% of the population. Software developers have long known that about 80% of the programming effort goes into roughly 20% of the code. On the Web, 80% of the Web's links point to only about 15% of the totality of web pages.

Power-law distributions are abundant in nature [426]. There are a few large earthquakes but many small ones, there are a few very heavily populated cities but most are lightly populated, and there are only a few very large sized companies yet many companies of small size. In books (and texts, in general) a few words such as "of," "and," and "the" are very frequent yet many words are relatively rare (this is known as *Zipf's law*). In bibliometrics, a few authors receive many citations but most authors receive only a few citations (this is known as *Lotka's law*).

There have been several power-law distributions that have been observed on the Web. To name a few (i) many web pages have only one or two incoming links but a few sites (such as Google, Yahoo, and Amazon) have an enormous number of incoming links, (ii) most web sites are small (in the number of web pages they contain) but there are a few very large web sites, and (iii) on any given day many web sites receive a few visitors but there are a few that receive a huge number of daily visitors (such as Google, Yahoo, and Amazon) [10].

Power-law distributions are also known as scale-free and heavy-tailed (or long-tailed or fat-tailed) distributions. The term *scale-free* refers to the fact that power-law distributions look the same at all scales. For example, if we observe web sites having only between 10 and 100 incoming links, they would be distributed in the same way as web sites having between 100 and 1000 incoming links. In practice, this means that if a distribution obeys a power law, then detecting the power law at a given range of values allows prediction of its values outside the range. This characteristic, of having the same properties at all scales, is also known as *self-similar* or *fractal* behavior. The term *heavy-tailed* and its synonyms is an indication of the, small but significant, fraction of entities in the "tail" of the distribution that have a large value.

9.6.1 Detecting Power-Law Distributions

Recall that the degree distribution of a network records, for each i, how many nodes have degree i. This applies to a undirected network; in a directed network, we must consider either the indegree or the outdegree distribution. Assume for the moment that we are interested in the degree distribution of the web graph.

By examining the degree distribution of a network, we can distinguish between a random network and a scale-free (or power-law) network. The degree distribution of a random network is binomial, since each link (which is bidirectional in a undirected network) is present with probability p and absent with probability $1 - p$. If the number of nodes in the network is large enough, then the degree distribution can be approximated by a normal distribution. On the other hand, in a scale-free network, the degree distribution is a power law.

So, how do we detect power-law distributions. Let us consider the indegree distribution of the web graph as of May 1999 [108]. A method that is often used is to plot the data on a logarithmic scale (such a plot is called a *log–log plot*) and then to check whether it is a straight line using a linear regression tool. If this is the case, then the distribution is a power law. A log–log plot of the indegree distribution is a plot of the logarithm of the number of web pages against the logarithm of the indegree, as shown in Fig. 9.7. In the figure, a straight line with slope 2.105, which is a very good fit to the data, is superimposed on the data, so the indegree distribution of the web graph is seen to be a power law. Log–log plots can be problematic, since in some cases the head of the distribution (i.e., the left part of the plot) does not appear to follow a power-law distribution, and the tail of the distribution (i.e., the right part of the plot) is often messy making it difficult to position the slope of the regression line.

How to best fit a power-law distribution is still a matter of ongoing research [260]. One way to get around the messy tail is to use a technique called *logarithmic binning*. The data is collected into bins, in such a way that the bin sizes increase exponentially. So, the first bin covers the range with the single value 1, the second bin the range 2–3, the third bin the range 4–7, and so on. The bins

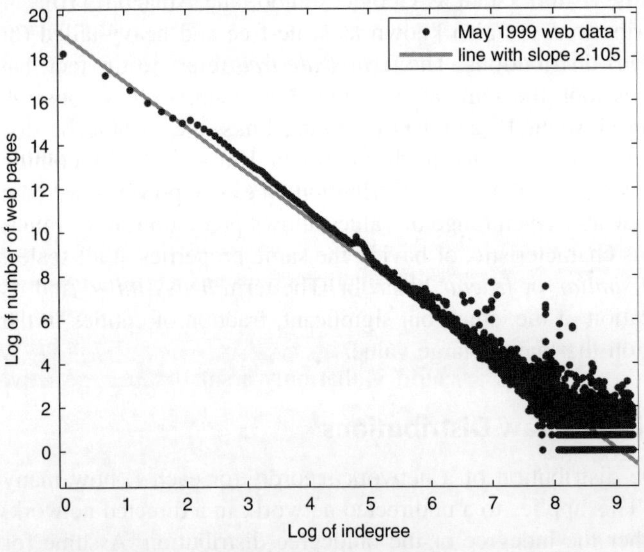

Figure 9.7 Web inlink data from May 1999.

are then normalized by dividing the number of data points in each bin by the width of the bin. Once the data is preprocessed in this manner, we proceed to plot it on a log–log scale, so that the widths of the bins appear to be even, and then carry out linear regression as before.

9.6.2 Power-Law Distributions in the Internet

We mention some other power-law distributions that are present in the applications running over the Internet. The indegree distribution of the Gnutella P2P network is a power law with exponent 2.3 [588], and the indegree distribution of blogspace is also a power law with exponent 2.1 as observed in the 2002 study of blogspace mentioned in Section 9.5.

A study of 50,000 users of an IM system was carried out in 2002 [614]. The nodes of the network are its users and there is link from one user to another, if the latter user is on the contact list of the former. The indegree distribution of this social network is a power law with exponent 2.2.

A study in 2002 of an e-mail network consisting of nearly 60,000 e-mail addresses was carried out in a university environment [199]. In this social network, the nodes are e-mail addresses (including external addresses, in addition to internal university accounts), and there is a link between two nodes if an e-mail was exchanged between them, so the network is considered as undirected. The degree distribution of this network is a power law with exponent 1.8, and when only internal addresses are considered the exponent of the power-law distribution is 1.32.

It appears that many of the power-law degree distributions in network applications running over the Internet have exponents between 2 and 3. One characteristic of these distributions is that their average value is finite (since the exponent is greater than 2) but their variance is infinite (since their exponent is less than or equal to 3). Systems having infinite variance can exhibit large fluctuations over time. In practice, this means that although, typically most web pages have a small number of inlinks, a small but significant number, such as Google, Yahoo, and Amazon have millions of inlinks.

It is interesting to note that the e-mail network has an exponential cutoff, which means that the indegree values decay exponentially beyond a certain value. In addition, the degree distribution of collaboration networks, where the nodes are researchers and the links denote coauthorship of a scientific paper between two researchers, is also typically power-law distributions with an exponential cutoff [497]. The cutoff point can be viewed as a physical constraint on the system, as after all there is a limit on the number of papers a scientist can publish in his or her life. Another explanation for the cutoff is that only a small subset of active scientists are potential collaborators [483].

9.6.3 A Law of Surfing and a Law of Participation

An interesting question is whether any general characteristics emerge from web surfing patterns created by users when following links trying to satisfy their information needs. As there are millions of users surfing the Web at any given time, it is impossible, in this context, to look at individual surfing traces, rather, it is more fruitful to model users' behavior as a stochastic process (i.e., one involving chance).

One way of understanding surfing is to assume that each page has a "value" to the user, which is a function of the information gleaned from the page with respect to the "goal" of his or her navigation session. This value of the click leading to the next page is related to the previous page browsed in a Markovian fashion. In this model, the user will continue surfing if the expected cost, to the user, of continuing is smaller than the expected gain obtained from future information in pages which will be browsed. (The cost to the user is normally measured in terms of the time spent to gain the information sought after.) The number of links followed, on an average, is the critical parameter of surfing. On the basis of this model, it can be established that the probability of surfing when following L links is proportional to $1/L^{1.5}$; that is, it is a power-law distribution with exponent 1.5.

This "law of surfing" was validated on several data sets, including a sample of AOL users during five days at the end of 1997 [317]. It was also observed that, although the law of surfing still holds for different topics of users' information need, the mode of the distribution (i.e., its most frequent value) is dependent on the topic. This implies that the price users are willing to pay for the information, in terms of the length of the trail they are likely to follow, depends on what they are looking for. An information provider can take advantage of this situation to design the trail length accordingly; for example, in an e-commerce site longer trails can present more "temptations" to potential customers [14].

The law of surfing does not take into account the topology of the portion of the web graph being navigated. This aspect can be taken into account by assuming that users are navigating within a Markov chain representing the portion of the web graph, where longer trails are less probable than shorter trails. This makes sense as the probability of a trail is related to the cost of the trail, that is, to the length of time it takes to follow the trail, which is related to the length of the trail. Again, it can be shown that a power-law distribution, which is proportional to the length of the trail being navigated, is derived for the probability of surfing [417].

A comparative law of voting can be found in peer production systems, where people create, share, and rate content. One such popular site, Digg (www.digg.com), is oriented toward sharing news stories although links to other content such as images, videos, and podcasts can also be shared. Users vote on submitted content and, essentially, the most popular ones, within a certain time period, are promoted to the front page and displayed in order of popularity.

Wilkinson [683] calls such systems, which have become an important part of the social web, *coactive*. He has shown that such coactive systems obey a law of participation, where the probability that a person stops contributing varies inversely with the number of contributions he or she has made. This rule leads to a power-law distribution for the number of contributions per person, implying that a small number of people account for most of the contributions. It also implies that the power-law exponent is proportional to the effort required to make a contribution. Wilkinson showed that this law holds for several other coactive sites including edits on Wikipedia.

9.6.4 The Evolution of the Web via Preferential Attachment

What is the mechanism by which a network evolves into a scale-free one? In particular, how can the growth of the Web, as a network, be understood, and why did it evolve in the way it did? Moreover, how can such a model describing the evolution of the Web, be used to make predictions about the future growth of the Web?

Recent seminal research by Barabasi *et al.* [55], building on earlier research by Nobel prize laureate, Herbert Simon in 1955 [609] and Derek de Solla Price in 1976 [179], presents one answer to how a scale-free network may evolve.

Let us illustrate the ideas using the indegree distribution of the web graph as an example. There are two mechanisms which explain the evolution of the network. The first is the *growth* of the network: the network is continuously expanding by new pages and links being added to the system. To simplify the formalism, we can view the process as happening at discrete time steps, when at each step one of two events may occur: (i) a page may be added with probability p or (ii) an inlink may be added to an existing node with probability $1 - p$. When a node is added it is assumed that it has one inlink, say from a randomly chosen existing node, and when a link is added to an existing node, this node is chosen through a second fundamental mechanism.

This mechanism, called *preferential attachment*, means that the node receiving the new inlink is chosen in proportion to the number of inlinks that the node already has. So, a node having twice as many inlinks than a second node is twice as likely to receive the new link than the second node. Figure 9.8 depicts a scale-free network with 130 nodes constructed using Albert and Barabasi's preferential attachment mechanism.

To illustrate the preferential attachment of both inlinks and outlinks, consider the evolution of the small network shown in Fig. 9.9. A new node is added to the network at step 1. At step 2 a node is chosen randomly, and this node connects to the new node. At step 3, a node is chosen preferentially according to the number of its inlinks and the new node connects to this node. Finally, at step 4, a node is chosen preferentially according to its outlinks, a second node is chosen preferentially according to its inlinks, and the first node connects to the second.

These mechanisms can be expressed in terms of difference equations and their solution for large networks results in a power-law distribution with exponent $1 + \varrho$ for the indegree, where $\varrho = 1/(1 - p)$; a similar power-law distribution can be obtained for the outdegree. Thus, in this model, the power-law exponent depends on the rate at which the network grows. In practice, pure preferential attachment does not necessarily occur; that is, sometime we link to popular sites but at other time there are different considerations, for example, when we link to a colleague's site or to a site that we find interesting. This can be modeled by modifying the choice of node to link to, to be a mixture of preferential attachment and uniform random chance (i.e., all nodes have equal chance of being linked to)

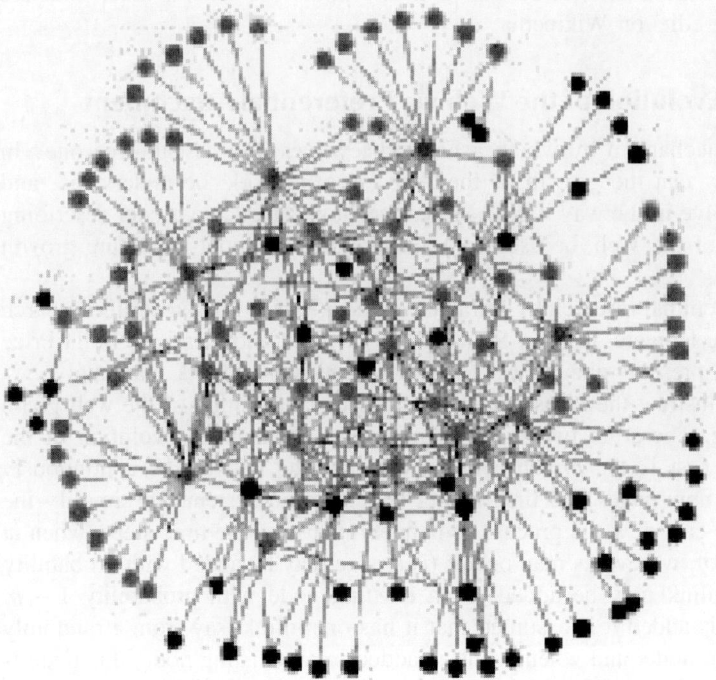

Figure 9.8 Scale-free network with 130 nodes. (Source: Center for Complex Network Research (CCNR). www.nd.edu/~networks/Linked/exp_scale.gif.)

[418]. As long as there is a preferential element present the distribution is a power law, where the exponent increases with the increase of the random component. In the extreme case when the choice is purely random, the distribution becomes exponential.

The mechanism of preferential attachment is not new, and has been known under different names. Some of these are the "rich get richer" phenomenon in economics, the "Matthew effect" in sociology, according to Gospel Matthew [467], and "cumulative advantage" in bibliometrics.

In the preferential attachment model, there is a correlation between the age of a node and its indegree; in economics this is referred to as the *first mover advantage*. That is, the older the web page the more likely it will have more inlinks. Although many of the older web sites such as Yahoo and Amazon have maintained their lead, many more have stagnated or disappeared, and newcomers such as Google and Facebook have arrived on the scene and managed to become very popular, as measured by their number of inlinks.

To deal with these departures from the basic evolutionary model, several extensions can be added. First, deletions of links [216] and nodes [215] can be added to the model to make it more realistic. Deletion of links does not change the distribution as such (it is still a power law), but it allows us to model

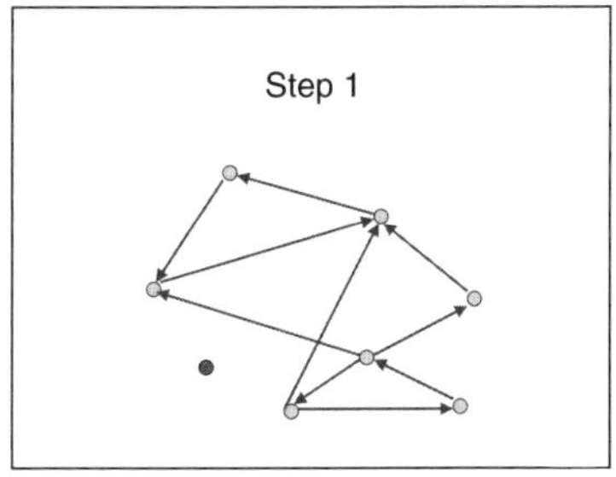

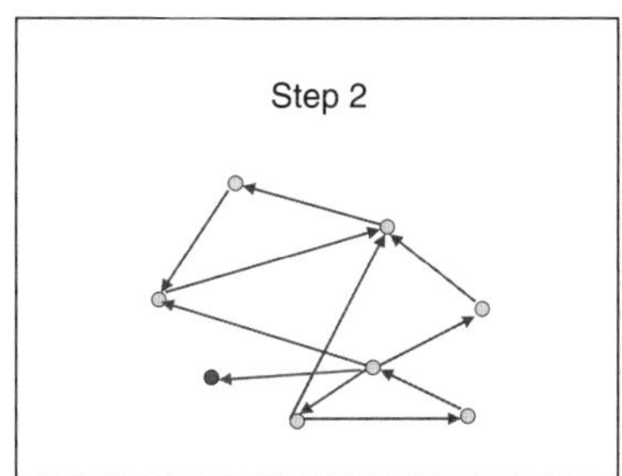

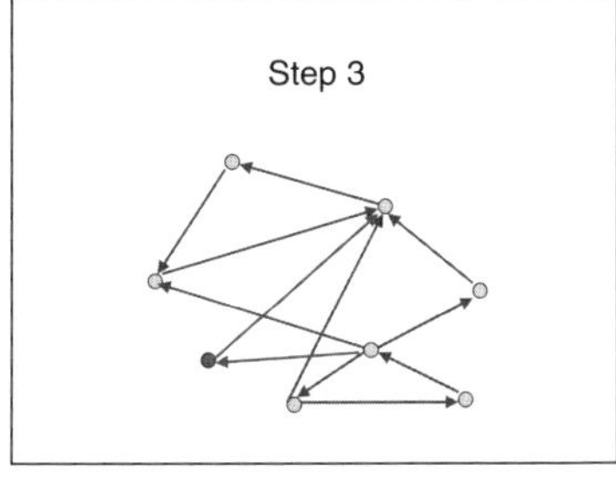

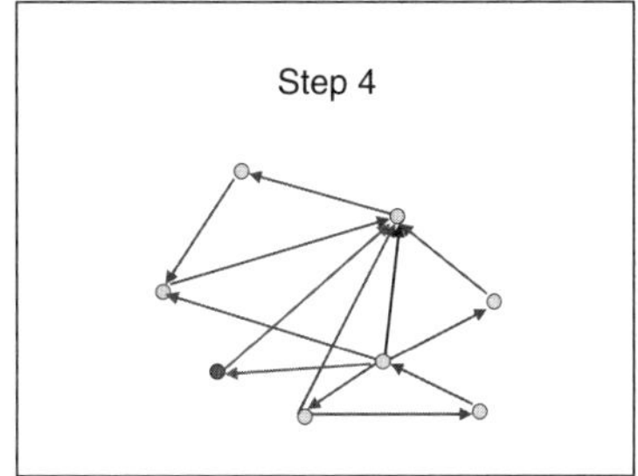

Figure 9.9 Example of network growth and preferential attachment.

reality more accurately. On the other hand, deletion of node allows to detect a possible exponential cutoff in the power-law indegree distribution, which has been observed in scientific collaboration networks but not yet in the web graph.

Still, these extensions do not explain why Google has become so popular, despite having started up late in 1998. To explain this we can assume that each node comes with a fixed "fitness"; the higher the fitness the more chance it has of receiving an inlink. The modification to the basic model is that a node is now chosen in proportion to the number of inlinks it has multiplied by its fitness [83]. In this way, a young node with high fitness will be able to compete with old nodes with low fitness, in proportion to the ratio of their fitness values.

The resulting distribution depends on the probability distribution that fitness values are chosen from. For example, in the case of a uniform distribution (all fitness values are equally likely), the indegree distribution is a power law, where the "fit-get-rich," that is, fit nodes obtain inlinks at a higher rate than unfit nodes. What is interesting is that for distributions with infinite support (i.e., having an infinite set of values such that the probability of all values outside this set is zero) we have a "winner-take-all" situation, were almost all nodes have a single link to the single winner node.

9.6.5 The Evolution of the Web as a Multiplicative Process

An alternative mechanism to generate a power-law distribution is via a *multiplicative process* [475]. To explain the mechanism, consider the distribution of the number of pages in a web site. In order to describe the process underlying the growth of a web site, it is reasonable to assume that there are day-to-day fluctuations in its size, and that the number of pages a site gains or loses is a random proportion of its current size; this mechanism is known as *multiplicative growth*. In absolute terms, larger sites normally gain or lose more pages than a smaller site. In order to obtain a power-law distribution, two further aspects are considered [316].

During the first years since the inception of the Web, its growth has been exponential and even with the growth slowing down, there are still many more "young" sites than "older" ones. This can be accounted for in the model by having sites appear at different times, and increasing the rate at which they appear as time goes by. In this way the few older sites can grow in size to produce the long tail of the distribution, as more and more new sites appear on the scene. Multiplicative growth combined with this aspect results in a power-law distribution after a sufficiently long growth period. In this variation of the growth process, there is clearly a correlation between size and age.

The second aspect to consider is that some sites grow faster than others, even if they appear at the same time. As in the first case, combining this aspect with multiplicative growth leads to a power-law distribution. The growth rate of a site can be viewed as a form of fitness, as discussed above, thus providing an explanation why relatively "young" sites may become larger and better connected than some "old" and established sites. In this variation of the growth process, it is clear that there need not be a correlation between size and age [9].

In summary, combining multiplicative growth with one or both of the above aspects will result in the distribution of the size of web sites being a power law. Both aspects make sense in the context of the Web, and help us understand the ubiquity of power laws found in web data.

9.6.6 The Evolution of the Web via HOT

Another rather appealing mechanism by which power-law distributions may emerge is called *highly optimized tolerance* (HOT) [193]. The idea behind HOT is that power-law distributions are the result of robust design of complex systems. In particular, optimizing a design objective in the presence of uncertainty and specified constraints can lead to a power-law distribution.

One example of a HOT system is the design of the layout of a web site, in terms of partitioning the space into files of different sizes. There is a constraint on the overall size of the site, on the maximum number of files that the site can be partitioned into, and a constraint specifying that smaller files are more popular (in terms of number of clicks) than larger ones. The design objective is to optimize the average file size download during a user's navigation session. The distribution of file sizes in the resulting optimized web site is a power law. A problem with HOT is that it does not necessarily prescribe a method of how to achieve the optimal design. One heuristic for the web site design problem is to split a file if it is popular and large, and to merge files if they are unpopular and small.

A related method is called *heuristically optimized trade-offs (HOT)* [209], which is a model for network growth leading to a power-law degree distribution for a wide range of its parameters. The model works by constructing a network on the unit square as follows. At each time step, a new node arrives and is placed uniformly randomly on the unit square. It then connects to an existing node that minimizes a weighted sum of two objectives. The first objective is to minimize the Euclidean distance to the node (multiplied by a weighting parameter α, which may be a function of the number of nodes in the network), and the second is to maximize the centrality of the node it is connecting to (recalling that centrality minimizes the distance to other nodes in the network).

In the special case, where the center of the network is fixed as the initial node that is placed in the network, the objective is intuitively to connect to a node that minimizes the distance of the new node from the initial node. In this case, the degree distribution resulting from the optimization problem can be solved analytically, but experiments with the model have shown it to be robust with respect to more general definitions of centrality. There are three situations to consider depending on the value of α.

- In the first case, when α is less than some constant, the resulting network is a star, since all new nodes prefer to connect to the initial node.
- In the second case, when α grows at least as fast as the square root of the number of nodes in the network, the degree distribution of the network is exponential, since the preference is to link to locally close nodes.
- In the third case, when α is in between the above two cases, the degree distribution is a power law.

Thus, a power-law distribution arises via an optimization process with conflicting local and global objectives. Figure 9.10, from Ref. 209, depicts the first 10,000 nodes of a HOT network having a total of 100,000 nodes with $\alpha = 20$. The log–log plot of the cumulative degree distribution of this network is shown in Fig. 9.11, also from Ref. 209. It can be seen that the degree distribution is a power law with an exponential cutoff beyond a certain degree.

9.6.7 Small-World Networks

In Section 9.1, there was a preliminary discussion of the small-world property. We now turn to the description of the type of networks that may support this property, known as *small-world networks*.

A small-world network is one in which the average distance among nodes is small—typically logarithmic in the number of nodes in the network, as is the case in a random network—and whose clustering coefficient is much larger than that of a random graph of the same density [496].

In a random graph, each link, taken from the set of all possible links, is present with a fixed probability p; thus, given that A is connected to both B and C, does not have an effect on the probability that B and C will be connected, that is, this probability is still p. This implies that the clustering coefficient of a

Figure 9.10 First 10,000 nodes of a HOT network with 100,000 nodes and $\alpha = 10$.

random graph is p. In a small-world network, if A is connected to both B and C, then there is an increased probability that B and C will be connected, and therefore the clustering coefficient is typically much larger than p. For example, in the movie actor collaboration network, the clustering coefficient is 0.79, which is much larger than the value, 0.00027, that it would have on a random graph with p evaluated as the ratio of the average number of collaborations of an actor to the number of actors in the network.

An alternative definition of the clustering coefficient, based on the notion of a triangle, is the ratio of three times the number of triples in the network to the number of connected triples in the network. A *connected triple* is a set of three nodes with at least two edges between them such as A, B, and C with edges between A and B, and between B and C. In other words, the clustering coefficient is the fraction of connected triples that are triangles. The ratio is multiplied by three, since there are three connected triples for each triangle.

In a seminal paper [674] Watts and Strogatz, showed how to construct a small-world network on a regular lattice. The construction starts from a one-dimensional lattice (a ring) and an average degree of nodes, say z. It then connects each node in the lattice to its z closest neighbors, as shown in Fig. 9.12a, from Ref. 674, with $z = 4$. We then iterate through all the links in this lattice and

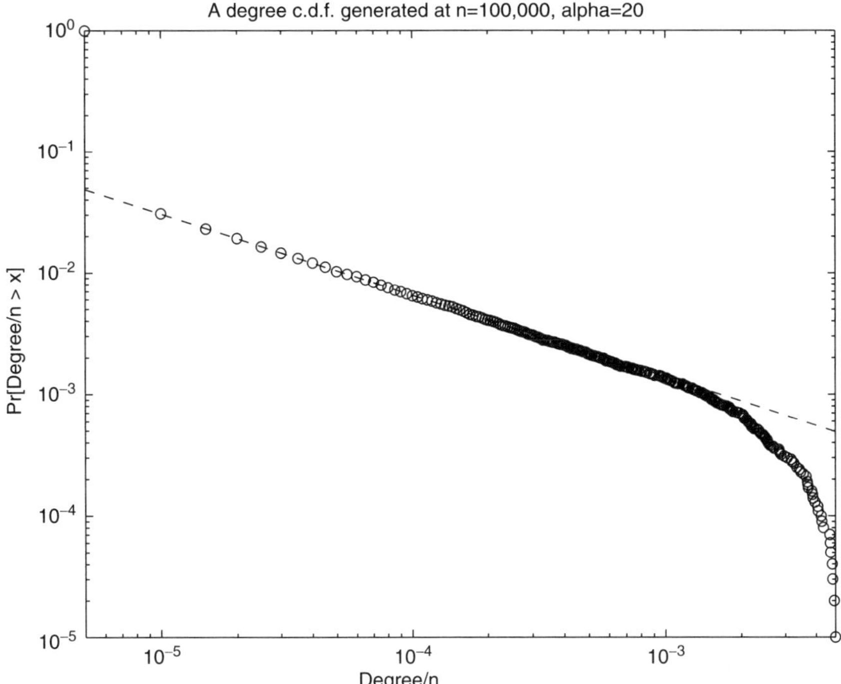

Figure 9.11 Log–log plot for the cumulative degree distribution of the network shown in Fig. 9.10.

with some probability, called the *rewiring probability*, we *rewire* one of its ends to connect to another node in the lattice chosen uniformly at random. For small rewiring probability, we obtain a small-world network, as shown in Fig. 9.12b, while in the extreme situation shown in Fig. 9.12c, when the rewiring probability is 1, we have a completely random lattice. (An alternative construction of a small-world network is to add new links between pairs of nodes chosen uniformly at random rather than to rewire existing links. The advantage of this model is that it is not possible for any region of the network to become disconnected from the rest of the network, as is possible with the original construction.)

We denote the clustering coefficient given rewiring probability p as $C(p)$ and the average distance given p as $L(p)$, noting that these values are maximal when $p = 0$ and minimal when $p = 1$. Watts and Strogatz conducted simulations using their network construction method, varying the rewiring probability from 0 to 1, and plotted $C(p)/C(0)$ and $L(p)/L(0)$ against p obtaining the plots shown in Fig. 9.13, from Ref. 674. The region of the rewiring probability when $C(p)/C(0)$ is "large" (much larger than for a random network) and $L(p)/L(0)$ is "small" (almost as small as for a random network) is the region where small-world networks emerge. The interesting discovery is that by rewiring only a small fraction of the links, thus creating a few shortcuts between nodes that would otherwise be distant, a small-world network emerges.

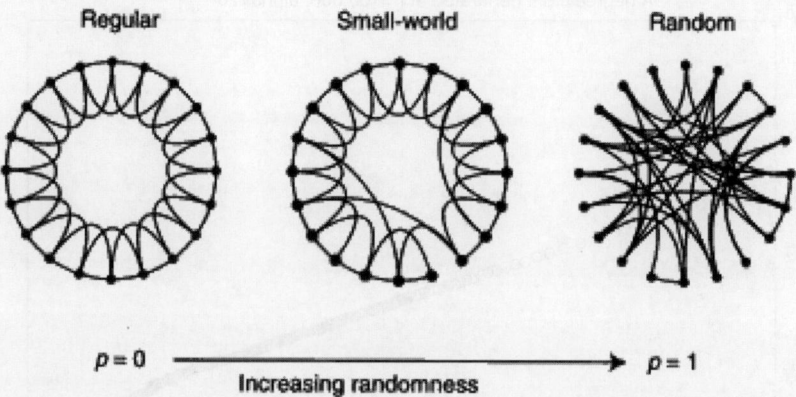

Figure 9.12 The emergence of a small-world network: (a) regular, (b) small world, and (c) random.

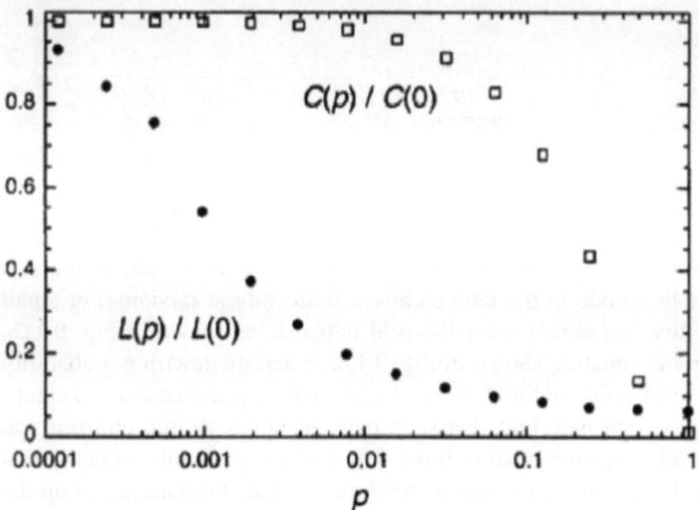

Figure 9.13 Average distance and clustering coefficient for the network construction shown in Fig. 9.12.

Although the above construction of a small-world network is somewhat artificial, it proves the existence of such types of networks, and opens the door for understanding real-world networks. The following are the three classes of real-world small networks that have been recognized [28]:

1. Networks with power-law degree distributions, that is, scale-free networks such as the Web.
2. Networks with power-law degree distributions having an exponential cutoff such as the movie actors network and scientific collaboration networks.

3. Networks whose degree distributions have an exponentially decaying tail, as opposed to a long tail, such as the electric power grid of Southern California, the network of world airports, and the neural network of a worm.

The average distance in scale-free networks is typically logarithmic, yet it does not immediately follow that the clustering coefficient of a scale-free network will be as large as it should be in order for it to be classified as a small-world network.

Analysis of a crawl of many web sites was used to compute their clustering coefficient and average distance [6]. The value of the clustering coefficient of a web site was found to be 0.1078, which is much larger than 0.00023, the value it would have on a random graph with the same degree, and the average distance between nodes in a web site was found to be 3.1, indicating that web sites are indeed small-world networks.

To obtain a high clustering coefficient in a scale-free network, an additional mechanism, called *triad formation*, can be added to the evolution of the network as follows. After a node, say v, preferentially attaches itself to another node, say w, an additional link is added from v to a random neighbor of w [307]. Triad formation maintains the power-law distribution of the network, while increasing the clustering coefficient. To have control on the level of clustering, triad formation can be carried out after a preferential attachment step only with a certain probability, say q.

Small-world properties have also been found in file swapping P2P networks. The *data sharing graph* is a network in which the nodes are users and the links connect users who have similar interests. In this context, similarity means that the intersection of their requests to download files is larger than some threshold over a given period of time. Analysis of the data sharing graph of Kazaa over a period of 5 days in 2003 showed that its degree distribution follows a power law, and that it is a small-world network, since the average distances between nodes is logarithmic in the size of the graph, and the clustering coefficient is much larger than it would have been in a random graph with the same degree [320].

Transportation networks such as train networks can also be analyzed from the small-world perspective. Instead of trying to measure average distance and clustering, it is possible to measure *efficiency* and *cost* of the network, which have the following meaning. In a transportation network we are interested in the geographical distances between connected stations, so the links can be weighted according to these distances, obtaining a *weighted network*. Also, it is customary in a weighted network to set the distance between two stations that are not connected as infinity. The efficiency in communication between two stations is assumed to be inversely proportional to the shortest distance between them, so that if no path exists between the two their efficiency is zero. The *global efficiency* of the network is the average efficiency between stations. The *local efficiency* of a station is defined as the average efficiency between all neighbors of this station, and the local efficiency of the network is defined as the average local efficiency of all stations. Global efficiency corresponds to the average distance and local efficiency corresponds to the clustering coefficient. Small-world transportation systems are networks with both high global and local efficiencies, normalized to be percentages.

Analysis of the Boston underground transportation system has shown the global efficiency to be 63%, while the local efficiency was shown to be only 3% [404]. So, this system is globally efficient but locally inefficient. So, transportation systems are not small-world networks. Commuters using this system can get from one station to another with few intermediate stations in between but the system is not fault tolerant. When a station is closed it has drastic local effects in the connection between the neighbors of the closed station.

To understand why such networks are locally inefficient, it is convenient to consider another important metric for these types of networks, that is, the *cost*. It is defined as the ratio of the total length of the network, computed by adding up the distances between all connected stations, to the maximum length the network could have (which is the sum of distances between all distinct pairs, whether connected or not). The cost of the Boston underground was shown to have the value of 0.2%. So, increasing the number of connections increases the local efficiency, and thus the fault tolerance of the network, but this comes at a cost which may not be affordable. The priority in transportation networks seems to be achieving high global efficiency at a low cost. An additional consideration here is that a system, such as the underground, is supported by a wider transportation system such as the bus system, which taken together may increase the local efficiency of the network, so that it becomes a small-world network.

9.6.8 The Robustness and Vulnerability of a Scale-Free Network

One way to measure the connectivity of a network is in terms of the existence of a *giant component*. Informally, the giant component is a substantial connected part of the network. More specifically, the largest connected component of a network is referred to as a *giant component*, if its size is a positive fraction of the size of the network, and this fraction is maintained throughout the growth of the network. What this means is that when a giant component exists its size is monotonically increasing with the size of the network.

In random networks a phase transition occurs in the network causing the appearance of a giant component, when the average degree of a node is greater than one. In scale-free networks the situation is different. As long as the power-law exponent of the degree distribution is less than 3 (i.e., the variance of the degree distribution is infinite), the giant component is always present for large enough networks [158].

These observations regarding the giant component have implications for the robustness of the Web (and, in general, the Internet) against breakdown of its nodes [23]. There are two situations to consider, one is random failure of nodes and the other is an attack, targeted to cause failure at specific well-connected nodes.

We measure robustness by the connectivity of the network, and as long as the network maintains a giant component we consider the network to be resilient against the breakdown or attack. The intuition behind this is that the network will become dysfunctional only when it becomes fragmented and the communication is broken between the various fragments. The *threshold value* is the proportion of nodes that need to be removed in order to fragment the network.

The first result is that scale-free networks, whose degree distribution is a power law with exponent less than 3, are extremely robust against random attacks. Even after the removal of a large percentage of random nodes, the giant component will still remain intact. The reason for this is that in power-law networks most of the nodes have a few connections, and it is extremely unlikely that random failure will occur at a few well-connected nodes. In fact, it can be shown that the threshold value for scale-free networks approaches 100%, as the size of the network increases. Random networks are not as resilient to such attacks, as their threshold value has an abrupt drop to zero, when the average degree falls below one.

On the one hand, scale-free networks are vulnerable against an attack targeted at its well-connected nodes. In this case, the removal of just a few well-connected nodes can cause the giant component to become fragmented. For the Web, deletion of roughly 5% of the well-connected nodes will cause the collapse of the network. So, in the case of a targeted attack, a scale-free network is much more vulnerable than a random network.

The Love Bug virus (May 2000) was spread through an e-mail, which when opened would cause damage to the documents on the infected computer. The virus further spread by sending copies of itself to people in the address book of Microsoft Outlook Express, if installed on the infected computer. Within four days of its inception it managed to infect 78 million computers, eventually causing about 10 billion dollars worth of damage. Although an antivirus program, to eliminate this virus, was made publicly available, the virus was not completely eradicated even a year after it was let loose. In general, the characteristic life of a computer virus is between 6 and 14 months, despite the availability of antivirus software within days of the virus appearing.

When a node is connected to an infected node it becomes infected with a certain probability and is cured with another probability, so the *spreading rate* of a virus is taken to be the ratio of these two probabilities. In random graphs, a virus has a positive *epidemic threshold*, beyond which the virus spreads throughout the network and becomes persistent, and below which the virus dies exponentially fast [367].

Surprisingly, in scale-free networks, the epidemic threshold is zero, implying that infection of even a small part of the network may cause the virus to persist and spread [532]. What happens is that in a scale-free network it is likely that the virus will spread to a well-connected node, and once such a node is infected, it passes the virus to its neighbors causing it to spread throughout the network. The reason that the virus is likely to spread to a well-connected node is, again, due to the fact that power-law distributions with exponents less than 3 have infinite variance. It can be shown that, on an average, for such networks the number of nodes two steps away from a given node depends not only on the average number of connections but also on the variance of the number of connections, which in practice will be finite but still "large" [498].

This analysis suggests that in scale-free networks random immunization will not be effective, since most nodes have a small number of connections, and the well-connected nodes are less likely to be immunized, maintaining the endemic state in which the virus is still persistent in the network. In scale-free networks, only complete immunization guarantees the eradication of the virus, due to the absence of an epidemic threshold.

In order to contain a virus in scale-free networks, well-connected nodes should be immunized first. A targeted immunization strategy, which progressively immunizes the most well-connected nodes with a degree higher than some cutoff, substantially increases the network's tolerance to infections, while only treating a small fraction of the nodes [533]. Immunizing the well-connected nodes has the effect of fragmenting the network with respect to the ability of the virus to spread. There still remains the problem of identifying the well-connected nodes. An ingenious solution based on the above observation that a random node two steps away is more likely to be well connected is as follows. Choose a fraction of the nodes uniformly randomly and then for each one of these nodes immunize one of its neighbors, since it is more likely to be well connected. This strategy, called the *acquaintance immunization strategy*, is effective since it makes the immunization of well-connected nodes highly likely, without global knowledge of the network [159].

We end this section by mentioning that in the last few years there have been several books published, which describe the recent developments in the area of networks that we have touched upon. Three popular books are "Linked" by Barabási [54], "Nexus: Small Worlds and the Groudbreaking Science of Networks" by Buchanan [114], and "Six Degrees: The Science of the Connected Age" by Watts [672]. Several more technical books are "Evolution of Networks: From Biological Nets to the Internet and WWW" by Dorogovtsev and Mendes [191], "The Laws of the Web: Patterns in the Ecology of Information" by Huberman [315], "Evolution and Structure of the Internet A Statistical Physics Approach" by Pastor-Satorras and Vespognani [534], "The Structure and Dynamics of Networks" by Newman *et al.* [500], and "Dynamical Processes on Complex Networks" by Barrat *et al.* [57].

Several notable surveys on advances in social and computer networks are "Statistical mechanics of complex networks" by Albert and Barabási [22], "Evolution of networks" by Dorogovtsev and Mendes [190], "The structure and function of complex networks" by Newman [499], "Complex networks: Structure and dynamics" by Boccaletti *et al.* [86], and "Characterization of complex networks: A survey of measurements" by Costa *et al.* [163].

Interestingly enough *all* these authors have a background in physics, which is more than a mere coincidence; that is, not to say that physicists are the only ones working in this area. I encourage the reader to surf the Web for surveys in the areas of social and computer networks, as many of the authors have been putting the theory into practice by posting their research papers on the Web.

9.7 SEARCHING IN SOCIAL NETWORKS

The traditional way of finding information when navigating is to use maps, guides, and other aids such as a compass. As we have seen in Chapter 7, various navigation and orientation tools have been developed for web navigation based on the tools and metaphors from the real world.

9.7.1 Social Navigation

Social navigation [185] is a different form of navigation that helps you find your way by using information from other people who have been through the space.

Examples of social navigation from the real world are passing by a busy restaurant and deciding to go in, seeing a worn book on a bookshelf in the library and deciding to take it out, and hearing music on the radio and deciding to buy the album. In all these examples, we use traces or advice from other people's experiences to help us make decisions.

CF compares the interests one user to others in order to derive recommendations that help and encourage the user to make decisions. Social navigation is more general, in the sense that it allows a user to observe the traces of other users in places (web pages) they have visited, based on the activities they have done, which can range from just browsing some document, to being involved in a chat room topic or downloading an MP3 file. The trace can indicate the frequency and recency of the activity, for example, how many people downloaded the file and when. Features such as customer reviews of products and comments on news items are another form of trace we may stumble upon when we surf the Web.

In direct social navigation, the user will communicate directly with other users in the space they are navigating through. For example, a user may want to ask others "where did you go to from here" or " do you know how to get to some other place." The user may also be able to communicate with an artificial agent such as the wizard in Microsoft Office tools.

Indirect social navigation is more common on the Web, involving the observation of traces of users who have passed through the space. In order to support "traces," a web site must record the activities of users surfing the site, and provide tools that allow users to observe current and previous traces. In addition to implicit information collected when users surf a site, it is also possible to allow users to give explicit feedback such as rating and commenting on items they have inspected; as an example, weblogs normally allow for such feedback.

A form of social navigation that takes advantage of previous traces is called *history enriched navigation*. In this type of social navigation support, links can be annotated with frequency and recency information of the pages they link to, and with other information regarding these pages such as when they were last modified. Another idea is to add shortcuts to pages, which are new links to pages that were often visited from the current page. It is also possible to incorporate a recommender system, which helps people find information based on their personal profile and other people's experiences; this can be implemented using the techniques described in Section 9.4.

Educo [397] is an example of a learning environment that utilizes social navigation as part of its user interface. Its visual interface displays the document currently being browsed in its main window and a map of the learning space in a frame on the left-hand side of the main window. Each document in the space is represented as an icon, and each user is represented as a colored dot. A dot is shown next to the each document that a user is browsing, and when placing the mouse over a dot or an icon the tool gives current information about the user or document. For the benefit of its users, the interface is updated in real time. Different colors of dots represent different groups of users, and document icons become brighter when they are browsed more frequently, providing a form of history enriched navigation.

Other features of Educo are chat, commenting, newsgroups, search for documents and users, and an alarm facility, where the system watches for a condition set by the user and informs him or her when the condition is satisfied. For example, the alarm may refer to a document the student wishes to collaborate on, and the system will inform the student when someone else is browsing the document.

Social navigation can also be of use within an organization to augment web browsing. Context-aware proxy-based system (CAPS) is a system that tracks a group users within a web site using a proxy in the users' browser, and it recommends and annotates links through a user interface built on top of Google [605]. The interface to CAPS does not require any user input, it logs users' page accesses and the amount of time spent browsing the pages, and builds user profiles based on their home page.

Figure 9.14, from Ref. 605, shows the user interface of CAPS, for the query "context aware." The symbols "Known" and "Popular" near the first and second results indicate that the second result is popular, while the first is known, indicating that it is not as popular as the second. A pop-up is displayed when the mouse is moved over the result, showing the statistics for the result, as can be seen for the first result in the figure. At the top of the screen, we see a highlighted link that is recommended by the system as being relevant to the query.

9.7.2 Social Search Engines

A new breed of search engines that support social navigation (see Subsection 9.7.1) and user-generated content (see Section 9.10), called *social search engines*, has been developed, tested, and deployed. The basic idea is to share information from multiple users making similar searches, in order to influence the current search you have submitted. In this type of search engine, the information regarding previous searches within a related community of users is used either to modify the current query or to influence the ranking process.

The goal of the query modification method is to find similar queries, which were previously submitted, and to use this collective knowledge in order to modify the query in some way that better reflects its intended meaning. On the other hand, the method of reranking the search results for a query is to factor into the ranking process the popularity (i.e., number of hits) of the relevant pages.

Figure 9.14 User interface of the context-aware proxy-based system for the query "context-aware."

In this way, pages that are both relevant and popular will be ranked higher than pages that are relevant but unpopular.

Detecting related queries can be done via intersecting keywords, for example, "chess computer" and "chess software," but it could also be done by inspecting the degree to which their top-*n* search results intersect [256].

A more cautious way of providing the user with community-based search assistance for a given query is simply to display to the user the related queries alongside the unchanged search results for the user's original query. In this way, the community knowledge is a form of recommendation, and the user is then free to modify the original query and/or inspect results from related queries.

A straightforward way to factor community information into the query ranking algorithm is to monitor users' selection of web pages for queries. So, for a query such as "computer chess," the system can estimate the probability that a page P_i is selected, according to the clickthroughs recorded for that query [235]. This is essentially the same idea behind the popularity-based metrics discussed in Section 5.3. This idea has been implemented in the experimental I-Spy metasearch engine [234]. The method can be refined by clustering similar queries, for example, using TF–IDF as a similarity measure, and by clustering users into communities, for example, according to their interests, which can be gauged either explicitly or implicitly.

Social search engines come in several flavors.[204] The first type is *community search*, a typical example being community-based question answering (see Subsection 9.10.5), which harnesses users' expert knowledge to find answers to any question and making use of the wisdom of the crowds through a voting mechanism to establish the best answer.

The second type is *collaborative search*, where people work together to locate web resources through the use of search engines [480]. Collaborative search is enabled by a search interface that will invoke one or more searches during its use. One such tool is Microsoft's SearchTogether interface [481], which enables groups of remote users to synchronously or asynchronously collaborate when searching the Web. SearchTogether allows users to save search sessions, mark, rate and comment on viewed pages, and to divide the search labor among the group members when searching on a particular topic.

The third type is *collective search*, where we tap into the wisdom of the crowds to gain an impression of what other people are doing. Two examples of this type of search are real-time search (see Subsection 9.5.5), when we are searching a snapshot of the Web as it is evolving at this moment by tapping into current social network data and social tagging search (see Section 9.8), that takes advantage of the tags that users attach to web pages to search the part of the Web that users are interested in. Popularity of a resource is an important aspect of collective search (see Section 5.3). Popularity can be measured by user votes, clicks, and content they have shared or published.

The fourth type is *friend search*, where shared social data from friends and friends of friends can be searched. An example of this is Google social search, where social content can be mixed with traditional search results.[205] There is always an issue of privacy in such systems, which is addressed first by only presenting social search results when users are logged onto their Google account, and second by allowing users, through their profile, to decide which social data to make public for social search and which should remain private. The user can add or remove links on their profile at any time, and therefore have control on what information they are willing to share.

As an example of a commercial product, StumbleUpon (www.stumbleupon.com), launched in 2001 by Garrett Camp and Geoff Smith, is a social search and browsing tool for discovering web pages and sharing the ones you have visited with other users. It was acquired by eBay in 2007 and bought back by the

[204]3 Flavors of Social Search: What to Expect, by B. Evans, November 2009. www.readwriteweb.com/archives/3_flavors_of_social_search_what_to_expect.php.

[205]Introducing Google Social Search: I finally found my friend's New York blog!, by M. Heymans, October 2009. http://googleblog.blogspot.com/2009/10/introducing-google-social-search-i.html.

Figure 9.15 StumbleUpon toolbar.

founders in 2009, as, not being an eBay core business, it was not easy to develop synergies between the two. By early 2010, StumbleUpon had just under 9 million users and tens of millions of web pages that have been endorsed by its users.

The discovery and sharing process is enabled through the StumbleUpon toolbar, shown in Fig. 9.15, which is installed on the user's browser. Upon joining the network, a user profile is created for you and you are asked to specify your preferences from a list of about 500 interest topics. You can also specify your friends and discover similar users to yourself on the basis of the sites you have stumbled upon and given a thumbs up vote.

When you browse a web page you can rate it by clicking "I like it" (thumbs up) or "Not for me" (thumbs down) on the toolbar; the more people like a page, the higher its overall rating will be. Rating web pages also has a personalization effect in that it provides reinforcement of the topics that you prefer. At any time you can click on the "stumble" button, and it will present to you pages related to your preferred topics that are either highly rated or have been recommended to you by your friends. In addition, you can view the profile of the first person (or a friend of yours), say Joe, who recommended the page you have stumbled upon and shared it, and you can then add this person to your list of friends from whom you will get recommendations. The page review button allows you to read comments of other people on the web page you are browsing or to add your own comments to it, and the "share" button allows you to share the page with your friends and like-minded people.

9.7.3 Navigation Within Social Networks

We now turn to navigation in social networks. Milgram's small-world experiment can be described in terms of navigating from a source node to a chosen destination, where the navigator has very little global information about the network, and the choice of which link to follow is guided mainly by local information. Although we know that in small-world and scale-free networks, which are representative of social networks, the distance between nodes is typically small, that is, logarithmic in the size of the network, it is not clear how to find these short paths. Moreover, an important question that needs to be addressed is whether these paths can be found efficiently by local search strategies that examine only the neighbors or neighbors of neighbors of a node.

A simple breadth-first search (BFS) is a strategy that moves from a node to all of its neighbors before traversing any other node. BFS is an exhaustive strategy, since it will eventually visit all the nodes in the network. Recall that this is essentially the search mechanism of the P2P network Gnutella, with the TTL constraint on the depth of the search (see Section 9.3).

The key to improving BFS is to utilize the fact that in a scale-free network a random neighbor of a neighbor (i.e., a node two steps away from the current node) is more likely to be a well-connected node, than simply a random neighbor of a node. Reaching well-connected nodes will speed up the search as their degree depends on the variance of the number of connections, which is "large" in scale-free networks.

Thus, a simple improvement on BFS is to carry out a random walk on the network, making sure that we do not revisit nodes already visited. The random walk strategy, which moves from one node to the next by selecting a neighbor uniformly at random, will be biased in scale-free networks toward the high-degree, that is, well-connected, nodes. Actually, we can do better than a random walk search by choosing at each step the neighbor with the highest degree. This will bias the search even further toward the high-degree nodes, and further speed up the search. The time complexity of these strategies is sublinear in the size of the network. Simulations of the strategy that passes messages to high-degree nodes on the P2P network, Gnutella, assuming that each file is stored at a single peer only, resulted in 50% of the files being found in eight steps or less [11].

A promising approach that could improve search in P2P networks having power-law degree distributions is based on the facts that (i) high-degree nodes will most likely be in the giant component of the network and (ii) the diameter of the giant component is logarithmic in the size of the network [589]. The search algorithm tailored for P2P networks has three phases.

- In the first phase (caching), each peer caches his or her contents on all nodes visited along a short random walk on the network, where the length of the walk ensures that he/she visits a well-connected node with high probability; we note that the length of the walk depends on the exponent of the power-law degree distribution.
- In the second phase (query implantation), a peer starts a query by storing it at all nodes visited along a short random walk of the network, whose length is the same as in the first phase.
- In the third phase (giant component search), each node that received the query in the second phase initiates a broadcast search, as in Gnutella; however, it forwards the query to its neighbor with a fixed probability.

This fixed probability of forwarding a message depends on the likelihood of the message staying within the giant component of the network. If the exponent of the degree distribution is less than 3 and the network is large enough, then this probability can be small, that is, a node that has received the query need only broadcast it to a small proportion of its neighbors. Thereafter, due to the logarithmic length of the diameter of the giant component, the query will propagate through the network quickly.

Simulations using a snapshot of Gnutella have shown that this algorithm can reduce the overall traffic in the network by two to three orders of magnitude without compromising performance.

The search strategies we have just mentioned have no global knowledge of the network, and, in particular, no notion of how far away the target is from the current node. Having more than just local information on who your neighbors are can enhance search. When people are navigating within a social network, they often use information such as geographical or social distance from the target in choosing who to pass the message to. (Social distance may be determined according to different social dimensions such as occupation, position in organizational hierarchy, education, and age.) Global information such as geographical distance from the target often manifests itself in terms of the use of "long-range contacts," which act as shortcuts in the networks bringing you much closer to the target than you would be by just using your "close" neighbors.

9.7.4 Navigation Within Small-World Networks

In a small-world network, the shortcuts created by rewiring or adding links to the network provide "long-range links," which lead to the small average distance between nodes. Consider, for example, the small-world network constructed by rewiring a small number of links on a one-dimensional regular lattice, as shown in Fig. 9.12b. We know that short paths exist but they are hard to find. The reason for this is that the rewired links connect to nodes chosen uniformly at random, and so there is no notion of distance that a searcher can use to choose between the different neighbors of a node.

A more complex structure is the two-dimensional lattice or grid, where each node has exactly four neighbors. In such a lattice, distance can be measured in terms of the "city block distance," also known as the *manhattan distance*. As with the one-dimensional lattice, adding random shortcuts, as shown in Fig. 9.16, will create short paths but they will not be easy to find.

Rather than adding long-range links uniformly at random, Kleinberg [376] suggested that when a shortcut is chosen, the probability that it will connect to another node should decrease with the distance between the nodes. In particular, he considered the probability of long-range links to be proportional to $1/d^{\tau}$, where τ is the dimension of the lattice and d is the distance between the nodes. It can be shown that when creating long-range links in this way, the probability that the distance, d, between the end points of any long-range link lies in the range, $x \leq d \leq 2x$, is independent of x. (It also follows that in the above, inequality 2 can be replaced by any other constant.) Therefore, such a lattice is equally likely to have long-range links at all distance scales, which gives rise to the efficient local search algorithm we now introduce.

A search algorithm is said to be a *decentralized algorithm*, if its knowledge at any given node is limited to (i) its local contacts, that is, the neighbors of the node on the underlying lattice; (ii) its long-range contacts, that is, the shortcuts that were added to the node; and (iii) the grid locations, that is, coordinates, of all its contacts, the nodes it has already visited and the target node; this information can be used to compute distances of nodes from the target. A "greedy" algorithm is a decentralized algorithm that moves (or forwards the message) to the neighboring node that is closest to the target node.

The remarkable result is that the greedy algorithm is efficient, in terms of the time it takes to reach the target if and only if $\tau = 2$. Efficient in this case

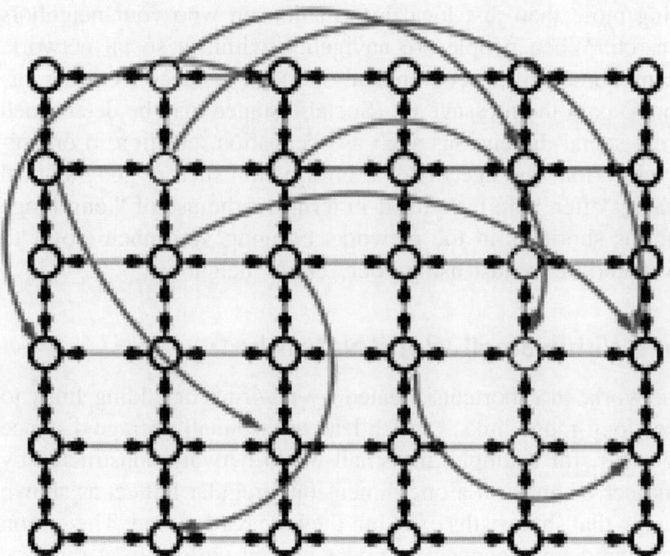

Figure 9.16 A two-dimensional lattice with random shortcuts. (Source: The Mathematics of Networks: The Small-World Phenomenon and Decentralized Search, by J. Kleinberg, Figure 9.1, Siam News, April 2004. www.siam.org/news/news.php?id=214.)

means that the path length is a polynomial in the logarithm of the network size. In particular, Kleinberg showed the path length of the greedy algorithm to be a quadratic in the logarithm of the network size. (This result can be generalized to any lattice dimension, in which case we would have that τ is the dimension of the lattice.)

The intuition behind this result is that when $\tau < 2$ there are too many shortcuts to nodes that are far away from the source node, and when $\tau > 2$ there too many shortcuts to nodes that are close to the source node.

This result could be useful in improving the performance of query answering in P2P networks [698]. The idea is that peers can cache the contents of neighboring peers, including the contents of a few long-range contacts. It was shown that maintaining such a small-world cache replacement scheme outperforms the standard least recently used cache replacement policy.

An extension of the greedy algorithm that assumes slightly more knowledge than a decentralized algorithm is the neighbor-of-neighbor greedy (NoN-greedy) algorithm [452]. Instead of just knowledge of the neighbors of a node, it assumes that the algorithm also has the knowledge of the neighbors of the neighbors (i.e., of the nodes two steps away) from the current node being visited, including their long-range contacts, as shown in Fig. 9.17. Using this knowledge, the NoN-greedy algorithm chooses to move to the neighbor of a neighbor that is closest to the target node, routed through the neighbor leading to it. The result obtained is that the NoN-greedy algorithm is more efficient than the greedy algorithm, which is validated with simulation results.

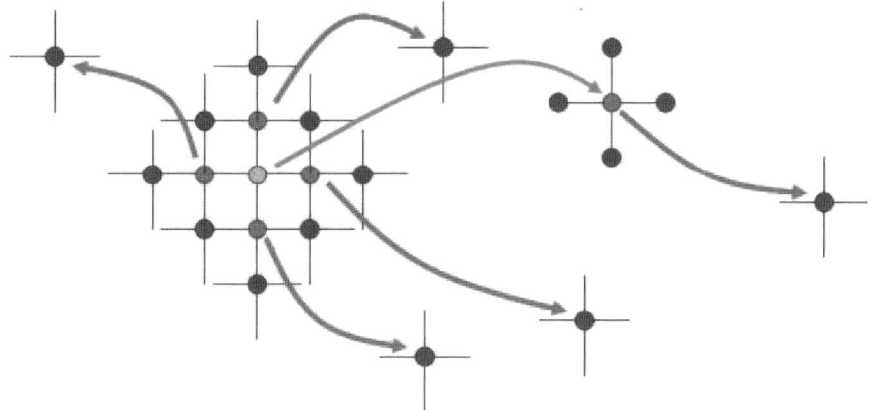

Figure 9.17 The local knowledge including the neighbors of a neighbor. (Source: Lookup in small worlds: A survey, by P. Fraigniaud. www.liafa.jussieu.fr/~asalgodis/AS1105/Fraigniaud_Pierre.ppt.)

Further speedup to the greedy algorithm can be achieved based on the idea that searching using two criteria such as geographic and social distance is much faster than searching using only one criterion such as geographic distance.

The additional knowledge an algorithm now has for each node is a set of long-range links, called the *awareness set*. In the greedy algorithm, the awareness set of a node is simply the long-range links of the node, and in the NoN-greedy algorithm the awareness set is augmented by all the links of the neighbors of the node. The *indirect greedy algorithm*, as it is called, has two phases, which are repeated until the target node is reached [232]. In the first phase, the algorithm selects the link, say $u \rightarrow v$, from its awareness set combined with the set of links from the source node to its neighbors, such that v is the closest node to the target. In the second phase, it uses the greedy algorithm to move from the source node to the node closest to u, which was chosen during the first phase.

For the indirect greedy algorithm to converge, its awareness set must be *monotone*; that is, the long-range link chosen at phase one of the algorithm must be present in the awareness set of the node chosen by the algorithm during phase two, unless this long-range link is a neighbor of the source node. We observe that if the awareness set of a node contains the long-range contacts of a fixed number of its closest nodes, then it is monotone. Although the presence of an awareness set improves the performance of the search relative to the greedy algorithm, once the awareness set increases beyond a certain limit its performance degrades. In particular, if the awareness set contains all the long-range contacts in the network, it would not perform better than the greedy algorithm.

As we have mentioned above, people often use more than one criterion when searching through a social network. It has been observed that, in practice, people use both geographic and social distances when deciding who to pass the message to. Although useful, the lattice model used as the network structure in the above algorithms is not realistic as a model of a social network. Building on these observations, Watts *et al.* [673] have devised a more general model, where proximity between actors in the network can be measured according to different criteria. On the basis of the notion of affiliation networks that have links between actors and the groups they belong to, actors assume an *identity* consisting of the groups that they belong to according to different social criteria, that is, the different affiliations they have. Each criteria such as location or occupation is organized into a hierarchy. The top level of the hierarchy is very general and the bottom level very specific. So, for example, if we are specializing in web site design, we belong to a bottom level group of other people specializing in the same area. The distance between two individuals in a hierarchy is measured as the height of their lowest common ancestor. So, the distance between two actors in the same group is one, and the distance between actors in sibling groups is two; a sibling group to those specializing in web site design may be a group specializing in web site development. Although we may be close to an actor in one hierarchy, we may be far from this actor in another. For example, we may both be web site designers (distance one in the occupation hierarchy) but live in distant locations (high distance in the location hierarchy). In the context of this model, we call the smallest distance between two actors, over all the possible affiliations they both have, their *social distance*.

As an example, we recast this model in terms of locating pages in the web graph. In this model, web pages are the actors in the social network, and the destination web pages on the other side of their outlinks are their network neighbors. Each web page can have several semantic categories attached to it; these are the set of affiliations, or attributes, of the page. For example, the Department's home page may be categorized both in terms of its subject area, that is, computer science, and in terms of its location within the University of London, implying that the page belongs to two groups of web pages according to these two different criteria. We assume that it is possible to measure similarity between pairs of pages within an ontology, for example, within a category of the Open Directory structure. The similarity between two pages within a category can be defined as the least number of levels needed to reach a common ancestor category; other similarity measures, say involving textual similarity, are also possible. The social distance between two pages, each having several attributes, is the smallest distance over all common attributes that the two pages may have. So, for example, the distance between the Department of Computer Science and a noncomputing department within the University of London may be one, while the distance between the Department of Computer Science and another department of Computing outside the University of London may be greater than one due to different research area specializations.

In order to construct a social network, the probability of a link between two actors, as a function of their social distance τ, is set to be proportional to $1/\exp(d\tau)$, where exp is the exponential function, d is the social distance, and τ is a tunable parameter as in the lattice model. Note that when $\tau = 0$, the connections are random, and when τ is large close local connections get the highest probability.

Simulations under this model have shown that as long as $\tau > 0$ and the number of affiliations of an actor is greater than one, ideally two or three, then a greedy algorithm that chooses to follow the link to a neighbor who is closest to the target in terms of social distance finds the target quickly. By "quickly" in this context it means that the target is reached within a predetermined maximum number of steps with high probability.

9.7.5 Testing Navigation Strategies in Social Networks

To test the models of navigation in social networks, Adamic and Adar [8] carried out experiments within an e-mail network and an online student social network.

In the e-mail network, the local strategy of following the best connected neighbor, that is, the one with the highest degree, did not perform well. The average number of steps to reach the target was 40 compared to the average distance of three in the network as a whole. The reason for the bad performance is that the degree distribution of the e-mail network under consideration was closer to that of a random network rather than to a scale-free network. The second strategy used was the greedy algorithm, with the measure of distance being proximity within the organizational hierarchy. This strategy fared well, the average number of steps being about five. The third strategy used the greedy algorithm with the measure of distance being physical proximity within the organization. This strategy did not perform as well as the second one, with the average number of steps being 12.

In the online student network, the local strategies were less successful, although a strategy combining several attributes to form a social distance performed better than the one following the best connected neighbor. The reason for this was mainly due to the data being incomplete, with many of the actors listing none or only few of their friends. Another factor was that many of the attributes were binary, thus only allowing to discriminate between close and near. Examples of such attributes are whether the students were in the same year or not, whether they were in the same department or not, whether they were both undergraduate or graduate or one of each, or whether they were living in the same halls of residence or not.

Overall, these experiments show that local search strategies can be effective in practice as predicted by the models we have described, but real-world networks do not seem to be as structured as the theoretical ones.

9.8 SOCIAL TAGGING AND BOOKMARKING

As we will see in Section 9.10, Web 2.0 is about the social web and how users can take an active role in the creation, annotation, and sharing of content. But, what about finding the content we are interested in? Although search engines are very successful in this task, they still lack in their understanding of the user's intent, which is why automated personalization and recommendation systems are being developed. Still, manually tagging the content with keywords, which act as a memory aid for future retrieval, can be very useful to the users. Moreover, sharing tags with other users transforms a personal activity into a social one, and can also be viewed as an extension of browser bookmarking facility to the social arena.

A Pew Internet report, based on a daily tracking survey of a sample of 2373 American adult internet users during December 2006, found that 28% of these users tagged online content such as photos, news stories, or blog posts, and on a typical day 7% of these tag content [552].

We mention a few of the many social tagging sites that have sprung up since 2000.

9.8.1 Flickr – Sharing Your Photos

One of the best known social tagging sites is Flickr (www.flickr.com), where photos can be managed, shared, and tagged. It was launched in 2004 by Caterina Fake and Stewart Butterfield and acquired by Yahoo in 2005.

Flickr contains a rich source of tagged images with different types of information including name of photographer, time, geolocation, and a variety of textual annotations such as subject, occasion, and genre. An "interestingness" measure is used to rank images (www.flickr.com/explore/interesting), which takes into account their popularity and the tags assigned to them. Flickr can also cluster images through tags using a relatedness metric based on tag co-occurrences. So, for instance, the tag "jaguar" as an animal co-occurs with "zoo" and "cat" while as a vehicle it co-occurs with "auto" and "car." Photos have a strong spatial element attached to them, so it is useful to be able to ascertain whether we can associate a tag with a place [559]. For example, tags such as "airport," "museum," and "NY marathon" have coherent place semantics while tags such as "dog," "food," and "red" do not generally represent places. Rattenbury and Naaman [559] demonstrate that place semantics can be assigned to tags of geolocated photos (i.e., those having latitude and longitude coordinates as part of their metadata) by employing the usage distribution for each tag, which is the set of coordinates associated with the tag. In particular, when the usage distribution of a tag shows bursty behavior, that is, the usage peaks over a small number of nearby locations, then the tag can be assumed to have place semantics.

9.8.2 YouTube – Broadcast Yourself

YouTube (www.youtube.com) is a video sharing application that has become one of the most popular sites on the Web. It is a popular culture phenomenon, with 20 hours of video being uploaded to YouTube every minute as of mid-2009.[206] It was launched in 2005 by Chad Hurley, Steve Chen, and Jawed Karim, and acquired by Google in 2006 for the sum of $1.65 billion. In January 2009, 100.9 million viewers watched 6.3 billion YouTube videos in the United States (about

[206]Zoinks! 20 Hours of Video Uploaded Every Minute! www.youtube.com/blog?entry=on4-EmafA5MA.

62.4 videos per viewer).[207] As of late 2009, YouTube has been serving over one billion videos per day, which is an indicator of the scalability problems facing YouTube.[208]

As with photos, social tagging of videos is potentially very useful, since in the case of video there is a larger semantic gap, than for single images, between the low-level features of a video and the high-level content description of the video [247]. Apart from the tags that are added by the person who uploaded the video, the metadata available for a video also includes a title and description of the content. (Note that in Flickr users may allow others to tag their photos, while on YouTube the tags are added only by the person who uploaded the video.) On an average, a video has less than a handful of tags, but it seems that increasing the number of tags to over a handful will increase the number of views the video will have [280]. (Increasing the length of the title and description, up to a point, will also increase views.) Thus the metadata including the tags play a key role in the ease of finding a video and thus have an impact on the number of views. Most videos tends to have their largest number of views in the first few days after they were uploaded to the system, and then the number of views it acquires tends to decrease with time.

YouTube videos and their tags provide a rich source of training data for machine learning algorithms to automatically add tags to videos [650]. As tags generally represent high-level concepts that are present in the videos, this type of learning is a step in addressing the semantic gap mentioned above. The system learns a probabilistic model that can estimate the conditional probability of a tag given a video. In order to do so, the video is segmented into keyframes and several features are defined for each frame to obtain a conditional probability of a tag given a feature in a frame. The frames are then integrated in a *feature pipeline* that gives the probability of a tag given a feature in the video, and finally these pipelines are combined to obtain the conditional probability of a tag being present given the video. The feature pipelines that have been used include color, texture, motion, and a bag of visual word descriptors based on local patches of pixels within a frame. (We note that machine learning can also be deployed to automatically annotate photos, and although easier than video annotation, it is still a very challenging task [427]; see http://alipr.com.)

Being a celebrity of YouTube transcends the realm of the Internet. The story of amateur guitarist with online alias "funtwo" is a case in hand. He posted a video of Canon Rock (arranged by another Korean guitarist, "JerryC") on a Korean music site. In the video he is playing the guitar in a room, his face being hidden by a baseball cap. Shortly after that, at the end of 2005, a YouTube member, "guitar90," posted the 5 mins and 20 secs video on his site. It became an instant hit spreading like fire through the Internet, and, as of early 2010, it is still one of the most popular clips on YouTube with over 69 million views.

[207]YouTube Surpasses 100 Million U.S. Viewers for the First Time. www.comscore.com/Press_Events/Press_Releases/2009/3/YouTube_Surpasses_100_Million_US_Viewers.

[208]Y,000,000,000uTube, by Chad Hurley, October 2009. http://youtube-global.blogspot.com/2009/10/y000000000utube.html.

Eventually, the identity of "funtwo" was discovered; he is a Korean, who was studying Computer Science at Auckland New Zealand, and taught himself to play the guitar. He has posted some more videos since the original one, and has in the meanwhile acquired celebrity status (there is even a Wikipedia page about him).

9.8.3 Delicious for Social Bookmarking

Another well-known site is Delicious (http://delicious.com), which is a web page social bookmarking tool. It was launched in 2003 by Joshua Schachter and acquired by Yahoo in 2005. In Delicious, a resource is a URL, which can be tagged by several users, as opposed to a Flickr photo or a YouTube video, which is "owned" by the user who uploaded it and thus essentially tagged only by this user and possibly by his or her circle of friends.

The nature of Delicious resources is of course very general as a URL can address any type of content including, amongst others, traditional HTML web pages, PDF files, images and videos.

Social bookmarking sites such as Delicious are not immune to spam, when, for example, many bookmarks are uploaded with the same set of tags and all point to the same or only few domains, or bookmarks are uploaded with an unreasonably large number of tags to make the resources more visible. A machine learning approach to such a problem is to determine a set of relevant features and train a classifier (or a bunch of classifiers) to ascertain through evaluation which features should carry the most weight in identifying tag spam. In Ref. 389, features were identified relating to the four categories of profile (e.g., name and e-mail address), activity (e.g., number of tags and number of bookmarks), location (e.g., number of users in the same domain and number of spam users with the same IP), and semantic information (e.g., ratio of tags on black list and co-occurrence of tags with known spammers). These features were evaluated with well-known machine learning methods and showed promising results.

9.8.4 Communities Within Content Sharing Sites

Research has shown that Delicious users are biased toward technology-oriented topics such as blogs, design, software, and programming [186]. On the other hand, Flickr tags describe features of photos such as location, color, or context, and there are no topic biases as such. In YouTube, tags generally describe the genre of the clip and affective responses, and as in Flickr the videos cover a large range of topics. In Delicious, the core activity is bookmarking, that is, storing, retrieving, and sharing resources, and thus community structure in Delicious can be defined by tag overlap. In Flickr, there seem to be two broad communities, one of professional photographers seeking feedback and the other of amateurs interested in sharing photos with a subcommunity of family and friends. The community structure in YouTube revolves around 12 broad categories rather than around friends; the dominant categories are music, entertainment, comedy, and sports covering over 60% of the videos [142].

As with many other social tagging sites, power-law distributions are abundant [678]. For example, as of 2008, in Delicious, the top 1% of users added 22% of all bookmarks and the top 10% contributed 62%. Moreover, 39% of all bookmarks link to the top 1% of URLs and 61% to the top 10%; in addition, 80% of the URLs appear only once. Popularity of bookmarks is fleeting as URLs that become popular receive most of their posts very quickly and the number of posts decreases sharply shortly afterward. Bookmarked URLs are generally more popular than a random sample of URLs as they receive more user clicks on search results, as was demonstrated in Ref. 381 by inspecting a search engine query log.

9.8.5 Sharing Scholarly References

We also mention that scholarly references can also be organized by asocial tagging service such as in CiteULike (www.citeulike.org). It was launched in 2004 by Kevin Emamy and Richard Cameron, and a collaboration with the publisher Springer was announced in 2008. In addition, e-commerce vendors such as Amazon.com have incorporated user tagging into their product pages.

9.8.6 Folksonomy

The collection of tags that are used to organize the bookmarks in a social tagging system has come to be known as a "folksonomy." The term *folksonomy* was coined by Thomas Vander Wal in 2004 as a combination of folk (meaning people) and taxonomy (meaning a scheme of classification).[209]

Clay Shirky argues that a taxonomy based on a fixed set of categories such as the Yahoo Directory (http://dir.yahoo.com) and the Open Directory (www.dmoz.org) are not optimized for web usage, because there is no fixed way in which to organize the Web so that each web resource belongs to a single or a small set of categories implied by a taxonomy.[210] The Web is an emergent and dynamic structure with a massive number of uncoordinated users and an enormous amount of varied content, so the controlled vocabulary of a taxonomy with a fixed number of categories is not flexible enough to predict the labels or tags that users may assign to resources. In such a folksonomy, the semantics are in the users who tagged the resources and not in the system. The system does not understand the semantics of tags as it does when there is a controlled vocabulary, but it can still provide recommendations based on co-occurrences of tags.

Gruber [270] argues that there is much benefit to be gained from sharing of tags across applications such as Delicious, Flickr, and YouTube, and suggests the core concepts involved in tagging. The concepts included are the tagger (person tagging), the tagged object (e.g., a URL), the application in which the tag was

[209]Thomas Vander Wal, Folksonomy. http://vanderwal.net/folksonomy.html.

[210]Clay Shirky, Ontology is Overrated: Categories, Links, and Tags. www.shirky.com/writings/ontology_overrated.html.

defined, and other information such as the time the tag assertion was made and the rating given to the tag, which can be positive or negative.

Folksonomies share the inherent problems of all uncontrolled vocabularies such as ambiguity (different users apply tags to objects in different ways), polysemy (a word having more than one meaning), synonymy (more than one word having the same meaning), and basic level variation (related terms that describe an object varying from being very specific, e.g., cheetah, to very general, e.g., animal). Spiteri [626] analyzed tags from three popular tagging sites by applying the National Information Standards Organization guidelines for construction of controlled vocabularies. She found that the tags correspond closely to a number of guidelines pertaining to the structure of terms, namely, the types of concepts (predominantly representing things), the predominance of single word terms and the use of nouns, the use of recognized spellings, and the use of mainly alphabetic characters. Despite this, there is inconsistency in the use of plural forms, difficulty in creating multiterm tags in Delicious, and incidences of ambiguous tags (e.g., Ajax (asynchronous JavaScript and XML) is a Web 2.0 technology but also a European football team).

Heymann [301] compared the controlled vocabulary of the Library of Congress Subject Headings (LCSH) and the folksonomy defined by user tags in LibraryThing (www.librarything.com), which is a social bookmarking site for cataloging books. It was found that approximately half of the LCSH keywords describing books are also used as tags and most of the other keywords have related tags, where relatedness is computed using Wikipedia explicit semantic analysis (ESA) [239]. (Wikipedia ESA computes relatedness using vector similarity of weighted vectors constructed with a TF–IDF scheme pertaining to terms that appear in Wikipedia articles. The weighted vectors that are compared are those pertaining to the tags we wish to relate.) Although the overlap of keywords and tags was high, there was no agreement between the experts (using LCSH keywords) and users (using tags within LibraryThing) on how to apply the shared keywords to individual books. Assuming that users know best how they would like to describe an object, it is reasonable to prefer users' tags to experts' keywords.

9.8.7 Tag Clouds

A tag cloud (also known as a word cloud) is a popular method to visualize textual data, where the importance of each word in the text is highlighted by its font, size, and/or color (117, 660). The importance of a word may simply be its number of occurrences in the text, that is, its frequency, but, in general, it is a weight attached to the word. The words in a tag cloud are usually, but not exclusively, presented alphabetically, and are arranged as a continuous list rather than as a table. In a social tagging scenario, the words are tags that can be clicked on to get the relevant tagged content. Examples of tag clouds from Flickr and Delicious tags are shown in Figs 9.18 and 9.19, respectively. As another example, Wordle (www.wordle.net), created by IBM researcher Jonathan Feinberg, creates aesthetic word clouds, as shown in Fig. 9.20.

Figure 9.18 Tag cloud of all time popular tags on Flickr; June 24, 2009. (Source: Reproduced with permission from Yahoo! Inc. © 2010 by Yahoo! Inc., FLICKR (www.flickr.com), and the FLICKR logo are registered trademarks of Yahoo! Inc.)

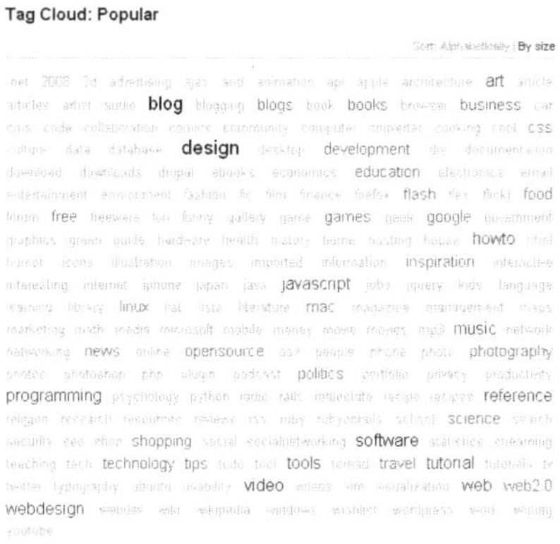

Figure 9.19 Tag cloud of popular tags on Delicious; June 24, 2009. (Source: Reproduced with permission from Yahoo! Inc. © 2010 by Yahoo! Inc., DELICIOUS (http://delicious.com), the DELICIOUS logo are registered trademarks of Yahoo! Inc.)

There is some debate on whether tag clouds are the best way to show word frequency information [292]. Simpler ways such as a standard column-based list of words ordered by frequency may be clearer than displaying the words in a continuous stream. Alternatively, a standard visualization of word frequency such as a bar chart would increase the accuracy of the presentation, as font and size are not necessarily the best way to depict frequency. Another issue is that although it is easy to find popular tags in a tag cloud, it is hard to find less popular ones that may be almost hidden. Moreover, it is difficult to see semantically related topics (e.g., Windows and Linux) in tag clouds, as these will most likely not occur in alphabetical order. Still, it is not yet clear how semantically clustered tag clouds can provide improvements over the alphabetically ordered clouds in search tasks for finding specific tags [596].

Despite these perceived shortcoming, tag clouds are popular. It can be argued that tag clouds signify collaborative social activity and give the visitor an idea of what is popular on the site. Thus, they are more of a social tool than of a data analysis tool.

9.8.8 Tag Search and Browsing

An important question is whether social bookmarking data can be used to augment web search [302], and a related question is how does searching a social

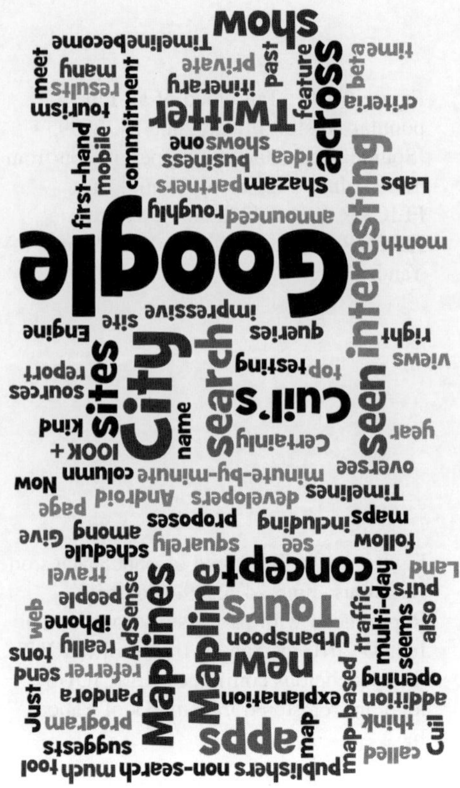

Figure 9.20 Wordle tag cloud of Search Engine Land RSS feeds; June 24, 2009.

bookmarking site compare with mainstream web search [388]. Traditionally, web search engines use three data sources: page content, link structure, and usage data from query logs. The fourth type of data which is made available through social bookmarking is user-generated content as exemplified by the user tags and bookmarks (which we will assume are represented as URLs).

Looking specifically at Delicious, it roughly covered, as of 2008, about 150 million URLs [678], which is only a small fraction of the Web as a whole, approximated at about 600 billion pages. Heymann *et al.* [302] sampled queries from a query log of a major search and found that 9% of the top 100 search engine results are covered by Delicious URLs, and when considering the top 10 results the coverage increases to 19%. Given that Delicious covers only a small fraction of the Web, this is an encouraging result regarding popular queries. One explanation for the this high overlap is that taggers use search engines to find relevant bookmarks [388]. Another way in which social bookmarking could be useful in search is through the tags. Here, tags that overlap with queries can help users find relevant pages, and related tags may help in query suggestion and refinement. One difference that stands out between web search and social search is that in web search many of the queries are navigational, where the user is looking for a single web page, for example, a home page of a specific site,

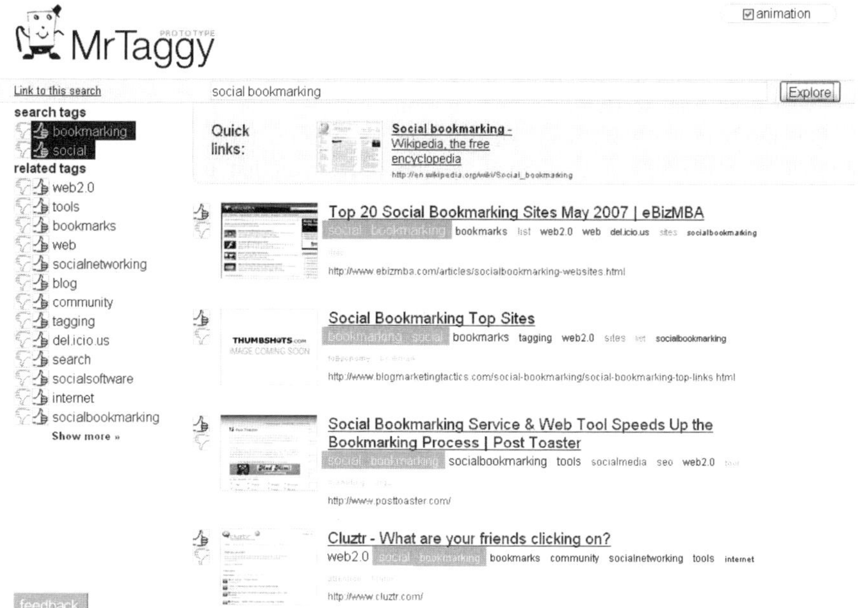

Figure 9.21 MrTaggy's search results for the query "social bookmarking."

while in social search the user is generally interested in browsing a page on a particular topic, which is more informational.

Tagging can also be used as the basis for a social browsing tool such as StumbleUpon (www.stumbleupon.com) discussed in Section 9.7.2 and a search engine such as MrTaggy (http://mrtaggy.com). MrTaggy is an experimental search engine launched in 2009 by The Augmented Social Cognition Research Group at PARC, which crawls and searches the web tag space (144, 356); MrTaggy does not index the text on a web page as it is only interested in the tags and corresponding URLs. Search results for the query "social bookmarking" is shown in Fig. 9.21. The interface gives users the opportunity to give feedback on tags and pages by clicking on the thumbs up or down icon to the left of a page or a tag.

The blog search engine Technorati (www.technorati.com) also uses tags in its search process, and encourages blog authors to add tags to their posts to make it easier for others to find the posts.

Another feature that can be useful in social bookmarking systems is tag recommendation, which assists users in finding appropriate tags. Three types of algorithms for tag recommendation have been suggested [338]. The first method is an adaptation of CF as presented in Section 9.4, where the items to be recommended are either the resources or the tags; when recommending a resource we are effectively recommending the tags describing the resource. The second method is an adaptation of PageRank, called *FolkRank*, where the underlying network containing undirected edges for each, user, resource and tag triple, is weighted by the number of times each pair (user, resource), (user, tag) or (resource, tag) occurs. The third method is based on popularity, simply recommending the most popular tags, or a mixture of popularity, for a given user and resource, recommending the tag that maximizes the sum of the number of other users who tagged the resource with that tag plus the number of other resources tagged by the user with that tag. Recommending the most popular tags is outperformed by the other methods, while FolkRank is the best performer. On the other hand, the most popular mixture approach proved to be better than the CF approach, and is much cheaper to compute than FolkRank.

Tag prediction can be viewed as a content-based approach to tag recommendation. The problem here is given a resource, say a URL, can we predict the relevant tags that apply to it using the knowledge we already have about resources that have already been tagged as training data for a classifier. Heymann *et al.* [303] carried out an experiment for predicting the top 100 tags from Delicious given the information from the URLs that were tagged. In particular, three different features were used for each URL, that is, its page text, anchor text of inlinks to the URL, and surrounding text from pages that link to and are linked from the URL including the page of the URL itself. The best feature in prediction was page text, followed by anchor text, and in the third place surrounding text. For all three features, the results showed that if only small recall is needed, say 10%, then the precision can reach above 90%. On the other hand, the precision-recall break even point, at which the precision equals the recall, was 60% for page text, 58% for anchor text, and only 51% for surrounding text. As about 55% of the tags appear only once [678], recall is heavily limited for rare tags.

9.8.9 The Efficiency of Tagging

To understand the efficiency of tagging, we can look to Information Theory [145]. Central to Information Theory is the notion of entropy which measures the average amount of information of an object in terms of its probability distribution. So, for example, the entropy of tags, denoted by $H(T)$, is defined as the negative sum over all tags of the product of the probability of each tag and the logarithm of the probability of the tag; $H(R)$ and $H(U)$ can similarly be defined as the entropy of resources and users, respectively. Analysis of Delicious showed that $H(T)$ was initially increasing but seems to have reached a plateau. This implies that initially it was probable that users would add new tags to resources but it has become increasingly hard to do so, and it is more likely that an already popular tag will be added to newly tagged resources (note that in Delicious a resource can be tagged many times). The entropy of resources, $H(R)$, is increasing over time, that is, it is becoming increasingly hard to navigate to a resource with tags acting as navigation aids. In addition, the entropy of users, $H(U)$, is also increasing, so it is harder to predict which user is tagging which resource. The conditional entropies are even more telling, for example, $H(R|T)$ is the conditional entropy of resources given the set of tags, which asks the following question: given that the set of tags is known, how much uncertainty is there regarding the resource set? It seems that $H(R|T)$ is increasing rapidly, implying the tags are becoming harder to use since they are tagging too many resources. The conditional entropy $H(T|R)$ is also increasing, so over time the number of tags is increasing or the tag distribution is becoming more uniform over the resources. Either way it is becoming more difficult for users to specify tags for resources. The conditional entropy $H(R|U)$ initially increased and then reached a plateau, implying that users are increasingly more likely to tag existing documents. On the one hand, the conditional entropy $H(U|R)$ is linearly increasing, showing that it is increasingly hard to find experts on a set of resources. Similarly, the conditional entropy $H(T|U)$ is increasing, but only gradually, so it is getting slightly harder for a user to specify tags that users are interested in. On the other hand, the conditional entropy $H(U|T)$ is increasing rapidly, so it is also increasingly harder to find experts on a set of tags.

To conclude, the set of tags is becoming more diverse over time and it is harder to direct users to resources matching these tags. It is also becoming harder for users to provide meaningful and discriminating tags for resources. The folksonomy emerging from the tag set both describes the resources and provides a way to navigate them. It seems that this is becoming less efficient as the tag set is becoming more saturated. The implication is that as the corpus grows more tags are needed to describe individual resources. (This is also true for web search as the Web continues to grow.)

9.8.10 Clustering and Classifying Tags

Clustering in this context is the problem of partitioning a set of web resources into groups of similar resources. In the case of the social bookmarking site Delicious, the resources are web documents, for Flickrs they are images, and for YouTube they are videos. The question in this context is how can the tags improve clustering? Ramage *et al.* [555] have shown that the k-means algorithm (see Section 7.2.4) can be used to cluster Delicious web documents using the vector representation for words in documents and for tags. The words and tags are weighted independently and thereafter combined into a single vector. This model provides better clusters than just using the words in documents or the tags separately.

It is also useful to consider classifying tags into a predefined set of semantic categories [518]. A generic method is to use an available corpus of classified phrases or documents from, say Wikipedia, the Open Directory, or WordNet[211] to which the tags can be mapped to and then classified using the set of existing categories for the corpus under consideration.

[211]WordNet is a large lexical database for English, which groups words into synonyms, provides short and general definitions, and records semantic relationships between the synonym groups; see http://wordnet.princeton.edu.

9.9 OPINION MINING

A Pew Internet report, based on a daily tracking survey of a sample of 2400 American adult internet users during August 2007, found that two thirds of internet users have shopped online, but at the same time 75% do not like giving their credit card number or personal information online [308]. Moreover, 43% of users are frustrated by the lack of information when trying to find out about or buy products online, 35% have found some information confusing during their research or shopping, and 30% have been overwhelmed by the amount of information they have had to digest during the online shopping process. Overall, 58% of internet users have experienced at least one of these three negative feelings during online shopping. It was also found that 81% of user do online research before buying a product, and 30% have posted a comment or a review about a product they have bought.

A study conducted in October 2007 found that more than three-quarters of internet users are significantly influenced by online consumer reviews when making a purchase.[212] The study also revealed that consumers were willing to pay at least 20% more for services receiving an"excellent" (5-star) rating than for the same service receiving only a"good" (4-star) rating. Users noted that they are more influenced by reviews of fellow consumers rather than those generated by professionals.

All this information points to the fact that there are substantial information needs from consumers to analyze product information and reviews, and to present them in digestible form. (This information need goes beyond e-commerce, for example, many people use the Web to gather political information, and many potential students use the Web to help them make a decision at which university they would like to study.)

Opinion mining and sentiment analysis is the activity of mining for opinions in user-generated textual content, as opposed to dealing with facts which is what search engines do [435, Chapter 11; 526]. Apart from delivering opinions from diverse sources to individual web users, it has applications in business intelligence (e.g., what are users saying about our products?), ad placement next to user-generated content (e.g., if the user's sentiment is positive toward a product it can then be advertised), and providing a general search facility for opinions.

There are numerous comparison shopping sites (such as the eBay subsidiary Shopping.com, www.shopping.com) that allow users to search for products, which are then compared in terms of their price. The product comparison normally also includes detailed product information and reviews from all the e-commerce sites that are selling the product. Opinion mining goes beyond comparison shopping in that it analyzes users' textual content to automatically infer sentiment, rather than just aggregate the information as comparison shopping agents do.

[212]Online Consumer-Generated Reviews Have Significant Impact on Offline Purchase Behavior. www.comscore.com/Press_Events/Press_Releases/2007/11/Online_Consumer_Reviews_Impact_Offline_Purchasing_Behavior.

There are three important mining tasks on texts that express opinions:

1. Feature-based opinion mining and summarization, which looks at the sentence level of a text to discover what aspects of an object, for example, a product, did people like or dislike.
2. Sentiment classification, which treats the problem as a text document classification problem with three classes: positive, negative, or neutral. (If the 5-star system is used, then there will be five classes, giving a finer-grained sentiment analysis.)
3. Comparative sentence and relation extraction, which allows the comparison of one object to one or more similar ones; for example, is laptop A better than laptop B.

9.9.1 Feature-Based Opinion Mining

One way to use the results from opinion mining is to produce feature-based summaries of the product under review. This works in three steps: (i) mine the product features in the customer reviews, (ii) identify the opinion sentences in each review, and (iii) summarize the results [313].

In step (i) a natural language processor performs part-of-speech tagging on the review; features are normally nouns or noun phrases. In order to identify features for which many customers have expressed opinion, frequent itemsets are identified; a frequent itemset is a set of words or a phrase that occurs together in many sentences.

Next, opinion words are extracted from sentences, where opinion words are taken in this task to be the adjectives. The justification for this is that research has shown that there is high correlation between adjectives and expressing subjective opinions. Thus, a product sentence is one that has one or more features and one or more opinion words, and for each feature its nearest opinion word is taken as its effective opinion. In order to identify the orientation of the opinion as positive or negative, WordNet (http://wordnet.princeton.edu) can be used to identify synonyms and antonyms of each adjective, together with a seed set of adjectives with known orientations with which it is matched against.

An opinion sentence is one that contains one or more opinions. In order to predict in (ii) the orientation of opinion sentences as positive or negative, the dominant orientation of opinion words in the sentence is taken. If this is neutral, then the effective opinions are counted per feature and if more features have a positive or negative orientation then the sentence is considered as positive or negative. If this measure is still neutral, then the orientation of the previous sentence is used.

In step (iii), for each discovered feature, related opinion sentences are put into positive and negative categories according to the orientation of the opinion sentences found in the previous step. The features can then be ranked according to their frequencies in the reviews. An evaluation of this method in Ref. 313 showed it to be promising. One way to improve the method is to use more sophisticated natural language processing methods such as pronoun resolution, and better detection of opinion words or phrases that are not necessarily adjectives.

9.9.2 Sentiment Classification

Given, say a movie or book review, sentiment classification determines whether the orientation of the review is positive or negative. In sentiment classification, as opposed to topic-based classification, the important words to detect are positive and negative opinion words such as "great," "excellent," "bad," or "worst."

A method that classifies customer reviews was described in Ref. 648. As in feature-based opinion mining, the first step is to mine opinion words and phrases from the review; in this context, an opinion phrase is two consecutive words one of which is likely to be an opinion word. Once this is done, the strength of semantic association between the two words in each extracted phrase is estimated as the mutual information between the words in the phrase. (The mutual information between two words is the logarithm of the ratio of their co-occurrence probability and the product of their individual probabilities. Note that the product of their probabilities is the probability that they co-occur if they are statistically independent, and thus the mutual information is a measure of the degree of statistical dependence between the two words.)

The semantic orientation of an opinion phrase is then computed as the difference between the mutual information of the phrase and the positive reference word "excellent," and the mutual information of the phrase and the negative reference word "poor." The probabilities here are estimated by issuing queries to a web search engine and computing the probabilities by counting the number of results returned. Queries are submitted for each reference word on their own and for each reference word together with the phrase. The average semantic orientation of all the opinion phrases extracted from the review is then computed, and the review is classified as positive if the computed average is positive.

An alternative approach, with competitive results, is to use a standard classification method such as naive Bayes (see Section 3.2.2) for the task [527]. As opposed to Turney's method described above [648], which is unsupervised (i.e., it does not need any classified reviews for training), methods such as naive Bayes are supervised (i.e., they need training data). So, the advantage of naive Bayes is that it does not rely on natural language processing to extract opinion phrases, but its disadvantage is that it needs sufficient training data for the classification to be successful.

In this case, naive Bayes would use the positive opinion training reviews to build a probability distribution of the words in these reviews, and a different probability distribution for the words in the negative opinion training reviews. For a large enough set of training data, we would expect, in the positive examples, that the probability of positive opinion words will be high and the probability of negative opinion words will be low; the converse should be true for the negative examples. Interestingly, Pang *et al.* [527] showed that naive Bayes performed as well in this task, when instead of computing the frequency of occurrence of words in documents only binary values were used to record the absence or presence of words in the documents.

There are, of course, many complications of which we mention two [526]. One is the use of negation, that is, "not good" is the opposite of "good" and needs to be detected. Another is that sentiment classification can be influenced by the domain of objects to which it is applied. As an example, the sentence "go and read the book" indicates a positive opinion when reviewing a book but a negative one when reviewing a movie. There is also the hard problem of detecting review spam, which is a fake review whose intention is to promote or damage a product's reputation.

9.9.3 Comparative Sentence and Relation Extraction

A typical opinion sentence is "book A is great," while a typical comparative sentence is "book A is better than book B." A comparative sentence is expressed as a relation between two objects that is extracted from the sentence. Examples of comparative relations are "better," "cheaper," "faster," and "equal." Comparative mining can proceed in two steps [343]. In the first step, comparative sentences are identified and in the second step the comparative relation in the sentence is extracted, assuming there is only one such relation in the sentence.

9.10 WEB 2.0 AND COLLECTIVE INTELLIGENCE

As I am writing about Web 2.0, there is already talk about its successor Web 3.0. Only time will tell what Web 3.0 will actually entail. Will it be the long awaited semantic web, heralded since 1998, by Tim Berners-Lee, the founder of the Web, "as the web of data with meaning in the sense that a computer program can learn enough about what the data means to process it." (In fact, there is some confusion and debate about the meaning of the phrase "semantic web," which is briefly addressed in the concluding chapter.) Another attempt at predicting what Web 3.0 will be is that it will bring about the successful marriage of artificial intelligence and the Web. In any case even when Web 3.0 arrives, it is not clear whether it will subsume Web 2.0.

So, what is Web 2.0? One definition is that it is a bunch of web technologies that have driven the Web forward since the new millennium and the collapse of the dot-com bubble. It is not clear who coined the term Web 2.0, but it became mainstream following Tim O'Reilly's seminal article on what Web 2.0 entails [514]. To promote Web 2.0 and look beyond it, the Web 2.0 Summit (formerly named Web 2.0 Conference, www.web2summit.com) is an annual gathering that started in 2004 as a forum for presenting and discussing innovations that are shaping the Web and its future and how these are related to the world around us.

Beyond the buzzwords that are associated with Web 2.0, it is about users taking an active role in shaping the Web. In more concrete terms, users can create new content, share it, link to it, search for it, tag it, and modify it. To give you a feeling of what Web 2.0 is about, we list a few of the top

Web 2.0 sites as of early 2010: Delicious (social bookmarking, http://delicious.com), eBay (online auctions, www.ebay.com), Facebook and MySpace (social networking, www.facebook.com and www.myspace.com), Digg (social news, www.digg.com), Flickr (photo sharing, www.flickr.com), Twitter (microblogging, www.twitter.com), Wikipedia (collaborative authoring, www.wikipedia.org), and Youtube (video sharing, www.youtube.com).

Michael Wesch gives a clear and thought provoking explanation of Web 2.0 in an under 5 mins Youtube video called, Web 2.0 . . . The Machine is Us/ing Us.[213] In the video, Wesch explores the evolution of media from text and hypertext to social media. He explains how HTML has evolved from a tool for writing hypertext, where form (structural and stylistics elements) and content are inseparable to XML, where form and content are separable by using cascading style sheets (CSS). This enables data to be exported in a simple format and syndicated via RSS. Through blogs and other tools, users can upload content to the Web; the content is not restricted to text and can also be image, audio and video, or any other format that can be digitized. Content can now be created, tagged, exchanged, and "mashed" together to create new content. The users (Us) are now responsible for organizing the Web, leading Wesch to state that "we are the web" and "the machine is Us." Web 2.0 is linking people that are creating, sharing, trading, and collaborating with the aid of the tools and web sites such as those mentioned above. The word *prosumer*, which combines both producer and consumer, describes the role of a Web 2.0 user.

We now dig a bit deeper and look at the technologies that underpin Web 2.0 and those that have come to the fore as a result. One of the most succinct definitions of Web 2.0 is that of viewing the Web as a platform. On the one hand, the Web has become a software development and content delivery platform, and, on the other hand, it is serving as a social media platform.

9.10.1 Ajax

From a technological point of view one of the key enablers of Web 2.0 is Ajax[214]. In a traditional web application, most user actions will trigger an HTTP request from the web server and once a web page is returned the effect in the browser will be to refresh itself with the returned page. In an Ajax application when the user interacts with the web page, the data is retrieved from the server asynchronously in the background without the need to reload the web page. So, when using Ajax, a web page can be updated smoothly as the user interacts with the page without the need for the user to wait for the page to reload. A much quoted example of the use of Ajax is in Google suggest (http://labs.google.com/suggestfaq.html), which updates query suggestions as the query is typed into the search box, but you can find Ajax applications in many web sites that display up-to-date information or demand some user interaction. The asynchronous retrieval is done via

[213]Michael Wesch, "Web 2.0 . . . The Machine is Us/ing Us". www.youtube.com/watch?v=NLlGopyXT_g.

[214]J. Garrett, Ajax: A new approach to web applications. http://adaptivepath.com/ideas/essays/archives/000385.php.

an XMLHTTPRequest[215] that makes a background HTTP request and receives data from a server without interfering with the user behavior. JavaScript binds everything together and is used to display the results.

We will now discuss several other technologies, namely, syndication, open APIs, mashups, widgets, and the concept of software as a service (SaaS), which are all Web 2.0 enabling.

9.10.2 Syndication

Syndication (making web site content available to users) has been widely adopted by content providers (for example, delivering news), blogs (publicizing their content), and generally companies who wish to publish up-to-date information about their business. Several formats have been designed to enable the syndication of web feed, the most known being RSS (www.rssboard.org/rss-specification), and the less widely deployed alternative Atom format (www.atomenabled.org) [513]. Both these formats specify feeds in XML, but there are some differences between them. The motivation for developing Atom was to address some of the limitations and perceived flaws of RSS such as the specification of how the content is encoded and support for different language contexts. The feed icon, shown in Fig. 9.22, has by now become the standard for identifying RSS and Atom feeds on web pages.

In order to capture the multitude of feeds that are available, feed aggregators collect feeds from multiple sources into a single collection. The aggregation may be automatic as in Google News (http://news.google.com) but often trusted human editors play a central role in the aggregation, providing a high-quality information filter. Digg (http://digg.com) is an example of social aggregation of news items, where users submit articles and user votes (i.e., popularity) decide which articles are displayed on the front page of the site. On the other hand, Bloglines (www.bloglines.com) is a subscription-based news aggregator; it was acquired by Ask Jeeves in February 2005. Users of Bloglines can subscribe and read their favorite feeds on their desktop or on a mobile device.

Web feed management systems provide tools for publishers and content providers to syndicate and manage their feeds. One such web feed management system is FeedBurner, which was acquired by Google in June 2007. FeedBurner provides tools for managing and publishing feeds including advertising in feeds.

Figure 9.22 The RSS logo.

[215]The XMLHttpRequest Object, W3C Working Draft 15 April 2008. www.w3.org/TR/XMLHttp-Request

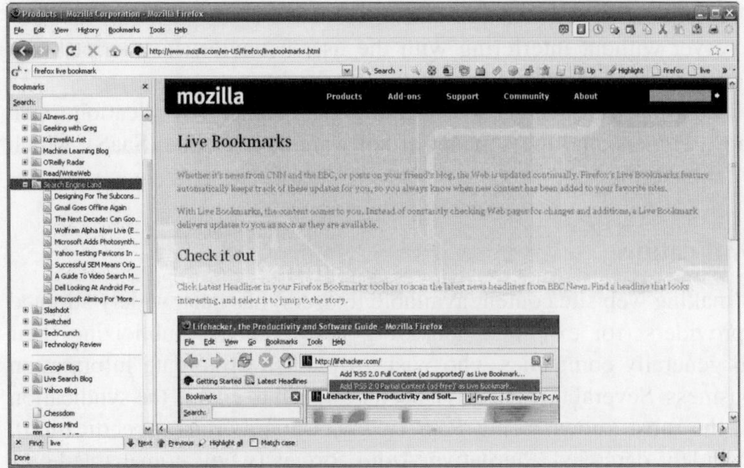

Figure 9.23 Live bookmarks in Firefox.

It has also become important to allow users to subscribe to web feeds through their browser. For example, the live bookmarks feature in Firefox, shown in Fig. 9.23, does just that. When an RSS feed is available, the icon will appear on the right side of the location bar. The user can then subscribe to the feed by adding it to his or her live bookmarks. To keep the information up-to-date, the feed is refreshed periodically by the browser.

9.10.3 Open APIs, Mashups, and Widgets

An *open API* is an API that is open to developers, enabling communication between an application and a web site. For example, the Google Maps API (http://code.google.com/apis/maps) allows developers to manipulate, add content to and embed maps in a web site. Open APIs exist for many Web 2.0 sites as a means of allowing developers to create applications that make use of their content. Combining or remixing data from several APIs to create an integrated application is called a *mashup* [691]. A site that keeps track of the latest open APIs and mashups is Programmableweb (www.programmableweb.com); as of early 2010, it listed about 1600 APIs and over 4500 mashups, with new ones being added to the site every day.

HousingMaps (www.housingmaps.com), Weatherbonk (www.weatherbonk.com), HealthMap (www.healthmap.org), and Newsmap (www.newsmap.jp) are typical examples of mashups. HousingMaps is a mashup of Google Maps and housings ads from Craiglist (www.craigslist.org), making it easier to find a place to buy or rent in a given area. (Craiglist is a network of online communities, featuring online classified advertisements. It is an extremely popular site, getting more than 50 million new ads every month and having over 20 billion monthly page views as of early 2010.[216].) Weatherbonk is a mashup of Google Maps and

[216]Craiglist online community, about > factsheet. www.craigslist.org/about/factsheet.

Figure 9.24 Treemap visualization of news. (Source: NewsMap, by M. Weskamp. www.newsmap.jp.)

real time weather information coming from personal homes and schools as well as from national weather services. HealthMap is a mashup combining Google Maps and health information from disparate sources to present a global view of the state of infectious diseases and their effect on human and animal health. Using Google Maps and other map APIs in applications has become a prolific source for mashups.[217] Another mashup is Newsmap combining information from the Google News aggregation service, using the treemap visualization algorithm (www.cs.umd.edu/hcil/treemap); see Fig. 9.24.

Mashups are about simplicity, usability, and ease of access. To speed up mashup development and reduce the programming effort involved, several tools have been developed. One such tool is Yahoo Pipes (http://pipes.yahoo.com), which allows users to combine feeds from various sources to create a mashup. It also supports geocoding information; that is, finding location names within the feed and browsing the locations on an interactive map.

A widget, also commonly known as an app, is a program that can be embedded on a computer be it a desktop or a mobile device or on a web page [407]. These are important for deployment of Web 2.0 software as it allows programs to be independent from the traditional browser and makes the distribution of web-based application much easier. Third party widgets are an important mechanism of enhancing the user experience in social networks such as Facebook and MySpace, and provide a means for companies to advertise their products on these sites. On mobile devices, such as cell phones, widgets are set to become a major platform for the delivery of web content and for connecting users to web services such as social networks. The potential list of widgets for mobile phones is endless and ranges from news headlines, transport information, your local weather,

[217]Google Maps Mania (www.googlemapsmania.blogspot.com) is a blog that tracks mashups that are influenced by Google Maps.

entertainment, finance, music, photos, video, games, to almost anything you can think of that might be useful for a mobile phone user.

9.10.4 Software as a Service

Web 2.0 is also transforming the way software is being deployed from the conventional shrink-wrapped software (SWS), which is developed, sold as a package, and deployed in-house, to SaaS, where software is hosted on the vendors' web servers and delivered to customers who use it on demand over the Internet.

SaaS is related to the much hyped concept of *cloud computing* [121], where computing services are delivered over the Internet; the computing resources may be geographically distributed, may come from a multitude of computing systems and are delivered to a variety of devices. (The cloud refers to the Internet as a distributed delivery platform and comes from network diagrams where the Internet is often depicted as a"cloud.") Many of us already use cloud services in our day-to-day work such as web-based e-mail, social networking, and online collaboration tools.[218].

SaaS refers to the situation where companies, rather than directly licensing software that is important to their business, pay a service provider for the usage of the software over the Internet. SaaS alleviates the need to install and maintain the full range of applications on the customers' computers. It also means that the customer does not need a separate license for each software package being used and may thus reduce licensing costs. SaaS is normally associated with cost and maintenance business software such as CRM solutions as delivered by one of the leading SaaS providers (as of 2010), salesforce.com. In a typical scenario, a salesman can access the software online, on demand, anytime and anywhere as long as a connection to the Internet can be made; in some cases, a lightweight version of the software is made available for offline work, and when a connection is reestablished then the work can be synchronized with the online version.

SaaS is a multibillion dollar business (as of 2010) and is forecast to increase. Still there are some concerns about SaaS such as quality of service, reliability, network speed, security, and problems with customer lock-in that make it imperative to have a viable exit strategy. There is also the problem of customization for individual clients, which may be resolved with an appropriate API. Another concern raised is that the SaaS model has been historically volatile and dependent both on external economic factors and technological innovation [124]. (It is important to note that some of the concerns with SaaS are also true for the traditional software licensing model.)

Examples of big internet companies providing cloud services are Amazon (Amazon Web Services, http://aws.amazon.com), Microsoft (Azure Services Platform, www.microsoft.com/azure), and Google (Google Apps, http://apps.google.com).

[218]As an example of online collaboration tools, Cisco WebEx (www.webex.com) proves services that support webinars, online training, online events, collaborative online meetings, and online presentations.

9.10.5 Collective Intelligence

We now examine the concept of *collective intelligence* as being central to the Web 2.0 paradigm. Collective intelligence may be defined as the emergence of new ideas as a result of a group effort, noting that the members of the group may or may not collaborate, coordinate, or share information. For example, as we have seen in CF, the user obtains recommendations based on the opinions of other users but this is achieved without any formal collaboration between the users. However, there are scenarios when some coordination is necessary, as in the situation when a consensus among editors collaborating on a Wikipedia article is needed to resolve some dispute.

A wiki (a Hawiian word meaning "fast") is a collection of web pages that allows anyone to contribute to the collection or modify their content. Wikipedia and the open source wiki software package, MediaWiki (www.mediawiki.org), is the most visible example of a wiki and its implementation, but there are many other wikis on the Web, some of which are open only to users within a particular enterprise. Wikis can be viewed as a form of collective intelligence, where knowledge is aggregated by collaborative effort. In this respect there is even a wiki on collective intelligence hosted by MIT.[219] It provides a survey of the field, aiming to summarize what is known, provide references to sources of further information, and suggest possibilities for future directions. So, through the wisdom of the crowds, we can learn more about collective intelligence.

Another example of collective intelligence that harnesses expert knowledge is community question answering (CQA). A user of a CQA site posts a question and members of the community respond with answers to the question. In Yahoo Answers (12, 277) (http://answers.yahoo.com), which is the largest English language CQA site as of early 2010, the question answering process proceeds as follows. A user posts a question in one of the 25 top-level categories. Once there are enough answers to the question, the user who asked the question can choose the best answer to the question and the community can also vote on what they think the best answer is. After a certain period of time since the question was asked it becomes resolved, and is available for searching. Users can then add comments and ratings to the best and other answers that were provided.

CQA sites such as Yahoo Answers, Baidu Knows [689] (the largest Chinese CQA site, http://zhidao.baidu.com), and Naver's Knowledge Search [493] (the largest Korean CQA site, http://kin.naver.com) have become increasingly popular. As of 2009, Yahoo Answers had approximately 23 million resolved questions, Baidu Knows had over 47 million question and answers, and Naver's Knowledge Search had over 95 million questions and answers. There is a wide range of question types, from factual information, to advice seeking, opinion gathering, discussion, and task oriented (how do I do something?).

Participating in these communities is rewarded by virtual points for various activities; for example, a number of points are awarded for posting the best answer and fewer for providing an answer or voting on an answer. The reasons

[219]Handbook of Collective Intelligence. http://scripts.mit.edu/~cci/HCI/index.php?title=Main_Page.

that people participate in the community are varied; some common reasons are gaining points, altruism and the wish to help others and share knowledge, to gain or maintain understanding of a topic, to relieve boredom and kill time, because it is fun and entertaining, and to promote a business or opinion. (To get a good feel of peoples' motives you can query Yahoo Answers with the question "What is your motivation for answering questions?".)

The quality of questions and answers also vary significantly. Even if a question is relevant, answers can be of poor quality due to several reasons such as limited knowledge, spam, or limited time to answer the question. (As an aside we note that it has been shown that the quality of answers increases when there is a financial reward for answering a question, as was the case in Google Answers, which operated between 2001 and 2006 [283]. As mentioned above, in the case of CQA the rewards for participation are not financial.)

There have been several attempts to automate the process of detecting high-quality answers and user expertise (81, 634). A machine learning algorithm can make use of several features to detect an expert. These include number of answers provided, number of categories the user is the top contributor, proportion of best answers, average answer length (better answers are typically longer), and number of community votes obtained. Another method is to adapt the HITS hubs and authorities ranking algorithm (described in Section 5.2.7) to measuring the question quality (hubness) and answering expertise (authoritativeness) of users. The idea being that, in this case, the mutual reinforcement principle of the algorithm is that a good question is more likely to be answered by an expert, and conversely, a poor question is less likely to be answered by an expert, if at all. Results from experiments have shown that automated methods for recognizing quality answers can be effective in retrieving quality answers from the growing database of questions and answers.

Collective intelligence is related to the wisdom of the crowds [633], where under the right circumstances groups of people are smarter than the best expert in the group. A common application of the wisdom of the crowds is a *prediction market* (also known as an *information market*), which is a market established to aggregate knowledge and opinions about the likelihood of future events in order to make predictions about these events [538]. The payoff of a contract in a prediction market is associated with the outcome of a future event such as who will win an election. On the other hand, the price of a contract in the market is linked to the market's consensus probability that the event attached to the contract will, in fact, happen.

Another related activity is that of *crowdsourcing* [310],[220] which is the act of taking a job traditionally performed by a designated agent (usually an employee) and outsourcing it to an undefined, generally large group of people in the form of an open call, generally using the Internet. Online communities such as social networks are often the building blocks for crowdsourcing. As an example, iStockphoto (www.istockphoto.com) is an online company selling low-price (micropayment) royalty-free stock photography, animations, and video

[220]Jeff Howe on Crowdsourcing, www.youtube.com/watch?v=TCM7w1lUltk.

clips. Anyone can submit a photo to the site and, if approved, will earn a small share of the profits each time the photo is downloaded. iStockPhoto had over 3 million registered users as of 2008 who share ideas through forums. The business model of iStochphoto is based on the crowdsourcing of photographers, mainly amateur, to provide a marketplace for their work.

Amazon's Mechanical Turk (www.mturk.com) is a marketplace for businesses to submit tasks that require human intelligence and workers to perform these tasks and to be paid for them. The idea is to employ humans to do relatively simple tasks that are difficult or cannot be carried out by computers. As of late 2009, the Mechanical Turks utilized 400,000 workers in more than 100 countries, on about 60,000 human intelligence tasks (HITs).[221]

One potential problem with this approach is that the tasks are not carried out properly, especially if the responses that are provided by the humans are not verifiable. Experiments carried out by Kittur *et al.* [374] showed that special care needs to be taken in the formulation of the tasks, in order to get high-quality results; this is especially important when the user measurements are subjective or qualitative. It is important to have verifiable questions, where answering them accurately requires as much effort as random or malicious completion.

(The Mechanical Turk was inspired by the chess playing automaton constructed in the late eighteenth century, which appeared to play a strong game of chess. Actually, it was operated by a master strength chess player hidden inside the machine [629].)

9.10.6 Algorithms for Collective Intelligence

Collective intelligence also has a algorithmic component that enables programs to take advantage of the enormous amounts of data collected from users (599, 20). These algorithms generally come from the fields of web data mining and machine learning, allowing programs to group, interpret, summarize, and find patterns in data, and to learn from the data and make inferences from it. We mention some of the algorithms that have been instrumental in programming Web 2.0 features that collect, interact with, and act on user-generated data.

CF (discussed in Section 9.4) is used by many online retails such as Amazon.com to recommend products and media. Clustering and classification are used for grouping and categorizing data items and users. In clustering (for example, hierarchical, discussed in Section 7.2.4, or k-means, discussed in Section 6.3.3), the grouping is carried out through a similarity matrix. For example, e-commerce customers can be clustered by similar buying habits and demographic patterns, and web pages can be clustered according to similar content. Once the similarity matrix is established, the clustering algorithm is automatic and the clusters may be visualized to aid the interpretation of the results. In classification (for example, naive Bayes, discussed in Section 3.2.2, or other methods used in web page classification such as using decision trees to detect link spam, discussed in

[221]Amazon.com Pushes Benefits Of Crowdsourcing, by N. Kolakowski, November 2009. www.eweekeurope.co.uk/news/amazon-com-pushes-benefits-of-crowdsourcing-2422.

Section 5.2.13), the objects are divided into predefined classes. For example, web pages are often classified into topics such as art, entertainment, news, science, shopping, technology, and sports. Classification is normally carried out in two steps, training and testing. During the training phase, examples of objects and their correct classes are presented to the learning algorithm, which uses this information to construct a classifier. During the testing phase, the classifier applies its learnt knowledge to add class labels to other objects without seeing their labels. A successful classifier will not only maximize the number of objects to which it attaches a correct label (known as *true positives*) but it will also minimize the number of objects to which it attaches an incorrect label (known as *false positives*).

A widely used open source Java toolkit for data mining toolkit is Weka (www.cs.waikato.ac.nz/ml/weka). Weka contains machine learning algorithms and preprocessing tools. Weka also contains a graphical user interface, which allows users to explore data sets, apply algorithms to them, and visualize the results.

The phenomenon of social tagging (see Section 9.8) and the taxonomies arising from user-defined tags (known as *folksonomies*) are a by-product of Web 2.0 user-generated content. To leverage this information, tags can be used for making recommendations, for personalization of the content, and for enhancing search through a social search mechanism. In this context, tag clouds stand out as having been specifically developed to assist users to dynamically navigate within a folksonomy.

Finally, we mention that the massive amount of user-generated data has also provided the impetus for developing algorithms for opinion mining and sentiment analysis (see Section 9.9). In general, many of the search and navigation technologies presented in the previous sections are relevant to making Web 2.0 work in practice.

The last two subsections review two of the most popular and influential Web 2.0 web sites, Wikipedia (www.wikipedia.org) and eBay (www.ebay.com).

9.10.7 Wikipedia — The World's Largest Encyclopedia

Wikipedia (www.wikipedia.org) was founded in 2001 by Jimmy Wales and Larry Sanger, and, as of early 2010, had over 14 million articles in 272 languages; the English version has about 3.15 million articles and its closest rival in German has about 1 million articles followed by just under 900,000 French articles. (You can, of course, get full details of the history of Wikipedia and the current statistics from the Wikipedia:Statistics entry.) Wikipedia content is licensed under the GNU Free documentation licence (see www.gnu.org/licences), which is a free licence in the spirit of open source software; the software that drives Wikipedia is also open source.

A Pew Internet report, based on a daily tracking survey of a sample of 2220 American adult internet users between February and March 2007, found that 36% of these adults consult Wikipedia [553]. They also found that young adults and broadband users have been earlier adopters of Wikipedia.

A Becta[222] report, based on a 2008 study of approximately 2600 11–16-year-old students in the United Kingdom, investigated the use of Web 2.0 tools for learning in formal education [442]. While many students were familiar with a range of Web 2.0 technologies, few were engaged in sophisticated activities such as producing and publishing content for wider consumption. One of the questions asked was for the students to suggest, in order of preference, up to three web sites they used to find information to assist them in schoolwork and homework. Out of 1556 respondents, about 57% prefers to use Wikipedia. This is interesting, since less than 20% prefers to use search engines for this task.

In order to cater for secondary schools, there is even a hand-checked selection of about 5500 Wikipedia articles that can all fit on a DVD, targeted at the UK National Curriculum (see http://schools-wikipedia.org). Open resources such as this one, which are distributed worldwide, are valuable and increasingly used in schools.

Although there is some controversy regarding the reliability of Wikipedia, it is far more popular among well educated than among those with lower levels of education. It turns out that the use of Wikipedia is more popular than other web activities such as online shopping. There are several possible reasons why Wikipedia is so popular. First, it is the sheer volume of information in Wikipedia and its wide coverage of topics, including current events and popular culture. Second, the use of search engines has grown, and because Wikipedia articles often appear on the first results page of search engines, they are more likely to be viewed than other pages appearing further down the search engine ranking. Another factor is the convenience of finding knowledge-based information such as science information in Wikipedia. In many cases, it gives a quick and mostly accurate description, say of a mathematical formula, that can be verified with other sources if necessary.

The growth rate of Wikipedia (as of the Web itself) was initially exponential, and this was indeed the case until mid-2006, with the content approximately doubling yearly between 2002 and 2006. A more realistic growth model is the logistic S-curve model [478], where after initial exponential growth, the growth slows down until it eventually reaches a steady state of no or very little additional growth. A plot of the number of articles on the English Wikipedia and logistic extrapolations to a maximum of 3, 3.5, and 4 million articles are shown in Fig. 9.25. As the growth rate, in 2009, was still strong at about 1500 articles a day, the logistic growth is probably slowing more gradually than the predictions in Fig. 9.25, and could be expected to continue until the size of Wikipedia reaches about 10 million articles at or just beyond 2025.

We now briefly describe how Wikipedia works [42] (see http://howwikipediaworks.com). Wikipedia is organized according to a set of categories that describe the topic an article belongs to. As with every bit of Wikipedia content, the details are fully described within Wikipedia and there are guidelines for assigning a page to a category or subcategory. An article is a page containing

[222]Becta (www.becta.org.uk) is a UK government agency leading the national drive to ensure the effective and innovative use of technology throughout learning.

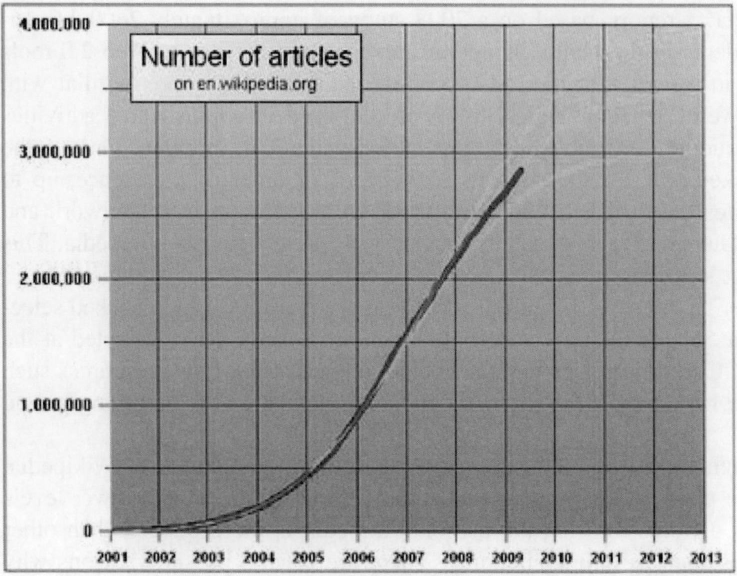

Figure 9.25 The growth of English Wikipedia based on a logistic growth model.[223]

encyclopedic information. There are also nonarticle pages, the most important being talk pages, one for each article, for discussing the content of articles and suggested changes. In addition, there are user pages for editors to describe themselves. Other types of pages are policy and guidelines, community discussion, and help pages.

Wikipedia includes various types of content in its article pages. The most common include the following:

1. traditional encyclopedic content;
2. notable people, that is, people who are known within their major field of endeavor, including fictional characters (about 20% of articles were listed as biographies by the end of 2007);
3. places, including countries, cities, major geographical features, cities, and towns;
4. media, that is, movies, television shows, books, music albums, and video games, to name a few;
5. companies and organizations—these are factual articles about the most known corporations;
6. computer software and hardware;
7. current events, for example, the 9/11 attack in 2001 or the US presidential elections in 2008.

[223]Source: Number of articles on en.wikipedia.org and extrapolations. http://commons.wikimedia.org/wiki/File:Enwikipedialin.PNG.

Anyone is allowed to add content to Wikipedia; that is, you do not need to have a Wikipedia account to edit a page. On the other hand, to create a new article the user must be registered but can still remain anonymous by registering under a pseudonym; a registered user is a Wikipedia editor. Higher up the Wikipedia hierarchy are *administrators* (known as admins or sysops), who have entrusted access to restricted technical features that help with the maintenance of the system. For example, admins can protect (prevent or restrict a page from being edited), delete (remove a page), or block (disallow a user to edit a page) a page, and also undo these actions. A smaller group are the *bureaucrats* that have the authority to turn other users into administrators but cannot revoke their status. Bureaucrats can also grant and revoke an account's *bot* status, where a bot is an automated or semiautomated tool that carries some repetitive or mundane task in maintaining Wikipedia's pages. While there are only about 30 bureaucrats, there are about 1000 administrators. Users are granted bureaucrat status by community consensus. At the top of the hierarchy are the *stewards*, who are users with complete rights to change all users' rights and groups. They are elected roughly on an annual basis by the global Wikimedia community and appointed from the elected candidates by the board of trustees of the Wikimedia Foundation; there are about 40 stewards. The Wikimedia Foundation is a nonprofit organization that oversees the Wikimedia projects, including Wikipedia.

Not all types of content is allowed in Wikipedia. There are some basic principles determining what content is allowed, governed by fair-use, and monitored by the community of editors. Three policies are central to the way Wikipedia work. They are as follows:

1. Verifiability from reliable outside sources that are cited in the article.
2. No original research, that is, the content should have been published elsewhere prior to inclusion of the article.
3. Neutral point of view, that is, objectivity of the content. This means that all points of view should be taken into account in the article.

Anyone can contribute to most pages, still a few pages are restricted such as key pages, for example, Wikipedia's main pages. When a new page is submitted it goes live without any intermediate authorization. Other contributors review new articles, and an article that does not conform to the policies is deleted. Alternatively, an article may be edited to make it conform to the policies. Only Wikipedia administrators can delete articles. Before an article is deleted it is proposed by anyone for deletion and discussed in the light of Wikipedia policies. The following are the common reasons for deletion:

- spam like posting such as an advertisement;
- too specialist and judged as not notable;
- bad writing should not be a reason for deletion rather than cleanup, but well-written articles are less likely to be deleted.

Vandalism is the act of editing Wikipedia content with the intent of compromising it. Vandelism is not tolerated, and pages that are vandalized may be protected at any give time if the vandalism cannot easily be removed. A fundamental concept in Wikipedia is to assume "good faith," that is, that people contributing to the project are trying to help it and not to harm it. Thus, a good faith effort, even if misguided or not given careful consideration, is not vandalism and is dealt with in the normal Wikipedia way.

When two or more editors try to impose their view on an article by changing the content back and forth we have an *edit war*. This is the most common type of dispute in Wikipedia. There is no formal process for resolving disagreement. Arriving at a consensus through regular discussion is the preferred solution. If this is not possible, an administrator can intervene and halt the war by protecting the disputed pages for a given time from reedits by the editors involved in the dispute. If this does not work when the protection is lifted, there is a mediation process to try and reach a practical compromise. If also this does not work, there is a final and binding arbitration process carried out by a formal elected body of editors. The arbitration process may result in editors being banned from the site for a specified period or even indefinitely due to destructive of disruptive behavior.

There are some common objections to the Wikipedia model.

- Wikipedia is an ongoing project and a majority of articles, although useful, are incomplete.
- Misinformation is a real possibility in Wikipedia. More common than deliberate misinformation are missing key aspects of the topic or mistakes made unmaliciously.
- Academic respectability; Wikipedia has a mixed reputation with educators. It is not only the questionable accuracy of content but also encouraging students to do their own research.
- Lack of respect to expert and authoritative opinions. An expert has the same privileges as any other editor. Expertise is manifested through the editing and discussion process. This is in opposition to the encyclopedic tradition.
- Openness to amateur editors. Not all Wikipedia editors are amateur, and in fact many of them are academic. Yet the world's largest encyclopedia could not have been created without widespread participation.

A survey carried out by Nature comparing Wikipedia to Encyclopedia Britannica (www.britannica.com), the oldest English language encyclopedia still in print since 1768, caused quite a stir [253]. It seems that both encyclopedias contain about the same number of errors per article (at least in the science category which was the one tested). Obviously, Wikipedia would benefit if experts had written the articles, and surely some of the articles are indeed written by experts in the field, still Wikipedia's mechanisms have proven to work well in practice.

9.10.8 eBay – The World's Largest Online Trading Community

Originally founded as AuctionWeb in 1995 by Pierre Omidyar, in the early days of the Web, it has become almost synonymous with online auctions and is one of the most popular sites on the Web. The volumes it handles are enormous, with 83.6 billion active users worldwide, trading $60 billion per year, 120 million items for sale in 50,000 categories and over 2 billion pageviews per day, as of 2009.[224]

In distinction from other e-commerce sites, the business model of eBay is unique as it could not have existed without the Internet. It is more of a marketplace where people can both buy and sell rather than just a selling platform. The growth of eBay has been steady but not as fast as that of its e-commerce rival, Amazon.com. The reason for this is that eBay's focus is on profitability and acting as an efficient intermediary between sellers and buyers, while Amazon had focused on rapid growth and expansion at the expense of profits. The growth of eBay has been steady since its inception, but, by 2005 eBay's, growth was slowing down as it became increasingly harder to find bargains on eBay due to the growth of fixed price e-commerce retailers such as Amazon offering low prices and free shipping, and buyers increasingly making use of comparison shopping sites. As of 2009, eBay has been increasing its fixed price listings by cutting its fees for fixed price items but keeping the fees of auctioned items at a higher price.

The acquisition of the online payment e-commerce site PayPal (www.paypal.com), in 2002, made strategic sense as it was the payment method of choice for eBay customers and it was competing with its alternative payment methods at the time. Its acquisition, in 2005, of the internet telephony service Skype (www.skype.com) is less clear, but it is evident that it has increased eBay's user base and competitive edge. Skype has had an impressive growth curve, and as of 2009, it had over 40 million active users per day, and over 440 million registered users.

We will now briefly explain the mechanics of buying items on eBay.[225] On eBay, items can be sold either by auction or at a fixed price. We will concentrate on auctioned items, as selling items at a fixed price is similar to Amazon's Marketplace, where Amazon (or in this case eBay) act as a third party for a seller. When an item is auctioned it has a fixed duration attached to it, by which time the item is either sold or may be relisted by the seller with a new duration attached to it. Auctions such as on eBay that end at a specific time are called *hard close* auctions. In contrast, in a *soft close* auction such as on uBid (www.ubid.com), if there are any bids within a certain time before the official end of the auction (10 mins on uBid), then the auction is extended until there are no bids for a

[224]Best Practices for scaling websites, lessons from eBay. Presentation by Randy Shoup, eBay Distinguished Architect, QCon, Enterprise Software Development Conference, Beijing, April 2009.

[225]Detailed tutorials on how eBay works can be found at the eBay university learning center; see http://pages.ebay.com/education.

continuous period (10 mins on uBid). This gives bidders ample opportunity to respond to higher bids when bids are made in the last minute.

An item on auction has a *starting price* of at least $0.99 specified by the seller, and the bidding starts from that price. A buyer can then place a bid for the item, or, when there is a *Buy it Now* option, can purchase it instantly at a set price without bidding. In addition to placing a bid, a buyer may specify a maximum amount he or she is willing to pay, and if there is a higher bid than the one he or she placed, then eBay will automatically increase the bid by a specified increment above the current highest bid, as long as this amount is not more than the maximum amount the buyer is willing to pay; this automated feature is called *proxy bidding*. For example, assume Bob's bid of $25 is the highest, and he is then outbid by Iris who bids $26. Then, if Bob's maximum is say $30, eBay will automatically post a new bid for Bob to the value of $27. If Iris then outbids Bob by placing a bid of $30, then the system will post a bid of $30 for Bob, but although his bid matches that of Iris, she put her bid in first and is therefore the current highest bidder. In this case, when someone else places a bid that is the same or higher than Bob's maximum bid, the system will notify Bob and he can then decide whether to increase his maximum bid. At any stage of an auction the only public knowledge is the second highest bid, and at the end of the auction the winner pays the second highest price plus a specified minimum bid increment.

As a general rule, bids cannot be retracted or cancelled. Once you place a bid you agree to pay for the item if you are the winner of the auction. However, there are special cases when a bid can be retracted such as entering the wrong bid amount by mistake due to a typing error, not being able to reach the seller by phone or by e-mail, or when the seller has changed the description of the item during an auction.

On the other hand, a seller has the right to end the auction before it is finished and cancel the bids on the item, when, for example, the item is no longer available as described or there was some error in the listing. When a listing is removed, the seller has the alternative option to sell the item to the current highest bidder if there is one. Although the item has been removed, the seller is still obliged to pay eBay the listing fees. It is not permitted on eBay to end an auction in order to avoid selling an item that did not meet a desired sale price, and abuse of this option may be investigated by eBay. A seller can also block specified buyers from their listings, and cancel current bids in cases such as when a bidder contacts the seller to retract a bid or when the seller is not able to contact the bidder. In general, eBay does not encourage the seller to cancel bids during an auction.

Another factor which needs to be taken into account is whether the item has a *reserve price*, which is the minimum price the seller is willing to accept for the item. (The reserve price is hidden from the bidders but they will know that there is a reserve price and whether it has already been met; when a seller receives an inquiry from a buyer he or she may reveal the reserve price to him or her.)

We note that eBay is a variation on a second-price auction, where the winner pays the second highest price bid (as in the influential Vickrey auction), as opposed to a first-price auction, where the winner pays the highest price bid (as in the traditional English auction) [630].

There are several determinants of the final price of an item in an online auction [443]. On eBay, after a transaction is completed both buyers and sellers can leave feedback about each other. Positive feedback increases a member's feedback profile by one, negative feedback decreases it by one, while neutral feedback does not effect the feedback profile; members can also leave a short comment with their feedback. Positive feedback ratings for a seller from other buyers has a positive effect on the price an item is sold for, but negative feedback has an even larger influence on the price, this time in decreasing the price. It turns out that the longer auctions tend to fetch higher prices and the same is true for weekend auctions in comparison to auctions that take place on weekdays. Another determinant of the price is the presence of a reserve price, which tends to increase the final price, as long as the reserve price is not too high [309]. This result may seem puzzling as a reserve price may be a deterrent for some bidders to enter the auction. However, the reserve price may be acting as a competing bidder, at least until the reserve price has been met. It was also found that charging a high shipping cost while having a low reserve price leads to a higher number of participating bidders and higher revenues when the shipping charge is not excessive [309].

Another interesting phenomenon observed in online auction is herding, when bidders are more likely to join an auction with more existing bids [610]. Moreover, when the starting price is low, an auction is more likely to receive additional bids. However, this herding behavior is nonrational, as, when there is a winning bid in a low-bid starting auction, it is likely to be higher than that in similar auctions with high starting bids. Despite this, on an average, the seller's expected revenue is the same for both high and low starting bids, since in low starting price auctions there is an additional risk of selling the item at a loss. Finally, the researchers found that experienced bidders are less likely to bid on low-price starting auctions, which is the rational action.

As a result of an eBay auction having a fixed duration, *sniping*, that is last minute bidding just before the auction ends, is possible [578]. The intuition behind sniping is that it softens the competition by not allowing time for counter bids which may raise the final price. In this way, the sniper hopes to purchase the item at a lower final price (which is the second highest price), by taking advantage of the proxy biding mechanism where the initial price may be low and is increased in incremental steps. For this reason, sellers generally object to sniping. A second motivation for sniping is that it avoids *price wars*, where competing bidders incrementally increase their bids in response to each others bid.

In addition, a bidder may have some private information about the value of the item that he or she does not wish to disclose by early bidding; for example, this may be knowledge about the true worth of an antique on sale. By sniping, the bidder may profit from this information without allowing other bidders to respond in time. This may account for the empirical finding that experts are more likely to snipe (682, 677), and suggests that sniping may be more prevalent in high price auctions. We emphasize that sniping is only a viable strategy because the auction finishes at a fixed time. The risk of sniping is that the bid is too late and does not go through due to network traffic, and of course the snipe bid may be too low to win.

Sniping does not break eBay's auction rules. According to the eBay help pages, "Sniping is part of the eBay experience, and all bids placed before a listing ends are valid, even if they're placed one second before the listing ends.". Sniping can be done manually or with the aid of sniping software, either installed on the user machine or delivered as a service over the Web that will do the bidding on your behalf.

Fraud is an ongoing problem on internet auctions and is also a major concern for law enforcement agencies [246]. According to the Internet Crime Complaint Centre (www.ic3.gov), auction fraud accounted for approximately 25.5% of consumer complaints in 2008, and the total loss from all referred cases of internet crime was $264.6 million, which is up from $239.1 million in reported losses from 2007. The most common reported offences were nondelivered merchandize, delivered but inferior or damaged merchandize and nonpayment for merchandize purchased, comprising 32.9% of all internet crime referred complaints. To combat fraud, it is necessary for individuals to take preventive measures and to be aware of the pitfalls and the best practices they should use in order to protect oneself against the types of fraud that may occur; see eBay security center (http://pages.ebay.com/securitycenter) for detailed information on the subject.

A common form of auction fraud is shill bidding. This occurs when fake bids are introduced by the seller or someone acting on his or her behalf in order to artificially increase the final price of an item. The account from which the shill biding is carried out is called a *shill account*. Shill bidding is fraudulent and prohibited on eBay. Under their shilling policy, eBay also prohibits any bids by individuals such as family members or employees who may have some knowledge about the item's worth which is not common knowledge.

Shill bidding if often used to uncover the value of the highest bid and make use of this information to increase the price of the item by making a bid which matches this bid. One such strategy is the discover-and-stop bidding method [206], where the shill bidder incrementally pushes up the price until the highest bid is discovered and then stops. This strategy is effective if the highest bid is not at an incremental price of a proxy bid. For example, if the highest bid is $10, the second highest bid is $5.50 and the increment is $1, then once the price reaches $10 the shill bidder knows the highest bid has been reached, otherwise it would have changed to $10.50. Another effective strategy involves canceling a high shill bid once it becomes the highest bid, so that the second highest bid will then become the highest. It is evident that these strategies are not effective against sniping, and thus last minute bids are a rational response to this type of shill bidding, which is only successful if there are any early bids [56]. Of course, shill bidding will still drive the price up, and in case the shill, that is, the seller, wins, the item can be resold in a subsequent auction. The seller still incurs eBay's listing fee and the time spent bidding, so shilling does not always pay even if the bidder is not caught. Shilling can also be carried out by a software agent, who acts on the shill's behalf [646]. The agent follows a set of directives that maximize the chance of increasing the highest bid price, while avoiding winning the auction. Useful directive are (i) bid the minimum amount that is required to reveal the highest bid; (ii) bid quickly after a rival bid to maximize the time left for other bidders to raise their bid; (iii) do not bid too close to the end of the auction as it risks winning; (iv) bid only until a target price has been attained, for example, when the seller's reserve price has been reached; and (iv) bid only when there are a sufficient number of buyers bidding for the item relative to the end time of the auction. These directives can also help in the development of techniques to detect shilling.

Auction fraud breaks the element of trust which is central in a system such as eBay, based on online transactions. The reputation system of eBay, based on the feedback profile, helps to address the trust problem by providing information to potential buyers about the quality of sellers, at least as perceived by the feedback they have obtained [563]. Fraudsters often collude to boost their reputations by manipulating the feedback system, which motivates the development of fraud detection methods beyond reputation systems. One way in which the feedback system has been gamed is by sellers offering items that cost almost nothing, say a penny, offering in return to give positive feedback and hoping also to get positive feedback for themselves [111]; note that penny transactions incur a loss to the seller as they still have to pay eBay's listing fee. This scheme can work as feedback is agnostic to the amount of a sale, and the details of transactions for which feedback was made is only available for 90 days after the sale. Although such practices are prohibited by eBay, they do not necessarily deter fraudsters. Once their rating is established they are in a position of trust and can sell expensive items and defraud sellers.

The textual feedback in the form of comments that eBay buyers leave about their transactions provides important information about the types of complaints about sellers [269]. These indicate that the main types of fraud are nondelivery of items and misrepresentation of items, that is, when the seller deceives buyers about the true value of the item. A fraud detection algorithm that makes use of the feedback profiles and other information about possible fraudulent behavior could thus enhance the accuracy of a reputation system. Such an algorithm could typically make use of the social network of sellers and buyers, where there is an edge between two nodes whenever a transaction was made between the two users, represented by the nodes, and the strength of the tie between the two nodes is captured by the number of transactions between them. Nodes can have three states fraud, accomplice or honest, where both fraud and accomplice nodes are suspected of fraud but the difference between them is that accomplices behaved legally gaining reputation from honest nodes to boost the reputation of fraud nodes. The algorithm suggested by Zhang *et al.* [702] is based on Bayesian belief propagation. Initially, some nodes may be identified as belonging to one of the three states, and then, a Bayesian approximation algorithm incrementally determines the probability of nodes being of one of the types, using message passing along the edges making use of the sum and product rules of probability [394]. The output of the algorithm gives a belief of each node, which is the probability that the node is in each state [702].

In a single day, the number of bids buyers place in a single category and the number of auctions that a buyer bids on, both follow a power-law distribution [686]. This implies that while most buyers place a few bids there are several buyers placing a large number of bids on possibly different items, and while most buyers participate in a few auctions there are several buyers who participate in many auctions. It seems that the auctions are dominated by a small number of highly active *power buyers* who are responsible for the fat tail in the power-law distribution. It turns out that power buyers win auctions more frequently and are also more likely to pay less for the items they won. There are also *power sellers* as the total number of items offered by a given seller also follows a power-law distribution [494]. On the other hand, the total number of bidders participating in a single auction and the total number of bids in an auction follow an exponential distribution (686, 494). This indicates that the vast majority of auction have only a few bidders and a only small number of bids.

Using an evolutionary model for buyers in auctions with preferential bidding, where a buyer making frequent bids up to a certain time is more likely to make another bid in the next time interval, it has been shown that the number of bidders who make k bids up to time t follows a power-law distribution and that sniping, that is, making the first bid in the last minute, is a winning strategy for this model [687].

Benford's law, known as the *first-digit law* [221], is an interesting phenomenon that occurs in nature. If we observe the first digit of a collection of numbers—tally the numbers in which each digit from 1 to 9 is first, and find that the distribution of these tallies is logarithmic rather than uniform—then we have discovered an instance of Benford's law. (The distribution is logarithmic if the probability of the leading digit d is $\log((d+1)/d)$, where logarithms are in the base 10, and the distribution is uniform when the probability of the first digit d is 1/9.) Some examples of Benford's law are population sizes, areas of countries, the closing prices of a range of stocks and numbers reported in tax returns. Well, the closing prices of certain eBay auctions also closely follow Benford's law [252]. This may be useful in detecting fraudulent behavior in certain auctions by testing its departure from Benford's law, in a similar way that it has been useful in detecting tax evaders [505].

CHAPTER SUMMARY

- A social network links people together rather than documents, as does the Web. Despite this, the Web can also be viewed as a social network, since through its links it provides an electronic communication medium between people who can transform real social networks into virtual ones, and it enables people and organizations to make connections by linking to each other.

- Milgram's small-world experiment resulted in the famous hypothesis that any two individuals are separated by "six degrees of freedom." A modern day equivalent to Milgram's experiments using e-mail to pass on messages, confirmed Milgram's hypothesis for completed chains, attributing the low completion rate to random failure.
- Examples of social networks are collaboration graphs, IM, and e-mail networks, and a web site's social web, where the links are between people's home pages.
- During 2003, there was a surge in social network start-ups. The number of social network users has grown exponentially since then, and by late 2009 there were over a billion users worldwide. Some target young adults who can meet people who are friends of their friends up to four degrees away, while others aim to connect professionals and businesses. Yet another type of social network evaluates the relationships between the people inside a company and between its customers and contacts.
- Social network analysis is an established field that is concerned with metrics that measure the relationships between actors in a network. The basic metrics and terminology have been introduced. The fundamental concepts of relation, tie (strong and weak), triangle, geodesic, degree distribution, and clustering coefficient, have been defined. Three measures of actor centrality, degree centrality, closeness centrality and betweenness centrality, have been introduced.
- Web communities are collections of web pages that are focused on a particular topic or theme. Several methods have been proposed that employ link analysis to efficiently identify web communities, based on the structure of the web graph.
- P2P networks can be viewed as social networks between cooperating computers over the Internet. In a P2P network, the distinction between clients and servers breaks down; the computers in the network can act as both a client and a server depending on the circumstance. P2P networks have been mainly utilized for file sharing activities. The architecture of a P2P network can be centralized (for example, Napster), decentralized (for example, Gnutella), or hybrid (for example, Kazaa). To avoid free riding, incentives, such as reputation, currency, and barter, need to be provided in P2P systems.
- Notable P2P methods are DHTs that provide a method for locating content in a P2P system; BitTorrent, which is a protocol for distributing large amounts of data by sharing the load among several computers by having them upload pieces of the data to each other; and JXTA search, which is a set of open source protocols for P2P communication between devices connected to a network.
- CF has been deployed on a very large scale by Amazon.com. It is based on the idea that if two people are similar in some respect, for example, they have a similar taste in books, then they can recommend to each other

books they have read and enjoyed. The process of recommendation may be automated by asking users to explicitly rate items or instead using implicit indicators, such as the purchase of an item.

- There have been several approaches to implementing CF. In the user-based approach, like-minded users are determined by their similarity in ratings on overlapping items. Once these are established, recommendations are made for items that the active user has not rated, based on the ratings of like-minded users. In the item-based approach, the system matches similar items that have been co-rated, rather than matching similar users, and in the model-based approach the probability that a user will like an item is evaluated, for instance using a naive Bayes classifier. Content-based recommendation systems base their predictions on a profile of the user's interests.
- Content-based and CF systems can be combined, by using content-based filtering to fill in pseudoratings for items rated by one user but not the other.
- The the MAE and RMSE are the most common metrics used to evaluate collaborative filtering systems.
- The issue of scalability of a recommendation system such as that used by Amamzon.com is crucial, and can be achieved by preprocessing, offline, the similarity between co-rated items.
- The Netflix prize stimulated a lot of innovative research in CF between 2007 and 2009, and has made the results accessible to other researchers. One lesson from the competition was that the most successful entries resulted from combining several prediction models into a single model. Improvements to the nearest-neighbor approach and latent factor models also proved to be major components of the winning submissions.
- A weblog (or blog) is a frequently updated web site composed of entries appearing in reverse chronological order. Blogs have become a popular form of online personal journalism. Creating links from one blog to other blogs and sites is known as *blogrolling*, and these links have the power to influence the ranking, on search engines, of the linked sites. The space of weblogs, known as *blogspace*, is being studied in order to monitor its evolution and the ideas that are currently being debated and are popular on the Web.
- The real-time web refers to the snapshot of the Web as it is evolving. One source of real-time web data comes from microblogging. This is a form of blogging where each entry is a short snippet of text, a single photo or a short video.
- Power-law distributions, also known as *scale-free distributions*, are abundant in nature and have also been observed on the Web. For example, the number of inlinks to web pages, the size of web sites, the number of visitors to web sites on any given day, the number of links surfers follow (known as the *law of surfing*), and the number of contributions a person makes in

peer production systems (known as the *law of voting*), all follow a power-law distribution. There are several techniques, such as linear regression on a log–log plot of the data, used to detect power laws, but the best way to fit a power law is still an ongoing research problem.

- What are the mechanisms by which the Web may have evolved into a scale-free network?

  One explanation is that there are two mechanisms: growth (the Web is expanding) and preferential attachment (pages receive new inlinks in proportion to the number of inlinks they already have), which together cause the network to be scale-free. An alternative explanation is that the Web is evolving as a multiplicative process. Looking at the evolution of the size of web sites, multiplicative growth implies that the size of a site fluctuates on a day-to-day basis in proportion to its current size. This mechanism combined with a mechanism that ensures that there are many more young sites than older ones, or with one in which some sites grow faster than others, leads to a power-law distribution. A third explanation is based on the idea that power-law distributions can result for an optimized design objective in the presence of uncertainty and some specified constraints.
- A small-world network is one in which the average distance among nodes is typically logarithmic in the number of nodes in the network, and whose clustering coefficient is much larger than that of a random graph of the same density. Many real-world networks including web sites, P2P networks, collaboration networks, and the network of world airports have been shown to be small-world networks.
- Scale-free networks have been shown to be robust against random attack; yet, vulnerable to an attack targeted against its well-connected nodes. This has implications regarding the spread and immunization strategies of viruses in scale-free networks.
- Social navigation is a form of navigation, where surfers use information from others that have passed through the space, to help them find their way. Social search engines support social navigation by sharing information between users, who have submitted similar queries.
- Several local strategies have been proposed for navigation in social and P2P networks. Breadth-first-search is a simple strategy that visits the neighbors' node before traversing any other nodes. This strategy can be improved by choosing at each step to move to the highest degree node that has not already been visited. A further improvement that takes into account the scale-free characteristics of the network distributes the search among several nodes, which are visited along a short random walk of the network.
- Although in small-world networks the average distance between any two nodes is short, this does not imply that a short path can be efficiently found using a local search strategy. In fact, in two-dimensional lattices with long-range links, short paths can be found by a decentralized algorithm only in the case when the probability of a long-range link from any node is proportional to the inverse of the squared distance from the node. The algorithm

used is a greedy one, which moves, at each step, to the neighboring node closest to the target. The greedy algorithm can be improved upon by having knowledge of nodes that are two steps away from the current node. This extra knowledge is utilized by choosing the neighbor of a neighbor who is closest to the target.

- In practice, when choosing which neighbor to pass on the message to, apart from geographic distance, people take into account additional social criteria such as similarity in occupation. This observation can be used to devise a model, which is more general than the lattice one, in which search can be carried out efficiently by choosing to move to the closest neighbor across all known social criteria.
- Social tagging and bookmarking, which involve tagging content with keywords, act as memory aids for individuals and as a social activity when the tags are shared. Notable social tagging sites are Flickr for sharing photos, YouTube for broadcasting yourself, and Delicious for social bookmarking of web pages.
- A folksonomy is a collection of tags used to organize the content in a social tagging system. It implies a taxonomy based on the way folks, that is, people, organize the content. There is an ongoing debate on the merits of a folksonomy compared to a taxonomy based on a fixed set of categories such as in the Yahoo Directory and the Open Directory.
- A tag cloud is a popular method of visualizing textual data by highlighting words within the text signifying their importance. There is some debate on whether a tag cloud is the best way of showing word frequency information, say compared to a bar chart.
- Tags can be useful to augment social search and browsing, as well as in tag recommendation. The set of tags is becoming more diverse over time and it is harder to direct users to resources matching these tags. Moreover, it is becoming harder for users to provide meaningful and discriminating tags for resources. As the volume of content grows, more tags are needed to describe the available resources. Thus the folksonomy arising from tags seems to be less efficient over time. Clustering and classifying tags can be more useful methods for grouping content than grouping the content based on individual tags.
- Opinion mining and sentiment analysis is the activity of mining for opinions in user-generated textual content as opposed to dealing with just facts as traditional search engines do. Three important opinion mining tasks are feature-based mining and summarization, sentiment classification, treating the problem as a classification problem, and comparative sentence and relation extraction.
- Web 2.0 can be viewed as a collection of technologies that has driven the Web forward since the dot-com bust. On a deeper level, Web 2.0 is about giving users the ability to create, share, link, tag, and modify web content. Influential technologies in this respect have been Ajax, RSS syndication, open APIs, mashups, and widgets.

- SaaS is a model for remote hosting of software, and delivery of this software to customers, on demand, through the Internet. SaaS alleviates the need to install and maintain the full range of applications on customers' computers and the need to have a separate licence for each software package. It allows access to the software online, on demand, anytime and anywhere.
- Collective intelligence is central to the Web 2.0 paradigm, referring to the emergence of new ideas as a result of a group effect. Collective intelligence is related to the concept of the "wisdom of the crowds," where a group of people can be smarter than the best expert in the group. There is also an algorithmic component to collective intelligence that enables programs to take advantage of the massive amount of data collected from users. The algorithms generally come from the fields of data mining and machine learning, allowing programs to group, interpret, summarize, find patterns and make inference from data.
- Case studies of Wikipedia, the world's largest encyclopedia, which is a massive collaborative effort, and eBay, the world's largest online trading community, which is a marketplace where people can both buy and sell goods through an online auction mechanism, have been presented.

EXERCISES

9.1. (Explore). Voice over Internet Protocol (VoIP) is a technology that enables users to hold phone conversations over the Internet. Using a hybrid P2P approach, Skype (www.skype.com) have developed software that enables users with broadband connections to use internet telephony [89].

What problems do you think the P2P software has to overcome for such a system to be workable?

9.2. (Explore). In P2P networks, the efficiency, reliability, and robustness of the topology are essential. In decentralized P2P networks, the topologies are *ad hoc*, and depend on the peers who are online at the time of connection.

An idea to improve on current P2P protocols is to make them adaptive, based on the following two notions [162]. The first is that a peer should connect only to peers from which he/she is likely to download satisfactory files. The second is that to estimate the likelihood of a successful download, a peer may use his or her past interaction history with other peers.

Suggest an efficient decentralized P2P protocol taking these two notions into account, and explain why it will be more robust to malicious attacks on the network.

9.3. (Discuss). TiVo (www.tivo.com) is a CF recommendation system for television [25]. A TiVo client is a combination of hardware and software. The hardware contains a hard-disk on which TV shows can be recorded, enabling customers to view shows at their convenience and in their preferred order.

TiVo's CF system is item based, and to overcome the first-rater problem it uses a Bayesian content-based classifier. TiVo has two types of rating: explicit and implicit. An explicit rating involves a thumbs up or down in the range of -3 (dislikes) to $+3$ (likes), and an implicit rating when the user records a previously unrated show.

TiVo's CF system works as follows: (i) The client uploads its entire thumbs ratings of shows every so many days, which replaces all previous ratings for this client. (ii)

Periodically, the server computes a fresh set of correlated pairs of shows from all its users ratings. (iii) Every so many days, the client downloads the fresh set of correlated pairs from the server. (iv) The CF algorithm that makes predictions is run on the client.

Describe the differences between TiVo's CF system and a standard item-based CF system, explaining why you think TiVo decided to implement their system in this way.

9.4. (Miniproject). Implement an algorithm to compute the degree distribution of a network from its specification as a collection of nodes and links.

Analyze the degree distribution, the average distance between nodes, the diameter, and the clustering coefficient of a small web site of your choice.

How do you think the fact that you are analyzing a small network effects the measurements?

9.5. (Miniproject). Analyze the degree distribution, average distance between nodes, the diameter, and clustering coefficient of a known transportation network such as the London underground or the Boston subway.

Discuss how real-world networks differ from virtual ones.

9.6. (Explore). Social search engines emphasize in their ranking algorithm the popularity of queries, as measured by the clickthroughs of its user base.

Conduct an evaluation of a social search engine you have discovered, by choosing several queries and recording how their results change over a period of a week.

Compare your findings with results for the same queries submitted to a conventional web search engine at the same time.

9.7. (Discuss). Comparison shopping [667] has become a very useful service for consumers. Often when comparing products, users read reviews of the product to help them make a decision.

Discuss how opinion mining can assist users of comparison shopping services to browse through product reviews.

How do you think search engines can make use of opinion mining to enhance searches for product reviews [314]?

9.8. (Explore). Explore how crowdsourcing may be applied in the context of software development, software testing, and project management.

Can you find any start-ups that are making use of crowdsourcing in these areas?

CHAPTER 10

THE FUTURE OF WEB SEARCH AND NAVIGATION

"With great powers come great responsibility."

— Spider-Man's uncle

WE HAVE provided an extensive introduction to web search and navigation technologies, including coverage of these technologies in the context of the mobile web and the impact that social networks are having on the way in which we interact with the Web.

Many of the tools that we use today for interacting with the Web have only been deployed on such a massive scale since the mid-1990s, when the Web took off, and we can therefore expect many additional improvements as time goes by.

Although, currently, search engine technology is in a much more stable state than it was during the late 1990s, it cannot be considered a mature technology in the same sense as, say, relational database technology is. The same can be said for the navigation tools that are currently on offer. Much of the progress will be evolutionary, with many of the tools presented in the book being further developed and improved.

It is hard to predict where the revolution that mobile computing has already started will take us. With the ubiquity of mobile devices, a variety of opportunities present themselves. The commodity that the Web allows us to obtain or to share is *information* in its many forms, and being connected to the Web through a desktop, a laptop, a mobile phone, or any other internet-enabled device gives us the "potential power" that comes with being part of the global information society. This potential power can be realized only if we can make sense of and filter the information accessible to us, and this is where search and navigation tools present themselves.

As web users, we have become accustomed to adapting to new ways of information seeking, as new tools become available, but the time has come for the machine to adapt to our preferences and interests, in order to give us a more personalized view of the Web.

An Introduction to Search Engines and Web Navigation, by Mark Levene

Predictive analytic technologies and recommendation systems incorporate machine learning and social networking techniques in order to help us deal with the "paradox of choice," where we have many possible choices and no easy way to distinguish between them [173]. These techniques, based on a feedback loop between a business and a customer, are extensively used on the Web in the creation, marketing, and selling of "cultural products," such as books, music, and video. It is safe to predict that these techniques will be improved and gain broad market acceptance.

The semantic web [78],[226] mentioned in Chapter 1, holds the promise to improve the interaction between users and the Web by providing the interfaces and languages whereby the information can be expressed in a machine digestible format [600]. Much has been said and written about the semantic web and its enabling language, RDF [544]. In a nutshell, RDF is a language for expressing human-readable and machine-processable metadata that uses XML [259] as a lower level common syntax for processing and exchanging fragments of RDF. One of the important aspects of the semantic web is that it allows the separation of content from its presentation. To take advantage of semantic web data, say in RDF format, new browser capabilities need to be developed. One such RDF-based information management environment is Haystack [548], whose user interface supports conventional browsing tools, in addition to multiple presentation styles, called *views*.

One of the core ideas of the semantic web is the ability to use different ontologies according to the specific vocabularies needed for different applications. The OWL web ontology language is a family of knowledge representation languages for authoring ontologies that enable this aspect of the semantic web. At the end of the day, it is the need for these semantic web technologies in real-world applications and the availability of development tools that will drive them out of the research labs. One such development tool is the open source ontology editor, Protégé (http://protege.stanford.edu), which can be used to construct, visualize, and reason about ontologies. Examples of significant applications for the semantic web are in biomedical research and healthcare [341]. Other examples that we have already looked at in the context of the social web are the ubiquitous RSS format (see Section 9.10.2) and the FOAF ontology (see Section 9.1.5).

As mentioned in Section 9.10 on Web 2.0, the semantic web may well coincide with its successor (Web 3.0), which may attempt to inject artificial intelligence into the Web. There is still some skepticism about the semantic web [327] as, so far, its academic promise has been greater than its impact on industry, but this may change as semantic web technologies are adopted in more applications.

The technologies we have presented in this book are to a large degree orthogonal from those that underpin the semantic web. As the semantic web matures, search and navigation tools will be able to take advantage of the new

[226]W3C Semantic Web Activity. www.w3.org/2001/sw.

wealth of available metadata, but this will not change the fundamental way in which search engines work.

We can expect many improvements to current practices; we mention a few of these: (i) integration of multimedia information in the form of text, audio, images, and video; (ii) advances in natural language understanding technologies in the context of search; (iii) large-scale personalization of search and navigation using machine learning techniques; (iv) novel user interfaces and visualization methods; (v) more effective distributed search strategies in P2P systems; (vi) improved distributed models of crawling the web, which will involve more cooperation between search engines and web sites; (vii) search engines as data miners and trend detectors; (viii) new and refined metrics for measuring relevance of information to users, possibly borrowing from social network analysis; (ix) making hidden web databases accessible through search engines; and (x) the realization of the mobile web and location-aware services.

At the time of writing this book, web search is still, to a large degree, a separate activity from *desktop search*—the term used for searching information which resides on a user's computer and managed by the operating system's file storage (this may include e-mail and other user data) [161,441]. This may change as Microsoft continues to integrate search within the Windows operating system.[227] Microsoft obviously has a grip on users' desktop (assuming they are using windows), but this will not stop other players in the search engine space competing for an integrated web and desktop search tool.

Google has done just that with their desktop search tool (http://desktop.google.com) that searches your e-mail, files on your hard disk, web pages you have viewed, your online chats, and more.[228] Once the tool is installed, searching can be done from a Google desktop home page, which has the options to search your desktop, as well as searching the Web in the usual way with desktop results displayed together with web search results. Yahoo[229] was also providing desktop search to compete with Google and Microsoft Search, but has subsequently discontinued offering a free desktop product.

Web search is not a very "sticky" activity and users will shift their loyalties as soon as a new tool is released which better satisfies their information needs. One way in which a search engine may gain control over an industry standard is through proprietary APIs that can be used in commercial tools [217]. It is possible that the search engine wars will tip toward the search engine whose platform gets adopted in the many software tools that search both surface and deep web information, including the provision for paid placement advertising. In order to win the standards wars, search engines will have to release open APIs

[227] Windows Search. www.microsoft.com/windows/products/winfamily/desktopsearch/default.mspx.

[228] Google Desktop Search Launched, by D. Sullivan, October 2004. http://searchenginewatch.com/searchday/article.php/3421651.

[229] Yahoo launches desktop search, by C. Sherman, January 2005. http://searchenginewatch.com/searchday/article.php/3457011.

across as many platforms as possible and do everything they can to make their APIs the industry standard.

Looking into the future, the next natural step will be to create a search engine for the real world [103]; that is, one which has knowledge of the location of real-world objects. Moreover, links to web pages having information about these objects will be established. In one scenario, we are standing in front of a historical building and through location awareness, we can find information on the Web about the building. In another scenario, we are in a museum and when standing next to an artifact we would like to find out about it. At an individual level, we may also want to hold an index of the location of our personal objects, and get the search engine to locate them and store information about them. Setting up the infrastructure for such a tool will take time as all searchable objects will need to be tagged using a technology such as RFID (radio frequency identification) [669].

There is a huge potential for collective problem solving on the Web through distributed computations [300]. Owing to the inherently distributive nature of the Web and the massive number of computers that are connected as a result, it is possible to carry out distributed computation on a global scale. As an example, the ChessBrain project [352] aims to explore distributed computation in the context of playing chess over the Internet by exploiting the power of as many connected machines as possible. The idea is for a super-peer node to split up the computation, which in this case aims to find the "best" move, by delegating to the peer nodes smaller computing tasks that can be computed quickly. Projects such as this one are just the tip of the iceberg on what can be done through distributed computation on the Web.

Looking further into the future, we observe that the Web is a self-organizing system, having no central entity guiding its evolution [225]. Despite its highly distributive nature, many regularities emerge in the structure of the Web—in the way in which we search and navigate the web and in the communities that are formed on the Web. The knowledge encapsulated in the Web is a mirror of the collective knowledge that has been made available on the Web, and, as with many self-organizing systems, the sum is greater than its parts.

It is important to mention Cybercrime, which has become a fertile ground for Cybercriminals who use the Web to serve malicious content that can compromise users' machines [546]. The increased complexity and vulnerability of the browser is one of the key security loopholes, where usability and security are often at odds with each other. Browsers should be aggressive in patching security vulnerabilities and put in place systems for detecting, reporting, and responding to any security flaws. Moreover, search engines that crawl the Web can identify potentially malicious web sites in order to secure their search results.

As an addendum, we mention brain scanning studies using functional magnetic resonance imaging (MRI) that have shown a pattern of increased brain activity when searching the Internet for information, compared to a traditional reading task. Interestingly, those with no prior web searching experience had much less brain activity when surfing the Internet than those who were web-savvy [612]. However, after a period of web search training, the levels of brain activity of the less savvy users increased and were similar to those of the web-savvy users [613].

Herther [299] describes the current generation as "digital natives" compared to the older "digital immigrants" whose digital roots are not as strong. Yet, the brain is flexible and we never lose the ability to adapt and learn, so cognitive training and being involved in stimulating and challenging activities, which may involve surfing the Net, can be cognitively beneficial.

BIBLIOGRAPHY

1. Abiteboul S, Preda M, Cobena G. Adaptive online page importance computation. In: Proceedings of the International World Wide Web Conference (WWW). Budapest; 2003. pp. 280–290.
2. Abrams D, Baecker R, Chignell MH. Information archiving with bookmarks: personal web space construction and organization. In: Proceedings of the Conference on Human Factors in Computing Systems (CHI). Los Angeles (CA); 1998. pp. 41–48.
3. Abrams Z, Keerthi SS, Mendelevitch O, Tomlin JA. Ad delivery with budgeted advertisers: a comprehensive LP approach. J Electron Commer Res 2002; 9:16–32.
4. Abrams Z, Vee E. Personalized ad delivery when ads fatigue: an approximation algorithm. In: Proceedings of the Workshop on Internet and Network Economics (WINE). San Diego (CA); 2007. pp. 535–540.
5. Adam D. The counting house. Nature 2002; 415:726–729.
6. Adamic LA. The small world web. In: Proceedings of the European Conference on Research and Advanced Technology for Digital Libraries (ECDL). Paris; 1999. pp. 443–452.
7. Adamic LA, Adar E. Friends and neighbours on the web. Soc Networks 2003; 25:211–230.
8. Adamic LA, Adar E. How to search a social network? Condens Matter Arch 2003; 27:187–203. See http://arxiv.org/abs/cond-mat/0310120.
9. Adamic LA, Huberman BA. Technical comment: power-law distribution of the world wide web. Science 2000; 287: 2115a.
10. Adamic LA, Huberman BA. Zipf's law and the internet. Glottometrics 2002; 3:143–150.
11. Adamic LA, Lukose RM, Huberman BA. Local search in unstructured networks. In: Bornholdt S, Schuster HG, editors. Handbook of graphs and networks: from the genome to the internet. Berlin: Wiley-VCH; 2002. pp. 295–317.
12. Adamic LA, Zhang J, Bakshy E, Ackerman MS. Knowledge sharing and Yahoo Answers: everyone knows something. In: Proceedings of the International World Wide Web Conference (WWW). Beijing; 2008. pp. 665–674.
13. Adar E, Adamic LA, Zhang L, Lukose RM. Implicit structure and the dynamics of blogspace. In: Proceedings of the International Workshop on the Weblogging Ecosystem: Aggregation, Analysis and Dynamics, Held in conjunction with the International World Wide Web Conference (WWW). New York; 2004. See www.blogpulse.com/www2004-workshop.html.
14. Adar E, Huberman BA. The economics of surfing. Q J Electron Commer 2000; 1:203–214.

An Introduction to Search Engines and Web Navigation, by Mark Levene

15. Adar E, Huberman BA. Free riding on Gnutella. First Monday 2000; 5(10).
16. Agarwal N, Athey S, Yang D. Skewed bidding in pay-per-action auctions for online advertising. Am Econ Rev 2009; 99:441–447.
17. Agichtein E, Lawrence S, Gravano L. Learning to find answers to questions on the web. ACM Trans Internet Technol (TOIT) 2004; 4:129–162.
18. Agresti A. An introduction to categorical data analysis, Wiley Series in Probability and Statistics. 2nd ed. Hoboken (NJ): John Wiley & Sons, Inc.; 2007.
19. Aizen J, Huttenlocher D, Kleinberg J, Novak A. Traffic-based feedback on the web. Proc Natl Acad Sci U S A 2004; 101:5254–5260.
20. Alag S. Collective intelligence in action. Greenwhich (CT): Manning Publications; 2009.
21. Alam H, Hartono R, Kumar A, Rahman F, Tarnikova Y, Wilcox C. Web page summarization for handheld devices: a natural language approach. In: Proceedings of the International Conference on Document Analysis and Recognition (ICDAR), Volume II. Edinburgh; 2003. pp. 1153–1157.
22. Albert R, Barabási A-L. Statistical mechanics of complex networks. Rev Mod Phys 2002; 74:47–97.
23. Albert R, Jeong H, Barabási A-L. Error and attack tolerance of complex networks. Nature 2000; 406:378–382.
24. Aldous DJ. Reorganizing large web sites. Am Math Mon 2001; 108:16–27.
25. Ali K, van Stam W. TiVo: making show recommendations using a distributed collaborative filtering architecture. In: Proceedings of the ACM SIGKDD International Conference on Knowledge Discovery and Data Mining (KDD). Seatle (WA); 2004. pp. 394–401
26. Allan J. Introduction to topic detection and tracking. In: Allan J, editor. Topic detection and tracking: event-based information organization. Norwell (MA): Kluwer Academic Publishers; 2002. pp. 1–16.
27. Alreck PL, Settle RB. Consumer reactions to online behavioural tracking and targeting. Database Mark Customer Strategy Manage 2007; 15:11–23.
28. Amaral LAN, Scala A, Barthélémy M, Stanley HE. Classes of small-world networks. Proc Natl Acad Sci U S A 2000; 97:11149–11152.
29. Amento B, Terveen LG, Hill WC. Does "authority" mean quality? Predicting expert quality ratings of web documents. In: Proceedings of the International Conference on Research and Development in Information Retrieval (SIGIR). Athens; 2000. pp. 296–303.
30. Andersen R, Borgs C, Chayes JT, Hopcroft JE, Jain K, Mirrokni VS, Teng S-H. Robust PageRank and locally computable spam detection features. In: Proceedings of the International Workshop on Adversarial Information Retrieval on the Web (AIRWeb). Held in conjunction with the International World Wide Web Conference (WWW). Beijing; 2008. pp. 69–76.
31. Anderson CR, Domingos P, Weld DS. Adaptive web navigation for wireless devices. In: Proceedings of the International Joint Conference on Artificial Intelligence (IJCAI). Seattle (WA); 2001. pp. 879–884.
32. Anick P, Kantamneni RG. A longitudinal study of real-time search assistance adoption. In: Proceedings of the International Conference on Research and Development in Information Retrieval (SIGIR). Singapore; 2008. pp. 701–702.

33. Anick P, Murthi V, Sebastian S. Similar term discovery using web search. In: Proceedings of the International Language Resources and Evaluation (LREC). Marrakech, Morocco; 2008. pp. 1209–1213.

34. Aridor Y, Carmel D, Maarek YS, Soffer A, Lempel R. Knowledge encapsulation for focused search from pervasive devices. In: Proceedings of the International World Wide Web Conference (WWW). Hong Kong; 2001. pp. 754–763.

35. Ashbrook D, Starner T. Using GPS to learn significant locations and predict movement across multiple users. Pers Ubiquit Comput 2003; 5:275–286.

36. Ashkan A, Clarke CLA. Term-based commercial intent analysis. In: Proceedings of the International Conference on Research and Development in Information Retrieval (SIGIR). Boston (MA); 2009. pp. 800–801.

37. Aslam JA, Savell R. Models for metasearch. In: Proceedings of the International Conference on Research and Development in Information Retrieval (SIGIR). New Orleans (LO); 2001. pp. 276–284.

38. Aslam JA, Savell R. On the effectiveness of evaluating retrieval systems in the absence of relevance judgments. In: Proceedings of the International Conference on Research and Development in Information Retrieval (SIGIR). Toronto; 2003. pp. 361–362.

39. August KG, Hansen MH, Shriver E. Mobile web searching. Bell Labs Tech J 2002; 6:84–98.

40. Avrachenkov K, Litvak N. The effect of new links of Google pagerank. Stoch Models 2006; 22:319–331.

41. Avrachenkov K, Litvak N, Nemirovsky D, Osipova N. Monte carlo methods in pagerank computation: when one iteration is sufficient. SIAM J Numer Anal 2007; 45:890–904.

42. Ayers P, Matthews C, Yates B. How Wikipedia works: and how you can be a part of it. San Francisco (CA): No Starch Press; 2008.

43. Babaioff M, Chuang J, Feldman M. Incentives in peer-to-peer systems. In: Nisan N, Roughgarden T, Tardos E, Vazirani VV, editors. Algorithmic game theory. Cambridge: Cambridge University Press; 2007. pp. 593–611.

44. Baeza-Yates RA, Castillo C, Saint-Jean F. Web dynamics, structure, and page quality. In: Levene M, Poulovassilis A, editors. Web dynamics. Berlin: Springer-Verlag; 2004. pp. 93–109.

45. Baeza-Yates RA, Ribeiro-Neto B. Modern information retrieval. Reading (MA): ACM Press Books in Conjunction with Addison-Wesley; 1999.

46. Baldi P, Frasconi P, Smyth P. Modeling the internet and the web: probabilistic algorithms. Chichester: John Wiley & Sons, Ltd.; 2003.

47. Bar-Ilan J. Search engine ability to cope with the changing web. In: Levene M, Poulovassilis A, editors. Web dynamics. Berlin: Springer-Verlag; 2004. pp. 195–215.

48. Bar-Ilan J. Informetrics at the beginning of the 21st century—A review. Journal of Informetr 2008; 2:1–52.

49. Bar-Ilan J, Gutman T. How do search engines handle non-english queries? - A case study. In: Proceedings of the International World Wide Web Conference (WWW). Budapest; 2003. pp. 78–87.

50. Bar-Ilan J, Gutman T. How do search engines respond to some non-English queries? J Inf Sci 2005; 31:13–28.

51. Bar-Ilan J, Levene M, Mat-Hassan M. Methods for evaluating dynamic changes in search engine rankings: a case study. J Doc 2006; 62:708–729.
52. Bar-Ilan J, Mat-Hassan M, Levene M. Methods for comparing rankings of search engine results. Comput Netw 2006; 50:1448–1463.
53. Bar-Ilan J, Zhu Z, Levene M. Topic-specific analysis of search queries. In: Proceedings of the Workshop on Web Search Click Data (WSCD). Held in conjunction with the ACM International Conference on Web Search and Data Mining. Barcelona; 2009.
54. Barabási A-L. Linked: the new science of networks. Cambridge (MA): Perseus Publishing; 2002.
55. Barabási A-L, Albert R, Jeong H. Scale-free characteristics of random networks: the topology of the world-wide web. Physica A 2000; 281:69–77.
56. Barbaro S, Bracht B. Shilling, squeezing sniping: explaining late bidding in online second-price auctions. Working paper, Economics. Germany: University of Mainz; 2006.
57. Barrat A, Barthélemy M, Vespignani A. Dynamical processes on complex networks. Cambridge: Cambridge University Press; 2008.
58. Barroso LA, Dean J, Hölzle U. Web search for a planet: the Google cluster architecture. IEEE Micro 2003; 23:22–28.
59. Batagelj V. Notes on blockmodeling. Soc Netw 1997; 19:143–155.
60. Batagelj V, Mrvar A. Some analyses of Erdös collaboration graph. Soc Netw 2000; 22:173–186.
61. Batagelj V, Mrvar A. Pajek analysis and visualization for large networks. In: Jünger M, Mutzel P, editors. Graph drawing software: mathematics and visualization. Berlin: Springer-Verlag; 2004. pp. 77–103.
62. Baykan E, Henzinger MR, Marian L, Weber I. Purely URL-based topic classification. In: Proceedings of the International World Wide Web Conference (WWW). Madrid; 2009. pp. 1109–1100.
63. Becchetti L, Castillo C, Donato D, Baeza-Yates R, Leonardi S. Link analysis for web spam detection. ACM Trans Web 2008; 2:1–2.
64. Bedord J. Ebooks hit critical mass: where do libraries fit with oprah? Online Mag 2009; 33:14–18.
65. Beeferman D, Berger A. Agglomerative clustering of a search engine query log. In: Proceedings of the ACM SIGKDD International Conference on Knowledge Discovery and Data Mining (KDD). Boston (MA); 2000. pp. 407–416.
66. Beitzel SM, Jensen EC, Chowdhury A, Frieder O, Grossman D. Temporal analysis of a very large topically categorized web query log. J Am Soc Inf Sci Technol (JASIST) 2007; 58:166–178.
67. Beitzel SM, Jensen EC, Lewis DD, Chowdhury A, Frieder O. Automatic classification of web queries using very large unlabeled query logs. ACM Trans Inf Syst (TOIS) 2007; 25:1–9.
68. Belew RK. Finding out about: a cognitive perspective on search engine techology and the WWW. Cambridge: Cambridge University Press; 2000.
69. Bell RM, Bennett J, Koren Y, Volinsky C. The million dollar programming prize. IEEE Spectr 2009; 46:28–33.

70. Bell RM, Koren Y. Scalable collaborative filtering with jointly derived neighborhood interpolation weights. In: Proceedings of the IEEE International Conference on Data Mining (ICDM). Omaha (NE); 2007. pp. 43–52.
71. Bell RM, Koren Y, Volinsky C. Chasing $1,000,000: how we won the Netflix progress prize. ASA Stat Comput Graph Newsl 2007; 18:4–12.
72. Bell RM, Koren Y, Volinsky C. Matrix factorization techniques for recommender systems. IEEE Comput 2009; 42:30–37.
73. Benczúr AA, Csalogány K, Sarlós T, Uher M. SpamRank—fully automatic link spam detection. In: Proceedings of the International Workshop on Adversarial Information Retrieval on the Web (AIRWeb). Held in conjunction with the International World Wide Web Conference (WWW). Chiba; 2005. pp. 25–38.
74. Bennett J, Lanning S. The Netflix prize. In: Proceedings of the KDD Cup and Workshop 2007. San Jose (CA); 2007. pp. 3–6.
75. Berberich K, Vazirgiannis M, Weikum G. T-Rank: time-aware authority ranking. In: Proceedings of the International Workshop on Algorithms and Models for the Web-Graph (WAW). Rome; 2004. pp. 131–142.
76. Bergman MK. White paper: the deep web: surfacing hidden value. J Electron Publishing 2001; 7. See www.journalofelectronicpublishing.org/.
77. Berners-Lee T. Weaving the web. London: Orion Books; 1999.
78. Berners-Lee T, Hendler J, Lassila O. The semantic web. Sci Am 2001; 284:35–43.
79. Bernstein M. Patterns of hypertext. In: Proceedings of the ACM Conference on Hypertext. Pittsburg (PA); 1998. pp. 21–29.
80. Bhargava HK, Feng J. The impact of sponsored results on the quality of information gatekeepers. In: Proceedings of the International Conference on Electronic Commerce (ICEC). Minneapolis (MN); 2007. pp. 147–152.
81. Bian J, Liu Y, Zhou D, Agichtein E, Zha H. Learning to recognize reliable users and content in social media with coupled mutual reinforcement. In: Proceedings of the International World Wide Web Conference (WWW). Madrid; 2009. pp. 51–60.
82. Bianchini M, Gori M, Scarselli F. Inside PageRank. ACM Trans Internet Technol (TOIT) 2005; 5:92–128.
83. Bianconi G, Barabási A-L. Competition and multiscaling in evolving networks. Europhys Lett 2001; 54:436–442.
84. Bilenko M, White RW, Richardson M, Murray GC. Talking the talk vs. walking the walk: salience of information needs in querying vs. browsing. In: Proceedings of the International Conference on Research and Development in Information Retrieval (SIGIR). Singapore; 2008. pp. 705–706.
85. Billsus D, Pazzani MJ. User modeling for adaptive news access. User Modeling and User-Adapted Interaction. 2000; 10:147–180.
86. Boccaletti S, Latora V, Moreno Y, Chavez M, Hwang D-U. Complex networks: structure and dynamics. Phys Rep 2006; 424:175–308.
87. Bohnert F, Zukerman I, Berkovsky S, Baldwin T, Sonenberg Liz. Using interest and transition models to predict visitor locations in museums. AI Commun 2008; 21:195–202.
88. Bollobás B. Random graphs. 2nd ed. Cambridge: Cambridge University Press; 2001.
89. Bonfiglio D, Mellia M, Meo M, Rossi D. Detailed analysis of Skype traffic. IEEE Trans Multimedia 2009; 11:117–127.

90. Borges J, Levene M. Data mining of user navigation patterns. In: Masand B, Spiliopoulou M, editors. Web usage analysis and user profiling, Lecture Notes in Artificial Intelligence (LNAI 1836). Berlin: Springer-Verlag; 2000. pp. 92–111.
91. Borges J, Levene M. A fine grained heuristic to capture web navigation patterns. SIGKDD Explor 2000; 2:40–50.
92. Borges J, Levene M. An heuristic to capture longer user web navigation patterns. In: Proceedings of the International Conference on Electronic Commerce and Web Technologies (EC-Web). Greenwich; 2000. pp. 155–164.
93. Borges J, Levene M. Ranking pages by topology and popularity within web sites. World Wide Web 2006; 9:301–316.
94. Borges J, Levene M. Evaluating variable length Markov chain models for analysis of user web navigation sessions. IEEE Trans Knowl Data Eng 2007; 19:441–452.
95. Borodin A, Roberts GO, Rosenthal JS, Tsaparas P. Link analysis ranking: algorithms, theory, and experiments. ACM Trans Internet Technol (TOIT) 2005; 5:231–297.
96. Boyd DM. Friendster and publicly articulated social networking. In: Proceedings of the Conference on Human Factors in Computing Systems (CHI). Vienna; 2004. pp. 1279–1282.
97. Boyd DM, Ellison NB. Social network sites: definition, history, and scholarship. J Comput-Med Commun 2007; 13: 11.
98. Brachman RJ. Systems that know what they're doing. IEEE Intell Syst 2002; 17:67–71.
99. Brandes U. Drawing on physical analogies. In: Kaufmann M, Wagner D, editors. Drawing graphs: methods and models. Berlin: Springer-Verlag; 2001. Chapter 4. pp. 71–86.
100. Branigan S, Burch H, Cheswick B, Wojcik F. What can you do with traceroute? IEEE Internet Comput 2001; 5: 96.
101. Brauen TL. Document vector modification. In: Salton G, editor. The SMART retrieval system—experiments in automatic document processing. Englewood Cliffs (NJ): Prentice Hall; 1971. Chapter 24. pp. 456–484.
102. Breese JS, Heckerman D, Kadie C. Empirical analysis of predicitve algorithms for collaborative filtering. In: Proceedings of the Conference on Uncertainty in Artificial Intelligence (UAI). Madison (WI); 1998. pp. 43–52.
103. Brewer EA. When everything is searchable. Commun ACM 2001; 44:53–54.
104. Brill E, Dumais S, Banko M. An analysis of the AskMSR question-answering system. In: Proceedings of the Conference on Empirical Methods in Natural Language Processing (EMNLP). Philadelphia (PA); 2002. pp. 257–264.
105. Brin S, Page L. The anatomy of a large-scale hypertextual web search engine. In: Proceedings of the International World Wide Web Conference (WWW). Brisbane; 1998. pp. 107–117.
106. Broder A. Taxonomy of web search. SIGIR Forum Fall 2002; 36.
107. Broder A, Fontura M, Josifovski V, Kumar RR, Motwani RR, Nabar SS, Panigrahy R, Tomkins A, Xu Y. Estimating corpus size via queries. In: Proceedings of the ACM International Conference on Information and Knowledge Management (CIKM). Arlington (VA); 2006. pp. 594–603.
108. Broder A, Kumar R, Maghoul F, Raghavan P, Rajagopalan A, Stata R, Tomkins A, Wiener J. Graph structure in the web. Comput Netw 2000; 33:309–320.

109. Brooks N. Sponsored search: how much are you paying for your customers' navigational behavior? Technical report. Atlas Institute; 2007.

110. Brown DJ. Web search considered hamrful. ACM Queue 2004; 2:84–85.

111. Brown J, Morgan J. Reputation in online auctions: the market for trust. J Ind Econ 2006; 49:61–81.

112. Brusilovsky P, Nejdl W. Adaptive hypermedia and adaptive web. In: Singh MP, editor. Practical handbook of internet computing. Baton Rouge (FL): Chapman Hall & CRC Press; 2004. Chapter 2.

113. Brusilovsky P, Rizzo R. Map-based access to multiple educational online resources from mobile wireless devices. In: Proceedings of the International Symposium on Mobile Human-Computer Interaction. Pisa; 2002. pp. 404–408.

114. Buchanan M. Nexus: small worlds and the groudbreaking science of networks. New York: W.W. Norton & Company; 2002.

115. Buckley F, Harary F. Distance in graphs. Redwood City (CA): Addison-Wesley; 1990.

116. Bucklin RE, Lattin JM, Ansari A, Gupta S, Bell D, Coupey E, Little JDC, Mela C, Montgomery A, Steckel J. Choice and the internet: from clickstream to research stream. Mark Lett 2002; 13:245–258.

117. Bumgardner J. Building tag clouds in perl and PHP. Sebastopol (CA): O'Reilly; 2006.

118. Burges CJC, Shaked T, Renshaw E, Lazier A, Deeds M, Hamilton N, Hullender GN. Learning to rank using gradient descent. In: Proceedings of the International Conference on Machine Learning (ICML). Bonn; 2005. pp. 85–96.

119. Bush V. As we may think. Atl Mon 1945; 176:101–108.

120. Buyukkokten O, Kaljuvee O, Garcia-Molina H, Paepcke A, Winograd T. Efficient web browsing on handheld devices using page and form summarization. ACM Trans Inf Syst (TOIS) 2002; 20:85–115.

121. Buyya R, Yeoa CS, Venugopala S, Broberg J, Brandic I. Cloud computing and emerging IT platforms: vision, hype, and reality for delivering computing as the 5th utility. Future Gener Comput Syst 2009; 25:599–616.

122. Cadez I, Heckerman D, Meek C, Smyth P, White S. Model-based clustering and visualization of navigation patterns on a web site. Data Min Knowl Discov 2003; 7:399–424.

123. Cafarella M, Cutting D. Building nutch: open source. ACM Queue 2004; 2:54–61.

124. Campbell-Kelly M. Historical reflections: the rise, fall, and resurrection of software as a service. Commun ACM 2009; 52:28–30.

125. Cao J, Chan KM, Shea GY-K, Guo M. Location-aware information retrieval for mobile computing. In: Proceedings of the International Conference on Embedded and Unbiquitous Computing (EUC). Aizu-Wakamatsu City; 2004. pp. 450–459.

126. Carpineto C, Osiński S, Romano G, Weiss D. A survey of web clustering engines. ACM Comput Surv (CSUR) 2009; 41:1–17.

127. Carreira R, Crato JM, Gonçalves D, Jorge JA. Evaluating adaptive user profiles for news classification. In: Proceedings of the International Conference on Intelligent User Interfaces (IUI). Medeira, Funchal; 2004. pp. 206–212.

128. Chakrabarti S. Mining the web: discovering knowledge from hypertext data. San Francisco (CA): Morgan Kaufmann; 2003.

129. Chakrabarti S, Batterywala Y. Mining themes from bookmarks. In: Proceedings of the Workshop on Text Mining. Held in conjunction with the ACM SIGKDD International Conference on Knowledge Discovery and Data Mining (KDD). Boston (MA); 2000.

130. Chakrabarti S, Dom B, Kumar SR, Raghavan P, Rajagopalan S, Tomkins A, Gibson D, Kleinberg JM. Mining the web's link structure. IEEE Comput 1999; 32:60–67.

131. Chakrabarti S, Dom B, Kumar SR, Raghavan P, Rajagopalan S, Tomkins A, Kleinberg JM, Gibson D. Hypersearching the web by members of the clever project team. Sci Am 1999; 280:54–60.

132. Chakrabarti D, Kumar R, Punera K. Quicklink selection for navigational query results. In: Proceedings of the International World Wide Web Conference (WWW). Madrid; 2009. pp. 391–400.

133. Chakrabarti S, Srivastava S, Subramanyam M, Tiwari M. Using Memex to archive and mine community web browsing experience. Comput Netw 2000; 33:669–684.

134. Chang F, Dean J, Ghemawat S, Hsieh WC, Wallach DA, Burrows M, Chandra T, Fikes A, Gruber RE. Bigtable: a distributed storage system for structured data. ACM Trans Comput Syst 2008; 26:1–4.

135. Chau M, Fang X, Yang CC. Web searching in chinese: a study of a search engine in Hong Kong. J Am Soc Inf Sci Technol (JASIST) 2007; 58:1044–1054.

136. Chen H, Dumais S. Bring order to the web: automatically categorizing search results. In: Proceedings of the Conference on Human Factors in Computing Systems (CHI). The Hague, The Netherlands; 2000. pp. 145–152.

137. Chen H, Mohapatra P. A novel navigation and transmission technique for mobile handheld devices. Technical Report CSE-2003-1. Computer Science, University of California, Davis; 2003.

138. Chen Q, Li M, Zhou M. Improving query spelling correction using web search results. In: Proceedings of the Conference on Empirical Methods in Natural Language Processing (EMNLP). Prague; 2007. pp. 181–189.

139. Chen ALP, Liu CC, Kuo TCT. Content-based video data retrieval. Proc Natl Sci Counc ROC(A) 1999; 123:449–465.

140. Chen Y, Ma W-Y, Zhang H-J. Detecting web page structure for adaptive viewing on small form factor devices. In: Proceedings of the International World Wide Web Conference (WWW). Budapest; 2003. pp. 225–233.

141. Chen Z, Wenyin L, Li M, Zhang H. iFind: a web image search engine. In: Proceedings of the International Conference on Research and Development in Information Retrieval (SIGIR). New Orleans (LO); 2001. p. 450.

142. Cheng X, Dale C, Liu J. Statistics and social network of YouTube videos. In: Proceedings of the International Workshop on Quality of Service (IWQoS). Enschede, The Netherlands; 2008. pp. 229–238.

143. Chi E. Improving web site usability through visualization. IEEE Internet Comput 2002; 6:64–71.

144. Chi EH. Information seeking can be social. IEEE Comput 2009; 42:42–46.

145. Chi EH, Mytkowicz T. Understanding the efficiency of social tagging systems using information theory. In: Proceedings of the ACM Conference on Hypertext and Hypermedia (HYPERTEXT). Pittsburgh (PA); 2008. pp. 81–88.

146. Chi EH, Rosien A, Supattanasiri G, Williams A, Royer C, Chow C, Robles E, Dalal B, Chen J, Cousins S. The Bloodhound project: automating discovery of web usability issues using the InfoScent simulator. In: Proceedings of the Conference on Human Factors in Computing Systems (CHI). Fort Lauderdale (FL); 2003. pp. 505–512.
147. Choi H, Varian H. Predicting the present with Google Trends. Research paper, Google. 2009. Available at http://googleresearch.blogspot.com/2009/04/predicting-present-with-google-trends.html.
148. Chowdhury A, Soboroff I. Automatic evaluation of world wide web search services. In: Proceedings of the International Conference on Research and Development in Information Retrieval (SIGIR). McLean (VA); 2002. pp. 421–422.
149. Chu S, Chen J, Wu Z, Chu C-HH, Raghavan V. A treemap-based result interface for search engine users. In: Proceedings of Symposium on Human Interface, Held in conjunction with HCI International Conference. Beijing; 2007. pp. 401–410.
150. Church K, Gale W. Document frequency (IDF): a measure of deviation from poisson. In: Proceedings of the Workshop on Very Large Corpora. Cambridge (MA); 1995. pp. 121–130.
151. Cisco. Cisco visual networking index: Global mobile data traffic forecast update. White paper, Jan 2009.
152. Clark J. Deconstructing "You've Got Blog". In: Rodzvilla J, editor. We've got blog: how weblogs are changing our culture. Cambridge (MA): Perseus Press; 2002. pp. 57–68.
153. Clifton B. Advanced web metrics with google analytics. Indianapolis (IN): John Wiley & Sons, Inc.; 2008.
154. Clishain T, Dornfest R. Google hacks. 3rd ed. Sebastopol (CA): O'Reilly; 2006.
155. Cockburn A, Greenberg S, Jones S, McKenzie B, Moyle M. Improving web page revisitation: analysis, design and evaluation. IT & Soc 2003; 1:159–183. Special issue on web navigation.
156. Cohen B. Incentives build robustness in BitTorrent. Technical report. http://bittorrent.com/, 2003. Available at http://bittorrent.com/documentation.html.
157. Cohen J. Embedded speech recognition applications in mobile phones: Status, trends, and challenges. In: Proceedings of the International IEEE Conference on Acoustics, Speech and Signal Processing (ICASSP). Las Vegas (NV); March/April 2008. pp. 5352–5355.
158. Cohen R, Erez K, ben Avraham D, Havlin S. Resilience of the internet to random breakdowns. Phys Rev Lett 2000; 85:4626–4628.
159. Cohen R, Havlin S, ben Avraham D. Efficient immunization strategies for computer networks and populations. Phys Rev Lett 2003; 91:247901–1–4.
160. Cohen D, Herscovici M, Petruschka Y, Maarek YS, Soffer A, Newbold D. Personalized pocket directories for mobile devices. In: Proceedings of the International World Wide Web Conference (WWW). Honolulu (HI); 2002. pp. 627–638.
161. Cole B. Search engines tackle the desktop. IEEE Comput 2005; 38:14–17.
162. Condie T, Garcia-Molina H, Kamvar SD. Adaptive peer-to-peer topologies. In: Proceedings of the International Conference on Peer-to-Peer Computing (P2P). Zurich; 2004. pp. 53–62.
163. Costa FL, Rodrigues FA, Travieso G, Villas Boas PR. Characterization of complex networks: a survey of measurements. Adv Phys 2008; 56:167–242.

164. Croft B, Metzler D, Strohman T. Search engines: information retrieval in practice. Upper Saddle River (NJ): Addison-Wesley, Pearson Education; 2009.

165. Cucerzan S, Brill E. Spelling correction as an iterative process that exploits the collective knowledge of web users. In: Proceedings of the Conference on Empirical Methods in Natural Language Processing (EMNLP). Barcelona; 2004. pp. 293–300.

166. Cugini J, Scholtz J. VISVIP: 3D visualization of paths through web sites. In: Proceedings of the Web-Based Information Visualization DEXA Workshop. Florence; 1999. pp. 259–263. VISVIP home page is at www.itl.nist.gov/iaui/vvrg/cugini/webmet/visvip/vv-home.html.

167. Culliss G. The direct hit popularity engine technology. White paper, Direct Hit. 1999. Available at http://web.archive.org/web/20010619013748/www.direct-hit.com/about/products/technology_whitepaper.html.

168. Culotta A, Bekkerman R, McCallum A. Extracting social networks and contact information from email and the web. In: Proceedings of the Conference on Email and Anti-Spam (CEAS). Mountain View (CA); 2004.

169. Cusumano MA, Yoffie DB. Competing for internet time: lessons from netscape and its battle with microsoft. New York: Touchstone; 2000.

170. Czyzowicz J, Kranakis E, Krizanc D, Pelc A, Martin MV. Enhancing hyperlink structure for improving web performance. J Web Eng 2003; 1:93–127.

171. Daswani N, Mysen C, Rao V, Weis S, Gharachorloo K, Ghosemajumder S. Online advertising fraud. In: Jakobsson M, Ramzan Z, editors. Crimeware: understanding new attacks and defenses. Indianapolis (IN): Addison-Wesley Professional; 2008. Chapter 11.

172. Datta R, Joshi D, Li J, Wand JZ. Image retrieval: ideas, influences, and trends of the new age. ACM Comput Surv (CSUR) 2008; 40:1–5.

173. Davenport TH, Harris JG. What people want (and how to predict it). MIT Sloan Manage Rev 2009; 50:23–31.

174. Davison BD. Recognizing nepotistic links on the web. AAAI-2000 Workshop on Artificial Intelligence for Web Search, Technical Report WS-00-01, AAAI Press; 2000.

175. Davison BD. Topical locality in the web. In: Proceedings of the International Conference on Research and Development in Information Retrieval (SIGIR). Athens; 2000. pp. 272–279.

176. Davison BD, Gerasoulis A, Kleisouris K, Lu Y, Seo H-J, Wang W, Wu B. DiscoWeb: discovering web communities via link analysis. In: Poster Proceedings of the International World Wide Web Conference (WWW). Amsterdam; 1999.

177. de Bruijn O. M-RSVP: a solution for mobile internet browsing. In: Proceedings of the Workshop on Mobile Search, Held in conjunction with the International World Wide Web Conference (WWW). Honolulu (HI); 2002.

178. de Freitas S, Levene M. Evaluating the development of wearable devices, personal data assistants and the use of other mobile devices in further and higher education institutions. JISC Technology and Standards Watch Report: Wearable Technology TSW 03-05, June 2003. Available at www.jisc.ac.uk/index.cfm?name=techwatch_report_0305.

179. de Solla Price D. A general theory of bibliometric and other cumulative advantage processes. J Am Soc Inf Sci 1976; 27:292–306.

180. Dean J. Challenges in building large-scale information retrieval systems. In: Proceedings of the ACM International Conference on Web Search and Data Mining (WSDM). Barcelona; 2009. Invited talk.

181. Dean J, Ghemawat S. MapReduce: simplified data processing on large clusters. Commun ACM 2008; 51:107–113.

182. Dean J, Henzinger MR. Finding related pages in the world wide web. Comput Netw 1999; 31:1467–1479.

183. Deshpande M, Karypis G. Item-based top-n recommendation algorithms. ACM Trans Inf Syst (TOIS) 2004; 22:143–177.

184. Diaz A. Through the Google goggles: sociopolitical bias in search engine design. In: Spink A, Zimmer M, editors. Web search: multidisciplinary perspectives. Berlin: Springer-Verlag; 2008. pp. 11–34.

185. Dieberger A, Dourish P, Höök K, Resnick P, Wexelblat A. Social navigation. Interactions 2000; 7:36–45.

186. Ding Y, Jacob ElinK, Caverlee J, Fried M, Zhang Z. Profiling social networks: a social tagging perspective. D-Lib Mag 2009; 15. Available at www.dlib.org/dlib/march09/ding/03ding.html.

187. Djuknic GM, Richton RE. Geolocation and assisted GPS. IEEE Computer 2001; 34:123–125.

188. Dodds PS, Muhamad R, Watts DJ. An experimental study of search in global social networks. Science 2003; 301:827–829.

189. Dodge M, Kitchin R. Mapping cyberspace. London: Routledge; 2001.

190. Dorogovtsev SN, Mendes JFF. Evolution of networks. Adv Phys 2002; 51:1079–1187.

191. Dorogovtsev SN, Mendes JFF. Evolution of networks: from biological nets to the internet and WWW. Cambridge: Cambridge University Press; 2003.

192. Dou Z, Song R, Wen J-R, Yuan X. Evaluating the effectiveness of personalized web search. IEEE Trans Knowl Data Eng 2009; 21:1178–1190.

193. Doyle J, Carlson JM. Power laws, highly optimized tolerance, and generalized source coding. Phys Rev Lett 2000; 84:5656–5659.

194. Dumais ST, Cutrell E, Cadiz JJ, Jancke G, Sarin R, Robbins DC. Stuff I've seen: a system for personal information retrieval and re-use. In: Proceedings of the International Conference on Research and Development in Information Retrieval (SIGIR). Toronto; 2003. pp. 72–79.

195. Dunlop MD, Masters MM. Pickup usability dominates: a brief history of mobile text entry research and adoption. Int J Mob Hum Comput Interact 2009; 1:42–59.

196. Duri S, Cole A, Munson J, Christensen J. An approach to providing a seamless end-user experience for location-aware applications. In: Proceedings of the International Workshop on Mobile commerce. Held in conjunction with the International Conference on Mobile Computing and Networking. Rome; 2001. pp. 20–25.

197. Eagle N, Pentland A. Reality mining: sensing complex social systems. Pers Ubiquit Comput 2006; 10:255–268.

198. Eagle N, Pentland A. Eigenbehaviors: identifying structure in routine. Behav Ecol Sociobiol 2009; 63:1057–1066.

199. Ebel H, Mielsch L-I, Bornholdt S. Scale-free topology of e-mail networks. Phys Rev E 2002; 66:035103(R)–1–4.

200. Edelman B. Securing online advertising: rustlers and sheriffs in the new wild west. In: Oram A, Viega J, editors. Beautiful security: leading security experts explain how they think. Sebastopol (CA): O'Reilly; 2009. Chapter 6. pp. 89–105.

201. Edelman B, Ostrovsky M, Schwarz M. Internet advertising and the generalized second-price auction: selling billions of dollars worth of. Am Econ Rev 2007; 97:242–259.

202. Eick SG. Visualizing online activity. Commun ACM 2001; 44:45–50.

203. Eisenberg B, Novo J. The Marketer's Coomon Sense Guide to E-metrics. Brooklyn (NY): Future Now; 2002.

204. Engelbart DC. The click heard around the world. Wired 2004; 12:158–161. Told to writer K. Jordan.

205. Engelbart DC, English WK. A research center for augmenting human intellect. In: Proceedings of AFIPS Fall Joint Computer Conference. San Francisco (CA); 1968. pp. 395–3410.

206. Engelberg J, Williams J. Ebays proxy bidding: a license to shill. J Econ Behav Organ 2009; 72:509–526.

207. Etzioni O, Banko M, Soderland S, Weld DS. Open information extraction from the web. Commun ACM 2008; 51:68–74.

208. Evans M, Hastings N, Peacock B. Statistical distributions. 3rd ed. New York: John Wiley & Sons, Inc.; 2000.

209. Fabrikant A, Koutsoupias E, Papadimitriou CH. Heuristically optimized trade-offs: a new paradigm for power laws in the internet. In: Proceedings of the International Colloquium on Automata, Languages and Programming (ICALP). Malaga; 2002. pages pp. 110–122.

210. Fagin R, Kumar R, McCurley KS, Novak J, Sivakumar D, Tomlin JA, Williamson DP. Searching the workplace web. In: Proceedings of the International World Wide Web Conference (WWW). Budapest; 2003. pp. 366–375.

211. Fain DC, Pedersen JO. Sponsored search: a brief history. In: Proceedings of the Workshop Sponsored Search Auctions. Held in conjunction with the ACM Conference on Electronic Commerce (EC). Ann Arbor, MI; 2006.

212. Feder M, Merhav N, Gutman M. Universal prediction of individual sequences. IEEE Trans Inf Theory 1992; 38:1258–1270.

213. Feldman S. Unpuzzling search: Best practices from Mondosoft study. IDC Bulletin \#27867, IDC, Aug 2002.

214. Feng J, Bhargava HK, Pennock D. Implementing sponsored search in web search engines: computational evaluation of alternative mechanisms. INFORMS J Comput 2007; 19:137–148.

215. Fenner TI, Levene M, Loizou G. A stochastic evolutionary model exhibiting power-law behaviour with an exponential cutoff. Condens Matter Arch 2002, cond-mat/0209463. Available at http://arxiv.org/abs/cond-mat/0209463; to appear in Physica A 2005.

216. Fenner TI, Levene M, Loizou G. A stochastic model for the evolution of the web allowing link deletion. Condens Matter Arch 2003, cond-mat/0304316. Available at http://arxiv.org/abs/cond-mat/0304316; to appear in ACM Trans Internet Technol (TOIT) 2006;6 May.

217. Ferguson CH. What's next for Google? Technol Rev 2005; 108:38–46.

218. Fetterly D, Manasse M, Najork M. On the evolution of clusters of near-duplicate web pages. J Web Eng 2004; 2:228–246.
219. Fetterly D, Manasse M, Najork M. Spam, damn spam and statistics. In: Proceedings of the International Workshop on the Web and Databases (WebDB). Held in conjunction with the ACM SIGMOD/PODS International Conference. Paris; 2004. pp. 1–6.
220. Fetterly D, Manasse M, Najork M, Wiener J. A large-scale study of the evolution of web pages. In: Proceedings of the International World Wide Web Conference (WWW). Budapest; 2003. pp. 669–678.
221. Fewster R. A simple explanation of Benfords law. Am Stat 2009; 63(1): 26–32.
222. Fink J, Kobsa A. User modeling for city tours. Artif Intell Rev 2002; 18:33–74.
223. Fitzgerald M. Internetworking. Technol Rev 2004; 107:44–49.
224. Fitzgerald B, Wood SE. Social data analysis at Swivel: lessons learned & next steps. In: Proceedings of the Workshop on Social Data Analysis, Held in conjunction with the Conference on Human Factors in Computing Systems (CHI). Florence; 2008.
225. Flake GW, Pennock DM. Self-organization, self-regulation, and self-similarity on the fractal web. In: Introduced by Clarke AC, editor. The colours of inifnity. Bath: Clear Books; 2004. pp. 96–127.
226. Flake GW, Tsioutsiouliklis K, Zhukov L. Methods for mining web communities: bibliometric, spectral, and flow. In: Levene M, Poulovassilis A, editors. Web dynamics. Berlin: Springer-Verlag; 2004. pp. 45–68.
227. Fogaras D, Rácz B, Csalogány K, Sarlós T. Towards scaling fully personalized PageRank: algorithms, lower bounds, and experiments. Internet Math 2005; 2:333–358.
228. Foote J. An overview of audio information retrieval. Multimedia Syst 1999; 7:2–10.
229. Fortunato S, Boguná M, Flammini A, Menczer F. Approximating PageRank from in-degree. In: Proceedings of the International Workshop on Algorithms and Models for the Web-Graph (WAW). Banff, Canada; 2006. pp. 59–71.
230. Fortunato S, Flammini A, Menczer F, Vespignani A. Topical interests and the mitigation of search engine bias. Proc Natl Acad Sci U S A 2006; 103:12684–12689.
231. Fox S, Zickuhr K, Smith A. Twitter and status updating, fall 2009. Technical report, Pew Internet & American Life Project, Oct 2009.
232. Fraigniaud P, Gavoille C, Paul C. Eclecticism shrinks even small worlds. In: Proceedings of the ACM Symposium on the Principles of Distributed Computing (PODC). St. John's, Newfoundland; 2004. pp. 169–178.
233. Freeman LC. Centrality in social networks: conceptual clarification. Soc Netw 1978/79; 1:215–239.
234. Freyne J, Farzan R, Brusilovsky P, Smyth B, Coyle M. Collecting community wisdom: integrating social search & social navigation. In: Proceeding of the International Conference on Intelligent User Interfaces (IUI). Honolulu (HI); 2007. pp. 52–61.
235. Freyne J, Smyth B, Coyle M, Balfe E, Briggs P. Further experiments on collaborative ranking in community-based web search. Artif Intell Rev 2004; 21:229–252.
236. Funk JL. The mobile internet: how japan dialled up and the west disconnected. Hong Kong: ISI Publications; 2001.
237. Funkhouser T, Min P, Kazhdan M, Chen J, Halderman A, Dobkin D, Jacobs D. A search engine for 3D models. ACM Trans Graph (TOG) 2003; 22:83–105.

238. Furnas GW. Effective view navigation. In: Proceedings of the Conference on Human Factors in Computing Systems (CHI). Atlanta, Georgia; 1997. pp. 367–374.

239. Gabrilovich E, Markovitch S. Computing semantic relatedness using Wikipedia-based explicit semantic analysis. In: Proceedings of the International Joint Conference on Artificial Intelligence (IJCAI). Hyderabad, India; 2007. pp. 1606–1611.

240. Galitsky B. Natural language question answering system: technique of semantic headers, International Series on Advanced Intelligence. Adelaide: Advanced Knowledge International; 2003.

241. Gan Q, Attenberg J, Markowetz A, Suel T. Analysis of geographic queries in a search engine log. In: Proceedings of the International Workshop on Location and the Web, Held in conjunction with the International World Wide Web Conference (WWW). Beijing; 2008. pp. 49–56.

242. Gandhi M, Jakobsson M, Ratkiewicz J. Badvertisements: stealthy click-fraud with unwitting accessories. J Digit Forensic Pract 2006; 1:131–142.

243. Garfield E. It's a small world after all. Essays Inf Sci 1979; 4:299–304.

244. Garton L, Haythornthwaite C, Wellman B. Studying online social networks. J Comput Med Commun Web Q 1997; 3, Available at http://jcmc.indiana.edu/vol3/issue1/garton.html.

245. Gauch S, Wang G, Gomez M. Profusion: intelligent fusion from multiple, distributed search engines. J Univ Comput Sci 1996; 2:637–649.

246. Gavish B, Tucci CL. Reducing internet auction fraud. Commun ACM 2008; 51:89–97.

247. Geisler G, Burns S. Tagging video: conventions and strategies of the YouTube community. In: Poster Proceedings of the ACM/IEEE-CS Joint Conference on Digital Libraries (JCDL). Vancouver (BC); 2007. p. 480.

248. Geller NL. On the citation influence methodology of Pinski and Narin. Inf Process Manage 1978; 14:93–95.

249. Gevers T, Smeulders AWM. Content-based image retrieval: an overview. In: Medioni G, Kang SB, editors. Emerging topics in computer vision. Englewood Cliffs (NJ): Prentice Hall; 2004. Chapter 8.

250. Gharachorloo K. Click fraud: anecdotes from the front line. In: Proceedings of the Workshop on Ad Fraud. Stanford (CA); 2007.

251. Ghemawat S, Gobioff H, Leung S-T. The Google file system. In: Proceedings of the ACM Symposium on Operating Systems Principles SOSP). Bolton Landing (NY); 2003. pp. 29–43.

252. Giles DE. Benfords law and naturally occurring prices in certain ebaY auctions. Appl Econ Lett 2007; 14:157–161.

253. Giles J. Internet encyclopaedias go head to head. Nature 2005; 438:900–901.

254. Ginsberg J, Mohebbi MH, Patel RS, Brammer L, Smolinski MS, Brilliant L. Detecting influenza epidemics using search engine query data. Nature 2009; 457:1012–1014.

255. Girvan M, Newman MEJ. Community structure in social and biological networks. Proc Natl Acad Sci U S A 2002; 99:7821–7826.

256. Glance NS. Community search assistant. In: Proceeding of the International Conference on Intelligent User Interfaces (IUI). Santa Fe (NM); 2001. pp. 91–96.

257. Glance NS, Hurst M, Tomokiyo T. BlogPulse: automated trend discovery for weblogs. In: Proceedings of the International Workshop on the Weblogging Ecosystem: Aggregation, Analysis and Dynamics, Held in conjunction with the International World Wide Web Conference (WWW). New York; 2004. Available at www.blogpulse.com/www2004-workshop.html.

258. Glover EJ, Lawrence S, Gordon MD, Birmingham WP, Giles CL. Web search—your way. Commun ACM 2001; 44:97–102.

259. Goldfarb CF, Prescod P. The XML handbook. 5th ed. Englewood Cliffs (NJ): Prentice Hall; 2003.

260. Goldstein ML, Morris SA, Yen GG. Problem with fitting to the power-law distribution. Eur Phys J B 2004; 41:255–258.

261. Golub GH, Van Loan CF. Matrix computations. Johns Hopkins Studies in Mathematical Sciences. 3rd ed. Baltimore (MD): The Johns Hopkins University Press; 1996.

262. Gonçalves B, Meiss M, Ramasco JJ, Flammini A, Menczer F. Remembering what we like: toward an agent-based model of web traffic. In: Proceedings of the ACM International Conference on Web Search and Data Mining (WSDM Late Breaking-Results). Barcelona; 2009.

263. Good NS, Krekelberg A. Usability and privacy: a study of kazaa P2P file-sharing. In: Proceedings of the Conference on Human Factors in Computing Systems (CHI). Fort Lauderdale (FL); 2003. pp. 137–144.

264. Goodman J, Gray PD, Khammampad K, Brewster SA. Using landmarks to support older people in navigation. In: Proceedings of the International Symposium on Mobile Human-Computer Interaction. Glasgow; 2004. pp. 38–48.

265. Gori M, Witten I. The bubble of web visibility. Commun ACM 2005; 48:115–117.

266. Granovetter M. The strength of weak ties. Am J Sociol 1973; 78:1360–1380.

267. Gravano L, Hatzivassiloglou V, Lichtenstein R. Categorizing web queries according to geographical locality. In: Proceedings of the ACM International Conference on Information and Knowledge Management (CIKM). New Orleans (LO); 2003. pp. 325–333.

268. Green DC. Search engine marketing: why it matters. Bus Inf Rev 2003; 20:195–202.

269. Gregg DG, Scott JE. A typology of complaints about eBay sellers. Commun ACM 2008; 51:69–74.

270. Gruber T. Ontology of folksonomy: a mash-up of apples and oranges. Int J Semant Web Inf Syst 2007; 3:1–11.

271. Gruhl D, Chavet L, Gibson D, Meyer J, Pattanayak P, Tomkins A, Zien J. How to build a WebFountain: an architecture for very large-scale text analytics. IBM Syst J 2004; 43:64–77.

272. Gulli A, Signorini A. The indexable web is more than 11.5 billion pages. In: Poster Proceedings of the International World Wide Web Conference (WWW). Chiba; 2005. pp. 902–903.

273. Gupta T, Garg S, Mahanti A, Carlsson N, Arlitt M. Characterization of FriendFeed A web-based social aggregation service. In: Proceedings of AAAI International Conference on Weblogs and Social Media (ICWSM). San Jose (CA); 2009.

274. Gyöngyi Z, Garcia-Molina H. Link spam alliances. In: Proceedings of the International Conference on Very Large Data Bases (VLDB). Trondheim; 2005. pp. 517–528.

275. Gyöngyi Z, Garcia-Molina H. Spam: It's not just the inboxes anymore. IEEE Comput 2005; 38:28–34.

276. Gyöngyi Z, Garcia-Molina H, Pedersen J. Comabting web spam with TrustRank. In: Proceedings of the International Conference on Very Large Data Bases (VLDB). Toronto; 2004. pp. 576–587.

277. Gyöngyi Z, Koutrika G, Pedersen J, Garcia-Molina H. Questioning Yahoo! Answers. In: Proceedings of the Workshop on Question Answering on the Web (QAWeb). Held in conjunction with the International World Wide Web Conference (WWW). Beijing; 2008.

278. Hagen PR, Manning H, Paul Y. Must search stink? Forrester report. Forrester; 2000.

279. Haigh J. Taking chances: winning with probability. Oxford: Oxford University Press; 2003.

280. Halvey M, Keane MT. Analysis of online video search and sharing. In: Proceedings of the ACM Conference on Hypertext and Hypermedia (HYPERTEXT). Manchester; 2007. pp. 217–226.

281. Hand DJ, Yu K. Idiot's Bayes—Not so stupid after all? Int Stat Rev 2001; 69:385–398.

282. Harary F. Status and contrastatus. Sociometry 1959; 22:23–43.

283. Harper FM, Raban D, Rafaeli S, Konstan JA. Predictors of answer quality in online Q&A sites. In: Proceedings of the Conference on Human Factors in Computing Systems (CHI). Florence; 2008. pp. 865–874.

284. Hartley T, Burgess N. Models of spatial cognition. In: Nadel L, editor. MacMillan Encyclopaedia of cognitive science. London: Nature Publlishing Group; 2002.

285. Harzing AWK, van der Wal R. Google scholar as a new source for citation analysis. Ethics Sci Environ Polit (ESEP) 2008; 8:61–73.

286. Haveliwala TH. Topic-sensitive PageRank: a context-sensitive ranking algorithm for web search. IEEE Trans Knowl Data Eng 2003; 15:784–796.

287. Haveliwala T, Kamvar S, Jeh G. Analytical comparison of approaches to personalizing PageRank. Stanford university technical report. Department of Computer Science, Stanford University: Stanford; 2003. Available at http://dbpubs.stanford.edu:8090/pub/2003-35.

288. Hawking D. Challenges in enterpise search. In: Proceedings of the Australasian Database Conference (ADC). Dunedin; 2004. pp. 15–24.

289. Hawking D, Craswell N, Bailey P, Griffiths K. Measuring search engine quality. Inf Retr 2001; 4:33–59.

290. He B, Patel M, Zhang Z, Chang KC-C. Accessing the deep web. Commun ACM 2007; 50:95–101.

291. Hearst MA. Next generation web search: setting our sites. Bull Tech Comm Data Eng 2000; 23:38–48. Special Issue on Next-Generation Web Search.

292. Hearst MA, Rosner D. Tag clouds: data analysis tool or social signaller? In: Proceedings of the Hawaii International Conference on System Sciences (HICSS). Waikoloa (HI); 2008. p. 160.

293. Heer J, Viégas FB, Wattenberg M. Voyagers and voyeurs: supporting asynchronous collaborative visualization. Commun ACM 2009; 52:87–97.

294. Henzinger MR. Hyperlink analysis for the web. IEEE Internet Comput 2001; 5:45–50.

295. Henzinger MR. Indexing the web: a challenge for supercomputing. In: International Supercomputing Conference. Heidelberg; 2002. Invited talk.

296. Herlocker JL, Konstan JA, Borchers A, Riedl J. Am algorithmic framework for performing collaborative filtering. In: Proceedings of the International Conference on Research and Development in Information Retrieval (SIGIR). Berkeley (CA); 1999. pp. 230–237.

297. Herlocker JL, Konstan JA, Terveen LG, Riedl JT. Evaluating collaborative filtering recommender systems. ACM Trans Inf Syst (TOIS) 2004; 22:5–53.

298. Hernandez EA. War of the mobile browsers. IEEE Pervasive Comput 2009; 8:82–85.

299. Herther NK. Digital natives and immigrants: what brain research tells us. Online Mag 2009; 33:15–21.

300. Heylighen F. Collective intelligence and its implementation on the web: algorithms to develop a collective mental map. Comput Math Organ Theory 1999; 5:253–280.

301. Heymann P, Garcia-Molina H. Contrasting controlled vocabulary and tagging: experts choose the right names to label the wrong things. In: Proceedings of the ACM International Conference on Web Search and Data Mining (WSDM Late Breaking-Results). Barcelona; 2009.

302. Heymann P, Koutrika G, Garcia-Molina H. Can social bookmarking improve web search? In: Proceedings of the ACM International Conference on Web Search and Data Mining (WSDM). Stanford (CA); 2008. pp. 195–206.

303. Heymann P, Ramage D, Garcia-Molina H. Social tag prediction. In: Proceedings of the International Conference on Research and Development in Information Retrieval (SIGIR). Singapore; 2008. pp. 531–538.

304. Hildebrandt W, Katz B, Lin J. Answering definition questions using multiple knowledge sources. In: Proceedings of the Human Language Technology Conference (HLT). Boston (MA); 2004. pp. 49–56.

305. Hinman LM. Searching ethics: the role of search engines in the construction and distribution of knowledge. In: Spink A, Zimmer M, edtiors. Web Search: multidisciplinary perspectives. Berlin: Springer-Verlag; 2008. pp. 67–76.

306. Holland JH. Emergence from chaos to order. Oxford: Oxford University Press; 1998.

307. Holme P, Kim BJ. Growing scale-free networks with tunable clustering. Phys Rev E 2002; 65:026107–0261–4.

308. Horrigan JB. Online shopping. Technical report. Pew Internet & American Life Project, 2008.

309. Hossain T, Morgan J. Plus shipping and handling: revenue (non) equivalence in field experiments on eBay. Adv Econ Anal Policy 2006; 6:Article 3.

310. Howe J. Crowdsourcing: how the power of the crowd is driving the future of business. New York: Random House; 2008.

311. Howe AE, Dreilinger D. Experiences with selecting search engines using metasearch. ACM Trans Inf Syst (TOIS) 1997; 15:195–222.

312. Hu J, Bagga A. Categorizing images in web documents. IEEE Mulitmedia 2004; 11:22–33.

313. Hu M, Liu B. Mining and summarizing customer reviews. In: Proceedings of the ACM SIGKDD International Conference on Knowledge Discovery and Data Mining (KDD). Seatle (WA); 2004. pp. 168–177.

314. Huang S, Shen D, Feng W, Baudin C, Zhang Y. Improving product review search experiences on general search engines. In: Proceedings of the International Conference on Electronic Commerce (ICEC). Taipei; 2009. pp. 107–116.
315. Huberman BA. The laws of the web: patterns in the ecology of information. Cambridge (MA): MIT Press; 2001.
316. Huberman BA, Adamic LA. Growth dynamics of the world wide web. Nature 1999; 401: 131.
317. Huberman BA, Pirolli PLT, Pitkow JE, Lukose RM. Strong regularities in world wide web surfing. Science 1998; 280:95–97.
318. Hughes D, Coulson G, Walkerdine J. Free riding on gnutella revisited: the bell tolls? IEEE Distrib Syst Online 2005; 6.
319. Hussherr F-X, Dréze X. Internet advertising: is anybody watching. J Interact Mark 2003; 17:8–23.
320. Iamnitchi A, Ripeanu M, Foster I. Small-world file-sharing communities. Comput Res Rep 2003; cs.DS/0307036 Available at http://arxiv.org/abs/cs.DC/0307036.
321. Ide E. New experiments in relevance feedback. In: Salton G, editor. The SMART retrieval system—experiments in automatic document processing. Englewood Cliffs (NJ): Prentice Hall; 1971. Chapter 16. pp. 337–354.
322. Immorlica N, Jain K, Mahdian M, Talwar K. Click fraud resistant methods for learning click-through rates. In: Proceedings of the Workshop on Internet and Network Economics (WINE). Hong Kong; 2005. pp. 150–161.
323. Introna L, Nissenbaum H. Defining the web: the politics of search engines. IEEE Comput 2000; 33:54–62.
324. Ishii K. Internet use via mobile phone in Japan. Telecommun Policy 2004; 28:43–58.
325. Jacó P. Savvy searching: Google scholar revisited. Online Inf Rev 2008; 32:102–114.
326. Jain AK, Dubes RC. Algorithms for clustering data. Englewood Cliffs (NJ): Prentice Hall; 1988.
327. Janev V, Vraneč S. Semantic web technologies: ready for adoption? IT Prof 2009; 11:8–16.
328. Jansen BJ. Operators not needed? The impact of query structure on web searching results. In: Proceedings of the International Conference of the Information Resource Management Association. Philadelphia (PA); 2003. pp. 814–817.
329. Jansen BJ, Booth DL, Spink A. Determining the informational, navigational, and transactional intent of Web queries. Inf Process Manage 2008; 44:1251–1266.
330. Jansen BJ, Brown A, Resnick M. Factors relating to the decision to click on a sponsored link. Decis Support Syst 2007; 44:46–59.
331. Jansen BJ, Mullen T. Sponsored search: an overview of the concept, history, and technology. Int J Electron Bus 2008; 6:114–131.
332. Jansen BJ, Spink A. An analysis of web documents retrieved and viewed. In: Proceedings of the International Conference on Internet Computing. Las Vegas (NV); 2003. pp. 65–69.
333. Jansen BJ, Spink A. An analysis of web searching by european AlltheWeb.com users. Inf Process Manage 2005; 41:361–381.
334. Jansen BJ, Spink A. Investigating customer click through behaviour with integrated sponsored and nonsponsored results. Int J Internet Mark Advert 2009; 5:74–94.

335. Jansen BJ, Spink A, Koshman S. Web searcher interaction with the Dogpile.com metasearch engine. J Am Soc Inf Sci Technol (JASIST) 2007; 58:744–755.

336. Jansen BJ, Zhang M, Sobel K, Chowdury A. Twitter power: tweets as electronic word of mouth. J Am Soc Inf Sci Technol (JASIST) 2009; 60:2169–2188.

337. Järvelin K, Kekäläinen J. Cumulated gain-based evaluation of IR techniques. ACM Trans Inf Syst (TOIS) 2002; 20:422–446.

338. Jäschke R, Marinho L, Hotho A, Schmidt-Thieme L, Stumme G. Tag recommendations in social bookmarking systems. AI Commun 2008; 21:231–247.

339. Java A, Song X, Finin T, Tseng B. Why we twitter: an analysis of a microblogging community. In: Goebel R, Siekmann J, Wahlster W, editors. Advances in web mining and web usage analysis. Lecture Notes in Artificial Intelligence (LNAI 5439). Berlin: Springer-Verlag; 2009. pp. 118–138.

340. Jeh G, Widom J. Scaling personalized web search. In: Proceedings of the International World Wide Web Conference (WWW). Budapest; 2003. pp. 271–279.

341. Jepsen TC. Just what is an ontology, anyway? IT Prof 2009; 11:22–27.

342. Jindal A, Crutchfield C, Goel S, Kolluri R, Jain R. The mobile web is structurally different. In: Proceedings of the IEEE Global Internet Symposium. Phoenix (AZ); 2008.

343. Jindal N, Liu B. Mining comparative sentences and relations. In: Proceedings of the National Conference on Artificial Intelligence (AAAI). Boston (MA); 2006.

344. Jing Y, Baluja S. VisualRank: applying PageRank to large-scale image search. IEEE Trans Pattern Anal Mach Intell 2008; 30:1–14.

345. Joachims T. Optimizing search engines using clickthrough data. In: Proceedings of the ACM SIGKDD International Conference on Knowledge Discovery and Data Mining (KDD). Edmonton (AB); 2002. pp. 133–142.

346. Jolliffe IT. Principal component analysis. 2nd ed. Berlin: Springer-Verlag; 2002.

347. Jones M, Buchanan G, Mohd-Nasir N. An evaluation of WebTwig–a site outliner for handheld web access. In: Proceedings of the International Symposium on Handheld and Ubiquitous Computing. Karlsruhe; 1999. pp. 343–345.

348. Jones M, Buchanan G, Thimbleby H. Sorting out searching on small screen devices. In: Proceedings of the International Symposium on Mobile Human-Computer Interaction. Pisa; 2002. pp. 81–94.

349. Jones M, Jain P, Buchanan G, Marsden G. Using a mobile device to vary the pace of search. In: Proceedings of the International Symposium on Mobile Human-Computer Interaction. Udine; 2003. pp. 390–394.

350. Jones S, Jones M, Deo S. Using keyphrases as search result surrogates on small screen devices. Pers Ubiquitous Comput 2004; 8:55–58.

351. Jung JJ, Jo G. Extracting user interests from bookmarks on the web. In: Proceeding of the Pacific-Asia Conference on the Advances in Knowledge Discovery and Data Mining (PAKDD). Seoul; 2003. pp. 203–208.

352. Justiniano C, Frayn CM. The ChessBrain project: a global effort to build the world's largest chess supercomputer. Int Comput Games Assoc (ICGA) J 2003; 26:132–138.

353. Kaasten S, Greenberg S. Integrating back, history and bookmarks in web browsers. In: Proceedings of the Conference on Human Factors in Computing Systems (CHI). Seattle (WA); 2001. pp. 379–380.

354. Kaasten S, Greenberg S, Edwards C. How people recognize previously seen web pages from titles, URLs and thumbnails. In: Proceedings of the BCS Human Computer Interaction Conference. London; 2002. pp. 247–265.

355. Kahn P, Lenk K, Kaczmarek P. Applications of isometric projection for visualizing web sites. Inf Des J 2001; 10:221–228.

356. Kammerer Y, Nairn R, Pirolli P, Chi EH. Signpost from the masses: learning effects in an exploratory social tag search browser. In: Proceedings of the Conference on Human Factors in Computing Systems (CHI). Boston (MA); 2009. 625–634.

357. Kamvar M, Baluja S. Deciphering trends in mobile search. IEEE Comput 2007; 40:58–62.

358. Kamvar M, Baluja S. Query suggestions for mobile search: understanding usage patterns. In: Proceedings of the Conference on Human Factors in Computing Systems (CHI). Florence; 2008. pp. 1013–1016.

359. Kamvar S, Haveliwala T, Manning C, Golub G. Exploiting the block structure of the web for computing PageRank. Stanford University Technical Report. Department of Computer Science, Stanford University; 2003. Available at http://ilpubs.stanford.edu:8090/579.

360. Kamvar M, Kellar M, Patel R, Xu Y. Computers and iphones and mobile phones, oh my!: a logs-based comparison of search users on different devices. In: Proceedings of the International World Wide Web Conference (WWW). Madrid; 2009. pp. 801–810.

361. Karlson AK, Robertson GG, Robbins DC, Czerwinski M, Smith G. FaThumb: a facet-based interface for mobile search. In: Proceedings of the Conference on Human Factors in Computing Systems (CHI). Montreal; 2006. pp. 711–720.

362. Katz B. Annotating the world wide web using natural language. In: Proceedings of the RIAO Conference on Computer Assisted Information Searching on the Internet. Montreal; 1997.

363. Kawai H, Akamine S, Kida K, Matsuda K, Fukushima T. Development and evaluation of the WithAir mobile search engine. In: Poster Proceedings of the International World Wide Web Conference (WWW). Honolulu; 2002.

364. Keenoy K, Levene M. Personalisation of web search. In: Anand SS, Mobasher B, editors. Intelligent techniques for web personalization (ITWP). Lecture Notes in Computer Science (LNCS). Berlin: Springer-Verlag; 2005. pp. 201–228.

365. Kemeny JG, Snell JL. Finite Markov Chains. Princeton (NJ): D. Van Nostrand; 1960.

366. Kemp C, Ramamohanarao K. Long-term learning for web search engines. In: Proceeding of the European Conference on Principles of Data Mining and Knowledge Discovery (PKDD). Helsinki; 2002. pp. 263–274.

367. Kephart JO, Sorkin GB, Chess DM, White SR. Fighting computer viruses. Sci Am 1977; 277:88–93.

368. Kherfi ML, Ziou D, Bernardi A. Image retrieval from the world wide web: issues, techniques, and systems. ACM Comput Surv (CSUR) 2004; 36:35–67.

369. Khopkar Y, Spink A, Giles CL, Shah P, Debnath S. Search engine personalization: an exploratory study. First Monday 2003; 8(7). See http://firstmonday.org.

370. Kim H, Hirtle SC. Spatial metaphors and disorientation in hypertext browsing. Behav Inf Technol 1995; 14:239–250.

371. Kim MW, Kim EJ, Ryu JW. A collaborative recommendation based on neural networks. In: Proceedings of the International Conference on Database Systems for Advanced Applications (DASFAA). Jeju Island; 2004. pp. 425–430.

372. Kim S, Zhang B-T. Genetic mining of html structures for effective web-document retrieval. Appl Intell 2003; 618:243–256.

373. Kimball A, Michels-Slettvet S, Bisciglia C. Cluster computing for web-scale data processing. In: Proceedings of the Technical Symposium on Computer Science Education (SIGCSE). Portland (OR); 2008. pp. 116–120.

374. Kittur A, Chi EH, Suh B. Crowdsourcing user studies with Mechanical Turk. In: Proceedings of the Conference on Human Factors in Computing Systems (CHI). Florence; 2008. pp. 453–456.

375. Kitza W. Inside hypercard. Bonn: Addison-Wessley; 1988.

376. Kleinberg J. Navigation in a small world. Nature 2000; 406: 845.

377. Kleinberg J. Bursty and hierarchical structure in streams. Data Min Knowl Discov 2003; 7:373–397.

378. Kleinberg JM. Authoritative sources in a hyperlinked environment. J ACM 1999; 46:604–632.

379. Kleinfeld JS. Could it be a big world after? The "six degrees of separation myth". Society 2002; 39:61–66.

380. Kohavi R, Parekh R. Ten supplementary analyses to improve e-commerce web sites. In: Proceedings of the WebKDD Workshop: Webmining as a Premise to Effective and Intelligent Web Applications. Held in conjunction with the ACM SIGKDD International Conference on Knowledge Discovery and Data Mining (KDD). Washington (DC); 2003.

381. Kolay S, Dasdan A. The value of socially tagged URLs for a search engine. In: Poster Proceedings of the International World Wide Web Conference (WWW). Madrid; 2009. pp. 1023–1024.

382. Konstan JA, Miller BN, Maltz D, Herlocker JL, Gordon LR, Riedl J. GroupLens: applying collaborative filtering to Usenet news. Commun ACM 1997; 40:77–87.

383. Koren Y. Factorization meets the neighborhood: a multifaceted collaborative filtering model. In: Proceedings of the ACM SIGKDD International Conference on Knowledge Discovery and Data Mining (KDD). Las Vegas (NV); 2008. pp. 426–434.

384. Koren Y. Collaborative filtering with temporal dynamics. In: Proceedings of the ACM SIGKDD International Conference on Knowledge Discovery and Data Mining (KDD). Paris; 2009. pp. 447–456.

385. Kosala R, Blockeel H. Web mining research: a survey. SIGKDD Explor 2000; 2:1–15.

386. Koshman S, Spink A, Jansen BJ. Web searching on the Vivisimo search engine. J Am Soc Inf Sci Technol (JASIST) 2006; 57:1875–1887.

387. Kovacevic M, Diligenti M, Gori M, Milutinovic VM. Recognition of common areas in a web page using visual information: a possible application in a page classification. In: Proceedings of the IEEE International Conference on Data Mining (ICDM). Maebashi City; 2002. pp. 250–257.

388. Krause B, Hotho A, Stumme G. A comparison of social bookmarking with traditional search. In: Proceedings of the European Conference on IR Research (ECIR). Glasgow; 2008. pp. 101–113.

389. Krause B, Schmitz C, Hotho A, Stumme G. The anti-social tagger–detecting spam in social bookmarking systems. In: Proceedings of the International Workshop on Adversarial Information Retrieval on the Web (AIRWeb). Held in conjunction with the International World Wide Web Conference (WWW). Beijing; 2008. pp. 61–68.

390. Krebs V. The social life of routers, applying knowledge of human networks to the design of computer networks. Internet Protoc J 2000; 3:14–25.

391. Krikke J. Graphics applications over the wireless web: Japan sets the pace. IEEE Comput Graph Appl 2001; 21:9–15. Available at www.computer.org/cga/homepage/wwaps.htm.

392. Krishnamurthy B, Gill P, Arlitt M. A few chirps about twitter. In: Proceedings of the workshop on Online Social Networks (WOSN). Seatle (WA); 2008. pp. 19–24.

393. Krishnan V, Raj R. Web spam detection with Anti-Trust Rank. In: Proceedings of the International Workshop on Adversarial Information Retrieval on the Web (AIRWeb). Held in conjunction with the International World Wide Web Conference (WWW). Seatle (WA); 2006. pp. 37–40.

394. Kschischang FR, Frey BJ, Loeliger H-A. Factor graphs and the sum-product algorithm. IEEE Trans Inf Theory 2001; 47:498–519.

395. Kumar R, Novak J, Raghavan P, Tomkins A. On the bursty evolution of Blogspace. In: Proceedings of the International World Wide Web Conference (WWW). Budapest; 2003. pp. 568–576.

396. Kumar R, Raghavan P, Rajagopalan S, Sivakumar D, Tomkins A, Upfal E. The web as a graph. In: Proceedings of the ACM Symposium on Principles of Database Systems. Dallas (TX); 2000. pp. 1–10.

397. Kurhila J, Miettinen M, Nokelailnen P, Terri H. Educo–a collaborative learning environment based on social navigation. In: Proceeding of the International Conference of Adaptive Hypermedia and Adaptive Web-Based Systems (AH). Malaga; 2002. pp. 242–252.

398. Kwok C, Etzioni O, Weld DS. Scaling question answering to the web. ACM Trans Inf Syst (TOIS) 2001; 19:242–262.

399. Labrou Y, Finin TW. Yahoo! as an ontology: using yahoo! categories to describe documents. In: Proceedings of the ACM International Conference on Information and Knowledge Management (CIKM). Kansas City (MI); 1999. pp. 180–187.

400. Laffey D. Paid search: the innovation that changed the web. Bus Horiz 2007; 50:211–218.

401. Lai W-C, Chang E, Cheng K-T. An anatomy of a large-scale image search engine. In: Poster Proceedings of the International World Wide Web Conference (WWW). Honolulu (HI); 2002.

402. Lamping J, Rao R. The hyperbolic browser: a focus+context technique for visualizing large hierarchies. J Vis Lang Comput 1996; 7:33–55.

403. Langville AN, Meyer CD. Fiddling with PageRank. Technical Report CRSC Tech Report CRSC-TR03-34. The Center for Research in Scientific Computation, North Carolina State University; 2003. Available at http://meyer.math.ncsu.edu/Meyer/PS_Files/FiddlingPageRank.pdf.

404. Latora V, Marchiori M. Is the Boston underground a small-world network? Physica A 2002; 314:109–113.

405. Lawrence S, Giles CL. Searching the world wide web. Science 1998; 280:98–100. Available at www.neci.nec.com/lawrence/websize.html.

406. Lawrence S, Giles CL. Accessibility of information on the web. Nature 1999; 400:107–109. Available at www.neci.nec.com/lawrence/websize.html.
407. Lawton G. These are not your father's widgets. IEEE Comput 2007; 40:10–13.
408. Lazar J, Bessiere K, Robinson J, Cepraru I, Shneiderman B. Help! I'm lost: user frustration in web navigation. IT&Soc 2003; 1:18–26. Special issue on web navigation.
409. Lazarinis F, Ferro JV, Tait J. Improving non-english web searching. SIGIR Forum 2007; 41:72–76.
410. Lazarinis F, Vilares J, Tait J, Efthimiadis EN. Current research issues and trends in non-English web searching. Inf Retr 2009; 12:230–250.
411. Lee JH. Analyses of multiple evidence combination. In: Proceedings of the International Conference on Research and Development in Information Retrieval (SIGIR). Philadelphia (PA); 1997. pp. 267–276.
412. Lee H-C. Metasearch via the co-citation graph. In: Proceedings of the International Conference on Internet Computing. Las Vegas (NV); 2003. pp. 24–30.
413. Leibowitz N, Ripeanu M, Wiezbicki A. Deconstructing the Kazaa network. In: Proceedings of the IEEE Workshop on Internet Applications. San Jose (CA); 2003. pp. 112–120.
414. Lempel R, Moran S. SALSA: the stochastic approach for link-structure analysis. ACM Trans Inf Syst (TOIS) 2001; 19:131–160.
415. Lempel R, Moran S. Predictive caching and prefetching of query results in search engines. In: Proceedings of the International World Wide Web Conference (WWW). Budapest; 2003. pp. 19–28.
416. Lempel R, Soffer A. PicASHOW: pictorial authority search by hyperlinks on the web. ACM Trans Inf Syst (TOIS) 2003; 20:1–24.
417. Levene M, Borges J, Loizou G. Zipf's law for web surfers. Knowl Inf Syst 2001; 3:120–129.
418. Levene M, Fenner TI, Loizou G, Wheeldon R. A stochastic model for the evolution of the Web. Comput Netw 2002; 39:277–287.
419. Levene M, Loizou G. A correpondence between variable relations and three-valued propositional logic. Int J Comput Math 1995; 55:29–38.
420. Levene M, Loizou G. A guided tour of relational databases and beyond. London: Springer-Verlag; 1999.
421. Levene M, Loizou G. Web interaction and the navigation problem in hypertext. In: Kent A, Williams JG, Hall CM, editors. Encyclopedia of microcomputers. New York: Marcel Dekker; 2002. pp. 381–398.
422. Levene M, Loizou G. Computing the entropy of user navigation in the web. Int J Inf Technol Decis Making 2003; 2:459–476.
423. Levene M, Wheeldon R. Navigating the world wide web. In: Levene M, Poulovassilis A, editors. Web dynamics. Berlin: Springer-Verlag; 2004. pp. 117–151.
424. Lew MS. Next-generation web searches for visual content. IEEE Comput 2000; 33:46–53.
425. Lewis JR, Commarford PM. Developing a voice-spelling alphabet for PDAs. IBM Syst J 2003; 42:624–638.
426. Li W. Zipf's law everywhere. Glottometrics 2003; 5:14–21.
427. Li J, Wang JZ. Real-time computerized annotation of pictures. IEEE Trans Pattern Anal Mach Intell 2008; 30:985–1002.

428. Liang J, Kumar R, Ross KW. Understanding Kazaa. Technical report. Brooklyn (NY): Department of Computer and Information Science, Polytechnic University; 2004.

429. Lin J. An exploration of the principles underlying redundancy-based factoid question answering. ACM Trans Inf Syst (TOIS) 2007; 25:1–6.

430. Lin W, Alvarez SA, Ruiz C. Efficient adaptive-support association rule mining for recommender systems. Data Min Knowl Discov 2002; 6:85–105.

431. Lin W-H, Jin R, Hauptmann AG. Web image retrieval re-ranking with relevance model. In: Proceedings of the International Conference on Web Intelligence (WI). Halifax; 2003. pp. 242–248.

432. Linden G, Meek C, Chickering M. The pollution effect: optimizing keyword auctions by favoring relevant advertising. In: Proceedings of the Workshop Ad Auctions. Stanford (CA); 2009.

433. Linden G, Smith B, York J. Amazon.com recommendations: item-to-item collaborative filtering. IEEE Internet Comput 2003; 7:76–80.

434. Lita LV, Hunt WA, Nyberg E. Resource analysis for question answering. In: Proceedings of the Annual Meeting of the Association for Computational Linguistics (ACL). Barcelona; 2004. pp. 162–165.

435. Liu B. Web data mining: exploring hyperlinks, content and usage data. Berlin: Springer-Verlag; 2007.

436. Liu T-Y. Learning to rank for information retrieval. Found Trends Inf Retr 2009; 3:225–231.

437. Liu Y, Gao B, Liu T-Y, Zhang Y, Ma Z, He S, Li H. BrowseRank: letting web users vote for page importance. In: Proceedings of the International Conference on Research and Development in Information Retrieval (SIGIR). Singapore; 2008. pp. 451–458.

438. Lorigo L, Haridasan M, Brynjarsdóttir H, Xia L, Joachims T, Gay G, Granka L, Pellacini F, Pan B. Eye tracking and online search: lessons learned and challenges ahead. J Am Soc Inf Sci Technol (JASIST) 2008; 59:1041–1052.

439. Losee RM. Term dependence: a basis for luhn and zipf models. J Am Soc Inf Sci Technol (JASIST) 2001; 52:1019–1025.

440. Lowe DG. Distinctive image features from scale-invariant keypoints. Int J Comput Vis 2008; 60:91–110.

441. Lu C-T, Subramanya SM, Wu SHY. Performance evaluation of desktop search engines. In: Proceedings of IEEE International Conference on Information Reuse and Integration. Las Vegas (NV); 2007. pp. 110–115.

442. Luckin R, Clark W, Graber R, Logan K, Mee A, Oliver M. Do web 2.0 tools really open the door to learning? Practices, perceptions and profiles of 11-16 year old learners. Learn Media Technol 2009; 34:87–104.

443. Lucking-Reiley D, Bryanz D, Prasad N, Reeves D. Pennies from eBay: the determinants of price in online auctions. J Ind Econ 2007; 55:223–233.

444. Luhn HP. The automatic creation of literature abstracts. IBM J Res Dev 1958; 2:158–165.

445. Ma H, Chandrasekar R, Quirk C. Page hunt: improving search engines using human computation games. In: Proceedings of the International Conference on Research and Development in Information Retrieval (SIGIR). Boston (MA); 2009. pp. 746–747.

446. MacKenzie IS. KSPC (keystrokes per character) as a characteristic of text entry techniques. In: Proceedings of the International Symposium on Mobile Human-Computer Interaction. Pisa; 2002. pp. 195–210.

447. MacKenzie IS, Kober H, Smith D, Jones T, Skepner Eugene. LetterWise: prefix-based disambiguation for mobile text input. In: Proceedings of the ACM Symposium on User Interface Software and Technology (UIST). Orlando (FL); 2001. pp. 111–120.

448. Mahdian M, Tomak K. Pay-per-action model for online advertising. Int J Electron Commer 2008; 13:113–128.

449. Makridakis SG, Wheelwright SC, Hyndman RJ, editors. Forecating: methods and applications. 3rd ed. New York: John Wiley & Sons, Inc.; 1998.

450. Mango T, Sable C. A comparison of signal-based music recommendation to genre labels, collaborative filtering, musicological analysis, human recommendation, and random baseline. In: Proceedings of the International Conference on Music Information Retrieval (ISMIR). Philadelphia (PA); 2008. pp. 161–166.

451. Mani I, Maybury MT, editors. Advances in automatic text summarization. Cambridge (MA): MIT Press; 1999.

452. Manku GS, Naor M, Wieder U. Know thy neighbor's neighbor: the power of lookahead in randomized P2P networks. In: Proceedings of the ACM symposium on the Theory of Computing (STOC). Chicago (IL); 2004. pp. 54–63.

453. Manning CD, Raghavan P, Schütze H. Introduction to information retrieval. Cambridge: Cambridge University Press; 2008.

454. Markowitz A, Brinkhoff T, Seeger B. Geographic information retrieval. In: Proceedings of the International Workshop on Web Dynamics. Held in conjunction with the International World Wide Web Conference (WWW). New York; 2004. Available at www.dcs.bbk.ac.uk/webdyn3.

455. Marmanis H, Babenko D. Algorithms of the intelligent web. Greenwhich (CT): Manning Publications; 2009.

456. Mat-Hassan M, Levene M. Can navigational assistance improve search experience: a user study. First Monday 2001; 6(9). See http://firstmonday.org.

457. Mat-Hassan M, Levene M. Associating search and navigation behaviour through log analysis. J Am Soc Inf Sci Technol (JASIST) 2005; 56:913–934.

458. Mathieu F, Bouklit M. The effect of the back button in a random walk: application for PageRank. In: Poster Proceedings of the International World Wide Web Conference (WWW). New York; 2004. pp. 370–371.

459. May P. Mobile commerce: opportunities, applications, and technologies of wireles business (Breakthroughs in Application Development). Cambridge: Cambridge University Press; 2001.

460. Maymounkov P, Maziéres D. Kademlia: a peer-to-peer information system based on the XOR metric. In: Proceedings of the Internation Workshop on Peer-to-Peer Systems (IPTPS). Cambridge (MA); 2002. pp. 53–65.

461. McCallum A. Information extraction: distilling structured data from unstructured tex. ACM Queue 2005; 3:48–57.

462. McEneaney JE. Graphic and numerical methods to assess navigation in hypertext. Int J Hum Comput Stud 2001; 55:761–786.

463. Mehta A, Saberi A, Vazirani U, Vazirani V. Adwords and generalized online matching. J ACM 2007; 54:1–22.

464. Meiss M, Menczer F, Fortunato S, Flammini A, Vespignani A. Ranking web sites with real user traffic. In: Proceedings of the ACM International Conference on Web Search and Data Mining (WSDM). Stanford (CA); 2008. pp. 65–75.

465. Melville P, Mooney RJ, Nagarajan R. Content-boosted collaborative filtering for improving recommendations. In: Proceedings of the National Conference on Artificial Intelligence (AAAI). Edmonton; 2002. pp. 187–192.

466. Meng W, Yu C, Liu K-L. Building efficient and effective metasearch engines. ACM Comput Surv (CSUR) 2002; 34:48–89.

467. Merton RK. The Matthew effect in science: the reward and communication systems of science are considered. Science 1968; 159:53–63.

468. Metwally A, Agrawal D, El Abbadi A, Zheng Q. On hit inflation techniques and detection in streams of web advertising networks. In: Proceedings of the International Conference on Distributed Computing Systems (ICDCS). Toronto; 2007. p. 52.

469. Metwally A, Emekçi F, Agrawal D, El Abbadi A. SLEUTH: single-publisher attack detection using correlation hunting. In: Proceedings of the International Conference on Very Large Data Bases (VLDB). Auckland; 2008. pp. 1217–1228.

470. Milic-Frayling N, Sommerer R, Rodden K, Blackwell AF. SmartView and Search-Mobil: providing overview and detail in handheld browsing. In: Proceedings of the International Workshop on Mobile and Ubiquitous Information Access. Udine; 2003. pp. 158–171.

471. Miller BN, Konstan JA, Riedl J. PocketLens: toward a personal recommender system. ACM Trans Inf Syst (TOIS) 2004; 22:437–476.

472. Mitchell M. An introduction to genetic algorithms. Cambridge (MA): MIT Press; 1998.

473. Mitchell T. Machine learning. New York: McGraw-Hill; 1997.

474. Mitra M, Singhal A, Buckley C. Improving automatic query expansion. In: Proceedings of the International Conference on Research and Development in Information Retrieval (SIGIR). Melbourne; 1998. pp. 206–214.

475. Mitzenmacher M. A brief history of generative models for power law and lognormal distributions. Internet Math 2003; 1:226–251.

476. Miyahara K, Pazzani MJ. Collaborative filtering with the simple Bayesian classifier. In: Proceedings of the Pacific Rim International Conference on Artificial Intelligence (PRICAI). Melbourne; 2000. pp. 679–689.

477. Mobasher B. Web usage mining and personalization. In: Singh MP, editor. Practical handbook of internet computing. Baton Rouge (FL): Chapman Hall & CRC Press; 2004. Chapter 16.

478. Modis T. From my perspective: strengths and weaknesses of S-curves. Technol Forecast Soc Change 2007; 74:886–872.

479. Montague M, Aslam AJ. Condorcet fusion for improved retrieval. In: Proceedings of the International Conference on Research and Development in Information Retrieval (SIGIR). McLean (VA); 2002. pp. 538–548.

480. Morris MR. A survey of collaborative web search practices. In: Proceedings of the Conference on Human Factors in Computing Systems (CHI). Florence; 2008. pp. 1657–1660.

481. Morris MR, Horvitz E. SearchTogether: an interface for collaborative web search. In: Proceedings of the ACM Symposium on User Interface Software and Technology (UIST). Newport (RI); 2007. pp. 3–12.

482. Mortensen T, Walker J. Blogging thoughts: personal publication as an online research tool. In: Morrison A, editor. Researching ICTs in Context. InterMedia Report 3/2002. University of Oslo; 2002. pp. 249–279.

483. Mossa S, Barthélémy M, Stanley HE, Amaral LAN. Truncation power law behavior in "scale-free" network models due to information filtering. Phys Rev Lett 2002; 88:138701-1-4.

484. Mukherjea S, Foley JD. Showing the context of nodes in the world-wide web. In: Proceedings of the Conference on Human Factors in Computing Systems (CHI). Denver (CO); 1995. pp. 326–327.

485. Mukherjee R, Mao J. Enterprise search: tough stuff. ACM Queue 2004; 2:37–46.

486. Müller H, Müller W, Marchand-Maillet S, Pun T, Squire D. Strategies for positive and negative relevance feedback in image retrieval. In: Proceedings of the International Conference on Pattern Recognition (ICPR). Barcelona; 2000. pp. 5043–5046.

487. Murray BH, Moore A. Sizing the internet. White paper. Cyveillance; 2000.

488. Murray GC, Teevan J. Query log analysis: social and technological challenges. SIGIR Forum 2007; 41:112–120.

489. Najork M. Comparing the effectiveness of HITS and SALSA. In: Proceedings of the ACM International Conference on Information and Knowledge Management (CIKM). Lisbon; 2007. pp. 157–164.

490. Najork M, Craswell N. Efficient and effective link analysis with precomputed SALSA maps. In: Proceedings of the ACM International Conference on Information and Knowledge Management (CIKM). Napa Valley (CA); 2008. pp. 53–62.

491. Najork M, Heydon A. High-performance web crawling. In: Abello J, Pardalos PM, Resende MGC, editors. Handbook of massive data sets. Norwell (MA): Kluwer Academic Publishers; 2002. pp. 25–45.

492. Najork M, Wiener JL. Breadth-first crawling yields high-quality pages. In: Proceedings of the International World Wide Web Conference (WWW). Hong Kong; 2001. pp. 114–118.

493. Nam KK, Ackerman MS, Adamic LA. Questions in, knowledge in? A study of Naver's question answering community. In: Proceedings of the Conference on Human Factors in Computing Systems (CHI). Boston (MA); 2009. pp. 779–788.

494. Namazi A, Schadschneider A. Statistical properties of online auctions. Int J Mod Phys C 2006; 17:1485–1493.

495. Nelson T. Xanalogical structure, needed now more than ever: parallel documents, deep links to content, deep versioning, and deep re-use. ACM Comput Surv (CSUR) 1999; 31: 32. Article No.33.

496. Newman MEJ. Models of the small world. J Stat Phys 2000; 101:819–841.

497. Newman MEJ. The structure of scientific collaboration networks. Proc Natl Acad Sci U S A 2001; 98:404–409.

498. Newman MEJ. Ego-centered networks and the ripple effect. Soc Netw 2003; 25:83–95.

499. Newman MEJ. The structure and function of complex networks. SIAM Rev 2003; 45:167–256.

500. Newman M, Barabási A-L, Watts DJ. The structure and dynamics of networks. Princeton (NJ): Princeton University Press; 2006.

501. Niederst J. Wed design in a nutshell: a desktop quick reference. 2nd ed. Sebastopol (CA): O'Reilly; 2001.

502. Nielsen J. The art of navigating through hypertext. Commun ACM 1990; 33:296–310.

503. Nielsen J. Hypertext and hypermedia. San Diego (CA): Academic Press; 1990.

504. Nielsen J. Designing web usability: the practice of simplicity. Indianapolis (IN): New Riders Publishing; 2000.

505. Nigrini MJ. A taxpayer compliance application of Benford's law. J Am Tax Assoc 1996; 18:72–91.

506. Notess GR. On the net, bookmarklets, favelets, and keymarks: shortcuts galore. Online Mag 2003; 27:38–40. Available at www.infotoday.com/online/jul03/OnTheNet.shtml.

507. Notess GR. On the net, toolbars: trash or treasures? Online Mag 2004; 28:41–43. Available at www.infotoday.com/online/jan04/OnTheNet.shtml.

508. Ntoulas A, Najork M, Manasse M, Fetterly D. Detecting spam web pages through content analysis. In: Proceedings of the International World Wide Web Conference (WWW). Edinburgh; 2006. pp. 83–92.

509. Nyce JM, Kahn P, editors. From Memex to hypertext: Vannevar Bush and the mind's machine. San Diego (CA): Academic Press; 1991.

510. Obendorf H, Weinreich H. Comparing link marker visualization techniques–changes in reading behavior. In: Proceedings of the International World Wide Web Conference (WWW). Budapest; 2003. pp. 736–745.

511. O'Hara K. Understanding geocaching practices and motivations. In: Proceedings of the Conference on Human Factors in Computing Systems (CHI). Florence; 2008. pp. 1177–1186.

512. O'Neill ET, Lavoie BF, Bennett R. Trends in the evolution of the public web 1998–2002. D-Lib Mag 2003; 9. Available at www.dlib.org/dlib/april03/lavoie/04lavoie.html.

513. Orchard L. Hacking RSS and atom (ExtremeTech). Chichester: John Wiley & Sons, Ltd.; 2005.

514. O'Reilly T. What is web 2.0: Design patterns and business models for the next generation of software. 2005. Available at www.oreillynet.com/pub/a/oreilly/tim/news/2005/09/30/what-is-web-20.html.

515. Oren A, editor. Peer-to-peer computing: harnessing the power of disruptive technologies. Sebattopol (CA): O'Reilly; 2001.

516. Oren T. Memex: getting back on the trail. In: Nyce JM, Kahn P, editors. From Memex to Hypertext: Vannevar Bush and the mind's machine. San Diego (CA): Academic Press; 1991. pp. 319–338.

517. Osinski S. Improving quality of search results clustering with approximate matrix factorisations. In: Proceedings of the European Conference on IR Research (ECIR). London; 2006. pp. 167–178.

518. Overell SE, Sigurbjörnsson B, van Zwol R. Classifying tags using open content resources. In: Proceedings of the ACM International Conference on Web Search and Data Mining (WSDM). Barcelona; 2009. pp. 64–73.

519. Owens L, Brown M, Poore K, Nicolson N. The Forrester Wave: enterprise search, Q2 2008. Technical report. Forrester; 2008.

520. Ozmutlu S, Spink A, Ozmutlu HC. A day in the life of web searching: an exploratory study. Inf Process Manage 2004; 40:319–345.

521. Oztekin BU, Ertöz L, Kumar V, Srivastava J. Usage aware PageRank. In: Poster Proceedings of the International World Wide Web Conference (WWW). Budapest; 2003.
522. Page L, Brin S, Motwani R, Winograd T. The PageRank citation ranking: bringing order to the web. Stanford digital library technologies project technical report, Department of Computer Science, Stanford University. 1998. Available at http://ilpubs.stanford.edu:8090/422.
523. Pagendarm M, Schaumburg H. Why are users banner-blind? The impact of navigation style on the perception of web banners. J Digit Inf 2001; 2(1). See http://journals.tdl.org/jodi.
524. Pandey S, Roy S, Olston C, Cho J, Chakrabarti S. Shuffling a stacked deck: the case for partially randomized ranking of search engine results. In: Proceedings of the International Conference on Very Large Data Bases (VLDB). Trondheim; 2005. pp. 781–792.
525. Pandit S, Olsten C. Navigation-aided retrieval. In: Proceedings of the International World Wide Web Conference (WWW). Banff; 2007. pp. 391–400.
526. Pang B, Lee L. Opinion mining and sentiment analysis. Found Trends Inf Retr 2008; 2:1–135.
527. Pang B, Lee L, Vaithyanathan S. Thumbs up? Sentiment classification using machine learning techniques. In: Proceedings of the Conference on Empirical Methods in Natural Language Processing (EMNLP). Philadelphia (PA); 2002. pp. 79–86.
528. Pant G, Srinivasan P, Menczer F. Crawling the web. In: Levene M, Poulovassilis A, editors. Web dynamics. Berlin: Springer-Verlag; 2004. pp. 153–177.
529. Papadogkonas D, Roussos G, Levene M. Analysis, ranking and prediction in pervasive computing trails. In: Proceedings of the International Conference on Intelligent Environments (IET). Seattle (WA); 2008. pp. 1–8.
530. Park S. Analysis of characteristics and trends of Web queries submitted to NAVER, a major Korean search engine. Libr Inf Sci Res 2009; 31:126–133.
531. Park S, Lee JH, Bae HJ. End user searching: a Web log analysis of NAVER, a major Korean search engine. Libr Inf Sci Res 2005; 27:203–221.
532. Pastor-Satorras R, Vespognani A. Epidemic spreading in scale-free networks. Phys Rev Lett 2001; 86:3200–3203.
533. Pastor-Satorras R, Vespognani A. Immunisation of complex networks. Phys Rev E 2001; 65:036104–1–4.
534. Pastor-Satorras R, Vespognani A. Evolution and structure of the Internet: a statistical physics approach. Cambridge: Cambridge University Press; 2004.
535. Patel N, Clawson J, Starner T. A model of two-thumb chording on a phone keypad. In: Proceedings of the Conference on Human-Computer Interaction with Mobile Devices and Services (MobileHCI). Bonn; 2009.
536. Paterek A. Improving regularized singular value decomposition for collaborative filtering. In: Proceedings of the KDD Cup and Workshop 2007. San Jose (CA); 2007. pp. 39–42.
537. Pavlovych A, Stuerzlinger W. Less-Tap: a fast and easy-to-learn text input technique for phones. In: Proceedings of the Graphics Interface Conference. Halifax, Nova Scotia; 2003. pp. 97–104.
538. Pennock DM, Sami R. Computational aspects of prediction markets. In: Nisan N, Roughgarden T, Tardos E, Vazirani VV, editors. Algorithmic game theory. Cambridge: Cambridge University Press; 2007. pp. 651–675.

539. Perkowitz M, Etzioni O. Towards adaptive web sites: conceptual framework and case study. Artif Intell 2000; 118:245–275.
540. Perkowitz M, Philipose M, Fishkin KP, Patterson DJ. Mining models of human activities from the web. In: Proceedings of the International World Wide Web Conference (WWW). New York; 2004. pp. 573–582.
541. Peterson D, Levene M. Trail records and navigational learning. Lond Rev Educ 2003; 1:207–216.
542. Pitkow JE, Schütze H, Cass TA, Cooley R, Turnbull D, Edmonds A, Adar E, Breuel TM. Personalized search. Commun ACM 2002; 45:50–55.
543. Polikar R. Ensemble based systems in decision making. IEEE Circuits Syst Mag 2006; 6:21–45.
544. Powers S. Practical RDF, Sebastopol (CA): O'Reilly; 2003.
545. Pringle G, Allison L, Dowe DL. What is a tall poppy among web pages? Comput Netw ISDN Syst 1998; 30:369–377.
546. Provos N, Rajab MA, Mavrommatis P. Cybercrime 2.0: when the cloud turns dark. ACM Queue 2009; 7:46–53.
547. Qi X, Davison BD. Web page classification: features and algorithms. ACM Comput Surv (CSUR) 2009; 41: 12:1–12.
548. Quan DA, Karger R. How to make a semantic web browser. In: Proceedings of the International World Wide Web Conference (WWW). New York; 2004. pp. 255–265.
549. Raghavan P, Kumar R, Rajagopalan S, Tomkins A. The web and social networks. IEEE Comput 2002; 35:32–36.
550. Radovanović M, Ivanović M. CatS: a classification-powered meta-search engine. Volume 23, Advances in Web Intelligence and Data Mining, Studies in Computional Intelligence. Berlin: Springer-Verlag; 2006. pp. 191–200.
551. Raento M, Oulasvirta A, Eagle N. Smartphones: an emerging tool for social scientists. Sociol Methods Res 2009; 37:426–454.
552. Rainie L. Tagging. Technical report. Pew Internet & American Life Project. 2007.
553. Rainie L, Tancer B. A profile of Wikipedia users. Technical report. Pew Internet & American Life Project. 2007.
554. Rajaraman A. Kosmix: exploring the deep web using taxonomies and categorization. Bull Tech Comm Data Eng 2009; 32:12–19.
555. Ramage D, Heymann P, Manning CD, Garcia-Molina H. Clustering the tagged web. In: Proceedings of the ACM International Conference on Web Search and Data Mining (WSDM). Barcelona; 2009. pp. 54–63.
556. Randall KH, Stata R, Wiener JL, Wickremesinghe R. The link databases:fast access to graphs of the web. In: Proceedings of the Data Compression Conference (DCC). Snowbird, Utah; 2002. pp. 122–131.
557. Raper J, Gartner G, Karimi H, Rizos C. Applications of location-based services: a selected review. J Location Based Serv 2007; 1:89–111.
558. Rappoport A. Search query spellchecking. In: Proceedings of the Workshop on Best Practices and Future Visions for Search User Interfaces. Held in conjunction with the Conference on Human Factors in Computing (CHI). Fort Lauderdale (FL); 2003.
559. Rattenbury T, Naaman M. Methods for extracting place semantics from Flickr tags. ACM Trans Web 2009; 3:1–1.
560. Read K, Maurer F. Developing mobile wireless application. IEEE Internet Comput 2003; 7:81–86.

561. Reed RD, Marks RJ II. Neural smithing: supervised learning in feedforward artificial neural networks. Cambridge (MA): MIT Press; 1999.

562. Renda ME, Straccia U. Web metasearch: Rank vs. score based rank aggregation methods. In: Proceedings of the ACM Symposium on Applied Computing (SAC). Melbourne (FL); 2003. pp. 841–846.

563. Resnick P, Zeckhauser R, Swanson J, Lockwood K. The value of reputation on eBay: a controlled experiment. Exp Econ 2006; 9:79–101.

564. Richardon M, Domingos P. Combining link and content information in web search. In: Levene M, Poulovassilis A, editors. Web dynamics. Berlin: Springer-Verlag; 2004. pp. 179–193.

565. Richardson M. Learning about the world through long-term query logs. ACM Trans Web 2007; 2:1–21.

566. Richardson M, Dominowska E, Rango R. Predicting clicks: estimating the click-through rate for new ads. In: Proceedings of the International World Wide Web Conference (WWW). Banff; 2007. pp. 521–529.

567. Richardson M, Prakash A, Brill E. Beyond PageRank: machine learning for static ranking. In: Proceedings of the International World Wide Web Conference (WWW). Edinburgh; 2006. pp. 707–715.

568. Riedl J, Konstan J. Word of Mouse: the marketing power of collaborative filtering. New York: Warner Books; 2002.

569. Ripeanu M, Iamnitchi A, Foster I. Mapping the Gnutella network. IEEE Internet Comput 2002; 6:50–57.

570. Rissanen J. Survey of research towards robust peer-to-peer networks: search methods. Comput Netw 2006; 50:3485–3521.

571. Rivadeneira W, Bederson B. A study of search result clustering interfaces: comparing textual and zoomable user interfaces. Technical Report HCIL-2003-36, CS-TR-4682, Human-Computer Interaction Lab, University of Maryland. 2003. Available at http://hcil.cs.umd.edu/trs/2003-36/2003-36.pdf.

572. Rivlin E, Botafogo R, Shneiderman B. Navigating in hyperspace: designing a structure-based toolbox. Commun ACM 1994; 37:87–96.

573. Rocchio JJ. Relevance feedback information retrieval. In: Salton G, editors. The SMART retrieval system–experiments in automatic document processing. Englewood Cliffs (NJ): Prentice Hall; 1971. Chapter 14. pp. 313–323.

574. Rodzvilla J, editor. We've got blog: how weblogs are changing our culture. Cambridge (MA); 2002.

575. Rokach L, Maimon O. Volume 69, Data mining with decision trees: theory and applications, Machine Learning Perception and Artificial Intelligence. Singapore: World Scientific; 2008.

576. Rose DE, Levinson D. Understanding user goals in web search. In: Proceedings of the International World Wide Web Conference (WWW). New York; 2004. pp. 13–19.

577. Ross SM. Stochastic processes. 2nd ed. New York: John Wiley & Sons, Inc.; 1996.

578. Roth AE, Ockenfels A. Last-minute bidding and the rules for ending second-price auctions: evidence from eBay and Amazon auctions on the internet. Am Econ Rev 2002; 92:1093–1103.

579. Roto V. Search on mobile phones. J Am Soc Inf Sci Technol (JASIST) 2006; 57:834–837.

580. Rui Y, Huang TS, Chang S-F. Image retrieval: current techniques, promising directions, and open issues. J Vis Commun Image Represent 1999; 10:39–62.

581. Ruvini J-D. Adapting to the user's internet strategy on small devices. In: Proceeding of the International Conference on Intelligent User Interfaces (IUI). Miami (FL); 2003. pp. 284–286.

582. Ryabko BY, Topsoe F. On asymptotically optimal methods of prediction and adaptive coding for Markov sources. J Complex 2002; 18:224–241.

583. Salton G, McGill MJ. Introduction to modern information retrieval. New York: McGraw-Hill; 1983.

584. Samuel AL. Some studies in machine learning using the game of checkers. IBM J Res Dev 1959; 3:210–229. Available at www.research.ibm.com/journal/rd/441/samuel.pdf.

585. Sanderson M, Kohler J. Analysing geographic queries. In: Proceedings of the Workshop on Geographic information Retrieval. Held in conjunction with the International Conference on Research and Development in Information Retrieval (SIGIR). Sheffield; 2004. Available at www.geo.unizh.ch/rsp/gir.

586. Santini S, Jain R. Similarity queries in image databases. In: Proceedings of the Conference on Computer Vision and Pattern Recognition (CVPR). San Francisco (CA); 1996. pp. 646–651.

587. Sarawagi S. Information extraction. Foundations and trends in information retrieval 2007; 1:261–337.

588. Saroiu S, Gummadi S, Gribble SD. Measuring and analyzing the characteristics of Napster and Gnutella hosts. Multimedia Syst 2003; 9:170–184.

589. Sarshar N, Boykin PO, Roychowdhury V. Scalable percolation search in power law networks. Condens Matter Arch 2004, cond-mat/0406152, June Available at http://arxiv.org/abs/cond-mat/0406152.

590. Sarwar B, Karyis G, Konstan J, Riedl J. Analysis of recommendation algorithms for e-commerce. In: Proceedings of the ACM Conference on Electronic Commerce (EC). Minneapolis (MN); 2000. pp. 158–167.

591. Sarwar B, Karypis G, Konstan J, Riedl J. Item-based collaborative filtering recommendation algorithms. In: Proceedings of the International World Wide Web Conference (WWW). Hong Kong; 2001. pp. 285–295.

592. Schaale A, Wulf-Mathies C, Lieberman-Schmidt S. A new approach to relevancy in internet searching—the "Vox Populi Algorithm". The Computing Research Repository 2003, cs.DS/0308039, Available at http://arxiv.org/abs/cs.DS/0308039.

593. Schafer JB, Konstan JA, Riedl J. E-commerce recommendation applications. Data Min Knowl Discov 2001; 5:115–153.

594. Schechter S, Krishnan M, Smith MD. Using path profiles to predict HTTP requests. Comput Netw ISDN Syst 1998; 30:457–467.

595. Schonfeld U, Shivakumar N. Sitemaps: above and beyond the crawl of duty. In: Proceedings of the International World Wide Web Conference (WWW). Madrid; 2009. pp. 991–1000.

596. Schrammel J, Leitner M, Tscheligi M. Semantically structured tag clouds: an empirical evaluation of clustered presentation approaches. In: Proceedings of the Conference on Human Factors in Computing Systems (CHI). Boston (MA); 2009. pp. 2037–2040.

597. Scott J. Social network analysis: a handbook. 2nd ed. London: Sage Publications; 2000.

598. Sculley D, Malkin R, Basu S, Bayardo RJ. Predicting bounce rates in sponsored search advertisements. In: Proceedings of the ACM SIGKDD International Conference on Knowledge Discovery and Data Mining (KDD). Paris; 2009. pp. 1325–1334.

599. Segaran T. Programming collective intelligence. Sebastopol (CA): O'Reilly; 2007.

600. Segaran T, Evans C, Taylor J. Programming the semantic web. Sebastopol (CA): O'Reilly; 2009.

601. Selberg E, Etzioni O. The Metacrawler architecture for resource aggregation on the web. IEEE Exp 1997; 12:11–14.

602. Sellen AJ, Murphy R. The future of the mobile internet: lessons from looking at web use. Technical Report HPL-2002-230, Information Infrastructure Laboratory, HP Laboratories, Bristol; 2002. Available at www.hpl.hp.com/techreports/2002/HPL-2002-230.html.

603. Shannon CE. A mathematical theory of communication. Bell Syst Tech J 1948; 27:379–423, 623–656.

604. Shardanand U, Maes P. Social information filtering algorithms for automating "word of mouth". In: Proceedings of the Conference on Human Factors in Computing Systems (CHI). Denver (CO); 1995. pp. 210–217.

605. Sharon T, Lieberman H, Selker T. A zero-input interface for leveraging group experience in web browsing. In: Proceeding of the International Conference on Intelligent User Interfaces (IUI). Miami (FL); 2003. pp. 290–292.

606. Shen D, Chen Z, Yang Q, Zeng H-J, Zhang B, Lu Y, Ma W-Y. Web-page classification through summarization. In: Proceedings of the International Conference on Research and Development in Information Retrieval (SIGIR). Sheffield; 2004. pp. 242–249.

607. Shermen C, Price G. The invisible web: uncovering information sources search engines can't see. Medford (NJ): CyberAge Books; 2001.

608. Silverstein C, Henzinger MR, Marais H, Moricz M. Analysis of a very large web search engine query log. SIGIR Forum 1999; 33:6–12.

609. Simon HA. On a class of skew distribution functions. Biometrika 1955; 42:425–440.

610. Simonsohn U, Ariely D. When rational sellers face nonrational buyers: evidence from herding on eBay. Manage Sci 2008; 54:1624–1637.

611. Small HG. Co-citation in the scientific literature: a new measure of the relationship between two documents. J Am Soc Inf Sci 1973; 24:265–269.

612. Small GW, Moody TD, Siddarth P, Bookheimer SY. Your brain on Google: patterns of cerebral activation during internet searching. Am J Geriatr Psychiatry 2009; 17:116–126.

613. Small G, Vorgan G iBrain: surviving the technological alteration of the modern mind. New York: HarperCollins; 2008.

614. Smith RD. Instant messaging as a scale-free network. Condens Matter Arch 2002, cond-mat/0206378, Available at http://arxiv.org/abs/cond-mat/0206378.

615. Smyth B, Cotter P. MP^3—mobile portals, profiles and personalisation. In: Levene M, Poulovassilis A, editors. Web dynamics. Berlin: Springer-Verlag; 2004. pp. 411–433.

616. Soboroff I. Do TREC web collections look like the web? SIGIR Forum Fall 2002; 36.

617. Soboroff I, Nicholas C, Cahan P. Ranking retrieval systems without relevance judgments. In: Proceedings of the International Conference on Research and Development in Information Retrieval (SIGIR). New Orleans (LO); 2001. pp. 66–73.

618. Soltani A, Canty S, Mayo Q, Thomas L, Hoofnagle CJ. Flash cookies and privacy. SSRN eLibr 2009, Available at http://ssrn.com/abstract=1446862.

619. Song R, Liu H, Wen J-R, Ma W-Y. Learning block importance models for web pages. In: Proceedings of the International World Wide Web Conference (WWW). New York; 2004. pp. 203–211.

620. Spence R. Information visualization. Harlow: ACM Press Books in conjunction with Addison-Wesley; 2000.

621. Spence R. Rapid, serial and visual: a presentation technique with potential. Inf Vis 2002; 1:13–19.

622. Spiliopoulou M, Mobasher B, Berendt B, Nakagawa M. A framework for the evaluation of session reconstruction heuristics in web usage analysis. INFORMS J Comput 2003; 15:171–190. Spring Special Issue on Mining Web-Based Data for E-Business Applications.

623. Spink A, Jansen BJ, Blakely C, Koshman S. A study of results overlap and uniqueness among major web search engines. Inf Process Manage 2006; 42:1379–1391.

624. Spink A, Jansen BJ, Ozmultu HC. Use of query reformulation and relevance feedback by excite users. Internet Res Electron Netw Appl Policy 2000; 10:317–328.

625. Spink A, Jansen BJ, Wolfram D, Saracevic T. From e-sex to e-commerce: web search changes. IEEE Comput 2002; 35:107–109.

626. Spiteri LF. The structure and form of folksonomy tags: the road to the public library catalogs. Inf Technol Libr 2007; 26:13–25.

627. Staab S, Werthner H. Intelligent systems for tourism. IEEE Intell Syst 2002; 17:53–66.

628. Stamou S, Ntoulas A. Search personalization through query and page topical analysis. User Model User-adapt Interact 2009; 19:5–33.

629. Standage T. The mechanical turk: the true story of the chess-playing machine that fooled the world. London: Penguin; 2004.

630. Steiglitz K. Snipers, shills, and sharks: “EBay” and human behavior. Princeton (NJ): Princeton University Press; 2007.

631. Sterne J. WebKDD in the business world. In: Proceedings of the WebKDD Workshop: Webmining as a Premise to Effective and Intelligent Web Applications. Held in conjunction with the ACM SIGKDD International Conference on Knowledge Discovery and Data Mining (KDD). Washington (DC); 2003. Invited talk.

632. Stirling IA. Topic mapping for context, searching for content. Online Mag 2003; 27:28–33.

633. Surowiecki J. The wisdom of the crowds: why the many are smarter than the few. London: Abacus; 2004.

634. Suryanto MA, Lim EP, Sun A, Chiang RHL. Quality-aware collaborative question answering: methods and evaluation. In: Proceedings of the ACM International Conference on Web Search and Data Mining (WSDM). Barcelona; 2009. pp. 142–151.

635. Sutton C, McCallum A. An introduction to conditional random fields for relational learning. In: Getoor L, Taskar B, editors. Introduction to statistical relational learning. Cambridge (MA): MIT Press; 2007. Chapter 4. pp. 108–143.

636. Sydow M. Random surfer with back step. In: Poster Proceedings of the International World Wide Web Conference (WWW). New York; 2004. pp. 352–353.

637. Takács G, Pilászy I, Németh B, Tikk D. Major components of the gravity recommendation system. SIGKDD Explor 2007; 9:80–83.

638. Takács G, Pilászy I, Németh B, Tikk D. Scalable collaborative filtering approaches for large recommender systems. J Mach Learn Res (JMLR) 2009; 10:623–656.

639. Takano H, Winograd T. Dynamic bookmarks for the WWW. In: Proceedings of the ACM Conference on Hypertext and Hypermedia (HYPERTEXT). Pittsburgh (PA); 1998. pp. 297–298.

640. Talbot D. Search me: inside the launch of Wolfram's new "computational knowledge engine". Technol Rev 2009; 112:32–39.

641. Tepper M. The rise of social software. netWorker 2003; 7:18–23.

642. Thakor MV, Borsuk W, Kalamas M. Hotlists and web browsing behavior—an empirical investigation. J Bus Res 2004; 57:776–786.

643. Thao C, Munson EV. A relevance model for web image search. In: Proceedings of the International Workshop on Web Document Analysis (WDA). Held in conjunction with the International Conference on Document Analysis and Recognition (ICDAR). Edinburgh; 2003.

644. Thurow S. Search engine visibility. 2nd ed. Indianapolis (IN): New Riders Publishing; 2007. Available at www.searchenginesbook.com.

645. Tochtermann K, Dittrich G. Fishing for clarity in hyperdocuments with enhanced fisheye-views. In: Proceedings of the European Conference on Hypertext Technology. Milan; 1992. pp. 212–221.

646. Trevathan J, Read W. A simple shill bidding agent. In: Proceedings of the International Conference on Information Technology (ITNG). Washington (DC); 2007. pp. 766–771.

647. Trigg RH. From trailblazing to guided tours: the legacy of vannevar Bush's vision of hypertext use. In: Nyce JM, Kahn P, editors. From Memex to hypertext: Vannevar Bush and the mind's machine. San Diego (CA): Academic Press; 1991. pp. 353–367.

648. Turney PD. Thumbs up or thumbs down? Semantic orientation applied to unsupervised classification of reviews. In: Proceedings of the Annual Meeting of the Association for Computational Linguistics (ACL). Philadelphia (PA); 2002. pp. 417–424.

649. Tyler JR, Wilkinson DM, Huberman BA. Email as spectroscopy: automated discovery of community structure within organizations. In: Wenger E, Huysman M, Wulf V, editors. Communities and technologies. Norwell (MA): Kluwer Academic Publishers; 2003. pp. 81–96.

650. Ulges A, Schulze C, Keysers D, Breuel TM. A system that learns to tag videos by watching Youtube. In: Proceedings of the International Conference on Computer Vision Systems (CVPR). Santorini; 2008. pp. 415–424.

651. Upstill T, Craswell N, Hawking D. A case study in search & searchability. In: Procedings of the Australasian Document Computing Symposium. Sydney; 2002.

652. Upstill T, Craswell N, Hawking D. Query-independent evidence in home page finding. ACM Trans Inf Syst (TOIS) 2003; 21:286–313.

653. Urstadt B. Social networking is not a business. Technol Rev 2008; 111:35–43.

654. Van Couvering E. The history of the internet search engine: navigational media and the traffic commodity. In: Spink A, Zimmer M, editors. Web search: multidisciplinary perspectives. Berlin: Springer-Verlag; 2008. pp. 177–208.

655. van Rijsbergen CJ. Information retrieval. London: Butterworths; 1979. Available at www.dcs.gla.ac.uk/Keith/Preface.html.

656. van Zaanen M, Mollá D. Named entity recogniser for question answering. In: Proceedings of Conference of the Pacific Association for Computational Linguistics (PACLING). Melbourne; 2007.

657. Vaughan-Nichols SJ. Will mobile computing's future be location, location, location? IEEE Comput 2009; 42:14–17.

658. Vertanen K, Kristensson PO. Parakeet: a continuous speech recognition system for mobile touch-screen device. In: Proceedings of the International Conference on Intelligent User Interfaces (IUI). Sanibel Island (FL); 2009. pp. 237–246.

659. Vidmar D, Anderson C. History of internet search tools. In: Kent A, Williams JG, Hall CM, editors. Encyclopedia of microcomputers. New York: Marcel Dekker; 2002. pp. 133–148.

660. Viégas FB, Wattenberg M. Tag clouds and the case for vernacular visualization. Interactions 2008; 15:49–52.

661. Viégas FB, Wattenberg M, van Ham F, Kriss J, McKeon M. Many Eyes: a site for visualization at internet scale. IEEE Trans Vis Comput Graph (TVCG) 2007; 13:1121–1128.

662. Volkovich Y, Litvak N, Donato D. Determining factors behind the PageRank log-log plot. In: Proceedings of the International Workshop on Algorithms and Models for the Web-Graph (WAW). San Diego (CA); 2007. pp. 108–123.

663. von Ahn L, Blum M, Langford J. Telling humans and computers apart automatically. Commun ACM 2004; 47:56–60.

664. von Ahn L, Maurer B, McMillen C, Abraham D, Blum M. reCAPTCHA: human-based character recognition via web security measures. Science 2008; 321:1465–1468.

665. Voorhees EM. Overview of trec 2002. NIST Special Publication SP 500-251, Text Retrieval Conference (TREC). Nov 2002. Available at http://trec.nist.gov/pubs/trec11/t11/_proceedings.html.

666. Walker J. Links and power: the political economy of linking on the web. In: Proceedings of the ACM Conference on Hypertext and Hypermedia (HYPERTEXT). College Park (MD); 2002. pp. 72–73.

667. Wan Y. Comparison-shopping services and agent design: an overview. In: Wan Y, editor. Comparison-shopping services and agent designs. Hershey (PA): Information Science Reference, IGI Global; 2009. Chapter 1. pp. 1–18.

668. Wang A. The Shazam music recognition service. Commun ACM 2006; 49:44–48.

669. Want R. RFID a key to automating everything. Sci Am 2003; 290:56–65.

670. Waterhouse S, Doolin DM, G Kahn, Faybishenko Y. Distributed search in P2P networks. IEEE Internet Comput 2002; 6:68–72.

671. Watters C, Amoudi G. GeoSearcher: location-based ranking of search engine results. J Am Soc Inf Sci Technol (JASIST) 2003; 52:140–151.

672. Watts DJ. Six degrees: the science of the connected age. London: William Heinemann; 2003.

673. Watts DJ, Dodds PS, Newman MEJ. Identity and search in social networks. Science 2002; 296:1302–1305.

674. Watts DJ, Strogatz SH. Collective dynamics of 'small-world' networks. Nature 1998; 393:440–442.

675. Weinreich H, Lamersdorf W. Concepts for improved visualization of web link attributes. Comput Netw 2000; 33:403–416.

676. Wellman B. Computer networks as social networks. Science 2001; 293:2031–2034.

677. Wenyan H, Bolivar A. Online auctions efficiency: a survey of eBay auctions. In: Proceedings of the International World Wide Web Conference (WWW). Beijing; 2008. pp. 925–933.

678. Wetzker R, Zimmermann C, Bauckhage C. Analyzing social bookmarking bystems: a del.icio.us cookbook. In: Proceedings of the Mining Social Data Workshop, Held in conjunction with the European Conference on Artificial Intelligence (ECAI). Patras; 2008. pp. 26–30.

679. Wheeldon R, Levene M. The best trail algorithm for adaptive navigation in the world-wide-web. In: Proceedings of the Latin American Web Congress. Santiago; 2003. pp. 166–178.

680. White GC, Anderson DR, Burnham KP, Otis DL. Capture-recapture and removal methods for sampling closed populations. Report LA-8787-NERP. Los Alamos (NM): Los Alamos National Laboratory; 1982. p. 235.

681. White HD, McCain KW. Bibliometrics. In: Williams ME, editor. Volume 24, Annual review of information science and technology (ARIST). Amsterdam: Elsevier Science Publishers; 1989. pp. 119–186.

682. Wilcox RT. Experts and amateurs: the role of experience in internet auctions. Mark Lett 2000; 11:363–374.

683. Wilkinson DM. Strong regularities in online peer production. In: Proceedings of the ACM Conference on Electronic Commerce (EC). Chicago (IL); 2008. pp. 302–309.

684. Xie Y, O'Hallaron D. Locality in search engine queries and its implications for caching. In: Proceedings of the Annual Joint Conference of the IEEE Computer and Communications Societies. New York; 2002. pp. 1238–1247.

685. Yan J, Liu N, Wang G, Zhang W, Jiang Y, Chen Z. How much can behavioral targeting help online advertising? In: Proceedings of the International World Wide Web Conference (WWW). Madrid; 2009. pp. 261–270.

686. Yang I, Jeong H, Kahng B, Barabási A-L. Emerging behavior in electronic bidding. Physic Rev E 2003; 68:016102–1–016102–5.

687. Yang I, Kahng B. Bidding process in online auctions and winning strategy: rate equation approach. Phys Rev E 2006; 73:067101–1–067101–4.

688. Yang B, Qian W, Zhou A. Using wide table to manage web data: a survey. Front Comput Sci China 2008; 2:211–223.

689. Yang J, Wei X. Seeking and offering expertise across categories: a sustainable mechanism works for Baidu Knows. In: Proceedings of AAAI International Conference on Weblogs and Social Media (ICWSM). San Jose (CA); 2009.

690. Yeh T, Tollmar K, Darrell T. IDeixis: image-based deixis for finding location-based information. In: Proceedings of the Conference on Human Factors in Computing Systems (CHI). Vienna; 2004. pp. 781–782.

691. Yu J, Casati F, Daniel F. Understanding mashup development. IEEE Internet Comput 2008; 12:44–52.

692. Yu PS, Li X, Liu B. On the temporal dimension of search. In: Poster Proceedings of the International World Wide Web Conference (WWW). New York; 2004. pp. 448–449.

693. Zamir O, Etzioni O. Grouper: a dynamic clustering interface to web search results. Comput Netw 1999; 31:1361–1374.

694. Zaphiris P. Depth vs. breadth in the arrangement of web links. In: Proceedings of the Meeting of the Human Factors and Ergonomics Society. San Diego (CA); 2000. pp. 133–144.

695. Zdziarski JA. Ending spam: Bayesian content filtering and the art of statistical language classification. San Francisco (CA): No Starch Press; 2005.

696. Zeinalipour-Yazdi D, Kalogeraki V, Gunopulos D. Information retrieval techniques for peer-to-peer networks. IEEE Comput Sci Eng 2004; 6:20–26.

697. Zhang H, Chen Z, Li M, Su Z. Relevance feedback and learning in content-based image search. World Wide Web Internet Web Inf Syst 2003; 6:131–155.

698. Zhang H, Goel A, Govindan R. Using the small-world model to improve Freenet performance. In: Proceedings of the Joint Conference of the IEEE Computer and Communications Societies (Infocom); Volume 3. New York; 2002. pp. 1228–1237.

699. Zhang Y, Jansen BJ, Spink A. Time series analysis of a web search engine transaction log. Inf Process Manage 2009; 45:230–245.

700. Zhang Y, Moffat A. Some observations on user search behavior. In: Proceedings of the Australian Document Computing Symposium. Brisbane; 2006. pp. 1–8.

701. Zhang J, Van Alstyne M. SWIM: fostering social network based information search. In: Proceedings of the Conference on Human Factors in Computing Systems (CHI). Vienna; 2004. p. 1568.

702. Zhang B, Zhou Y, Faloutsos C. Toward a comprehensive model in internet auction fraud detection. In: Proceedings of the Hawaii International Conference on System Sciences (HICSS). Waikoloa (HI); 2008. p. 79.

703. Zhou B, Pei J. Link spam target detection using page farms. ACM Trans Knowl Discov Data 2009; 3:13: 1–38.

704. Zhu Z, Cox IJ, Levene M. Ranked-listed or categorized results in IR: 2 is better than 1. In: Proceedings of the International Conference on Natural Language and Information Systems (NLDB). London; 2008. pp. 111–123.

705. Zhu Z, Levene M, Cox IJ. Query classification using asymmetric learning. In: Proceedings of the International Conference on Applications of Digital Information and Web Technologies (ICADIWT). London; 2009. pp. 518–524.

706. Zimmerman J, Dimitrova N, Agnihotri L, Janevski A, Nikolovska L. MyInfo: a personal news interface. In: Proceedings of the Conference on Human Factors in Computing Systems (CHI). Fort Lauderdale (FL); 2003. pp. 898–899.

707. Zittrain J. The future of the internet and how to stop it. New Haven (CT): Yale University Press; 2008.

INDEX

An Introduction to Search Engines and Web Navigation, by Mark Levene